THE
PORTABLE MBA
IN MARKETING

The Portable MBA Series

Forthcoming Titles

THE PORTABLE MBA IN MARKETING

Second Edition

Charles D. Schewe
Alexander Watson Hiam

John Wiley & Sons, Inc.

New York • Chichester • Weinheim • Brisbane • Singapore • Toronto

This publication is designed to provide accurate and authoritative information in regard to the subject matter covered. It is sold with the understanding that the publisher is not engaged in rendering professional services. If professional advice or other expert assistance is required, the services of a competent professional person should be sought.

ISBN: 0-471-19367-4

Printed in the United States of America.

10 9 8 7 6 5 4 3 2 1

DEDICATION

Dedicated to Sara Christie Schewe, age 20, who was killed on a treacherous road in India one black night, March 27, 1996. We miss you terribly!

FOREWORD

I have been thinking and writing a lot about the importance of customer service—and I have come to believe that the secret to competitive success is to give customers service so far above their expectations it becomes legendary. Many managers are rediscovering the power of positive word-of-mouth and realizing that to generate it you have to deliver *more* than customers expect. Your attention to customer needs and problems can differentiate what would otherwise be a commodity product and lead to larger market share and profits. It's that simple—and that difficult. It's difficult because many companies are not used to a 100 percent focus on adding value for their customers. They are not used to listening well, trusting their employees, and making continuous improvements, yet these are the keys to competitive success today.

Here is a book that may become a legend in its own right because it shows how managers can achieve competitive success by building on the core concepts of marketing. The authors argue that the marketing concept is at the root of all the exciting new directions in management, and they show readers how to nurture their service and quality efforts and many other programs with the concepts and tools of marketing.

One of the most basic principles I teach in my service workshops is that if you're not getting better, you're getting worse. Continuous improvement means that you have to continually find ways to do things better, faster, different, to be a leader in your industry. Where do new ideas for continuous improvement come from? This book shows how ideas can be stimulated by looking at the entire corporation (not just the marketing department!) from the customer's perspective. Schewe and Hiam use the term "marketing imagination" to describe the powerful force this perspective creates, and the unexpected benefits it produces for customers.

One way to look at this is to draw a box representing the product. Around this box is a second, larger box. It represents everything the customers expect to be bundled with that product—local distribution, timely repairs, and a warranty, for example. This second box is what's expected, so it is the price of admission. But you don't win the game just by getting onto the playing field. So now you have to draw a third, even larger box, this one representing what is *possible*. Many things are possible that the customer may not expect, may not even have imagined. But your task as a manager is to figure out how to deliver these extras. It is in the third box that markets are won and lost, that the battle for U.S. companies to regain leadership of industries like consumer electronics, textiles, and automobiles is fought. This book maps the terrain and defines the strategies and tactics for competing in the third box.

In fact, *The Portable MBA in Marketing* is a fine illustration of the strategy of giving what's possible, rather than just what customers expect. As readers, we expect this book to present the MBA marketing curriculum and make it relevant to managers. It does this, more than adequately, but it goes far beyond the expected by showing how any manager, in any department, can create positive change and achieve competitive advantage by applying the marketing concept. In the effort to give more than readers expect, the authors may have rewritten the marketing curriculum forever. This is not just marketing at the MBA level; this is the *new* marketing, and I think it will serve as a user's manual for the quiet revolution that is now percolating in U.S. businesses.

I want to end this foreword with another observation from my work on customer service with all sorts of organizations: I believe that listening is one of the most underutilized skills in business today. Your best resources for information about your business are your customers, your suppliers, and your employees. You need to track costs and read the accounting reports, sure, but you won't ever find a source of competitive advantage in them. And how do you listen better? In part, this means gathering more and better information, and again I recommend this book for both the basic principles and for new ideas and insights on the whole subject of marketing information. And in part, it means listening with commitment.

There is a big difference between commitment and interest. Most managers are interested in what their customers, suppliers, and employees think and feel. But I'm not sure how many managers are *fully committed* to hearing what they have to say and acting on it. So ultimately better listening comes down to commitment, and that's an eight inch job; it's all in your head. When managers start working on that job, all sorts of incredible achievements are possible. You've already taken the first step; that's why you are reading this book. I recommend making the study of marketing—and rethinking what the marketing concept means in your work—a top priority when you do your One Minute Goal Setting.

Years ago in *The One Minute Manager* I wrote that 80 percent of your really important results will come from 20 percent of your goals, which means you shouldn't waste time on any but the three to six most important goals. But these goals deserve full attention, and you should track your performance on them carefully. Well, I don't know what every reader's top few goals are right now, but I can guess they generally have to do with improving business performance, rising to competitive challenges, and striving for excellence in management. What I *do* know is that developing and applying your marketing imagination ought to be among those goals because it is very likely to help you achieve them.

KEN BLANCHARD
Co-author of
The One Minute Manager

ACKNOWLEDGMENTS

This book owes much to those marketing experts who taught us at Northwestern University, The University of Michigan, and The University of California at Berkeley. We heartily thank them for the knowledge they brought us and for laying the foundations in marketing upon which this book rises.

We also offer thanks to our current teachers—the many clients and students who have shared their questions and challenges with us. They continue to "push the envelope," keeping the field of marketing relevant and vital.

We sharpened our writing teeth on past books focusing on marketing. We want to acknowledge the publishers that gave us so many opportunities to ply our trade in the written word, including McGraw-Hill, Random House, Worth Publishing, Prentice-Hall, and IDG Books Worldwide. Without them, this book would not be as polished as it now is.

And a special thanks to Tom Peters who gave one of us a "personal seminar with Tom Peters" at a time of deep emotional trauma that provided the vision to make this revised book happen. His encouragement has been most supportive . . . and we sincerely thank him for that.

Special thanks are due to Happi Cramer of Word for Word who smilingly made the manuscript black print on white paper . . . and to Amy Scalese who copyedited the first draft without even one murmur of complaint about the work and to Nancy Marcus Land of Publications Development Company who diligently copyedited and managed the production of the final draft. We also wish to acknowledge the influence and support of the editors at John Wiley & Sons, especially Renana Meyers who oversaw putting this revision to bed. Thanks also to Robert Desideri for inspiring the For Your Imagination features you'll find in each chapter of this new edition.

And, of course, we thank our families—especially our wives, Anne and Heather—for standing by us as we spent the countless hours of time that could have been spent with them. But they too saw the vision of what this could be. Without all these wonderful people, this book just could not have happened, and we are grateful to them all.

C.D.S.
A.W.H.

ABOUT THE AUTHORS

Charles D. Schewe is Professor of Marketing at the University of Massachusetts at Amherst as well as principal in Lifestage Matrix Marketing. Schewe received his Ph.D. (1972) from the Kellogg Graduate School of Management at Northwestern University and his M.B.A. (1965) and B.A. (1964) from the University of Michigan. In 1979, he was a Fulbright-Hays Scholar at the University of Lund, in Sweden, where he frequently is a visiting professor.

Schewe has advised numerous companies in strategic planning, competitive intelligence, marketing research, customer service, and competitive positioning. His client engagements have included Kellogg's, Spalding Sports Worldwide, International Business Machines, Kmart, RJR Nabisco, Kraft General Foods, Prudential Bache, Grand Metropolitan, Lucky Stores, and Procter & Gamble. Over the past two decades, Schewe has focused on understanding the marketing management implications of our aging population and assisted numerous manufacturers and retailers targeting the 50+ population. From this knowledge base, he has worked as Executive Consultant to Age Wave, Inc., a San Francisco-based consulting firm specializing in offering counsel on the implications of the Aging of America. While working at Age Wave, Schewe met Geoffrey Meredith, with whom he started Lifestage Matrix Marketing in 1994.

Schewe has spoken extensively and internationally to executive groups on marketing topics within his areas of expertise. He has given numerous keynote addresses to large and small audiences in such varied industries as credit unions, senior living communities, building supplies, and polyurethane. He has authored over fifty articles in academic journals such as the *Journal of Marketing,* the *Journal of Marketing Research, Business Horizons, Marketing Management,* and the *Journal of Consumer Marketing.* His recent articles in *American Demographics* have been quoted and referenced widely. He is frequently featured in newspapers, magazines, and trade publications nationwide. He, along with Alex Hiam, is the author of *Exploring the World of*

Business (Worth Publishers, 1996), co-authored with Ken Blanchard, author of *The One Minute Manager.*

Lifestage Matrix Marketing, 23 Ash Lane, Amherst, MA 01002, (413) 256-0914, www.lifestagemarketing.com.

Alexander Watson Hiam is a consultant, speaker and trainer, and author of popular titles such as *Marketing for Dummies, The Vest-Pocket CEO, The Manager's Pocket Guide to Creativity, The Entrepreneur's Complete Sourcebook, The Vest-Pocket Marketer,* and *Closing the Quality Gap: Lessons from America's Leading Companies.* He has taught marketing and advertising courses at business schools and served for four years on the faculty of the Marketing Department at the University of Massachusetts at Amherst before leaving to devote full time to his private practice. He currently runs Alexander Hiam & Associates, a consulting business in Amherst, Massachusetts, that provides assistance and support for marketers and general managers in planning, business growth, strategy research and development, and service quality measurement and improvement for more than a decade. He also facilitates product and concept development processes for clients and provides training in areas such as innovation and creativity.

In addition, Hiam develops and markets training and assessment materials and software in the areas of leadership, sales, change management, negotiation, and other business topics for his Human Interactions Assessment & Management brand. For example, the Flex Style Negotiating workshop and assessments, available through HRD Press, are used in the corporate training market.

Hiam has worked with a wide range of organizations, including The American Management Association, Bank of America, Bausch & Lomb, The Conference Board, Digital Equipment Corp., IntelliCorp., General Motors, Hewlett Packard, Hoechst Celanese Corp., JIAN, Kellogg Company, Mass Mutual Life Insurance Co., Pilot Software, Texas Instruments, The Vermont Country Store, UOL Inc., and Whirlpool Corp. He received his A.B. from Harvard College and M.B.A. in marketing from University of California's Berkeley's Haas School of Business.

Alexander Hiam & Associates, 69 South Pleasant Street, Suite 204, Amherst, MA 01002, (413) 253-3658.

CONTENTS

INTRODUCTION

In Greek mythology, Icarus and his father escape from the island of Crete by fabricating wings for themselves of wax and feathers. But the exhilaration of soaring over the ocean goes to Icarus' head and he flies higher and higher, until finally his wings are melted by the heat of the sun and he falls to his death in the sea.

Does this ancient story have any relevance to modern business? We fear so. Because the financial success of any business is truly as wondrous a thing as the flight of Icarus. If you've ever tried to start a company or even to launch a brand new product, you'll agree that it is an amazing thing to do successfully. Everything must be in alignment for a business concept to take flight. A great many things can and do derail even the best-sounding ideas. After all, more than 10,000 businesses fail each year in the United States alone, and the failure rate for new product introductions is more than 75 percent.

Like Icarus, no one in business should take their flight for granted. It is only the good will and enthusiastic support of our customers that keep us aloft. Take your customers for granted and you're dead.

Yet as we consider recent trends in business, we are reminded of another inheritance from ancient Greece—*hubris*. One dictionary defines it as "exaggerated pride or self-confidence often resulting in retribution." That's what did Icarus in, and it threatens many businesses today. We see too many instances in which companies treat their past successes as a right to future success. Overconfidence is a fatal attitude in business, as in flying. Yet many managers and many organizations lose sight of their customers for months or years at a time, focusing instead on the bottom line or their own financial and strategic goals.

What's wrong with the bottom line? Or financial and strategic goals? Nothing, in fact, they are essentials, but only as long as they are kept in their proper context—as the *end result* of customers' purchase decisions. If customers begin to favor purchase options other than yours, then your strategies are history and the bottom line is too. That's why we believe business success begins with happy customers . . . preferably many of them!

1

When we wrote the introduction to the first edition of this book, in the beginning of the 1990s, we were able to say with confidence that "all the important new directions in management thought and practice are marketing oriented." Industry was in the midst of an exciting discovery process in which quality teams were springing up by the thousands to champion customer needs and new measures of customer satisfaction and quality were taking their place alongside profitability and return on investment as key strategic indicators. It was an exciting period of exploration in which many employees and managers discovered the power of a customer orientation, including many from beyond the traditional boundaries of the marketing function. And it culminated in the reemergence of American businesses in the global arena. Today, we take for granted a general parity between the quality of U.S. and Japanese-made automobiles, for example. Yet it was not very long ago that U.S. auto makers were viewed as has-beens in the quality wars.

The turnaround in the fortunes of U.S. businesses is a happy thing for many of our readers, who, like us, are enjoying the fruits of a robust economy. We were pleased to have been able to play some small role as consultants and authors in the tremendous efforts to turn around U.S. business over the last decade. Yet we worry that the current period of prosperity has caused most of us to take our eyes off the ball.

Or, to return to the Icarus analogy, to lose sight of our limitations and put ourselves at risk of new and even greater failure. Icarus was escaping from a prison on the island of Crete when he died. And our current prosperity is a similarly miraculous escape from the threatening economic pressures of the 1980s. Might we too forget what lofted us from that prison and brought us to our current height? Surely it was a fanatical dedication to pleasing the customer—the sort of dedication that seems sadly lacking in today's typical headline stories of mergers, acquisitions, and downsizings. The cost of forgetting the customer is to be forgotten by the customer. And that is the beginning of the end for any business, no matter how large and powerful it may be.

And so it is an especially good time to rediscover marketing. The field of marketing contains within it all anyone needs to find customers, figure out how to please them, and let them know what you have to offer. (The rest is up to them.) Whether your interest is in a formal marketing task—we call that marketing with a big M—or in general management with an eye to gaining and keeping customers—that's marketing with a small m—you have come to the right place. The marketing curriculum of the modern business school covers the essential concepts and practices needed to "find a need and fill it," as the pundits sometimes sum up the marketing task. And in this book, we supplement that curriculum with a healthy dose of our real-world marketing experience from our client work and past experiences in marketing management.

The marketing perspective is a source of never-ending inspiration, a place to return again and again for those ideas and strategies that keep you afloat in the stormy winds of the competitive marketplace. We welcome those readers new to the field with a promise that the marketing orientation will be a rich and endless source of inspirations and strategies for success. And for those of you who, like us, are revisiting the roots of marketing for refocus and renewal, we offer a hearty "Welcome back!" This second edition should offer you enough fresh material to make the return visit more than worth your while.

PART ONE

REDISCOVERING THE MARKETING CONCEPT

As this book goes to print, we are just returning from a two-day brainstorming session with staff from several leading U.S. consumer-products companies. Our goal: To develop winning new breakfast-cereal concepts for adults. To do so, we first gathered extensive information about the preferences and attitudes of people from several cohorts—The Depression, the Post-War, and the baby boomers. Then we met in the middle of the desert in Arizona to "get out of the box" and develop hundreds of novel concepts. From these, we now must select and refine a dozen, to send on for many rounds of customer testing and development. With luck and the blessing of the customer, one or two successful new products may eventually arise from this elaborate and exhausting process and take their place on the crowded cereal shelves of your supermarket.

Investigating. Imagining. Testing through surveys, panels, and focus groups of customers. Tinkering and reinventing. Retesting. It takes a lot of these activities to develop something as seemingly simple as a new and better cereal. *Anything* you try to do for the customer must leap similar hurdles. It is no easy thing to please customers. They already have so many choices. If you wish to sway even one purchase decision in a new direction, you must discover and communicate something of unique value to customers.

It all comes down to customers. Without their active approval, no new product concept will sell, no store will attract shoppers, no catalog will generate a response, no Web site will log many visitors. To succeed in business, you must, first and foremost, focus on *what you will do for your customer.*

This seems an obvious point. Yet many a company, many an employee, loses sight of it. Today, we are (hopefully) emerging from a period of corporate introspection. Many executives have steered their organizations down the productivity path in an attempt to squeeze more results from fewer employees. Sometimes the short-term results of automation, exporting of jobs, and downsizing are highly profitable. But in the long run, it is all for naught if the customer is forgotten.

And indeed, it appears that many businesses *are* forgetting their customers. Customer satisfaction with products and services is slipping—down every year since we published the first edition of this book. The quality revolution has lost its momentum, and a new era of hard-nosed executives are returning to a get-tough approach to business. The trouble is, customers are the toughest people in the world. If they don't like your offerings or your attitude, they can downsize even the biggest company in a hurry.

It is time, no, *past* time to return our corporate attention to findings ways of giving the customer more for less, rather than of taking more for less. It is time to rediscover the customer. In this first part of our book, we will show you how.

1 THE ESSENCE OF MARKETING

The Customer First, Last, and Always

Nothing is worthwhile unless it touches the customer.

—Edgar Woolard, CEO, DuPont[1]

As companies have downsized and tried to deliver services with fewer employees, customer satisfaction has fallen dramatically.

—American Society for Quality Control, reporting on the American Customer Satisfaction Index

There was a time when companies had never heard of marketing. Either they sold products or they didn't sell them, depending on the success of the salespeople or retailers who were charged with making the sale. But even though the fundamental idea of marketing—*to focus on how to better satisfy consumers*—has been with us in a formal way only since the 1950s, the message itself is timeless. You do not need a formal marketing department to "do" marketing, since it is most fundamentally a way of looking at your business. It is looking at your business from your customer's point of view—not always a flattering perspective.

In fact, many businesses today still do not do formal marketing. The roadside vegetable stand has no marketing department, and does not need one. Nor do many larger local businesses, and most entrepreneurial successes only add marketing departments after they've made their first million. But whether or not there is a formal marketing department, every organization must do marketing to survive—and must do it exceptionally well to thrive.

5

IF MODERN MANAGEMENT IS SO EFFECTIVE, WHY AREN'T CUSTOMERS *SATISFIED?*

Marketing is now a well-recognized component of business success, a cornerstone of modern management. You won't find a president or chief executive officer who disagrees with the sentiment of Edgar Woolard, quoted on page 5, that nothing is worthwhile unless it touches the customer. Without satisfied customers, you lose business to your competitors. Without the ability to satisfy customers, you fail to attract new business.

The logic is simple but powerful (Exhibit 1.1). There are only two possible sources of business revenues: selling to new customers or selling to repeat customers. And since repeat customers are generally easier and more profitable to work with—an issue we will return to many times—you generally want to maximize customer satisfaction and insure a high rate of retention. Thus to succeed, a business needs to attract new customers, then make sure they are sufficiently satisfied to come back again and again.

It is no wonder that businesses devote so much time, attention, and money to activities designed to attract and retain customers. To attract them, they redesign their products, lower prices, develop new ad campaigns, seek faster and more convenient ways to distribute the products to customers, and so forth—the options are limited only by your marketing imagination.

Similarly, to retain customers, businesses invest in improved customer service, warranties, and guarantees; the reliability and quality of their products; and anything else they think might help. For example, the entire total quality management revolution is no more nor less than a story about how to retain customers in the face of stiff competition. Innovations as far removed from marketing as the production line are still part of the customer satisfaction equation because they can affect the customer's experience just as much as (and often more than) traditional marketing elements like

EXHIBIT 1.1.   The marketing effectiveness grid.

	Low — Customer retention — High	
High **Customer attraction** **Low**	**Partial failure** New customers replace lost customers.	**Success** Sales and profits grow at maximum possible rate.
	Total failure Sales fall as customers leave.	**Partial failure** Sales slow or fall due to lack of new customers.

the brand name, ads, and packaging. And many companies, both in the United States and abroad, have made great leaps in product quality and process redesign in the struggle to satisfy customers.

As authors we have often documented the success stories of this revolution, and as consultants we have had many interesting opportunities to join in the struggle to improve products, services, and business processes along with the more conventional elements of marketing. We are therefore especially concerned to see that overall customer satisfaction in the United States is *dropping* rather than rising in the late 1990s. This finding comes from a relatively new initiative (sponsored by the American Society for Quality Control) to track customer satisfaction through an annual survey. The survey examines attitudes toward 200 major companies in 33 different industries. The result? Declines each year since the first survey in 1994. Between 1994 and 1997, the customer satisfaction index fell 5.1 percent. Some of the biggest declines in satisfaction occurred in the service sector and in the transportation, communications, and utilities sectors. On average, just 71 percent of customers are satisfied—leaving a startling 29 percent ready to jump when the opportunity arises.[2]

Why are customers increasingly unhappy with the products and services they consume? Why are so many customers disloyal and eager to jump ship? What we think is happening is this: The dramatic investments in customer satisfaction that accompanied the total quality management movement have given way to a new emphasis on cost-cutting.

In the many customer satisfaction studies we performed or analyzed in the 1980s and early 1990s, we generally saw evidence of *increasing* satisfaction. It was the urgent goal of most of our clients. But goals have shifted and many other initiatives have arisen to compete for management's increasingly divided attention: Change management, downsizing, reengineering, teamwork, outsourcing, mergers and acquisitions, going global, and much more. Many companies have allowed customer satisfaction to slip. As a result, they neither attract customers nor retain them as effectively as they did even five years ago.

As we write, economists are grudgingly admitting the economy looks remarkably healthy. We have to sound a note of warning, however. It is our conviction that this heady growth of the mid-to-late 1990s is in large part a harvesting of investments made five and ten years before—and cannot be sustained unless companies return to that earlier focus on customer satisfaction.

Professor Claes Forrnell of the University of Michigan Graduate School of Business, where the annual survey is conducted, warns that "Cost cutting rather than revenue growth has led to high corporate earnings," and that "Corporate downsizing may have helped bottom lines and stockholders in the short-term, but it hasn't helped customers."[3] In the short-term, stockholders and customers have competing agendas. But in the long-term, their interests are aligned, for without progress in customer attraction and (especially) retention, no company can deliver long-term earnings to its shareholders.

We undertake this second edition of a classic book on modern marketing with some trepidation. The daily business headlines are full of optimism, but the long-term indicators leave us with a sense of foreboding. The current popularity of the chainsaw approach to business management threatens to return us to the dark days of dissatisfied customers and narrow profit margins—and it threatens the long-term prosperity of many of today's leading brands and businesses. The smart thing to do for anyone in business today, we are convinced, is to swim *against* this stream. Now is a great time to rediscover the marketing concept, to rediscover customers, to be one of the pioneers of the next wave of customer-oriented management. The innovators who lead this return to their business roots will be the big winners of the next decade. Those who wait will be the losers.

We will reexamine earlier marketing success stories to draw inspiration from prior periods of emphasis on customer satisfaction. Many—really, all—of today's leading businesses achieved their stature by innovating in what they did for their customers, as the following case illustrates. And if they don't return to their roots, somebody else will.

Case Study: The L.L. Bean Strategy

L.L. Bean had no marketing department in 1912 when it first began mailing catalogs (they were called circulars back then). Nonetheless, unlike many catalog retailers that have failed in the interim, L.L. Bean had a clear vision of the marketing concept. The 1912 catalog contained the following message from founder Leon Leonwood Bean:

> I do not consider a sale complete until goods are worn out and customer still satisfied. We will thank anyone to return goods that are not perfectly satisfactory.
>
> Should the person reading this notice know of anyone who is not satisfied with our goods, I will consider it a favor to be notified.
>
> Above all things we wish to avoid having a dissatisfied customer.[4]

Was this guy nuts? Some people thought so, and many managers would still hesitate to apply L.L. Bean's guarantee to their businesses. How many businesses advertise, as L.L. Bean does today, that "We'll accept returns at any time for any reason. Your purchase will be replaced, or we will refund your money or credit your credit card." The very thought strikes fear into many managers' hearts because it requires that they trust their customers. But trusting the customer is certainly part of the ephemeral essence of marketing: If you can't trust them, why should they trust you?

Marketing is the sum total of activities that keep a company focused on its customers and, with good management and a little luck, ensure that the company's offerings are valued by its customers. At the roadside vegetable stand, marketing includes a host of decisions concerning location, pricing, the choice of vegetables to grow, and the quantities to offer. It might also include issues such as whether to switch to organic produce, whether and where to post signs or run ads to attract customers, and how to handle complaints and returns. It certainly includes the decision as to whether you can trust your customers, for many farm stands work on an honor system with an open cash box!

No marketing department exists in this type of business because the principals are best suited to handling marketing decisions and activities themselves, and, mercifully, because the business is simply not large enough to justify specialization and division of labor and the bureaucracy it often brings. However, the management of a successful roadside stand is of necessity marketing-oriented, as is any other business, whether for-profit or not-for-profit, unless it is so protected by regulation or economic monopoly that it can afford to ignore its customers. It is difficult to find examples of such protected organizations, especially over the long run, because they simply do not prosper.

The U.S. Postal Service may be an exception. It has, after all, a protected partial monopoly. Nevertheless, it seems to do a decent job of moving millions of pieces of mail to their intended destinations. Before firms such as Federal Express and United Parcel Service began competing with it, most people would have given the Postal Service high marks.

However, the fact that private companies now carry mail faster and more reliably illustrates an important essence of marketing-oriented management that was missing at the Postal Service: the drive to find new ways to satisfy customers, even if customers have not already envisioned and demanded them. Fred Smith knew mail could be delivered overnight, even though the Postal Service and its customers did not. Although Smith's company, Federal Express, cannot by law deliver mail to mailboxes, it can and does hand deliver mail overnight at a lower cost and more reliably than the Postal Service. The U.S. Postal Service has recently made gains in the overnight letter market by using its letter carriers to sign up small business accounts for its express mail service. Where there is marketing imagination and a willingness to look at the business from the customer's perspective, there is always hope.

This drive to innovate and improve upon current service standards is a natural outgrowth of the sincere conviction that "a customer is the most important person in this office," as Leon Bean warned his employees in 1912. None of his employees would have written the following letter, sent by a U.S. Postal Service manager to a customer—whom they didn't know was writing a book on marketing at the time. After waiting 25 minutes in line at a post office, Alex had filed a customer complaint card and this is the response:

Dear Mr. Heam:

This letter is to acknowledge receipt of your consumer service card. I wish to apologize for any inconvenience you experienced due to the line at the University Drive Post Office. As in any business, we experience peak times of the day, early morning, late afternoon, which requires some amount of delay time to our customers. I'd like to assure you that this is not a situation we wish to put our customers through. Every effort is made to anticipate such times and schedule employees accordingly.

In an effort to save you time in the future, I am enclosing a stamps by mail envelope. This service will provide stamps through mail delivery for you and will make it unnecessary to come to the Post Office. Our vending machines in the lobby area are also available from 5:30 A.M. to 5:30 P.M. A new scale device in our lobby area can provide you with information as to costs and available services.

Thank you for taking the time to express your concerns to us. Your business is important to the Postal Service and every effort will be made to improve delays in the future.

Sincerely,

xxx xxxxxx

Acting Window Supervisor
Amherst Post Office
Amherst, MA 01002-9998

At first, this looks like a good marketing effort: A personal letter or apology, signed by a manager, is sent to a customer after the customer complains. No doubt this letter is the outgrowth of one of the many customer service programs that have taken seed across the nation. On closer reading, however, the letter is an example of how *not* to do marketing.

The letter opens with a misspelling of the customer's name, clearly starting off on the wrong foot. (How much do you value my business if you don't bother to spell my name correctly?) The writer then explains that it is difficult to staff the post office properly. But customers do not care why service is bad—this is not the customer's problem. Most significantly, the second paragraph, despite its polite tone, makes very clear that the Postal Service does not want the customer to come to the post office in the future. You wouldn't have to wait if you didn't bother us by coming here in the first place is the solution this letter offers: "Ah, wouldn't it be peaceful around here if it weren't for those irritating customers," one imagines the managers grumbling.

The acid test of a marketing-oriented organization is whether the managers blame their customers or look within their organization for the cause when something goes wrong. (Sure, you can always find a way to blame the customer, but that won't lead to the growth in sales and profits associated with marketing success.) The Postal Service employee who responded to the complaint flunks this acid test of the marketing concept. Despite its progress, this organization still has a way to go before it can better Federal Express and its other challenging competitors. John West, Federal Express' manager of quality improvement, explains the philosophy necessary for success in this competitive service industry when he says, "We won't be happy until we have 100 percent customer satisfaction and on-time delivery."[5]

The difference between good and bad marketing can be subtle. Although West's statement does not seem very different from the Postal Service's response—"I'd like to assure you that this is not a situation we wish to put our customers through"—the structure of these two statements is worlds apart. West's quote uses "won't," short for the definitive "will not," whereas the Postal Service employee used "I'd," short for the conditional "I would"—implied, *"if I could."* This choice of words unintentionally betrays a lack of conviction, an unwillingness to take on the responsibility for customer satisfaction.

Why split hairs? Because many people and many managers think U.S. organizations have already adopted the marketing concept, whereas in fact its essence is still missing at most companies.

DO YOU *REALLY* BELIEVE THE CUSTOMER IS RIGHT?

The view that the consumer is the focal point of the firm is the fundamental principle of the marketing concept—captured in the slogan, "The customer is always right." Here are some other slogans that express this point of view:

"We Do It All for You."

"You're the Boss."

"Nobody-Else-Like-You Service."

"Chosen #1 in People Pleasin."

"The Customer Is King."

It is far easier to put the marketing concept into a slogan than into practice. In fact, often consumers feel more like serfs than kings or queens. Poor service, low product quality, inconvenient locations, rude salespeople, excessively high prices, and other frustrations suffered by consumers attest to the fact that companies are still struggling to apply the marketing concept in full. Most firms are not yet truly customer-oriented, which is why customer satisfaction is falling.

For every customer-is-right slogan there are a dozen company-is-god slogans. Most advertising is shamelessly self-congratulatory. Here are a few examples from the display ads in a recent copy of *Fortune* magazine:

"World Leaders in Insurance and Financial Services."

"The Complete Networking Solution."

"On Top of the World."

"The Road You Should Be On."

"The Ultimate Driving Machine."

"The Worldwide Leader."

Even if you don't print an egotistical message in your ads, it is easy to fall into this frame of mind—and hard to maintain the humility of the "customer-is-always-right" perspective. Ask yourself if you really believe customers are always right—all customers. No matter what they do. Even if they act stupid, criticize your business unfairly, or are obviously wrong in their assertions.

Is the customer who forgets to read the instructions right when he or she breaks your product? Is the customer who stops doing business with you because of the mistaken belief that your company uses prison labor right? Is the customer who gets mad and calls you names on the telephone right? In truth, almost all employees do not really believe their customers are *always* right. They know that slogan, maybe even say it, but they cannot "walk the talk." They cannot really take this slogan as a philosophy of business, a way of life. They say things like, "Sure the customer is always right—except sometimes they don't know what they're saying." Or "Some customers are right—but we don't really need to do business with everyone." Or, "We try to do what the customer wants, unless it's too expensive." The unwritten slogan, the one that shapes our behavior in most businesses, is, "Customers are usually right, especially when they agree with us."

This is a sensible, rational interpretation of the marketing concept, and we certainly don't blame you if you agree with it. You are *our* customer, after all! But we also have a goal for you—to convince you that the customer *is* always right. And we intend to accomplish this goal by the end of the book.

The marketing concept is something you have to adopt on many levels, emotionally as well as rationally, before it can do you much good. People who have decided to act as if the customer is always right have a different approach to business. It's not that they literally chose to lose every argument with customers. Or that they think they can ask customers how to run their business. It's that they chose to *accept responsibility* for customer satisfaction. And that means they do not blame customers, but instead look within themselves and their companies whenever they fail to attract a new customer or retain an old one. This willingness to look within, to take on the blame and responsibility, is incredibly empowering. It opens up the marketing imagination, freeing you to seek new and better ways to serve customers.

The distinction between lip service and adoption of the marketing concept is a subtle one, and it is often hard to tell at first glance whether a person or company has truly adopted the marketing concept. But when push comes to shove, the distinction becomes clear. Critical events in which customers are either attracted or repelled are where we all show our true convictions—and where it is clear whether we truly believe the customer is always right.

For instance, let's say you are in charge of marketing for a credit card provider, and you discover that a small minority of customers are inactive. They just don't seem to use their cards at all. No activity for, say, the last four months. What will you do about this? The answer to this, as to all critical events in the relationships between marketers and customers, depends entirely upon whether you truly accept the marketing concept or just pay it lip service. Because what you do, how you see the situation, depends upon how you instinctively assign causality for the problem. Are customers not using the card because of something about *them,* or something about *you?*

As you might have noticed, Alex likes to collect examples of customer service, such as the letter from his local post office that was quoted above. And he happens to have a letter from a leading credit card provider in his files, received after he had stopped using the card for a few months due to some customer service problems. Here is how that company's customer service manager tackled the problem:

Dear Alexander W. Hiam:

We have noticed that you have not been using your account. We hope that this is not a sign of dissatisfaction with the service that °°°°°° has provided to you in the past.

In order to service our active accounts in the most efficient manner, we find it necessary to close the inactive credit card accounts in our files. If you have not already done so, please take a moment to destroy all credit cards and Charge-It Checks with the account number listed above.

Sincerely,

xxx xxxxxx
Customer Service Manager

FOR YOUR IMAGINATION

Whack, Whirl, Vrooom!

What do golf balls, polyurethane printer drums, and diesel engines have in common? Not much at first glance. But to the marketer, they share one overwhelmingly important characteristic. *None of them will sell unless the customer is happy.*

The growing importance of customer satisfaction in every business was brought home to us recently when we received almost simultaneous requests from the Polyurethane Manufacturers Association and Commins Engine for help in designing measures of customer satisfaction. And, in spite of the differences between these industries, the benchmark measures are very much the same. A happy customer is a happy customer, regardless of the product or service involved.

Of course, that explains the similarity between printer drums and engines. What about golf balls? The reason for that is a little more personal. Some years ago now, we were involved in extensive studies of quality and customer service for Spalding, and so when we hear the words "customer service," a little golf ball-shaped lightbulb goes off in our heads.

And you know, the golf ball is a pretty good symbol of customer service. Because winning the loyalty of a customer through the excellence of your service is a lot like playing a tough golf course. The holes are awfully small, the grass awfully wide. Even if you make a hole in one, you can lose the game unless each stroke is carefully made so as to keep you moving toward the next hole.

Customer relations are like that too. The little things count. Most of the time, you are way out there on the fairway and it is easy to lose sight of the next hole. But you *have* to keep moving toward it. And in marketing, you can only win by "securing" the next customer through the excellence of your service. How do you know if you've reached this goal?

By measuring the customer's attitude toward you. With benchmarks like the ones we suggested to our clients. Here are seven of them. As you read them, ask yourself how well you would rate, say, your health care provider, long distance telephone company, or auto manufacturer on these questions. If you are like the average consumer, you will find that the marketer you rate has not made a hole in one. In fact, odds are they are stuck in a sand trap.

Try Our "7×7" Survey for the Company of Your Choice

1 = Strongly Disagree   7 = Strongly Agree

1 2 3 4 5 6 7   I am highly satisfied with all aspects of customer service.

1 2 3 4 5 6 7   I definitely will make more purchases from this company in the future.

(continued)

1 2 3 4 5 6 7   I commonly recommend this company to other customers.

1 2 3 4 5 6 7   This company is highly responsive to customer needs.

1 2 3 4 5 6 7   This company's service is faster than typical of the industry.

1 2 3 4 5 6 7   This company's employees are helpful and cooperative.

1 2 3 4 5 6 7   This company is good at resolving problems for customers.

Their overall score = _____ out of a possible 49 points. (If score is lower than 43, you are an insecure customer who might defect before the next purchase.)

Does the author of this note and her company believe that the root causes of customer satisfaction lie within the company? Certainly not. While the author "hopes" the company's failure to retain Alex's business is "not a sign of dissatisfaction," she does not bother asking if it is. Nor does she take any steps to retain Alex's business. Instead, she instructs him to destroy his card. Once again, that little voice seems to be saying, "Wouldn't it be nice around here if we could just get rid of those pesky customers." It always does when one hasn't truly adopted the marketing concept. And the result is always customer *dis*satisfaction.

By the way, this letter illustrates another sure indicator of the "false customer orientation" problem so common in business: the use of the Royal We. The Queen of England is grammatically entitled to refer to herself as "We." But not marketers. Whenever you hear "we" in place of "I," you know that someone has unconsciously deposed the customer and made themselves and their company king instead.

QUALITY MARKETING?

Perhaps the distinction between good and poor marketing is hard for most of us to make because real customer-driven management and its results—excellent products and service—are so rare we hardly know them. Professor Peter Senge of the Massachusetts Institute of Technology's (MIT) Sloan School of Management argues that "Most Americans don't know good service. They haven't had it."[6] That's what the low and falling customer satisfaction data tell us, too. And it agrees with the finding from another in-depth study of consumer behavior (in a wide variety of industries): that only 10 percent of U.S. consumers are fully loyal to a single brand.[7]

In the 1980s, some U.S. companies learned what the marketing concept truly means by watching their Japanese rivals. The Japanese companies' passionate pursuit of customer-defined product and service quality gave them an edge over domestic competitors in the U.S. markets. Japan's enthusiastic pursuit of its country's Deming Award for quality spawned the Malcolm Baldrige National Quality Award in the United States. But the Japanese concept of quality has not remained static, as Senge explains:

Japanese firms' view of serving the customer has evolved. In the early years of total quality, the focus was on "fitness to standard," making a product reliably so that it would do what its designers intended it to do and what the firm told its customer it would do. Then came a focus on "fitness to need," understanding better what the customer wanted and then providing products that reliably met those needs. Today, leading edge firms seek to understand and meet the "latent need" of the customer—what customers might truly value but have never experienced or would never think to ask for.[8]

From fitness to standard, to fitness to need, and now to fitness to latent need, the Japanese version of the marketing concept has proved a moving target for U.S. businesses. The irony is that it all started in the United States. W. Edwards Deming, of Japan's Deming Prize, is American, but at first U.S. companies would not listen to him. Early pioneers such as Leon Bean also knew about fitness to latent need. Bean didn't invent the special Bean boot, with leather upper and rubber lower parts, because customers asked for it, but because he knew they needed a new kind of boot that gave both the comfort of leather and the waterproof quality of rubber. L.L. Bean listens well to its customers—this is what fitness to standard demands—but it goes beyond this to address customer needs in a creative manner. That's something you cannot do if you focus on your company's greatness instead of your customer's importance.

We call this drive to visualize better solutions for customers the marketing imagination, and it is as essential to the marketing concept as are good products and service and a willingness to listen and respond to customers. Fred Smith's marketing imagination created overnight parcel service. Mazda's marketing imagination inspired the successful Miata. As a Detroit executive explained to Peter Senge, "You could never produce the Mazda Miata solely from market research. It required a leap of imagination to see what the customer might want."[9] This is why Senge believes that "Most changes don't come from listening to the customer. Most major innovations come from some 'crazy people' in the organization who have an idea for something that will work and add value."[10] Thus, how a company manages innovation and how it manages all its employees becomes a part of the essence of marketing. Good marketing is not as easy as simply listening to the customer. But it may be the best way for U.S. companies to regain their leadership in marketing and management. U.S. companies are the original innovators in this area. As Paul Allaire, CEO of Xerox, put it, "We're never going to outdiscipline the Japanese on quality. To win, we need to find ways to capture the creative and innovative spirit of the American worker. That's the real organizational challenge."[11]

Also essential is the basic strategic vision a company sets for itself—its self-image. The U.S. Postal Service sees its task as moving mail around, and this it does with great gusto. But Federal Express sees its task as satisfying each and every customer, so it is far more able to take a customer complaint or problem seriously than is the Postal Service. While the U.S. Postal Service collects, but does not learn from, customer complaints through the relatively passive medium of complaint forms, Federal Express actively seeks information about problems through 2,100 customer interviews every quarter of the year.

What Federal Express has learned from its customer interviews since beginning the process in 1985 is regularly incorporated into its Service Quality Indicator, the measure by which every employee's performance is evaluated daily.[12] Because of its customer-oriented vision of itself, Federal Express is able to learn from what it hears customers say, whereas many companies do not.

To truly adopt the marketing concept, an organization must go beyond listening to its customers. It must apply its own imagination to what it hears the customers saying. But the process is slow and difficult. The process requires dramatic changes, even for companies that already stand out as leaders. Which explains why Allaire of Xerox says, "I have to change the company substantially to be more market driven."[13]

We stated that a company's basic strategic vision is relevant to its marketing concept. The reverse is true as well. This thought was presented most forcefully by Theodore Levitt in a 1960 article called "Marketing Myopia."[14] He observed that, because the railroads saw themselves as in the business of laying track instead of transporting goods and people, they passed over opportunities to profit from new technologies such as autos and trucks, airplanes, and even telephones. Thus, the railroads declined even though the demand for passenger and freight transportation grew. Similarly, because the oil companies refused to pursue natural gas, renegade executives left to start competing gas companies. Companies often miss growth opportunities by failing to define themselves in terms of the benefit they provide to customers.

As long as companies view their business creatively and from the customer's perspective, they will find opportunities to grow and prosper. According to Levitt, "Every major industry was once a growth industry. . . . In every case, the reason growth is threatened, slowed, or stopped is not because the market is saturated. It is because there has been a failure of management." He continues, "In truth, there is no such thing as a growth industry, I believe. There are only companies organized and operated to create and capitalize on growth opportunities."[15]

THE TWIN PERILS OF MARKETING MYOPIA AND MARKETING MANIA

In his 1975 retrospective commentary, Levitt observed that his 1960 article had done both good and bad. Although many companies broadened their vision most profitably—from oil company to energy company, for example—others developed what he calls "marketing mania," becoming "obsessively responsive to every fleeting whim of the customer."[16] Uncontrolled brand and line extensions, compulsive redrawing of organization charts, and riotous growth of sales and marketing departments are not the answer. The marketing concept does not call for more marketing; what it demands is better management. If a company satisfies all its customers all of the time, it will need less of those expensive, traditional ad campaigns that generally are designed to replace lost customers. But some companies fail to grasp this essential point.

This dichotomy of views leads to two interpretations of the chapter's opening quote from DuPont's CEO—"Nothing is worthwhile unless it touches the customer"—because a touch can be welcome or unwelcome. The fact that the number of telemarketers grows dramatically each year—and now numbers in the many millions—is evidence that many managers believe more touch is what the marketing concept requires. The corresponding fact that "the Direct Marketing Association has counted roughly 1,000 new state bills on telemarketing . . . about one-third of which would curb unsolicited sales calls,"[17] is strong evidence that customers do not appreciate unwanted touches. Companies need to touch, and be touched by, their customers, but the *quality* of this contact is (or ought to be) the key concern of marketing.

Steven Star, director of the Marketing Center at MIT's Sloan School, argues that this may be the central challenge of marketing. He writes, "If you think for a moment about the process of trying to practice the marketing concept carefully, you quickly see how things will necessarily go wrong."[18] The following, according to Star, summarizes how they go wrong: "No matter how specialized our media, how carefully computerized our audience data, how sophisticated our protocols of market analysis, there remain, as always, major misfits among products, audiences, messages, and media." The result is usually that for every targeted customer who welcomes the touch of a marketing program, many more "frustrated, distracted, or irritated customers" are touched more or less accidentally as an artifact of the program's implementation. (Star's article is illustrated by a cartoon of a bald-headed man on the street, surrounded by billboards and taxi and bus posters, all advertising hair sprays.)

From the company's perspective, this misfit between message and audience is a costly waste and, quite possibly, a source of consumer ill will. From the customer's perspective, it is also costly, but more because of the increasing din of misdirected marketing messages it creates than because of any tangible impact. If you believe, as Leon Bean did, that "the customer is the most important person" in your company, the last thing you want to do is shout something at customers that they don't want or need to hear.

When looked at from these multiple perspectives, marketing seems at once more challenging and more essential than it is usually thought to be. The essence of the marketing concept is difficult to grasp and even more difficult to implement. But implementing it is a practical necessity, both broadly, in how the organization defines and organizes itself, and more narrowly, in how the managers conceive of and implement specific marketing programs.

THE TOOLS OF MARKETING

Program design and implementation are constrained by the tools available to management. These tools are conventionally thought of as including the "four Ps"—product, price, place, and promotion—although, as we discuss next, the implementation of the marketing concept may require additional elements. How these elements of the marketing mix are utilized is the general issue in development of a marketing program.

Product

The focal point of the marketing mix is the product. A product includes more than a good or service that is designed, produced, and offered for sale. It includes all the planning that precedes actual production; it includes research and development; and it includes all the services that accompany the product, such as installation and maintenance. Consider videocassette recorders (VCRs). Buyers found that several steps were involved in installing and programming a VCR, and that the instruction booklets often were not much help. When Sony became aware of this problem, it began making a VCR with a set of synthesized vocal instructions that guided the user through the installation and operation procedures. This instructional mode was as much a part of the product as was the actual machine.

Price

Price is the cost, or what the buyer must give up, to receive the product. Although price usually means an amount of money, some exchanges involve the giving of goods and services by both parties. Price is not static. For example, the price of a VCR was high when introduced, but fell as competition intensified and manufacturers learned to produce machines at lower cost.

Place

Place, or distribution, involves making sure that the product is available where and when it is wanted. Marketers can choose among many ways of moving products to consumers. They may choose among different types of outlets and store locations. Distribution also involves decisions such as how much inventory to hold, how to transport goods, and where to locate warehouses. Manufacturers initially placed VCRs in retail stores that sold TVs, but now catalogs and discounters also carry VCRs.

Promotion

Promotion is perhaps the element most visible to consumers. Promotion is the broad term used to describe the entire field of sales communication—advertising, personal selling, sales promotion, and public relations. These activities result in consumer awareness of a product's existence, as well as knowledge about its unique and desirable features. In short, promotion informs and persuades, and sometimes irritates, as Steven Star observed. When VCRs were first introduced, press coverage was very important in educating consumers. Now competing manufacturers advertise to build brand image and trumpet new features, while retailers use sales promotions and in-store selling to encourage purchase.

Imagination

This is a vital tool, one that gives the marketer the power to use the other tools effectively. It takes marketing imagination to make the marketing concept work. One often has to innovate and create new ways to retain customers. If the customer doesn't seem right from a rational perspective, then it takes an act of imagination in order to *make* the customer right.

Thus imagination and creativity make up the foundations of all successful marketing; they can be found between the lines of every business success story. Take WorldCom, an innovative telephone company that offered customers a menu of telecommunications services, including long distance, local calling, and Internet services. From the customer's perspective, telephone companies are in the communications business, not the business of operating any specific type of line. Free of the marketing myopia of its competitors, WorldCom outstripped them all in revenue and profit growth, providing its investors with an average 53 percent gain in total returns each year between 1986 and 1996; which makes it the third most profitable investment of all the Fortune 1,000 during that decade.[19]

A MARKETING MIX FOR TODAY

Dick Berry, a professor from the University of Wisconsin–Madison, surveyed a sample of marketing managers, customer service managers, product managers, and senior executives to find out which marketing variables they consider to be the most important. He started with the four *P*s, breaking each into subcategories, and added an S to represent customer service elements of the marketing mix and two Cs to represent customer sensitivity and convenience. Some marketers argue that customer service deserves as much attention in planning as do the four *P*s. Fortune's 1991 special issue on the hottest ideas for the 1990s featured the idea that managers should market every product as though it is a service. According to this concept, there are no products, only services. This means, for example, that Xerox should focus on the quality of the service performed by and with its photocopiers, rather than on the machine itself.

Berry analyzed his results to identify the elements of the marketing mix that managers currently consider most important and ranked them by importance. The three new items on this list—the S and two Cs—as well as the traditional four *P*s all have to do with how the company responds to and serves its customers. Below are the seven elements of the marketing mix, as ranked in Berry's study from most to least important:[20]

1. Customer sensitivity—Employee attitude, customer treatment, and response to customers.
2. Product—Product quality, reliability, and features.
3. Customer convenience—Availability to the customer, customer convenience, and selling.
4. Service—Postsale service, presale service, and customer convenience in obtaining service.
5. Price—Price charged, pricing terms, and pricing offers.
6. Place—Provider accessibility, provider facilities, pricing terms, and availability to customer.
7. Promotion—Advertising, publicity, selling, presale services, and pricing offers.

Note that Berry's respondents ranked customer sensitivity—a variable that was not even considered in the traditional four *P*s structure—as the most important variable in the marketing mix. To manage sensitivity to customers, the marketer needs to manage the attitudes of all employees whose work affects the customers. Berry's survey results expand our vision of what a marketing program consists of: It must now involve almost everyone in the business. It takes everyone to make sure the customer *feels* right. The additional items—the two Cs and the S—need to pervade a company's use of the traditional four *P*s in a way that is not traditional in U.S. business. Just as imagination is critical to the effective use of the four *P*s, so too is this sensitivity to the customer perspective. Marketing imagination and customer sensitivity are two sides of the same coin.

INFORMATION TO FUEL THE MARKETING IMAGINATION

We have now seen what makes up the practice of marketing. Let's look at yet another perspective, one that boils all this down to the essence of marketing. To obtain that customer sensitivity that Professor Berry says in so critical to marketing, the marketer needs to have information. Renowned guru Peter Drucker takes it a step further when he says that information is any firm's greatest asset. From a marketing perspective, information gathering, assembling, and disseminating is at the crux of effective marketing. Good marketing begins with knowledge that the marketing function within the organization accumulates and uses information to plan the activities of marketing, the four *P*s. This is the overall theme of Chapters 2 through 8 that you will be reading next.

What is done with this information? Marketers lay their plans for executing the four *P*s based on this information. The product must conform to the wants and desires of the customer, it must be priced to meet the value seen by the customer, it must be located in the right place as dictated by the customer, and be promoted to reflect the match between what the customer is looking for and what the product offers. And if imagination is involved, it too can rest on the information the marketer accumulates.

EXHIBIT 1.2.   The essence of marketing.

Each of these four *P*s activities really is an outflow of information from the organization. Each of these activities is sensed by the market and interpreted . . . or perceived . . . in some way. In short, this is information emanating from the marketer. The product represents value from its form, its shape . . . from its smell and taste, perhaps. The price is information about the value embedded in the product. Distribution, or place, informs the customer about the availability of the product. And promotion by its very nature is information transferred. So in this way, the execution of marketing represents information out from the firm. (See Exhibit 1.2 on page 20.) Information, then, is the essence of marketing . . . information is at the root of preparation and planning and also of the implementation of marketing activities. Chapters 9 through 12 reflect the information outflow in the process of marketing.

The decisions that make up the marketing mix, when implemented, are the basis for providing satisfaction to consumers in a particular market segment. Satisfaction comes from an exchange. But an exchange takes place only when each party will receive greater satisfaction from what is received than from what is given up. In other words, the price paid by the buyer must be equal to or less than the total satisfaction obtainable from the bundle of benefits received. If the buyer perceives the price to be greater than the benefits received, the value of those benefits is not "worth" the cost and the exchange will not happen.

Marketers can manipulate price, product, place, or promotion. They can lower the price (or make it appear lower; we will discuss psychological pricing later) and/or increase the degree of satisfaction offered (through better goods and services, more convenient distribution, and/or more effective promotion). They can also stimulate exchanges through advertising, promotions, and other marketing techniques. And, perhaps most important, they can apply their marketing imagination and customer sensitivity to the search for new, innovative offerings for their customers.

There are two ways to look at this exchange. The most obvious and common view is distributive: The buyer and seller cut up a pie, and each tries to get a bigger piece. In this approach, the company worries about recovering its costs plus a decent margin, while the customer tries to get the best price possible. The other view tries to give both parties more by making the pie bigger. Marketing imagination and constant improvement on the part of the seller engender more commitment and trust in the buyer by adding value beyond what was expected. If any single perspective can be said to capture the essence of marketing, this is it.

Paul Allaire of Xerox has said, "If we do what's right for the customer, our market share and return on assets will take care of themselves."[21] This is an unusual statement in that it reflects a remarkable faith in the marketing concept. Many CEOs assume that the marketing department will take care of customers, and that their own job is to take care of the bottom line. But managers with Allaire's insight see everything differently. For example, Henry Ford, speaking long before the fall of Detroit said, "We have never considered any costs as fixed. Therefore, we first reduce the price to the point where we believe more sales will result. Then we go ahead and try to make the prices. We do not bother about costs. The new price forces the costs down."[22]

The "don't bother about prices" view starts with a desirable price and believing (it has to be a matter of faith) that the company can learn to make the desired product for that price. Perhaps the essence of marketing is that simple—attack everything backward, from the customer's perspective instead of the company's, and have faith that you can rise to the challenges this perspective creates. Although Ford Motors rose to greatness on the strength of this perspective, the vision was eventually lost, allowing foreign auto makers to champion the consumer's cause. Now Ford is struggling to regain the vision—and its status—through a grueling total quality program. Perhaps the essence of marketing is also that difficult, for it is easy to lose this vision, to come down with marketing myopia, and to spend all one's time squinting at accounting reports instead of listening and imagining on behalf of the customer. Have you contracted marketing myopia? You'll know by how you answer the question, "Is the customer *really* always right?"

2 MARKETING AND STRATEGY

Using Tested Concepts and New Ideas for Marketing Strategy

If the purpose of strategy is to gain competitive advantage, then by implication theories of strategy should be continually in flux. Any new insight that obtains wide currency . . . loses value in providing additional competitive advantage . . . This self-destructive aspect of strategic insight . . . has received limited attention, as has the attendant need to be continually innovative and creative.

—Paul Schoemaker,
Graduate School of Business.
University of Chicago[1]

If there's a hell for planners, over the portal will be carved the term "cash cow."

—Stephen Hardis,
Vice President of Planning,
Eaton Corporation[2]

If theories of strategic planning should be "continually in flux," as Paul Schoemaker observes in the first of our opening quotes, then all is well with the world. Because there cannot be any field more turbulent or unstable in the entire management panoply than strategic planning and its alter ego, marketing planning.

"Strategic planning is dead; long live strategic planning!" seems like an appropriate way to begin this chapter, for it is necessary both to mark the passing of the old strategic planning and to note the exciting emergence of entirely new approaches, much as the succession of kings was once heralded. But the problem is, nobody seems quite sure who the rightful heir to the throne will be.

Since its birth in the 1950s and 1960s, strategic planning reigned by giving managers a new and exciting set of more marketing-oriented tools for analysis, planning, and control. Innovators such as the Boston Consulting Group and General Electric discovered the wisdom of identifying opportunities based on market analysis rather than solely on financial analysis, and their philosophy and techniques spread rapidly throughout the 1970s and into the 1980s. But strategic planning's growth stalled in the 1980s, with many companies abandoning their large planning staffs and forsaking more complex analytical methods and planning processes, and by the beginning of the 1990s, it was moribund. When Gary Reiner of the Boston Consulting Group wrote in 1989 that "planning is passe," it was clear that a succession was imminent.[3] The problem was that the old king had left no legitimate offspring, so managers must find their own. They face the daunting task of planning in the face of great uncertainty and rapid change, and without any simple prescriptions guaranteed to do the trick. As Michael Porter of the Harvard Business School sees it, "The state of practice in this area is very primitive."[4]

What has replaced the orderly strategic planning cycles of the 1980s? The experts offer many answers, but no single approach has been sufficiently successful to rein in peace for very long. David Aaker of the Haas School of Business at U.C. Berkeley believes that strategic market management displaced strategic planning in the mid-1980s because "the planning cycle is inadequate to deal with the rapid rate of change that can occur in a firm's external environment." And he characterizes this new market-driven approach to strategy as being highly responsive to the "strategic surprises and fast-developing threats" of the modern marketplace.[5]

Strategic market management is like a new, faster, and more flexible strategic planning in that it encourages "real-time" response to external changes, rather than tying an organization's rate of change to its annual planning cycle. In theory, at least, this rapid-response approach to strategy should keep businesses on or above the pace of change in their markets, allowing them to anticipate, even lead change.

But the most popular form of business strategy in the 1990s is the massive "restructuring" that is generally accompanied by a major downsizing and a closing of facilities and/or sell-off of subsidiaries or brands. The daily financial news should provide you with fresh examples whenever you read this chapter. Here's just one typical example from *The Wall Street Journal* on the day we wrote this paragraph:

> Tool and hardware maker Stanley Works swung to a second-quarter loss because of a charge for a restructuring program that includes closing 53 of its 123 plants and eliminating about 4,500 jobs, or 24 percent of the company's workforce.[6]

The popularity of this sort of massive restructuring, with its deep cuts of product lines, divisions, facilities, and people, is the strongest possible evidence that strategic planning as practiced today is unable to anticipate and prepare for change. If companies grew and changed along with their markets, they would never get so profoundly out of alignment as to necessitate closing a third of their plants or firing a fourth of their people.

The failure of formal planning processes to anticipate important changes and align the organization with them in advance led Henry Mintzberg, a strategy expert from McGill University, to title his major review of the field *The Rise and Fall of Strategic Planning*. The king is dead. Long live the new king . . . whoever he may be!

THE 1980S: A TURNING POINT FOR MARKETING AND STRATEGY

If any single factor can be blamed for the death of strategic planning, it must be the failure of the U.S. economy to compete globally during the 1980s. This economic bottleneck in the United States forced a reexamination of every aspect of business management. And even though the economy rebounded in the 1990s, that examination revealed too many warts for anyone to want to return to business as usual. The failure of conventional strategies and management methods became painfully obvious in the 1980s as the trade imbalance in categories such as autos, machine tools, consumer electronics, semiconductors, and textiles took a nasty turn for the worse on the economist's charts. A report from MIT's Commission on Industrial Productivity summed up management's initial response to the problem:

> The decline of the U.S. economy puzzles most Americans. The qualities and talents that gave rise to the dynamism of the postwar years must surely be present still in the national character, and yet American industry seems to have lost much of its vigor. In looking for ways to reverse the decline, it is only natural to turn to the methods that succeeded in the golden years of growth and innovation. Many business managers have adopted just this strategy. The results, unfortunately, are rather like those of a man who keeps striking the same match because it worked fine the first time.[7]

This failure to measure up to global competition left the people at Xerox looking through their pockets for another book of matches. Xerox's story is an excellent illustration of what is happening to planning in U.S. businesses at this critical turning point in history. In 1974, Xerox had a stunning 86 percent world market share for photocopiers. What could possibly go wrong? As discussed shortly, conventional planning models assume that strength and profits flow from strong market shares. But as new competitors, such as Ricoh and Canon, entered the market, Xerox fell back, all the way to a 17 percent market share in 1984.[8] If strategic planning really was king, Xerox's managers would have been beheaded! The company began to climb back out of its hole in the latter half of the 1980s, regaining lost share and improving quality. Along the way, Xerox invented new ways of planning and implementing strategy, and adopted many of the best techniques used by its Japanese competitors. We'll start with a quick review of the planning models that led companies such as Xerox into so much trouble.

It is easy to dismiss the old approach to planning as worthless, but this is not fair. Managers today cannot ignore the old wisdom, but they also cannot rely on it to provide competitive advantage. One must know yesterday's techniques to play the game, and must pioneer tomorrow's techniques to win it. One must realize that the changing environment requires new tools, and the old tools by nature lose their edge when everyone learns to use them. As this chapter's opening quote suggests, there is a sort of arms race in strategy, with the advantage going to the innovators. But, although "smart missiles" may now carry the day, it would still be folly to enter the battlefield without a rifle. Business strategy is similar: Today's planners must master both the old and the new. (And then, most likely, invent something of their own anyway. But more on that later!)

STRATEGIES AND TACTICS: THE CORNERSTONES OF CONVENTIONAL PLANNING

Strategy is conventionally thought of as the overall game plan or blueprint that guides the organization toward achieving its objectives. Tactics are the detailed, individual activities that the organization undertakes to carry out the strategy. They specify how the elements of the marketing mix—the four *P*s discussed in Chapter 1—will be allocated, and they allocate manufacturing, capital, people, and other resources as needed.

With the help of a strategic plan, members of the organization can develop tactical plans that are much more detailed than the strategic plan. A written plan permits others to evaluate the reasoning and assumptions that underlie the firm's objectives. The plan helps to coordinate the activities that must be implemented to carry out the plan. It also serves as a control device: Actual results can be compared with the intended results outlined in the plan, and adjustments can be made if necessary. This formal view of the plan has not been entirely abandoned, but managers today are more likely to see vision or mission as driving the company, above strategy in the strategy-tactics hierarchy. They also may allow more leeway for employees than formal tactics and controls once did.

Marketing plays an important role in the firm's strategic plan by providing specific information about the firm's current market position and its opportunities for future market positions. Marketing also participates in the organization's planning process by developing specific strategies and tactics for products, customers, distribution channels, and the like. These will be incorporated in varying degrees into the organization's formal strategic plan, and will also form a stand-alone marketing plan to be followed by people in sales, product development, and other functions.

The process of strategic planning rests on assumptions held by the planner. Assumptions concerning expected responses to marketing actions will shape the marketing strategy and tactics. Assessment of the outcomes allows the planner to validate those assumptions or create new ones. The importance of sound assumptions cannot be overemphasized.

Feedback provides the basis for evaluating and revising assumptions. Learning by feedback comes through experiencing the plan-execution-feedback process illustrated in Exhibit 2.1.

EXHIBIT 2.1.   Learning through feedback at American Express.

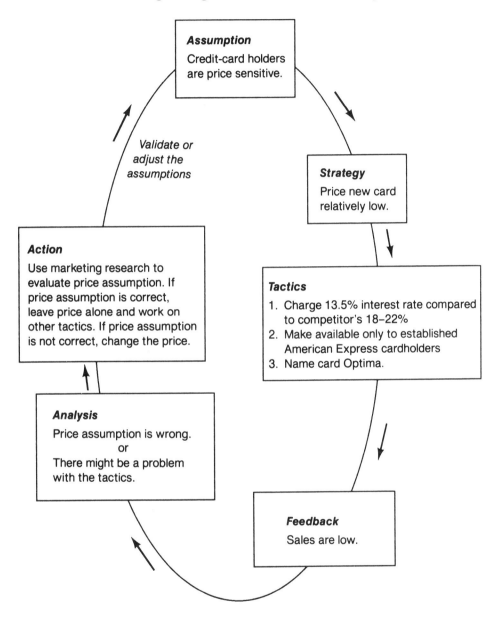

In the top-down approach, which was once the norm for most companies, the task of charting an overall strategy for an organization rests mainly with top management. That strategy then guides the decision making of managers at each organizational level. Many firms now employ bottom-up planning, in which plans developed at the lower levels of the organization are blended into a master strategic plan. Such a plan may turn out to be more marketing oriented than a plan formulated by the top-down method, mostly because it is created by those in daily touch with the customers, the competitors, and the realities of operation. As a *Fortune* article pointed out, the strategic watchwords for the first half of the 1990s were "focus and flexibility." Focus means determining what you do best and building on it. It originates at the top. Flexibility means drafting several possible scenarios for the future so the organization can be ready to explore opportunities as they arise without having to shoot from the hip, and it also means giving the bottom enough freedom to be truly flexible.[9]

THE STRATEGIC MARKET PLANNING PROCESS

The strategic planning process traditionally starts with the setting of objectives for the organization as a whole and continues with the development of marketing goals that reflect those objectives. Next, the strategic planner conducts the situation analysis, beginning with an in-depth look at the environmental trends that will affect the organization. The planner can be said to be looking outward through a "strategic window," viewing the present and predicting the future. Then the planner looks inward through the strategic window to analyze the organization's strengths and weaknesses. A key purpose of this step is to assess the firm's distinctive competencies, that is, what it can do better than other firms.

These two steps, external and internal analysis, are the cornerstones of traditional strategic market planning. They provide the information base from which the rest of the process follows—at least in a top-down approach to planning, which is what the traditional model entails. The situation analysis may also lead to adjustments to inappropriate corporate or marketing objectives. (This remains true today, although the nature of the analysis is changing rapidly.)

After completing these two fact-finding steps, the planner generates alternative plans or strategic options. The planner then chooses the option or set of options that best matches each market opportunity with the strengths of the organization. This is a crucial step because the organization's distinctive competencies may be only occasionally and briefly aligned with those required by a dynamic external environment. Strategic planners must be ready to seize upon such opportunities as they arise. In the rest of this chapter, we will present information on how each of these steps in market planning is traditionally performed—along with ideas about how they are changing and how they need to continue to change in order to keep strategies relevant and vital.

DRIVERS OF STRATEGY: VISION, MISSION, AND OBJECTIVES

Who are we and why are we here? Such questions may baffle philosophers for centuries, but businesses and their employees don't have the luxury of debating them forever. In business, we must resolve the fundamental questions, establish their operating values and principles and seize upon a mission. Otherwise we cannot get around to the urgent necessity to *do* something. As Will Rogers once said, "Even if you're on the right track, you'll get run over if you just sit there."

The well-springs of marketing strategy are at the top of the organization, where the senior executives are expected to earn their bloated paychecks by establishing a bold, profitable vision and mission.

When Howard Schultz of Starbucks says, "We will dominate every place coffee is sold," he is articulating a mission that his people can readily translate into marketing strategies.[10] With this mission in mind, it is obvious, for example, that the Starbucks brand of coffee must be marketed in grocery stores, not just through the Starbucks chain of stores.

From the corporate mission, the organization (in conventional planning) is supposed to develop a set of objectives that will direct it over a 3- to 5-year period. These objectives are generally stated in terms of sales growth, market share improvement, profits, innovation, acquisitions, and risk reduction. (In the new strategic planning, however, the validity of long-term forecasts and plans is no longer taken for granted; the environment changes too rapidly. More on that in a moment.)

From general corporate objectives flow more specific marketing goals. These goals may focus on overall sales increases, but usually they are somewhat more detailed, calling for sales increases by product class, geographic region, or type of customer. It is generally assumed that market share improvement translates into higher sales volume, and higher volume means lower production costs and higher profits. Thus, marketing goals are often expressed in terms of improvement in market share, or the percentage of the total market served by the company. Market share is the chief measure of how well an organization is doing relative to its competitors.

Strategic market planning takes its direction from the overall organizational goals. Although we often think of an organization as simply setting targets for sales, profits, return on investment, and the like, organizations usually have broader, less measurable objectives. An organization is, or ought to be, guided by the invisible hand of its purpose or mission. In this sense, the mission of computer companies is to provide information, and that of telephone companies is to facilitate communication. Rather than considering itself a copier company, Xerox sees itself as an "office of the future" company. Some organizations have even more abstract missions: Consulting firms can be seen as providing education, museums as preserving a cultural heritage, and so on. These missions guide the organization's marketing efforts and shape its strategies and plans.

The corporate mission depends on how the organization defines its business. That definition is based on the answers to two questions: "What business are we in?" and "What business should we be in?"

Sometimes too broad a business definition can create problems for an organization. For example, Levi Strauss, a leader in the apparel industry, added many new lines throughout the 1970s, including sportswear, youth wear, and ski clothes. In a 1979 talk to securities analysts, the company's president stated that Levi Strauss should be looked upon "as a consumer-products company that just happens to be in the garment business." As one worried analyst told *Fortune,* "If they ever really start to believe that, it's trouble." Such a broad business definition would allow the company to add a whole range of products with which it has no marketing experience—cereals, automobiles, detergents, watches, and so on.[11]

Although it did not take such a wildly divergent approach, Levi Strauss did move into higher priced, more fashion-oriented lines. And the skeptical analyst apparently was correct. The period from 1980 to 1982 produced a 10 percent drop in sales for Levi Strauss and a 76 percent plunge in net income. In 1982, the company eliminated many of its upscale product lines and returned to its emphasis on mid-priced, middle-class-oriented apparel, especially its well-known jeans. Its president then told *BusinessWeek,* "We've realized that just putting Levi's name on something isn't enough to gain instant marketing acceptance."[12] Now it sees itself as an "adaptable" company, able to take advantage of opportunities to which its distinctive competencies are applicable. For example, with the apparent emergence of a global generation of teens with similar tastes and values, Levi Strauss has been quick to try its hand at global marketing. It sells a 1960s style across the planet, and it is even gaining popularity in the United States.[13]

The company's product mix is now somewhere between the narrow jeans-only strategy of its early years and the unfocused consumer-products focus of the early 1980s. New products generally have some tie-in with the jeans identity and market, meaning that it makes sense to consumers for Levi Strauss to sell them. The current star of its product line illustrates this point. Dockers is a line of casual slacks for men, made from a cotton twill that is softer and more comfortable than denim. It is targeted at aging baby boomers, the same customers who made jeans a runaway success in the 1960s and 1970s. According to Alan Millstein, editor of *Fashion Network Report,* "Levi Strauss really understood the forty-something generation," who "have been living off beer, pretzels, and microwave popcorn. Their waistlines have expanded . . . and they can't fit into their jeans."[14] But they can fit into Dockers, and the success of this product fueled a surge in Levi Strauss' income in 1991 and laid the foundations for Levi Strauss' expansion into the growing market for casual office clothes during the mid-to-late 1990s.

Three Secrets of Strategic Success: Focus, Focus, and Focus

The Levi Strauss story teaches another important strategic lesson—the importance of focus. And focus. And focus! It is hard enough in a competitive market to do even one thing really well, well enough that you attract and retain customers better than competitors. When companies have a clear focus, they are trying to do one thing well, which at least gives them a fighting chance. As soon as their mission begins to sprout "ands," they are at risk of doing nothing well. That is certainly a point Andrew Grove, president and CEO of Intel Corporation, takes to heart. He argues that it takes every erg of energy in your organization to do a good job pursuing one strategic aim, especially in the face of aggressive and competent competition. Without exquisite focus, the resources and energy of the organization will be spread a mile wide—and an inch deep. If you're wrong, you will fail. But most companies don't fail because they are wrong; most fail because they don't commit themselves. They fritter away their momentum and their valuable resources while attempting to make a decision. The great danger is standing still.[15]

Do You Know Your Way?

The focus principle (or should we call it the "focus-focus-focus principle"?) is close cousin to the "don't-get-lost" principle of marketing strategy. Sure, you should always try to give customers what they want and need—but within your abilities. If you allow the search for hot new marketing ideas to take you too far from your core competencies, you can lose your focus and wander in the strategic desert. Getting lost is a sure-fire way to lose your focus.

Despite the wisdom of customer-oriented market definitions, it can be very dangerous to move into unfamiliar territory, as Anheuser-Busch discovered along with Levi Strauss in the 1980s. Anheuser-Busch's management felt that its single-minded emphasis on the domestic beer business did not give it any way to use the excess cash it generated. As a result, the company redefined itself as a global food and beverage business and introduced the premium-priced Eagle brand of pretzels, corn curls, tortilla chips, and nuts. It also increased emphasis on its Dewey Stevens, a diet wine cooler; low-alcohol LA; and soda and bottled waters. The company's focus was on making better use of the firm's distinctive competency in beer distribution and developing new products for its existing markets.

By 1988, the company was retrenching heavily, having put up for sale its three bottled water products and its California winery. "The beer guys weren't wine or water guys," said a former company executive. The company "didn't know how to sell the stuff properly."[16] And in the wine cooler market, where all products are already perceived as "light," Anheuser-Busch could not establish a foothold. Perhaps the greatest trouble spot, however, rested with the company's Eagle brand of snacks. On top of tremendous capital expense for the start-up, Eagle managed to lose several million dollars each year following its inception.

A more recent example is provided by Starbucks Coffee Company, which made fast work of the coffee market by creating the largest chain of cafes in the United States during the 1990s. As this book heads for the printer, Starbucks is going in a new direction—the supermarket shelves. Procter & Gamble (P&G) Company's Folgers brand is the leader in supermarket sales of coffee beans, followed by Kraft Foods' Maxwell House. But not for long in the view of Starbucks' president Howard Schultz. He too sees the marketing implications of his mission, which says Starbucks has to be the dominant force in the coffee business.[17]

Is Starbucks making a classic marketing blunder? Will it lose its way in the battle for supermarket shelves—as many contenders have over the years? Is this new battleground too different from the old one, a dangerous loss of focus? Or is Schultz right that the company can beat out P&G and Kraft at their own game because of the growing value of the Starbucks' brand name? Only time will tell—but we are willing to guess. We bet you won't find Starbucks dominating shelf space or register receipts at the average grocery store in the year 2000. And we suspect the expansion of its chain of cafes may slow as management diverts attention to the grocery store battle instead. But we have to hedge this bet with the comment that some of the greatest strategic breakthroughs sounded far more hair-brained than this strategy does at inception—you can never be sure. Starbucks just might pull off a coup in the coffee aisle. But we will be surprised if they do!

The many cases in which marketers got burned by overextending lead us to sound a cautionary note—it can be hubris to pursue unfamiliar products and markets, even if the customer demand is clearly there. There appear to be practical constraints on how far afield a company should go in pursuit of the marketing concept. However, to be fair, a single-minded focus on a firm's familiar products and technology also can land it in big trouble. Remember Levitt's marketing myopia described in Chapter 1: When cars and trucks came along, railroad companies ignored them—and entered a long, slow decline. Why? Because they saw themselves as specializing in laying track rather than in transporting people and freight.

Maybe it would be as bad a mistake for Starbucks to see itself in the coffee store business instead of the coffee business. Are they really in the *restaurant* business? (Hmm. Got to think about that one.) There is often a fine line between the sort of marketing myopia that doomed the railroads and the overconfidence of an Anheuser-Busch (or Starbucks). The success of Levi's Dockers illustrates the importance of expansion that *makes sense to the customers.* Another product line for established customers is a safer bet than something totally new to the company, and smart strategists pursue the safe bets whenever there are any to be found.

STRATEGY AS A FOCUS RATHER THAN A PLAN

One reason strategic planning will never die is that without a strategy of *some* sort, there can be no clear focus. Many organizations are resuscitating strategic planning, in spite of their inability to see very far into their futures. But the role of strategic planning is fundamentally different. Let's look at this interesting transition.

In most industries today, events are so fast-paced and unpredictable that nobody can write a plan or create a forecast worth the paper its printed on. H. Igor Ansoff has documented this change in an extensive series of studies. Ansoff's formal title is Distinguished Professor of Strategic Management at the United States University in San Diego—but many people in the marketing field refer to him as "the father of strategic planning" because of his important work in the development of this field. In recent years, his work has provided perhaps the strongest documentation that many of the conventional planning methods are antiquated. Most striking is his measurement of what he terms the turbulence level of a business's external environment. Here is Ansoff's turbulence scale:

Turbulence Level	Name	Description
1	Repetitive	No change
2	Expanding	Slow incremental change
3	Changing	Fast incremental change
4	Discontinuous	Discontinuous, predictable change
5	Surprising	Discontinuous, unpredictable change

Further, he has demonstrated in a range of studies that "a company's profitability is optimized when a company's strategy and management capability both match the turbulence in the company's environment."[18] This means, for example, that if your organization used to face a turbulence level of 3 but now faces a level 4.5 environment—a transition typical of most industries over the last two decades—then the old strategies and management approaches will lead to failure today just as surely as they led to success yesterday. In the high-turbulence environments most businesses now face, Ansoff finds that entrepreneurial and creative strategies work, while reactive and anticipatory strategies do not. Yet conventional planning cycles, in which data is gathered, numbers crunched, forecasts generated, and long-term strategies formulated, are generally reactive or at best anticipatory. Not entrepreneurial, and rarely creative.

Which is why, as we observed earlier, formal planning processes were downsized almost out of existence in many companies. And why Tom Peters, that most popular of management gurus, wrote that "madness *is* afoot" and advised managers that, in order to thrive on the chaos around them, they should abandon their long-range strategic plan in exchange for "a strategic mind-set" so as to be able to foster "internal stability in order to encourage the pursuit of constant change."[19] In other words, strategic planning as usual is dead.

But strategic planning is experiencing something of a rebirth in the late 1990s. (As Mark Twain once said, "The reports of my death are greatly exaggerated.") Perhaps the most striking symbol of this rebirth is the rising stature of strategic planning in what was supposed to be its replacement—total quality management. And this is seen nowhere more clearly than in the annual judging criteria for the Malcolm Baldrige National Quality Award. These criteria are modified every year in an effort to provide a better standard for the management processes of U.S. firms, and lately strategic planning has emerged as a key component of the criteria. According to Vicki Spagnol, a member of the award's board of examiners, "In recent years, Category 2, Strategic Planning, has undergone significant evolution, which has expanded its scope and made it more central to the overall criteria." She summarizes the change as follows, "The scope of planning was broadened from planning for quality and operational improvements to developing an overall business strategy. Greater emphasis was also placed on translating strategy into action-oriented 'key business drivers,' which could be used to deploy strategy throughout the organization."[20] Why bring strategic planning out of moth balls, especially when many people argue it is what led to the *need* for new approaches like total quality management and reengineering in the first place? Because, in Spagnol's words, "The faster the rate of change, the more important it is to understand the dynamics of the marketplace and to have a strategy that will enable an organization to outperform its competition over the long haul." Fast change makes a good strategy more essential than ever. But—and here is the paradox—fast change (and the high turbulence with which it is typically associated) makes coming up with a good long-term strategy almost impossible. Whatever knowledge base the strategy rests on will be antiquated by new events before the implementation is half-way complete. How do you resolve this paradox—this great need for good strategy in conditions which make it terribly hard to design good strategy?

The most successful answer—and the key to strategic planning's rebirth—seems to be to use strategy as a source of focus and direction, not as a blueprint. Listen to Steve Roemereman, vice president and strategy manager of Texas Instruments' Defense Systems & Electronics business (which won the Baldrige Award in 1992):

> Most of those companies that had a great decade did it not by planning out forty great quarters. They had a strategic plan, and then they executed forty great quarters more or less along the lines of the plan. Their people knew where the company was going, and the shared knowledge made it easier to get good quarterly performance.[21]

In other words, the strategic plan gave everyone a common focus, a vision of where the company wanted to go. And then everyone did whatever seemed necessary to get there. The role of this plan, then, is to provide focus rather than direction, to give a common purpose rather than to give specific instructions. The entrepreneurial, creative elements aren't in the plan. They have to be provided by the people who implement it. Nobody can forecast those. But without some agreement on where the entrepreneurship and creativity is supposed to take you, everyone would pull in different directions.

In order for strategic plans to perform this focusing role effectively, everyone must have what is coming to be called a *line of sight,* which is a clear view of the connections between their own work and the big picture of the organization's strategy. Without it, they cannot improvise without losing the tune. The American Society for Training and Development reported that the goal alignment provided by such lines of sight "has a significant impact on employee performance" because it "enables employees to see how their work helps the company succeed."[22] Thus strategy still has a vital role—perhaps an even more vital role—because in turbulent markets it may be the only constant, the only clear beacon to aim for, amid the chaos.

Market Share as a Strategic Goal

A great many marketing missions and objectives rest on the assumption that a dominant share of your market is a sure-fire recipe for success. Think again about the Starbucks mission—"to dominate every place coffee is sold." This is in fact a market share objective, and it makes sense only if there is some payoff for holding a dominant share of markets.

Because of the importance of assumptions about market share, a group of professors with the Strategic Planning Institute (SPI) has assembled a highly detailed database of information on the performance of thousands of individual businesses and business units over four years or more. It tracks the standard financial measures, plus many of the marketing and strategy variables thought to drive financial performance. In this Profit Impact of Marketing Strategy (PIMS) database, two striking trends appear. First, on average, market share and return on investment (ROI) vary together. A smaller share is typically associated with lower ROI, and vice versa. In fact, the relationship is virtually a straight line, varying from an average ROI of 11 percent for businesses with market shares of 10 percent or less, up to an ROI of 40 percent for businesses with shares of 50 percent or more. Professors Buzzell and Gale write that:

> The primary reason for the market share–profitability linkage, apart from the connection with relative quality, is that larger share businesses benefit from scale economies. They simply have lower per-unit costs than their smaller competitors. These cost advantages are typically much smaller than those once claimed by overenthusiastic proponents of "experience curve pricing strategies," but they are nevertheless substantial and are directly reflected in higher profit margins.[23]

Second, as their brief aside about quality hinted, the data also show a clear relationship between quality relative to competitors, as perceived by customers, and both market share and ROI. The data support the arguments of quality advocates that there does not need to be a trade-off between quality and cost. Higher quality seems to be associated with higher share and lower costs (thus higher margins and ROI) in actual operating data from thousands of companies.

So what happened to Xerox? If firms gain 3.5 points of ROI for every 10 points of market share on average, as the PIMS database indicates, Xerox's 86 percent share in 1974 should have given it a greater than 25 percent lead in ROI over its closest competitors. How could anyone possibly afford to challenge Xerox? This is exactly what its management assumed, and what many leaders in other industries assumed as well. (The U.S. auto industry is a classic example.) But this assumption ignores the impact of quality. Higher profits do not guarantee dominance—it depends on how you spend them! Xerox did not use its cost advantage to maintain its leadership in quality and product superiority, and customers do not share planners' regard for market position.

Market share represents customers' past purchases, not their future purchases—something planners tend to overlook—and if a better product comes along, future purchases will not remain consistent with past purchases. Market share is a good objective for management, but it is not an impenetrable shield against competitors, as Xerox learned.

THE SITUATION ANALYSIS

In the next step of strategic planning—the situation analysis—planners traditionally analyze information about the firm's environment, especially its customers and competitors. This environmental scanning involves looking at the present state of the environment and forecasting trends in its various aspects. Planners also look inward and analyze their organization's strengths and weaknesses. They assess not only tangible, observable resources, but also intangible resources, such as the skills of personnel and the company's image. The focus then shifts to matching the opportunities that exist in the environment with the firm's particular strengths. The outcome of this analysis is an understanding of how to take advantage of the opportunities by using the distinctive competencies of the organization. It may also require some revision of previously set goals. This crucial step in the strategic market planning process may utilize analytical tools such as the Boston Consulting Group's growth-share matrix, which will be discussed shortly. It also draws on an organization's ongoing efforts to monitor its business environment.

Environmental Scanning

A navigator would not plot a course without first establishing the ship's position and examining a chart with care. Nor should a manager develop strategy without examining the environment. As a practical matter, it is essential to simultaneously monitor the business environment and develop and refine strategy on an ongoing basis.

But what do we mean by the business environment? In the world of strategic planning, this term encompasses any and all important events—and even undercurrents that might lead to future events—in a wide range of areas. Classically, an environmental scan looks for both opportunities and threats, and does so in the following areas:

- The social/cultural environment, including the beliefs, values, and norms of behavior that are learned and shared by people in the business's environment.

- The competitive environment, including changes and objectives at established competitors, plus any and all new competitive threats from entrepreneurs, foreign companies expanding into the market, and so forth.

- The technological environment, including any and all new technologies that might impact the products and/or processes of the industry or related industries.

- The economic environment, including any trends that might affect the company directly, plus all that affect consumers and their spending patters.

- The political/legal environment, including any legislation that might alter the rules of the game in the firm's industry and markets. (Anyone in health care right now is used to worrying about this factor!)

- The natural environment, including the natural resources the business and its customers depend on, any surprises the weather may dish up, and issues concerning the firm's environmental impact and how to minimize it.

As the breadth of this list makes clear, any full-blown situational analysis must cover a broad range of issues. It is a demanding research project. And yet, even when done carefully and thoroughly, such scanning may fail to reveal the most important threats and opportunities in today's highly turbulent business environments. The most exciting and important new directions are often difficult to tease out of the mass of data and piles of reports. Managers and marketers must learn to listen for weak signals as well as strong ones. And, increasingly, the eyes, ears, and instincts of the entire organization are required to find and amplify these weak signals in time for appropriate action. That is why Henry Mintzberg refers to modern strategies as "emergent." They may spring up, like weeds, from unexpected sources anywhere in the organization, or even beyond its doors in the network of suppliers and distributors surrounding it. Scanning can no longer be left to a centralized planning staff—it is so important that everyone needs to be involved.

The Organization—Looking Inside the Strategic Window

Once the external environment has been analyzed, planners traditionally examine the firm's resources, both tangible and, often more important, intangible. Planners should thoroughly review the tangibles—the firm's financial resources, production and distribution systems, and the like. They also should analyze intangible resources, such as the company's image and culture, the creative and administrative talent of its personnel, employee attitudes toward the company, and the company's vulnerability to competition. These intangibles, though difficult to assess, can make the difference between success and failure.

Does Starbucks have the core competencies and financial deep pockets needed to go head to head with leading consumer brand marketers in a battle for grocery store market share? We don't know for sure, but if we had to make the decision, we would start with a brutally honest examination of the organization itself.

PORTFOLIO ANALYSIS: IS IT READY FOR A REBIRTH?

Perhaps no company has contributed more to the "old" strategic market planning than General Electric (GE). In the 1970s, GE reorganized its forty-eight divisions and nine product lines into strategic business units (SBUs). Each SBU consists of one or more products, brands, company divisions, or market segments that have something in common, such as the same distribution system, similar customers, or the same basic technology. At the same time, each SBU has its own mission, its own distinct set of competitors, and its own strategic plan. About 20 percent of the largest manufacturing firms in the United States have adopted the SBU system. Recently, for example, Campbell's Soup Company established eight SBUs: soups, beverages, pet foods, frozen foods, fresh produce, main meals, grocery, and food service. The SBU structure's great merit is that it defines the company according to the markets it serves—one SBU per market. Smaller companies are often focused on a single market, but larger ones easily lose their marketing orientation without the SBU structure to force it.

The Boston Consulting Group (BCG) suggested in the 1970s that SBUs should be managed as a portfolio the way financial investments are managed (Exhibit 2.2a). Different SBUs may have different missions, but all work together to achieve the organization's

EXHIBIT 2.2a.   The BCG portfolio matrix.

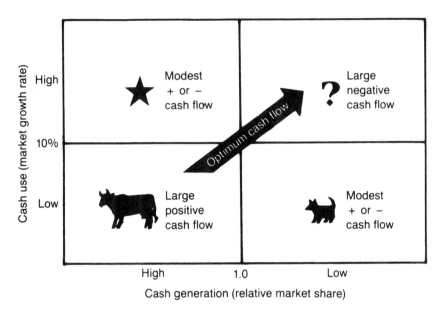

overall objectives. Top management decides which business units or brands to build up, maintain, phase down, or eliminate. In short, the organization is continually attempting to improve its portfolio of SBUs by divesting itself of units that do not perform well and, at the same time, acquiring promising new ones (Exhibit 2.2b).

The BCG approach focuses on three factors: market growth, the SBU's relative market share, and cash flow. An SBU's relative market share is determined by dividing its market share by that of its largest competitor. Thus, if Gillette's razors-and-blades

EXHIBIT 2.2b.   Possible changes in the portfolio over time.

Product dynamics:
"success" sequence

Product sales growth rate

"Success"
Sequence

*

?

S

Relative market share

Product dynamics:
"disaster" sequence

Product sales growth rate

*

?

"Disaster"
Sequence

X

S   X

Relative market share

SBU has a 65 percent share of that market while Schick, its largest competitor, has 16 percent and BIC has 11 percent,[24] their relative market shares are:

Gillette	4.1	(65%/16%)
Schick	0.3	(16%/65%)
BIC	0.2	(11%/65%)

The dividing line between high and low relative market share is set at 1. Only the market leader can lie to the left of this point. The more dominant the leader's share, the stronger its position in the marketplace.

SBUs are categorized by the amount of cash they generate, resulting in the following four categories:

1. *Stars*—These SBUs are in industries with high sales growth rates, and they have a high relative market share. The stars are the leaders in their markets. They need continual inputs of cash to maintain their high growth rates. Eventually that growth will slow and they will become cash cows.

2. *Cash cows*—Cash cows are SBUs with a higher market share than competitors in a low-growth market. They have high sales volume and low costs. Thus, they generate more cash than they need; the excess cash can be used to support other SBUs. At Gillette, the razors-and-blades SBU generated 32 percent of the company's 1989 sales revenues, but 64 percent of its profits. Profit margins on this SBU were a whopping 34.7 percent, compared with 15.2 percent for stationary products and 6.9 percent for toiletries.[25] Domestic beer is a cash cow for Anheuser-Busch, supporting the new product lines discussed earlier.

3. *Question marks*—These high-growth, low-market-share SBUs are problems for management because their future direction is uncertain. They require a lot of cash simply to maintain their position, let alone increase their market share. Management must decide whether to pour in enough cash to make them into leaders; if not, these SBUs probably will be phased out of the portfolio.

4. *Dogs*—Dogs are low-growth, low-market-share SBUs. They may provide enough cash to support themselves, but they are not a substantial source of funds. Such SBUs often are in the process of entering a particular market or phasing out of it. Either way, their position is below average.

The distribution of an organization's SBUs in the different categories provides a profile of the firm's health. But such an analysis also needs to consider the direction in which each SBU is moving. Organizations prefer to turn question marks into stars and, as growth slows, into cash cows that can be used to fund other question marks. This is precisely the sequence that occurred at Gillette, where the excess cash from the razor blade business was funneled into disposable lighters. Eventually Gillette's Cricket lighter became a star.

The portfolio approach aids in the setting of marketing strategies. The following basic strategies are closely related to this approach:

- *Build*—This strategy is appropriate for question marks if they are to grow into stars. The firm invests heavily to improve product quality, develop promotional campaigns, or subsidize price reductions—all in an effort to beat the competition.

- *Hold*—This strategy is used to protect cash cows and stars that are strongly entrenched. The market leader simply defends its market share and maintains customer loyalty.

- *Harvest*—When the future looks dim for a weak cash cow, a dog, or even a question mark, the best strategy may be to harvest as much profit from it as possible before letting it go. Marketing (especially promotion) and research and development expenditures are curtailed; economies of production are emphasized; and customer services are reduced. In short, all costs are lowered as the SBU is "milked" of its cash-generating potential.

- *Divest*—When a dog or question mark has no future, it is sold off or dropped from the portfolio because the cash needed to fund it can be used better elsewhere.

Competitive Position Matrix

The matrix can be modified to analyze the position of products relative to their competitors. In Exhibit 2.3, the top ten beer brands are plotted using 1990 data. The market growth rate is not used, because it is the same for every brand in this market (total 1990 U.S. beer sales grew 3.1 percent over 1989, but were flat for the three previous years). Instead, the growth in each brand's sales is used to show which grew faster. Sometimes, as in this illustration, each brand's growth is made relative to the growth of the market to show whether its share is growing or shrinking. (To do this, divide a brand's annual revenue growth or unit growth by the market's annual growth, or by dividing current market share by last year's market share to find the percentage of change in market share, as in Exhibit 2.3.)

Exhibit 2.4 shows the data we used to create a competitive position matrix for the U.S. beer market. This kind of analysis can show the market in a new light. The leader in sales, Budweiser, had a strong relative market share, but was weak on the growth dimension of the matrix—its share was slipping. The hot brands were Coors Light and Miller Genuine Draft, which gained a significant share in 1990. The cash flow implications of the BCG matrix do not necessarily apply, however, because competing brands may be owned by different companies. This analysis can be taken a step farther by identifying each brand's brewer and comparing the company portfolios, or by plotting companies instead of brands. One could learn, for example, that Anheuser-Busch had the largest share, 43.4 percent, and that its sales grew 7 percent, more than twice as fast as the total market. Also, one would find that brewer's share is closely related to performance. The top three—Anheuser-Busch, Miller, and Coors—were responsible for all the market growth in 1990. (Of course, you would

EXHIBIT 2.3.   Competitive position matrix for leading beer brands, 1990.

```
           Why is no brand                          MILLER
           in this quadrant?                        G.D.
    20

    15

                                            COORS
    10                                      LIGHT
                                                 BUD
     5                                        LIGHT
Growth
  in   0                            MILLER      MILW'S
Market                              LITE          BEST
Share  -5  BUD                           BUSCH
 (%)
    -10                                     OLD MILW.

    -15                                   MILLER H.L.

                                                COORS

     3           1              .5              .1
```

◀——— Relative Share of Market (Log Scale)

EXHIBIT 2.4.   Competitive position analysis.

Brand	1990 Share of Shipments	1989 Share of Shipments	% Change in Share	Relative Market Share, 1990
Budweiser[a]	25.2%	25.9%	−2.7%	2.40
Miller Lite	10.5	10.5	0	.42
Coors Light	6.2	5.6	10.7	.25
Bud Light	6.1	5.7	7.2	.24
Busch	4.6	4.8	−4.2	.18
Milwaukee's Best	3.6	3.6	0	.14
Old Milwaukee	3.3	3.6	−8.3	.13
Miller High Life	3.2	3.8	−15.8	.13
Miller Genuine Draft	3.0	2.4	25.0	.12
Coors	2.2	2.7	−18.5	.09

[a] Calculations:

   $25.2/25.9 = 0.97; 0.97 − .1 = 0.027 \times 100 = −2.7\%$
   $25.2/10.5 = 2.4$

need to update these statistics to the latest available before making any "real world" decisions about how to market a brand of beer, or any other product!)

One might also plot a matrix that compares light and regular beers, which would indicate that, of the top 25 brands, the only light beer to lose share in this sample period was Old Milwaukee Light. Altogether, light beers in 1990 had about a 30 percent market share and annual growth of 12.5 percent. And some background reading on the beer industry would reveal that Old Milwaukee Light's sliding share reflected the financial problems of its parent brewer, Stroh, which cut Old Milwaukee's advertising and other marketing expenses in 1989 in an effort to harvest profits from its brands and thus lost 12 percent of its volume. This analysis would indicate that light beers are currently the high performers of the beer market.

This example illustrates a fundamental principle of the new strategic planning: The firm must use available techniques and information creatively to gain new insights into its position and opportunities. It is not enough to crank out the same old matrices that were used last year, even if they are as venerable as the BCG matrix. It is important to ask intelligent questions ("Are light beers fueling the growth in the beer industry?" "Is the leading brand losing share?"), and to take a creative approach to analysis to answer such questions clearly. The firm that asks an intelligent question before its competitors do may be able to seize an opportunity first.[26]

It is fair to say that nobody uses the BCG matrix as the cornerstone of planning any more. It exists only in the textbooks littering the nation's business schools. And yet there is a fundamental wisdom to this planning model that should not be ignored. Perhaps it even makes sense to bring the tool back again—at least in modified form.

The strongest argument for the BCG matrix is that market growth rates and market shares are still good indicators of strategic potential. After all, which do you think will do better, all else being equal: A brand with low share in a mature, slow-growth market, or one with high share in a dynamic, fast-growth market? You see— there *is* something worth saving about it after all!

The continued relevance of the BCG approach is underscored by a recent "breakthrough" contribution to the strategy literature from two top people at Bain & Company, which bills itself as an international strategy-consulting firm. The authors of the Bain study examine the conventional wisdom which "holds that market share drives profitability" by examining profitability and other variables in a wide selection of consumer products. Their finding? Surprise! "Instead, a brand's profitability is driven by both market share and the nature of the category, or product market, in which the brand competes." Specifically, "A brand's relative market share has a different impact on profitability depending on whether the overall category is dominated by premium brands or by value brands to begin with."[27] To put this finding in the context of the BCG matrix, it turns out that in the competitive consumer products markets of the United States in the 1990s:

- Relative market share is still an important predictor of ROI,
- But it is still mediated by the attractiveness of the market,

- However, market growth rate seems less important than whether the market is brand or price oriented.

Note the qualifier here—that the attractiveness of the market, while still a key to returns, is *not* well represented by market growth rate. This may reflect the sad reality that most of the brands in the study are in similarly mature, slow-growth markets. But whatever the reason, the point is that a matrix approach to predicting future success would work today, as long as you modified the matrix by substituting a premium brands-versus-discount brands variable for the slow-versus-high growth variable of the original matrix. Otherwise, the portfolio approach's reliance on a market share variable and a market attractiveness variable *is still sound.*

We want to expose you more deeply to this school of strategic planning by showing you variants on the BCG model that permit the user greater control over the variables, thus making it easy to adapt the model to changing market conditions.

The GE Business Screen

GE developed a more flexible, multidimensional matrix on the theory that the portfolio approach should not be limited to relative market share and market growth. Too great an emphasis on these two variables may mask many other factors that make a business or brand attractive and indicate its strengths. Also, relative share is of greatest importance where economies of scale and "experience curve" effects give the largest producer a significant cost advantage. (An experience curve reflects a decline in unit costs as more units are produced; it is the result of learning or "experience" in contrast to straight economies of scale.) Yet the experience curve does not always apply. As a result of such insights, many strategic planners have gone beyond the BCG approach to other approaches that rely on multiple measures of a firm's ability to compete successfully. One of the first and best known of these alternative approaches is the investment opportunity chart or business screen developed by GE.[28]

In the business screen approach, a strategic business unit (SBU) is classified according to how well it rates on certain success measures, referred to as its business strength. The industries in which SBUs operate are classified on the basis of measures of opportunity, referred to as industry attractiveness. Among the measures of business strength are the SBU's product quality, price sensitivity, knowledge of the market, technological capability, image, and so on, whereas industry attractiveness is measured by factors such as intensity of competition, seasonality of sales, legal constraints, importance of technological change, and the like (Exhibit 2.5). Not all these factors can be measured as objectively and precisely as market growth, relative market share, and cash flow. On the other hand, the GE method offers much greater flexibility and comprehensiveness than the BCG approach.

The business screen is used in the following way: The nine cells shown in the illustration are placed in three zones. GE colored these zones green, yellow, and red; hence, this is often called the stoplight approach. The three zones at the upper left indicate industries that are attractive and match the SBUs' strengths. They have a

EXHIBIT 2.5.   The GE business screen.

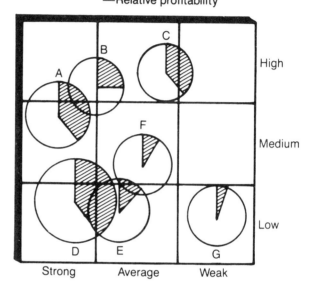

Business strength
—Domestic market share
—World share
—Share growth
—Share relative to leading competitor
—Product quality
—Technology skills
—Cost efficiency
—Marketing skills
—Relative profitability

Industry attractiveness
—Market size
—Growth
—Profitability
—Cyclicality
—Government regulation
—World scope
—Technology requirements

High

Medium

Low

Strong   Average   Weak

"green light" for investment. The three cells along the diagonal indicate industries of medium interest. They have a "yellow light" to denote caution; usually these SBUs warrant a strategy geared toward maintaining their present market share. The three cells at the lower right show weak SBUs for which a harvesting or divesting strategy may be the best option. The circles A through G represent the SBUs; their size is in proportion to the size of the industries in which they compete. The pie slices represent each SBU's market share within its industry.

The GE business screen's history is representative of the history of strategic planning. Developed in the 1970s by William Rothschild at GE with Mike Allen of the consulting firm McKinsey & Company, the tool was carefully—and laboriously—applied in annual planning and forecasting by GE's large central planning staff. Now, however, according to GE spokesman Bruce Bunch, the business screen "takes too much time" and is not used at GE any more.[29] In fact, neither GE nor McKinsey will claim ownership of it today (in response to inquiries concerning permission to reproduce it for publication). Once the heir apparent of the strategy throne, this method is a homeless orphan! (It remains a standard in the business school curriculum and important for the concepts it represents, even though it is no longer in widespread use.)

What happened? The SBUs of GE and many other firms that were identified as winners according to the business screen were not necessarily better than other SBUs. They ought to have been—nobody could dispute that these represented great business opportunities. However, GE line managers did not necessarily know how to pursue the opportunities, and someone else—perhaps someone from Europe or Japan—might have pursued an opportunity more effectively. The model leaves out the *focus-focus-focus factor* after all.

As a result of problems in implementing strategies produced with such matrices, bigger companies, GE included, pushed planning back to the line managers and cut central staff. For example, in 1984, Michael Naylor, General Motor's director of strategic planning, declared that "planning is the responsibility of every line manager," and added that "the role of the planner is to be a catalyst for change—not to do the planning for each business unit."[30]

The case of GE's Major Appliance Business Group is instructive. The group's central planning staff numbered in the 50s at the beginning of the 1950s. Although some of the planners' calls were right—for example, they identified the Japanese threat back in the 1970s—operating managers resisted the growing authority of planning staff and tended to ignore them. They insisted on ignoring Japan and treating Sears as their major competitor, for example. In other cases, planners were dead wrong—their focus on numbers blinded them to realities of implementation. As GE's Roger Schipke concluded when he took over the major appliance group (and booted out planners) in 1982, "An awful lot of conclusions were drawn by that group somewhat in isolation. We had a lot of bad assumptions leading to some bad strategies."[31]

BusinessWeek performed an interesting study in 1984, tracking a random sample of 33 planning strategies described in the magazine in 1979 and 1980. The tally: 19 clear failures and only 14 clear successes.[32] A lot of planners lost their jobs that year!

STRATEGIC PLANNING AND PROCESS REDESIGN

So what does GE do now? Its circuit breaker business provides a good example. This stagnant SBU in a mature industry would have flunked all the screening tests, but with a billion in yearly revenues, it hardly seemed appropriate to divest it and leave the market to competitors Seimens and Westinghouse. Besides, if any lesson had come out of the old planning models, it was that profits did not necessarily come from high-share, high-growth SBUs. (As Stephen Hardis, Eaton Corporation's vice president of planning, put it, "It's great to say, 'Why don't we all go into growth businesses?' But those are not all highly profitable. If there's a hell for planners, over the portal will be carved the term cash cow.")[33] Instead of divesting, GE consolidated operations—from six circuit breaker plants to only one (in Salisbury, North Carolina).[34] Solving this problem in just one location seemed like enough of a challenge.

Then management assessed the problem, but not in the conventional way, by asking planning staff and consultants for a report. Instead they formed an interdisciplinary team with specialists from manufacturing, marketing, and design, and asked them to figure out how to make the manufacturing process profitable. The group decided to compete on the basis of speed, and adopted the goal of reducing manufacturing time from three weeks to three days.

This radical change could not be accomplished given the existing process, in which GE engineers designed a unique box for each customer using a selection from GE's 28,000 parts, then factory workers assembled the boxes by hand. So the team redesigned the product line, paring parts to 1,275 while still allowing customers the ability to customize their boxes. Next the team developed an expert computer system that could automatically convert customer requirements into instructions for the factory machines. This eliminated the engineers and the delay needed for custom designing. The team also added more machines, increasing the automation of the production process.

Finally, the team tackled personnel problems on the factory floor. The key issue was delays associated with decision making. According to a *Fortune* reporter:

> The solution was to get rid of all line supervisors and quality inspectors, reducing the organizational layers between worker and plant manager from three to one. Everything those middle managers used to handle—vacation scheduling, quality, work rules—became the responsibility of the 129 workers on the floor, who are divided into teams of 15 to 20. And what do you know: The more responsibility GE gave its workers, the faster problems got solved and decisions made.[35]

Because of these changes at GE, costs dropped, quality improved, and customers believed they had more features from which to choose. Delivery was made in three days, as hoped; the backlog shrunk from two months to two days; employee morale was up; and market share was growing despite the flat market. The 1989 statistics, for example, were quite amazing: Productivity was up 20 percent, and ROI was above 20 percent. But it was not easy to turn this dog into a star; the project began in 1985, four eventful years before the stunning results we report. Everything had to change, from product line through production process to corporate structure and culture. Not every line manager is capable of leading such a transformation, but it definitely takes a line manager to do it. No central planning staff would undertake such goals, or succeed if it did. Still, the new planning approaches are tougher on management. Managers must champion change; they must be willing to push authority down into the organization; and they must learn to use, and work in, teams. As GE's Roger Schipke puts it, "Now it's a question of 'Can they develop a strategy for their business?' Some will make that cut, some won't." When he took over the major appliance group, only one of the four top managers reporting to him made that cut. The others were fired.[36]

Success with the new planning approach also requires reducing the barriers between company and customer—touching customers and listening in the proactive sense described in Chapter 1. For example, GE now promotes an answer center in TV ads and on product packaging. Staffed 24 hours a day, the center may be reached via a toll-free call. Several million calls are logged annually. Frank Sonenberg of Ernst & Young's Consulting Group says that, "By making information easily available to consumers [General Electric] builds brand loyalty in a tough competitive field."[37]

Planning to Be the Best

In the old strategic planning, goals often reflected desired financial returns or conventional wisdom about what was reasonable in the circumstances. But the Japanese competitors did not play by the same rules. They saw nothing wrong with tilting at entrenched leaders in photocopiers or autos, for example, even though entering the U.S. markets for these products meant violating the prescriptions of the BCG and GE portfolio models. And GE's circuit breaker business went way beyond conventional expectations, making such radical improvements that it was able to grow profits, quality, and share despite a no-growth market. Where do goals such as these come from, and how can they be implemented when the more modest goals of the old strategic planning were so often missed? The case of Xerox will help answer these critical questions.

In 1983, when Xerox CEO David Kearns decided to stem the flood of competition, he announced the beginning of a total quality campaign. To the uninitiated, total quality sounds like tougher quality control, more inspections. It is not. Total quality programs eliminate quality inspection and focus on doing it right the first time. ("It" may be fitness to standard, fitness to need, or fitness to latent need, as discussed in Chapter 1.) This means every person must do his or her job right, or stop the process if he or she does something wrong. Total quality involves suppliers and distributors as well. (McAlpin Industries, a Xerox supplier, now sends its managers to a Xerox quality course, designs its parts with a Xerox team, and endures Xerox auditors on its factory floor.)[38] Total quality touches every process in the company, from manufacturing processes to sales and customer service processes. To accomplish total quality, Xerox puts in charge those people who know each process best: the front-line workers.

This type of program involves a big change for most companies—a change in corporate culture. Employee initiative must be encouraged, and employees can no longer be punished for mistakes. They will not report them otherwise. Employees must be trained in the statistical methods needed to monitor and improve the quality of their own work. And they must learn to work together in teams to solve problems or think of ways to work better.

The first move Kearns made to kick off Xerox's quality program was an appeal to the company's 100,000 workers—the task of championing customer needs would fall to them.[39] And they have proven more than able to meet such challenges. For example, in 1990, a team of people from sales, distribution, and accounting determined how to save Xerox $200 million in inventory costs.[40]

Perhaps the hardest part of changing the corporate culture is admitting openly what is wrong with the old one. Whatever is wrong, however, is at the root of any problems and must be grubbed out. The old culture becomes a conservative force, preventing employees and managers from focusing on customer needs and limiting the rate of organizational learning and change. At Fuji Xerox, the company's total quality program began by admitting that there were some rather serious problems, and that they were systemic rather than the fault of any one manager or group. Hideki Kaihatsu, one of Fuji Xerox's directors, explains:

> The first step was to understand the problems facing the company and why these problems occurred. This soul-searching analysis revealed many surprising facts:
>
> - Our leadership had become fragmented and inconsistent.
> - Our managers had become complacent, arrogant, and had lost their sense of urgency.
> - We did not pay close enough attention to customer requirements.
> - We found our product development process particularly sloppy and not acceptable.
> - We depended too much upon U.S. design capability.
> - The product development process was slow and there was little cross-functional cooperation.
> - We did not recognize the value of maintaining strong bonds with our suppliers.[41]

In the days of the old strategic planning, a manager's career could have been ruined for coming forward with even one of these criticisms. In fact, that's one reason consulting firms flourished: When one knew the messenger would be killed, one was eager to hire someone else to deliver the message, regardless of price! But Xerox's disastrous performance forced its managers to put these games behind them and take an honest look at their company. The result was an almost incredible list of major problems.

Solving them was not as simple, however, as setting the solutions as strategic goals. How could change be accomplished, and how much change was a reasonable goal? How could the goals be broken down into smaller, more attainable tasks? The answers could not be found within Xerox; the needed changes were too radical. But surely they could be found somewhere; there were undoubtedly companies that could provide role models, companies that were the best at each of the individual processes Xerox had to rebuild. With this realization in mind, Xerox created one of the most important of the new planning techniques: benchmarking.

Case Study: Benchmarking at Xerox

Benchmarking began at Xerox in 1979 as a way to analyze competing products. According to Robert Camp of U.S. Marketing for Xerox's Business Services, "Selected product comparisons were made; operating capabilities and features of competing copying machines were compared; mechanical components were taken apart and scrutinized."[42] This reverse engineering of competing products was a natural response to the inroads made by Japanese competitors. But with Xerox's quality program, benchmarking was extended beyond product comparisons, to include process comparisons and companies from other industries.

For example, Xerox used L.L. Bean for benchmarking. Camp tells the story:

> When (we) first informed our management that we were going to
> assess ourselves against L.L. Bean. There was disbelief. But we
> had much to learn from them. The L.L. Bean statistics that dealt
> with their warehouse order picking . . . showed that they were
> able to do it almost three times faster than Xerox.[43]

This meant that L.L. Bean could fill customer orders faster than Xerox.
When Xerox adopted a computerized system like L.L. Bean used, one
that "made a conscious effort to sort the orders and minimize the
picker's travel distance" according to Camp, Xerox also was able to
fill orders faster. This is an example of what Xerox now calls "functional benchmarking." The following are the definitions of the four
benchmarking methods Xerox uses:

1. *Internal benchmarking* compares a company's operations with
   an internal exemplar, for example, a plant that has innovated successfully in certain areas.

2. *Competitive benchmarking* makes comparisons with individual
   competitors; reverse engineering of a competing product is one
   example.

3. *Functional benchmarking* is when "we compare function against
   function across wide sections of different industry types," as in
   the L.L. Bean comparison.

4. *Generic benchmarking* looks at fundamental business processes
   that tend to be the same in every industry, such as taking orders,
   servicing customers, and developing strategies. For these generic
   practices, Xerox "looks at a wide cross-section" from different industries "to make sure that we have in fact identified those industry best practices," again according to Camp.

The benchmarking process in its various forms gives Xerox a
practical way to set radical goals—the company simply finds some
other company that is the best in a certain (often narrow) area, and
studies how the company became best. CEO Kearns of Xerox defines
it succinctly as "the continuous process of measuring products, services and practices against the toughest competitors or those companies recognized as industry leaders."[44] It must be a continuous
process, according to Kearns, because "we realize we are in a race
without a finish line. As we improve, so does our competition."[45]
Xerox cannot afford to become complacent, and the new planning
tools give the company the ability to compete effectively in the current environment. Kearns adds that "Five years ago, we would have
found this disheartening. Today we find it invigorating."[46]

The Learning Organization

In the days when strategic planning meant plotting a bunch of growth-share matrices,
it was widely assumed that organizational learning occurred in lockstep with the

number of units produced. As more units were produced by a firm, it became more proficient at producing them and costs dropped correspondingly. This was one reason why BCG plotted relative market share on its matrix. The firm that held the largest share had presumably produced more units, and therefore had learned how to lower costs the farthest. Now that the Japanese have demonstrated both that a low-share competitor can learn faster and that learning can improve quality as well as reduce cost, U.S. managers are forced to rethink their whole notion of learning. In the emerging view, the kind of changes made by both GE and Xerox are successful because they greatly increase the rate of organizational learning.

Ray Stata of Analog Devises has argued that an organization's rate of learning is the key to its competitiveness. Specifically, he argues that "At Analog Devises, and many other U.S. companies, product and process innovation are not the primary bottleneck to progress. The bottleneck is management innovation."[47] After deciding to tackle the issue of management innovation at Analog Devises, Stata discovered that organizational learning drove management innovation, "I see organizational learning as the principal process by which management innovation occurs. In fact, I would argue that the rate at which individuals and organizations learn may become the only sustainable competitive advantage."[48] This conclusion focused his attention on how to use the strategic planning process and a total quality program to increase the rate of learning in his company. Incidentally, how he arrived at his conclusions is an example of the new approaches managers are beginning to take in their quest for organizational learning. Stata joined a group of managers working with two MIT professors to develop and exchange ideas in this field.[49] For example, Stata's recognition of the key role played by organizational learning can be traced to the influence of fellow group member Arie deGeus, director of group planning at Shell International.

A learning organization is an adaptive organization. It is able to rethink its structure and function and redefine itself in response to market challenges and customer needs. The need for faster and smarter change is obvious: Many managers believe adaptability is the key to success, and are making it the cornerstone of their strategy. This requires pushing both authority and initiative down into the organization, encouraging people to think harder and learn quicker—and giving them the freedom to do so. But as Stata also observes, "Organizations can learn only as fast as the slowest link learns,"[50] and, in many cases, the slowest link is management.

The Learning Manager

In 1983, around the time Xerox began its total quality drive, Professor Elliot Carlisle of University of Massachusetts at Amherst wrote a story—a parable actually—about a harried manager who bumps into a successful mentor-like manager on an airplane and learns from him a new way of thinking about management. Here is what the mentor had to say about thinking:

> "You know," he mused, "when you get right down to it, it's almost impossible to get any real thinking done at work. Not just because of interruptions, but almost more importantly, the whole psychological and physical environment in which managers work

tends to discourage contemplation and encourage activity. The higher the level in an organization, the more critical is the role of reflection and the less important that of activity, but so often we've become conditioned on the way up through the ranks. How many bosses would give a word of encouragement to a subordinate if they were to come upon him sitting at his desk, chair tipped back, foot resting on an open drawer, and staring into space with an abstract expression on his face? They'd be far more likely to ask him what the hell he's doing, and if the unfortunate replied, 'Thinking,' he'd probably be advised to stop thinking and get back to work."[51]

Although there is now widespread recognition of the need to think harder—and, on the other side of the coin, to learn and adapt more quickly—managers still suffer from that conditioning referred to in the quote. In fact, this conditioning is stronger the higher up you go in the organization. According to Harvard Business School professor Chris Argyris:

> Any company that aspires to succeed in the tougher business environment of the 1990s must first resolve a basic dilemma: success in the marketplace increasingly depends on learning, yet most people don't know how to learn. What's more, those members of the organization that many assume to be the best at learning are, in fact, not very good at it. I am talking about the well-educated, high-powered, high-commitment professionals who occupy key leadership positions in the modern corporation.[52]

In this view, it is senior management that stands in the way of organizational learning and adaptability, and thus in the way of success in the marketplace. The problem, according to Argyris, is that people habitually reason defensively, unconsciously protecting themselves, maintaining their control, and suppressing conflict and negative views. Their behavior blinds them and their organizations to challenges and opportunities that truly open-minded, productive reasoning and learning would reveal. Thus effective, lasting change in any organization must start at the top with self-examination and behavioral change by the leaders.

The effects of the new strategic planning and the market challenges that drive it put this issue front and center. As Rosabeth Moss Kanter, another Harvard Business School professor, sees it, "Competitive pressures are forcing corporations to adopt new flexible strategies and structures." And this is forcing changes in the nature of management's work:

> The old bases of managerial authority are eroding, and new tools of leadership are taking their place. Managers whose power derived from hierarchy and who were accustomed to a limited area of personal control are learning to shift their perspectives and widen their horizons. The new managerial work consists of looking outside a defined area of responsibility to sense opportunities and of forming project teams drawn from any relevant sphere to address them. It involves communication and collaboration across functions, across divisions, and across companies. . . . Thus rank, title, or official charter will be less important factors in success at the managerial work than having the knowledge, skills, and sensitivity to mobilize people and motivate them to do their best.[53]

An example of this concept in action is provided by Raymond Gilmartin, CEO of medical equipment maker Becton-Dickinson, "We're creating a hierarchy of ideas. You say, 'This is the right thing to do here,' not 'We're going to do this because I'm boss.'" This means the vision still comes from the top, but strategies well up from Becton-Dickinson's 15 divisions, and Gilmartin must be content to sit back and let this more informal approach to strategy work.[54]

When GE pushed down planning to the line managers, this was not simply the outcome of a struggle for authority between corporate staff and operating divisions (as many saw it at the time). It was the beginning of the transformation of managerial work that Kanter speaks of. And when, in words that proved prophetic, Michael Naylor of GE declared in 1984 that line managers had to be catalysts of change through their planning, he was anticipating the new strategic role of the manager. This role requires flexibility and rapid learning, and it requires that managers teach these traits to others, for these are the traits that a company needs today to identify and implement successful strategies.

Xerox's benchmarking is an example of adaptable, accelerated learning, in that it casts a broad net in the effort to learn how to do something better. The fact is that Xerox can learn from L.L. Bean, and vice versa—insight can and must come from all available sources. The truly interesting thing about the new strategies is the way they are pushing (in some cases, dragging) management along this path. As the new strategic planning unfolds in the 1990s, two things are bound to become clear. First, it is management (starting at the top) that is the greatest obstacle to change, and that can become the greatest catalyst. (Stata's quest led Analog Devises to superior performance, logging an incredible 50 percent improvement in product failure rates every three to six months, for example.) Second, the entire thrust of the many new strategic directions and organizational changes is toward the marketing concept. Managerial companies are struggling to learn and adapt in order to serve customers better—better than they did before, better than their customers expect, and better than their competitors do.

This implies a never-ending process, and never-ending change. It is a frightening thought—this notion of chasing a moving finish line—and it takes strategy well beyond the bounds of yesterday's comfortable matrices. Yesterday's solutions become today's problems. Take Xerox's benchmarking against L.L. Bean to speed up delivery of products. It was an exciting innovation in the copier business last year, but this year Xerox is already looking beyond it. Although Xerox learned to deliver products faster than its competitors, studies showed that customer satisfaction was still suboptimal—only 70 percent. The problem was that customers wanted to know exactly when their copiers would arrive. Speed was fine, but uncertainty remained a problem. A new team was convened, with people from distribution, accounting, sales, and so forth, and a new solution developed. Xerox now tracks the progress of every copier through the distribution process so that salespeople can tell customers exactly when they will receive their products, thus providing speed and predictability. Now customer satisfaction with product delivery measures at 90 percent instead of 70 percent.

But satisfaction still is short of 100 percent, and if it ever reaches 100 percent, competitors may innovate and push it down—satisfaction is, after all, a relative concept. So Xerox cannot stop now—it must search for and explore the next frontier. This is the nature of the new strategic planning. As PepsiCo's CEO, Wayne Calloway, explains, "The worst rule of management is 'If it ain't broke, don't fix it.' In today's economy, if it ain't broke, you might as well break it yourself, because it soon will be."[55]

FINDING THE RIGHT STRATEGY FOR *YOUR* BUSINESS

In the beginning of this chapter we mentioned Henry Mintzberg's important book, *The Rise and Fall of Strategic Planning.* He reaches an interesting conclusion on page 397 of it, one we want to reproduce here in case you don't make it to the end of his book any time soon: "Organizations differ, just as do animals; it makes no more sense to prescribe one kind of planning for all organizations than it does to describe one kind of housing for all animals."[56] Dozens of planning methods and approaches have flashed before your eyes as you read this chapter. And believe us, there are many, many more should you care to pursue the planning literature in greater depth! Which, if any, are appropriate to your ways of thinking and the needs of your organization? Possibly, none. At most, one or two in any given situation. It is a terrible (though common) mistake to think that one can "do" planning just by force-fitting a handful of famous methodologies to one's business. Sure, it helps to know what they are and how they work. But in the end, it is up to you and your fellow planners and marketers to sniff the wind and chose your own path. Perhaps—as is more often the case than we so-called experts like to believe—that path will be largely of your own design, not ours.

In our client work, we've noticed that many of the best strategies arise when people trust their instincts and create their own planning processes. Formal situation analysis and planning can provide helpful inputs to this more natural, organic approach to planning—*but they are not substitutes for it.* Mintzberg seems to be describing the same phenomenon when he writes (of the case studies conducted from McGill) that:

> We found strategy making to be a complex, interactive, and evolutionary process, best described as one of adaptive learning. . . . The process was often significantly emergent. . . . Indeed, strategies appeared in all kinds of strange ways in the organizations studied. Many of the most important seemed to grow up from the "grass roots" (much as weeds that might appear in a garden are later found to bear useful fruit), rather than all having to be imposed from the top down, in "hothouse" style.[57]

Strategies as weeds. What an interesting metaphor! And how many of us, especially in the context of established business organizations, are willing and able to give weeds room to grow? All too few, which is one reason why many of the best new strategies in any industry are executed by entrepreneurs, working outside the boundaries of the established market leaders. Listen to another expert on strategy, Dineh Mohajer, founder of Hard Candy—although she might laugh at our describing her as a strategy expert. But actions speak louder than words (or laughs), and this successful executive founded a nail polish company in her teens and grew it from zero to $10 million is sales in just two years by providing new, fun colors that were not available in the product lines of the giants of her industry. Here is how she and her young partners develop their home-run marketing strategies:

> We do whatever we like. We don't do marketing research or anything like that. I'm not even sure what that is—that's how much we don't do it. We just go with our gut because that's what brought us here.[58]

Had she taken her ideas to a market leader, they would probably have been treated like weeds. But now the market leaders are scrambling to imitate this successful strategy.

The question is, can you recognize the next big idea in your market and nurture its growth? We opened the chapter with the search for the new king of strategy and the unsettling news that no heir apparent is in sight. We close on the same thought, with the added insight that it is perhaps best this way. Rather than propose our own candidate, we urge you to find your own. If it is different from everybody else's, so much the better. Maybe your strategy will be unique, too.

The king is dead. Thank goodness! Now maybe we can create a democratic model of strategic planning.

3 THE INTERNATIONAL CHALLENGE

Planting Your Flag Abroad—and Helping It Take Root

These are the trenches. This is where we compete head-on.

—Horace Whittlesey, general manager
for China, American Standard Inc.[1]

A water closet is a water closet. The trick is in setting up the best distribution system and marketing campaign.

—Koichi Noda, president of Toto Ltd.'s China Unit[2]

It's very simple, really. As the vast nation of China begins to adopt western-style plumbing, it is also beginning to adopt sit-down toilets. And that is a revolution worthy of more than a little red book, as any foreign business traveler visiting China will agree. There is something, well, unappealing, about having to squat over an open hole in the floor of a public restroom—especially when it is overflowing with the ubiquitous raw sewage that inevitably plagues any facility used by tens of thousand of people a day. There must be a better way.

At least, that's what the visionaries at two of the world's leading toilet manufacturers think. American Standard, the U.S. leader, is pushing hard to open up the Chinese market, and its units are now in use in many new apartment and office buildings in China. But Toto Ltd., a leading Japanese maker, is also pushing into China in a big way. It's head to head (pun intended) competition as they jockey for a dominant share of what may prove the biggest and fastest-growing market for toilets in the world.

Which will win? Both make similar products, designed to be inexpensive and light enough to import, and to use the minimum water in a nation so densely populated that the average citizen traditionally used less fresh water in a day than the average American or Japanese citizen discards with a single flush. And both manufacture for the Chinese market in nearby Thailand and other Asian countries where inexpensive labor keeps prices appropriate for the Chinese market. So the biggest differences between the rivals are in how they market their similar products within China—distribution strategies, sales, advertising, building relationships with big purchasers, and obtaining major contracts to supply new developments. As Toto's Noda puts it in his opening quote for this chapter, "The trick is in setting up the best distribution system and marketing campaign."

Or is it? There are many subtleties when it comes to international marketing. You can, for instance, invest in the biggest and best distribution system and the flashiest advertising campaign, and still blow it big time. Take Nike's effort to gain a dominant share of European soccer shoe and clothing markets, heralded with bold ads declaring, "Barricade your stadiums. Hide your trophies. Invest in some deodorant. As Asia and Latin America have been crushed, so shall Europe . . . The world has been warned." This in-your-face attitude is part of Nike's brash, American personality—but it doesn't always work in other cultures. That campaign was not a success, and now Nike is trying to find a more diplomatic approach to the European soccer market. According to Philip Knight, Nike's president, "Now we have to add a sort of United Nations side, which is a little bit difficult."[3] Even the biggest and boldest of global brands can stumble in foreign markets. Each market is unique, each nation's culture subtle and multifaceted, and each country has different marketing conditions, from local competition to consumer buying habits and behavior patterns. In China, it is in part an educational effort to sell a sit-down toilet, for many people have never used one. In the United States, toilet makers and marketers haven't had to educate consumers about how to use their product for a long, long time. A shift of focus, a new perspective, is necessary to succeed in the Chinese market. American Standard is off to a good start, though, and may end up the winner.

On the other hand, we won't be surprised to hear some day that an unexpected third rival has arisen to dominate both American Standard and Toto in the Chinese market. Who? We're not exactly sure, but we can give you a few clues. First, it will be a Chinese-based competitor. Second, it will adopt the modern designs and production methods of American Standard and Toto. And third, it will adapt them in subtle ways, so as to make the product cheaper and more suitable for the local market.

This is just our best guess; we don't actually market toilets in China. However, we do recognize a familiar pattern in this story of leading foreign rivals in a rapidly developing market—one that often ends up pitting the global brands against emerging national brands in the long run.

It is a difficult thing to make a permanent home for your products in someone else's country—but it *can* be done, as we will see in this chapter. And for many U.S. companies especially, foreign markets have been a key source of revenue and profit growth in recent years. A run in U.S. exports began in the first half of the 1990s, with a

52 percent gain in dollar sales between 1990 and 1995. The growth continued at roughly the same rate into the late 1990s, moderated only by the relative strength of the U.S. dollar. For many U.S. companies, the 1990s have been the international decade, the time when they discovered how to turn a trickle of foreign sales into a flood.

For Whirlpool, the U.S.-based appliance maker, the last decade has been one of transformation—from a national company with a minor interest in exporting, to one that is increasingly global in its operations and philosophy. Whirlpool's story—an international marketing success—began with a clear realization that future growth would have to come from abroad. According to its CEO, David Whitwam, in the mid-1980s, they began a process to transform Whirlpool from a successful, largely domestic, fairly conservative company into a world leader in the appliance industry. They initiated this transformation because they saw a "no growth," difficult future in the mature, highly competitive U.S. marketplace. Today, Whirlpool manufactures in eleven countries and markets their products in more than 120 countries. They are number one in North America and all of Latin America, number three in Europe, and the largest Western producer and marketer in Asia.[4] But you don't have to be a giant like Whirlpool to profit from international marketing. Many of the biggest gains in U.S. exports are coming from small and mid-sized companies, ones that never had the time to think about foreign markets before. For many of them, the 1980s was a rough

---

FOR YOUR IMAGINATION

Flying Pigeon Bicycles

The Flying Pigeon Bicycle Company is one of China's largest bicycle manufacturers—and one of the first state-controlled manufacturers in that country to attempt the transition to a marketing orientation. Its flight away from a strict production orientation and toward its customers' desires is a migration that will have to be made by hundreds of state-run manufacturers in China, the Russian republics, what was East Germany, Poland, Hungary, Czechoslovakia, Bulgaria, and Yugoslavia. (Little in the way of reform is expected, however, in Romania or Albania.) The barriers these businesses face are similar in many respects to those faced by Western businesses operating in these countries.

Henry Ford's dictum that "They can have cars any color they like as long as it's black," didn't last long in the face of competition from other automakers. Today, we take for granted the diversity of colors and styles available to consumers. But Flying Pigeon bicycles have always been black—until September 1990, that is, when an unsold inventory of two million black bicycles convinced managers that making more of the same was not a good idea. Nobody wanted to buy black bikes anymore. Thus, Flying Pigeon introduced yellow and red bicycles and entered, albeit in low gear, the modern age of marketing. According to *U.S. News and World Report*, "This simple innovation helped Flying Pigeon's sales take off."[5]

---

wake-up call, as their home markets began to be flooded with imports from Asian and Latin American producers who beat them on either quality, or price—or, too often, both. It took a while, but this new, global competition gradually changed the average U.S. marketer's perspective.

At first, the outside world loomed large as a growing threat to domestic markets—which it still is. Then, for many, a second level of realization was reached—they began to see the globalization of their markets not just as a threat, but as an incredible opportunity. Take family-owned Red Spot Paint & Varnish Company of Evansville, Indiana. This auto paint manufacturer's international sales grew from almost nothing to 20 percent of total sales in less than a decade. The owner and president used to handle international orders at his own desk on Saturday mornings. Now an entire department is needed to keep up with the company's growing international business.[6]

THE RANGE OF OPTIONS IN INTERNATIONAL MARKETING

If a U.S. company decides to start selling its products in China (or any other foreign country), how should it proceed? There are a variety of ways in which a firm can become involved in international marketing. Exhibit 3.1 shows that the degree of a firm's involvement in foreign markets can range from casual to total. Perhaps the most common form of involvement, at least for U.S. firms, is casual. The firm does not actively seek international trade and is not particularly sensitive to the needs of international markets. A small German toy manufacturer that sells its products at the 400-year-old Nuremberg Christmas market (where buyers come from all over the world) is a casual international marketer. If a French buyer contacts the manufacturer, the toymaker

EXHIBIT 3.1.   Degrees of involvement in international marketing.

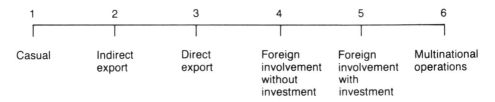

1. Not actively seeking international trade.
2. Sells to domestic customers, some of which sell internationally.
3. The firm itself sells to international customers.
4. Uses funds of partners in host countries to establish production facilities there.
5. Uses own funds to establish production facilities in host countries.
6. Views the world as a set of markets and sources of supply.

may be willing to fill a one-time order, but it is unlikely to systematically examine international market opportunities as part of a long-term strategy.

Somewhat less casual is the involvement of the indirect exporter, which sells mainly to domestic customers, some of whom might be in the export business. Some organizations serve as the export department for other, less involved firms. Such organizations are known as export merchants or export brokers. These firms may be used on a one-time or continuing basis, depending on the preferences of the manufacturing company.

The various forms of direct export represent a greater degree of a company's involvement in international marketing. A firm may have an export department or may sell to an import house in another country; in either case, the company views international markets as a long-term opportunity for sales and profits. Many organizations do not advance past the direct export level of commitment. Indeed, for small and medium-sized organizations, this may be the best strategy.

Next on the continuum between casual and total involvement is foreign involvement without investment. A company might license the sale of a product, set up a franchise organization, or enter into a contract with foreign nationals to produce the product abroad or manage the marketing of it. AT&T, for example, entered into a reciprocal agreement with Compagnie Generale d'Electricite (CGE) in which AT&T would help the French firm sell its digital telephone switches in the United States. AT&T also agreed to purchase $200 million worth of CGE equipment over a four-year period. In return, AT&T gained 16 percent of the French telephone switch market, about $150 million in annual sales, by having the French company market its product in France.

Foreign investment represents an even greater degree of commitment to international marketing. Once a market becomes important enough or a company is offered sufficient incentive by a host country, the firm may decide to invest its own capital in physical facilities abroad. There are many forms of foreign investment, ranging from joint ventures to complete ownership. Joint ventures are strategically beneficial in helping companies penetrate distribution networks in new countries and in helping defray the cost of massive development and production projects. In South America, Ford and West Germany's Volkswagen have formed Autolatina; this organization will produce both VWs and Fords on the same assembly line in a factory previously owned by Ford. To be successful, joint ventures should bring together complementary skills from each partner.

The greatest involvement in international marketing is that of multinational corporations (MNCs), which do not distinguish between domestic and foreign markets. A multinational corporation is based in one country, called the parent country, and produces goods and/or services in one or more countries, called host countries. MNCs make all decisions within a global framework, viewing the world as a set of alternative markets, sources of supply, and locations for productive and distributive facilities. Such companies work toward developing standardized products that can be altered to meet the unique demands of different countries. IBM follows this strategy. Said an

IBM executive, "Our overall concept is to develop a worldwide product line. Each development lab has responsibility for a product from cradle to grave. It is also responsible for identifying customer requirements all around the world, irrespective of the lab location. What is important is that the concept of adaptability is built into the product."[7] Hence, IBM can adjust products to match local markets. Its keyboards, for instance, are all modifiable to meet different language needs. Europe alone needs 20 such keyboards.

An interesting problem arises in staffing the overseas offices of multinational companies. If they hire only local people, managers fear, they do not really have an international business because each local office is separated by language, culture, and a lack of experience in the company's headquarters or other foreign offices. There is no over-arching corporate culture. The tendency, therefore, is to staff at least the key management positions with people from the "home country," creating a truly global class of marketers and managers. But this too has its problems. For starters, it is costly. The average three-year international posting costs the company upwards of $1 million. And 50 percent of those sent on overseas assignments don't make it through their entire term—they jump ship or request a transfer back to the home office.[8] Culture shock and the separation from family and friends can take a heavy toll. Furthermore, if companies staff their foreign operations too heavily from home, they fail to take advantage of the local talent and local knowledge available in any foreign labor pool. Thus, the staffing of multinationals is complicated by the need to strike a delicate balance between maintaining continuity throughout the corporation, on the one hand, and adapting to local conditions on the other.

Flag-Planting or True Globalization?

Becoming a global company entails far more than opening offices abroad. It is a way of life, one in which the entire world is viewed as a source of opportunities and threats; one in which the globe is scoured routinely in the search for the best place to perform each business function. Whirlpool exemplifies this philosophy in its approach to global marketing. That's why David Whitwam, CEO of Whirlpool, sees more than one approach to the multinational strategy—but only one "right" approach. He argues that, in fact, most international manufacturers aren't truly global:

> They're what I call flag planters. They may have acquired or established businesses all over the world, but their regional or national divisions still operate as autonomous entities. In this day and age, you can't run a business that way and expect to gain a long-term competitive advantage. To me, "competitive advantage" means having the best technologies and processes for designing, manufacturing, selling, and servicing your products at the lowest possible costs. Our vision at Whirlpool is to integrate our geographical businesses wherever possible, so that our most advanced expertise in any given area—whether it's refrigeration technology, financial reporting systems, or distribution strategy—isn't confined to one location or one division.[9]

The casual international company, although common enough, cannot truly compete globally. It cannot meet the challenge of international markets on a sustainable basis. Thus, companies that start with a casual involvement often progress through the continuum—perhaps even developing the kind of global integration of operations that now characterizes Whirlpool. To get serious about international marketing, you need to think and act like a multinational (MNC). If your firm is too small to open offices abroad on its own nickel, then it can do so through partnerships and joint ventures—becoming a "virtual" multinational. Scale is less important than attitude!

But how exactly should the MNC think and act? A simple answer is impossible. The international environment is challenging and strategy must be responsive to it. Furthermore, the optimal global strategy is currently a matter of fierce debate. We must examine both the environment and strategy to answer the question. And because governments play a major role in the environment, we will start with their role.

THE GLOBAL ENVIRONMENT

Governments control the rules of international trade, making them a bigger part of the global business environment than most managers expect. Government policies determine not only what procedures must be followed in importing and exporting foods and services, but also what goods may be traded and even who will be allowed to engage in international trade.

As multinational corporations grow in both size and power, there is some concern that they may be beyond the control of any government. Although no single agency has power over international trade, certain roles that governments can and do play have a major influence on how trade is carried out. Among these are the role of buyer in international markets and that of supporter and regulator of international trade.

Governments themselves buy products. They purchase industrial products such as airplanes, tanks, oil refineries, and typewriters. Many governments have some form of "buy national" policy, requiring their agencies to purchase goods and services in domestic markets whenever possible. However, for products that are not manufactured domestically, the government market represents a large opportunity for foreign firms.

Governments as Regulators and Supporters

Governments also formulate policies that regulate the international marketing efforts of both domestic and foreign firms. Such policies can have far-reaching effects. For example, the government may set tariffs (i.e., taxes) on certain imported goods, which raises the prices paid for those goods by the ultimate consumer. Governments also regulate trade, either explicitly or implicitly. In the United States, the government is often said to have "no policy toward trade," whereas in fact it does. However, U.S. policy does not often directly support the international marketing activities of a U.S. company. Rather, it attempts to establish "rules of the game" that will allow companies based in the United States to compete fairly in international markets. Other governments, such as that of Japan and Korea, have an explicit policy of aggressively supporting exports.

The Impact of Government Policies

The most visible and controversial international trade policy today is protectionism, or the erection of trade barriers in an attempt to protect domestic industries from foreign competition. Such barriers can take a variety of forms; the most common are tariffs and quotas. There are three types of tariffs: specific, ad valorem, and mixed. A specific tariff is based on the number of items exported or imported. An ad valorem tariff is based on the value of the product; a 20 percent ad valorem tax on a $3,000 motorcycle would result in a tax of $600. Mixed tariffs combine the other two types, as in a $50 tax on each item plus 20 percent of its value. Tariffs have generally lost their bite as a protection measure. Among the world's trading countries, the monetary value of tariffs now amounts to only about 5 percent of the value of the goods that carry tariffs, compared to about 50 percent in 1933.

A quota is a specific limit on the number of items of a particular kind that may be imported. A more extreme form of quota is an embargo, which totally bans imports in designated categories or from certain countries. Other barriers to trade are administrative in nature, such as requiring emission controls on all imported cars.

As a result of the dramatic climb of the U.S. trade deficit in the mid-1980s, the call for measures to protect domestic industries gained widespread support. Although the deficit is greatly reduced now, and a free market philosophy is far more popular as a result, various trade sanctions are still an important feature of international trade. Surprisingly, U.S. penalties associated with trade sanctions affect trade and investment with 35 countries according to the National Association of Manufacturers—indicating that there are still substantial teeth to U.S. trade laws.[10] And approximately a fifth of goods imported to the United States are under some kind of special protection, roughly double the proportion of the early 1980s.

The pursuit of trade protection is a consuming passion for some companies and their executives. For example, Lee Iacocca, chairman and CEO of Chrysler Corporation, says:

> For years, I've been telling anyone who would listen that we're heading for economic disaster with a U.S. market that is wide open to the Japanese market while the Japanese market remains effectively closed to us. That's only possible because the U.S. government is wide open to the Japanese while their government is closed to us. . . . Americans have always been able to make themselves heard in Washington. But now they are being drowned out by more powerful voices from Japan.[11]

Bolstering the manufacturing base (with its positive effect on the trade deficit) is only one reason behind the pressure for protectionism. It is estimated that over two million U.S. jobs are lost each year as a result of foreign competition. However, enacting protectionist measures is not all positive; once legislated, they are difficult to retract. The U.S. glassware industry, for example, has been protected since 1922, the dairy industry since 1953, and textiles since 1957. Prices to consumers for protected goods can rise as supply is limited. When the Japanese had an import quota imposed on automobile imports to the United States in the early 1980s, they chose to export more expensive models. In fact, the quota probably forced them to do so, as the only way to increase revenues when volume is restricted is to increase price, which means learning to make better cars.[12]

Trade barriers may limit consumer choice as well as elevate consumer prices. Most damaging, however, barriers can provide artificial isolation from world markets and world competitors; protected firms tend to learn and change more slowly, becoming less competitive over time. This slow change is more likely in a larger country than a smaller one, because the firms in a smaller country tend to look outward for growth and to engage in global competition out of necessity.

The United States is not alone in building trade barriers. Italy has defined its import laws so restrictively that only a few thousand Japanese automobiles have been sold there since 1957. France makes all Japanese videotape recorders that come into the country through an out-of-the-way customs office in Poitiers. Brazil disallows import licenses for most products produced domestically.

In 1978, China initiated an "open-door" policy as part of its economic reform program. Until recently, U.S. companies have tried unsuccessfully to grab a share of the Chinese consumer market of one billion people. Chinese trade officials sought foreigners to invest in export industries or high-technology projects. Consumer companies such as Coca-Cola Company and Kentucky Fried Chicken Corporation were limited to licensing and low profits. But gradually China's attitude changed and political logjams for foreign trade were lifted. For example, the Chinese no longer demand majority or at least 50-50 ownership. China also sees more value in low-technology imports. As a result, U.S. companies rushed to the Chinese mainland. Procter & Gamble began a $10 million project to produce laundry and personal-care products in Canton. RJR-Nabisco began to sell its Ritz Crackers in China. Chinese consumers are beginning to buy Agree shampoo, Raid insect killer, Band-Aids, and Bausch & Lomb contact lenses.

The activities of foreign firms in China came to a precipitous halt after the massacre of Chinese student protesters in Tiananmen Square on June 4, 1989. Non-Chinese staff was withdrawn and business activity ceased temporarily. Foreign firms put growth plans on hold while waiting to see the full extent of the government clampdown. By now, however, most Japanese and U.S. firms that do business in China have resumed their operations in full—regardless of recent reports that political repression and human rights abuses are as widespread as ever by the Chinese regime. U.S. firms often prefer to look the other way, hoping that the internal abuses of foreign governments won't affect them. Yet in the long run, as their international activities expand, they cannot escape the internal climate of countries like China because many of their customers and employees must live with the country's legal and political conditions, even if the top executives do not.

Governments also affect international trade through the agreements they reach with one another. Perhaps the most important international trade pact is the General Agreement on Tariffs and Trade (GATT). Established in 1948 under United Nations auspices, GATT binds ninety of the world's trading nations (and about 95 percent of world trade) to mutual agreements that set limits on both tariff and nontariff barriers. Each decade since GATT was created, special sessions (called "rounds") have been convened to discuss current problems in international trade.

Billed as the most important U.S. trade agreement in the past two decades, the U.S.-Canada Free Trade Agreement phases out all tariffs and quotas between the two countries by 1999. This pact is intended to improve each country's GNP, employment, and consumer spending. So far, economists, executives, and labor unions are still arguing over whether its impact is good or bad—but regardless of who wins these arguments, it is now clear that the North American Free Trade Agreement (NAFTA) will increase the volume of international trade within the region.

Other multinational trading agreements exist. At one extreme is "most favored nation" status, in which special treatment is given to a specific trading partner, or set of trading partners, in connection with specific products. The United States, for example, gives developing nations limited duty-free (i.e., tariff-free) access to certain markets. Under a trade program for developing economies called the Generalized System of Preferences (GSP), 140 countries are given GSP status, resulting in exemption for $15 billion of their exports. In 1988, Asia's "Four Tigers"—South Korea, Taiwan, Hong Kong, and Singapore—were removed from GSP status; their exports to the United States resulted in $37 billion of the 1987 U.S. trade deficit, up from $6.1 billion in 1981. Meanwhile, these countries have been resisting opening their markets to U.S. products.

At the other extreme from most favored nation status is the economic cooperation among several nations, such as is found in the European Economic Community (EEC), which was formed in 1957 by six countries and has since expanded to embrace most of western Europe. In a sweeping program, the EEC is wiping away a sea of red tape, regulation, and fiscal restriction that has grown over the decades to protect member nations. By the end of 1992, the 320 million consumers of the twelve countries were supposed to be unified into one market regulated by a common set of trade laws. In effect, people, products, and services could move across country borders with the same ease that they move among the state borders in the United States. Soon to come, according to plan: a single currency. But things never go exactly as planned; problems still exist with the currency plan, and numerous other debates continue to plague the effort to create a single trade zone. Nonetheless it will happen, and that means continued changes of importance to marketers everywhere.

It is expected that protectionist regulations will be raised to favor member nations and insulate the EEC from outsiders, especially Japan and the United States. However, foreign companies already firmly entrenched in the EEC nations will fare well. Furthermore, a recent surge in foreign investments, joint ventures, and even mergers within EEC nations is a strategic move by foreign companies to establish themselves in the EEC. With Europe becoming one, vast economies of scale may become available to marketers. Transportation will be quicker and less expensive without the border stops, fewer product alterations will be needed as product requirements are leveled, and much advertising will become standardized across nations.

On a broader scale, the ability to engage in international marketing at all is contingent upon the permission of the governments involved. In the early 1980s, for example, Caterpillar had a major contract to work on a gas pipeline in the former Soviet Union. The Reagan administration demanded the cancellation of that contract, primarily in response to the Soviet invasion of Afghanistan. Large portions of the contract were reassigned to Japanese competitors. Coca-Cola Company left India when the government demanded that the company turn over its secret formula to an Indian company. However, because India has a population of 800 million and annual sales of 2.4 billion bottles of name-brand soft drinks, PepsiCo agreed in 1988 to tough conditions imposed by the Indian government to gain entry to India. PepsiCo agreed to export five times the value of components imported to India. Failure to comply will result in none of its profits being allowed out of the country. In defense of the company's decision to enter India, the president of PepsiCo International indicated, "We're willing to go so far with India because we wanted to make sure we get an early entry while the market is developing. The Indian middle class is beginning to emerge, and we see that as a big growth market."[13] Such examples point up the importance of uncontrollable environmental forces in international marketing, a subject that is discussed in detail in the next section.

THE LOCAL ENVIRONMENT

The most obvious problems in global marketing result from language, laws and restrictions, time zones, customs inspections, transportation, and customary business practices. For instance, haggling is never done by the Dutch, often by Brazilians, and always by the Chinese. Financing and currency swings can also cause trouble. Because exporting entails abnormally high overhead, many private banks are not willing to bankroll beginning exporters. And the volatility of currencies can deeply affect profitability. When the dollar soared in the early 1980s, many companies became financially traumatized; in the later 1980s, many companies recouped their losses as the dollar's strength changed.

To develop an international marketing strategy, a company needs to assess five major areas: economic, cultural, technological, political/legal, and geographic environments.

The Economic Environment

In Manila, Marlboro cigarettes are sold singly, not by the pack or carton. "It's too expensive to buy the whole pack, so I get a few at a time," explained a Filipino taxi driver.[14] The point of this example is that if consumers cannot afford a company's products, the company does not necessarily have to ignore that market. Instead, it can reorganize its marketing mix to take limited economic resources into account. Product and price adjustments may be useful in marketing to consumers in affluent nations as well. For example, Mercedes-Benz cars are priced higher in the United States than in Germany, where they are made. The cars carry a premium image in the United States and are given a premium price to match.

These examples emphasize the importance of a country's level of economic development. Countries are frequently classified based on gross domestic product per capita into three economic categories: less developed, developing, and highly developed. The differences among these categories are considerable. For example, the least developed countries have per capita GNPs of less than $400, whereas the most highly developed ones may have per capita GNPs of over $110,000.

The economic gap between the poorest and richest nations is widening as economic growth is offset by rapid population growth. Except for Asia, with its newly industrialized countries, less developed countries have made much less progress than the industrialized nations.

Nations that have achieved a long-term record of economic growth are classified as "developing." Examples include Brazil, India, and Taiwan. India, where food once accounted for 25 percent of total imports, now produces its own and even exports grain to Russia.

Still other countries are classified as highly developed. Many of these are members of the Organization for Economic Co-Operation and Development (OECD), which was formed after World War II to provide a forum for discussion of the economic relationships among member nations. Together, the OECD nations (which include most of Western Europe, New Zealand, Australia, Canada, the United Kingdom, Turkey, and the United States) account for well over 70 percent of world trade and have shown the most consistent growth patterns over the years. Their export growth has been higher than the world average, in contrast to that of less developed countries, whose export growth is only about 10 percent of the world average.[15]

But for U.S. exporters, the developing countries often represent the greatest opportunities. Their rising economies and growing populations combine to create new, growth markets for products such as Whirlpool's household appliances that face far more mature, slow-growth markets in developed countries. That is why more than 40 percent of U.S. exports of manufactured goods go to developing countries. Yet, ironically, far less is known about the needs and behaviors of consumers in developing countries than in developed countries. For most marketers, then, the fastest-growing global markets are also their greatest marketing blind spots.[16]

Learning to Dance in Developing Countries

The fact is that more than two-thirds of the world's population lives in the developing nations—an enormous market, highly attractive to marketers, but also difficult to master and sometimes difficult even to enter.

Perhaps the greatest challenge facing marketers is the low level of disposable income in many of those countries. The per capita income in many developing countries is less than $200 per year. Low or negative economic growth rates, coupled with high birthrates, result in a situation in which fewer economic resources must be allocated among more people. This leaves very little to be spent on imported goods on a per capita basis. However, many companies see developing countries as a major source of growth markets in the future.

To overcome the difficulties of marketing in developing countries around the world, marketers can use a four-step model of the market entry process that is designed to help them succeed in developing countries. The model has come to be called the A-B-C-D paradigm by experts on the topic, and it says that marketers of consumer goods need to go through the following stages in order to succeed in any local market:

- *A. Access.* The first step involves getting the product or service to the right consumers in ways that are appropriate to the culture. This gives them access to it—but does not guarantee they will use that access to buy it.

- *B. Buying behavior.* In this second stage of market development, the international marketer focuses on understanding buyer behavior within the local culture, concentrating on issues such as how the brand is perceived and what must be done to create brand loyalty.

- *C. Consumption characteristics.* In this, the third stage of development, the marketer focuses on understanding the overall consumption patterns, asking questions such as "Why does this group of consumers buy that type of product in large quantities, while others don't?" Social class, the nature of the local culture, and other factors help explain the unique consumption patterns of any developing country.

- *D. Disposal.* In the fourth stage, the marketer begins to think about packaging, recycling, and other issues that help reduce the costs of the product to the local society and consumer. Growing environmental consciousness makes the disposal of the product more important in developing countries than most marketers realize. As marketers focus on disposal issues, they should also become more conscious of the broader social impact of their business on the country and its people. This final stage involves a transition to a responsible citizenship role in the developing country. The international marketer is no longer an outsider trying to "milk" the country for sales, but increasingly a citizen in its own right, concerned about the long-term development and success of the nation and its people and natural environment.[17] With this integration into the local scene, the company is finally "at one" with its market and able to understand fully what local customers want and need.

The Cultural Environment[18]

Culture may be thought of as a set of shared learned behaviors based on group values. Among the elements of culture are language, religion, values and attitudes, ethics, education, and social organization.[19]

The importance of cultural factors to a firm that engages in international marketing can be seen in the following example. A company marketing baby food in Sweden, which has a 99 percent literacy rate, could advertise the product in various magazines and newspapers, perhaps including information about the product's nutritional content. In Yemen, however, where the literacy rate is about 30 percent, an approach based on the use of visual media, such as posters, would be more appropriate. Even then, the company might run into problems. One company that hoped to market baby food in central Africa put a picture of a cute baby from a local tribe on the jar. Consumers responded all right, but not in the way the company expected. The literacy rate in the area was practically zero, and consumers had come to expect that the picture on the package represented its contents. They concluded that the baby food jars contained processed baby!

The baby food didn't sell, of course. But behind that failure is more than bad luck—there is a lack of interest in the critical social factors. To avoid stupid mistakes, and to find opportunity in the unique culture of each country and market, managers need to acquire deep, personal knowledge of a culture. If they can't do this personally, they need to hire people from the culture and rely on their expertise.

Language

Language is perhaps the most important element of culture from the standpoint of international marketers. Chevrolet once attempted to introduce its Nova into Spanish-speaking countries. In Spanish, however, the word nova means "It doesn't go." Needless to say, Chevrolet's venture was not a success. A similar problem arose for a German exporter of chocolates, which introduced its product to the U.S. market under the brand name Zit. Such stories are amusing, but it is important to realize that both companies incurred substantial losses as a result of these mistakes. They could modify their brands, but such changes take time and money while leaving the market open to competitors.

Edward T. Hall's concept of the "silent language" of time and space is indicative of another source of problems for unwary international marketers.[20] In India, "time is a river;" whereas in the United States, "time is money." The notions of deadlines and delivery dates are very different in the two cultures. Space also is viewed differently in different cultures. U.S. marketers sometimes feel uncomfortable when negotiating with Jordanian counterparts because Jordanians tend to stand closer to others than is generally considered acceptable in the United States.

Religion

Religion and ethics play key roles in people's responses to marketing activities. An example is the reaction of consumers in Saudi Arabia to an airline ad showing a female flight attendant serving champagne to smiling business people. This ad violated at least two norms related to the Moslem religion: the appropriate roles for women and the prohibition of alcoholic beverages. It was seen by Saudis as an attempt to change their religious values and eventually had to be canceled.

Values and Attitudes

Cultures differ in their values and attitudes toward work, success, clothing, food, music, sex, social status, honesty, the rights of others, and much else. For example, attitudes toward personal care—and hence personal-care products—vary considerably. Pepsodent's claim that its toothpaste helps create white teeth did not go over well in parts of Southeast Asia where people chew betel nuts to stain their teeth.

| **FOR YOUR IMAGINATION** |

Buy Our Product. It Sucks!

Some of our favorite marketing jokes are actually other people's marketing mistakes. Which is, we know, a bit hard-hearted. But other people's mistakes *can* be pretty amusing. And here are some of the funniest, compiled from the Internet and sent to us by Daniel Blanchard, director of network systems and services at U. Mass Amherst's Office of Information Technologies.

- Scandinavian vacuum manufacturer Electrolux used the following slogan for a U.S. ad campaign: "Nothing sucks like Electrolux."

- The name Coca-Cola, when first translated to Chinese, came out as Ke-kou-ke-la—which some people read as meaning "bite of the wax tadpole" and others saw as "female horse stuffed with wax." (It all depends on the tone, or how you pronounce each syllable—a complexity we don't plan to master anytime soon.) Now they use Ko-kou-ko-le, which they hope will be read as "happiness in the mouth."

- Another Chinese blunder: Kentucky Fried Chicken's translation of its "Finger-lickin' good" slogan came out as "eat your fingers off."

- Why didn't the Ford Pinto, a best-seller in the United States, succeed in Brazil? Maybe because pinto was slang for "tiny male genitals." It sold better when renamed Corcel, which means horse. *All* of the horse, not just one part of it.

- You think Ford got in trouble? What about Frank Purdue, the U.S. chicken magnate. His photo appeared on billboards in Mexico with a rough translation of his U.S. slogan. Instead of saying "It takes a tough man to make a tender chicken," the ads read, "It takes a hard man to make a chicken aroused."

- More trouble with slang. Hunt-Wesson translated its Big John brand name into Canadian French as Gros Jos, only to learn this was slang for "big breasts." Oops.

Values and attitudes are frequently translated into rules of conduct and sometimes into laws that can directly affect international marketing. The ban on comparative advertising in Germany, for example, causes problems for U.S. advertisers that are used to claiming their products are stronger, faster, or cheaper than those of competitors. Unwritten rules of conduct are almost as important as formal laws. A gesture such as putting one's feet on one's desk can be interpreted quite differently in different cultures. In the United States, this action is taken as a sign of relaxation or contemplation. In most Middle Eastern countries, by contrast, it is considered in very poor taste. There, the sole of the foot or shoe is considered offensive because it comes into contact with the ground.

Ethics

When in Rome, do—or don't do—as the Romans do? Determining what constitutes ethical practices when conducting business at home is not always easy. When doing business on foreign turf, the question becomes even more difficult to resolve. A barrage of global actions by U.S. marketers have come under question. Multinational companies have striven to change deep-seated cultural values. For example, U.S. consumer products such as deodorants, toothpastes, fast foods, and breakfast cereals have been introduced and pushed in Third World countries where they were previously unknown. Birth control devices and infant formula to replace breast feeding have been marketed in many illiterate countries.

Is it ethical to attempt to change cultural values to obtain greater sales for U.S. companies? In most Third World countries, the per capita consumption of cigarettes is zooming. In such countries, advertising is not regulated; packaging is not mandated to include health warnings. U.S. tobacco companies have aggressively targeted these countries to offset the lack of growth in markets at home. Is this ethical marketing? (Is it even ethical to market a harmful product like cigarettes in *any* country? Such questions are often posed in business school classrooms, but too easily overlooked in real-world marketing.)

In the United States, bribery is considered unethical. But in parts of Asia, Africa, and the Middle East, certain forms of bribery are considered another cost of doing business. Gifts in the form of outright money, products, even services can be demanded of U.S. companies without a blush. For instance, executives wanting to operate in Qatar were requested to make a staggering $1.5 million "gift" to the country's minister of oil. An official of Indonesia's government-owned oil company asked U.S. suppliers for contributions to an Indonesian restaurant in New York City to "enhance" the Indonesian image in the United States. Ethical? Extortion? Or simply normal business practice?

America's aversion to bribery is mirrored in the law. In 1977, Congress enacted the Foreign Corrupt Practices Act which prohibits U.S. companies from "providing or even offering payments to foreign political parties, candidates, or officials with discretionary authority under circumstances that might induce recipients to misuse their positions to assist the company to obtain, maintain, or retain business." Corporations can be fined up to $1 million. Some foreign countries also have legislated against bribery. In Malaysia, long imprisonment can result from bribery. In the old Soviet Union, officials found guilty of accepting bribes could be executed. Yet in most countries where antibribery laws are on the books, deep-rooted traditions replace the law. Foreign companies have the option of treating the request as illegal or as local custom. In fact, in some cultures, what outwardly appears to be a bribe is truly local custom. The act may be a signal of intent to do business, or it may symbolize gratitude, friendship, or even a release of some obligation. In East Africa, for instance, a monetary gift called *zawadi* is generally requested and, as dictated by tradition, is used to provide a feast in the honor of the donor.

The ethical boundaries of non-Western practices are defined by laws, traditional commercial practices, and social norms. Violation may well rest with interpretation and with general business attitudes tempered by understanding of the local tradition. What may be viewed by Americans as bribery, begging, or blackmail may simply reflect local custom and be nothing more than cross-cultural courtesy or friendship building.[21]

Education

As shown in the baby food example, education and the resultant increase in literacy rates have an enormous impact on the options open to international marketers. Of the elements in the marketing mix, promotion is most affected by this aspect of culture. In India, for example, where the literacy rate is about 33 percent and television and other means of modern mass communication are not widespread, advertising objectives are often met through pictorial outdoor advertising (e.g., transit posters and billboards) and filmed commercials aired in movie theaters. In contrast, newspaper advertising is the largest sector of the advertising industry in the United States.

Social Organization

All societies have some kind of social-class structure. Members of a given class tend to behave in similar ways, especially when compared with members of other social classes. Comparing social classes across societies is difficult. A middle-class Frenchman and a middle-class German do not share the same values and preferences. However, people in the upper classes in most societies seem to be more similar to each other than to members of other classes within their own societies.[22] Interestingly, there may be a shift in this pattern with the emergence of a global generation of youth with many shared values and tastes; we discussed Levi Strauss' effort to court this new market in Chapter 2.

Social mobility, or movement from one social class to another, also varies considerably from one culture to another. In India, traditional Hindu religious values dictate that people accept their social status, at least for this lifetime. In the United States, by contrast, Judeo-Christian religious values encourage people to strive for higher social status in this lifetime. But people are seldom completely honest about social class and/or cannot always take such conventional wisdom for granted. Class mobility in the United States may be more limited than generally assumed, a point to which we'll discuss in Chapter 6. Meanwhile, mobility in India is increasing.

Members of the middle and upper classes are more likely than members of the lower classes to use imported products. This makes countries with large lower-class populations, such as Chile, less attractive to international marketers than countries with larger middle and upper classes, such as Sweden.

The Technological Environment

A nation's level of technology directly affects the assortment of goods and services that a marketer is able to sell there. For example, sales of mainframe computers in China are limited because buildings there are not cooled to the correct temperature range. Meanwhile, in India, water buffalo remain the dominant source of energy for farming. Obviously, the level of technology that prevails in some societies is lacking in others, and in still others, technological advances occur in fits and starts. Even the meaning of technology varies from one nation to another. The U.S. Agency for International Development (AID), which assists nations in their efforts to develop economically, once donated small tractors to farmers in a Latin American nation. When AID representatives returned a year later, they discovered that the tractors had not been maintained—the oil had not been changed, tune-ups had not been performed, and so on. The farmers had never heard of "preventive maintenance" and were quite surprised when the tractors stopped working. (This anecdote says as much about the assumptions of AID workers as it does about Latin American farmers.)

The Political and Legal Environments

Throughout this chapter, we have discussed instances of differences in the political and legal environments of various countries. Exhibit 3.2 illustrates the differences among various Western European countries in the regulation of advertising. Imagine the problems involved in developing an advertising campaign that would meet all these requirements and still deliver the desired message to the consumer. Fortunately, however, such regulations have begun to become standardized with the EEC unification of the European market. But on other continents, such differences persist. For this reason, many marketers prefer to work through local affiliates and/or global ad agencies such as the five largest global agencies (*Advertising Age*, April 21, 1997, p. 514):

Rank	Name	Headquarters
1	WPP Group	London
2	Omnicom Group	New York
3	Interpublic Group	New York
4	Dentsu	Tokyo
5	Young & Rubicam	New York

Governments frequently block investment by foreign firms. Many less developed nations view such investment as exploitive, because the return on the investment does not remain in the host country. But several countries with high levels of foreign debt have changed their policies and are aggressively seeking foreign investment.

Repatriation (i.e., transfer back) of profits from foreign countries also is restricted in some countries. To circumvent such restrictions, a strategy known as transfer pricing is sometimes used. This might occur, for example, when a firm in

EXHIBIT 3.2.   Pre-EC European regulations on advertising.

| | General Regulations | | Limitations of Specific Products | | |
Country	Comparative Advertising	Advertising to Children	Alcoholic Beverages	Tobacco	Drugs and Medicine
Germany	Banned	Voluntary for TV and radio	Voluntary limits by industry	Banned on TV and radio	Banned in all media
Italy	Direct comparisons banned; indirect OK if substantiated	Cannot show children eating	Some restrictions on TV ads	Banned in all media	Copy clearance needed
Netherlands	OK if comparison is fair and detailed	Voluntary restraints	Voluntary restraints on TV and radio	Voluntary restraints on TV and radio	None
Sweden	Banned if denigrating	Ban on showing children in danger	Voluntary control on ads for wine and hard liquor	Banned in all media	Prescription drug ads banned
Switzerland	None	None	Banned in all media	Banned in all media	Banned in all media
United Kingdom	Banned if denigrating	Voluntary rules designed to protect children	No commercials before 9 P.M.	Cigarette ads banned on TV and radio	Voluntary control

Source: Adapted from Courtland L. Bovee and William F. Arens, *Contemporary Advertising,* 3rd ed., Richard D. Irwin, Homewood, IL, 1988.

Switzerland has an affiliate in Argentina that is permitted to transfer only a certain amount of profit to the parent firm each year. The Swiss firm may therefore charge the affiliate $125 for a product that is normally priced at $100. The effect is to transfer an extra $25 of profit from the affiliate to the parent firm.

It is sometimes difficult to determine which country's laws govern an international contract; there is no international code or law in this area. Thus, most international contracts include a jurisdiction clause that specifies which set of laws will apply if a dispute arises. An often-quoted piece of advice for resolving such disputes is "negotiate, arbitrate, litigate;" that is, try to settle disputes out of court if at all possible, because court cases are even more lengthy and costly in an international dispute than in a domestic one.

Political issues are another major concern of international marketers. For example, Hong Kong's political status changed entirely in 1997, when it transferred from British to Chinese control. Although some large firms seem to view this political shift as an opportunity to penetrate Chinese markets more deeply, they are nervous about the possibilities of nationalization or expropriation. Nationalization occurs when a government takes over the ownership or management of a business organization. Expropriation is a more radical action in which the host country denies a foreign corporation the right to engage in business there and seizes its assets. When copper mines and plants in Latin America were expropriated in the 1970s, foreign-owned corporations lost millions of dollars worth of their assets. Confiscation is expropriation without compensation.

Geographic Environments

Products must sometimes be modified to accommodate differences in topography and climate. In Lesotho, a small, mountainous nation in southern Africa, breakfast cereals are sold in bags rather than boxes. Because products are delivered to Lesotho over very rough, unpaved roads, boxes tend to be damaged during shipment. Cereals packed in bags survive the trip without damage. Similarly, Quaker Oats uses special vacuum-sealed tins to protect its cereal products in hot, humid countries. Desert driving conditions in the Middle East require that cars be equipped with supplementary air filters and special clutches.

Natural resources are a major determinant of a nation's production potential. The United States has a variety of minerals, many navigable rivers, and a diverse climate. Thus, it can produce a wide assortment of goods and distribute them efficiently. This has allowed Americans to achieve a high standard of living without relying on imports and exports. Japan, on the other hand, faces a shortage of resources and has been forced to rely on imports and exports to survive economically.

STRATEGIC ALTERNATIVES

We have just described some of the external forces that shape success or failure when doing business in the global arena. Knowledge of these environments directly affects the determination of an appropriate global strategy. International marketing begins with the choice of an entry strategy. Once a company is established in a foreign market, other strategies can be employed to seek competitive success.

Global Entry Strategies

The easiest way to enter international markets is through exporting. Most commonly companies beginning exporting use indirect export. Little investment is needed. The company simply employs salespeople outside the company who provide various services plus international selling expertise. Most indirect exporting is done through domestic-based export merchants who buy domestic products and sell them abroad, and through domestic-based export agents who never own the goods but merely seek out foreign buyers for a commission. Some indirect exporting is done through cooperative organizations where many producers band together and collectively administer the exporting activities.

When the marketer's foreign business has grown sufficiently, the company will likely shift to direct export by setting up an export department or division. The exporter contacts foreign buyers and conducts the marketing activities. Such greater involvement may include the hiring of international manufacturers' representatives, overseas agents who sell related noncompetitive products for a small number of exporters. Alternatively, the exporting company could use import houses, merchants located abroad who buy directly from the exporter and resell to wholesalers, retailers, and industrial users in their countries. Because these import houses do not have exclusive territorial rights, an exporter might use a number of such import houses within a country. This, however, dilutes their loyalty to the exporter. Another alternative is to set up a sales office in the foreign country, staffed with salespeople from the home or foreign country. Because it entails actual presence on foreign soil, this alternative should be considered a form of investment.

Mead Corporation's coated board division has been a successful direct exporter. The company recently began building a new $500 million plant in Alabama to double its capacity to produce coated paperboard used in packaging. Most of the additional capacity is earmarked for Pacific Rim countries. To ensure meeting the local needs of Japanese customers, Mead signed an agreement with Seibu Saison Group, a $20 billion retailer, which will function as the sales representative. The deal will ensure that Mead knows the ultimate customer's wants and will be able to tailor boxes to specific products.

Investment without capital investment means joining with a foreign partner in some sort of arrangement that leads to some production abroad but without bearing the cost of that production. Licensing is an easy way to conduct global marketing. The licenser agrees with a licensee in the foreign country to allow the use of the licensor's production processes, trademark or brand name, patent, marketing know-how, or some other valued asset. In return, the licensee pays the licenser a fee or royalty. A.G. Spalding, the marketer of athletic goods, now has more sales revenue from licensing than from direct production of products. Gerber Company grabbed entry to Japan through licensing. However, because the licenser has less control over the licensee than with its own manufacturing, this strategy is rather risky. Sometimes the licensor finds that at the end of the contract, a direct competitor has been created. Constant innovation by the licensor is the best way to avoid this.

Popular with consumer goods, franchising has become a frequently used entry strategy. In a franchise, the franchiser contracts with a franchisee, as in licensing. The franchise agreement spells out the specific rights and responsibilities of each party. Generally, much more is involved than with licensing. Capital requirements, location restrictions, and merchandising programs are often set for the franchisee to ensure needed control. The franchiser in turn receives financial remuneration. Holiday Inn, McDonald's, and Kentucky Fried Chicken have expanded to foreign markets via franchising.

Production contracting involves agreeing with a local producer in the foreign country to make a product. Generally, the company retains the marketing activities, often through its foreign sales branches. Although a company cannot maintain good control over production, contracting provides quicker access to foreign markets than setting up one's own manufacturing facilities. Many Japanese companies have used this strategy to enter U.S. markets. Sapporo Breweries contracted with southern California's Hansen Foods to bottle soft drinks for sale in the United States, and Kirwin Brewery Company has an agreement with Molson Breweries of Canada to bottle Japanese beer for sale in the United States.

With management contracting, the domestic firm provides management skills and knowledge to the exporting firm in return for capital for the operation. Hilton and Marriott both operate many hotels in foreign countries using this strategy.

Joint venturing exists when foreign companies join together in a partnership in which they share ownership and control—and risk. Three options exist: The domestic company may buy a share in the existing operation of the foreign company, the foreign investor may buy an interest in the local company, or the two partners may form a completely new company. The joint venture is particularly effective when one party needs the financial, production, labor, or marketing expertise of the other partner. Some foreign governments demand joint venture, often offering less than 50 percent ownership to the foreigner, as a condition of entry.

In the quest for greater worldwide market share, joint venturing has become an increasingly popular strategy.[23] India's leather-processing subsidiary of Tata has joined with France's TFR to challenge the Italians' dominance in upscale leather goods. America's Caterpillar is teaming with Japan's Mitsubishi to manufacture enormous earth-moving equipment. Some joint ventures seek world dominance. Philips, the Dutch electronics conglomerate, has joint ventures with many partners to grab the lion's share of the optical disc market. The major alliance is with U.S. DuPont to develop, produce, and market optical storage media. Sometimes these joint ventures produce industries not feasible otherwise. South Korea's Jindo Corporation's joint venture with Siberian sable ranches received the blessing of the Soviet government (but may now have to be renegotiated with Siberian authorities, illustrating the impact political events can have on global strategy). Bringing Jindo's designers and stitchers together with the pelt producers created a $265 million annual fur business.

The greatest involvement comes with the direct investment in manufacturing abroad. When sufficient expertise in the foreign country exists and/or when the market appears large enough, the company may decide to build its own production plants. This strategy maintains control; creates jobs in the foreign country, which enhances the company's image politically and culturally; and builds relationships with the government, people, suppliers, and local distributors. However, this strategy exposes the company to greater risk from unstable governments, changing markets, and even possible expropriation.

But the latest trend in many industries is to access foreign producers in low-labor-cost countries in Asia and Latin America through buying agents and subcontractors. Behind big-name U.S. brands like Nike, Wal-Mart, Disney, and the many popular clothing designers are long, flexible supply chains reaching into the latest "hot" places to produce their products. A single U.S. company making sewn products such as clothes, shoes, or soccer balls may actually be doing business with dozens to hundreds of small factories in any single buying season.

The global race for the lowest possible production costs can lead to uncontrolled labor conditions in these lengthy supply chains. A growing number of exposes in the popular press have alerted U.S. consumers to the problem of sweatshop conditions in many of these factories. And it turns out that U.S. parents don't want to buy soccer balls for their children that are made by children under forced labor conditions in Pakistan. Nor do people want to wear clothes from The Gap that are made under unfair and unsafe conditions in Latin American sweatshops. The globalization race has thus created a new marketing problem for many companies, one that they are just now learning to deal with. According to a spokesperson for Verité, a non-profit that provides inspection and certification services for companies producing overseas, a growing number of U.S. companies are beginning to see the sweatshop issue as a key to their future success—or failure.[24]

EXHIBIT 3.3.   Risk factors and market concerns in international market entry strategies.

Alternative	Risk Factors			Market Concerns		
	Necessary Capital	Political/ Economic Risk	Adaptability to Trade Barriers	Stability of Relationships	Availability of Information	Control
Indirect export	VL	VL	L	VL	VL	VL
Direct export, export						
department	M	M	L	M	M	L
Sales representatives	L	L	L	L	M	M
Import house	VL	VL	L	L	L	VL
Sales office	M	M	M	M	H	M
Involvement without						
capital investment						
Licensing	L	M	H	L	L	VL
Franchising	M	L	M	M	H	M
Product contract	VL	H	M	M	M	L
Management contract	L	M	M	M	H	M
Involvement with						
capital investment						
Joint venture	M	M	H	M	H	H
Manufacturing						
abroad	H	H	H	H	H	H

VL = Very low; L = Low; M = Medium; H = High.

Weighing the Risks

Exhibit 3.3 summarizes the risks associated with each method of market entry, rating each from very low to high. The table also rates three areas of market concern associated with each method. Under Risk Factors, the heading Necessary Capital refers to the risk a firm encounters when it invests its own capital to support the strategy. Political/Economic Risk refers to the degree to which the strategy is vulnerable to political or economic pressures within the host country. Adaptability to Trade Barriers refers to the strategy's ability to respond to newly imposed trade barriers. Under Market Concerns, the heading Stability of Relationships examines the nature of the interaction between organizations in the host and home countries. For example, indirect exporting occurs on an ad hoc basis, with no thought to the long-term potential of that relationship, whereas joint ventures require partners that maintain a mutually rewarding relationship over the long run. Availability of Information refers to the marketing information required for the strategy to be successful. Finally, Control refers to the amount of influence the firm will have over marketing activities in the host country.

A brief look at Exhibit 3.3 shows that each method of market entry involves trade-offs between risk and market concerns. Indirect exports, for example, rate very low on all risk factors but also rate low in terms of the firm's ability to influence the market. In other words, if a firm sells its products to an export broker, the broker assumes the risks of international marketing, but the seller gives up control over how its product is marketed. On the other hand, the risks of establishing a manufacturing plant abroad are very high, but this method of market entry gives the marketer the greatest potential influence on the market.

Global Marketing Strategy

The degree of adaptation to local cultural and business conditions is one consideration in deciding on a strategy. One popular, though controversial, strategy is referred to as the global marketing strategy (GMS).[25] This approach has been defined as "selling the same product, the same way, everywhere."[26] GMS is based on the notion that consumers around the world are growing more and more similar and that a standardized product and marketing mix can achieve enormous economies, especially in advertising, packaging, and distribution because they would not be changed. The strategy is controversial because it seems to flaunt the many factors that make it difficult to move into a new national market, factors much of this chapter is dedicated to analyzing.

Proponents of this strategy believe that modern technology has created a commonalty among people around the world. Global travel and communication have exposed more and more people to products and services that they have heard about, actually seen, or even experienced—and now want. Although differences exist in consumer preferences, shopping behavior, cultural institutions, and promotional media, those who support GMS believe that these preferences and practices can and will change to be more similar. The general strategy of offering high-quality, lower priced products will prevail in any global market.

A few companies, such as Coca-Cola, McDonald's, Exxon, and recently Levi Strauss, have achieved great success through strategies that allow them to operate in a standardized fashion in diverse markets. The "Marlboro Man" advertising campaign has worked well around the world. Coca-Cola is the most recognized soft drink brand on this globe. Yet many companies have been unsuccessful in using this approach. Recall Nike's difficulties with its aggressive approach to the European soccer market, discussed in this chapter's opening pages. Many companies have therefore found it necessary to adapt their strategies to different markets. Exhibit 3.4 lists some factors that appear to affect the success of a global marketing strategy.

Okay, We'll Tell You What We Recommend

What is the answer, then—go international with a single global strategy and brand identity, or focus locally with individualized strategies and offerings? The answer is not yet clear—there are successes and failures in both cases—but it is beginning to appear that both strategies need to be implemented at once. This is the "think globally, act locally" strategy.

Honda is the third largest manufacturer of automobiles in the United States. Although it is a Japanese company, it has made such a large investment in U.S. operations that it is also a major U.S. manufacturer. It might be considered an extreme exemplar of the localization strategy. Hidea Sugiura, Honda's previous chairman (still an active adviser to the company) explains that, "More than 60 percent of our total sales take place outside of Japan; our products are marketed in well over 100 countries. Moreover, we manufacture products at 77 plants in 40 countries outside Japan."[27] Sugiura goes on to

EXHIBIT 3.4.   Factors influencing the success of a global marketing strategy.

	Favoring Global Strategy	Favoring Individualized Strategy
Environment		
Unique cultural factors affecting consumption	Not present	Present
Legal environment	Similar	Different
Geographic factors	Similar	Different
Government involvement in business	Laissez faire	Controlled
Attitude toward change	Flexible	Inflexible
Market characteristics		
Character of resident population		
Degree of urbanization	Largely urban	Largely rural
Size of total population	Very large	Small
Sophistication of marketing institutions	Sophisticated	Primitive
Product		
Breadth of market appeal	Narrow	Broad
Technical complexity of product	Simple	Technical
Cost of financial factors		
Level of R&D cost	High	Low
Importance of price	Important	Unimportant
Availability of investment capital	High	Low

explain that, "We place the utmost importance on localization—adapting our activities to those practiced in the countries where we operate. This overseas strategy consists of four concepts: localization of products, profit, production, and management."[28] This means that products are tailored to the needs of local markets, profits from local markets are reinvested (which often makes the difference between being a welcome or unwelcome guest in a foreign country), production occurs in major local markets, and authority and control are decentralized to the local management.

This strategy would be a recipe for disaster without a strong centralizing force to tie together every local market and keep the Honda mission and identity at the fore. At Honda, this comes from a transfer of corporate culture to the local enterprise. According to Sugiura, "It involves the transfer of a philosophy, that is, the corporate culture that constitutes the basis of technology and management, developed within a corporation since its founding."[29]

U.S. auto companies take the opposite approach, traditionally building most of their cars in the United States for export to foreign markets and not customizing the product or even the marketing message for the local market. U.S. cars with the steering wheel on the left are still offered in many foreign countries where traffic laws require one to drive on the left even though most cars have the wheel on the right. To these U.S. auto companies, Honda's incredibly localized strategy seems very appealing, but difficult to implement. From Honda's perspective, the centralized control over marketing and product development that Ford or Chrysler maintain no doubt seems efficient and simpler to manage.

This contrast appears in a study of many multinational corporations by professors Cristopher Bartlett and Sumantra Ghoshal, published in the University of California-Berkeley's California Management Review. They reported that,

> In the course of a study of some of the world's leading Japanese, European, and American multinationals, we found that these globalizing and localizing forces are working simultaneously to transform many industries. But for historical reasons, few companies have built the organizational capabilities to respond equally to both of these forces.[30]

In other words, although both centralized and localized models have appealing features, it is difficult for managers to transform either model into the other. What the authors recommend instead is a linkage of central and local structures that combines strengths of each, allowing the company "to do what it must to survive in today's international environment—think globally and act locally."[31] To be effective, this hybrid approach needs to be characterized by:

- Interdependence between local operations through shared resources and responsibilities.

- Devices to force integration of operations among local units, for example, through communications and cooperation by managers.

- Strong, shared corporate identity and philosophy, such as Honda uses to keep its local operations focused on the central goals and mission.

Whirlpool also relies on a strong, shared corporate identity and philosophy to unify its many global operations. For instance, the company's employees are asked to focus on a set of four "value-creating objectives" that can be applied anywhere in the world. For instance, the list includes the following: "Our Worldwide Excellence System will deliver products and services that by measurement [in the local markets] exceed customer expectations and outperform all our competitors."[32]

Of the various characteristics needed for the hybrid approach, the operational interdependence of local units may be even more important than the unifying philosophy or culture. According to Bartlett and Ghoshal,

> Perhaps the most important requirement of the transnational organization is a need for the organizational configuration to be based on a principle of reciprocal dependence among units. Such an interdependence of resources and responsibilities breaks down the hierarchy between local and global interests by making the sharing of resources, ideas, and opportunities a self-enforcing norm.[33]

Perhaps the simplest way to state this principle is to say that the organization needs to be designed so that local managers work with local managers from other countries, not merely their own. This is the essence of thinking globally but acting locally.

Other Strategic Options

In addition to a GMS or an individualized approach, other strategies are open to international marketers. One of these is called modular marketing, a centrally coordinated strategy that is carried out in local units or modules. The modules may be either demographic or geographic. They may even cross national boundaries. This approach is used by Procter & Gamble in selling soap. A soap with the same chemical properties may be marketed in the Western European module and the Asian module using the same basic advertising theme (cleanliness), but the soap may be positioned differently according to the cultural meaning and importance of cleanliness in each module. The packaging may also appeal to different cultural traits through the colors and artwork used.

Another strategic option for international marketers is the use/need approach.[34] In this strategy, the product mix and the promotional mix are either extended (used in the same manner) or adapted (modified) according to an evaluation of whether the product use and the need being served are the same or different in various markets. Thus, bicycles sold in China or Holland might be physically similar to bicycles sold in the United States, but the manner in which they are promoted would be quite different because the needs they satisfy are different. In China and Holland, a bike is needed for transportation; in the United States, the chief need satisfied is recreation. In this situation, a single, global strategy is unrealistic. A more localized approach that takes into account local use and need would therefore be appropriate. Products would have to differ dramatically between transportation- and recreation-oriented bicycle markets.

GLOBAL COMPETITIVENESS: THE BIG-PICTURE ISSUE FOR MARKETERS

Sometimes the issue for global marketers is broader than how to take one brand or company into one foreign market at a time. What if your industry in your country is, overall, simply not capable of competing against rivals from another country? Perhaps these foreign competitors seem to have a cost advantage, or to always beat you to the punch on technical advances. If so, then it takes more than good marketing to make you competitive. First, you must figure out how to level the global playing field so that your company and nation are more competitive globally. And to address issues of global competitiveness, you need to understand why disparities between the industries of different countries arise in the first place. That's a tall order—one many economists spend their lives disagreeing over—but we think one model in particular is probably most relevant to the real-world marketer.

The findings of Michael Porter of Harvard Business School are perhaps especially relevant, as they share a philosophical perspective with the "think globally, act locally" strategy discussed previously. Porter spent four years studying the market share trends of ten countries in hundreds of separate industries. He found, for example, that between 1978 and 1985, the United States increased its share by 15 percent or more in 82 industries, but lost 15 percent or more of its share in 97 others, producing a net loss. What is particularly interesting about his findings is his explanation of why these trends occurred. Competitive advantage occurs, according to Porter, when an industry has four conditions that are favorable to successful business development in that industry:[35]

1. *Factor conditions*—The natural resources needed in the industry and the ability to turn them into a specialized advantage (the resources do not help competitiveness if many other countries also have them).

2. *Demand conditions*—A large, sophisticated domestic market to spur innovation and development in the industry.

3. *Related and supporting industries*—According to Porter, "An industry striding toward the top needs worldclass suppliers" and strong indirect competitors that, together, can form what he calls an industrial cluster in which accelerated innovation occurs. (Silicon Valley is an obvious example.)

4. *Company strategy, structure, and rivalry*—The factors that determine how a company is "created, organized, and managed." For example, a highly competitive domestic industry will tend to produce companies that are more competitive on the global level.

Porter's findings are relevant to government policymakers, but we are especially interested in their implications for managers. For example, what do they say about the U.S. computer industry? It has favorable factor conditions, such as a highly educated workforce (although national policy has not focused on maintaining this advantage). It has favorable demand conditions, with a large, sophisticated, and demanding U.S. consumer base. It also has fierce, sophisticated rivals to provide domestic competition.

So what could be wrong? Does it have the critical mass of related and supporting industries that Porter talks of? Do the industrial clusters of Silicon Valley and Boston's Route 128 fill this role adequately? Perhaps not. Ferguson's findings seem to point to a weakness in this area, one that is not immediately obvious because it is happening under the surface. More and more Silicon Valley companies are sourcing critical components overseas, and doing the bare minimum of assembly here. This means that the power of this industrial cluster is fading, and it no longer contains a critical mass of related companies, all innovating and competing together to advance the computer industry.

What should U.S. companies do to remain competitive worldwide? Some of the success factors Porter identifies are difficult for individual companies to control—how do you single-handedly create an industrial cluster, or keep one from losing its vitality? But perhaps even a problem of this magnitude can be addressed. Firms often make some headway on such issues through trade groups and lobbying efforts, providing they agree that the issue deserves their attention.

Foreign Success Begins at *Home!*

At the level of the individual firm, Porter interprets the results as indicating a need to build global strategy on a firm "home-base" strategy. By this, he means that "a company has only one home base for each particular business, and its health is essential to the company's capacity to prosper in the long run."[36] The home base should be the country and location that provides the four critical success factors an industry needs, as defined on page 82, and the company's strategy should be designed to be closely tied to this home base. Porter explains that "Today's competitive advantage is a matter of knowledge and skill. These are shaped by local institutions, local values, local suppliers, local customers. . . . The capacity to compete globally arises from the advantages created at home."[37] This means, for example, that although in the short run a company might achieve cost advantages by buying products from abroad, in the long run it will become less competitive because it will no longer have the advantage of capable home-base suppliers. The company's management must both select a good home base and nurture that home base so that it will in turn nurture the company for global competition.

Porter's arguments could be taken as a conservative call for fully centralized management of multinationals. They are not. On the marketing side, to be successful, companies need to maintain a local presence and know thoroughly a country's culture, values, and needs. This means acting locally, through vertical integration into the foreign country for distribution, even for production in many cases. But this must be balanced by a dynamic home base, one that ensures a long-term supply of leading-edge innovations and that allows the company to lead the market in the effort to give customers more for their dollar—or yen. Honda's successful local strategy is based on a strong Japanese home industry, and much of Honda's know-how, ideas, and components come from Japan, even though many of its cars and motorcycles are built overseas.

When Porter's arguments concerning the need for a strong home base are considered, we can conclude that three strategic components seem essential to a company's global competitiveness. First, as discussed earlier, the firm must have a global vision. It must think globally and have sufficient mechanisms to ensure that local managers rub shoulders—and share ideas—with other managers on a global as well as a local level. Second, also as discussed earlier, a strong local presence in each foreign market is essential. This is the "act locally" component of the multinational's strategy. Third, the company must pick a domestic home base for each of its industries that can give the company home-base advantages in each industry. This strategy is not simple to follow—it is much more complex than the strategies required to succeed in a domestic market. But, then again, the problem of how to achieve global leadership is not a simple one!

PART TWO

ACHIEVING MARKETING INSIGHT

When we do marketing research or strategy consulting for our clients, we try to avoid the technicalities of these complex subjects. Sure, technical matters matter. You don't want to use the wrong analytical technique or write a misleading survey question. But the big picture is easily lost in such details.

The big picture is startlingly simple—and yet most of the people we work with in business are surprised when we explain our view of it, and startled to discover they have been overlooking something so important.

The big picture is this. You stand in one of three positions relative to all that nasty competition out there. First, you may be behind them because you don't know something important about your market or customers that they do. That we call *information disadvantage.* If you have an information disadvantage, no new tactics or strategies will succeed, no matter how clever you think they are or how hard you try to implement them. So the bottom line is, to avoid certain failure you must make sure you don't have an information disadvantage.

The second position—and the most common one—is *information parity.* It means you know roughly as much as your competitors do about your market and customers. Information parity keeps you from losing big-time, and is a good minimum standard for anyone in business. But when you share a knowledge base with your competitors, you are unable to beat them to the punch. You can hold steady in the fight for customer loyalty, but you cannot gain significant new ground because it is hard to imagine things your competition hasn't already thought of.

Most companies struggle in this difficult parity position. It's a natural result of doing the same kinds of things that your competitors do. If you use similar sources of information, or if you produce new products, or design new marketing programs through similar processes, then you will never come up with anything that's very original or exciting to your customers. Information parity leads to similar products and encourages customers to buy on the basis of price. Not much fun for marketers!

The third possible position is the only really fun and profitable one. We call it *information leadership,* and it gives you the advantage of some insights that your competitors don't have. Not yet. Whenever you find a fresh new way of looking at customer behaviors and needs, or a new approach to designing your products or processes, you can do things that excite your customers and madden your competitors. So the name of the game in business and in marketing is to maintain an information advantage and use it to offer customers something new and different, something more useful or fun, something of greater value in their minds than anything the competition can do.

How? It's not simple, but it is attainable. To find out how, read on.

4 MARKETING RESEARCH AND INFORMATION

The Search for Customer Insight

A desk is a dangerous place from which to view the world.

—*John Le Carré*

We become slaves to demographics, to market research, to focus groups. We produce what the numbers tell us to produce. And gradually, in this dizzying chase, our senses lose feeling and our instincts dim, corroded by safe action.

—*Barry Diller, CEO, Fox Broadcasting*[1]

The marketing research industry worldwide is measured in billions of dollars. Many large companies budget millions for their surveys and studies. For example, Maryanne E. Rasmussen, senior vice president of Quality, American Express Travel Related Services Company, says "We spend hundreds of millions of dollars trying to figure out what the customer wants."

It is vital to know what your customers want, and to know it more clearly and quickly than your competitors do. Such insights fuel innovations in all aspects of business and are the root of all business growth and success. This chapter is going to cue up many of the staple techniques of marketing research to help you improve your insight into customer needs and wants.

In spite of the billions spent on research, in spite of a huge, multifaceted research industry (see Exhibit 4.1), in spite of an incredible arsenal of sophisticated statistical and psychological methods—it can be remarkably difficult to figure out what customers *really* want.

87

EXHIBIT 4.1.   The research cornucopia.

Specialized Research Areas	Examples of Research Providers
Advertising effectiveness	Audits & Surveys Worldwide, New York, (212) 627-9700 NFO Research, Inc., Greenwich, CT, (203) 629-8888
Ad copy evaluation	Research International, New York, (212) 679-2500
Asian markets	MRD Co., El Cerrito, CA, (510) 525-9675
Brand evaluation	Burke Customer Satisfaction Associates (BCSA), Cincinnati, OH, (800) 264-9970 Brand Consulting Group, Southfield, MI, (810) 559-2100 The Landis Group, West Palm Beach, FL, (407) 684-3636
Food & beverages	GFK/Sofema International, 10 Rue Lionel Terray, Rueil Malmaison Cedex 92500, France, 3-31-47-14-44-00 Creative & Response Research Services, Chicago, (312) 828-9200
Business-to-business marketing	Burke Customer Satisfaction Associates (BCSA), Cincinnati, OH, (800) 264-9970 Industrial Market Research Co., Whittier, CA, (310) 698-2341
Competitor intelligence	The Becker Research Co., Rocky Hill, NJ, (609) 951-8570
Consumer products	The BASES Group, Covington, KY, (606) 655-6000 Research International, New York, (212) 679-2500
Controlled store testing	Capstone Research, Inc., Lyndhurst, NJ, (201) 939-0600
Copy testing	NFO Research, Inc., Greenwich, CT, (203) 629-8888
Corporate image research	I.D. ENTITY, Brea, CA, (800) 355-9817
Customer satisfaction	BCSA, Cincinnati, OH, (800) 264-9970 The Blackstone Group, Chicago, IL, (312) 419-0400 Polaris Marketing Research, Atlanta, GA, (404) 816-0353
Data collection and processing	Data Recognition Corp., Minnetonka, MN, (612) 935-5900
Demographic analysis	Data Mapping Services, Akron, OH, (216) 929-1353

EXHIBIT 4.1. *(Continued)*

Specialized Research Areas	Examples of Research Providers
Ethnic markets	Hispanic Market Connections (HMC), Los Altos, CA, (415) 965-3859
Eye tracking	Perception Research Services, Fort Lee, NJ, (201) 346-1600 Toronto Focus, Toronto, Ontario, Canada, (416) 250-3611
Focus groups	Roanoke Focus Group Centre, Roanoke, VA, (703) 342-5364 Manhattan Opinion Center, New York, (212) 557-3085
In-store interviewing	Audits & Surveys Worldwide, New York, (212) 627-9700
Mail surveys	Questar Service Quality Research, Eagan, MN, (612) 688-0089
Market segmentation/structure	SERS, Chicago, IL, (312) 828-0702
Media studies	The Arbitron Company, New York, (212) 887-1300 BAI, Tarrytown, NY, (914) 332-5300
Mystery shopping	Capstone Research, Fairfield, NJ, (201) 939-0600
Name testing	NameQuest, Carefree, AZ, (602) 488-9660
New product research	The BASES Group, Covington, KY, (606) 655-6000 SERS, Chicago, IL, (312) 828-0702
Package design	Perception Research Services, Fort Lee, NJ, (201) 346-1600
Simulated test markets	The BASES Group, Covington, KY, (606) 655-6000
Store audits	O'Connor Survey Service, Knoxville, TN, (615) 525-9989
Survey processing	Scantron Corp., Tustin, CA, (714) 259-8887
Test marketing	Maritz Marketing Research, Fenton, MO, (314) 827-1610

This chapter's opening quote from Barry Diller epitomizes a growing backlash against conventional marketing research methods. It reflects the rising frustration of managers who have all the statistics and surveys their desks can handle without collapsing, but still lack fresh insights into their customers, products, and markets. Instead of illuminating, those stacks of research reports often cloud the picture. It is easy for marketing researchers to count and measure every tree, but awfully hard for them to describe the forest.

As we showed in the diagram on page 20, you can think of the marketing process as hinging upon the quantity and quality of the information it brings in. Information is marketing's greatest asset. Most of this chapter is going to look at formal processes for creating a rich in-flow of information. But the backlash against marketing research reflects a little-understood issue—that this information flow really has two very different roles and must be managed with an eye to both.

On the one hand, much of routine research and information-gathering fulfills a fairly simple (if time-consuming) role: to maintain information parity with competitors in your industry. Should you fail to do so, should *they* know more about your customers and markets than *you* do, you're going to be at a disadvantage. (You can't afford an information deficit. Anything that can be an asset can also be a liability.) Thus, you will find that competitors in any industry tend to do similar types of research and to budget similar amounts for their research—just as they do for advertising or product development or any other essential marketing function. They survey their customers, evaluate the effectiveness of different ad media, and so forth, just to make sure they keep up with the trends and don't overlook any obvious opportunities or problems.

On the other hand, parity is not enough. Ask your boss or your shareholders if you don't believe us. So how do you increase your revenues, boost your market share, or squeeze more profits out of your sales? The answers must flow from some fresh insight. The second key role of information is to give your firm an information *advantage*, to gain an insight that will allow you to introduce an exciting new product or try a new approach to distribution or service. Business breakthroughs are built on information advantages and the clearer views they offer of the marketing landscape—as represented by the peak of the information pyramid in Exhibit 4.2. When Barry Diller complains that his firm's senses are dulled by too much research, he's highlighting a problem: Conventional approaches to information-gathering get in the way of your information advantage, instead of helping you achieve it. If you aren't careful, you can easily spend your entire budget on fancy surveys and studies that fail to give you any information advantage at all.

Perhaps you also remember the American Express TV commercial in which a successful young businesswoman breaks in her new credit card by taking her (also successful) husband to dinner. It aired nationally for a short time, but was pulled after tests suggested that some people found the ad intimidating. In an interesting study, Ogilvy & Mather, the ad agency handling this campaign, asked consumers to imagine that they were *talking* with American Express cards.

One subject in the study imagined the American Express card saying, "You're not really my type—you can't keep up."[2] Ogilvy shifted to "a more laid-back crew of cardholders. Still handsome, still elegant, but in more relaxed settings—two people off on a spontaneous vacation, for instance," as Forbes described it.

Decisions like this, based on detailed consumer information, are not uncommon at American Express (Amex). The company takes advantage of its regular contacts with cardholders to amass a great deal of information about them. For example, their computers are reported to maintain, with weekly updates, 450 pieces of information about each cardholder.[3] The customer database now totals an incredible 500 billion

EXHIBIT 4.2.   The information pyramid.

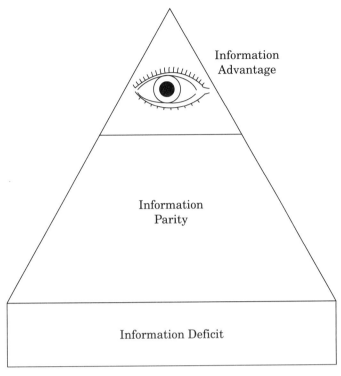

Information Advantage

Information Parity

Information Deficit

Source: Alexander Hiam & Associates.

bytes of data—too much for anything but the most sophisticated parallel computer processors to handle.[4] Amex uses its customer information to target specific groups of customers for ancillary sales of everything from magazine subscriptions and stereo equipment to gas grills. Amex marketers identify women who buy most of their dresses at Saks Fifth Avenue, and then offer them discounts on shoes at that store as a reward for using their Amex cards.[5]

Many success stories in marketing are based on successful acquisition and interpretation of marketing information. But useful information can be hard to obtain. Managers often complain about the marketing information available to them. Does Amex truly need all 450 pieces of information it collects about each cardholder? Why, with all this information, did the company not know its advertisement was a flop until Ogilvy & Mather asked viewers to talk to their cards?

Managers frequently complain that information is scattered throughout the company and hard to find, or that it arrives too late to be useful. They also worry about the accuracy of their marketing information. These complaints reflect the essential role of marketing information, and the frustration managers experience when they must make decisions based on imperfect information.

To overcome many of these problems and to increase the value and quantity of information, managers can pursue the following strategies:

- Increase the sources of information.
- Reduce error.
- Design studies better.
- Report information more clearly.
- Manage the company's marketing information system more aggressively.
- Seek innovative research methods.

The latter strategy is perhaps the hottest one right now in marketing because it offers new insights into customers, the possibility of information advantages upon which to build real marketplace advantages.

For example, one of our clients, the CEO of a cable television company, favors what he calls "walking-the-dog" research. By this he means research in which marketers make casual inquiries as they encounter people during their daily routines. He can sometimes learn more of value to his business by walking his dog than by reading the formal research reports his firm commissions. A surprising amount of valuable information can come from such casual conversations—including many insights that you wouldn't have thought to ask about in a formal survey.

Informal research by actual decision makers rather than research specialists is the latest fashion in marketing. When Louis Gretna became CEO at IBM with the task of reversing its downward slide in 1993, he refused to make any marketing or strategic decisions for the first six months. Instead, he spent six months wandering the world in continuous conversations with customers, suppliers, distributors, and anyone else who might have valuable insights for turning IBM around. Breakfast meetings with customers, followed by plant visits, then lunches with still more customers, and on and on until late every evening.

| FOR YOUR IMAGINATION |

Innovative Listening at HP

"The listening process is the process by which we develop an understanding of customer needs, and our goal in changing the process is to develop a clearer and more imaginative understanding of those needs. A key to success is to use multiple channels in order to hear more and more varied inputs concerning customer perceptions and needs.

It is not enough to conduct standard marketing research any more. Our listening process now uses three main channels: customer research, market watchers, and advisory councils. By listening in all three channels, we gain a three-dimensional picture of the customer's perception that supports an imaginative approach to defining and meeting customer needs."

—Manuel F. Diaz, vice president, Worldwide Sales and Marketing, Hewlett Packard Computer Systems Organization[6]

Most people thought he was crazy. But now they're not so sure—and many other managers are beginning to follow suit. IBM's stock, which reached an 18-year-low of $40.62 at the time Gerstner took over, is up 400 percent as of this writing, and IBM's competitors are shocked at the strength of its rebound in all its major markets.[7]

IBM was one of the first companies to jump onto this new direction in research, but others are following. A recent article in the *Harvard Business Review* is titled, "Spend a Day in the Life of Your Customers."[8] Even one day devoted to shadowing a customer is something new for many managers, but if Gerstner can do it for six months, one day can't hurt!

SOURCES OF INFORMATION

Numerous sources of information exist—many more than most marketers use. Some sources provide formal information, such as a carefully written report describing survey results, whereas others present information informally. But all are valuable. The following are some categories of marketing information:

Books and periodicals.

Consultants and research firms.

Customers.

Friends inside your company.

Friends outside your company.

Grapevine.

Marketing information system (company's internal records).

Marketing research.

Other managers.

Public documents from competitors.

Staff.

Subordinates.

Superiors.

Suppliers.

Surfing the web.

Walking your dog.

Customers are often the most valuable source, and most marketing research focuses on them. But other sources, from employees to competitors, can also be useful.

Informal Sources

American Express, Sony, Whirlpool, Procter & Gamble, and many other companies have begun to solicit complaints from customers as a supplement to the formal customer surveys they conduct. General Electric's (GE) answer center in Louisville, Kentucky, handles three million calls via the company's toll-free number each year, and about 10 percent of them are complaints. The complaints are used by marketing to identify problems and improve products and service. Twenty-five percent of the callers ask for help with prepurchase decisions, giving GE a chance to influence 500,000 purchases. American Express spends $150 million annually to help customers with problems. The communication lines, data banks, computers, personnel, and specialized training that go into this operation produce a tremendous amount of marketing information for use in decision making. Coca-Cola's (800) GET-COKE number logged more than 12,000 calls a day when New Coke replaced the old formula in 1985. Ninety percent were complaints, and Coke Classic was reinstated soon after.

Informal information from customer complaint lines and centers is sometimes supplemented by information from other sources. United Airlines decided to provide better flight information because a company executive overheard passengers discussing their difficulties. Montgomery Ward lowered its prices when its chairman discovered many of his employees shopping at Kmart. At Minnesota Mining & Manufacturing (3M), the salesforce is the main source of new product ideas. When its salespeople saw workers in automobile factories choking on the dust produced by dry sandpaper, 3M developed a sandpaper that could be used wet. The firm also came up with disposable surgical staples and Steri-Strip, a tape for closing incisions, as a result of its salespeople's observations of problems that occurred in operating rooms.

Formal Sources

Formal sources are those that follow specified procedures, which increases their accuracy in some cases and makes it much easier to assess their reliability in all cases. Formal systems usually start with a manager's information request, then collect and analyze raw data to answer the manager's question. Formal sources include primary sources (or original sources), such as customers, and secondary sources, which report on information already gathered from primary sources. Most of this chapter focuses on formal sources.

Often-Missed Sources

Are you overlooking good sources of information? The following is a list of sources most commonly overlooked by managers:

- *Government patent filings*—Watching such data discloses potential technological advancement within a firm's industry.

- *Competitors' annual reports*—In an attempt to enhance stockholders' image of the firm, the annual report may disclose new technology in research and development or other useful information.

- *Competitors' employment ads*—Such ads may suggest a competitor's technical and marketing directions.

- *Professional associations and meetings*—The competitors' products, research and development, and management philosophy are often disclosed in displays, brochures, scientific papers, and speeches.

- *Various governmental agencies*—Under the 1966 Freedom of Information Act, many federal agencies must provide requested documents, files, or other records, such as the Federal Drug Administration's inspection reports of competitors' plants, competitors' cost data in a competitive bid, and reports filed with the Federal Trade Commission to support advertising claims.

- *Newspaper and magazine reports*—Tracking events at competitors' sites and in the industry and environment as a whole. It is often worthwhile to assign someone the task of clipping articles and compiling a weekly circular of the important ones.

- *Casual conversations with customers, salespeople, distributors, suppliers, and industry experts, individually or in groups*—Most marketing people are so busy with the tasks cued up in their in boxes that they fail to get out and soak up informal information from these sources. Don't forget to walk your dog!

THE ROLE OF RESEARCH

American Express uses its customer research to "divine the preferences of its card members and potential card members, primarily by surveying them relentlessly and extensively refining and test marketing new ideas." Amex knows, for example, just which card enhancements—automatic car-rental insurance, 24-hour phone lines for service—really make a difference to customers but don't break the bank to provide.[9] Furthermore, Amex uses its marketing information to segment customers into groups based on lifestyle and income. They pitch different products and services to each group. Customer research also provides the foundation for Amex's quality program, which aims to improve customer service through efforts such as employee training performed at its Quality University in Phoenix.

At Fingerhut, a consumer products catalog company in Minnetonka, Minnesota, researchers mine a database of 1,400 pieces of information about each of its 13 million customers to predict consumer behavior. For example, Fingerhut has discovered that children's birthdays provide a great opportunity for customized marketing appeals. They mine data about a child's age, preferences, and birth date for their magic moment birthday fliers, one for each month of the year. A personalized message is included, such as "Here's wishing Sally a happy birthday in May. With your order, you'll get special birthday gifts for her, PLUS three other free gifts."[10] It's a remarkably effective appeal.

Research plays many roles at Fingerhut, as it does at most companies. It is important to understand thoroughly the role of research in marketing. Too many people are confused about research, and too few take full advantage of the marketing information it can provide. In the following sections, we answer basic questions in an effort to pin down the role of research in modern business.

What?

Marketing research focuses on understanding customers. This usually involves asking them questions and interpreting their answers. Questions are asked and answers found through systematic, objective research that focuses on gathering information relevant to a specific marketing problem.

It is essential that marketing research be:

- *Systematic*—The research needs to be a planned, well-organized process. Even informal research should have a goal and a method.
- *Objective*—The information must not be biased by the researcher or the research process.
- *Useful*—The process needs to produce information that helps managers make decisions.
- *Specific*—The information should focus on a specific problem.
- *Decision oriented*—When gathered, the information should result in a decision. Otherwise it was a waste of time and money.

Why?

Most companies perform research to identify the characteristics of the market and to measure market potential. Research is also commonly used to support short-range and long-range forecasts, and to study competitive products and develop or evaluate new products. Exhibit 4.1 listed many other research topics without being exhaustive. There are as many whys as there are problems to solve. No two research projects are exactly alike because no two problems are identical.

Who?

Formal marketing research dates back to the 1920s. It is now used in a large majority of medium and large companies. Use of marketing research has grown substantially in recent years, and it is spreading to many not-for-profit and service organizations. Since 1970, the number of financial service companies conducting research has grown from negligible to over 70 percent. Research is performed by marketing departments, and also with increasing frequency by product development, customer service, quality management, and other customer-oriented functions. And with the rise of informal research, managers are getting into the act—talking with customers and others in their markets. In short, anyone can do marketing research—and most of us ought to be doing more of it.

How Much?

On average, businesses spend from 25 to 50 percent of their marketing research budgets on the services of specialized research firms. A single customer survey may cost as little as $10,000, but many cost a great deal more. A focus group, run by an expert facilitator and using the one-way observational glass and videotaping features of a professional facility, may cost $5,000 or more. In-house information gathering can also be expensive: GE's telephone answer center, for instance, costs $8 million per year.

The Role of Specialists

Most research is performed by specialist research firms and purchased by marketing departments, on either an as—is or a customized basis. There are three types of research firms. Syndicated services compile specific types of data for sale to marketers. For example, A. C. Nielsen Company, the world's largest marketing research firm, provides demographic profiles of television audiences. The American Research Bureau provides both television and radio audience data, whereas Simmons Market Research Bureau and Target Group Index do the same for magazine readership. These and other syndicated firms provide significant amounts of useful information.

The custom research firm designs a customized study in collaboration with the client, collects the information, and provides a report (and presentation if desired) for the client firm. Although the research staffs of these companies include statisticians, psychologists, and experts in survey design, one cannot expect direct access to the most expert staff without a specific request.

The final category of commercial research suppliers is the specialty line supplier. Such firms specialize in one aspect of the research process. Perhaps the most common firm of this type is the field interview firm, which specializes in personal interviewing. If a company has considerable in-house expertise in research, it may subcontract portions of a study to specialty research firms and do the rest in-house. Some full-service custom research firms use these specialty line suppliers as subcontractors as well.

The ten largest research firms in the United States, based on a survey of the top 100 research companies by *Advertising Age* magazine in the Spring of 1997, are:

Company	Headquarters	Global Research Revenues, 1996 (millions)
Information Resources Inc.	Chicago	$344.6
Nielson Media Research	Westport, CN	319.4
IMS	Westport, CN	316.5
AC Nielsen Corp.	Stamford, CN	286.5
SRI International	Menlo Park, CA	280.7
VNU Marketing Information Services	New York	197.5
Arbitron Co.	New York	153.1
Westat Inc.	Rockville, MD	147.0
Gallup Organization	Princeton, NJ	135.8
MMRI (Maritz Marketing Research Inc.)	Fenton, MO	108.4

The importance of the research industry to marketers is demonstrated by some statistics from the *Advertising Age* study. The top 100 firms billed $4.04 billion annually in the United States in 1996, up 9.6 percent from the year before. And worldwide, the billings of the top 100 totaled an amazing $6.52 billion, up 9.9 percent over the year. Such is the value of information!

A company usually selects a research firm by identifying a handful of firms in the region that have some experience in similar studies and markets, describing the project to each in detail, and asking each to present a proposal and bid. The choice should be based not only on cost, but also on the competence and interest of the firm's personnel, their prior experience, and the quality of their study design and proposal. Small differences in key assumptions (e.g., response rate) can lead to very different price quotes, so compare assumptions and ask for explanations if the quotes differ dramatically.

Syndicated Marketing Research Services

It is always less expensive to purchase available information than to hire a firm for a custom study. The trade-off is that the available information may not be as relevant. However, a great deal of information is available from syndicated research firms, and it is essential to check with them before doing original research. The following is a list of the major syndicated research services and their products:

- *A.C. Nielsen Company, Northbrook, Illinois*—The specialty of Nielsen, the world's largest marketing/advertising research company, is monitoring TV program viewing. Its "audimeter" device is attached to 1,700 household TV sets throughout the nation. The company also provides syndicated and custom audits of retail product sales.

- *Arbitron Ratings Company, New York*—Focuses on measurement of radio and TV audiences in local markets. The company also offers a computerized program that provides audience data merged with information on viewer lifestyle.

- *Burke Marketing Research, Cincinnati*—Provides both syndicated research services and various customized services through its multiple divisions. It offers pre- and post-TV advertising copy testing and custom survey research, educational seminars, special market modeling, television campaign testing in controlled laboratory settings, and psychological measurement of reactions to advertising. (It's Burke Customer Satisfaction Associates is a leading survey research provider.)

- *The Gallup Organization, Princeton*—Specializes in quantitative attitude and public-opinion research and provides syndicated surveys in the areas of packaged goods, video, and financial services.

- *IMS International, New York*—Syndicated audits in the pharmaceutical, medical, and health care industries throughout the world. The company tracks the movement of products through panels of doctors, drugstores, hospitals, medical laboratories, nursing homes, and the like.

- *Information Resources, Chicago*—Using its BehaviorScan system, collects product sales data via in-store scanner equipment; monitors buying behavior through a panel of households that use an identification card tied to the optical scanner; controls TV advertising to selected homes via cable to test the relationship of advertising to purchase behavior; and measures in-store promotions.

- *NFO Research, Toledo*—Tracks purchases of beverages, home furnishings, women's tailored apparel, and home computers and video games, using a fixed panel of 240,000 households.

- *Simmons Market Research Bureau, New York*—Conducts an annual survey of 19,000 adults regarding their media usage, purchase behavior, and demographic characteristics. These data are combined with the Dun & Bradstreet databank to produce measures of advertising effectiveness by geographic area.

- *Yankelovich, Skelly & White, New York*—Offers two widely used services: Monitor, a survey of opinions and trends in special segments of society, and Laboratory Test Market, a market simulation that evaluates new products in the planning stage.

A number of consulting and research firms produce occasional special reports on specific markets, either presold to a group of clients or sold as high-priced publications to an industry after publication (e.g., The Yankee Group of Boston produces detailed studies of the telecommunications and computer industries). Check with a research librarian and the research staff of relevant trade associations to find out what is available from these sources.

STAGES IN A MARKET RESEARCH PROJECT

If the information a company requires is unavailable from syndicated research firms, and no existing source of information provides an adequate substitute, then a customized research project is the only alternative. It is helpful to review the standard stages of research projects before planning a project. Analyze a project stage-by-stage to estimate the cost of research.

Research projects are usually managed by the marketing manager or research manager, but sometimes by a president, division manager, or other manager. This person should guide the project through the following stages:

1. Formulate the problem.
2. Determine information needs and sources.
3. Select the research technique.
4. Design the sample.
5. Process and analyze the data.
6. Report and use the data.

Skipping a stage is an easy way to run into trouble or produce information that is not helpful to management.

The first and last steps of the research process are the most critical. The last, reporting and using the information, is critical because it focuses on the action needed to make the decision and solve the problem. The first stage, formulating the problem, is often the most difficult task in the process. Marketers often have only a vague notion of what their problems are, but researchers need a concrete definition of the problem. The definition will guide the entire research process. An inaccurate definition of the problem will inhibit or even preclude proper use of the results.

Stage 1: Formulate the Problem

Define the problem. A problem is identified when something other than the usual happens. For instance, the New England Aquarium in Boston, one of the region's most frequently visited attractions, recently found attendance down after a period of rapid growth. This was not the problem, however; it was a symptom. It was a sign to management that something was wrong and needed attention. The problem was eventually diagnosed as the museum's inability to attract visitors from the local community.

The researcher and manager need to work together to define the problem correctly. The decision maker should describe the action that will be taken on the basis of the research results. This forces him or her to focus on information that will be useful rather than simply nice to have. The researcher needs to understand the events that brought the problem to management's attention—this helps the researcher get a better understanding of the problem.

When the New England Aquarium's managers realized they needed to focus on local visitors, for example, they were able to give researchers a clear definition of the problem and the decisions that research should support. Research was used to find out how local visitors differed from other visitors and to support the scheduling and marketing of special events, programs, and exhibit openings to match visitor preferences.

Set specific objectives. Once the problem has been defined, the actual goals of the research project can be set. Those goals should be stated in very precise terms, because they will guide the rest of the research process. Moreover, they must be stated in such a way that specific action can be taken on the basis of research findings. In the aquarium study, for example, the following objectives were stated:

1. To know whether different types of people attend on weekends versus weekdays.

2. To determine what affects their decision to visit the aquarium.

3. To find out whether visitors differ from season to season.

4. To learn what percentage of visitors come from the Boston area versus out-of-town.

The analysis of objectives can be taken even further. It is often helpful to add to the list of objectives a short description of the decisions affected by each objective, and possibly to outline likely actions for several different research outcomes. The more thought given to the decisions that management might make, the more action-oriented the research can be. It is at this first stage, formulating the problem, that the usefulness of the study is usually determined. A problem formulation that is not action-oriented will probably yield marketing information that management will later complain was "nice to know," rather than *necessary* to know. "Need-to-know" information should be the ultimate goal of every research project.

Stage 2: Determine Information Needs and Sources

In the aquarium study, the marketing manager might hypothesize that more families visit the museum on weekends than during the week. This hypothesis flows from a discussion of Objective 1. It seems reasonable, but to act on it, the hypothesis must be proved or disproved. The aquarium could commission the researcher to collect data on whether visitors are attending alone or with other people and, in the latter case, whether those people are members of the visitor's family. The marketing manager might also ask the following questions:

- Are more children coming on weekdays than on weekends?
- What are the educational levels of visitors who come at different times of the week?
- What percentage of weekday visitors are from Boston-area colleges?

At this point, the researcher should conduct an informal investigation to answer these questions. Likely sources of information include people both inside and outside the organization, including various managers, salespeople, and customers. Hanging around the aquarium and talking to visitors could provide some answers and could help in deciding what additional information should be sought. For example, tourists who travel more than 500 miles might be hoping for a glimpse of a live whale. Without such information, the researcher might not become aware of the need to focus on this particular attraction.

Caution! Check secondary sources. It is tempting at this stage to begin primary research. But the project manager should check secondary sources first. Company sales records and other internal sources may be helpful. Some useful reports can be easily obtained from industrial trade associations and the government. For the aquarium project, the National Association of Museums provided demographic data on visitors to museums throughout the United States. This secondary source indicated the kinds of visitor characteristics the aquarium should focus on in its research.

Stage 3: Select the Research Technique

If the researcher and manager decide that there is not enough information available to solve the problem, and that the research problem is important enough to justify spending additional money and time, they may choose to collect primary data. The first step along this path is taken by the researcher, who must develop a research design that specifies the kind of research and how it will be conducted. One key decision is the research method to employ. A good place to start is to decide whether the research is primarily descriptive or causal in its focus (simpler observational methods are more likely to work with descriptive studies than with causal studies).

Descriptive studies focus on demographic information about markets and their composition. The aquarium study provides a good example. In that case, the manager wanted to find out where visitors came from, and compare that data by day of the week and season of the year.

Causal studies are required when the problem demands exploration of the cause-and-effect relationships between various phenomena. For example, what is the effect on attendance when the aquarium increases its advertising? Will weekend visitors come during the week if the weekend admission fee is raised? In addition to deciding whether the study should be descriptive or causal, the manager and researcher need to select one of the following three methods: observation, experiment, or survey.

Observation

In observational studies, the researchers do not actually interact with the subjects. Toy companies often use the observational method when deciding whether to market certain products. Fisher-Price, for example, runs an on-site nursery school where designers observe children through one-way mirrors. They watch for things such as general interest, safety features, and ease of play. The true test of a toy is its "play value," that is, whether the child plays with a new toy for a few minutes and then goes back to an old favorite or whether the new toy is interesting enough to be used repeatedly.

There are many observational techniques. Two Detroit companies, Urban Science Applications and R. L. Polk, collect license plate numbers at shopping center parking lots. These are fed into a computer and compared with auto registration data to show where the shopping center's customers live. Such a study showed Taubman Company, a shopping center developer, which customer groups were not coming to its centers. A direct-mail campaign aimed at those groups increased sales by 40 percent at one San Francisco area center.

Other observational techniques involve the use of mechanical devices, such as counting machines, cameras, and recorders. As mentioned earlier, A. C. Nielsen plants an audimeter in selected homes to record when the TV set is in use and which programs are being watched. This is the source of the widely used Nielsen popularity ratings. AGB Television Research has a similar product. Marketers usually refer to these types of studies as "people meters." Along similar lines, Chicago-based Information Resources has developed BehaviorScan, which monitors store purchases by people who agree to carry special shopper identification cards. The success of such experiments has led stores to introduce membership clubs in which most of their customers carry scanable I.D. cards. You may have one in your wallet for the grocery store nearest your home. As purchases are made, the point-of-sale equipment records the information and assigns it to your household.

| **FOR YOUR IMAGINATION** |

What Can You Do with a Trash Bag, a Camcorder, and a Pair of Scissors?

Gain amazing insights into customer behavior!

Sometimes an alternative research method using one of these tools is just the thing. For example, if you don't have good census data on a U.S. neighborhood but want to find out how many children live in it, you could collect the garbage and count how many toys and children's clothes were thrown away during the last week. According to research by the Garbage Project, an initiative of the U.S. Census Bureau's Center for Survey Methods Research, the average kid throws out 2.52 toys and toy packages per weak, and 0.87 items of clothing and clothes packages. And you could also learn quite a bit about the preferences and lifestyles of the households those kids live in. Is the trash full of status brand names or not? Does it include lots of waste food or very little? Does the trash include containers of products that were promoted in the last few weeks—indicating high sensitivity to promotions? Researchers at the University of Arizona are finding useful ways to profile households based on their trash.[11]

Don't feel like mucking around in a dumpster? How about videotaping consumers as they shop for or make use of products? That's what the folks at E-Lab did when they wanted to find out how often children rather than parents push baby strollers. The results of the "guerilla video" footage E-Lab shot revealed that kids often push strollers—and led to some new design concepts for a stroller manufacturer. In another study, E-Lab researchers handed out disposable cameras to people and asked them to photograph their audio equipment in order to gather clues as to the usage behaviors and contexts of use. According to John Cain of E-Lab, something is often missing from conventional research. He defines it as "information about real behavior in real situations."[12]

Wondering what to do with those scissors? Well, Professor Gerald Zaltman of Harvard Business School gives them to consumers, and asks them to create collages of magazine photographs to represent their feelings toward products. Then he brings them into his lab to explain their artwork—and often learns something new about the product as a result. For example, when DuPont, which supplies material to many pantyhose manufacturers, wanted to learn more about women's attitudes toward their hose, Zaltman used this method. Glenda Green, a marketing research manager at DuPont, explains the results, "As we kept probing into the emotions behind the choice of photos, the women finally began admitting that hose made them feel sensual, sexy, and more attractive to men. There's no way anyone would admit that in a focus group."[13] And that insight has implications for product development as well as marketing—for example, a more durable material might sound practical, but it won't fly unless it looks and feels sexy, too.

Sherlock Holmes learned much about his subjects without using any of the modern research techniques. Some market researchers employ very simple but often ignored observational techniques. For instance, an attraction such as the New England Aquarium might like to know which exhibits people visit first. They could find out by surveying customers or, more simply, by observing the dirt patterns on the floors on a snowy day. During the summer months, scuff marks on a polished floor might provide the same information. Libraries can use circulation figures to decide what kinds of books to add to their collections.

If observational techniques will help achieve research objectives, they definitely should be used. It is almost always less expensive to observe than to run an experiment or to question people.

Experiment

Let's go back to that grocery store I.D. card in your wallet for a moment. Some marketers are using a checkout counter system from Catalina Marketing Corp. of Anaheim, California, that generates coupons based on what you buy. For example, Nabisco can hire Catalina to have this system give you a coupon for Nabisco's Chips Ahoy cookies if you buy a competitor's brand instead. The idea is to match the coupons with users of competing brands in order to encourage them to switch to Nabisco next time.[14]

Think about the kind of data a marketer like Nabisco generates from Catalina's system—detailed histories of the responses of individual consumers to individually targeted coupon offers. With that sort of data, marketers can run experiments to find out how best to lure customers from competing brands to their own. Will you try a new brand for $0.35 off, or will it take $0.50? You may not know—but in the end, Nabisco will. Experimental approaches such as this are less common than other research methods, but can be of great importance, too.

In a controlled experiment, the effect of a particular variable is measured. The researcher makes changes in the conditions experienced by a test group (usually customers) with respect to a variable (e.g., the amount or type of advertising). The results are compared to those of a control group that did not experience the change; in this way, the effect of the change can be measured.

In a laboratory experiment, people are brought to a specific location and given the experimental treatment. In such settings, it is easier to eliminate outside influences that might cause invalid conclusions. The laboratory can be equipped with one-way mirrors, recorders, videotapes, and the like. For example, one group of consumers watches a series of commercials in a movie theater. A second group then watches the same series, except that one commercial is different. Both groups are asked to rate the commercials. Differences between the two sets of ratings can be ascribed to the effects of the different commercials.

Field experiments are much harder to conduct than laboratory experiments because it is more difficult to hold extraneous factors constant. For instance, how can a researcher testing the effect of a price reduction regulate competitors' advertising?

Moreover, it is often hard to gain the attention, interest, or cooperation of respondents. Also, it may be difficult to measure the relevant variable, such as how many sales of the product actually resulted from the price reduction rather than from friends' suggestions, advertising, or plain luck. Despite these drawbacks, field experiments are used more often than laboratory experiments.

Information Resources' BehaviorScan provides a good example of field experimentation. This system has been set up in several small cities. In each city, purchase data are collected from 12,000 households that have cable television service. On the basis of their purchase behavior, certain households receive specific commercials whereas others do not. Each household's subsequent buying behavior is monitored and related to the commercials seen.

Survey

Questionnaires and surveys are used when personal information is needed. Observing people under natural or experimental conditions reveals only what they do. Surveys are required to learn what they think. However, people do not always tell the researcher what they are thinking—they do not necessarily even know what they think—so survey technique must wrestle with the issue of how accurately subjects can report their thoughts and feelings. There are three major survey techniques: the personal interview, the telephone interview, and the mail interview.

The personal interview is a perennial favorite of interviewers because it allows face-to-face interaction with respondents. The interviewer can explain complex questions; use audiovisual aids, such as records, pictures, diagrams, and actual products; and can spend more time with the respondent. Face-to-face contact builds confidence and usually permits in-depth probing by the researcher.

On the negative side, personal interviews (especially in-home interviews) can be expensive. Moreover, the presence of the interviewer can introduce two kinds of bias. On the one hand, some respondents may alter their responses so as to appear in a positive light. On the other hand, the way in which the question is presented, the tone of voice, or even the body language of the interviewer can influence the answers given. Extensive training of interviewers is the best antidote to the latter problem.

Today the shopping mall intercept has largely supplanted the in-home interview. In this technique, interviewers approach or "intercept" people as they pass a particular spot in a shopping mall. This technique is very popular: A survey of major consumer goods and service companies by Market Facts found that 90 percent of them use this technique—it was surpassed only by telephone interviewing.

Another popular technique is the focus group, also used by 90 percent of consumer goods and service companies. Groups of 8 to 10 people are brought together to offer their views on an issue, idea, or product. We frequently employ focus groups in our client work to test new concepts for products or ads, for example. These informal sessions are conducted by a moderator, who structures the discussion by asking specific questions. One major use of focus groups has been in the early stage of research, when the researcher wants to gain greater insight into the problem. For example, a computer company might want to know whether users of personal computers (PCs) are concerned about the amount of random access memory (RAM) available to them. Through a focus group session, the company might learn that people tend to think in terms of the number of pages of text a machine can hold. The company could then develop a survey that asks a larger sample of PC users questions about the number of pages their computer could hold, rather than the number of bytes of RAM—and the researchers would be more likely to obtain meaningful responses as a result. This technique can be very helpful in refining a problem definition, learning what further questions to ask, determining how they should be phrased, and even learning what answers to expect. Focus group sessions often are held in front of a one-way mirror and recorded on camera or tape. Managers can sit behind the mirror to observe the session or review the tape later.

Much can be learned from conducting three focus groups on the same topic. The small group sizes tend to produce significant variation among groups. If findings from the second group differ from the first, the third group can act as a tiebreaker. One should not expect quantitative results from a focus group, or believe them if they are offered.

The telephone interview is the most frequently used method of marketing research. It is the fastest and has a relatively high response rate—mostly because it involves little effort by the respondent. Although people are more likely to hang up than to close the door on an interviewer, the response rate is significantly higher for telephone interviews than for mail surveys. Telephone interviewing eliminates the high cost of travel, and is often the least expensive survey method. With the use of WATS, even national surveys can be cost-effective. An advantage of telephone interviewing is that it allows the interviewer to probe. Respondents generally are willing to participate for a period of 10 to 20 minutes, particularly when the caller indicates the length of time the interview will take when the call begins.

On the other hand, telephone interviews do not allow for observation or audiovisual aids. Moreover, when there is no face-to-face contact, the respondent feels anonymous. This promotes less rapport between researcher and respondent, leading to more difficulty in obtaining personal information such as the respondent's age and income. Also, the potential respondents are limited to those with telephone numbers listed in a directory, which excludes a significant percentage of U.S. households. Certain groups of people in the United States are more likely than others to have unlisted numbers—notably blacks, people aged 16 to 34, those who live in the West, and residents of metropolitan areas. As a result, responses to telephone surveys are automatically biased against these groups. A number of techniques can be used to avoid this problem. In random-digit dialing, the caller adds four random numbers to a telephone prefix. In plus-one sampling, numbers are taken from a directory, but one digit is changed. These methods allow the researcher to reach any phone number that is operating, regardless of whether it is in the directory.

Telephone interviewers can now use computer-assisted telephone interviewing (CATI). In CATI, answers are entered directly into the computer, eliminating the cost, time, and errors of manually coding data. Computer systems also make it possible to design more elaborate and flexible surveys. It is advisable to use a research firm with this capability.

Honda did a wonderful telephone research project in which its factory workers took phone breaks to call recent purchasers of Accord automobiles. In three months, the workers managed to talk with almost half of the customers who bought the latest models. They asked customers if they were happy with the cars, and probed for ideas and possible improvements. The study generated useful ideas for marketers and product designers, helped factory workers improve product quality, and created an emotional link between the people who made the cars and those who drove them.[15]

The mail survey is the least flexible data collection technique. Because the questionnaire must be highly structured and standardized, it provides little room for probing. This drawback can be overcome to some degree by asking open-ended questions. However, questionnaires must be short and easy to complete to keep the amount of effort required of the respondent to a minimum.

USAA, a Texas-based financial services firm, uses mail surveys to obtain feedback about its insurance, banking, and mutual fund products. Many of its target customers are military officers and their families, a specialized market segment that often has unique perceptions and desires, so USAA mails a half-million multiple-choice surveys to them each year.[16]

Because the mail survey is standardized, interviewer bias is reduced or eliminated. Moreover, questionnaires can be returned anonymously, allowing some respondents to be more frank than they would be in a personal interview. One frequently encountered problem is that the appropriate mailing list can be difficult or impossible to obtain. Perhaps the greatest disadvantage of mail surveys is their low response rates—often less than 20 percent. This creates concern about the answers that would have come from people who did not respond—nonresponse error can be high. However, mail surveys are sometimes less costly than telephone surveys and are always less costly than personal interviews.

Techniques for increasing mail response rates include notifying people that they will be receiving a questionnaire (via mailgrams, postcards, phone calls, or letters), personalizing the questionnaire package, offering monetary or gift incentives, including a self-addressed return envelope, and sending a follow-up letter or postcard one to three weeks after the questionnaire mailing. For consumer surveys, the follow-up letter and a prepaid monetary incentive have been found most effective. Many marketing research studies now consist of a preliminary phone call, followed by a mailed questionnaire, followed by another phone call.

USAA reports a remarkable 60 percent response rate to its annual customer surveys. Why? There are probably two reasons. First, the company has long-term relationships with its customers, maintained through strong customer service. (If customers like your firm, they are more willing to help it out.) And second, customers see results from the surveys, such as new products designed to customers' requests.

A variation of the mail survey is the consumer panel, in which people are given some form of remuneration for participating in an ongoing study. These individuals receive a series of questionnaires or keep detailed records of their purchase behavior. This technique allows researchers to track brand loyalty, the effectiveness of advertising campaigns, and rates of consumption of products and brands.

See the Appendix at the end of this chapter for details of how to design survey questions.

Stage 4: Sample Design

An important part of the research process is selecting the respondents. The choice of respondents will influence the types of questions asked, as well as the methods used to ask them. It usually is unrealistic and unnecessary to include every possible respondent in a survey. Instead, researchers select a sample of respondents who represent the population being surveyed. (A population includes all the individuals who have a particular characteristic about which conclusions will be drawn.) Sampling offers researchers a number of benefits that would not be available if the entire population were surveyed. In conducting personal interviews, for example, researchers can save both time and money through sampling, since fewer respondents are interviewed. Moreover, sampling can actually be more accurate than surveying the whole population. In many cases, it is virtually impossible to interview an entire population—imagine trying to talk to all the tennis players in the United States. Because respondents' thoughts, impressions, and feelings can change, by the time the last member of the population is interviewed, many of those already spoken to may have changed their minds.

There are two basic kinds of sampling procedures: probability sampling, in which all members of the population have a known chance of being included in the sample, and nonprobability sampling, in which respondents are selected partly on the basis of researchers' judgment. Probability sampling is done according to statistical rules that leave no room for judgment on the part of the researcher or interviewer. (Note that we said each member of the population has a *known* chance of being selected for the sample; this is not the same as having an *equal* chance. With a known chance, the researcher can calculate the probability of a certain person's being selected.) We discuss three probability sampling techniques: simple random sampling, stratified random sampling, and area (cluster) sampling.

In *simple random sampling*, researchers obtain a complete list of the members of the population and choose the sample in a random fashion. For example, the names of all the individuals in the population might be written on cards and mixed thoroughly in a barrel. The researchers then choose the sample by pulling out cards without looking or otherwise influencing the choice. This gives every member of the population not only a known, but also an equal, chance of being included in the sample.

In the *stratified random sampling* technique, the total population is divided into subgroups, or strata, each of which is treated like a simple random sample. This approach is often followed when certain subgroups of the population might have an unusual impact on the results. For instance, suppose the research objective is to determine the average amount of time people spend playing tennis. Those who have higher incomes than the general tennis-playing population are more likely to play year-round and to do so indoors. Thus, to ensure that the sample does not reflect too many year-round players, the researchers might divide all tennis players into groups based on income or indoor club membership. They could then use simple random sampling to select individuals from each of the strata.

In many cases, it is difficult to obtain a list of the total population, but data about specific geographic areas, such as city blocks, can easily be obtained from the U.S. Census Bureau. An area (cluster) sample is chosen by simply taking a random sample of the geographic areas on the list. Then each household in the geographic unit is interviewed, or a second random sample is taken from each of the geographic units and those households are interviewed.

In *nonprobability sampling*, the selection of the sample is based to some extent on the researchers' judgment. There is no known chance of any particular person's being selected. Nonprobability sampling is used when probability sampling is not possible—when no list of the population exists, when the population is not stable over time, and so on. We examine three nonprobability sampling techniques: convenience sampling, judgment sampling, and quota sampling.

As the name implies, convenience samples are selected to suit the convenience of the researchers. Examples include asking people to volunteer to test products, using the mall intercept method discussed earlier, using students as subjects in an experiment, and conducting "on-the-street" interviews on television. Convenience samples are almost always used in the new informal "walk-the-dog" types of customer research as well. In all these cases, either the sample members volunteer out of interest in the project, or researchers select them because they are available. However, with such samples, it is unclear exactly what population is represented; the members of the desired population do not all have an equal or known chance of participating. Thus it often makes sense to use convenience samples for insight-generating research, then follow them up with statistical samples if it is necessary to validate the insights.

In the *judgment sampling* technique, samples are selected on the basis of criteria that the researchers believe will result in a group that is representative of the population being surveyed. In test marketing a new product, for example, researchers may turn to the U.S. Census Bureau to make a judgment about which cities are similar to national markets.

Quota sampling is a special form of judgment sampling. In this case, researchers take specific steps to obtain a sample that is like the overall population in terms of some specified characteristic or set of characteristics. For example, an interviewer may be instructed to select half the sample from people over 30 and half from people under 30 because the researcher knows that the population is divided in half at the 30-year mark. Moreover, this simple example uses only one characteristic. To get a truly representative sample of a population, researchers must use a number of characteristics, making effective quota sampling very difficult.

Stage 5: Process and Analyze the Data

What do the results mean? Do they answer your questions? Do they give you insights into how to improve your marketing efforts? Perhaps—but not until you ferret out the answers. The most powerful results are those that can be reduced to a simple statistic or picture in order to dramatize an important point. And so analysis plays a critical role in the research process.

Consider the diagram in Exhibit 4.3. It is used by research firm Burke Customer Satisfaction Associates to explain the results of customer satisfaction surveys. It shows how three different statistical measures can be combined to identify those customers that are most secure, or unlikely to defect to your competitors. It is a simple and compelling diagram, one that helps Burke clients understand a critical relationship in what might otherwise appear as three unrelated tables of statistics about answers that measure customer loyalty, satisfaction, and advocacy.

Marketing researchers use a variety of statistical techniques to turn raw data into useful information. First, they tabulate the data, or count the frequency of each type of response. In doing so, they produce three different kinds of numbers: the

EXHIBIT 4.3.   Secure versus vulnerable customers.

Customer Satisfaction
(very satisfied)

Secure
Customers

Customer Loyalty   Customer Advocacy
(Definitely Would Continue) (Definitely Would Recommend)

Reproduced from *The Portable Conference on Change Management,* Alexander Hiam (Ed.), 1997, HRD Press, Inc. © Burke Customer Satisfaction Associates.

mode, the median, and the mean. These simple statistics provide the foundation of more advanced statistical analysis. The mode is the number that occurs most frequently. The median is the middle number; it divides a list in half so that 50 percent are above the median and 50 percent are below it. The mean, or average, is the sum of all the numbers divided by the number of scores. These calculations are illustrated in Exhibit 4.4, using data from research on family size in a suburban neighborhood.

The next step is to cross-classify the data, that is, to look for frequencies of responses by different categories of respondents. Finally, more sophisticated analytical techniques can be used to extract further information from the data. These techniques can be complex, and special training in data analysis is needed to use them properly. For example, statistical tests may be performed to determine whether a result is explainable simply due to the error that is likely to occur by chance, or whether the result is attributable to some determining cause. Generous use of graphs and tables is helpful in conveying this information. Recommendations for action should also be included, to help consumers of the research results see the links between study results and real-world decisions and activities.

Stage 6: Report and Use the Information

In the final step of the research process, the researchers prepare a report. The report should explain the research process and indicate any problems that occurred along the way, such as low response rates. It should be written for the marketing managers who will use the results of the research. The first part of the report should present a summary of the findings so that the readers can quickly see what conclusions have

EXHIBIT 4.4. Mode, median, and mean calculations.

Question:	How many children do you have?					
	1	2	3	4	5	6 or more
Results:	(Population of 200 families)					
	1	2	3	4	5	6 or more
	55	45	50	35	10	5
Mode:	1 child					
Median:	Between 2 and 3—50 percent have 2 or fewer and 50 percent have 3 or more					
Mean:	$55 \times 1 = \ 55$					
	$45 \times 2 = \ 90$					
	$50 \times 3 = 150$					
	$35 \times 4 = 140$					
	$10 \times 5 = \ 50$					
	$\ 5 \times 6 = \ 30$					
	$515/200 = 2.575$ children per family					

EXHIBIT 4.5. Actual marketing report.

Recommendations (Based upon results of an initial (1980) and follow-up (1981) telephone survey of public transit attitudes and awareness in Kalamazoo, Michigan)

Target Advertising Featuring the Benefits of Riding the Bus to:	Target Advertising to *Nonriders* Outlining the Fare Structure for Riding the Bus	Target Advertising to *Nonriders* Emphasizing How Close Bus Stops Are to Certain Kalamazoo Area Residents	Target Advertising to *Nonriders* Emphasizing Frequency of Bus Service, *i.e.,* How Often the Bus Comes by
• *Males* for "work," "personal business," "school," and "when I don't have a car/when car is in garage" purposes . . . *Females* for "personal business," "shopping," and "visits or recreation" uses. Radio spots could feature male and female announcers.			
Reason: There was an increase in the number of *males* and *females* who used the bus for the purposes mentioned above.	*Reason:* a 12% increase among *nonriders* who did not know the cost for a ride on the bus.	*Reason:* 48% of *nonriders* in both surveys, who live 1 to 2 blocks from the nearest bus route, chose not to use the bus during the last year.	*Reason:* Approximately seven out of 10 *nonriders* were initially unaware of the frequency of bus service, and remained so during follow-up interviewing.
Question 6 (p. 36 of report)	Question 10 (p. 16 of report)	Question 12 (p. 24 of report)	Question 14 (p. 17 of report)
Service improvements (where feasible) in the areas of more convenient routes and more courteous drivers.	• *Change negative attitudes that bus riding is inconvenient (via news stories for particularly good or unusual service).* • *Point out comparative costs of auto use versus public transit.*	*Target advertising to nonriders who own only one car.* *The message: "take the bus and save the family car for use by other members of the household."*	*Continue using "other" media and "radio" advertising in addition to newspaper and television advertising.*
Reason: An increase among certain Kalamazoo area *bus riders* and *nonriders* who reported a need for the improvements mentioned above.	*Reason:* More than nine out of 10 *nonriders* in both surveys reported "car" as their usual means of transportation.	*Reason:* Approximately one-third of *nonriders* in both surveys reported having only one automobile in their household.	*Reason:* Follow-up results for "other" media show a higher percentage of recall over initial survey results for *heavy* and *other* users, and for *nonriders.* Similar results were found for *moderate* users regarding recall of "radio" advertising.
Question 20 (p. 33–35 of report)	Question 34 (p. 25 of report)	Question 35 (p. 26 of report)	Conclusions (p. 51–54 of report)

Nancy L. Frederick's "2-Part Report Format Attracts Attention of Research Users," *Marketing News,* May 13, 1983, p. 18.

been reached. Generous use of graphs and tables is helpful in conveying this information. Recommendations for action should be included.

Exhibit 4.5, taken from an actual marketing report, shows concise, easy-to-read recommendations that were presented to the Kalamazoo Metro Transit system by a marketing research team. This example features four recommendations, each backed up by research endings. The recommendations are referenced to the numbers of the questions asked in the survey and to the page numbers of the report that provide further details. This is a good example of effective interpretation and presentation of marketing information.

CONCLUSIONS

The many options for gathering market research and the complex, five-stage process for conducting original (or primary) research make this a difficult topic to understand. Add a little math anxiety, and most managers find it positively repellent. Perhaps this is why research is left to specialists at most companies. Firms usually delegate research to a research manager, who in turn subcontracts all major studies to specialized research firms. In other cases, firms rely on their advertising agency's research department to design studies and hire the appropriate researchers.

In either case, the arm's-length relationship between research and general business management is potentially unhealthy. The more closely involved the entire marketing department and the entire management team are in the generation and interpretation of marketing information, the closer to the customer the company can be. A desk is a dangerous place from which to view marketing, and those who wait for the research reports to hit their desks may miss important insights that they could easily have gained by getting involved in the formal research process early on—or even better, by trying some informal research of their own. This point is illustrated by American Express' efforts to improve the quality of its services.

American Express uses dozens of unusual research techniques to further refine its understanding of customer desires and its measurement of service quality. According to Maryanne Rasmussen, senior vice president of quality at Travel-Related Services:

> We spend hundreds of millions of dollars trying to find out what the customer wants. One sophisticated external customer satisfaction market research program is our transaction-based surveys. We consider a transaction every contact a customer has with us—telephone calls, billing inquiries, a charge authorization question. This is the most difficult element to measure. Companies can determine customer expectations, measure transaction time, and analyze error rates. But we go beyond that through unique transaction-based surveys we focus on how customers perceive a particular single contact with us.[17]

When Amex learns that customers are frustrated with a specific kind of contact, the company translates this finding into specific goals and actions aimed at improving that contact. For example, each general manager is expected to set annual goals for improving customer service. The transaction-oriented customer surveys are used to maintain a "worldwide service tracking index" for each market in which the company competes, and general managers set their goals according to this index. This means customers write the managers' report cards.

Amex also brings marketing information into the management process through the use of regular "on-site business reviews" by Rasmussen's group of quality specialists. The several-week audits look at strategy and marketing plans and, most importantly, focus on the quality of customer service. For example, the auditors read customer correspondence and "ask employees from all levels of the organization what they believe affects internal and external customer quality."[18]

Efforts such as these are beginning to break down the traditional boundaries between research and other marketing functions, and to move marketing information into a more central position in the management of a business. This is an appropriate trend from the customer's perspective, as the marketing information generally represents customer needs. But it requires managers to work with, and understand, marketing information—and, we hope, makes the effort you have put into digesting this chapter all the more worthwhile.

A word of caution is also in order, however: The innovative efforts of companies such as American Express are producing new practices in the field of market research that do not always fit the standard categories and descriptors. Rasmussen's transaction-based surveys and service tracking index are both innovations, and neither has been clearly described in the marketing literature to date. And you won't find "walking-the-dog" research in the indexes of any marketing textbooks!

A hands-on knowledge of marketing research and a willingness to innovate helps managers at companies such as American Express improve products and services and outcompete rivals. It gives them the ability to go beyond information parity to achieve significant information advantages.

APPENDIX: SPECIAL TOPICS IN MARKETING RESEARCH[19]

International Marketing Research

Undertaking marketing research in the burgeoning international arena adds a layer of complexity to the process. Three particularly annoying problems exist: studying many markets, locating secondary data, and collecting primary data.[20] A study replicated in many countries increases the costs and problems. Although some economies are conducive to multiple uses of the research design, these are offset by increased implementation costs—for example, multiple-interviewer recruitment and training, questionnaire translation, and acquisition of population lists. Each country's differences must be factored into the study. For example, a study in one country resulted in the respondents being 64 percent women, whereas in another they were 80 percent men.[21] This sampling problem creates havoc with cross-cultural comparisons. In Lesotho, respondents holding up their thumb and first finger in response to a question about household size would be counted as two by an American interviewer. However, in Lesotho, people start counting on the little finger and continue over the thumb to represent six. Thus the actual answer would be seven. Such peculiarities multiply the problems of international marketing research.

Secondary data sources are much less available in many foreign nations, and statistical data are often unreliable. Most governments conduct censuses, but the quality varies. Laos and Oman never have, however, and Zaire took its last census in the 1950s. Because probability sampling is severely limited, most international studies employ convenience samples. Furthermore, cross-cultural comparisons are limited because secondary sources offer different measures. Classifications are different, and base years are seldom the same. Such terms as *wholesaler* or *commercial vehicle* can also vary in meaning by country.

A company trying to collect its own data meets with "people problems." Language is an obvious difficulty. Not all English words exist in other languages. The different dialects within a country can further complicate translation. In Zaire, for example, the official language is French; however, most Zairians speak one of four *lingua francas* of the country, and they use their tribal language when speaking of emotional issues. Translation of questionnaires for international use is not a simple operation. One technique that is used is *backtranslation,* in which a questionnaire is translated into a second language and then translated back into the original language. The two versions are compared and any inconsistencies resolved in drafting the final version. Coupled with the use of local researchers, this technique can be very effective.

Primary data collection is also confounded by social differences between countries. In many nations, the household includes grandparents and aunts and uncles. This complicates isolating decision makers and key influencers. The role of women around the globe also is not uniform. In Muslim countries, a woman may not be allowed to talk to a male interviewer if her husband is not present, and in many countries, women cannot work as interviewers. Obtaining responses is still another problem. Literacy, reluctance to talk about personal concerns, and even differences in thought patterns all add to the challenge of conducting global marketing research.

It is easy to see international marketing research as a problem. Although it presents many challenges, it also can provide interesting cultural insights and can be a source of ideas and opportunities for marketers. Sometimes it puts researchers in touch with interesting research techniques from other countries. For example, the "antenna shops" used for new-product research in Japan may soon be imported into the United States. Major Japanese manufacturers, from Sony to Nissan, have opened their own stores to have direct access to shoppers and their opinions. Matsushita Electric Industrial Company's antenna shop, Works, does not even sell products. Instead, customers come in to talk about the novel product ideas that the store displays. This antenna store played a central role in the development of the new Musica from Panasonic, a telephone/answering machine/alarm clock combination. The idea of antenna stores is gaining momentum in Japan, and there is even an antenna restaurant, run by Japan's largest fish-processing company, Nissui.[22] Perhaps U.S. companies will add this technique to their marketing research portfolio.

Marketing Information Systems

The recognition that successful marketing requires useful information has given rise to widespread use of what is called a *marketing information system* (MIS): "A set of procedures and methods for regular, planned collection, analysis, and presentation of information for use in making marketing decisions."[23] Although MIS often uses a computer, one is not always necessary. What is necessary is the planned, orderly, and continuous collection, analysis, and presentation of the correct information for marketing decisions. Thus, a library with its reference sources or an employee armed with a file cabinet can be considered a marketing information system.

The concept of an MIS can be all marketers—not merely by large firms such as Procter & Gamble or American Airlines, but also by a local grocery store or a small restaurant. The purpose of an MIS is to provide the information needed for decision making so that the use of guesswork can be reduced. These may sound like the same comments that could be made about marketing research, but the two are not synonymous. In fact, MIS and marketing research differ in a number of ways. First, marketing research generally focuses on one problem at a time, and information is collected for the sole purpose of solving that problem. In contrast, an MIS continuously collects and stores data that may be relevant to a variety of problems. Perhaps more important, the MIS provides information that can alert marketers to possible future problems. In this sense, the MIS functions as both a crisis preventer and a problem solver. (American Express' routinely updated record of 450 facts per cardmember is an MIS. The company's one-time study of what consumers imagined American Express cards would say to them was marketing research.)

Another difference between marketing research and MIS arises from how data are collected. In most cases, data for marketing research come from external sources, such as consumers, competitors, and the government. The MIS, by contrast, relies more heavily on data generated within the firm (e.g., sales and accounting data). Much of the original data in the MIS remain "raw" until they are combined or analyzed in some meaningful manner. Then the information is presented to decision makers in the form of reports. Often information obtained through marketing research is stored in the MIS as well.

The following are components of the computerized MIS:

- *Data bank*—Stores raw data that come in from both the external environment and internal records.
- *Statistical bank*—Offers statistical techniques to be used in analyzing data.
- *Model bank*—Contains mathematical marketing models that show relationships among various marketing activities, environmental forces, and desired outcomes.
- *Display unit*—Permits the user to communicate with the system.

IMS International provides a good example of a global MIS. The company developed sales management systems (SMSs) to provide pharmaceutical companies with access via telephone lines to data such as prescriptions filled in drugstores, number of sales presentations made to physicians, medical journal circulation figures, monthly sales volumes of major pharmaceutical products by brand, and number of product samples sent. Data are collected from a worldwide panel of 100,000 physicians, drug wholesalers, and drugstore chains. All data are maintained for each physician market segment and identified by medical specialty, age, and region where doctors' practices are located. In addition to retrieving data, the SMS user can run statistical programs or use a complex model to identify sales increases due to changes in promotional methods. Various marketing programs can be tested and the anticipated volume of new prescriptions determined. Thus, the usefulness of the system depends on the interaction among its various components.

Marketing Intelligence Systems

The marketing intelligence system is the set of activities whose purpose is to monitor the external environment for emerging trends or events. In practice, it often focuses on what competitors are doing. Marketing intelligence is gathered in many ways. Salespeople can be trained to notice, track, and report relevant changes. Wholesalers, retailers, and sales representatives are prime sources of intelligence, as are suppliers. Some companies even have specialists devoted to gathering intelligence. In addition, outside data agencies collect and sell valuable information. Market Research Corporation of America, for example, maintains a panel of 7,500 households and can supply weekly information on competitors' market shares, product package sizes, prices, and promotional deals. The Chicago Hospital Association provides the occupancy rates of all its member hospitals. Companies can also obtain information from government agencies by requesting it under the Freedom of Information Act. For instance, by scanning competitors' bids on government contracts, one can learn their bidding strategies and costs. However, it should be noted that the requests themselves are public documents, so competitors can monitor attempts to obtain information about their bids!

The growth in global marketing strategies has been accompanied by a growth in the need for international marketing intelligence systems. A coherent global strategy rests on a foundation of solid business information. Many sources for foreign intelligence are readily available right here in the United States. Special foreign newspaper subscription services exist. Overseas Courier ships Japanese periodicals worldwide; German News Company is a similar source for European print media. Foreign trade organizations and international chambers of commerce are also excellent resources. Foreign brokerage houses, many of which are in New York City, provide analytic reports on their country's international environment, and developing global communication networks is becoming a top priority as firms expand their market boundaries.

Strategic Intelligence . . . or Unethical Spying?

Today it is not money that makes the world go around, but information. Successful global and domestic marketing strategies are built on a solid base of business information. Generally, managers from other industrialized nations tend to be better informed than U.S. managers. Before entering a market, the Japanese, for instance, studiously analyze the country to be entered, gathering intelligence about language, key environmental trends, technologies in vogue, and the cultural values. To keep abreast, British executives reportedly read three times as many newspapers as U.S. managers. Strategic intelligence is the backbone of effective global strategies, as it is of domestic marketing strategies.

Ethically borderline methods are sometimes used to capture competitive insights. Public document scanning, bogus job interviews with in-depth grilling of applicants, even piecing together of torn memos from corporate trash are part of the growing game of corporate sleuthing. Consultants are hired or seminars taken to ensure effective snooping. Some detectives act as reporters in quest of corporate stores. Others, using a technique of "benchmarking," literally tear competitor's products apart looking at how they achieve the quality they provide. Even observing non-competitors helps. Xerox, for example, has dramatically improved its order handling process by studying the mail-order champion, direct mail cataloguer L.L. Bean. Other companies visit Japanese competitors, finding them surprisingly open about their plans. Said one executive after visiting a Japanese competitor, "It was sort of like them telling us, this is how we are going to kill you. Get ready."

Other methods used by corporate sleuths include:

- *Plant tours*—Firms often give tours of their plants to the public or to potential clients. Observation of the plant can be a dead giveaway.

- *Analysis of help wanted ads*—Help wanted ads are, in effect, press releases. The kinds of people a company wants to hire are potent clues as to what it will be up to next.

- *Buying competitors' garbage*—Once trash has left a competitor's premises, it is legally classified as abandoned property. Sometimes valuable information is thrown out in the trash. Smart competitors shred any documents that contain information that could be used by rivals.

Criminal action proceedings can occur when corporate intelligence exceeds legal limits. Procter & Gamble sued Frito-Lay, Keebler, and Nabisco for allegedly stealing its patented recipe for soft-center chewy cookies. In the suit, P&G claimed that Keebler took photographs of its plant from an airplane, that a Frito-Lay intelligence agent posed as a customer to gain entry to a secret sales meeting, and that Nabisco's spy sneaked by a security guard to get into a kitchen where "secret cookie-making technology was being used."

This kind of intelligence gathering rings of "007" tactics. However, improper sleuthing is unnecessary, because other approaches are quite ethical and substitute creativity for ethical transgressions. One consultant was used by the Internal Revenue Service to estimate the revenues of a house of prostitution; he resorted to using the data on restroom paper towel usage obtained from the brothel's supplier, which he was able to correlate with revenues. A Japanese company measured the amount of rust on the train tracks coming out of a competitor's plant—and estimated the factory's production. Also creative are the suggestions offered by intelligence trainers on how not to let out important information. They suggest that businesses flag sensitive information not for public or competitive consumption, and that executives should not work on airplanes where others can uncover secrets by reading over one's shoulder.

Marketing Decision Support Systems

The marketing decision support system (MDSS) is defined as "a coordinated collection of data, models, analytic tools, and computing power by which an organization gathers information from the environment and turns it into a basis for action."[24] This sophisticated system focuses on the marketing decision itself. The manager is viewed as a strategist who must perceive and analyze the environment, consider strategic options, and choose the best one available. The emphasis is on analysis. The MIS answers such questions as "What were sales of Brand X in September?" and "Did we meet our marketing budget?" The MDSS carries the analysis further to include cause and effect: "What changes in our competitor's marketing mix may have caused sales to change?" The MDSS also asks "What would happen if?" questions. In short, the MDSS amplifies the skills of the manager by eliminating certain barriers to problem solving.

To aid managers in coding, analyzing, and reporting data, some generalized commercial programs have been developed. One such program is Acustar, designed and developed by Tymeshare of Stamford, Connecticut. Acustar automatically integrates data from different sources, both external and internal. Adjustments are made to accommodate the fact that different sources collect data for different time periods (e.g., by week versus by month); then the data are stored in data banks or files. Within the files, information is held mostly by product, geographic area, and brand. Acustar is only one of the available commercial decision support services. A. C. Nielsen has INF°ACT, a time-sharing service that helps clients make use of its database. Information Resources offers EXPRESS, a computer language that allows integration of varied data sources and access to statistical analysis. Many other such services are likely to become available as technological advances continue to make it easier to collect, store, and combine information in highly sophisticated ways.

Guide to Questionnaire Design

Designing a questionnaire is an art; much creativity may be needed. Fortunately, there are some established principles for developing successful questionnaires.

The questions should be directly related to the research objectives. Every questionnaire item must be capable of being translated into a specific decision that will aid in solving the problem. All questions should be as easy to answer as possible. For example, checklists are more convenient to answer than open-ended questions. Personal questions, such as the respondent's age, should be asked only if necessary and put in the form of a range rather than an exact figure. Care should be taken to use simple and unambiguous words and phrases. (How would one interpret the information that most consumers find Pert shampoo "good"?) Finally, the earlier questions should not influence the answers to later questions. (Five questions asking for an evaluation of Saab automobiles might well affect the answer to the later question, "What is your favorite European automobile?").

Before the questionnaire is used, it must be pretested. This involves showing people the draft questionnaire and having them explain to the researcher what each question means to them. Many hidden problems can be uncovered in this way. For instance, a soup company may want to know what kinds of soup its customers prefer. It may design its questionnaire to ask, "What kind of soup do you like?" Through pretesting, it might discover that instead of naming beef barley or chicken noodle, respondents are likely to give such answers as "Mom's," "homemade," "hot," "any kind I don't have to make myself," or "Hector's Diner"!

As part of the questionnaire design process, researchers must decide which questioning technique to use. If they are seeking very simple information—such as whether the respondent is male or female—they can use a simple, direct question. But when they need to learn about respondents' feelings, attitudes, opinions, intentions, or motivations, they may find that simple, direct questions will not obtain the desired information. In that case, the researchers must use an indirect approach.

The questioning techniques used in marketing research can be divided into two kinds: structured and unstructured. *Structured questions* usually limit respondents to a specific set of replies. Examples include multiple-choice questions and simple checklists with a question such as "Which of the following brands of detergent do you think cleans well?" Structured questions are easier to use than unstructured questions. They require less skill on the part of the interviewer, and the data they yield are more easily analyzed. *Unstructured questions* give respondents more freedom. Often they do not set a limit on the length of responses, and they may not provide specific directions for replies. Some unstructured questions are designed only to get respondents to talk about a given subject. However, such questions require skilled interviewers, and it is difficult to analyze and compare the responses. (See Exhibits 4.6 and 4.7.)

EXHIBIT 4.6.   Structured questioning techniques.

1. *Likert Scale*

Presents respondents with a number of provocative statements and asks them the extent to which they agree or disagree with each statement. Quantitatively measures respondents' attitudes toward different products, brands, and so on.

Example

Following are a series of statements about tennis rackets. Please indicate the extent of your agreement or disagreement with each statement. Be sure to "X" one number for each statement.

Definitely disagree	Generally disagree	Moderately disagree
1	2	3
Moderately agree	Generally agree	Definitely agree
4	5	6

1. I spend a lot of time shopping for price when I buy a tennis racket.   1 2 3 4 5 6

2. I believe carbon fiber gives better control than aluminum.   1 2 3 4 5 6

3. No racket priced below $69.00 will last long.   1 2 3 4 5 6

2. *Semantic Differential*

Determines the connotative meanings of words and the intensity of those meanings as perceived by respondents. A scale is inscribed between two bipolar words (such as *good/bad* and *hot/cold*); respondents select the point that represents the direction and intensity of their feelings. Identifies words with favorable or unfavorable connotations.

Example

Spalding Tennis Racket

Durable					Nondurable
Bad					Good
Stylish					Nonstylish
Inexpensive					Expensive

(continued)

EXHIBIT 4.6. *(Continued)*

3. *Word Association*

Respondents are given a list of words and are asked to match each word with one of their own choosing. Answers are usually timed. Provokes quick, unrestrained answers that reveal strongest attitudes. First answer is important.

Example

What is the first word that comes to mind when you hear the following?

Spalding

_____

Oversized tennis racket

_____

Boris Becker

_____

Carbon filter tennis racket

_____

4. *Sentence Completion*

Respondents are shown the first parts of incomplete sentences and are asked to complete them. Requires respondents to take a position or express an attitude. Provides an unrestrained response; first answer is considered most revealing.

Example

1. When I purchase a can of tennis balls, the most important consideration in that decision is

_____

_____

2. If I were given a Spalding tennis racket as a gift, I would feel like

_____

_____

EXHIBIT 4.6.   *(Continued)*

5. *Importance Scale*

Rates the importance of some characteristic or set of characteristics from "not at all important" to "extremely important."

Example

How important are each of the following features in determining which tennis racket to purchase?

	Not at All Important 1	Somewhat Unimportant 2	Unimportant 3	Neither Important nor Unimportant 4	Important 5	Somewhat Important 6	Extremely Important 7
Balance	1	2	3	4	5	6	7
Texture of grip	1	2	3	4	5	6	7
Flexibility	1	2	3	4	5	6	7
Weight	1	2	3	4	5	6	7
Appearance	1	2	3	4	5	6	7

6. *Rating Scale*

Rates something on a scale from "Extremely Bad" to "Excellent."

Example

Rate the following types of tennis rackets on the following characteristics:

	Extremely Bad 1	Very Bad 2	Bad 3	Neither Bad nor Good 4	Good 5	Very Good 6	Excellent 7
Graphite							
Flexibility	1	2	3	4	5	6	7
Weight	1	2	3	4	5	6	7
Power	1	2	3	4	5	6	7
Ceramic							
Flexibility	1	2	3	4	5	6	7
Price	1	2	3	4	5	6	7
Weight	1	2	3	4	5	6	7

EXHIBIT 4.7. Unstructured questioning techniques.

1. Story Completion

Example

An extension of the sentence—completion approach (Exhibit 5.3), but less structured. Repondents are given the beginning of a story and are asked to complete it. Details of the story may be vague to avoid influencing responses. In completing the story, respondents reveal concerns, preferences, attitudes, and other important aspects of purchasing behavior.

Last weekend, Jim and I were trying to decide where to go for an outing. When I suggested the New England Aquarium, Jim remembered his last visit there. Now you complete the story.

2. Picture Frustration

Example

Respondents are asked to identify with cartoon characters by supplying dialog that reflects their feelings about the situation pictured. Gets at deep-seated, subconscious feelings. Analysis requires well-trained, skillful interpreter.

Fill in the empty balloon.

I was thinking of going to the aquarium instead of the science museum.

3. Thematic Apperception Test (TAT)

Example

An extension of the picture–frustration approach. Respondents are shown an even more ambiguous picture or series of pictures and are asked to explain the scene, tell what is happening, and describe the characters. Sometimes respondents are asked to make up a story about what is happening now and what may happen in the future. Reveals hidden feelings and suppressed desires. Requires a skilled technician to give the test, which must be interpreted by a psychologist.

Now make up a story about what these two people are doing. Make up any kind of story you want.

MUSEUM OF SCIENCE

4. Open–Ended Question

Example

A question that respondents can answer any way they wish.

What is the most important attraction at the New England Aquarium?

5 PROFILING MARKETS AND FORECASTING SALES

The Art and Science behind the Numbers

College dorms will burst at the seams. The apparel and music businesses could awake from their slumbers. Auto accidents—and insurance rates—will likely climb. So could violent crime. Brace for it: a "youthquake" of proportions not seen since the baby boomers donned love beads. The members of Generation Y, now in grade school, will hit their teen years just as the next century dawns.

—*The Wall Street Journal*[1]

In the twentieth century, it is sheer folly to disregard demographics. The basic assumption must be that populations are Inherently unstable and subject to sudden sharp changes—and that they are the first environmental factor that a decision maker, whether businessman or politician, analyzes and thinks through.

—*Peter F. Drucker*[2]

When we wrote the first edition of this book, in the beginning of the 1990s, the personal computer (PC) was just beginning to become a popular household appliance. Forecasts varied, but everyone expected the PC to win a central spot in at least the more affluent households by the end of the decade. As it turned out, the most optimistic forecasts were right, PCs are in something less than 40 percent of American households.[3]

The PC is now a staple of middle-income households in the United States and most European countries. Compaq and other leading marketers make the majority of sales to households and have learned to adapt their designs to the game-playing and Internet-surfing consumers who use their machines late into the night. Market leaders in the PC industry are an almost entirely new group of companies since we wrote the first edition. Why? Because in spite of the heady—and potentially profitable—growth of this market, there have been so many unexpected changes that many companies have failed to ride the wave. Although technology is hard to anticipate, the *hardest* thing is to anticipate *who* will want to use your products, and *for what*. The PC market is no longer predominantly driven by functional demands, for example. It is becoming an entertainment industry. And that's a change few would have bet their companies on ten years ago.

In a recent survey, 62 percent of male and 48 percent of female PC owners said they'd rather give up their dishwasher than their home computer.[4] The home computer has become an essential household appliance in less than a decade—one that is far more entertaining than the average dishwasher! This change creates new behavior patterns and a host of new needs and wants among consumers. Any forecasts for the year 2010? For example, what will teenagers want from their computers in the early 2000s? If your forecast turns out to be right, you could be the next Bill Gates. But if you bet wrong, you're history.

Every forecasting problem is unique, yet some simple principles nonetheless apply, as we will see in this chapter. For instance, take the acne medicine market—presumably quite a bit different from the market for home-use PCs, and yet the same people are the customers for both products. Both markets may be transformed by those Generation Y kids who will reach their teen years shortly.

So, how would you forecast sales of a top brand acne medicine? That's a tough one—but essential if you are in the business of marketing it.

You might look at the number of teenagers and discover that the number dropped in the 1980s as the baby boomers were displaced by a smaller number of young "baby busters." Today there are fewer teens as a result. But there are more young children, since baby boomers now have teenage children, so the number of teens will increase. There will be 30 million teenagers in the United States by 2006, the highest number since 1975.[5] Given these population trends, you might forecast slow current sales for your product, but with a gradually growing market that gets pretty hot around the turn of the century and peaks in 2006.

Another possibility is to look at the trends in skin problems. Dermatologists keep track of things like that, and young people have fewer today, it turns out. Combine that with the currently low number of teens and you are likely to forecast weak short-term sales for your product and its competitors.

Based on these data, sales should be way down right now, right? This scenario illustrates why forecasting is such a hazardous activity. Surprise! Baby busters buy more acne medicines even though they have fewer pimples. Surprise, again! Older consumers are buying more acne medicines, helping make up for the drop in teenagers. Caution: Sometimes it's hard to see where markets are heading.

If we'd been in charge of forecasting sales for Richardson-Vicks, the makers of Clearasil, we probably would have been dead wrong about sales in the 1990s. The company certainly was. Jody Phelps, the marketing manager handling Clearasil, explains, "The problem we expected never materialized."[6] The company waited nervously for a drop in Clearasil sales. Now the company is looking for sales growth as the number of teens grows again. But will they be right this time around? They will have to dig deeper than the simple population statistics upon which their previous forecasts were based.

To develop sound strategies to satisfy consumers' wants and needs, marketers must learn as much as possible about consumers. This learning process has three stages: description, understanding, and prediction. Before marketers can do anything about understanding and predicting consumer behavior, they need to be able to describe the market they plan to serve by answering questions such as, Who will buy? (For example, will parents as well as teenage children use acne medicines?) When will they buy? How will they buy? Where will they make their purchase? How often will they buy?

But this descriptive step results in only a two-dimensional sketch of the consumer. By seeking to understand consumers' purchase and usage behaviors, marketers can get a much more complete picture of the people whose needs they must satisfy. For example, maybe today's teens are more likely to use acne medicines daily, as a preventative, compared to previous generations who used them only when they (How to put it delicately?) needed treatment. And perhaps younger consumers, preteens, are more likely to model their behavior after teenagers today, and thus start using acne medicines earlier in life.

Such insights into consumer attitudes and behaviors give a more accurate, multidimensional portrait of the consumers in a chosen market—with which marketers can better predict consumers' reactions to their strategies and marketing programs. This chapter's focus—on population statistics—is just the first, descriptive step toward understanding your customers. You'll need to combine it with the Chapter 6's focus on consumer behavior to get a three-dimensional picture of your market.

The term *demographics* refers to statistics about a population: its size, location, and other characteristics. For example, a journal called *American Demographics* reports on trends in populations and markets in the United States (and, incidentally, is wonderful reading for anyone in business). Managers frequently analyze demographic trends to identify important changes in the markets they serve. In this chapter, we examine some demographic variables that help marketers describe consumers in general as well as particular markets. In the process, we discuss (in addition to acne medicines) why the baby boom is like a pig swallowed by a python, what makes Gerber think it is a good time to refocus on baby products, why many marketers forget to look at demographics, and what we can learn about the United States today by reading an 1890 census form. But we also must do a little math, review many statistics, and look at a variety of forecasting techniques to emerge with a leading-edge understanding of this important field.

We have used the term *market* frequently in the early chapters of this book. We loosely defined it as including both actual and potential buyers of a given product. Before we go on, it is necessary to define it more precisely.

A market consists of a group of people with unsatisfied wants and needs who are willing to exchange and have the ability to buy. The members of this group must be interested in buying and must possess the resources—money, goods, services—that might be given in an exchange.

The combination of desire to buy and ability to buy is referred to as *effective demand.* Markets—when identified precisely, as per the above definition—provide marketers with this all-important effective demand. Since sales are limited by effective demand, marketers need to devote more attention than most of us really do to the question of how to define our markets. Demographics gives us many tools for defining and anticipating shifts in the size and structure of these markets.

We said that markets are defined by three factors: they must include people with *unsatisfied wants and needs* who are *willing to exchange* and *have the ability to buy.* But one other factor is sometimes needed to explain a market fully. In some cases, people meet the three criteria just given, yet do not have the *authority* to make a purchase. Children with large trust funds but small allowances may want things, but be unable to buy them. It would be a mistake to market sports cars to them on the assumption that they are rich and therefore big spenders. Convicts in a penitentiary may have the desire and even the money to purchase certain items, yet they are prevented from doing so. It would be a mistake to market hacksaw blades to convicts (for more than one reason, but you get the point!). Neither category of people ought to be included in the definition of a market, any more than an employee who works for a large, wealthy company but lacks spending authority should be considered a likely prospect for expensive consulting services. Thus, we must qualify our definition of a market by noting that those without the authority to purchase lack the ability to buy, even if they appear to have sufficient financial resources to buy.

In this chapter, we focus on the first two components of a market—people and purchasing power. The third component, willingness to exchange, is a matter of understanding the most slippery of all marketing topics, human behavior and is the subject of Chapter 6. Insights into consumer behavior are that third dimension to market analysis. But you need a two-dimensional picture first. We will start by looking at demographics, the mass of statistics that helps marketers describe what is going on right now in their markets. We then examine forecasting, the various techniques whereby marketers try to anticipate what will happen in their markets tomorrow, based on what happened yesterday.

Forecasting is best viewed as a necessary evil—necessary because every business must plan for the future, and evil because no forecaster can predict the future with certainty (as the marketers of Clearasil learned). Therefore, before we proceed, it seems appropriate to offer some words of advice from C. Northcote Parkinson, the originator of Parkinson's law: "Heaven forbid that students should cease to read books on the science of public or business administration—provided only that these works are classified as fiction."[7] Our book should, of course, be considered an exception to that rule. But when it comes to forecasting, you will do well to remember that the field is as closely tied to fiction as to statistics. There are no sure forecasts—in fact, the only certainty is that the forecast will be wrong, and the key question is by how *much* it will be wrong.

DEMOGRAPHIC FACTORS

Demographics, the analysis of population statistics, seems pretty dry to most marketers. Few if any specialize in it. But demographics underlies almost every marketing program, and is often a source of potent insights and opportunities for marketers. Peter Drucker, the popular management guru, argues that demographic statistics are the single best source of business opportunity because they are often overlooked and because they can be forecast reliably.

If you know how many 1-year-olds there are today, for example, you can make a darn good guess how many 21-year-olds there will be in 20 years. (But you cannot be as certain about what they will do. For example, will they have large families and create another baby boom? Or will they marry late and have few children? Surveying them about their intentions would not be particularly useful at this date!)

One must follow the shifts in the numbers of Americans of different ages to understand why Gerber, the baby food producer, recently diversified into baby bottles, strollers, and humidifiers after scrambling for many years to find ways of diversifying out of baby products. (It went as far as packaging juice for adults in larger versions of its baby juice bottles, but they did not sell.) Its demographic analysis revealed that the number of potential buyers of such products is increasing, contrary to the general perception that, post-baby boom, the demand for baby products must be going down. These statistics are presented in a few pages, but first we will look briefly at the global picture.

Global and Domestic Populations

It took until the early 1800s for the world population to accumulate to 1 billion persons. In 1974, that number hit 4 billion; in 1995, it reached 5.7 billion; and in 2000, it is reaching 6.2 billion![8] By then, cities will hold half the world's population—a major shift from humanity's agricultural past.

The world's population growth is slowing, however, having peaked at just over 2 percent a year in the late 1960s. The present growth rate of 1.7 percent will result in the global population growth stopping, but not until the beginning of the twenty-second century. By then, the world's population is projected to total 11.6 billion. (This forecast rests on assumptions concerning future mortality and fertility rates—assumptions that could easily prove wrong. In the first edition of this book, we used the figure 10.6 billion, so you can see it has already been adjusted upward by demographers! And changes such as innovations in public health care could increase that forecast again.)

The vast majority of world population growth will occur in developing countries. For every child born in a developed country, 10 will be born in a developing country. The lion's share of the population (76 percent) now live in Africa, Asia (excluding Japan), and Latin America. In the year 2095, 8.8 billion of the world's 10.2 billion people will inhabit these areas. With a 3 percent growth rate, sub-Saharan Africa's growth is double that of the rest of the world, making it the fastest growing region in the world.

FOR YOUR IMAGINATION

Turkish Razor Blades?

Let's just say you want to forecast the market for razor blades in Turkey. Statistics on the number of adult men might be a good place to start—but not very! The problem is traditionally Turkish men "only got shaved to get married. Even then, you'd still leave the mustache," according to Turkish author Demitras Ceyhun. And traditions die hard. In 1993, 77 percent of Turkish men had mustaches—taking a significant bite out of that razor blade market. But a strange thing is happening. Men are increasingly favoring a Western-style clean-cut look, especially men who work in government or business. By 1997, the number of men with mustaches had fallen to 63 percent and counting.[9] Looks like a growth market for razor blades!

Asia now accounts for 59 percent of the world's population (up from 55 percent in our first edition, a remarkable change in less than a decade!). And Asia accounts for 70 percent of the population of the developing world. Latin America has slowed its growth rate, but faces large population booms in the near future as its large number of youths come into their family formation years. (Gerber, take note.)

Reflecting a definite shift in values away from family and to individual rights, birthrates in Western Europe have been falling. By the late 1980s, Austria, Denmark, Hungary, and West Germany slipped into a natural population decline with birthrates below the replacement fertility level of 2.1 children per woman. Eastern Europe seems to be following this trend as well.

The rapid growth in the populations of Asia, Africa, and Latin America means that the more prosperous consumers in these regions will be the main source of revenue growth for most European and North American marketers. From luxury products to essentials, export will be increasingly important. (*Everyone* take note.)

U.S. Demographics

In 1990, the population of the United States was 265 million. The total population is expected to be 271.2 million in 2000 and 282.5 million in 2050. Since the turn of the century, two distinct changes in the birthrate have had a substantial impact on the composition of the U.S. population, both present and future. From 1930 to 1945, because of the Depression and World War II, the birthrate was unusually low; from 1946 to 1964, it increased to an extremely high rate (the baby boom). After that, it dropped again. In 1988, American women bore an average of only 1.8 children, compared with an average of 3.8 in 1957. For three decades in a row, the rate of growth of the U.S. population has been slowing. In the 1970s, the population grew at its second-lowest rate in history.

While the overall birthrate in the United States remains low, births to women over 30 have been rising steadily for a decade, while births to women under 25 have been declining. One child in two is born to a woman over 30, compared with one in six in 1976. Two separate but related trends account for this. The over-30 age group is larger because the baby boom is getting older; hence, the "echo effect." In 1996, there were 32.4 million women between the ages of 30 and 44, compared with 17.7 million in 1970. Additionally, women are waiting until a later age before having their first child. The percentage of women aged 25 to 29 who are childless has risen from 31 percent in 1976 to 41 percent in 1988. Throughout the 1980s, first-time births accounted for over 40.7 percent of all births. This was the highest percentage of first-time births since the last golden age of child-bearing—the baby boom.

FOR YOUR IMAGINATION

How Do You Feel About Motherhood?

Before you read this sidebar, please answer the following question:

Do you agree that women should take care of running their homes and leave running the country up to men? ____ Yes ____ No

The baby boomers—people born between 1946 and 1964—are changing along with the rest of the U.S. population. In their youth, they were far more liberal than their parents: In 1974, only 17 percent of adult boomers described themselves as conservative. Yet today, 35 percent of boomers described themselves as conservative. They are far more likely to espouse centrist or conservative views on questions concerning government's role in social welfare, and are more likely today to feel that adultery is wrong than they were 20 years ago.[10]

But when it comes to women's role in the family, baby boomers are increasingly open-minded. They overwhelmingly disagree with the above question—feeling instead that women are just as welcome in the workplace as at home.

And this liberal attitude toward working women is held by far more baby boomers today than it was two decades ago. Eighty-nine percent disagreed with the above question in 1994, the last time the National Opinion Research Center at the University of Chicago asked them. Back in 1974, 75 percent disagreed—a significant majority, but still considerably less than the 1994 figure. So keep an eye on those baby boomers. They're growing up, and up. And their views on many issues are changing as a result. Any marketer or advertiser who fails to take note is likely to fail in their efforts to reach this lucrative market segment.

By the way, how did *you* answer that question—is your attitude in step with the vast majority of baby boomers, or do you hold contrary views?

Put on your forecasting hat for a moment. What does this mean for the makers of Clearasil? For colleges? For movie and TV producers? Can you see changes in U.S. society that this new "boomlet" of children explains—like Hollywood's current infatuation with feature movies using child or teen actors and plots that appeal to preteens?

The increase in first-time births is welcome to many marketers, because research has shown that parents and grandparents spend 10 times more on firstborn infants than on subsequent children. Parents spend some 25 percent of their income on firstborns. Such statistics are extremely helpful to some firms in their strategic planning. Gerber Products Company, for example, although it is best known for its food products for babies, has recently acquired Reliance Products, marketers of Nuk brand orthodontic bottle nipples and pacifiers; Century Products—car seats, walkers, and high chairs; Bilt-Rite Juvenile Products—playpens, carriages, and furniture; Walter Moyer—baby wear; Palo Alto Educational System—daycare centers; Hankscraft—vaporizers and humidifiers; and Nursery Originals—lamps, mobiles, and toys. Gerber expects first-time parents to purchase many of these items in the coming years. First-time parents often need other products and services, as well. They are likely to change their car-buying preferences, to remodel or purchase homes, to purchase insurance and medical services, to buy maternity wear, and to buy specialized books and magazines.

It is interesting to think of the many ways marketers are taking advantage of this opportunity. For example, the minivan is a relatively new product, invented to transport America's growing families. And it is now one of the best-selling categories of automobiles in the United States.

These first-time births are to a different type of parent than in prior boom periods. Today's first-time parents are older, better educated, more affluent ($35,000 + annual household income), more socially aware, and less concerned with being like their own parents. Statistics show that two-thirds of mothers return to work within the first three months after giving birth. This affects baby food marketers because parents are more likely to use prepared formulas and baby foods. Meanwhile, daycare centers and childcare services have expanded to meet the needs of dual-career couples.

America's Changing Age Structure

Exhibit 5.1 shows how the age structure of the U.S. population changed between 1986 and 1990, and how it is expected to change between 1990 and 2000. This information comes from the Bureau of the Census, a part of the U.S. Department of Commerce, and was extracted from a useful publication called the *Statistical Abstract of the United States* (which, like many demographic reports, can be ordered from the Government Printing Office in Washington, DC—and this one is usually stocked at local libraries, too).

Clearly, the largest group is the 25- to 44-year-olds. But can we tell from the table which are the fastest growing groups, and how fast they are growing? Probably not without a pocket calculator—which is exactly what should be used for examining demographics. It is often helpful to rework statistics to answer a specific question or test a hypothesis. For example, if all we want to know is whether there is more

EXHIBIT 5.1. Age structure of the U.S. population.

Age Range	Year	Number (in millions)	Percentage of Total
under 5	1986	18.1	7.5
	1990	18.4	7.4
	2000	16.9	6.3
5–17	1986	45.1	18.7
	1990	45.6	18.2
	2000	48.8	18.2
18–24	1986	27.7	11.5
	1990	26.1	10.4
	2000	25.2	9.4
25–44	1986	75.9	31.5
	1990	81.8	32.6
	2000	81.1	30.2
45–64	1986	45.1	18.6
	1990	46.9	18.7
	2000	61.4	22.9
65 and over	1986	29.2	12.1
	1990	31.6	12.6
	2000	34.9	13.0
Total	1986	241.1	100
	1990	250.4	100
	2000	268.3	100

growth in the numbers of young people, middle-aged people, or older people, we might want to combine the six age groups in this table into only three. To simplify the data even more, we could calculate the percentage of change in the numbers of each group from 1986 to 2000. (To do that, we divide the difference between starting and ending numbers by the ending number and multiply by 100 to find the percentage of change.) This reduces the information to only three numbers, which makes the table easier to read, but also sacrifices some of the detail (see Exhibit 5.2). (For example,

EXHIBIT 5.2. Growth of U.S. population, condensed into three groups.

Age Range	Percent Change, 1986–2000
Under 18	+3.9
18–44	+2.6
45 and over	+29.7

the rapid growth in the 45-and-over category might warrant closer attention, leading us to want to break it down further.)

From Exhibit 5.2, the most important trend pops right out. Our population is experiencing a rapid increase of older people, in contrast to minimal growth in the younger groups. If we break down the 45-and-over category further, we find growth of a whopping 36.3 percent in the 45- to 64-year-old group, and less rapid, but still striking, growth of 19.6 percent in the 65-and-over group. We might also think to ask where all these older people are coming from. Most Americans—and the majority of marketers—find these statistics a surprise. But you can be confident that Americans are not having older babies. The movement of the baby boomers into middle age is driving these statistics, and the trend has been predictable, if not widely anticipated, for decades.

Many companies are beginning to feel the effects of these trends, and the companies that follow demographic trends are already planning how to cope with the changes. For example, Levi Strauss introduced a line of roomier pants, Dockers, targeting 30-something men who have stopped playing football but are now watching it. And in 1996, Levi introduced trousers branded Slates, for the man over 50. And Johnson & Johnson is working both sides of the street: While it advertises its shampoo as appropriate for older people as well as babies, it also owns Ortho Pharmaceutical Corporation, one of the largest producers of contraceptives for people who want to avoid buying baby products.

In the following sections, we take a closer look at each of these age groups.

The Youth Market

Teenagers have long been a profitable market segment for producers of records, cosmetics, movies, clothing, and soft drinks. However, this market is dwindling right now, as we saw when we attempted to forecast the market for Clearasil in the opening pages of this chapter.

The Census Bureau reports that in 1995 that the number of teenagers in the United States was slightly over 10 percent of the population, down from 14 percent in 1975. Even so, teenagers numbered 23 million in 1990. And three out of five teenagers hold either a part- or full-time job. Adding teenagers' weekly earnings of about $600 million to their $80 million in allowances, marketers find the clout of the teen market at the cash register to be about $35 billion annually—nearly all of it spendable. There may be fewer teens right now, but they spend a lot more money than they used to!

And teens control a rising share of their households' spending. Forty billion dollars in family funds is spent by teenagers annually, mostly for groceries and household items.

Add to this the rising age of the Generation Y kids, and you have what looks like the beginning of an incredibly important teen market in the United States. When the number of Generation Y teens peeks at 30 million in 2006, that will be the largest it's been since 1975. And they will have the greatest buying power of any teen market ever.

In response to statistics such as these, Bausch and Lomb's Softlens division has featured teens in its television commercials and placed ads in magazines such as *Co-Ed* and *Tiger Beat*. Because 63 percent of teenage girls and 39 percent of teenage boys do some family grocery shopping, Nabisco and Nestle's advertise their food products on AVC-TV's "American Bandstand." Campbell's Chunky Soups produced a special MTV ad that shows a teenager lip-synching a popular song as he warms soup in his family's kitchen. Sara Lee cakes, the National Dairy Association, and Ralston Purina cat foods also advertise on the cable music video channel. Said a marketing researcher, "Typically, they'll [the parents] leave money and a note, 'Get two pounds of hamburger, a loaf of bread, soda, soup, and a box of Tide.' That leaves an awful lot of decision-making power in the hands of one teen."[11]

Marketers serving youth markets can look outside the United States for sizable numbers of youths in other countries. Kenya, for example, has a median age of only 14. In Europe, Portugal and Ireland are important youth markets, as are Singapore, Hong Kong, South Korea, Sri Lanka, Turkey, the Philippines, and China in Asia, and Reunion, Mauritius, Cape Verde, and trendsetter Egypt in Africa. The opportunities to serve the sometimes unique needs of these pockets of teenagers are fashioned by when they start to work, the trade climate for an infusion of U.S. goods, and the median income of youths, to name just a few determinants of success. In Costa Rica, for example, 20 percent of its 2.6 million inhabitants are between the ages of 15 and 24. Although the economy is rather stable, the GNP per capita is only $1,070 per year.

Advertising to Teens

Marketers' efforts to court teen buyers have changed the nature of advertising and sales promotions. Traditionally, most ads and other promotions aimed at adults—except toy advertising, which targeted young children. Now advertisers actively seek teen audiences for their messages, and as a result, television, radio, and print media are reinventing themselves to attract those lucrative teenage audiences their advertisers crave.

For example, the Nickelodeon TV network planned an interesting teen-oriented promotion for 1997 to help attract prime-time viewers. The promotion? A "Spot the Dot" game in which a red dot appears on the viewer's television screen with a secret message hidden inside. Decode the message and you might discover you've won one of 35,000 different prizes. To decode it, though, viewers need a special decoder distributed by Blockbuster Video (owned by Viacom, which also owns Nickelodeon). And, in a collaboration with Nintendo, Blockbuster also helped introduce the new Nintendo 64 product line in 1997 by making it available for rental.[12] Both Nintendo and Nickelodeon reach the teen market especially well, and teens are a growing force in the home video rental market, so these promotional collaborations make good sense to anyone following the demographic trends in the United States.

An interesting side effect of this rush to market to teenagers is that U.S. society seems to have turned cultural leadership over to its youth. Hot fashions, from clothing to music, are borrowed from teenagers. And if the trend continues, teen values and preferences will begin to shape social and political life more deeply as well. Even as the U.S. population ages, its attitudes and values may be shaped more strongly by teens than at any time since the 1960s. And how you feel about this teen influence depends to a large extent on your age. It's enough to make parents like us cringe!

Long-Term Fear: A Growing Underclass?

One demographic trend makes us pretty nervous about the future of America's youth. If you look behind the rosy picture of large numbers of fashion-oriented teen consumers, you can also catch a glimpse of another, less rosy demographic picture. In this picture, what you see is a growing number of poor children who lack the basic safety nets of a strong family life, good childhood education, and supportive social services within their communities. Samuel Preston, director of the Population Studies Center at the University of Pennsylvania, is worried about this issue. He points out that,

Twenty-two percent of American children currently live in poverty. That's 7 percentage points higher than in 1970, and higher overall than any comparable rates in a Western country or Japan. Our children have neither the strong families of Japan, where only 1 percent of births occur out of wedlock, nor the abundant state support provided in Europe. Many children are simply falling through the cracks. Reported and confirmed cases of child abuse and neglect are increasingly rapidly. For 5- to 24-year-olds, suicide and homicide rates have tripled since 1950.[13]

And Preston observes that voters are not likely to support programs designed to help the growing segment of impoverished children. Why? Demographics again. Voters living in households without young children don't usually support increased spending on children, and parents with children at home under 18 are less than 38 percent of the voting population. Short of a majority vote, for sure, and certainly far short of the two-thirds majority needed in most local elections to increase funding to school districts.

So if voters won't take care of the problem of childhood poverty, who will? Perhaps the responsibility will fall to the business community, since we have so much to gain from a prosperous new generation of consumers—and so much to lose if they fail to meet our rosy expectations.

The Baby Boomers

As noted earlier, the Depression and World War II combined to keep the U.S. birthrate very low during the 1930s and early 1940s. In 1990, as a result, a relatively small number of Americans were in the 45-to-60 age category. But the birthrate exploded in the years immediately after World War II, hit a peak in 1958, and stayed at that level until 1962. As a result, in 1990, there were 55 percent more people aged 30 to 44 in the United States than people aged 45 to 60. And now those baby boomers are in their forties and fifties, making middle age the biggest age group in the country.

The baby boom thus creates a demographic bulge—often likened to a pig swallowed by a python—that affects everything from the housing market to job opportunities.

Marketers and advertisers are rushing to position their products for the newly middle-aged baby boomer market. Take the Catera, a luxury sedan introduced by GM in 1996–1997 in an effort to turn baby boomers into Cadillac customers. Baby boomers' parents chose the Cadillac in middle age to show they'd arrived, but boomers weren't going for it. So GM studied boomers' attitudes and discovered, according to Catera brand manager Dave Nottoli, that "They don't place value on large cars. They prefer tighter suspensions and responsive handling. They want cars that are sporty, safe, luxurious, and long-lasting."[14]

Cadillac customers currently are an average of 66 years old. Can Catera win 45-year-old baby boomers with a smaller, sportier sedan than Cadillac offers—and thus help GM make the transition to the baby boomer market? At time of writing, the jury is still out. But you should be in a position to answer the question by the time this book makes it to you. Next time you go for a drive, see how many Cateras are on the road with you—and also check to see whether the drivers are in their forties or sixties. If they are in their sixties, then you'll know that the Catera has cannibalized Cadillac sales, switching older consumers to a less expensive product instead of attracting new, younger consumers.

Advertising to Baby Boomers

Baby boomers have spawned a number of trends that have revolutionized the way marketers satisfy needs and, especially, wants. The buying behavior of this key demographic segment has some important ramifications for marketers. Sometimes referred to as the "boutique generation," many two-income families use their affluence to indulge their taste for upscale products.

Boomers have already bought their first house and are probably raising a family—and discovering the vast needs that accompany these two major life changes. Thus, they are an ideal target market for the many marketers who sell goods and services to households with children. Additionally, the baby boom generation has a preference for premium goods and services, which has resulted in a dramatic increase in the number of small businesses catering to these tastes: upscale ice cream parlors, health clubs, fresh pasta and cheese stores, and gourmet cafes. The baby boomers are also the largest users of discount stockbrokers and automated teller machines.

A number of marketers are turning their attention to this segment. Soft drink companies are introducing older faces into their ads, as well as introducing new products. Pepsi Light, a diet soda with a slightly drier taste, is aimed at consumers aged 18 to 49.

A "Real Life, Real Answers" advertising campaign for John Hancock Mutual Life Insurance perfectly communicated with today's baby boomers. Showing everyday scenes such as a fortieth birthday party or a young parent telling his daughter about a recent raise, the ads created a brief financial profile of the person featured in the ad: "Age: 40, Salary (dual): $67,000, Home equity: $98,000." The theme of the campaign was that John Hancock understands your financial future.

It is interesting to examine television or magazine advertising for ads targeting baby boomers. Give it a try—grab the nearest general-interest magazine and flip through it for likely ads. Boomer ads generally speak to the life stages and challenges of middle age, as well as to the relatively liberal values and the concerns for future financial security that characterize today's boomers.[15] Find any yet? See, they're everywhere!

Changes in the age structure of the population are like glaciers—they change the market landscape, often at such a slow pace that people fail to notice the movement. One such change is the increasing age of the baby boomers. These consumers will be in their prime spending years by the year 2000, yet marketers are only now beginning to learn how to meet the wants and needs of a less youthful population segment. Many of the ads that target baby boomers fail to hit the bull's eye because they still treat boomers as young adults—while in reality they are now firmly into their middle age.

Cosmetics advertising, for instance, has always stressed the value of youth as a sign of beauty. But because the number of women between 35 and 44 grew by 56 percent in the 1990s, cosmetics firms are changing their tune. Cosmetics companies are introducing "anti-aging" skin care products that claim to hold back the ravages of time. Linda Evans (mid-40s) floats down a staircase in a Clairol ad to announce "Forty isn't fatal." And Joan Collins (early 60s) has her own line of perfume. There are similar products to help men grow older—and to help them avoid the realization that they are growing older. Hair dyes, hairpieces, skin care products, and health clubs are in great demand. John Forsythe (over 70) promotes his man's fragrance called Carrington. Marketers are recognizing that people over 49 spend more than others on travel, restaurant meals, and recreational vehicles. In fact, Coachmen Industries has taken away part of its recreational vehicle advertising budget from *Trailer Life* and allocated it to *Good Housekeeping, Popular Mechanics*, and other magazines that are popular among older subscribers.

Exhibit 5.3, an ad for investment counseling and financial management services from Babson-United Investment Advisors, is a good example of successful baby boomer advertising because it addresses real concerns of this group in a realistic manner. Their tag line—Strategies for the Individual—reflects a keen understanding of how boomers see themselves. And their service is designed to provide custom solutions to each client's unique needs. The ad also touches on aspects of the service that make it unique—what advertisers call its Unique Selling Proposition. For instance, the Babson-United advisors aren't brokers and don't make money from stock trades, so they have no bias toward getting clients to buy and sell often. And the firm's lengthy history in the industry is also used as a selling point, giving it the credibility boomers need for what they view as a very serious issue: how to plan for their up-coming retirement.

EXHIBIT 5.3.   What are your financial goals?

What Are Your Financial Goals?

Since 1904, Babson-United has provided objective, unbiased investment advice to individuals like you who have planned prudently to achieve a comfortable level of wealth.

Our focus is always on *your* goals. The strategies we suggest are completely objective and customized for *your* situation. Babson-United uses no formulas, applies no pre-programmed performance models to your portfolio.

Personal strategies, personal choices

Your Babson-United Personal Investment Counselor works with you to assess your current strengths and to suggest ways in which you can make your wealth work harder toward achieving your goals. We work from a long-term perspective and base our recommendations on a fundamentals approach to investing.

Throughout this process, *you* are the controlling partner. The choice to implement the strategies suggested by your Personal Investment Counselor is entirely yours.

Personal service

Your Babson-United Personal Investment Counselor is always available to work with other members of your investment team. Our relationship with you extends to your legal advisors, family fiduciaries, custodians, brokers and others chosen by you to help with your financial affairs.

And, as always, these relationships are discreet, confidential, and established only with your approval.

A simple phone call will tell you more

To discover how the services of a Babson-United Personal Investment Counselor can help you achieve your financial goals, please call John Holmberg at 888-223-7412 toll free.

When you call, please ask us to send you free preview issues of our weekly *United & Babson Investment Report*.

Strategies for the Individual

BABSON-UNITED INVESTMENT COUNSEL

A SERVICE OF BABSON-UNITED INVESTMENT ADVISORS, INC.
101 Prescott Street • Wellesley Hills, MA 02181 • Telephone: 781-235-0900 • FAX: 781-235-9450

The Elderly Market

The elderly age segment presents many opportunities for marketers. Today, 13 percent of the U.S. population is over 65—more than 33.5 million people, or about one in every nine Americans. With further improvements in medical knowledge and the aging of the baby boomers, that percentage will increase still further in the twenty-first century. Among the elderly, the fastest growing segment is the over-85 population—mostly because of improved medical techniques and medicines.

Today's elderly do not conform to the common stereotype of them as a relatively disadvantaged group. Most elderly people live in paid-for homes and have enough income to enjoy their leisure years. They are not physically infirm—only 5 percent live in nursing homes. And they are independent. Only 9 percent live with their children, compared with 31 percent in 1950. Financially, they are quite well off. The poverty rate of the elderly is 11 percent, compared with 15 percent for the population as a whole. Members of this segment prefer to spend their money rather than pass it on to their children. With an annual purchasing power estimated at $60 to $200 billion, senior citizens offer a market opportunity of sizable proportions.[16]

This mature segment has a thirst for services, particularly those focusing on the home—lawn care, home security, home maintenance, and the like. They have high levels of demand for travel, leisure activities, and health care services. The elderly are among the most frequent buyers of stocks, bonds, furs, jewelry, and expensive clothing.[17] They tend to prefer department stores over discount stores, and they like to be singled out and given special attention by store personnel. They do not seem to be price conscious and generally do not favor the use of food stamps, coupons, generic products, and unit pricing. The elderly are the prime users of mass media, especially television. They are the heaviest subscribers of newspapers and use them as guides to help them in their shopping.

Although these facts are well known, marketers have been reluctant to target this neglected market. Some of this reluctance is diminishing as marketers are becoming more aware of the tremendous opportunities open to them in this segment. For example, Price Chopper Discount Foods, a 53-store New York-based chain, runs free buses that provide round-trip transportation for elderly shoppers. Whirlpool Corporation has developed a line of washers and dryers with large-print instructions and dials to accommodate for diminished eyesight that accompanies aging. Take Time Fitness Centers, a Sunbelt chain, offers aerobic classes for the silver generation; its exercise program is conducted to the tranquil strains of Guy Lombardo and Glenn Miller rather than a driving disco beat. In sum, like other age groups, the elderly have unique needs that marketers must try to satisfy.

The explosion of elderly is not unique to the United States; all developed countries will be home to increasingly older populations. The world's oldest populations include Sweden (with 17 percent of its population aged 65 and older), West Germany (15 percent), and Denmark (15 percent). By the year 2025, every Western European country will have 18 percent or more of its population aged 65. Although this older segment does not constitute a significant share of developing countries' populations, it is important to note that in Brazil, Mexico, India, Indonesia, and the Philippines, the proportion of the population over age 65 will double between 1985 and 2025.

In Japan, the realization that those over 65 will grow from 10 percent presently to over 20 percent by 2025, as well as comprise a $1 trillion market, has perked up the interest of commercial endeavors. Many small service businesses have emerged to tend to housekeeping, bathing, and the equivalent of the U.S. Meals on Wheels. With average savings of $93,000, compared with $54,000 as a national average, Japanese oldsters are flocking to brokerage houses to improve their savings growth over the 1 percent passbook savings rate. Many U.S. companies are joint venturing to gain entrance to this burgeoning opportunity. Beverly Enterprises, a California retirement home developer, has joined with Japanese construction giant Shimuza Corporation to erect senior living communities.

Advertising to the Elderly

Please, *don't* use elderly models in ads aimed at the elderly. Charlie does a lot of consulting in how to market to older consumers, and he always uses the 80 percent rule, which states that your cognitive age—the age you *feel* you are and hence behave as— is 80 percent of your chronological age. That's a pretty big gap, and because it's a percentage, the gap gets bigger as we get older.

Advertisers need to portray their target customers as they see themselves, in other words, according to their cognitive, not chronological, ages. So if you want 70-year-olds to relate to your ad, for example, then you better use 56-year-old models!

But that's just the beginning. As one grows older, the central nervous system slows. Hence, information is processed more slowly. Older consumers find print promotions better than broadcast because they can control the pace at which the information is mentally ingested. Pictures are more easily processed than words—something good to know if you are creating an advertising campaign. Print size should be large, at least 12 point, and lots of white space should be left in presenting copy to add contrast. And the subtle innuendoes of communicating to older consumers go on and on. Some day we'll write a book on that interesting aspect of marketing!

Charlie's work on this age group is done through his firm, Lifestage Matrix Marketing, which, with his partner Geoffrey Meredith, is headquartered in Lafayette, California. His company studies the experiences we have that shape core attitudes and values of each of our cohorts. A cohort is the group of people you are born with and travel with through your life. A cohort is a smaller group than a generation, since generations are determined by when people have children—and members of the same generation are often radically different because they belong to different cohorts who experienced different events in their youth. (There may be several cohorts in a generation, which typically spans 25 years.)

The importance of this finding for marketing to everyone, but especially to the elderly, cannot be overstated. For starters, it teaches us that all elderly are not alike. Instead, you need to identify which cohort you want to target, and then tailor your advertising message and medium based on what that cohort prefers. Tricky stuff—but then, we never said marketing would be easy! We'll tell you more about how to use the cohort model in Chapter 7.

SOME CONTEMPORARY TRENDS

Populations are changing and they will continue to change. Some of the trends accompanying these changes have already drastically altered the fabric of U.S. society—and, hence, the nature of the marketplace. An analysis of these trends can yield fascinating insights into where society is today and where it may be headed. How marketers make use of this knowledge will have a significant effect on how society is served.

To begin with, the family in its traditional form is disappearing from the U.S. scene. In years past, the typical U.S. family consisted of a father who worked outside the home, a mother who took care of the home, and two children. Census data from 1980 show that only 7 percent of the then 82 million households in the United States fit that model. Thus, the greatest demographic changes concern how, and with whom, we live. These changes create and destroy many markets in each decade. Let's look at some of these interesting trends. The following sections describe some of the other major trends that are reshaping U.S. society.

Later Marriage

For men, the median age at first marriage is almost 27; for women, it is 25. (The figures we used in our first edition were 26 and 23.6, showing the rapid movement in this trend!) These figures are considerably higher than those of a decade earlier—yet close to the medians that existed in the earlier part of this century. Statistics tell us that 10 percent of young adults will never marry, double the rate that prevailed in the 1970s. In fact, college-educated women still single at age 35 have only a 5 percent chance of ever getting married. This trend has resulted in greater demand for apartments, recreational services, and sporty automobiles.

Fewer Children

We noted earlier in the chapter that the birthrate has been substantially lower in recent decades than it was earlier in the century. The number of families with three or more children under 18 has declined sharply since 1970—from 10.4 to 6.9 million. The average family size is now 3.2 for Whites, 3.7 for Blacks, and 3.9 for Hispanic Americans. Gerber and Beech-Nut (food), Fisher-Price (toys), and Parker Brothers (games) have all felt the pinch of this trend.

More Frequent Divorce

The United States has the highest divorce rate in the world. In the past few years, the divorce rate has leveled off after a dramatic surge in the 1970s. But demographers predict that 50 percent of first marriages and 60 percent of second marriages will end in divorce. As a result, the number of one-parent households has increased by 100 percent since 1970. Nine of ten one-parent families are maintained by the mother, but the proportion of single-parent families maintained by the father has more than doubled and is expected to increase as child custody and divorce laws are modified.

Greater Acceptance of POSSLQs

The 1980s witnessed a trend toward the formation of POSSLQs, or households made up of "persons of the opposite sex sharing living quarters" without being married. And in the 1990s, these households became socially acceptable. In Northern and Western Europe, cohabitation is increasingly accepted as normal, and there are indications that possibly as few as 50 to 60 percent of men and women in future generations will ever marry. In fact, the proportion of out-of-wedlock births has reached 45 to 46 percent in Denmark, Iceland, and Sweden. In those countries, the average age of women at first marriage is now higher than the average age at which they first give birth.

In the United States, almost half of Americans aged 25 to 35 have lived with someone of the opposite sex outside of marriage. This trend has become more acceptable with younger people. Although only 11 percent of Americans marrying between 1965 and 1974 had experienced this kind of living arrangement, 44 percent of those marrying between 1980 and 1984 had. Cohabitation is even more prevalent between marriages; 58 percent of recently remarried people had lived with someone of the opposite sex before remarrying. Sixty percent of those living together end up getting married. This kind of living arrangement is becoming increasingly tolerated in our society. Said a government demographer, "Cohabitation has not simply become increasingly common. If recent trends continue, it will soon be the majority experience."[18] However, the POSSLQ arrangement is transitory; most cohabiting couples marry or separate within a few years. Because partners in a POSSLQ are less committed to each other than partners in a marriage, such households are reluctant to purchase durable goods that would be difficult to dispose of if the relationship should end.

More People Living Alone

The Census Bureau has reported that 244.7 million single adults lived in the United States in 1995, up from 11 million in 1970.[19] To put that into context, 5 percent of the U.S. population lived alone in 1970, compared with 9 percent (almost double the share) in 1995.[20] If the share of single adults keeps rising at the same rate, soon all Americans will be single—which is pretty unlikely, but on the other hand, it's hard to guess when the trend might start slowing down. And interestingly, many, many of those who split up and leave their POSSLQ relationships return to live with their parents, creating what demographers refer to as the boomerang set.

Many sociologists and demographers believe that this rapid rise in the number of persons living alone constitutes a demographic revolution with far-reaching and unpredictable consequences. Certainly single adults go through very different life stages than those who marry and have children. (And by the way, the number of married couples without children is also rising.) That makes for a large and swelling number of households that don't spend a dime on baby food, diapers, Nintendo, or college tuition. But if you want to sell them anything for their own use, rather than for children, these households will have much more discretionary income to throw your way.[21]

Hallmark Cards provides unmarrieds with special greeting cards to commiserate by mail about the ebbs and flows of dating. Campbell's Soup Company has successfully marketed Le Menu frozen dinners and Swanson's Homestyle Recipe Entrees for singles. Pillsbury offers pint-sized cakes, microwavable in 10 minutes. Singles also can list preferred gifts at Bloomingdale's Self-Registry, a service similar to the traditional bridal registry.

More Women at Work

In 1995, 60.9 percent of U.S. women 16 years of age and older held jobs outside the home, compared with 32 percent in 1960 and 37 percent in 1970. Fifty-nine percent of working women are married, compared with 36 percent in 1940 and only 14 percent in 1890.[22] The female labor participation rate in the United States exceeds that of almost every other industrialized nation. Sweden, with 80 percent of women working, holds the highest ranking. In Japan, Hong Kong, and Taiwan, 55 percent of women aged 15 to 64 now work. Three-quarters of Chinese and Thai women in this age category work. Meanwhile, in West Germany, the participation rate has remained constant, at 38 percent, for the past decade. The full-time housewife has dramatically disappeared from the household scene in most developed countries. This forces, for instance, a retargeting for major appliance marketers around the world toward working husbands and wives.

The trend toward greater labor force participation by U.S. women is particularly significant because it affects many families with young children. Fifty-four percent of mothers with children under 17 have full- or part-time work outside of their homes. In addition to increasing the demand for childcare services, this trend boosts sales of briefcases, cars, credit cards, insurance, education, air travel, hotel rooms, and clothing. Companies are springing up to provide working parents with services ranging from take-out meals to after-school activities for their children. Reddi Maid in Chicago, for example, provides maids to serve breakfast, make the beds, touch up the bath and kitchen, and even fetch children from school and take them to the doctor. Knowing the importance of customer satisfaction, the maid will even call the day after a doctor's visit to inquire about the child's health! Established businesses also are changing their activities to meet the needs of working women. Hairdressers open earlier and close later. Hotels have increased their security procedures, and headwaiters have learned to ensure that no one bothers solitary female diners.

Advertising to Working Women and Their Daughters

Nike is one of many marketers to recognize an opportunity resulting from changes in women's attitudes toward themselves. Probably because of their influx into the workforce, women are more likely to have the self-confidence to tackle traditionally male activities, from buying a car to playing soccer. The U.S. women's soccer team is the best in the world at time of writing (let's not talk about the U.S. men's team), suggesting that U.S. women are leading a worldwide shift in gender-related behavior and self-perception.

And U.S. men are lagging behind this trend, still seeing women in more traditional and limiting ways—which is why the so-called "glass ceiling" in hiring still exists. Only 10 percent of the top jobs at the 500 largest U.S. companies are held by women![23]

Advertising needs to reflect women's increasing confidence in themselves and their rejection of traditional gender stereotypes if advertisers want to cash in on the growing buying power of women. That's why Nike has begun advertising on the theme that girls should participate in competitive sports just as much as boys do. A recent Nike ad by ad agency Wieden and Kennedy of Portland, Oregon, features girls explaining the benefits of playing sports:

> "I will like myself more; I will have more self-confidence if you let me play sports."

> "If you let me play, I will be 60 percent less likely to get breast cancer. I will suffer less depression if you let me play sports."

> "I will be more likely to leave a man who beats me. If you let me play, I will be less likely to get pregnant before I want to; I will learn what it means to be strong."[24]

These statements speak to both daughters and their parents, teachers, and coaches. Using demographic data, the advertisers have made a strong case for why girls should be encouraged to play sports—and, incidentally, why they will need to buy lots more Nike products than they used to!

Growing Ethnic and Racial Subcultures

The United States has been described both as a "melting pot" and as a "salad bowl," reflecting the many ethnic subcultures that coexist and mix within its boundaries. The ties of Americans to their many and varied ancestral backgrounds are strong, and modern life provides more opportunities than ever to learn about other people's cultural origins. A glance at the frozen food section of any supermarket offers proof enough: from blintzes to tacos to pizza, ethnic dishes of every variety compete for our attention.

The 1970s were clearly the "decade of the immigrant"—during the last three years of that decade, the number of immigrants to the United States surpassed the figure for any year since 1924. The greatest number of newcomers came from Asia— refugees from Southeast Asia; families from Korea, Taiwan, and the Fiji Islands; medical students from the Philippines. The total of Asian immigrants increased by 128 percent in the 1970s. Yet in absolute numbers—just over 5 million people—this segment is small. In this section, therefore, we look at two of the largest subcultural groups in the United States: Black Americans and Hispanic Americans.

There are nearly 32 million Black Americans, representing more than $200 billion in buying power. This group constitutes 13 percent of the population. Some general observations have been made about the buying behavior of this group. They include the following:

- Compared with White Americans, Blacks spend proportionately more of their income on clothing, home furnishings, transportation other than automobiles, and savings; they spend proportionately less on food, housing, medical care, automobile transportation, and insurance.

- Especially at the lowest income levels, Black consumers tend to do their food shopping close to home.

- At all income levels, Black women are at least as fashion conscious as White women, and this trait increases with income.

- Advertisements that use integrated models seem to have no adverse effects on either Blacks or Whites.

In their television viewing, Blacks show a greater preference than Whites for family entertainment and variety shows.[25]

But are such generalizations meaningful to marketers? In many cases, you will find that they are not. African-American consumers rarely constitute an appropriate target market, since they include people with diverse lifestyles and holding a wide range of attitudes. Race is probably an artificial social construct anyway, and it is especially artificial when you try to use it to predict consumer behavior. Be careful to define any target market in detail, rather than assuming that its buying preferences can be predicted solely by race!

The second largest subcultural group in the United States is the Hispanic minority. This group, numbering 27 million in 1995 (10.1 percent of the U.S. population and growing), is composed mainly of Mexican Americans, Puerto Ricans, and Cubans, and spends $140-plus billion annually. Having increased by 85 percent since 1980, this segment of the population is growing much faster than any other large segment. Looking for a growth market? Here it is!

The states with the largest Hispanic populations are California, Texas, New York, and Florida. On the average, members of this population are younger, have larger households, and are more loyal to church and family than the average U.S. citizen. Although they are poorer and have less schooling than the average American, their income and educational levels are increasing, as is their purchasing power. Like Black Americans, Hispanic Americans exhibit some distinctive buying patterns:

- Hispanic Americans spend more on food than members of other groups, mainly because of larger average family size.

- The Hispanic shopper feels lost in giant supermarkets and inhibited about asking questions of store personnel, yet Hispanics still do most of their shopping in large stores rather than in small shops.

- Hispanic consumers visit fast-food restaurants more frequently than non-Hispanic consumers do.
- Inhibited by difficulties with the English language, some Hispanic Americans are confused by multiple pricing and cents-off labels.
- Hispanics are highly brand loyal.[26]

Generalizations about minority markets can be dangerously simplistic, however. Among Hispanic Americans are many who speak English better than Spanish, for instance. Among Blacks, many do not fit the standard profile referred to above either. The marketer must focus intelligently on a specific target consumer when marketing to minorities, just as in any marketing effort.

In an increasing number of cases, *market segments cross ethnic and racial boundaries.* For example, Black graduates of Ivy League law schools may have more in common with their White classmates than with other Blacks when it comes to marketing many consumer durables. Tiger Woods appears at public events in conservative slacks and polo shirts when he's not wearing a green Master's blazer. He favors the kind of clothing found in a Land's End catalog, and even though that company does not target minorities specifically, it certainly wants to appeal to affluent consumers like Tiger Woods!

Advertising to Hispanic Consumers

A headlong rush for the Hispanic market has been mounted, and it takes many forms. For example, Spanish-language Satellite and cable television stations give advertisers growing access to Spanish-speaking Hispanics in the United States, and the California Egg commission now runs television infomercials in Spanish. They target Hispanics because their research shows that Hispanic households consume more eggs than the average U.S. household does.[27]

Advertising campaigns have also appeared featuring Latin athletes touting Miller Lite because it is *mas sabrosa* and no *Ilena.* Madge the manicurist pushes Palmolive to her clientele. To pitch their *pollo* and *hamburquesas,* Frank Perdue and Ronald McDonald are speaking Spanish. Aware that the family plays a very important part in the life of Hispanics, Ford Motor Company advertises its family vehicles, such as the four-door Tempo and Escort Wagon with the slogan *"De familia a familia"* ("From family to family"). American Telephone and Telegraph Company courts Hispanics by showing them longing for their relatives and picking up the telephone with the slogan "This close—only with AT&T." AT&T's market share among Hispanics is 12 percent higher than for the market as a whole.

Marketers are recognizing that the Hispanic market is far from homogeneous. Anheuser-Busch and Campbell Soup both vary the background music and Spanish voice-overs depending on whether their commercials will be aired in Mexican California, Cuban Florida, or Puerto Rican New York. Just like marketing in international markets, the sometimes subtle cultural differences must be accommodated. When Pacific Bell pushed its advertising agency to run Spanish ads suggesting that Hispanics make international calls on weekends to save as much as 50 percent, the agency pointed out that Hispanics do not want to feel cheap, particularly when it comes to the family. "If I waited until the rates went down to call home, that would be an insult," said the Hispanic advertising agency director.[28]

A Nation on the Move

Different geographic locations are often associated with different consumer preferences and rates of product usage. As a result, marketers need to be attuned to geographic population shifts, such as the following:

Region of United States	Percent Change in Population, 1990–1995
United States, Total	5.6
Mountain	14.5
South	7.5
Pacific	7.2
Midwest	3.6
Northeast	1.3

The difference between population growth in fast-growing regions and the lack of it in others amounts to millions of consumers gained or lost—and a major impact on the businesses in those regions! For example, a business operating in Nevada and other Mountain States could have gained hundreds of thousands of potential customers in the first half of the 1990s alone. (See the *Statistical Abstract of the United States,* published by the Department of Commerce each October, for the latest statistics if you wish to find fast-growing regions or states. And the annual *Economic Report of the President* also provides summary data on this topic. Both are shelved in the reference sections of most libraries.)

The Movement to the Suburbs

Within every region of the nation, there has been a steady movement out of cities and into suburbs. This trend, however, is less pronounced than it was in the two decades following World War II. Growth in the suburbs is expected to be held down by greater congestion; higher energy costs; increased crime, pollution, and racial tension; and housing shortages. Nevertheless, suburbia still dominates the nation's economic and social life. Beautiful shopping malls, sprawling office parks, and high-tech industrial centers have made the suburbs vibrant centers for jobs, shopping, and entertainment.

INCOME FACTORS: ABILITY TO BUY

Thus far in this chapter, we have focused on the "people" component of markets through our examination of demographics. However, people without money or some other means of making exchanges are not part of a market. In most situations, ability to buy is based on income. Before we look at this key determinant of buying behavior, however, we first look at two key factors that affect income: education and occupation. In general, the more education one has and the higher the prestige associated with one's occupation, the more income one can expect to receive.

Education, Occupation, and Income

The average education level in the United States has risen dramatically in the twentieth century, and this has major implications for marketers. In 1970, only 52 percent of Americans 25 years of age and over were high school graduates, and only 11 percent had graduated from college. Now more than 80 percent of those 25 years and older have finished high school, more than 33 percent have attended at least one year of college, and about 22 percent have completed four years of college.[29] Marketers, therefore, not only are called upon to satisfy a more sophisticated, wiser consumer, but also must meet a wider range of wants and needs. Better educated consumers are smarter in their buying behavior, and more likely to be well informed and choosy about the level of quality they receive. Education also affects the lifestyles and interests of consumers—and their income. People under 30 with a college degree will earn four times as much annual income as high school dropouts.[30]

The rate of unemployment is a significant factor in the amount of income consumers have available to spend. At time of writing—1997—unemployment is reaching record lows in the United States (in the 6 percent range). But another recession could reverse that trend. As the economy dips, unemployment rises. During 1981 and 1982, unemployment rates reached levels that had not been seen since the Great Depression of 1932; at the end of 1982, unemployment reached 11 percent, meaning one of every nine Americans looking for a job did not have one. During such depressed periods, purchases of many nonessential goods and services are curtailed. Sales of durable goods and luxury items suffer as people put off such purchases until their financial situation has improved. Today, fortunately, the rate of unemployment is delightfully low . . . but as noted earlier, conditions can change!

Disposable and Discretionary Income

Before 1930, the vast majority of U.S. households had low buying power—just above the subsistence level, in fact. Meanwhile, a small number of households, an elite pocket of the population, held a sizable amount of the total income. By 1960, this pattern had changed, and many people had substantial incomes. Throughout the 1960s and 1970s, median household income increased. But in the late 1970s, it turned downward, largely because of inflation.

Consumers' incomes take many forms, including wages and salaries, dividends, social security, and interest. Marketers are most concerned with disposable income, the amount of income available for spending after taxes have been deducted. To be meaningful, income figures must be stated in terms of real income, that is, income that has been adjusted for the effects of inflation. Disposable personal income per capita equaled $19,729 in 1995. Expressed in constant terms (taking out inflation), this figure represents a 5 percent increase in disposable income since 1990.

Marketers are also interested in discretionary income, the amount of disposable income left over after spending on the essentials or needs, such as food, clothing, transportation, shelter, and utilities. Because discretionary income goes toward satisfying wants rather than needs, it is far more difficult to predict how this income will be spent. Discretionary income is used to purchase luxuries such as boats, second homes, travel, and other top-of-the-line products.

Marketers must pay attention to how income is distributed, as well as to changes in total real income. The distribution of income in the United States is distinctly skewed. The top fifth of the population gets 43.7 percent of all income, while the bottom fifth receives 4.6 percent. Entrance to the top 20 percent requires an income of $53,000. The top 5 percent now get nearly two-thirds of their income from wages and salaries, compared with the dividends, trust funds, and capital gains source of the top 5 percent 25 years ago. Today's richest people have earned their wealth. These new rich are much more ostentatious than the older rich; they are the prime targets for marketers of $60,000 cars, $2,000 watches, and $3 million houses. In the middle income class are those with incomes around the typical U.S. family income of $29,458. This is a full 50 percent higher than the $19,500 average family income of 1960. At the bottom are the 13.5 percent who live below the official poverty level.

Although many people imagine that those on the top rungs of the income ladder live in ever-increasing luxury while those at the bottom fall into deeper financial misery, that picture is not quite true. Statistics show that 44 percent of people in the lowest fifth of incomes in 1971 had moved up and out in seven years—in fact, 6 percent made it to the top fifth. Meanwhile, half of those in the top 20 percent fell out of the top quintile, with 3.5 percent landing in the bottom fifth. The recessionary period the United States suffered in the early 1990s produced unprecedented layoffs of higher income, white-collar workers along with the layoffs of middle income and low income workers. Income mobility is remarkably high in the United States, with the exception that the very poor do not move out of the poverty level at high rates.

Forget the Middle Class: Go for the Poor and the Rich!

Some marketers see a new scenario emerging from income trends in the United States. The numbers that catch their eye are:

- The wealthiest fifth of the population has experienced income growth of 21 percent since 1980.
- The bottom 60 percent of the population by income has failed to increase its wealth over this same period.[31]

There is a growing mass market for low-priced goods and services—the ones Wal-Mart targets with so much success. At the same time, there is a growing market of wealthy consumers who are not very price sensitive—the ones that Tiffany targets. And there is less and less in the middle. Marketers need to make a choice. Go for a sophisticated, quality- or status-oriented buyer with plenty of disposable income? Or target the larger but increasingly impoverished Wal-Mart customers who are always looking for a deal?

If you fail to specialize in the rich or the poor, if you're brand is somewhere in the middle, offering a quality image and a middle-of-the-road price point, well, you may be chasing a disappearing middle-class consumer. Good luck!

Consumer Spending Patterns

It is not enough to understand trends in overall spending levels. They can help you understand who has how much money to spend. But they don't tell you how it will be spent. Yet there are significant trends in what people spend their money on as well.

Spending patterns for different product categories have changed over the years. The percentage spent on food, clothing, and personal care has been going down, while that spent on housing, transportation, medical care, and recreational pursuits has been increasing.

It does not take a genius to know that richer households spend greater amounts of money on goods and services than poorer ones. In the nineteenth century, a German statistician, Ernest Engel, explored the expenditure patterns of families as their wealth improved. He found that as family income increases, the percentage spent on food decreases, the percentage spent on housing and household operations is basically the same, and the percentage spent on all other categories as well as the amount saved increases.

Other studies have corroborated these results, which have since become known as Engel's Laws. Note that these laws refer to proportional changes in expenditures. As income increases, the absolute amounts spent increase in all categories. And recent U.S. patterns of spending on various categories of goods and services reflect these laws. Low income households spend 34 percent of their income on housing, middle income households spend 30 percent, and high income households spend 28 percent, for example—pretty close to a constant share of income, as Engel predicted. And food spending drops, also according to Engel's laws—from 19 percent of low income budgets to only 13 percent of high income budgets. This leaves proportionately more discretionary income in the budgets of wealthy households for consumer products, from home PCs to travel to fine clothing. And it also suggests that those Wal-Mart consumers, increasingly pinched by their static incomes, will be spending more of their incomes on food in the future.

THE FORECASTING CHALLENGE

At best, demographics provides a quantitative view of the marketplace as it is today. Why do we say "at best"? Because of the lag in the publication of demographic data, such data describe the *recent past* rather than the present. You may have noticed that the data we refer to in this chapter are, at best, current through 1997, and are sometimes several years older, reflecting the availability of information at the time of writing. Yet marketers are making decisions today that will be implemented tomorrow. They want to know the probable size of various market segments in the future, the effects of past demographic trends on the future composition of target markets, and expected sales in various markets.

In short, marketers want to look into a crystal ball and forecast the future composition of markets and future sales. Armed with sound forecasts about the future, marketers can make the right decisions today.

Predicting the future is no easy task. The U.S. government, some very sophisticated forecasters, and some of the largest companies use the latest techniques and employ the most highly skilled statisticians—yet forecasting is difficult even for them.

Not only that, but for marketers at least, forecasting is becoming a less exact science. Let us state that more strongly. However good your firm might have been at forecasting demand for its products this year, it will do a *worse* job next year. We guarantee it.

Why? Because of one simple confounding factor—more products. Each year, there are more and more products fighting for consumer attention and shelf (or catalog, or mailbox, or Internet) space. Production, distribution, and inventory plans are harder as a result, complicating the short-term forecasts of many marketers and increasing the amount of unwanted goods in inventories. And when short-term forecasts are inaccurate, long-term forecasts of market trends end up being even less accurate.[32]

Because so much forecasting is directed at predicting sales (in dollars or in units of product), our discussion here focuses on sales forecasts. Although marketers are also interested in forecasting demographic trends, they generally start with government forecasts when looking at these trends. When marketers do try to forecast population shifts, they use the same basic tools as in sales forecasting. Sales forecasting begins with a forecast for the entire industry, because conditions in an industry have such a great impact on the sales of any firm within that industry. Competition, consumer preferences, and other external forces affect the potential sales of any given firm.

From projected industry sales, the forecaster usually develops a sales potential forecast for the firm. Potential sales provide an absolute upper limit. Then forecasts are developed for specific products or markets; each product offered or market served is used as a basis for specialized forecasts. Such forecasts are made for the long-term (three to five years), the medium-term (one to three years), and the short-term (usually six months to one year).

Some Commonly Used Forecasting Techniques

Some forecasting methods are qualitative in that the prediction is based more on subjective opinions than on objective facts. (These techniques assume that opinions are based on accumulated experience, which can be viewed as a type of fact.) Other methods are quantitative—they involve mathematical manipulation of objective facts or observations. There are many sources of quantitative data. The government at all levels is a tremendous reservoir of data. There are also many commercial data sources, as discussed in Chapter 4. Industries have trade associations that collect and distribute many kinds of data. Also, companies have internal records from which they may obtain useful data. They can also collect data for forecasting purposes from suppliers, customers, salespeople, executives, and many other sources.

Simple Trend Analysis

In simple trend analysis, managers review historical data and use the rates of change to project future trends. For example, diet soft drink sales in the United States lost popularity in the early 1990s, and their overall share of the soda market fell from 30 percent to 24 percent between 1990 and 1997. Knowing only these two figures, what would you say their market share will be in 2000? If the trend continues in a straight line, it's fairly easy to guess, either by plotting share on a graph or crunching the numbers, that diet soft drinks will have about a 20 percent share of the U.S. soft drink market in the year 2000. A straight line connecting the 1990 and 1997 shares gets you to this 20 percent figure in the year 2000.

But will you be right? If you look at year-by-year changes in the market share of diet versus regular soft drinks, your confidence in that straight-line forecast may be shaken. Because diet sodas lost market share very rapidly in the late 1980s early 1990s, then leveled and began to regain share after 1992. Right now, diet's share of the soda market is growing slightly each year.[33] If you run a straight line through 1993–1997 sales, it gives you a very different forecast for the year 2000—something like 26 percent, instead of the 20 percent forecast from our first attempt. Which is right? Probably neither.

Forecasting demand from past sales figures alone is even harder than driving by looking in your rearview mirror. The straight-line projection is just the beginning of your trend analysis. You need to identify the factors that are likely to shift that line and include them in your model, too.

For example, advertisers are currently trying to reposition diet soft drinks, which have been sold on the basis of low calories and acceptable taste for many years. The latest idea is to position them as cool, as part of desirable baby boomer lifestyles, not just as a diet aid. But will this work? Yes, says Sergio Zima, marketing chief at Coca-Cola. He is working to "broaden the definition of Diet Coke." No, says Tom Pierce, president of consulting firm Bevmark in New York. He says, "You might get a spike in sales, but it'll fall back."[34] (What do *we* think? We're keeping our mouths shut on this one. If they can't agree, well, the odds of our being right are pretty darn slim!)

Trend analysis of various kinds is often applied to demographic data. For example, if family size has gotten consistently smaller in this country for many generations, it might seem reasonable to assume it would continue to shrink. This is exactly what demographers assumed in 1938. Peter Drucker describes what happened:

> The most prominent population experts called together by Franklin D. Roosevelt predicted unanimously in 1938 that the U.S. population would peak at around 140 million people in 1943 or 1944, and then slowly decline. The American population—with a

minimum of immigration—now stands at 240 million. For in 1949, without the slightest advance warning, the United States kicked off a "baby boom" that for 12 years produced families of record size, only to turn just as suddenly in 1960 (actually 1964) into a "baby bust," producing equally unprecedented small families.[35]

At the beginning of this chapter, we noted that the growth of the U.S. population has been slowing for three decades, and that the population is therefore expected to be 271.2 million in 2000 and 282.5 million in 2050. Will these forecasts prove accurate? They are basically advanced forms of trend analysis, so they depend on the continuation of trends in an expected direction. But demographers do not truly know what drives family size. Why did family size increase for the dozen years of the baby boom? And why did it drop again? It is interesting to note that the average Mexican parent has about three times as many children as do U.S. parents on the other side of the border. Combine this with the biggest trend in the U.S. population—the rapid increase in Hispanic households—and for all we know there might be a rebound in the number of children in U.S. families sometime in the early 2000s. That would confound all the population projections in a jiffy.

The importance of the baby boom on marketers today has been emphasized throughout this chapter. We also need to emphasize that we do not know how to predict a *future* baby boom with any accuracy. Knowing what one doesn't know is often the best defense when it comes to producing, or using, forecasts. In this example, because we do not really understand why family size varies, we must discount the future population forecasts. It might be more appropriate to use scenario analysis instead, as described shortly.

Market Share Analysis

Market share analysis starts with the assumption that the firm's market share will remain constant. Then, if the firm expects that total industry sales will grow by, say, 10 percent in the next year, it can expect that its sales will grow by 10 percent in that year.

This technique may be satisfactory in relatively stable industries. For example, over the past 10 years, Gillette has held 65 percent of the razor blade market. But when an industry is characterized by rapid change or growth, as is true of high-tech industries, the assumption that the firm's market share will remain constant could prove disastrous.

Test Marketing

Sometimes there are no historical data on which to base projections. An obvious example is the case of a new product. In such situations, firms often conduct test-marketing programs in which the product is introduced in a few specific markets. The firm uses the results to estimate total sales for the region in which the product will be introduced. The main problem with this approach is that political, economic, competitive, and other environmental conditions are not necessarily the same from one locality to the next. Furthermore, competitors often employ disruptive tactics, such as increasing their advertising, to distort test-market results. Sometimes competitors even investigate products brought out in test markets and use that information to improve their own products. This happened to Procter & Gamble when it introduced its new Duncan Hines softcenter cookies; by the time the cookies were distributed nationally, Nabisco, Frito-Lay, and Keebler all had introduced new and improved versions of their own cookies, thereby taking away P&G's taste advantage.

The Market Buildup Technique

The market buildup method is similar to test marketing in that the firm uses one of the other forecasting methods to gather information on a few specific market segments, and then aggregates them to arrive at a total sales forecast. Those segments may be based on geographic areas, age categories, ethnic groups, or even product uses. For instance, a maker of petroleum jelly may know that there are two basic types of users of its product: people who use it as a moisturizer and people who use it to remove makeup. The firm may first estimate sales for each segment and then aggregate them.

The Market Breakdown Approach

The market breakdown technique is the opposite of the buildup approach. In this case, the sales potential for some large unit—an entire industry, for example—is forecast using one or more of the other approaches. This figure is broken down into forecasts for smaller units, such as firms within the industry or individual product lines or market segments.

Consumer Surveys and Panel Discussions

It may be advantageous to contact consumers directly to find out how they would react to a planned change in a product or service. Purchase intentions, rate of consumption, and changes in brand loyalty are only some of the many kinds of information that can be obtained from consumer surveys and panels. (These techniques were discussed in Chapter 4.) On the basis of consumers' responses regarding intention to buy, the forecaster can create a quantitative measure of market potential. As long as proper sampling techniques have been used, the resultant estimate can be quite accurate.

Statistical Techniques

Market analysts can identify a variety of quantifiable factors that may influence the event they are attempting to forecast. Historical data are collected for each variable and fitted into a mathematical model. An example of such a technique is regression analysis. With the help of a computer, an equation is developed that shows how each variable affects the event being forecast. Then the analyst "plugs in" values for each variable to come up with a forecast. For example, a model for sales might be:

Units sold = 10,000 − 10,000 (Price) + 0.5 (Advertising expenditure)

The marketer plugs in the price of the item and the level of advertising, and the model predicts sales. If the price will be set at $10 and the firm plans to spend $500,000 on advertising, the equation will predict 160,000 units sold [10,000 − 10,000(10) + 0.5(500,000)]. Although this example has only two variables, price and advertising, the models developed by large corporations generally contain many more variables.

How might one develop such a model? These models usually are driven by a theoretical understanding of what factors drive sales. In our equation, price and advertising are assumed to drive sales. A more sophisticated model might add demographic factors, such as the change in the target market's population size; economic factors, such as interest rates; and competitor actions, such as price increases, advertising levels, and sales promotions. A model might even incorporate survey data on perceived quality of the product. Once data on all these factors have been collected for a number of historical periods, a linear regression or other statistical analysis might be performed on a computer to find shifts in sales levels that correspond to shifts in any of the factors thought to drive sales. The forecaster might start with one or two of the most obvious factors (as in the above formula), then keep adding factors until the computer program produced a formula that explained a large percentage of the historical variation in sales. This formula could then be applied to current data in an effort to forecast the future.

Advanced statistical modeling is now within reach of most marketers. Programs such as Lotus 1-2-3 make it fairly painless to perform the regression analysis needed to try out this method—but not completely painless. The user must review the basic concepts of statistical regression, then read the instructions and examples in the manual for the spreadsheet program. Even after mastering the technique, the forecaster may not be able to forecast sales with high accuracy. One of us spent several weeks some years ago on the formulation of a model to forecast purchase of freight services. When every possible factor had been quantified and added to the analysis, the model still explained only a little more than 50 percent of the variation in purchase of freight transportation services nationwide. This meant, for example, that to determine whether industry sales would go up or down in the next period, one would do just about as well as the model by simply flipping a coin. This was a disheartening realization after two weeks of number crunching!

Scenario Analysts

When using scenario analysis, researchers try to paint a subjective picture of several possible futures. One common approach generates three different pictures of the future: optimistic, pessimistic, and most likely. Each depicts an internally consistent situation in which several events are analyzed in terms of their effect on each other and on the future. Most often scenarios are developed for the purpose of establishing contingency plans for strategic management. Such plans indicate what the reaction should be if a particular event occurs.

Scenario building identifies cause-and-effect relationships and then follows them to their logical conclusions in much the same way that good science fiction writers do. Typically, scenario analysis begins with a question such as, "In the event that solar power is perfected, how will it affect the oil industry?" How far a scenario should look into the future depends on the industry in which the firm operates. A solar energy firm might want to look 20 years or more into the future, whereas a firm that produces fashion clothing may look a year ahead at most. Generally, scenario analysis is confined to forecasting aggregate conditions and is most accurate for long-term forecasts.[36]

The Delphi Technique

In the Delphi technique, a panel of experts is asked to assign rankings and probabilities to various factors that may influence future events. For example, the oil industry knows that hydrogen is potentially a very clean and efficient energy source and that the world's oceans provide a virtually limitless supply. The industry may want to determine the probability that in the next 20 years hydrogen could be extracted from water at a cost competitive with that of extracting oil, and if so, how that would affect the oil industry. It could assemble a panel of experts to answer these questions. The Delphi technique has several important characteristics. First, panel members remain anonymous and responses are submitted in writing. Second, panel members review one another's responses and give written feedback. Third, the process continues for several rounds until there is consensus or at least close agreement. It is hoped that the anonymity of panel members will increase the reliability and objectivity of the results.

Jury of Executive Opinion

In the jury of executive opinion technique, executives from various departments of a company are asked to estimate market potential and sales for several years into the future. They then try to reach a consensus. This method combines historical data and experienced judgment as bases for decision making. It is one of the oldest and simplest methods of forecasting and has the advantage of being able to be completed quickly.

Like trend analysis, however, this method has drawbacks. Environmental conditions change, and therefore historical data may not be useful in predicting the future. Moreover, some executives may be out of touch with the market and may overlook important factors. Depending on these conditions, this method may produce either very good or very poor results.

Salespeople's Estimates

Another method is similar to the jury of executive opinion, except that it is a "bottom-up" approach in that salespeople, rather than executives, are the source of the forecasts. Salespeople are asked to estimate sales in their own territories. These estimates are then aggregated to produce a total sales forecast. Salespeople are assumed to be more aware of buyers' wants and needs and their likely reactions to changes in the marketing mix. They may also have a feel for how consumers may react to changes in competitors' products. Again, this method has some limitations. Salespeople may be unaware of relevant changes in the nation's economic health or may not be aware of planned changes in their company's marketing mix or in the marketing programs of competitors. This method is very inexpensive to implement, however, and it can provide valuable information. For these reasons, salespeople's input should not be ignored.

Barometric Techniques

Barometric techniques involve the analysis of past trends to predict the future. John Naisbitt employed such a technique to identify the ten "megatrends" in his best-selling book by that name and the newer trends in his book on the future of the U.S. corporation.[37] Naisbitt's firm, the Naisbitt Group, receives 6,000 newspapers a month, from which news stories are clipped and classified by subject. The subject categories are then analyzed in terms of frequency of occurrence, and forecasts of future trends are based on the resulting data. Naisbitt's is one of several organizations that develop indices of trends as a barometer of things to come.

Composite Methods

In general, it is not wise for an organization to rely on only one technique in formulating its sales forecasts. All forecasting techniques have both strengths and weaknesses. Many firms, therefore, use several techniques simultaneously. If they all produce roughly the same results, greater confidence can be placed in the forecast than if only one technique were used. Similarly, if the use of several techniques fails to produce a consistent forecast, the firm should check its assumptions and the accuracy of its data.

READING BETWEEN THE LINES

Some people believe, as the old saying goes, that when all else fails, a person should read the directions. When it comes to understanding the demographic patterns that underlie markets, and when it comes to anticipating shifts in populations, markets, or product sales, working from the numbers is analogous to reading the directions. However, there are some fairly serious limitations to these directions. In fact, the majority of anecdotes in this chapter, from Clearasil's sales forecasts to Roosevelt's population projections, illustrate the dangers of taking the numbers literally. It is not enough to read from the directions.

Forecasting is as much art as science, and therefore it is probably more appropriate to say, "When all else fails, throw out the directions." Before we close this chapter, we want to dwell for a moment on what this means as a practical matter for managers and marketers.

For starters, it is important to look between the lines of population statistics or sales records for insight. Rather than expect a long-standing trend to continue, ask what might reverse it. Rather than market to the groups the data indicate exist, ask whether the survey or census collected data on the right kinds of groups. One study of why forecasts in high-tech industries usually go wrong concluded that the wrong people were usually surveyed.[38] Also look at the questions asked and the methodology used, and see whether they are biased by the values of the designers. Look at society, and make sure something new isn't going on that the demographers haven't gotten around to studying yet. Read between the lines, even if it means entering the world of fiction for awhile. Then go back to the world of hard numbers and test new ideas.

A simple example of the power of this approach is found in the U.S. census forms. Few people read the forms—only the data they collect. But the forms themselves tell a fascinating story about changed values and demographics, a story that is easily hidden by the mass of statistics. For example, the 1990 census form adds a number of questions and categories designed to collect information that the 1980 census did not:

- Two new categories are added to the relationship list—stepson/stepdaughter and grandchild.

- Space is allotted for Hispanic respondents to identify their background for the first time (i.e., if they are Mexican, Colombian, Dominican).

- The top value category for dwellings has been raised from $200,000 and over to $500,000 and over.

- A question is added to determine if monthly rents include any meals.

There are several explanations for these changes. The dramatic rise in divorce is leading to a growing number of stepchild relationships, and the combination of a growing number of very poor, an increase in single parents, and growth in the number of surviving elders has thrown childcare duties increasingly to the grandparents. The rapid increase in Hispanic populations from many countries of origin makes it more important to break down the group into subgroups. The price of houses keeps going up, and up, and up—and the growing gap between rich and poor means that wealthy respondents' houses go way off the old scale. Finally, the increase in elderly has led to a large number of special-care living arrangements in which food and other services are provided.

In a way, these four points at which the nation outgrew its old census form are the most striking and important of the changes that occurred over the decade. However, they are as much a matter of perception and values as they are a matter of statistical fact, an idea that might horrify the statistician, but is the marketer's bread and butter. For in the final analysis, it is the customers' perception of reality that determines what is bought and sold, not the statistician's perception.

To take this idea ten times farther, the 1890 census form differed even more dramatically from the 1990 form. When it asked women if they had children, it added a question to find out how many were still alive; a reflection of the high infant mortality rates of the time. One question asked whether the respondent was a "prisoner, convict, homeless child, or pauper," grouping categories that we would not care to lump to-gether today! The 1890 census takers were given very careful instructions concerning how to categorize Blacks: "The word 'black' should be used to describe those persons who have three-fourths or more black blood; 'mulatto,' those persons who have from three-eighths to five-eighths black blood; 'quadroon,' those persons who have one-fourth black blood; and 'octoroon,' those persons who have one-eighth or any trace of black blood." From these instructions, we can easily visualize a society so racist that the government felt it essential to quantify the extent of intermarriage between Blacks and Whites and to pigeonhole each person by the amount of "black blood" in his or her veins—even the expression is offensive today. The nature of work also has changed so dramatically that instructions concerning jobs such as livery stable keepers and tele-graph messenger boys stand in stark contrast to today's preponderance of more modern service professions.[39]

Another way to read between the lines of the forecasts and statistics is to ask *customers* what they think. The data may show that distinct Hispanic groups are emerging, but does this mean that a company should address each group separately in its marketing communications and product offerings? Do *they* see themselves as dis-tinct? If so, do they identify with the group as defined by the census, or do they have their own ideas about their group identity? A company had better make certain, or its marketing is liable to offend a great many potential customers.

Sometimes perceptions differ from the realities the statistics suggest. For ex-ample, Americans spend the largest amount of their money on housing, followed by transportation and then food. Based on these numbers, we might reasonably conclude that Americans are most concerned about paying for housing, followed by transporta-tion, followed by food.

Wrong. A Gallup Organization survey of 757 adults found that more people list "finding and paying for good health care" as their top concern over anything else, even though it ranks seventh in the list of expenditures, costing on average about one-sixth

EXHIBIT 5.4.   Share of spending vs. share of worry.

Item	Percentage of Total Spending*	Percentage of Respondents Who Worry about It Most
Housing	30%	17%
Transportation	22	NA
Food	16	NA
Personal insurance pensions	8	12
Apparel	5	NA
Entertainment	5	NA
Health care	5	21
Education	1	16
Day care for children	NA	9
Caring for elderly parents	NA	9

*For middle-income Americans.

of what Americans spend on housing.[40] Exhibit 5.4 contrasts the survey results with general spending statistics in order to illustrate the difference between what the numbers tell us and what consumers say. The two columns offer radically different perspectives on what household priorities are in the United States today.

If you are trying to decide whether to acquire a new product line in health care or in food services, and want to make sure you move into the market that is most important to Americans in the long run, you would have to use the statistics with caution. On the one hand, food accounts for a great deal more of the typical American's spending. On the other hand, Americans are not particularly worried about feeding themselves, but are most worried about finding and paying for good health care. Although the health care market is smaller in dollars spent, it is clearly much larger in need and opportunity. You might say that health care has a smaller share of spending but a higher share of worry.

It takes some creativity and insight to combine different kinds of numbers and ask different questions before you can reach a conclusion such as this one. If you come away from this chapter on profiling the market and forecasting sales with nothing else, be sure you take with you a willingness to read between the lines, to apply imagination and insight to the numbers. This is probably the marketer's most important skill.

It is a lesson Jody Phelps learned the hard way in her disastrous effort to forecast Clearasil sales, as we saw in the opening pages of this chapter. The costs of learning this lesson the hard way can be unusually high. But a good forecast is nonetheless an absolute necessity in marketing—provided that you remember it is pure fiction.

6 UNDERSTANDING BUYER BEHAVIOR

Customers on the Couch

The human being is a wanting animal and rarely reaches a state of complete satisfaction except for a short time. As one desire is satisfied, another pops up to take its place. When this is satisfied, still another comes into the foreground and so on. It is a characteristic of human beings throughout their whole lives that they are practically always desiring something.

—Abraham H. Maslow[1]

The more you know about the customer the better. You never know when a small fact might lead to a better product.

—R. Stephen Fountaine, vice president of market research, Kimberly-Clark Corporation

You're somewhat in the Ruffles camp. You must have confidence to dress that way, so flat chips aren't for you. You aren't taking a trip on the wild side, though; not exciting enough for jalapeno-flavored. Maybe on a Friday night you'll try cheddar to really step out. Bean dip too if you loosen up.

—Howard Davis, chairman of Frito-Lay's advertising agency, Tracy-Locke[2]

Imagine this. Your target customer is a female baby boomer, a women of 40 years of age who juggles a management job and family. You have designed a product line just right for her household. And now you have a chance to make the sale, because she is on her lunch break, shopping for a gift for her husband's birthday.

She has given herself a half-hour today to visit the mall nearest her office building. That's less than half the 66 minutes spent by visitors to U.S. shopping malls on average. Will she manage to find her way into the right store, right aisle, and right display, in order to find the product *you* market and select it for purchase? You hope so!

All goes well at first. She notices the appealing window displays and signs outside the store, and turns in to examine the merchandise. Browsing her way down an aisle, she encounters your product display and stops, interested. "Ah, I bet he'd like one of these!" she says to herself, leaning forward to examine a sample. But then something goes terribly wrong. It's hardly noticeable to the average observer, but more than enough to interrupt your customer's concentration. What happens is this. Another customer wanders down the same aisle and, because the aisle is so narrow, accidentally brushes against your target's rear end. Distracted, your would-be buyer begins to move down the aisle again, looking for other items. Then she glances at her watch, mutters "Darn, I'm going to be late for the staff meeting," and heads for the door.

No sale. Sorry. Another marketing exchange falls prey to consumer behavior. This particular problem—one of a seemingly infinite number of things that can go wrong—happens to be well studied by Paco Underhill, founder of Envirosell, a New York-based retail consulting firm. In thousands of hours of videotapes of shopper behavior, Underhill has identified a great many facts of relevance to marketers, including the observation that a woman shopper's probability of being converted from a browser to a buyer is inversely proportional to the likelihood of her being bumped while examining the merchandise.[3]

How could you have made that sale? Well, you might give more attention to where and how your products are displayed in retail stores. If aisles are narrow and crowded, then perhaps a free-standing island rack or an end-of-aisle display would eliminate what Underhill terms *le facteur bousculade*. And how about selecting a display location that is to the right of the doorway on the way into the store—since Underhill's research shows shoppers almost always turn right upon entering a store. Oh, but don't let them display your products *too* close to the door. If they fall into the shopper's decompression zone, the area just inside the door where shoppers slow down and refocus before beginning their shopping, then the displays will probably be ignored.

If demographics and forecasting are all about identifying the customer, consumer behavior is all about understanding that customer. And customer behavior can be remarkably complex, as our brief observations of this lunch-time shopper revealed. In many ways, understanding customer behavior is a far more difficult task than simply identifying your target customers. As the psychologist Abraham Maslow observed, people practically always desire something. But it takes a great deal of insight to know what they desire, when, and where.

Howard Davis has a clear understanding of chip desires. It comes from hundreds of hours of thought and research on the topic. In his chapter-opening quote, he is sizing up a visitor to his office at the ad agency Tracy-Locke based on a quick assessment of the man's clothing and appearance. Clues like boat shoes, khaki pants, red tie, plain blue shirt, navy socks, and a matching plastic pen provide the raw material for his Sherlock Holmes-style deductions. He thinks he can narrow down the visitor's preferences to only a few of Frito-Lay's 85 varieties of corn and potato chips. Is he right? Unfortunately, the journalist who reported this conversation did not say.[4]

But the odds of being right are strongly in Davis' favor because Tracy-Locke goes to incredible lengths to understand the personalities of each Frito-Lay brand and its users. The agency gets a head start from Frito-Lay, which operates an elaborate laboratory near Dallas dubbed the Potato Chip Pentagon. Staffed with close to 500 psychologists, chemists, and engineers, the lab studies everything from chip thickness to flavor patterns. For example, researchers have learned that people prefer their chips to break under approximately four pounds of pressure per square inch, and that they do not like the "Frito Breath" and "Dorito Breath" that people have after eating these chips. (Incidentally, Frito-Lay is experimenting with ways to reduce this effect.) The reason Frito-Lay invests so much in chip research comes down to a startlingly simple observation of human behavior. As Dennis Heard, senior vice president of technology, explains, "We have to be perfect; after all, no one really needs a potato chip."

Nonetheless, Howard Davis is determined to find out who wants chips, and which chips they want. To start with, the agency does consumer surveys to find out what people say they want (Frito-Lay's research queried a total of 500,000 people in a single year). But for some reason, people rarely tell the truth about their chip passions. Davis explains that "a lot of people who say they feed their families only alfalfa sprouts also eat potato chips." And careful tests have revealed that consumers actually eat about a third more chips at one sitting than they say they do. (How did they find this out? By giving people premeasured large bags of chips at a movie theater, then measuring the leftover chips afterward.) Perhaps people are not entirely honest about their chip behavior because chips are, with all that salt and fat, a somewhat unhealthy indulgence. And chip consumption is essentially a private affair—research shows that 65 percent of all chips are eaten in private.

Thus, Frito-Lay's survey research, psychographics, and other standard research must be supplemented with creative insight. The insight starts with projective research designed to learn more about consumers than they know about themselves. Respondents are shown photographs, for example, each depicting different people in different situations. Questions such as "Is this person likely to eat potato chips?" are used to get at underlying attitudes and values. (Some of the results are amusing: Someone with an umbrella is not likely to eat chips, whereas someone watching TV is very likely to.) Tracy-Locke combines the insights from this qualitative research with the mass of survey research to develop personality profiles, and then prepares videotapes portraying the types of people whom they expect to eat various types of chips. Each of these tapes comprises images collected from modern culture—bits of ads, movies, and television shows. The videos are then kept strictly under wraps, for use only by the agency's copywriters.

The public will never see these videos, but thanks to the diligence of a *Wall Street Journal* reporter, we can at least read a quick review of them:

> The videos reflect distinct personality differences among eaters of various snacks. Some examples: Lay's Potato Chips Consumers of these flat chips are seen as "affectionate, irresistible, casual and a fun member of the family." Scenes show bubbling

streams, puppies, flowers, a couple exchanging wedding vows, a farmer driving mules and a little girl stroking a cat. The music theme is the soft rock "Little Pink Houses" by John Cougar Mellencamp.

Ruffles Potato Chips Customers are depicted as "expressive, aware, confident enough to make a personal statement. Scenes show people getting into a BMW and other new cars, a man opening champagne, wind surfers, and a woman working out in a fashionable outfit. The music is from the fast-paced soundtrack from "Caddyshack."[5]

These videos are the culmination of an incredible effort to understand the people who eat chips. We don't even want to think about how much this effort costs Frito-Lay, and Frito-Lay does not want to reveal how much it costs either. But the results of the research pay handsomely. Americans eat more than six pounds of chips each in the average year, spending more than $4 billion in the process. And Frito-Lay's share of the market has grown from 25 percent a decade ago to 40 percent at present.[6] With pretax profit close to 20 percent of retail sales, it is difficult to visualize the potential earnings from this market! For example, a 1-percent gain in Frito-Lay's market share would be worth about $8 million in profits. The value of knowing your consumer's behavior a little better than the competitors can be incredibly high.

In this chapter, we examine the foundations of consumer behavior upon which programs such as Frito-Lay's are built. This requires reviewing a number of important concepts before we can apply them to the management task.

UNDERSTANDING EXCHANGE BEHAVIOR

Earlier in this book we defined the exchange process as involving two parties, each having an unsatisfied want or need and something to exchange. Frequently, however, there are more than two parties involved in an exchange. Instead of only one receiving party, as many as six parties, each with a different role, may be involved:

1. *Initiator*—The person who first recognizes an unsatisfied want or need.

2. *Influencer*—The individual who provides information about how the want or need may be satisfied.

3. *Decider*—The person who finally chooses an alternative that will satisfy the want or need.

4. *Buyer*—The purchaser of the product.

5. *Consumer*—The user of the product.

6. *Evaluator*—The individual who provides feedback on the chosen product's ability to satisfy.

Sometimes all these roles are filled by one person; at other times, different people enter the picture at each stage in the exchange process. Marketers must identify all the important people in any given purchase situation. (By the way, rather than trying to memorize terms such as these, try to *use* them. For example, think of cases in which you play each of these roles as consumers. You will find you have become familiar with the terms and remember them painlessly as a result. Now if you could only figure out how to create this kind of involvement among readers or viewers of your company's advertising!)

Understanding that modern-day mothers increasingly are working outside the home rather than in it, General Foods, a subsidiary of Philip Morris Company, is directing more of its marketing of food products toward children. A marketing manager told *The Wall Street Journal,* because "kids have more and more influence over food purchases, we felt we had to market increasingly toward children."[7] In one year's time, the proportion of Kool-Aid's advertising devoted to children jumped 200 percent. In addition to the time-honored roles of initiating, influencing, and evaluating, children are taking an increasing role in buying.

A kid-oriented promotion from H.J. Heinz Co., the ketchup makers, illustrates the incredible power children have gained over household purchases in the last decade. Their research showed that children are now dominating purchase decisions for their products, so they decided to reach out to children and increase their involvement with the company's Heinz Ketchup brand. Here's what they did. Heinz sponsored a contest in which children submitted designs for product labels. The contest was announced through print ads in magazines that used the headline, "Hey kids, wanna be famous?" Heinz also sent posters announcing the contest to art instructors at U.S. schools. The response? Approximately 60,000 children sent in submissions, and some now appear on Heinz products.[8]

In this chapter, we look at major influences on people's willingness to exchange, including culture, social class, reference groups, and family. Each of these can take one of three roles: It can act as an *initiator* (i.e., we see products that others have and want them for ourselves), an *influencer* (i.e., we talk with other people to obtain information that may help us satisfy our wants), or an *evaluator* (i.e., we look to others for approval of our buying behavior).

Culture

Culture is the most all-encompassing aspect of our social environment. It has been defined as "a complex of values, ideas, attitudes, and other meaningful symbols created by [human beings] to shape human behavior and the artifacts of that behavior as they are transmitted from one generation to the next."[9] As such, culture is the basic determinant of much of our decision-making and buying behavior. It has a lot to do with why some people prefer Lay's Potato Chips and others prefer Ruffles.

Each of us belongs to several cultural groups (see Exhibit 6.1). We are also members of smaller groups, subcultures within the larger society. These often reflect geographic, religious, or ethnic differences. For example, there are regional differences in taste for beer: New Yorkers seem to prefer a somewhat bitter beer, Californians like a lighter beer, and Texans prefer their beer chilled to 32 degrees.

Frito-Lay spends a great deal of time tailoring products and their distribution to the preferences of different regional subcultures. Vinegar-flavored chips sell in the Northeast, mesquite-flavored chips sell in the Southwest, and sour cream-flavored

EXHIBIT 6.1.   Cultural environment.

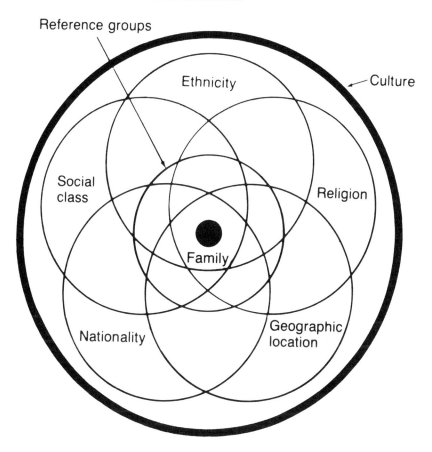

chips sell in the Midwest. This marketing approach might be viewed as simple opportunism—if a discrete regional market can be developed through regional product development and marketing, Frito-Lay can make more money and protect its market position better. But it also can be put into the context of the movement toward more customer-oriented marketing and management, a move that is beginning to change everything from manufacturing quality to customer service—and is bringing the customer into the loop earlier in the product development and planning process so that more focused offerings are now practical, even for behemoths such as Frito-Lay and its parent, PepsiCo.

Taken one step further, marketers can focus on subcultures as small as the neighborhood around a single grocery store. Firms such as Frito-Lay are now experimenting with customized product selections and in-store displays and promotions based on careful analysis of a store's neighborhood. The detailed data from scanners at checkout give companies the ability to see whether their experiments work.[10] Kraft also studies the purchases of individual households in search of interesting patterns. The data reveal "clusters of brands that are bought by segments of households," according to Lorraine Scarpa, senior vice president of marketing services at Kraft General Foods.[11] It also reveals other patterns—some likely the result of microcultures that can be reflected in decisions about which Kraft products to stock in which neighborhoods. Scarpa explains,

> In a group of 90 Kroger stores in Columbus, we looked at SKU [stock-keeping-unit] movement over a one-month period. The average stores stocked about 23,000 SKUs. 6,700 of those SKUs sold on a given day. 13,600 sold in a week. 17,500 sold in a month and 5,500 did not sell even once in 30 days! Are they the same 5,500 across the 90 stores? No! But a lot are, and when you manage your stores locally, you don't care that much—you just want them off your shelf.[12]

We've all noted the variations in what different grocery stores stock—sometimes it's a source of frustration that you can't find something that your local store stocks when you visit a store in a different town. Such variations might seem accidental to the consumer, but in fact they reflect the careful analysis of store-specific data.

The research firm Market Metrics in Lancaster, Pennsylvania, gathers data that include economic, social, and ethnic profiles; traffic patterns; per capita food expenditures; and information on store sales for each of 3,000 supermarkets.[13] Now marketers can take the kind of personality profiles that Tracy-Locke developed for Frito-Lay and match them with individual stores. For example, Coors Light Beer is targeted toward 21- to 34-year-old, male, middle to upper income, suburban or urban heads of households who belong to a health club, buy rock music, travel by plane, give parties and cookouts, rent videos, and are heavy television sports viewers.[14] This description is so specific that you could probably pick them out just by their clothing, as Howard Davis can with his potato chip profiles. The combination of this profile and store-specific information allows Coors to identify, for example, the three top stores for Coors Light: the Food Emporiums at 1498 York Avenue and First & 72nd Street, and the Gristedes Supermarket at 350 East 86th, all in New York City. This is a subculture of importance to Coors, but one that sociologists might find a bit odd because it is identified primarily by its preference for a specific brand of beer. From a marketing perspective, however, it is just as legitimate as any regional or ethnic subculture—and probably much more useful.

The Nature of Culture

Culture develops because we live together with other people in a society. Living with others creates the need to determine what behaviors are acceptable to all members of the group. To meet this need, groups develop rules of conduct, or norms. Norms are situation specific—they inform the members of a particular cultural group what behavior is correct in certain situations. For the Ruffles customer Howard Davis pegged in the chapter's opening quote, for example, wearing boat shoes with blue socks, khaki pants, and a red tie is no doubt accepted within his reference group or subculture, although it might be considered odd by other groups.

Underlying cultural norms are values, the deeply held beliefs and attitudes of the members of a particular society. Values give direction to the development of norms.

The process by which an individual learns cultural values and norms is called *socialization* or *enculturation*. We absorb cultural values, ideas, and attitudes primarily from our families, but also through the educational process and religious training. In later years, our behavior is refined by the influence of friends, peers, and the culture at large—everything from fine art to television—and even by marketers as they present ideas through their promotional campaigns. The constellation of attitudes and preferences that go into one of Frito-Lay's brand-user profiles reflects a common history of family, educational, and social influences. This constellation has a certain stability—they are a real reflection of our culture as experienced by a certain group of people.

Cultural norms are a shifting landscape. Today, the Ruffles consumer may wear blue socks with his boat shoes; tomorrow, boat shoes may be out and loafers in. However, the underlying values are more constant. The Ruffles eater's attitudes toward the importance of work, for example, are unlikely to change dramatically when he changes his shoes.

Although these values are more constant, they are not unchanging. When cultural values do shift, the impact on society, and on businesses in particular, is dramatic. And values do shift, only it happens so gradually that many marketers fail to take notice. One way to tune into the slower pace of value shifts is to track values by decade, rather than by year. What values were dominant in the 1960s? How do they compare with those of the 1950s—or with today's values? When looked at that way, values certainly do change.

Take Americans' attitudes toward luxury living and conspicuous consumption. It seems like a love of luxury alternates with a more frugal love of the simple life from decade to decade. And this swing of the value pendulum is reflected in a host of purchase preferences.

Two snapshots of U.S. consumers serve to illustrate this point. In the first snapshot, taken at the beginning of the 1990s, we see a shift away from luxury and self-indulgence as consumers begin to embrace the "simple life." *Time* magazine reported in the spring of 1991 that the United States was shifting toward simpler, home and family-oriented values; *Time*'s shopping list for the new simple life of the 1990s illustrates the impact of these values on marketers:

> Macaroni and cheese. Timex watches. Volunteer work. Insulated underwear. Savings accounts. Roseanne. Domestic beer. Local activism. Sleds. Pajamas. Sentimental movies. Primary colors. Mixed-breed dogs. Bicycles. Cloth diapers. Shopping at Wal-Mart. Small-town ways. Iceberg lettuce. Family reunions. Board games. Hang-it-yourself wallpaper. Push-it-yourself lawn mowers. Silly Putty.[15]

Behind these commercial symbols were a fundamental and significant change in values and lifestyles. Thousands of "dropout" managers such as Peter Lynch, who left his star position at Fidelity for family life, and Barry Blake, who left an executive position in the liquor industry to run an apple winery in Vermont, gave up the corporate chase of the 1980s for a more meaningful lifestyle.

What did this value shift mean for marketers? The researchers at ad agency Foote, Cone & Belding did not know, but they were determined to find out. To do so, they have moved undercover investigators into a small town in the Midwest (they won't say which one) to observe the simple life firsthand. According to one report, the researchers "are eavesdropping at school-board meetings, at the local cafe, and even at funerals (they say eulogies really sum up the town's values)."[16] According to Dan Fox, the project's director, they learned that "Everything that is important seems to be tied directly to children. And helping one's neighbors is not just something do-gooders do. It's all-pervasive."

But now let's flash-forward to another snapshot, this one taken in 1997. It reveals that the number of U.S. households with a net worth of at least $1 million rose 118 percent from 1992 to 1996.[17] There are more wealthy people every day, and they *are* getting richer. And these people like their luxuries. An annual survey of these rich consumers called the Mendelson Affluent Survey (by Mendelson Media Research, Inc.) finds that rich consumers are living the good life. They are far more likely to participate in activities such as tennis, sailing, and skiing, and to buy the expensive equipment these sports require. Other reports indicate that the BMW Z3 roadster, a flashy $35,000 two-seater nobody would describe as practical, is chocking up record sales.

Another study (by the NDP Group, Inc. of Port Washington, New York) finds that growth in spending by people with incomes of $70,000 or more outpaces spending growth in the rest of the U.S. population. In other words, not only are the rich getting richer, but they are also spending more each year.

Perhaps this is why some marketers declared that "status was back" by the mid-1990s. It seemed that the quest for the simple life was giving way again to the quest for the "finer" things of life. A *Brandweek* article declared that, "After years of retreat, affluent consumers are coming out of hibernation to indulge their appetites for the finer things."[18]

To kick off this seemingly major value shift, *Fortune* magazine did a story on "The Return of Luxury," citing rising sales for products like Dior Perfume (at $200 per ounce) and a Louis Vuitton Attache case that retails for $1,660.

Is the simple life now out again, and luxury back? Luxury products continue to sell well. But so do simple-life goods and services. One hypothesis is that the values in question are *both* on the upswing in the United States because of a growing economic disparity between the rich and the rest of us. If you take out the wealthy from demographic statistics, you find that household income for everybody else in the United States tends to stay steady or even fall from year to year. And if you are trying to raise a family on a falling income, you are more likely to see the appeal of a back-to-basics ethic than to pursue conspicuous consumption.

On the other hand, the pursuit of luxury may prove to be more democratic than we now think. It took more than millionaires to fuel the rapid growth of the gourmet coffee market, for example. Perhaps the free-spending ways of the wealthy are rubbing off on everybody else, and the United States will re-embrace luxury during the first decade of the new century. An alternative hypothesis is that the simple 1990s are out and a pursuit of luxury will dominate consumer spending in the next decade.

Which hypothesis is right? Such are the questions marketers must ask themselves in order to anticipate consumer tastes. We aren't sure, but we have a suspicion that the second hypothesis is the best bet—that the pursuit of luxury will gain in popularity among consumers, regardless of their incomes. Why? Well, it's that mysterious midwestern town. You see, while we can't swear to it, we suspect the researchers from Foote, Cone & Belding might have been studying the denizens of Wichita, Kansas. (If not, surely it was a town a lot like this one.) And if you haven't visited Wichita lately, you might not realize that it was featured in a 1997 *USA Today* cover story headlined, "Cigar-and-martini town echoes nation's prosperity."[19]

It seems that ordinary folk are packing into Mort's Cigar Bar nightly (it wasn't even in business back in 1991), and buying BMW roadsters from the local dealer at an amazing clip. Prosperity seems to have seized this dusty old town by the neck and tossed it into a new era. Perhaps the rest of the nation will follow.

Another, more long-term and predictable value shift of importance to U.S. businesses is the change in sexual mores. Society definitely views sex differently today than it did 40 years ago. Whereas in the past, sex was viewed primarily in terms of reproduction, this aspect of sex is given less attention today, and attitudes toward sexuality have become far less strict. Sexual values have changed in part as a result of birth control products, which, incidentally, are an excellent example of how products can and do drive even the most fundamental of cultural values. In the marketplace, these changes are reflected both in the goods and services offered, and in the promotional activities related to them. Few would argue that marketers have not kept pace with these changes in cultural values. Some marketers have used subtle sexual overtones to their advertising, such as the appeal, "All my men wear English Leather—or nothing at all." Other marketers test the outer limits of the U.S. value system: The highly suggestive and controversial Obsession perfume ads are examples. But these ads are probably not popular in Foote, Cone & Belding's secret Midwestern village. It will be interesting to see what impact the emerging constellation of simple-life values will have on the use of sex in advertising during the next decade.

In some cultures, the use of sex in advertising is more blatant. In Brazil, risqué advertising is the norm: In commercials for Playboy shampoo, a young couple is shown in bed, whereas another television ad shows two women talking about why people think they are homosexuals. In Japan, sexy ads are commonplace. Only three unwritten taboos exist: no frontal nudity, no depiction of sexual acts, and no advertising using sexual themes during the hours that children watch television. In Sweden, frontal nudity in ads is not only acceptable, but common. Yet the Swedish government, which distills and sells vodka nationwide, bans any form of advertising of hard liquor. In sharp contrast, in Malaysia, ads cannot show bare shoulders or armpits on female models, or touching, kissing, sexy clothing—or even blue jeans. Although the logic of cultural values sometimes escapes marketers, we must acknowledge the values nonetheless.

SOCIAL CLASS

Social classes are relatively permanent and homogeneous categories of people within a society; the members of a class have similar values, lifestyles, interests, and behavior. In some countries, social class is very defined and rigid. Over 3,000 subdivisions exist in India, and social mobility between classes or "castes" is impossible. In the United States, the social class system is appreciably more loose and flexible. An American's social class is determined by many factors. Generally, educational credentials and occupation are the most accurate indicators of social class. But one's social position is also affected by one's interpersonal skills, status aspirations, community involvement, cultural background, family history, recreational habits, and physical appearance.

People tend to look up to those in higher social classes, wanting many of their privileges and advantages. Many people in lower social classes try to emulate those in higher classes by buying similar goods and services, and their consumer behavior is therefore strongly influenced by their perception of social class. Thus, to the extent that a marketer can position a product so as to assist in the consumer's personal goal for upward class mobility, the marketer can add significant value to the product. This makes class an important topic for marketers. But it is also a confusing and potentially troubling subject, for notions of class structure have implications far beyond the world of marketing, and the very notion of a class-based society is controversial in the United States. For these reasons, it is especially interesting to take a look at the current debate over class.

The Class Debate

Benjamin DeMott, an English professor at Amherst College, refers to "the myth of classlessness." He argues that Americans suffer from the illusion that this country does not have a class-based society. In his view, Americans are restricted in their opportunities, especially their employment opportunities, by their class affiliations. In a book titled *The Imperial Middle: Why Americans Can't Think Straight about Class,* DeMott describes many "rationalizations that help to suppress consciousness of social differences."[20] If DeMott's theory is true—and it does seem to be at least near the bull's eye—it means that marketers must be cautious in the use of class-oriented appeals lest they touch on issues that consumers prefer to suppress. A company cannot simply say, "Hey, you're strictly lower middle class, but if you'll start eating potato chips with ridges, we can help you do something about it."

Others take issue with DeMott's thesis that class structure is a well-kept secret in the United States. Andrew Hacker, a professor of political science at Queens College, argues that "American society can be explained by privilege and inequality, even exploitation; but not necessarily by a system of classes. There is too much movement, too many crosscutting factors like race and religion."[21] Hacker reaches back to the vision of the nation's founders, quoting James Madison's prescription that "the society itself will be broken into so many parts, interests, and classes of citizens, that the rights of the minority will be in little danger from interested combinations of the majority." That vision is echoed eerily in a survey of social class by *Fortune* magazine which identifies an "apparent fragmentation of U.S. society into scores of distinct subcultures, each with unique tastes and yearnings of the sort that once distinguished broad social classes."[22]

Reference Groups

In addition to culture and social class, both of which are traditionally viewed as large aggregations of people, smaller groups also affect buyer behavior. A reference group is any set of people that influences an individual's attitudes or behavior. The group serves as a reference point in the individual's evaluation of his or her own behavior. There are many types of reference groups. Some, called primary groups, are small enough and intimate enough that all their members can communicate with one another face to face. Examples include the family, a group of close friends, and one's coworkers. Larger, less intimate secondary groups also influence our behavior. Trade unions, religious organizations, and professional associations are examples of such groups.

Some researchers have examined the influence of reference groups on purchases of various product categories, as well as of brands within those categories.[23] The researchers defined private products as those that other people are not aware that one has; public products are those that others know that one has and uses. Remember the statistic that 65 percent of chips are consumed in private? That makes chips closer to a private product—but not without a public side. Research shows that each category includes a variety of products and a wide range of prices. The nature of the product and its price do not seem to determine whether purchases of a particular product or brand are influenced by reference groups. However, the research indicates that when products or brands are socially visible and conspicuously consumed, our buying habits reflect the influence of our reference groups. No one has to know whether we buy a floor lamp or which brand we buy. But a new car is another matter—people notice.

OPINION LEADERS

Because of their special skills, intelligence, appearance, or gregarious personality, certain individuals within a reference group are viewed as experts and their opinions are trusted by other members of the group. These people often have a much greater impact on a company's sales than its advertising does, because they are perceived as more credible than company-sponsored promotion. Some people are looked to for information about personal computers, software, and peripheral equipment, yet they would not be considered an appropriate source of information about fashion clothing or sports equipment. These opinion leaders are exposed more than most people to the influence of the mass media (e.g., advertising), and they, in turn, influence others. (This is known as the two-step flow of communication.)

The Gillette Company's Paper Mate Division mailed 60,000 samples of its new Eraser Mate erasable-ink pens to opinion leaders such as U.S. senators, English teachers, baseball players, bankers, television news personalities, and advertising agency executives. When other consumers were interviewed shortly thereafter, 40 percent had heard of the product and 13 percent knew the brand name—before any advertising was done!

People belong to many reference groups, and marketers often have difficulty identifying the group that is most influential for a particular type of consumer. When this happens, they may turn to two other aspects of the individual's relationship to groups: role theory and self-image.

Role Theory

When Shakespeare wrote, "All the world's a stage, and all the men and women merely players," he effectively summed up role theory. Role theory recognizes that people conduct their lives by playing many roles. People look to others in their reference groups to learn which roles to play and how to play them. Role theory holds that for every position in society, there is a certain range of acceptable behaviors. An individual is expected to behave in a certain way to carry out the requirements of a given social position.

Behavior that is acceptable in one role may be unacceptable in another. For instance, a woman might occupy positions such as wife, mother, bridge club member, company executive, president of a neighborhood association, and tennis partner. Each position requires different behaviors, different skills, and different talents. Her position as a mediocre bridge player contrasts with her authoritative position as a mother and an executive, and with her prestige as head of the neighborhood association. Her performance in these roles is also affected by the fact that she must constantly change from one role to another during the course of a week or even a single day.

How a person performs in a given role is determined by role expectations; that is, the rights and privileges—and duties and responsibilities—that go with a role. As noted earlier, most people look to their reference groups to learn how they should behave. Thus, role expectations can be viewed as norms. Those who perform a role poorly may meet with the disapproval of other members of their reference group.

But role expectations change over time, creating interesting issues and opportunities for marketers. The changing role of men in household shopping is the subject of an amusing ad from Tandem Computers Incorporated. Their print ad is aimed at marketers and its purpose is to convince them they need to be doing data mining on Tandem equipment in order to gain a better understanding of their customers. That's what the body copy, the small print at the bottom, tells us. But what you see first in the ad is a photo of a big, beefy guy scowling at you, arms crossed, and dressed in nothing but a child's diaper.

The headline of the ad states, "AT 6:32 PM EVERY WEDNESDAY, OWEN BLY BUYS DIAPERS AND BEER." And the subhead advises marketers, "DO NOT JUDGE OWEN. ACCOMMODATE HIM."[24] Owen, like many fathers of young children, is taking a more active role in parenting than fathers used to. As a result, marketers need to recognize that he is as good a target for diaper ads as beer ads.

Yet the macho role is more likely to appear in ads aimed at men than the role of the nurturing father. So far, marketers have had trouble making the switch. Marketers may be behind the times in how we visualize the father's role in the average household. And that limits our ability to develop appropriate products and market them effectively. Many marketers still portray men, and especially fathers, as they did in earlier decades. But if men are seeing themselves more as Alan Aldas than Rambos, it's time for marketers to recognize a new role.

Self-Image

Each person has a mental picture of what he or she is like. This view, called real self-image, directs behavior. But it often happens that a person's real self-image is at odds with how others actually see that person. For instance, a business executive whose hair is turning gray may see that as a sign of diminishing youthfulness and vitality, whereas other people are amazed by his energy and competence. As a result of his real self-image, he may seek out such products as exercise equipment and hair coloring. Whether or not he actually needs these products, his real self-image influences his buying behavior.

Each person actually has three self-images. In addition to real self-image, people have a view of how they would like to be—ideal self-image—and a view of how they believe others see them—other's self-image. In comparing oneself with others, a person may wish to be better looking, more intelligent, healthier, wealthier, or happier. People also have a sense of the way they appear to others. These self-images also affect buying behavior.

For example, people who want to look rebellious may decide the most sophisticated way to do it is to purchase a leather jacket from Langlitz Leathers, which handmakes traditional motorcycle jackets in Portland, Oregon. But they'll have to be patient, because this small manufacturer makes only 1600 items a year and the current wait is about seven months. Nonetheless, some people are willing to wait, and to pay high prices, for one of these classic jackets. Customers range from ex-cons to Japanese executives to American stars like Bruce Springsteen and Sylvester Stallone. Anyone who's self-image is of a tough, Hell's Angel-type rebel—not a mall version but the authentic article—finds the Langlitz jacket irresistible.[25]

The Role of the Family

Family life is such an everyday, commonplace situation that it may seem unnecessary to discuss it. Yet some features of family living are very important to marketers—and they are not all obvious. One interesting feature of family structure is that most individuals are actually members of two families. The family a person is born into is the family of orientation; later, many people also marry and establish a family of procreation. This pattern results in a nuclear family, consisting of parents and children living together, and an extended family, which includes the nuclear family as well as aunts, uncles, grandparents, and in-laws. All these people influence a person's life and buying behavior.

In Chapter 5, we saw how this simple picture of the traditional family is disappearing as divorces have created many new forms of household. It is sometimes difficult to trace the household purchase influences—for example, imagine the complexity of a family in which children shuttle between two different houses, spreading their influence on purchases between both. In such cases, the nuclear family actually extends to more than one household.

Also of growing importance are female-headed single parent families—they make up 11 percent of U.S. households and are the fastest-growing type of household right now. These households may have some unique needs and pressures that marketers can address. However, marketers need to exercise caution in how they define the needs of the female-headed single parent family. For instance, researchers expected to find that these households used restaurants differently—perhaps more often—but they could not verify the hypothesis. Instead, the study found no significant differences in restaurant usage. Instead, eating habits seem to be embedded in culture, and therefore to characterize contraditional households as well as traditional ones. It would be a mistake to advertise a fast-food restaurant as catering to the needs of single parents since they probably don't see their needs as unique.[26]

People's membership in two families—nuclear and extended—has some definite effects on marketing. To begin with, most young couples start from scratch in purchasing housing, furniture, cars, and hundreds of other products. This creates a huge market to be served. Also, family life and structure are affected by many of the trends discussed in earlier chapters—fewer children, more women working outside the home, high divorce rates, greater geographic mobility, more single parents, more dual-income households, and increased leisure time.

The behavior of various family members at each stage of the purchase decision is of major importance to marketers. The members of a household are confronted with various decisions that reflect the needs of the family unit: Who will pay the bills? When will the grocery shopping be done? Who will wash the clothes? Three patterns of decision making in these areas have been noted:

1. *Husband dominated*—The husband has the greatest weight in the buying decision.

2. *Wife dominated*—The wife carries the greatest weight.

3. *Joint*—Both partners share about equally in the buying decision.

Who has more say in the purchase decision differs for various products and services. Joint decision making is most prevalent in decisions about vacations and housing. Life insurance tends to be the domain of the husband, whereas grocery purchases are usually the responsibility of the wife.[27] However, the relative influence of family members is changing. Husbands still dominate automobile purchase decisions, but they are influenced by their wives far more than they were a few decades ago.

Marketers keep looking for major changes in the shopping responsibilities of husbands and wives, but so far have not found them. Changes seem to come slowly. For example, baby boom couples still define spousal purchase responsibility according to the traditional classifications, with husbands dominating purchases of products like auto insurance and motor oil, and wives dominating purchases of food processors, living room sofas, and children's games. Advertising food processors to husbands is probably a waste of money.[28] Perhaps the continued strength of these traditional shopping roles reflects the finding that women and, to a greater extent, men, are strongly influenced by their parents in deciding what household tasks they will perform.[29]

Researchers have also examined the effect of egalitarianism, a balance of power between husband and wife. In the United States and most European countries, husbands and wives are more equal in their relationships than they used to be. In other countries, like China, husbands still hold considerably more power than the wives. You might expect egalitarianism to mean that either husband or wife might make a purchase decision, but that is not so. Instead, egalitarianism is associated with an increase in shared decision making. Even when one spouse initiates a purchase, the other is likely to get involved in the final decision.[30]

Knowing the relative influence of husbands and wives is basic to effective marketing; marketers need to target their messages toward the appropriate family member. For many products, such as toys, games, movies, and snacks, children can be a major force. Exhibit 6.2 shows the results of a study of children's influence on cereal purchases. One can see why Quaker Oats and Kellogg's direct much of their advertising toward children. At the same time, many critics argue that such directed advertising creates unnecessary wants in impressionable children, and thereby generates conflict within the family. A number of marketers of children's products have responded by curbing their pitches toward children, but many others have stepped up their marketing in order to take advantage of the strong influence of ads over children. Ethical and social issues are involved here, yet few marketers take the time to think them through. What do you think the right approach is?

EXHIBIT 6.2.   Influence of children on cereal purchases.

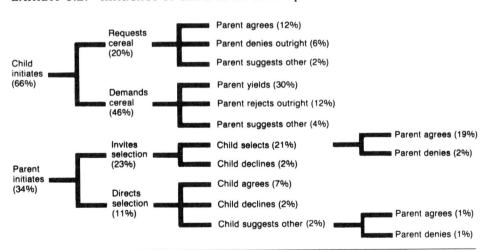

Source: Charles K. Atkin, "Observation of Parent–Child Interaction in Supermarket Decision Making," *Journal of Marketing,* 4(4), October 1978, pp. 41–45.

FOR YOUR IMAGINATION

Advertising to Firstborns?

Exhibit A: A change of strategy for Saab's U.S. advertising. In 1997, Saab's image changed "from rebel to leader, from quirky to purposeful and irreverent to confident." So says Saab's president and CEO, Joel Manby. To reposition Saab as a purposeful, confident leader, the Martin Agency (of Richmond, Virginia) developed ads emphasizing the car's fine engineering by comparing the car to the fighter jets that Saab also manufactures.[31]

Exhibit B: A breakthrough study by MIT scientist Frank J. Sulloway revealing that birth order—whether you were the oldest, youngest, or a middle child—shapes personality to a surprising degree. Firstborns, according to Sulloway, "identify with parents and authority," and are therefore "more likely to defend the status quo." They are "tough-minded," too.

In contrast, "later-borns are more likely to identify with the underdog and to challenge established order." They are more creative and radical. Especially last-borns, who Sulloway characterizes as "daring, zealous, and liberal."[32]

What do Exhibits A and B have to do with one another? Later-borns start revolutions and buy unconventional products, products that are characterized by Saab's *old* image: rebellious, quirky, and irreverent. But firstborns are more likely to see themselves reflected in Saab's *new* image, as a leader, purposeful, and confident. Whether Saab knows it or not (we think not), they are shifting their appeal from later-borns to firstborns.

And that may not be smart. The proportion of first-borns in any society is driven by the number of children per family. Big families mean few firstborns compared to later-borns, and vice versa. Baby boomers were the result of big families, at least by U.S. standards. Thus, only 32 percent of those born in the 1950s are firstborns. (By comparison, 41 percent of those born in the 1930s are firstborns because the Depression reduced family size.) Today's families are smaller—so there will be a high proportion of first-borns among Generation Y kids when they are old and wealthy enough to buy new Saabs. But that's not for quite a while. Right now, Saab's target market is the baby boomers, not their children.

Two-thirds of baby boomers are later-borns, not firstborns. Thus Saab's new positioning may appeal only to one-third of baby boomers. Is that enough? Only time will tell, but our best guess is that Saab will have to return to a more quirky, daring, and rebellious product image, embedded in its "Find Your Own Road" advertising campaign, in order to broaden its appeal among later-born boomers.

THE FAMILY LIFE CYCLE

A *Wall Street Journal* reporter profiled two different U.S. families, one with a household income of $150,000 per year, the other earning only $32,000 per year. What made these families news? Because, in spite of the five-fold difference in income, they seemed to have the same spending priorities. Both families try not to spend too much on consumer durables like TVs and VCRs or new furniture, and instead invest as much as they can in travel and activities—especially with their children.[33] Why? Because both families, in spite of their economic differences, are in the same stage— the parents have children of varying ages living at home with them. Where a family is in its life cycle has a tremendous influence over how it behaves—and therefore on how it shops.

As you are born into a family, grow older, and establish your own family, many changes in values and behavior occur. The differences that arise as people journey through the family life cycle are important to marketers. Developmentally, infants are totally dependent upon their parents, and do little beyond the house except, in some cases, attend nursery school. They need a wide variety of products, but play little role in their selection. These characteristics change rapidly and radically with age, however. One schema recognizes 16 discrete stages in the family life cycle, from infancy through young marrieds, young divorced, parents, and so forth, on to various middle-aged categories (married, not married; with or without children) and a variety of stages of later adulthood and retirement (see Exhibit 6.3).

Although this kind of descriptive effort can verge on the obvious, it is often an essential first step toward understanding the needs of a clearly defined target segment and focusing products and marketing messages on that segment. The fact is that people's needs and preferences change in important ways as they move through their own family life cycle. And it is also important to recognize that different people have different life cycles. In general, however, everyone in the same situation or stage will have in common a constellation of behaviors that create common needs and desires.

SITUATIONAL INFLUENCES

Thus far, we have emphasized the influence of other people on individual's purchase decisions. But other people are not the only outside influence; marketers must also recognize that the selection of a particular product or brand depends on how, when, and why the consumer is going to use it. These outside factors are called *situational* variables.

Consumers are influenced by the circumstances surrounding the purchase of a product. When a shopper looking for a favorite brand of potato chips is confronted with a change in price, an out-of-stock condition, or an attractive coupon on another brand, the favorite brand may lose out. Such possibilities have direct implications for a marketer's pricing, distribution, and sales promotion strategies.

EXHIBIT 6.3. Family lifestyle cycle stages.

Age Group	Age	Behavioral Characteristics	Products of Interest
Early childhood	Birth–5	Total dependency on parents; development of bones and muscles and use of locomotion; accident- and illness-prone; ego-centered; naps; accompanies guardian shopping; may attend nursery school.	Baby foods; cribs; clothes; toys; pediatric services; room vaporizers; breakfast cereals; candy; books; nursery schools.
Late childhood	6–12	Declining dependency on parents; slower and more uniform growth; vast development of thinking ability; peer competition; conscious of being evaluated by others; attends school.	Food; toys; clothes; lessons; medical and dental care; movies; candy uniforms; comic books.
Early adolescence	13–15	Onset of puberty; shifting of reference group from family to peers; concern with personal appearance; desire lot more independence; and transition to adulthood begin.	Junk food; comic books and magazines; movies; records; clothing; hobbies; grooming aids.
Late adolescence	16–18	Transition to adulthood continues; obtains working papers; obtains driver's license; concern with personal appearance increases; dating; active in organized sports; less reading for fun.	Gasoline; auto parts; typewriters; cameras; jewelry and trinkets; cigarettes; books and magazines; sporting goods.
Young singles	19–24	Entrance into labor market on a fulltime basis; entrance to college; interest in personal appearance remains high; increased dating; varying degrees of independence; activity in organized sports decreases.	Auto; clothing; dances; travel; toiletries; quick and easy-to-prepare foods.
Young marrieds	25–34	First marriage; transition to pair-centered behavior; financially optimistic; interest in personal appearance still high; learning to be homemakers, working wives, and husbands.	Home renting; furniture; major appliances; second auto; food; entertainment; small household items.
Young divorced, without children	28–34	Life style may revert back to young single; both males and females financially worse off than when married; most men and women will remarry.	Discos; therapists; clothing; auto; household goods; apartments.
Young parents	25–34	Transition to family-centered behavior; decline in social activities; companionship with spouse drops; leisure activities centered more at home.	Houses; home repair goods; health and nutrition foods; family games; healthcare services; early childhood products (see above).

EXHIBIT 6.3.   *(Continued)*

Age Group	Age	Behavioral Characteristics	Products of Interest
Young divorced, with children	28–34	Wife usually retains custody of children; husband provides child support; woman must look for employment; low discretionary income.	Child-care centers; household goods; condominiums.
Middle-aged, married with children	35–44	Family size at its peak; children in school; security-conscious; career advancements; picnics; pleasure drives.	Replacement of durables; insurance; books; sporting equipment; yard furniture; gifts.
Middle-aged, married without children	35–44	Small segment, but increasing in size; life style less hectic than when younger; emphasis on freedom and being "care-free."	Vacations; leisure-time services; athletic products; personal health-care services; party-related products.
Middle-aged, divorced without children	35–44	Small segment; major life style adjustment for both spouses; financial condition dependent on occupation and socioeconomic status; very unlikely ever to have children.	Self-help books; therapy; cruises; vacations; condominiums; household goods.
Middle-aged divorced with children	35–44	Life style changes are significant; some children may have resumed some responsibility for family's livelihood; divorced father has financial constraints; mother seeks employment if not already employed.	Condominiums; sports equipment; financial planning services.
Later adulthood	45–54	Children have left home; physical appearance changes; increased interest in appearance; community service; decline in strenuous activity; pair-centered.	Clothing; vacations; leisure-time services; food; gifts; personal health-care services.
Soon-to-be-retired	55–64	Physical appearance continues to decline; interests and activities generally continue to decline; pair-centered.	Gifts; slenderizing treatments; manicures and massages; luxuries; smaller homes.
Already retired	65 and older	Physical appearance continues its decline; mental abilities and health may decline; home-body and ego-centered behavior.	Drugs; dietetic canned foods; retirement communities; nursing home care; vacations; home care services.

Source: Adapted from Fred D. Reynolds and William D. Wells, *Consumer Behavior* (McGraw-Hill, New York, 1977); Patrick E. Murphy and William A. Staples, "A Modernized Family Life Cycle," *Journal of Consumer Research, 6,* June 1979, pp. 12–22. Reprinted by permission of the *Journal of Consumer Research.*

Consumers are also influenced by the consumption situation. The way the purchase is going to be consumed affects product and brand choices. The greeting card industry understands the importance of the consumption situation. The industry leaders, Hallmark, American Greetings, and Gibson, have designed cards that reflect the growing number of occasions for which greetings are typically offered. Now card givers can congratulate or sympathize with people for getting their driver's license, buying a new car, moving into a new home, obtaining a divorce, getting a job, losing a pet, or successfully completing a diet. The research for Frito-Lay in which respondents were asked whether people in the photographed situations would be likely to eat chips provided situational information of value in the development of new products and packages, the content and style of advertisements, and the management of product distribution. For example, if it were revealed in the study that people are likely to eat chips while driving home from work, an effort could be made to increase the availability of chips in vending machines at worksites.

Also of interest to the marketer is the communication situation. Where was a newspaper ad read—at home, on the train heading to work, at the newsstand, or late at night over America On Line? Was a television commercial viewed alone or with friends? Was the commercial aired during a program that was important to the consumer?

Situational factors such as these have definite implications for marketers. Market segmentation—how marketers define specific groups of consumers—is often influenced by the consumption situation. The paper towel market, for example, can be segmented on the basis of how the towels are used: heavy-duty uses (cleaning windows, washing cars, cleaning ovens), light-duty uses (napkins, placemats), and for cooking (drying fried potatoes, or covering a bowl in the microwave). Market analysis in terms of situational variables can uncover new marketing opportunities, and situational factors help direct promotional activities. In the case of paper towels, advertising to the light-duty segment would stress absorbency, whereas strength would be emphasized for the heavy-duty segment.

The Japanese have coined a term for marketing to situationists—TOP marketing, which stands for Time, Occasion, and Place. Japanese families, for instance, own multiple cameras, each for a different situation. Their sophisticated single-lens reflex 35-mm camera is reserved for weddings and overseas travel; a simple aim-and-shoot camera is for parties; and a weatherproof, underwater version is used for the beach and camping.

INDIVIDUAL INFLUENCES ON PURCHASE BEHAVIOR

We have covered a broad range of behavioral influences, including culture, class, reference group, and family, each of which can be vital to the success of a marketing effort. However, we have left out an important side of the equation, for all these factors are external to the individual. Learning what goes on *inside* people's heads and bodies is also important in understanding their behavior.

Studying the consumer's psychological side has been compared with looking inside a black box. Marketers can see the stimuli that precede behavior, and they can monitor the responses, but they cannot see what goes on inside the consumer's mind. For example, although Frito-Lay's researchers know the optimal thickness, diameter, and breaking point for a potato chip, they do not know why people have these preferences.

As consumers, we are bombarded with stimuli that lead to certain responses. In marketing terms, these stimuli include the marketing mix, competitors' marketing mixes, social influences, and the situation that prevails at any given time. On any given day, we are exposed to thousands of ads. After being exposed to certain stimuli, an individual may be motivated to seek more information, to buy, or to do nothing.

Even though they cannot directly observe the inner workings of the consumer's black box, marketers and behavioral scientists have come far in exploring the inner workings of consumers' minds. In the remainder of this chapter, we examine some research evidence on these phenomena and explore the problem-solving process consumers go through in making their purchase decisions.

Motivation

A motive is a need or want that is activated by a particular stimulus and initiates behavior toward some goal. We are filled with potential needs and wants; but only when they are aroused do they lead to actual behavior.

Motives generally are classified into two broad groups. Some motives are biogenic; they arise from physiological states of deprivation, such as lack of food, drink, sex, or bodily comfort. Others are psychogenic; they are psychological states of tension arising from the need or want for prestige, belonging, pride, recognition, and the like.

Consider Neutrogena skin care soap, the amber-colored, transparent bars that look attractive, smell nice, and do not irritate the face. At over $2 a bar, Neutrogena is billed as a mild soap for people who want healthy skin and are willing to pay a premium for it. This successful company understands both the biogenic and psychogenic motives that activate the consumer. As its president told *Forbes,* "What people think they're getting is what's important. With skin, half the problems are here," he said, touching his wrist, "and the other half are here," he added, pointing to his temple.[34]

Abraham Maslow has proposed a well-known five-level hierarchy of needs as a way of understanding motivation.[35] Basically, his theory states that a person has many kinds of needs with varying degrees of importance. The five levels of needs he has identified are shown in Exhibit 6.4.

A person focuses on satisfying the most important needs first. Those needs, according to Maslow's theory, are at the physiological level. The person then progresses to higher levels of the need hierarchy. Once a need has been satisfied, its motivating power ceases and the person is activated to satisfy the next most important need. For example, people who are very hungry seek only food. However, once they have eaten McDonald's Quarter Pounder with cheese or Burger King's Whopper, their focus turns to the need for safety. Need satisfaction is not as rigid a process as Maslow's

EXHIBIT 6.4. Maslow's hierarchy of needs.

Need for self-actualization: self-fulfillment

Esteem needs: self-respect, prestige, status

Social needs: affection, acceptance, belonging

Safety needs: security, protection, order

Physiological needs: sex, drink, shelter

model suggests. More than one need can be satisfied by the same action. Eating a five-course dinner (physiological) at the Four Seasons restaurant in Manhattan (esteem) with one's closest friends (social) is a good example.

A motivated person is ready to take action. Arousal has started the process that will result in behavior of some kind. But what shapes and influences that behavior? The answer lies in perception.

Perception

It is not reality that drives our behavior, but rather our perception of reality. This is the most commonly overlooked fact in the world of marketing. For example, it is easy to assume that, because your company sells a better product at a cheaper price, customers will go wild over it. But what makes it better? If it is not yet perceived as better by potential customers, then its quality is your perception, not theirs—and the market is your competitors', not yours!

Perception is the process by which a person attaches meaning to the various stimuli he or she encounters. Besides sensory impressions, perception involves an individual's own "filling in" of the picture on the basis of previous experiences. Very often a person perceives only what he or she wants to perceive; that is, people sometimes distort their sensory impressions.

For example, by now most Americans are aware of the dangers of sunburn and know you should use sunscreens to avoid this risk of skin cancer. As a result of major public health campaigns, sunburns were down and use of sunscreens up by the mid-1990s. And marketers in the suntan lotion business had made a rapid switch from tanning lotions to sunscreens in order to keep up with this trend toward protection instead of hard-core tanning. But then something happened. The late 1990s saw a resurgence in suntanning as college-age vacationers pursued the maximum tan, slathering baby oil, Vaseline, even motor oil on their skins before spending the day on a hot beach. The medical community is horrified, and so are marketers who assumed sunscreens were the way to go. But the growth in this market is in tanning lotions with dire health effects and names like Sizzle and Ultra Sun.[36]

Why are students on spring and summer breaks flaunting medical advice and courting sunstroke and melanoma? It's a perception thing.

While extreme tanning makes no sense to us, the risks must seem slim to those who do it, and the payoffs in peer admiration and enhanced self-image must be far greater than these perceived risks. Extreme tanners just don't see tanning the same way others do, and to understand their behavior you have to study their perception, not rely on your own.

It's hard enough to understand other people's perceptions. What if you want to *shape* those perceptions? For instance, how might you design ads to convince today's youth that extreme tanning is a dangerous activity?

To gain entry into consumers' perceptual arenas, marketers first must get their attention. And that's a difficult task in what one research study concluded is "the age of information overload." Why? Because the average U.S. resident is bombarded by hundreds of thousands of words and images daily from the mass media alone. For example, if you count the consumer's exposure to words from mass media, it comes to more than 60 per waking minute or one per second.[37]

Think of the last time you watched television. How many commercials can you recall? Probably not many; perhaps none. This is an example of selective perception. From the vast number of stimuli available in our complex world, we choose which ones we pay attention to. This is called *selective exposure*. We sift and funnel stimuli, paying attention to considerably fewer than we are exposed to and understanding even fewer. Finally, we remember only some of the ones we understand. This is called *selective retention*. In short, what we learn about our environment—what we perceive—is the outcome of a very selective process.

If you have raised children, you know that we learn early in life to ignore what our parents say—in fact, children appear to be selectively deaf. It is not a great leap for children as they grow up to become selectively deaf and blind to television commercials, for example, or even to zap them (no doubt many children would love to be able to use the television remote control to zap their parents as well). Marketers have been working long and hard to create advertisements that gain attention and are captivating enough to penetrate this selective perception. But it is an increasingly difficult task as the number of advertising messages per person increases daily. And now that we can zap television commercials so easily, it is estimated that exposure to commercials has dropped by 30 percent. (Nevertheless, the price paid by advertisers for airtime keeps going up!)

To counter this trend, advertisers use all kinds of gimmicks. In magazines, advertisers have used pop-ups, three-dimensional advertisements that stand up as readers turn the page, scent stripes, and even musical microchips to grab maximum impact. During the 1987 Christmas season, for example, Carillon Importers, and

Brown-Forman Beverage Company inserted a musical microchip in magazine ads for Absolut vodka and Canadian Mist whiskey that played Deck the Halls when the advertisement's page was opened. Because research indicates that "anything that startles—a loud noise, a flash of light—involuntarily triggers the brain to direct attention to the stimulus,"[38] some television ads have used surprise to grab the viewer's attention. For example, the early Bud Light commercials based on the line, "Don't just ask for a light . . . ," put on startling light shows to grab viewer attention and proved extremely memorable.

More recently, some television advertisers have used parodies of other ads to surprise and amuse consumers. For instance, Boston Market, a fast-food chain, ran an ad in 1997 that parodied fashion ads from firms like Calvin Klein. Shot in black and white, the ad shows a tall, thin model wandering along a barren beach and moaning, "How can I fill this empty void of emptiness?" Then, surprise!, a man jumps from behind a boulder with a far simpler solution than the fashion industry offers. His advice, "Eat something!"[39]

Sensory Thresholds

One of the more surprising results to come out of Frito-Lay's Potato Chip Pentagon is that consumers can detect, and will complain about, variations in chip thickness as small as 0.008 of an inch. (The standard for flat chips is 0.036 of an inch; for Ruffles, 0.091.) Apparently people like chips at the standard thickness and can tell with a high, and measurable, degree of accuracy when chips deviate from standard. But people do not necessarily detect other changes with as much sensitivity. For example, do you know what you last paid for a bag of potato chips, and do you think you would notice if the next one cost 10 percent more? This threshold is probably fairly high in light of the high profit margins in the chip industry.

Sensory thresholds, or limits, are obviously a key aspect of perception. Every human sensory process has an upper threshold, the point at which further increases in intensity will not be noticed, and a lower threshold, the point at which further decreases in intensity will not be noticed. What is of particular interest to marketers is the so-called difference threshold, that is, the smallest change in the intensity of a stimulus that can be noticed. Mercedes was surprised to learn that some consumers are extremely sensitive to vibration. But they are—and some of them have sued the company over their complaint that the steering wheels of their cars vibrate too much. Mercedes engineers don't see a problem, but since some of their customers do, Mercedes nonetheless *has* a problem.[40]

There are times when marketers do not want to exceed the difference threshold—Mercedes certainly wishes the vibrations in their S-class cars' steering wheels did not! In fact, the entire practice of downsizing is predicated on the consumer's inability to perceive small changes that do not exceed difference thresholds. Downsizing is one of the marketing terms not taught in MBA programs; in fact, it is almost a dirty word. Downsizing is the reduction of package size without a corresponding reduction in price, performed in such a way as to minimize the number of customers who notice it. For example, tuna fish cans held 6½ ounces of tuna for 30 years, until StarKist modified its can in 1990. It now holds ⅜ of an ounce less, but the price stayed the same.[41] This repackaging in effect gave StarKist a price increase of 5.8 percent without attracting consumer attention to it. Downsizing is essentially a deceptive practice; a simple price rise of this amount would undoubtedly have crossed the difference threshold of many StarKist buyers.

On the other hand, there are times when companies wish they *had* exceeded the difference threshold. Frito-Lay found itself in court over this issue when the gravelly voiced singer Tom Waits filed suit with the claim that a Tracy-Locke commercial for a spicy Frito-Lay corn chip featured an impersonation of his voice. The jury agreed that the singer in the commercial sounded like Tom Waits, and awarded Waits about $2.5 million in compensation.[42] That amounts to a lot of chips.

Difference thresholds likely vary depending upon the situation. A recent study of television advertising found that viewers evaluate dramas on the basis of how true to life they seem, whereas they evaluate argument-oriented ads based more on whether they seem factual and consistent than on whether they are true to life. This implies that viewers apply a different threshold for detecting consistency when viewing argument-oriented ads than when viewing ads that tell a story.[43] And a

---

FOR YOUR IMAGINATION

Get Me a Bottle of That Chardonnay with the Grape Leaf on It

If imitation is the sincerest form of flattery, then marketers often flatter leading brands. Pepsi is formulated to taste like Coke, and American automakers are rounding and shaping their sedans to look like luxury imports. Which is all well and good, unless the imitators are so similar that they fail to exceed consumers' sensory thresholds. Then it's a different matter—a matter for intellectual property lawyers and courtrooms.

Such is the fate of E. & J. Gallo Winery's Turning Leaf Chardonnay. It was introduced to compete with the highly successful Kendall-Jackson Chardonnay. And the Gallo knock-off is packaged so as to look similar to the Kendall-Jackson product. The bottles are the same shape and size, the labels similar in color and shape, and both feature a russet and green grape leaf. Gallo's Turning Leaf label is outlined with an elegant silver stripe, Kendall-Jackson's with a gold stripe. And of course they are from different and competing wineries. But Kendall-Jackson's owners and attorneys believe that the Gallo product is easily confused with their own, and that this accounts from the rapid success of the new competitor. Next time you have a chance to visit a store selling California Chardonnays, pop in and ask the clerk to show you the two bottles. And see whether you think the Gallo product could slip under the sensory threshold of a Kendall-Jackson customer. The courts didn't think so—and judged in favor of Gallo!

person's physical condition no doubt affects the difference threshold, which may explain the incredible claims the makers of cold medicines get away with. For example, one ad claims that "Only Dristan Sinus combines the leading decongestant with the modern pain reliever ibuprofen."[44] In fact, American Home Products manufactures both Dristan Sinus and CoAdvil—and they have the same active ingredients in the same doses. As a spokesperson for the company conceded, "In terms of chemicals, they're identical." This might be said for many of the other 85 brands of cold medicines on the U.S. market as well, but the fact is that a consumer with a terrible cold is not likely to worry about such details.

Learning

Closely tied to perception is learning, which may be defined as changes in our behavior that result from our experiences. Learning and perception are related because we can experience, and learn from, only what we perceive. Besides changes in physical behavior, learning includes changes in mental behavior, such as feelings, emotions, and personality. Learning in markets is ideally a two-way street, with consumers learning from product use experiences and marketing information, and with companies learning from customer research, the sales performance of their products, and other feedback. Furthermore, the company's learning can be beneficial to, and in tandem with, the consumer's learning, as when Hewlett Packard worked with customer groups to find out what people wanted in laser printers, then introduced a better, cheaper printer for owners of PCs. Hopefully this is the direction in which marketing is going. But it can also go the other way, with companies learning to take advantage of consumers, as downsizing takes advantage of difference thresholds. Think about these two options in the context of the quote from Henry Ford that we used to open this book, "The man who will use his skill and constructive imagination to see how much he can give for a dollar, instead of how little he can give for a dollar, is bound to succeed." Not every business uses marketing based on the objectives Ford articulated.

What do we learn, in general as individuals in society, and specifically in response to marketing efforts directed at us? We learn what objects are and what their functions are. We learn tastes—to like certain things such as spinach or Scotch. We also learn what is tasteful in clothes and in social behavior. And we learn wants and needs. We learn to want Ralph Lauren polo players on our clothes, and that excessive amounts of fat, sugar, and caffeine are not healthful. The list is endless. The point is that marketing plays a role in the learning process for every individual in a society.

Learning through Association

The process of building mental associations, or connections, is one form of learning. We build associations between two or more stimuli or between a stimulus and a response. Mental associations are a convenient way of understanding the information we receive.

Quaker State Oil Refining Corporation, the country's largest refiner and marketer of motor oil, knows the importance of mental associations. Quaker State consumers have unusually strong brand loyalty, stemming largely from their association of Quaker State with the so-called Penn-grade variety of crude oil, a light greenish crude that was used to refine the first motor oils used in the United States. The consumer's belief in the high quality of Pennsylvania motor oil is so widespread that many oil companies add green dye to their Texas or Middle Eastern crude-based oils.

In their efforts to create mental associations, marketers employ signs that communicate what the buyer can expect. Food marketers use the word "light" or "lite" to convey low calories. The scent of lemon is put into cleansers, furniture polishes, bath oils, and the like to communicate freshness. In the superpremium ice cream market, marketers use the Swedish-sounding Haagen-Dazs as a sign that their ice cream has a Scandinavian "all-natural" quality. In fact, the brand name Haagen-Dazs is not Swedish and has no meaning in any language.

Global marketers must be careful in choosing the correct signs to avoid creating a cross-cultural problem. McDonnell Douglas Corporation had to revise its television commercial to be shown in China because the Chinese government objected to footage of a plane flying into a map of China, a national symbol the Chinese do not want commercialized. Similarly, showing a man giving flowers to a woman in the United States is a sign of romance; in some Arab countries, it is a sign of death. The associations we attach to symbols such as these are often very powerful—but exactly which associations consumers will make when confronted with a symbol is sometimes a tricky issue. Focus group research can be informative in these cases.

The Learning Process

It is helpful to review some of the jargon of behaviorists, because these terms reveal a great deal about how the learning process works:

- A cue is an environmental stimulus that is perceived as a signal for action.
- A drive is a strong motivating tendency that arouses an organism toward a particular type of behavior. Usually it is synonymous with motive.
- A response is whatever occurs as a reaction to an aroused need.
- Reinforcement is the extent to which satisfaction is derived from a response.
- Retention is the extent to which one remembers what one has learned.

Although marketers cannot create drives within consumers, they can affect the amount of learning that takes place by the way they handle the cues that stimulate learning. The frequency with which cues are presented is one important factor. When consumers are exposed repeatedly to the same cue, they are more likely to remember it than when they are exposed to many cues at once. On the other hand, massive exposure to cues can lead to faster learning. Often marketers who are introducing a new product will expose consumers to frequent cues in large doses. Getting consumers to participate also enhances learning, which is why test-drives and free samples are so common in the world of marketing.

In general, the greater the reinforcement, the greater the learning. Total reinforcement, in which a reward is given each time a certain behavior occurs, results in faster learning. However, partial reinforcement, in which a reward is received for only some responses, leads to learning that is more difficult to extinguish. This can mean that once a brand has been used satisfactorily for some time, a single negative experience with that brand (partial reinforcement) may not change the opinion of the consumer.

Low-Involvement Learning

Recently marketers have noted that the way consumers learn depends on how much they care about or are interested in a given product. Automobile and home purchases are very important to the consumer, but most purchases are not. Bicycles, facial tissues, toothpaste, potato chips, and many other products show relatively low consumer involvement.[45] In the case of such low-involvement products, learning is done passively. Instead of actively seeking information to evaluate products before buying, consumers pick up pieces of information at random. Reference groups have little influence on product choice, at least for very low-involvement products, which are not likely to be related to the values of groups. Television is a good medium for conveying information to a passive audience, because its animation has attention-getting value and frequent repetition of commercials fosters the acquisition of random information. For example, Rold-Gold pretzel ads featured the personality of comedian Jason Alexander, "Seinfeld" co-star, more than anything specific in the line of product information. The ads are funny and attention getting. One shows the George character from the television show parachuting into the Superbowl. Putting a comedian in front of a passive audience turns out to be a good way to hold attention and slip in a little product awareness through the back door.

Memory

Information acquired by an individual undergoes a set of mental operations known as cognitive processes by the behavioral scientist. Two concepts are useful in this regard: *leveling* and *sharpening*. Leveling can be compared with forgetting: The information we retain becomes shorter and more concise. We tend to remember only certain aspects of an experience. For instance, when we think about a particular brand of aftershave lotion, we may recall its sting and not its pleasant scent. Sharpening is the opposite of leveling: Much of what we recall is more vivid and important than the event itself. The sting of the aftershave lotion may have been sharp, but not as intense or painful as we remember it to be, just as the strength of Dorito breath is probably not as strong as some consumers remember it to be.

Evaluative Criteria

Buyers and consumers can be viewed as decision makers. Their cues and drives create a perceived problem—a goal for the consumer. Consumers' goals are reflected in the evaluative criteria they apply when making a purchase decision. Some contemporary U.S. evaluative criteria are convenience, service, healthfulness, and quality. Some marketers are exploring the convenience criterion by, for example, packaging prewashed mixtures of salad greens.

Evaluative criteria also apply to noncommercial marketing. For instance, people who donate to charitable organizations expect their money to be put to a stated use. The choice of a political candidate depends on what the voter expects that person to do once he or she takes office. To provide satisfaction, marketers must know the consumer's evaluative criteria as thoroughly as possible. They must know how many criteria are involved, the importance of each, and the strength of each.

In some purchase situations, consumers may use only one criterion to make a decision. They may buy a pencil because it is available. In other situations, they may use many criteria. In buying a car, such features as style, safety, price, dependability, service, economy, color, accessories, and status may all be involved. On average, however, only five or six criteria come into play, and some of these may be far more important than others in the evaluation process. In the case of the car purchase, price, style, and economy may rank high on a consumer's list of priorities, whereas color may be less important. Finally, a particular criterion may be stronger in one exchange situation than in another. For instance, style may exert a stronger influence when one is buying a car than when one is buying a kitchen clock. Exhibit 6.5 shows the mental process that may be involved in buying an automobile. A number of strategies can emerge from analyses of evaluative criteria.

EXHIBIT 6.5. Evaluative criteria as applied to automobile purchases.

Criteria	Weight	Rating (Poor Match . . . Good Match)					Total
		1	2	3	4	5	
Style	10					X	50
Price	9				X		36
Economy	8				X		32
Dependability	6			X			18
Service	6				X		24
Accessories	4			X			12
Safety	3		X				6
Color	1	X					1
							179

If a marketer's brand matches a highly prized evaluative criterion, this can and should be communicated to the market. For instance, when the healthful effects of lower cholesterol became known to the public, Quaker Oats Company pushed in a print advertisement the cholesterol-lowering properties of its product: "You know by now that lowering your cholesterol level can lower your risk for heart trouble. Studies say that just 2 ounces of Quaker Oats a day, along with a low-fat, low cholesterol diet, can help lower your cholesterol almost 10%. Other studies say that's enough to reduce your risk of heart attack by nearly 20%." By the time this claim was determined to be false, or at least exaggerated, quite a number of consumers had increased their consumption of oatmeal. But please don't take the wrong lesson away from this story. It is always more effective (and ethical) to have a true story to tell. And if your product is not exceptional, you need to improve it.

If a marketer finds that its product is perceived as being poor on an important criterion, the marketer can attempt to improve the product's performance on that criterion. To combat its image as the purveyor of junk food, McDonald's confronted that negative perception with an advertising campaign stressing the nutritional value of the fast-food giant's menu. In the spring of 1991, McDonald's took a more substantive step toward improving its position on this criterion by introducing an innovative McLean Deluxe burger that is only 9-percent fat but still tastes (or is supposed to taste) like the typical 20-percent fat burger because it uses a carrageenan binder.[46] More recently, the company added chicken fajitas to its menu, which is an even healthier alternative. And in the mid-1990s, McDonald's discovered that adult consumers saw it as too kid-oriented, and so it undertook a series of new product introductions and promotions to fix this perceptual problem as well.

Another strategy is to make consumers aware of criteria they have not considered before. If successful, this strategy can redefine a market and catapult a brand to leadership. Such is the story of the sport drinks that rose to prominence in the 1990s. By adding nutrients or vitamins, beverage makers are able to claim that their products give consumers energy. Ginseng iced tea and AllSport sports drinks give you energy and enhance your performance, rather than simply quenching your thirst. Now that such drinks are popular, soda and juice makers have to face the fact that consumers evaluate beverages based on how they make you perform, not just on how they taste and whether they quench thirst.

Attitudes

Attitudes are our feelings of liking or disliking objects in our environment. Attitudes have three components: The cognitive component reflects one's evaluation of the characteristics of an object; the affective component is the emotional feeling of favorableness or unfavorableness that results from the evaluation; and the cognitive component is the resultant intention or tendency to act. In marketing terms, consumers have attitudes about products, brands, retail outlets, salespeople, and advertisements. Marketers obviously are interested in developing specific attitudes among consumers.

An important point for marketers to remember is that attitudes can develop only after consumers learn that an object exists and what its attributes are (the cognitive component). The affective or feeling component of an attitude is formed by perceiving information about an object and evaluating that information. Not before a lot of consumer education had taken place did attitudes form toward such products as wine coolers and Zima—both of which did not find consumer acceptance. Consumers' attitudes toward a product come from their assessment of the product's ability to meet their evaluative criteria. When we like a product, we tend to see only its good features; we selectively reject information about its weaker qualities. Thus, although our attitudes influence our behavior, our behavior (purchase and use of products, in this case) also affects our attitudes.

Marketers are concerned about consumers' attitudes because favorable attitudes lead to favorable exchange behavior. But marketers must also be concerned with consumers' intentions (the cognitive component). If favorable attitudes can be developed, consumers will intend to make a purchase, and this intention will lead to an actual purchase. In many cases, however, constraints intervene between attitudes and behavior, and may override the influence of attitudes. For example, a person may have a favorable attitude toward that BMW Z3 sports car, yet may not buy one. The reason may be simple: The car is too expensive. Or the person may feel that it is a waste to spend so much money on a car.

Much of what marketers do is directed toward the development of favorable attitudes, which depend on the topics we have discussed thus far. Exhibit 6.6 summarizes the steps in the development of attitudes that lead to exchange. Nothing can be bought or sold until the consumer moves through this process, step by step. The

EXHIBIT 6.6.   Attitude development steps.

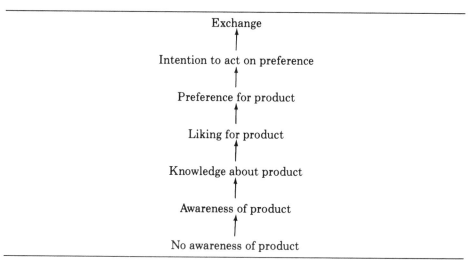

Source: Robert J. Lavidge and Gary Steiner, "A Model for Predictive Measurements of Advertising Effectiveness," *Journal of Marketing, 25*(4), October 1961, p. 61.

ultimate goal of marketing can therefore be seen as ensuring that consumers move through this process. Insight into the black box of human behavior is essential to this effort.

THE CONSUMER DECISION-MAKING PROCESS

In this chapter, we have examined several social, situational, and psychological concepts that add to marketers' understanding of consumers and their purchase behavior. It is wrong to assume that perception alone, or social class alone, or any of these concepts alone is enough to explain exchange behavior. In some cases, one or more of these concepts may dominate the exchange situation. But a more realistic view is that all these elements interact, as they seem to in the complex, multifaceted personality profiles that Howard Davis uses to sell different brands of potato chips for Frito-Lay, as discussed in the beginning of this chapter. What may seem to be an instantaneous decision by the buyer is actually a result of the interaction of mental and social phenomena. Next we take a closer look at the process by which consumers make purchase decisions.

Problem Recognition

The first step in the decision-making process is problem recognition. This occurs when the consumer perceives a difference between an actual state and an ideal state. You find that the battery in your wristwatch is not working; stepping on the scale reveals that you have gained two pounds during vacation; a particularly attractive person asks you to dinner on Saturday. All these events create problems that cry out for solutions. They create different levels of anxiety. Timex, Lean Cuisine, and Tommy Hilfiger have all provided ways of solving these kinds of problems.

Some problems are shelved until later, but others are attended to very quickly—especially those that reflect a large discrepancy between a real state and a desired state and those that touch off a key internal drive. When one realizes that one is shaving with the last blade in the pack, a particular behavior is likely to occur quite soon. The complexity of the decision also has an impact on the decision process. Buying another nine-pack of Gillette Sensor blades, a brand you have been loyal to for years, is quite a different matter from purchasing a personal computer, which involves considerations of user friendliness, memory capability, software availability, price, appearance, speed of response, peripheral equipment needs, service, and guarantee.

Marketers can uncover consumer problems by conducting marketing research. Problem recognition is at the root of good marketing and, clearly, at the heart of consumer decision making.

We both do a fair amount of business travel, and so we are painfully aware of the difficulties of hauling extra suits and ties, jogging shoes, and bulging files from airport to airport. And so are some luggage makers. The needs of the business traveler are a constant source of marketing innovations. One retailer even calls itself

Innovation Luggage, Inc. to let consumers know it specializes in new solutions to this age-old problem. Bag maker Travelpro of Boca Raton, Florida, specializes in suitcases with two wheels and a pull-up handle that take the weight off your shoulder. Many of them fit in the overhead racks of airplanes in recognition of another business traveler's need. And manufacturer Samsonite is going one better by introducing a suitcase with four wheels that is supposed to be even easier to wheel through busy airports.[47] The luggage industry's history is nothing more nor less than a constant search for solutions to consumers' travel problems.

Internal Information Search

When faced with a problem, the consumer first tries to recall any information he or she already has about possible solutions. What comes immediately to mind is termed the *evoked set.* Much of the communication engaged in by marketers is aimed at getting us to recall their products and brands when we have a particular problem. When you are hungry—think Snickers! When you have bad breath—think Scope! We search our memory for whatever bits of information about these possible solutions we have stored there. These are summoned and measured against the evaluative criteria we use to judge each possible solution to our problem. Generally, if we find a satisfactory solution among those in the evoked set, we make a decision based on our internal search.

Not all problems have satisfactory solutions in the evoked set. In such cases, we seek more information from sources outside our own memories. Certain circumstances influence the likelihood that we will search for more information. For example, some decisions are seen as riskier than others. The degree of perceived risk can dictate the amount of additional search in which we engage. Certain products by their nature are high in perceived risk—complex items (stereo equipment, computers), expensive goods (houses, typewriters), and high-involvement products (cars, clothing) are examples. When the consumer has limited knowledge about existing products and brands—when the consumer knows little about them and the proper evaluative criteria to use—more risk is felt and more information seeking takes place. Also, when the decision is very relevant to the consumer and high involvement exists, the consumer actively seeks further information from external sources.[48]

External Information Search

Sources of additional information can be either personal or nonpersonal. On the personal side, consumers turn to salespeople, friends, relatives, and opinion leaders—even doctors. Food marketers are using physician endorsements to capture sales. Procter & Gamble, for example, sends doctors brochures that outline the nutrition and health benefits of their products and counts on doctors to recommend them to their patients. Kellogg Company has used a physician in print advertisements to endorse its high-fiber cereals.

Nonpersonal sources are also key influences. Consumers turn to magazines, directories, and advertising to shed light on the alternatives available to them. Consider the choice of a personal computer—we have already noted the complexity of this decision. The software decision isn't any easier. For help in making these decisions, consumers are turning to a variety of nonpersonal sources. Many personal-computer magazines find that their software reviews are among their most popular articles, and a number of companies have issued massive directories that catalog thousands of programs.

The extent of a consumer's search for information depends on the perceived risk and uncertainty that surrounds the decision: The higher the risk and uncertainty, the greater the search. Studies have shown that better educated and higher income consumers conduct more extensive information searches,[49] as do those with lower self-confidence and greater anxiety.[50]

The Decision

Once the consumer has acquired information through internal and external searches, a choice can be made. Basically, one can do nothing, seek more information, or choose one of the known and considered alternatives. The decision not to buy may result when none of the alternatives appears to solve the problem satisfactorily—or, worse yet, when the purchase would create other problems. The desired choice may meet with social disapproval or cause financial strain, for instance. When uncertainty remains and there is no pressure to make a choice, the consumer may decide to seek additional information.

Postdecision Evaluation

Consumers do not stop with the purchase decision itself. They evaluate the amount of satisfaction they have derived from the decision. Such an evaluation cannot happen until the product has been consumed or used. Consumers' experiences are generally the strongest influence on what they believe about the product or brand and its attributes. A positive experience will strengthen positive beliefs, improve attitudes, and thereby increase the likelihood of repeat purchases. Furthermore, a satisfied customer can be a key influence on others.

Although satisfaction or dissatisfaction can come immediately with some products (as in downing a soft drink on a hot day), most purchase decisions are evaluated after a certain period of time. We have a natural tendency to assure ourselves that our decision was the best one. We need this assurance, because by choosing one alternative we have given up all the others. Each alternative had some positive attributes; those attributes have been passed up. This situation creates some degree of anxiety or postpurchase uneasiness, which is called cognitive dissonance.

People who have made a purchase decision use a variety of tactics to reduce or minimize cognitive dissonance. One approach is to seek more information that confirms the appropriateness of the decision. We perceive more ads now than we did before the purchase. We look for positive evaluations of our decision from peers. Postpurchase contact with consumers by marketers is particularly effective in reducing dissonance; among the techniques used for this purpose are letters of congratulation, guarantees, and toll-free customer complaint and problem-solving telephone lines. Consumers may also play down the advantages of the unchosen alternatives and emphasize those of the one they chose. In general, cognitive dissonance occurs more often when the purchase is important to the consumer and the alternatives that were not chosen are highly desirable.

The Big Picture

The consumer's decision-making process as we have presented it seems logical, yet some decisions seem not to fit this pattern. Many decisions, such as whether to buy chewing gum or a magazine, involve neither information seeking nor evaluation. Such decisions are habitual and routine, because the consumer has amassed much prior information and is satisfied with his or her past purchases. In other buying situations, the consumer has some knowledge of alternatives and their attributes, but a new brand comes on the market. In such cases, some information may be sought and added to what is already known. The greatest information-seeking effort is needed in cases that involve new problems or highly innovative solutions, such as cellular telephones and facsimile machines. The least effort generally comes with frequently used, low-priced items.

This decision-making process also can be interrupted at any time by external factors, such as the social influences noted earlier in this chapter. For example, the immediate problem of hunger may be squelched by the cultural value of wanting to look fit. Thus, you may forgo a snack as a result of reference group influence—perhaps someone mentioned that you were putting on a bit of weight—or you may skip dessert because of your ideal self-concept—you would like to be a lot thinner than you are. At the same time, other nonsocial situational factors may intervene—you are out of money, no food is available at the moment, and so on. Such interruptions can occur at any time in the decision-making process.

Frito-Lay recognizes this possibility and addresses it with a new line of "healthy" chips. Starting with test markets for low-oil Doritos and Ruffles Light,[51] the company went on to introduce a line of four light chips nationally. For some chip consumers, the urge to eat chips can be interrupted by thoughts of fat and salt. Through demographic research and the application of concepts of consumer behavior, Frito-Lay developed a profile of these people. Their demographics are "white-collar workers, 35 to 54 years old, earning more than $35,000." To target these consumers, Frito-Lay used the new store-specific databases to select stores with a high proportion of these customers. "By increasing promotional spending, running in-store taste programs and lobbying retailers to give more space to the pricier chips in the selected stores, Frito-Lay got the line off to a running start."[52]

But it is not always this easy. Marketers must remember that consumer behavior is complex and individualized. Although the models suggest logical, predictable behavior, in fact, behavior can be difficult to understand and predict. Understanding consumer behavior is more an art than a science, and it provides marketers with many of their greatest challenges and opportunities. Both the challenges and the opportunities arise from the essential fact that consumer behavior involves consumers, and consumers are people in all their complexity and individuality. Perhaps the only certainty is that people "are practically always desiring something," as stated by Maslow in the chapter's opening quote. The uncertainty arises when marketers need to decide exactly what consumers desire in any specific situation, as we have discussed. As the humorist Josh Billings used to say, "It's better to know nothing than to know what ain't so." Study consumer behavior to form hypotheses, but don't take them too seriously or you are very likely to find you know what ain't so!

7 SEGMENTATION, TARGETING, POSITIONING

From Mass Marketing to One-to-One with the Customer

The fifties and sixties were the heyday of mass marketing. There was one kind of Coca-Cola soft drink for the thirsty. One kind of Clairol hair dye for hair coloring. One kind of Holiday Inn motel for the traveler. The seventies became a decade of segmentation and line extension. It was followed in the early eighties by intensified niche marketing that sliced markets into smaller and smaller groups of consumers—each group with particular needs and wants to satisfy. By the mid-eighties, Robitussin was offering four kinds of medicine for four kinds of coughs. . . . From mass marketing to segmented marketing to niche marketing to tomorrow's world of one-to-one marketing—the transformation will be complete by the end of the eighties.

—Stan Rapp and Tom Collins, in MaxiMarketing, *1987*[1]

The old paradigm, a system of mass production, mass media, and mass marketing, is being replaced by a totally new paradigm, a one-to-one economic system. The 1:1 future will be characterized by customized production, individually addressable media, and 1:1 marketing, totally changing the rules of business competition and growth. Instead of market share, the goal of most business competition will be share of customer—one customer at a time.

—Don Peppers and Martha Rogers, in
The One to One Future, *1993*[2]

I call it the "spiderweb marketing strategy." Once they get your credit card number, they have you. The

199

> spiderweb technique involves making it so difficult to cancel the product or service that it's easier to just keep it.
>
> —*Scott Adams, in* The Dilbert Future, *1997*[3]

As the sequence of quotes above demonstrates, marketing has been chasing its own Holy Grail for the last two decades. The goal, according to many marketing experts, is to use high-tech database marketing to find and build personal, lasting relationships with *individual* customers.

No more masses of customers, moving like herds across the business landscape. That's too anonymous. It prevents you from customizing your offerings to individual needs, and makes your customer relationships so impersonal that competitors can easily steal those customers without your even knowing it. Instead, so the vision goes, the customer relationship should be like, well, like a personal relationship. With a lover, perhaps. At least that's what the cover of the popular book, *The One to One Future,* implies, for it shows two people in profile, nose to nose, evidently about to kiss.

It's a bold vision of a brave new world, one in which customers feel so much commitment to marketers that they happily stay loyal and even pay a premium to do so. And this vision has spawned a huge new industry in direct marketing—where marketers bypass retailers and other intermediaries and use individual media and computers to sell direct to the end user. But is the vision realistic? Do customers really want to kiss marketers?

Let's get real. This is the age of Dilbert. A new cynicism toward business pervades the land, fueled by unprecedented job layoffs and downsizing in the 1990s and continued reduction in the length of tenure of the average employee's job, both in the United States and abroad. And some of that cynicism people feel toward their employers rubs off on us marketers, too. So, what marketing gurus see as an exciting new one-to-one future with their customers may seem like an irritating spiderweb of intrusion from the customer perspective. Why should customers relish an involved, personal relationship with each of the hundreds of companies that produce each of the tens of thousands of goods and services they have the opportunity to buy in an average day?

When the gurus of direct marketing predicted that all marketers would be focusing their products and pitches on individual consumers by the 1990s, they were only partially correct. They didn't account for the Dilbert factor. And they certainly didn't put the retailers out of business. Yet, they did bring about a revolution of sorts in marketing. It turns out that they have perfected a high-tech marketing strategy that is based on a simple, low-tech principle of marketing: When you break smaller groups out of the big mass of customers, you can tailor your offerings to more specific customer needs and preferences. That's what this chapter is all about.

As a practical matter, one-to-one selling is not always a cost-effective way to market products and services. On the one hand, companies generally run into problems of scale when they try to break down their markets into ever-smaller groups. On the other hand, many products that were once designed and advertised to the entire country have now splintered into a variety of more specialized products and sales messages. So fragmentation of markets is a reality, and in some markets, that fragmentation has made it down to the level of the individual. It's up to you as a marketer to decide what level of fragmentation makes the most sense for your market and product—both from your profit perspective and from the customer's cynical perspective as well.

The revolution toward one-to-one marketing is not complete—if Dilbert has his way, it never will be—but the increasing power of computerized customer databases continues to drive marketing toward more narrowly focused products and marketing campaigns. At the root of this trend is the simple observation that no two consumers are alike.

This is easy to see in the consumer market. Think about all the material goods that your friends possess. No two individuals have the same set of possessions. Each person wants a unique combination of goods and services. Think about how numerous people are, how spread out over the country and the world they are, and how diverse their buying habits are. Meeting their needs is far from a trivial task. In their efforts to perform this task, marketers divide the market as a whole into smaller segments on the basis of some kind of similarity among consumers, such as age or sex, buying behavior, or psychological traits. Most managers believe that they cannot compete successfully in every market and that it is in their interest to focus on a few segments that seem more attractive than others. This is the basis of target marketing.

Porsche sent the following letter to potential customers, "Your preeminent position in society and your success as a doctor demonstrate that you pursue excellence in all things, a quality you share with Dr. Ferry Porsche, the creator of the original Porsche automobile. . . . Since you already own a luxurious European car, I would like to introduce you to another—the Porsche." The recipient may not have taken the bait, but he was bound to be surprised that Porsche knew he was a European-car-driving doctor. Steven Judge of Rapp Collins Marcoa, Porsche's direct-marketing agency, explains, "We've been successful in obtaining a great deal of information about our prospects, such as their profession, their income range, the type of cars they currently drive, where they live, and what type of neighborhood they live in." This research has allowed Porsche to select 300,000 likely prospects from an initial list of 80 million car owners. It cost the company 6 months and $250,000 to generate the list, but the benefits of targeting this segment will far outweigh the costs of development if it turns out, for example, that middle-aged male doctors who drive Mercedes, earn more than $150,000 per year, and live in affluent suburbs are very likely to buy Porsches.[4]

Before discussing market segmentation in detail, however, we need to consider a broader approach that marketers sometimes use. Instead of dividing the total market into smaller, more homogeneous segments, they may treat all consumers as one large group—an aggregate. Thus there are two basic strategies available to marketers: market aggregation and market segmentation. We examine the objectives, methods, costs, and benefits of each strategy.

MARKET AGGREGATION—THE STRATEGY OF MASS MARKETING

When marketers follow the strategy of market aggregation, also called mass marketing or undifferentiated marketing, the total market is not divided into segments. Rather, a single marketing program is used to offer the same product to all consumers. Because of the diversity of the consumers' wants and needs, the market aggregation approach will not completely satisfy every potential buyer. Marketers use this strategy when they believe enough consumers will buy the product as it is. This strategy has been used by marketers of standardized goods, such as sugar, many farm products, gasoline, salt, paint, and liquid bleach, as well as standardized services, such as dry cleaning, appliance repair, lawn maintenance, and house painting. It has also been used for some products that people may not think of as standardized, such as beer, cigarettes, coffee, and household cleansers.

The market aggregation approach is used when consumers perceive little or no difference between the products of different firms, that is, when competing products seem virtually the same physically and chemically. For this approach to be successful, therefore, a large number of people must have the same basic need or want. Also, the marketer must be able to design a single marketing mix that will satisfy various potential customers. If these two conditions are not met, mass marketing is doomed to failure.

Organizations that use the market aggregation approach realize that consumers may have different wants and needs, but they also believe that a sufficient number of consumers are similar enough to be treated as a homogeneous group. In short, consumers are expected to compromise by accepting a product that may not suit their needs perfectly. This approach is exemplified by Henry Ford's famous remark about potential buyers of his Model T. A firm believer in mass marketing, he is reported to have said that the market "can have any color it wants as long as it's black." Contrast this with the way Porsches are sold today.

The major advantage of the market aggregation strategy comes from lower production and marketing costs. Only one product is made and production techniques do not have to be changed for different models, styles, and the like. This is extremely efficient; Ford's Model T offered consumers more value for their money because standardized mass production lowered the cost of production. Advertising costs also may be lower because often only one advertising campaign is used.

Despite the advantages in terms of costs and efficiency, there are built-in dangers in the market aggregation strategy. By using an approach that may leave some consumers' wants unsatisfied, marketers expose themselves to challenges from competitors. This is especially true when the firm serves a large market. In trying to meet the entire market's needs reasonably well, marketers are vulnerable to competitors who satisfy those needs more precisely. Henry Ford was forced to offer a choice of colors when competitors started to.

Differentiating Your Offering

Marketers that use the market aggregation approach often employ promotion and other marketing activities to get consumers to perceive their product as different from and better than those of competitors. This strategy is known as product differentiation.[5] It involves creating a perception of uniqueness and superiority and, thus, a preference for a particular product. The actual product may not be different from competitors' products, but consumers believe it is different. To create that perception in the minds of consumers, marketers rely heavily on creating a positive image for the product or associating it with something that is valued by the consumer.

Consider the bath towel business. Can you honestly tell the difference between two bath towels? In recent years, towel manufacturers have created an industry in which consumers consider most bath towels as the same. Even designer brand sheets and towels have been sold at rock-bottom prices to bargain-seeking customers. In an effort to differentiate its products from those of competitors, Fieldcrest has begun marketing only its most fashionable, high-profit products under its corporate brand name. While most of its competitors sew their corporate names on all their products and sell them through all kinds of outlets—discount stores and mass merchandisers as well as prestigious department stores—Fieldcrest stitches its name only on its finest quality towels and markets them exclusively through department stores.

The chances of success with a differentiation strategy are greater under certain conditions. First, there should be some way for consumers to distinguish between the offerings of two or more competitors. The differences between Fords and Porsches are obvious, but can you tell one brand of sewing needle from another? Second, the differences between competing products should not be so small that they are trivial. Third, the consumer must care about the product; otherwise the differentiation strategy will not have much impact. Furthermore, the product features that are emphasized must be desired by a substantial portion of the population.

Product differentiation can be costly. Creating a difference in consumer perceptions often requires a major investment in promotion, packaging, branding, and the like. The marketer must be able to afford the expense that will be incurred by taking this approach. On the other hand, the rewards of this strategy, if it succeeds, can be substantial. Many consumers purchase the well-known Clorox brand of bleach over lower priced brands even though the products are chemically identical.

Over time, markets seem to move from a mass-marketing approach to increasing product differentiation, and ultimately to splintering into an increasing number of segments, and now into segments of one. Ford's Model T competed against a great many fewer competitors than Porsche does in today's auto market. Now that the auto market has splintered into dozens of regional, behavioral, and psychographic segments and many hundreds of product offerings, mass marketing is out of the question. The only way to get ahead in the auto market is to focus more narrowly and more accurately than the competitors—as Porsche is doing in its new direct-mail campaign. When this logic is extended to other products, it implies a competitive force pushing companies inexorably toward finer targets and more segments, presumably at ever-higher marketing costs. In fact, this does seem to be the case. There are certainly more products and more segments every year. Differentiated marketing is a difficult game to play, and the final moves are still unclear. Will the game really end in one-on-one marketing? The differences between business and personal relationships make this possibility unlikely. However, there is certainly room to maneuver between current efforts at segmented marketing and this one-to-one ideal.

A Revival of Mass Marketing?

Just to be controversial, we are going to make an unpopular forecast: that, far from a one-to-one future, we see a future in which mass marketing revives and takes its

---

FOR YOUR IMAGINATION

McMass Marketing

An interesting spin on mass marketing is offered by the *mass customization* strategy in which customized goods or services are mass marketed. How can that be? It's easier to explain by example, so we are going to give you a homework assignment. Walk into a McDonald's (or similar fast-food restaurant) and examine the menu, most likely displayed on a brightly lit board above the registers. No denying this restaurant markets to the masses and keeps its menu simple and limited to facilitate high-volume delivery to its millions of customers. That's mass marketing. But now step closer to the registers and listen to what people are ordering. In a few minutes, you can observe 10 or more customer orders. And if you do, you will notice something remarkable: in all likelihood, each order will be unique!

That's because even a small, standardized restaurant menu offers customers the potential for dozens of unique combinations of food and drink options. Restaurants are the classic example of mass customization, since they traditionally produce the product to order. But new examples are emerging rapidly these days—such as the use of "guest preference pads" at Ritz Carlton Hotels. (All employees carry these pads and take notes as they learn about a customer's preferences, so that the information can be stored in a database and used in future service interactions.)

If you can think of ways of producing a customized product or service to order in your industry, without raising prices or narrowing your appeal, then you too can adopt mass customization. We'll encounter additional examples of this new way to personalize mass marketing later on in the chapter.

---

place alongside other marketing strategies. In fact, we think we see clear evidence of a mass marketing revival already.

MARKET SEGMENTATION—THE STRATEGY OF SUBDIVIDING THE MARKET

When they choose to use a segmentation strategy, marketers view a particular market as consisting of many smaller parts whose members share certain characteristics. Market segmentation thus involves breaking down a large, heterogeneous market into small, more homogeneous segments as Porsche did when it targeted 300,000 of the 80 million U.S. car owners. Separate marketing programs, generally

EXHIBIT 7.1.   Basic product preference patterns.

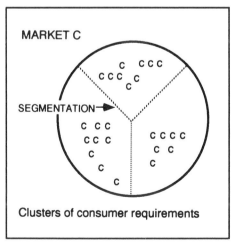

with a different product, are developed to meet each segment's particular needs. In this way, the company is able to provide a product and marketing mix that "fits" a relatively homogeneous part of the total market. As a result, market segmentation results in a better match between what the marketer offers and what the market desires.

This approach has its drawbacks, however. For one thing, research expenditures increase as more market segments are investigated. Production costs rise because production runs are shorter and the efficiency of mass production is lost. Finally, sales in one segment may be sacrificed as another segment is served—for example, Coca-Cola's addition of Cherry Coke cut into its sales of Mr. Pibb. On the whole, then, segmentation provides a better match between the product and the consumer, but not without substantial costs.

Markets can be broken down in many ways, as we'll discuss shortly. What marketers look for are distinctive groups of consumers within the total market. Sometimes there is no such group—that is, the market is totally homogeneous (Exhibit 7.1 on p. 205). At one extreme, for example, is the market for rubber bands. Because there are no (recognized) sets of consumers with different wants in this market, the market aggregation strategy is the proper approach. At the other extreme, carpenters, homebuilders, tailors, and furniture upholsterers face consumer demands that are highly diverse in that each individual has a unique set of requirements. The marketer can try to serve all, many, or some of those markets' diverse desires. As noted earlier, however, the costs are likely to be high; there is little opportunity for mass production standardization, which is one reason why houses and Porsches are so expensive.

For market segmentation to work well, marketers need to find a pattern of similarities in which consumer preferences form distinct clusters. Exhibit 7.1 shows different patterns of consumer needs. Only Market C offers the clusters of distinct groups that lend themselves to segmentation.

Effective Use of Market Segmentation

Market segmentation is not always the best strategy. For it to be effective, the marketer must answer the following questions:

1. Can the Market Be Identified and Measured?

Marketers must be able to identify which consumers are members of a particular market segment. There must be a shared characteristic that can be used to include or exclude consumers from the group, and that characteristic must be measurable. How can marketers identify and measure consumers whose vision is poor or whose scalps are itchy. These are difficult, perhaps impossible, traits to measure—yet marketers of contact lenses and shampoos probably wish they could do so.

Similarly, researchers have found that birth order (whether you are the oldest among siblings for example) influences your consumption behavior.[6] For example, firstborns show a proportionately greater tendency to achieve in life and as a consequence show greater interest in entrepreneurially oriented products such as business loans, and business start-up seminars. But let's say you wanted to send a direct mail promotion for a book on entrepreneurship to firstborns? It would be pretty hard to compile that list. The idea is not a practical one.

In contrast, Gaines Foods markets its Cycle dog food to clearly identified market segments. The company found that many dog owners think of their pets as four-footed humans with special needs. These owners respond favorably to Cycle because it is formulated to match their dog's age and activity pattern. Four products are marketed under the Cycle label, each designed to meet the needs of an identifiable segment: Cycle 1 for puppies, Cycle 2 for young adult dogs, Cycle 3 for overweight dogs, and Cycle 4 for older dogs. Dog food buyers know the age and condition of their dogs and can make the right choice at the store when Gaines labels its products in this manner.

2. Is the Segment Large Enough to Be Profitable?

Because market segmentation can be costly, unless a segment is large enough to generate a sales volume that will ensure a profit, it is not worthwhile to design a unique marketing program for that segment. Some segments are small yet have enough purchasing power to be profitable. For example, only about 10 percent of fur coats are sold to men, but this small segment's profit potential is very high.

One segment that is proving large enough to be profitable is people who are overweight and don't plan to do anything about it. In the United States, 62 million people are classified as overweight by the American Heart Association, and their numbers are growing faster than the population as a whole. That has supported a thriving diet industry for decades. But now some marketers have targeted those among the overweight who don't want to fight it anymore. Brand name magazines and catalogs with names like Amplestuff and BBW—for Big Beautiful Woman—are mining this new segment.

3. Is the Market Reachable?

For a segmentation strategy to succeed, marketers must be able to communicate effectively and efficiently with each segment chosen for attention. Some segments, even though they may be quite large, cannot be reached effectively. For example, potential buyers of inexpensive watches are not likely to read any one magazine or view any one television program. Thus, much of the promotion cost would be wasted in that it would be directed at people who are not interested in the product. Compare the ability of furniture companies to reach their market through magazines such as *Metropolitan Life* and *Better Homes and Gardens.* Sometimes direct marketing can be used to make a market reachable for the first time. Porsche's investment in list development gives it better access to its market than its competitors have.

Douglas Fugate, a marketing professor at Western Kentucky University, points out that homosexuals and lesbians in the United States make a difficult target market because they can be hard to reach. He writes that "In some cases, this can be accomplished through point-of-purchase promotions. For example, in South Miami Beach, restaurant owners place pink dots in store windows to alert vacationing homosexuals that their business is welcome." But, he finds, reaching larger audiences through electronic and print media is often more difficult because it requires the use of "readily identifiable encoding techniques such as same sex couples and avoidance of more conventional gender role behavior." Because media often reach both gay and straight consumers, "there is a risk of negative perceptual and economic pressure by the heterosexual community."[7]

In societies in which sexual orientation is the subject of strongly held values, segments defined even in part by sexual orientation are inevitably tricky to reach. Long-distance telephone companies are finding ways around this difficulty, however, as a promotion by MCI illustrates. The company developed a special promotional offer targeted at gay business owners, and used the membership list of the National Gay & Lesbian Business Alliance to distribute it. Problem solved.[8]

4. Is the Segment Responsive?

Unless a segment is likely to react to the marketing program, there is little reason to develop a unique program for that segment. Clearly, members of the segment must be willing to purchase the product in response to a particular marketing mix. For example, in a market known for flat sales, Orville Redenbacher found a responsive segment for his "gourmet popcorn," which claims to be lighter, fluffier, more tender, and bigger than ordinary popcorn. He markets to the segment that wants to pay more for better quality. Other popcorns, however, use mass marketing. There is probably no responsive segment of people looking for cheap popcorn, for example.

5. Is the Segment Expected Not to Change Quickly?

Designing and executing a marketing program aimed at a particular market segment takes time. For it to be profitable, the segment should be stable with respect to the wants and needs of its members over a considerable period of time. If it is not, the strategy chosen by the marketer may turn out to be inappropriate for that segment. Some markets, such as those for clothing and accessories, are known for their fickleness and must be approached with great care.

Potential Bases for Market Segmentation

How do you segment a market? This question is both complex and critical. It is complex because there are many possible ways to market a segment, and it is not always obvious which one to use. It is critical because how you segment the market often determines the success of your marketing strategy. Also, many new products arise from new ways of segmenting the market. Exhibit 7.2 lists many of the ways in which markets are segmented.

Creative approaches to segmentation offer considerable opportunity to the marketer. *Creative approaches to segmentation offer considerable opportunity to the marketer.*

EXHIBIT 7.2.   Commonly used bases for market segmentation.

Descriptive Bases

Demographic variables

Age	Under 6, 6–11, 12–19, 20–34, 35–49, 50–64, 65+
Gender	Male; female
Income	Under $5,000; $5,000–10,000; $10,001–20,000; $20,001–30,000; $30,001–50,000; over $50,000
Occupation	Managerial, professional, office worker, skilled trade, technical, homemaker, general laborer, student, sales, farmer, foreman, craftsman, public official
Education	Less than 8 years, 9–11 years, high school graduate, technical/ vocational school, 1–2 years college, 3–4 years college, college graduate, graduate or professional degree
Family size	1–2, 3, 4, 5+
Family life cycle	Young single; young married–no children; young married– youngest child under 6; young married–youngest child at least 6; older married with dependent children; older married with no children at home; older couple–retired; widow or widower
Religion	Catholic, Jewish, Protestant
Nationality	American, British, German, Chinese, Japanese, Italian, French, Spanish, Scandinavian, Latin American, Middle Eastern

Geographic variables

Region	Northeast, Midwest, West, Southwest, Southeast, Atlantic, Mountain
Density	Urban, surburban, rural
Climate	Warm, cold
Population	Under 5,000, 5,000–20,000, 20,001–50,000, 50,001–100,000, 100,001–250,000, 250,001–500,000, 500,001–1 million, over 1 million

Behavioral Bases

User status	Nonuser, ex-user, potential user, first-time user, regular user
Brand loyalty	Loyal, switcher
Usage rate	Heavy user, light user, nonuser
Benefits sought (toothpaste market)	Taste, decay prevention, brightness, plaque prevention, low price
Personality	Gregarious, achieving, egotistical, ambitious
Lifestyle (American men)	Quiet family man, traditionalist, discontented, ethical, highbrow, pleasure oriented, achiever, he-man, sophisticated
Social class	Upper, middle, lower
Occasion	Special, usual
Readiness to buy	Unaware, informed, interested, intending to buy

We want to make sure you think about that statement. You see, segmentation innovation is the best-kept secret of marketing. Most marketers pursue the same markets because they see the markets through the same eyes as their competitors. And thus they must play—and win or lose—by the same rules. Only those who find new ways of seeing their markets are able to change the rules, to play beyond the boundaries of the competitors' fields.

Therefore, we want you to study the following material on how markets are segmented carefully—and then do your best to rewrite it! Hopefully by the time we do a third edition of this book, your company's radical new segmentation strategies will force us to redo the whole chapter.

We are working with a number of clients who are engaged in segmentation innovations right now. They are re-defining customer segments based on cohorts—a new concept we explain at the end of this chapter.

Descriptive Bases for Market Segmentation

One of the most frequently used methods of subdividing a market is demographic or socioeconomic segmentation. Demographic variables include age, sex, family size, marital status, race, religion, and place of residence; socioeconomic characteristics include income, occupation, and education. These variables are most helpful in describing market segments because they are easy to measure and often prove to be good indicators of consumer wants, needs, preferences, and product usage. The following are some examples:

- Noting that the number of young adults aged 20 to 24 who have skin problems now exceeded the number of teenagers with such blemishes, Richardson-Vicks introduced Clearasil Adult Care. Adults are now an important market segment for acne medicine as we learned in Chapter 6.

- Learning that 15 percent of cookware customers are male, San Francisco-based Williams-Sonoma, a 26-store cookware chain, purchased mailing lists from men's magazines such as *Gentlemen's Quarterly* to boost its catalog sales.

- With the growth of older "silver" segments, Selchow and Richter markets a version of its Scrabble board game with tiles that are 50 percent larger than normal.

Geographic differences are another commonly used basis for market segmentation. In this case, a market is divided according to consumers' locations, which influence many of their needs and wants. Marketers use nations, states, regions, counties, cities, or even neighborhoods as bases for segmentation. For example, New Englanders scoop up an average of 23.1 quarts of ice cream a year, more than consumers in any other region. In the sunny Southeast, the average is only 11.57 quarts. What you drink may also be influenced by where you live. The South, with 32 percent of the population, accounts for 48 percent of tea consumption and only 21 percent of wine drinking. People in the Northeast, with 22 percent of the population, drink 19 percent of the tea and 30 percent of the wine.

Marketers going international are compelled to perform geographic segmentation. The traditional multinational segmentation approach has been to partition the world on political boundaries and to create a separate marketing mix for each country. With at least 125 countries in the world, however, the difficulty of treating each as an individual market can easily be seen. Many companies group nations into segments, but this is not always appropriate. Consider the Middle Eastern countries of Iran, Iraq, Saudi Arabia, Kuwait, the United Arab Emirates, Egypt, Syria, Israel, and Lebanon; they are all quite different. The Emirates, for instance, have no formal business laws, whereas the Egyptian legal system is very old and based on French law. Furthermore, these markets are all highly nationalistic in their cultures, creating even greater heterogeneity. Although they seem culturally similar to outsiders, they may view each other as different, and even as enemies—witness the Iran-Iraq war and Iraq's invasion of Kuwait. Although geographic segmentation based on grouping nations is often used to divide the world, it is not the best method; it overlooks many political and cultural differences among countries.

Behavioral Bases for Segmenting Markets

Descriptive variables can be a useful basis for dividing up markets; however, these variables do not get beneath the surface. Behavioral variables can give the marketer greater insight into the motivations of consumers in a particular market segment. Thus, behavioral variables can be a much more powerful means of segmenting markets than descriptive variables. They can be viewed as determining variables, whereas descriptive variables are qualifying variables, that is, variables that "qualify" a person to be a member of a certain market, but do not determine what he or she will buy.

One behavioral basis for market segmentation is user status. Some members of the market have never been users of the marketer's product or brand. These consumers represent a special challenge, because they must be persuaded to change their buying behavior—and they will tend to resist such a change. If the doctor who received the Porsche letter (described in the beginning of this chapter) has always favored restored MGs, it will be difficult to convince him another sports car is better. Then there are ex-users, those who have switched to another product or brand. This group also needs to have its perceptions changed—again, a difficult task. First-time users are another segment, one that is likely to be more responsive to marketing efforts.

With the percentage of women buyers of motorcycles growing from 7.5 to 10 percent of the market in the last decade, motorcycle marketers have taken steps to convert more of these traditional nonusers. The first step was to raise cycle consciousness through a nearly $1 million promotional campaign cosponsored by the four leading Japanese manufacturers: Honda, Yamaha Motor Corporation, Suzuki, and Kawasaki. The "Discover Today's Motorcycling" campaign's objective was to take the "motorcycle mama" image out of cycling and to show it as a leisure activity in line with the ideals of the women's movement. It seemed to work; in 1987, women purchased 21 percent of Kawasaki Motor's smaller sized 250 "Baby" Ninja model and 16 percent of Suzuki's more powerful 650 Savage bikes. (Yes, these shares of product sales are far higher than the 10 percent market share cited earlier because the Baby Ninja and 650 Savage are targeted at female buyers.)

In a more contemporary example, a wide variety of marketers are courting the adventurer in us—at least in the segment of adults in the United States who agree with the following statements:

- "I often crave excitement."
- "I like trying new things."
- "I like a lot of excitement in my life."

If you analyze survey data collected by Simmons Market Research Bureau's Choices System and SRI Consulting's VALS2 program, you can find out that 11.7 percent of the adult U.S. population agrees with all three statements. These people crave excitement, and thus are far more likely than most to take up dangerous sports like sky diving and bungee jumping.[9] As a result of the marketing efforts of firms like Primal Instinct, a Palo Alto company that helps people jump off hot air balloons, bridges, and cliffs, more and more consumers are trying such adventures.

Segments can also be based on brand loyalty—the marketer's favorite behavior! Some consumers are brand loyal. Others are constant switchers; their next purchase is totally unpredictable. Naturally, marketers would like consumers to be loyal to their brands. They entice consumers to try specific products through such strategies as free samples and cents-off deals in the hope that brand loyalty will develop. Such loyalty will happen when the fit between the attributes of the product or brand and the needs of the consumer is strong. Marketers also constantly attempt to maintain the loyalty of consumers who have already developed a preference for their brand. Postpurchase service and attention to product quality are ways of achieving this.

Segmentation by product usage involves distinguishing heavy users of a product or brand from light users and nonusers. Marketers who examine product usage rates often find the "80-20 principle" at work—20 percent of the market accounts for 80 percent of the sales. Although this rule of thumb cannot be applied to every product, it indicates the importance of a rather small group of buyers to the well-being of many firms.

Exhibit 7.3 shows the results of two studies, conducted 20 years apart, that examined purchase and consumption behavior for 16 categories of products. Users were assigned to the "light half" or the "heavy half" depending on whether their usage was low or above the median for the category. Certain product categories, such as cola, frozen orange juice, and bourbon, were found to contain segments in which one heavy-half household purchased as much as eight light-half households. This clearly illustrates the value of usage segmentation. (What is less clear to us is why the data also show a trend toward non-usage of toilet paper. Is it really true that 5 percent of U.S. consumers don't use it? Either people are stranger than we think, or there is something funny about the data. Actually, in marketing it's best to be a skeptic. Let's assume both are true—that people are weird *and* the data are no good!)

EXHIBIT 7.3. Examples of product usage segmentation.

Product	Light Half		Heavy Half		Nonusers	
	1962[a]	1982[b]	1962[a]	1982[b]	1962[a]	1982[b]
Soaps and detergents	19%	25%	80%	75%	2%	6%
Toilet tissue	26	29	74	71	2	5
Shampoo	19	21	81	79	18	6
Paper towels	17	25	83	75	34	10
Margarine	17	23	83	77	11	12
RTE cereals	13	20	87	80	4	14
Cake mixes	15	17	85	83	27	26
Frozen orange juice	11	16	89	84	28	32
Sausage	16	18	84	82	3	31
Cola	10	17	90	83	22	33
Hair fixative	12	19	88	81	54	47
Beer	12	13	88	87	67	59
Lemon and lime drink	9	13	91	87	42	61
Dog food	13	19	87	81	67	70
Hair tonic	13	25	87	75	52	78
Bourbon	11	5	89	95	59	80

[a] Chicago Tribune Panel Data.
[b] Simmons Study of Media and markets.
Source: Victor J. Cook, Jr., and William A. Mindak, "A Search for Constants: The 'Heavy User' Revisisted!" *Journal of Consumer Marketing, 1,* Spring 1984, p. 80.

The heavy half—those who are heavy users of the product—is especially attractive to many marketers because it is often relatively easy to identify and measure. For example, department stores can analyze the buying behavior of charge account customers, banks can assess how their services are used, and many syndicated services provide information about heavy users of consumer products.

An increasingly popular and extremely powerful approach to market segmentation is benefit segmentation. This approach focuses on the primary benefit that the consumer seeks. The marketer analyzes information about consumers' desires and translates that information into marketing programs that will satisfy those desires. This approach assumes that differences in benefits sought are the basic reason for the existence of different market segments. Although consumers seek as many benefits as possible from the products they buy, the value they attach to various benefits can differ significantly. That is, consumers do not often expect a product to provide many benefits all at once; rather, they are looking for one overriding benefit. Buyers of Levi's jeans seek "durability;" buyers of Elmer's Glue-All want "adhesion;" and buyers of Lego Toys' building blocks are looking for "possibilities." As a perceptive marketer once remarked, "Consumers do not buy three-quarter-inch drill bits; they buy three-quarter-inch holes." When using benefit segmentation, the marketer must identify the basic need that consumers seek to satisfy and apply this knowledge in developing the marketing mix. Selling Porsche on the basis of fuel economy would be a waste of time, regardless of how well the marketing program was executed.

A study of marketing managers found 65 percent agreeing that consumers' tastes for certain goods and services are becoming increasingly similar worldwide.[10] Consumers in different countries will differ demographically and culturally, but they may seek the same benefits. Nestle, for instance, found cat owners' concerns for feeding their pet the same throughout Europe. Focusing on the universally recognized independent nature of cats, Nestle created a pan-European campaign for its Friskies Dry Cat Food that stressed dry cat food as better than wet foods, given cats' indifference to eating (wet cat food dries before they finish it).

Personality segmentation has also been used to divide markets. The underlying concept is that if personality segments can be identified, products and brands can be given "personalities" that are consistent with those of the different personality segments. Marketers therefore have tried to use certain personality traits—dominant/passive, conservative/liberal, impulsive/thoughtful, and the like—to identify market segments. Most efforts along these lines have met with frustration, however; personality traits don't seem to be much help in understanding buying behavior.[11]

Recently marketers have looked at personality from a different angle and found a more promising way of identifying market segments. Called lifestyle or psychographic segmentation, this method divides the market into segments based on how consumers live, as reflected in their values, attitudes, and interests. Exhibit 7.4 offers some dimensions on which lifestyle is measured.

In researching the lifestyle patterns of consumers, marketers measure three things: activities, interests, and opinions. Opinions include beliefs, attitudes, or values. Stanford Research Institute (SRI) blended demographic and lifestyle variables (called VALS, for Values and Lifestyles) to create psychographic portraits of nine categories of Americans. SRI conducted a mail survey that drew responses from over 1,600 adults.

EXHIBIT 7.4.   Lifestyle dimensions.

Activities	Interests	Opinions
Work	Family	Themselves
Hobbies	Home	Social issues
Social events	Job	Politics
Vacation	Community	Business
Entertainment	Recreation	Economics
Club membership	Fashion	Education
Community	Food	Products
Shopping	Media	Future
Sports	Achievements	Culture

Source: Joseph T. Plummer, "The Concept and Application of Lifestyle Segmentation," *Journal of Marketing, 38,* January 1974, pp. 33–37.

Analysis of the data resulted in four broad categories of Americans—need-driven, outer directed, inner directed, and combined outer and inner—which were subdivided into nine lifestyle segments, each with a distinct set of values, needs, beliefs, drives, dreams, and special perspectives.[12] Recently, SRI updated VALS on the basis of a new survey, VALS2. These two surveys are especially popular with advertisers, although some marketers think they are a waste of time. (See the special discussion of VALS at the end of this chapter.)

Some evidence suggests that the VALS categories have counterparts in other countries.[13] Three cross-cultural psychographic segments have been identified: international sophisticates, semisophisticates, and provincials. The first segment has become increasingly important to global marketers, including the purveyors of such designer goods as Gucci, Louis Vuitton, Burberry, and Hermes.

Other Bases for Segmentation

Marketers sometimes employ social-class segmentation. As noted in Chapter 6, sociologists have suggested many ways of dividing the population into social classes; no one system is agreed upon by all. Yet at the basis of any breakdown of the population into classes is evidence of homogeneity in values, ideas, attitudes, lifestyles, and behavior within each class. The 300,000 recipients of the Porsche letter are no doubt similar in many ways. One way to view Porsche's strategy is as a class-based segmentation of the auto market.

West German household appliance manufacturer Braun AG has segmented the U.S. market on social class and targeted young, upscale "nouveau riche" consumers whose conspicuous consumption and deep pockets provide a match with its brand's high-quality performance and stylish European design. Priced 10 to 30 percent higher than U.S. counterparts, the appliances nonetheless sell well.

Occasions can also be used to segment markets. Certain occasions have special meanings. Significant events in our lives, such as graduation, marriage, and retirement, as well as holidays and other special events, often involve the use of special products. Candy, watches, flowers, and greeting cards can be marketed to segments based on special occasions. And Hallmark Cards is doing its level best to help make any day a special occasion by marketing a line of what the card industry terms "non-occasion cards," which further break down into any day and friendship cards. The idea is that many consumers feel there are too few occasions and too few opportunities to think of their friends and families. So why not make a non-occasion an occasion by sending an appropriate card?[14] Amazing how elastic a market segment can be if you have enough marketing imagination to stretch it!

Stage of buyer readiness is another helpful basis for segmentation. Sometimes consumers can be classified on the basis of how much they know about a product or brand and how interested they are in buying it. Some people are totally unaware of the product; others are aware of it; and still others are informed about it, interested in it, even intending to purchase it. Each stage requires a marketing program with a slightly different slant. For instance, the marketer needs to catch the attention of the unaware segment and make it aware. For those who intend to buy, the marketing program must emphasize price and other factors that will prompt them to buy the product.

Single versus Multivariable Segmentation

Segmentation can be based on one or more of the variables just described. Using only one basis for dividing a market is easier than using more than one; however, using one variable clearly is less precise than using more than one, since most markets are complex.

For example, beer drinkers can be broken down by age. Consumption is highest in the 18- to 24-year-old group; 61 percent reported in a survey that they drank beer during the last month. Next highest is the group aged 24 to 34 at 58 percent, then the 35 to 39 year olds at 44 percent. Only 25 percent of over-40s report drinking beer in the last month. With this data, the marketer could target younger people. But this is still a large, undifferentiated group.

The survey results also indicate that 83 percent of beer drinkers are men, and only 17 percent are women. By combining this data with the age data, the marketer could focus on younger men. Although the target is better focused, the group is still diverse.

The picture becomes clearer when market research data on the benefits consumers seek in beer are also included. For example, 76 percent care most about taste, and 5 percent about calories. Using benefits sought, age, and sex, the marketer can define much more specific segments. For example, a brand could be targeted at 18- to 24-year-old men who seek good taste in a beer—a smaller and more homogeneous segment than any based on only one or two of the variables.[15] A visual representation of this three-variable segment is provided in the "How Do You Like Your Beer?" diagram (Exhibit 7.5).

Steps in the Market Segmentation Process

Having explored the concept of market segmentation, we can now look at how marketers actually carry out this process. The six steps in the market segmentation process are discussed below.

1. Determine Market Boundaries

The first step is to define the market to be served. The marketing manager must keep in mind the business definition outlined in the strategic marketing plan. If the company is in the low-cost modular-housing business, for example, a different definition of the market should result than if the firm's focus is on luxury condominiums. The marketer should also consider the types of competition discussed in Chapter 2—generic, form, and brand. Given the broad definition of the firm's business, what are its generic competitors? In the low-cost modular-housing business, generic competition would come from trailer homes, apartments, rental houses, other low-cost houses, and

EXHIBIT 7.5. Segmenting the beer market.

a. Percentage of age segments who drank beer in the past month

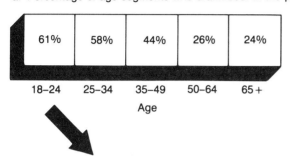

b. Percentage of men and women who drank beer in 1984

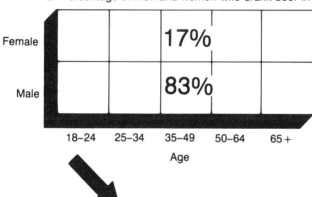

c. Percentage of men and women seeking various benefits

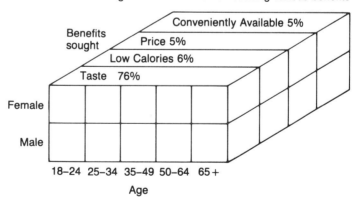

so on. Thinking about these questions forces the marketer to consider the basic wants and needs of the market to be segmented.

2. Decide Which Segmentation Variables to Use

We have discussed many variables that can be used to segment a market. An important step in the segmentation process is to sort through these variables and decide which are most likely to be useful. Sometimes marketers simply collect data on as many potentially useful variables as possible and then use data analysis to cluster people into segments. This "hunting expedition" approach is useful in some instances, particularly lifestyle segmentation, but in general it is more effective to select appropriate bases for segmentation in advance. Marketers have also found that product—specific variables are more closely tied to marketing decision making.

3. Collect and Analyze Segmentation Data

This step is the domain of marketing research. At this point, appropriate questionnaire items are developed and samples designed. Once the data have been collected, the marketer can use a wide range of analytical techniques to determine which segments of the market have the greatest within-segment homogeneity and between-segment heterogeneity. The entire process of market segmentation is focused on identifying groups whose members have the same unsatisfied wants and needs. Thus, the segments that emerge should be based on behavior-related variables such as benefits or lifestyles.

4. Develop a Profile of Each Segment

The next step is to select from the vast array of possible descriptive variables an appropriate set to fill in the portrait of the segment. Demographic and geographic variables create a more complete picture of each segment of the market. These variables should be related in some way to the actual buying behavior exhibited within the segment.

5. Target the Segments to Be Served

Now the marketer can look for opportunities. Which segments offer the most attractive opportunities? Where is the best fit between the organization's resources and those opportunities? How many and which segments should be pursued? The competitive situation and the firm's financial resources, special skills, unique technologies, image, objectives, and mission must be taken into consideration. The size of the market segment and its potential profitability must not be ignored.

6. Design a Marketing Plan

Once the segments to be served have been targeted, the marketer must decide how to go about serving them. The attributes of the product that appeal to the members of each segment must be identified. The segments served by competitors must also be identified, and then a strategy for getting the attention of consumers in each segment must be developed. The product's features must be designed or redesigned and the promotional campaign structured to create the image that the marketer intends.

SELECTING TARGET MARKETS

The market segmentation process identifies the segments that the marketer may choose to address. The marketer must evaluate those segments and decide which one or ones to serve. Most marketers would agree that they want to direct their efforts toward the segments that are potentially most profitable. Closely allied to profitability is response sensitivity, that is, the likelihood that a given segment will react to a marketing program with the desired buying behavior. However, research has shown that these bases for targeting are rarely used. Marketers often use the number of consumers in a segment as a basis for targeting that segment. A survey of consulting firms that conduct segmentation studies uncovered the following bases for targeting: "the best target had the heaviest users, these people are looking for product benefits our client's brand can deliver, and more women 18 to 34, the group the client has always gone after, were in this target segment than in any other."[16]

Although marketers often target the largest segment of the market, that segment does not always offer the best opportunity. Often the largest segment faces very heavy competition; often, too, consumers in that segment are very satisfied with competitors' products and brands. In many cases, the best choice is a segment that has been neglected by the competition—consumers who are likely to be dissatisfied with existing products and brands. The marketer that focuses on such segments has a better chance of success.

For example, companies like Green Tree Financial Company are making millions by lending money to people with bad credit histories. Now, that might seem like a dumb thing to do, since those who have defaulted on past loans are more likely than the average consumer to default again. But they are also desperate, because their poor credit history makes it all but impossible to get a conventional loan for a new car, mobile home, motorcycle, and other big-ticket items they may wish to purchase. And so lenders specializing in this segment have learned that they can get away with charging the highest interest rates legally allowable which gives them more than enough profit to make up for the higher default rate. Some people think it gives them too much profit—especially those having to pay the high interest rates. And perhaps the growing attractiveness of the poor-credit borrower segment will attract enough competition to lower those rates a bit, but in the meantime, this is a highly profitable segment for companies like Green Tree.[17]

When the marketer has evaluated the potential of each possible market segment, the next task is to decide how many and which segments will become the targets of the organization's marketing programs. The marketer has three target strategies from which to choose: concentration, differentiation, and atomization. (That is to say, there are currently three commonly used strategies. However, someone will eventually discover a new approach, and its novelty will provide an advantage. As you learn "truths" such as these, always look for creative ways to extend them.)

When marketers decide to serve a single market segment, they are pursuing a concentration strategy. Companies that have taken this approach include Primal Instinct, the bungee jump company that targets adventure lovers, and Porsche with its narrow focus on upper-class sports car drivers. The strategy is common among business-to-business marketers. For instance, there are many manufacturers that specialize in supplying component parts to auto makers—a pretty narrow market segment by any definition! A concentration strategy allows the marketer to direct all of its efforts toward satisfying a single group's desires.

This targeting strategy is not always best, however. It ties the firm to a single market segment; if that segment declines in size or consumer tastes change, the firm stands to lose. Not only will the company's financial resources be threatened, but the marketer's image may be tarnished as well. Furthermore, when a marketer becomes firmly focused on one segment, it may be unable to move into others. When Porsche introduced its 924S model in 1987 and priced it at $19,999 to appeal to middle-of-the-road buyers, the company's image was seriously hurt. Sales dipped 45 percent. In response, Porsche removed the low-end models and jacked up prices 23 percent to resecure its luxury, high-price image in the United States where it markets half of its annual production.

But the hurt to Porsche's image was deep. In 1992, sales were just one-fourth of their 1986 peak. It wasn't until 1997 when the Porsche mystique returned. Sales rebounded with Porsche's new Boxster sports car enjoying a one-year waiting list.

Most marketers that employ market segmentation find it profitable to direct their efforts toward several market segments. This is known as differentiated marketing, or the multisegment strategy. It involves varying the marketing mix through products, prices, promotional efforts, distribution arrangements, or a combination of these elements. Sometimes companies pursue different segments under different brand names, as The Limited does through its Lerner's subsidiary.

In a market *atomization* strategy, each individual consumer is treated as a unique market segment. Although forecasts suggesting that all consumer markets would be atomized by the 1990s proved false, this approach is popular among industrial firms. It is based on the idea that each customer has unique needs and concerns that the marketer must satisfy.

Atomization is traditionally used for certain consumer goods, including custom-built homes, tailor-made suits and shirts, and furniture reupholstering. And it is now being extended to many consumer products and services under the new rubrics of direct marketing and one-to-one marketing. We will provide a practical overview of the media strategies and database management techniques of the new direct marketers in a later chapter.

Alert readers quickly recognized the atomization strategy in the expert's forecasts of a switch to one-to-one marketing as quoted in this chapter's opener. However, their timetable for a complete switch to one-to-one marketing by the end of the 1980s proved incorrect. In a more recent book by direct marketing experts Stan Rapp and Tom Collins, *The Great Marketing Turnaround*, we found the prediction that "individualized marketing" will predominate by the end of the 1990s.[18] And many other experts are now hailing "micromarketing" with the same enthusiasm. Is the age of one-to-one marketing finally going to arrive? Well, you know we are skeptics at heart, but we can't help remarking that new information technologies are finally coming on line to take the atomization strategy farther than it has ever gone before. Scanner data from retail store registers now supports database mining capable of revealing individual preferences. And database marketing is certainly on the upswing, fueled in part by the emergence of the World Wide Web as a marketing medium.

Add all this up and you get an increasing move toward the atomization strategy, whether under this name or under the micromarketing, one-to-one marketing, mass customization, or individualized marketing banners. For example:

> Stash Tea Co. included a tiny ad for its catalog on its tea-bag wrappers. About 150,000 tea drinkers responded . . . many mentioning such personal details as their favorite brew. Stash . . . sent just a catalog to one group of customers. Another group received the catalog and a chatty note that used information that the customers had included in their letters.[19]

The result of this experiment in personalized marketing was three times as many responses from the group receiving both letter and catalog (30 percent versus 10 percent). The Porsche letter quoted in the beginning of the chapter is another example.

Here is an interesting example in which a service is customized over time to suit each individual user's needs precisely. The example comes from Individual, Inc., a Burlington, Mass. clipping service/research service. Customers who sign up for this company's First! service collaborate with a customer service representative to define key words for the company to use in its electronic searches of news stories and articles. That's not revolutionary, of course—many clipping services do the same. But then the company's software takes over, collecting relevance ratings for each clipping from the customer and analyzing those ratings to improve the search criteria every day. At first, customers rate roughly half the clipped articles as relevant to their interests, but after a month the software has perfected the search and 80 to 90 percent of all articles are rated as relevant to the individual client's interests.[20]

But not every effort toward atomization is a success. For example, Quaker Oats tried a series of coupon mailings to 18 million households, intending to track each household's response via a unique identity number on coupon bar codes so that future coupon mailings could be personalized to each household based on prior responses. But the high cost (and, one suspects, an underwhelming result) has put this program on hold.[21] Some practical obstacles do remain to truly personalized marketing, including in some cases a lack of imagination about how to implement this strategy.

In selecting a targeting strategy, the marketer must consider a number of factors. For instance, the firm's resources must be substantial if it plans to target several segments. Offering a wider selection of products and marketing programs greatly increases the costs of doing business. If resources are limited, a concentrated strategy may make more sense. A firm with a homogeneous product, perhaps a commodity, would be more likely to succeed using a concentrated strategy. Closely allied to product homogeneity is market homogeneity. If the market has the same basic wants, needs, and preferences, serving multiple segments may be difficult, if not impossible. Competitors' strategies must also be kept in mind. When competitors are employing a multisegment strategy, it may be appropriate to follow suit.

STRATEGIC POSITIONING

In Chapter 2, we saw how competitive activity can be likened to doing battle, complete with aggressors and defenders, attack plans, and actual assaults. The battlefield on which that warfare takes place has been said to be the mind of the consumer.[22] Consumers' behavior is guided by their perceptions of reality. Their interpretation of what they sense shapes their behavior. Marketers compete for consumers' attention by presenting various sensations that will allow them to arrive at a certain conclusion about a product or brand: Charmin is soft, Dove is for dry skin, Crest fights cavities. In this way, marketers' actions establish a distinct place for a product or brand in the minds of consumers. All the ways in which the marketer communicates with the consumer determine the psychological place that will be held by the product. Positioning, then, consists of all the actions taken by marketers to achieve this goal of managing the marketplace's perception.

Positioning Strategies

Strategic positioning is a result of communicated perceptions about a product or brand. It is different from image. Image is a global impression about a product, whereas a position assumes a reference point in the mind of the consumer, a point that is generally set in relation to the competition. The strategy is to find one or more characteristics that can be used to set apart the product or brand from competitors. Thus, in the highly fragmented shampoo market, which is overflowing with brands that promise body or control, renewed life for dull or damaged hair, elimination of split ends, and avoidance of dandruff, S.C. Johnson offered Agree, the shampoo that fights the "greasiest." This unique positioning strategy quickly gained Agree a 7 percent share of the shampoo market.

Effective marketers understand the value of establishing a solid position in the minds of consumers. The following sections discuss some alternatives among which marketers can choose in deciding on a positioning strategy.[23]

Product Attributes

The most frequently used approach to positioning attempts to associate a product with a specific feature or characteristic. Beers, for example, have been positioned against one another on the basis of lightness versus heaviness, imported versus domestic, light versus dark color, and the like. A company's own brands also can be positioned on the basis of product features—Miller High Life versus Miller Lite on the calorie dimension, Beck's Light versus Beck's Dark on the color dimension. A new product can be positioned on the basis of a feature that has been ignored by competitors. Other products can be positioned on the basis of existing features. Thus, whereas most paper towels have established positions on the basis of absorbency, Viva was introduced with the advertising slogan "keeps on working," pushing durability, and was followed closely by Brawny with its emphasis on strength.

Sometimes marketers attempt to broaden their market by positioning their brand with respect to two or more product features. Tylenol, for example, was advertised as "more powerful but safer" than aspirin. Although this strategy has been successful for Johnson & Johnson, marketers must not try to be all things to all people. If too many product characteristics are added to the positioning strategy, the market can become confused and the product's position can become cloudy.

In global marketing in which the brand image is standardized over many cultures, the features of "high tech, high touch" (function/emotion) seem to transcend cultural boundaries and provide a mechanism to position products in multicultural markets.[24] BMW is positioned worldwide as "The Ultimate Driving Machine," whereas print advertisements for VISA in Saudi Arabia and other places display the card with a backdrop of high-quality, high-price possessions. These extremes of high tech and high touch hit at universally understood appeals and can result in high involvement on the part of the consumer. The thrill of driving is known the world over, as is the desirability of owning gold and diamond jewelry.

Benefits, Problem Solutions, and Basic Needs

Closely allied to positioning on the basis of product features is positioning on the basis of the consumer's reason for buying the product. Yogurt has been positioned as "healthful," diet soft drinks as "keeping America trim," and light (i.e., low-calorie) beer as "less filling." Brands as well as products have been positioned in this way. Procter & Gamble introduced gender-specific disposable diapers in the United States, Europe, and Japan to solve what consumers indicated were the biggest problems with existing diapers—leakage at the waist for boys and at the legs for girls. The new diapers feature a "leak-guard zone" in the front for boys and in the middle for girls. "Boys and girls won't change, so we did," says a Belgian commercial. "Vive la différence."

Price and Quality

Marketers can gain a competitive advantage by offering products that are perceived as high in quality. A high price sometimes acts as a signal of quality. (Porsche's prices are predicated on this theory.) Often marketers offer more in terms of service, added features, or other advantages to warrant the higher price. Thus New Balance, the Boston-based athletic shoe company, offered the following print ad for its top-of-the-line 1300 running shoe: "Mortgage the house. The New Balance 1300 costs more ($130) than any running shoe you've probably ever owned. But, then, it offers more." The ad goes on to explain what the product offers in the way of added comfort and protection, finishing with: "The 1300. Proof that in running, it pays to dig deep."

Specific Use

Products can also be positioned on the basis of a special use. Gatorade has been positioned as a beverage for athletes who need to replace body fluids; AT&T has positioned itself as an emotional link to distant loved ones; and Campbell's has long spelled out for consumers the value of serving soup for lunch. Arm & Hammer has suggested numerous uses for its ubiquitous baking soda—it can be used not only as a baking ingredient, but as a toothpaste, a bath salt, and a deodorant for refrigerators, garbage cans, sink traps, and kitty litter boxes.

Product User

Numerous marketers have established a position for their brand or product by associating it with some well-known personality. Star athlete Bo Jackson ("Bo knows") has sold Nike sneakers; Jim Palmer has advertised Jockey underwear; and Bill Cosby has characteristically and comically touted Jell-O pudding pops. Such positioning is not limited to profit-driven firms. For example, a former president's wife lends her name to the Betty Ford Center in Rancho Mirage, California, a drug rehabilitation center, and publicly promotes its benefits.

Marketers also position products on the basis of user categories. In 1968, Oshkosh B'Gosh was a small Wisconsin clothing manufacturer with children's clothes making up only 15 percent of its sales. When a local mail-order house displayed in a catalog the company's bib overalls for children, 10,000 orders resulted. The next year Bloomingdale's and other children's specialty stores picked up the line. By 1988, the company's sales had increased 2,160 percent, with children's clothes accounting for 90 percent of sales.

Positioning against a Competitor

Another approach to positioning is to take an explicit or implicit stance against a competitor. When a competitor has a well-entrenched position, it can often be exploited by a direct reference to it. One of the classic examples of this approach is Avis' "We're Number Two. We try harder." The implication is that Hertz, the leader, has become "fat and flabby" and that Avis offers better service because it must to survive.

Comparative advertising has been used for years in the cola wars. Remember the Pepsi Challenge, in which Pepsi staged blind tastes against its arch-rival Coke in the United States in the 1970s? A majority of consumers favored Pepsi over Coke in these tests, which generated great footage for commercials and boosted Pepsi's market share. But this kind of gloves-off marketing is not as common in many other countries. Mexicans didn't take the Pepsi Challenge back in the 1970s, even though

Mexico is the world's second largest soda market and many ad campaigns run on both side of the border with only minor changes. So in 1996, Pepsi decided to try this same ploy in Mexico.

But secrecy was essential to avoid a counterattack by Coke, so television commercials for the Mexican Pepsi Challenge were filmed in Canada and plans for in-store booths were kept secret until the last possible minute. When the first commercial aired, inviting Mexicans to take the Pepsi Challenge, Coke was caught off guard. And within a few months, Pepsi was reporting a 13 percent jump in sales in targeted cities.[25]

Positioning in Relation to Other Kinds of Products

Some products are positioned in relation to particular classes of products. For example, granola bars are positioned in relation to candy bars, other snack foods, and even desserts. Stouffer's Lean Cuisine line of low-calorie dishes is positioned against dinner entrees. Lever Brothers' Caress hand soap, instead of being pitted against other toilet soaps, is positioned as a bath oil product.

Developing a Positioning Strategy

The development of a positioning strategy is highly dependent on the techniques of marketing research. The procedure for identifying an appropriate position involves a series of seven steps that have been refined and improved in recent years.

1. Determine the Relevant Product/Market

Many products are intended to satisfy more than one want or need. A candy bar, for example, is a source of energy, a snack, a dessert, a reward, and even a substitute for a meal. A product thus can be positioned in many different markets. The first step in positioning, therefore, is to list the possible wants and needs that the product may satisfy (i.e., the product/markets that might be served).

2. Identify the Competitors

An upscale beverage such as Perrier bottled water has a variety of competitors, including soft drinks, other natural spring waters, alcoholic beverages, beer, even tap water. Generally there are both primary and secondary competitors. Primary competitors are those that compete to satisfy the core need—other natural spring waters in Perrier's case. Secondary competitors are indirect competitors, those that do not come immediately to mind when one thinks about what the consumer wants or needs. Marketing research can be very valuable here. Consumers can be asked what products they use to meet a particular need: "When you come in hot and thirsty after engaging in some athletic event, what do you usually do to quench your thirst?"

3. Determine How Consumers Evaluate Options

When faced with a problem, people generally evaluate the possible solutions to see which one is most likely to satisfy their needs. The standards on which such an evaluation is based are the foundation on which product positions are built. The marketers must understand these standards and the relative importance of each one in the consumer's decision. Again, marketing research is needed.

4. Learn How Competitors Are Perceived

The marketer must also identify the positions held by competitors. Those positions could be based on product attributes, usage situations, or user groups. Exhibit 7.6 shows the positioning of various domestic and foreign automobiles along two dimensions: product attributes and user groups.

5. Identify Gaps in Positions Held

An analysis of the positions of competing products will often reveal areas in which there are many competitors. In Exhibit 7.6, for example, such a position is held by Lincoln, Cadillac, and Mercedes. A close inspection of the chart indicates, however, a gap in the lower right-hand corner. No one has provided a product that is reasonable in cost yet also has a high-spirited snazzy sports car appeal. This does not necessarily mean that efforts should be directed toward filling that gap; some analysis of the market segment represented by the gap must be made. That segment must meet the segmentation criteria of size, accessibility, identification, responsiveness, and stability.

EXHIBIT 7.6.   Perceptual map of brand images.

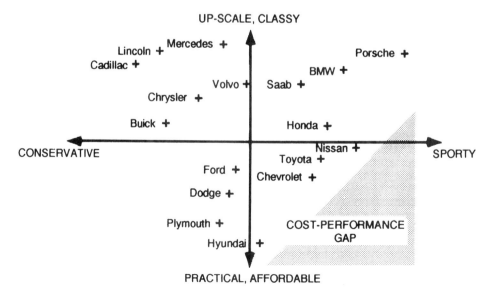

6. Plan and Carry Out the Positioning Strategy

Once the target market has been selected and the desired position determined, the marketer must design a program that ensures that every piece of information about the product or brand that is transmitted to the market will create the intended perception in the mind of the consumer. This means that the product's characteristics and price must be consistent with the desired position and that the outlets chosen to distribute the product must also communicate the appropriate message. The promotional campaign is at the center of the positioning strategy—the promotional messages must also convey the appropriate information to the market.

7. Monitor the Position

We have discussed how the environment in which marketers operate shifts over time. It is extremely important to make sure that the intended position is the one actually achieved by the product or brand. The actual position should be continually monitored and any needed adjustments made through changes in the marketing program.

TARGETING IN PRACTICE

We have focused thus far on the nuts and bolts of segmentation, targeting, and positioning. Taken together, they form three dimensions of the same picture, allowing the company to identify a group, target its marketing message on the group, and achieve a distinct position in that group's perception. Porsche's list development produced a segment of 300,000 car buyers out of the 80 million car owners in the United States. A careful analytical and creative process was required to develop a mailing and companion print advertising campaign that targeted this segment and strengthened Porsche's unique positioning relative to other sports cars.

Behind every successful segmentation, targeting, and positioning effort is an in-depth understanding of the segment. While the mass marketer can get away with only a general understanding of the customer, targeting demands a fuller acquaintance. The full range of analytical tools described in Part Two of this book must be applied in the effort to make a three-dimensional image of the targeted consumer pop from between the two-dimensional lines of the available marketing information.

This struggle to clarify the image of the customer is a recurring theme—both in modern management and within the pages of this book. Therefore, it seems fitting to end this chapter with three detailed examples of current efforts to bring the customer into better focus. In the first, the effort occurs at the neighborhood level, on the assumption that neighborhoods are characterized by common demographic and social attributes. In the second, the marketers focus on the value systems of consumers, trying to find useful patterns and groupings. In the third, the focus in on cohorts, the groups of people who share common values, attitudes and experiences because of when and where they grew up.

Marketing by Neighborhood

Thomaston, Georgia, is a city where people gobble up the National Enquirer; zero in on roller derby; and are prodigious buyers of curling irons, hair-setting lotions, and deviled ham. They worship Hardee's. And they are much like the folks in Tarboro, North Carolina, and those in Childersburg, Alabama. In sharp contrast is Huntington, New York, where new homes, new station wagons, country club membership, and electric toothbrushes and depilatories are the shoppers' rage.

Through its computer system Prizm, Claritas crunches census data on the 240,000 neighborhoods in the United States into 40 different prototypes that often very accurately profile life within them, including the purchase behavior exhibited, from amount of aspirin in the medicine chest to number of aboveground swimming pools. From this mountain of information, Claritas is able to show differences in what would seem to be very similar communities.

Consider the yuppie communities of what Claritas calls Young Suburbia—a subdivision of River Mist, northeast of Atlanta—and Young Influentials—Vinings, Georgia. People in predominately white-collar, baby-boomer communities play a lot of tennis, belong to health clubs, play backgammon, and purchase the same number of umbrellas. Yet many more River Mist yuppies have children than those in Vinings. This explains why people in Vinings buy three times as much Irish whiskey, take twice the number of cruises, and buy pregnancy tests, which are shunned in River Mist.

This kind of information is invaluable to marketers wanting to rifle their marketing campaigns. A marketing manager for Mountain Bell Telephone Company in Denver believed his best prospects for his call-waiting and call-forwarding services were Young Suburbanites and other parents: "Our internal analysis showed that kids were it." Prizm showed that his best potential customers were childless Young Influentials—ambitious, active, and hating to miss that critical phone call!

Not all of Claritas's insights have proven fruitful. Prizm was not helpful in marketing medical encyclopedias, for instance. Buyers tend to be hypochondriacs, and they live in all neighborhoods. When Pillsbury Company used Prizm to locate eaters of its Green Giant frozen corn on the cob, Prizm indicated that they were predominantly black. But with such a huge market, Pillsbury could not put coupons in everyone's mailbox as it hoped it could do. It needed a finer tuned analysis. Also, Prizm's geodemographic analysis offers little in the way of understanding the personal touches needed to meet demand. It merely creates assumptions about the "why" that drives marketplace behavior—assumptions that marketers have to test. Yet Prizm is still hailed as a giant step forward in market segmentation.

General Motors' Buick division, for example, uses Claritas to keep a sharp eye on market goings-on. Its Buick Electra, at one time a status symbol akin to the Cadillac, had dropped its presence in wealthy, upscale neighborhoods and become the prestige car in rural areas. Said a GM marketing researcher, [These rural people] "liked to buy cars for image and like them to be big, prestigious, bulky." So when GM brought out a shorter, sleeker Electra, the company was understandably worried. But Prizm showed Buick to be right on the money: The new model had success, to use

Prizm's terms, in the Furs and Station Wagon neighborhoods, in the Young Suburbias, and in the Pools and Patios, but lost ground in the Sharecropper neighborhoods.[26]

VALS and VALS2

Whereas Claritas divides the nation into 40 types of neighborhoods, SRI divides it into eight psychographic groups. This very different way to look at the nation is as powerful as Prizm when it comes to targeting products and services to specific consumer groups.

The original VALS, introduced in 1978, became the first psychographic segmentation system to be widely accepted in business. Many ad agencies use VALS to help them create fuller, more human targets than demographic statistics alone can provide, and a variety of marketers position their products to appeal to specific VALS segments. To create VALS, SRI drew on psychologist Abraham Maslow's classic hierarchy of needs (see Exhibit 6.4), dividing the U.S. population into nine segments. The bottom segment comprises the Survivors, who are focused on the most basic survival needs. At the top, as in Maslow's hierarchy, are the Integrateds. Two separate paths lead to the top. The outer-directed path moves from Belongers to Emulators and, just below Integrateds, the Achievers. The inner-directed path leads from I-Am-Me's, to Experientials, to the Societally Conscious.

What do these titles mean? They are defined briefly next. (Determine which group best describes you.)

Need-Driven Segment

- *Survivors*—Very poor, mostly elderly women. Purchases focus on necessities. Buy used cars, household cleaners, hot cereals. Total 7 million.
- *Sustainers*—Poor, angry, resentful. Majority under 35 and without high school education. Purchase cigarettes, pancake mixes, candy, canned soups at high rates. Total 12 million.

Outer-Directed Segment

- *Belongers*—Aging, traditional, patriotic, content. Purchase American cars. Buy homes, freezers, and recreation equipment at high rates; high-tech stuff at low rates. Half of the Belongers graduated from high school. Total 64 million.
- *Emulators*—Ambitious, competitive, ostentatious. Emulate people they see as richer and more successful than themselves. Purchase more foreign and specialty cars, also home electronics. Consume high rates of beer and vodka. Graduated from high school. Total 17 million.
- *Achievers*—Successful, materialistic, hardworking, middle aged. Include lawyers, doctors, and business managers. A quarter graduated from college. Purchase luxury and mid-sized cars, various home appliances, wines. Total 35 million.

Inner-Directed Segment

- *I-Am-Me's*—Young, impulsive, experimental, very active. A third have college degrees, and many are still students. Income fairly low. Buy used, foreign subcompact cars, bicycles, stereos, jeans, beer. Total 5 million.

- *Experientials*—Youthful, often artistic. Seeking direct experience, action, personal development. Over a third are college graduates. Fairly well off. Purchase new foreign cars, camping and sports equipment, wines, yogurt. Total 8 million.

- *Socially Conscious*—Concerned and mission oriented, often active in social and political issues. Mature and successful. Three-fourths have college degrees. Purchase foreign cars, dishwashers, food processors, exercise/camping equipment. Consume higher than average rates of alcohol and seafood. Total 20 million.

- *Integrateds*—Psychologically mature. Open-minded and understanding. Consumption is quite varied. Total 1 million.

Did you decide which group best describes you? If publishers marketed books using VALS (they don't), this book would probably be targeted at Achievers and at Emulators and Experientials as they begin to advance in their careers. The reason publishers don't use VALS is obvious when you think about how they distribute their products. Bookstores deliver to a broad cross-section of the book-buying public and do not collect any detailed information about their customers. A highly targeted marketing strategy for a book would run into trouble when it came time to distribute it, because bookstores cannot supply publishers with specific market segments. (The situation is different with professional books, which can be targeted at specific professional groups quite accurately through direct-mail solicitations. If the publisher advertised this book to you through the mail, it was because of your job title or magazine subscriptions, not your VALS classification.)

In fact, many marketers find it difficult to put the VALS typology into practice. Although it may be helpful to visualize the target consumer as fitting the Integrateds profile, it may be impossible, or at least impractical, to focus distribution and advertising efforts on the less than 2 percent of Americans who fit this profile. These people don't hang out at any particular mall or even read any specific magazine. (Newsstands are crowded with titles, but presumably not with Integrateds Life.) Easier by far are efforts to target larger VALS segments, such as the 40 percent of Americans who fit the profile of Belongers. But the larger categories also create problems for marketers. As Jane Fitzgibbon, a senior vice president at the ad agency Ogilvy and Mather, explains, marketers would often say, "If 40 percent are Belongers, why should we bother with the rest?" Other users found the variations in segment size a problem. For example, when WISH-TV in Indianapolis used VALS to profile its audience, it found that two-thirds fell into only two segments. This turned out to limit the kinds of advertisers the station could attract. In addition to these practical problems, SRI decided that "the link between values and lifestyles and purchasing choices seems less strong than it had been," as Edward Flesh, the director of SRI's VALS program, puts it. So SRI went back to the public with a survey of 2,500 people in 1988, and gave birth in 1989 to VALS2.

VALS2 uses eight psychographic groups of almost equal size. They are said to be based on "unchanging psychological stances" rather than the more changeable lifestyles and values of the earlier VALS groups. Although some of the names are similar, SRI insists that the new groups are completely different.

At the bottom of the scheme are the Strugglers who, like the Survivors of VALS, tend to be elderly and poor. At the top are the Actualizers, replacing the old Integrateds, and characterized by high self-esteem and high incomes. Between these two extremes are six groups, arrayed in a two-by-three matrix based on whether they have high or low resources (economic, social, and psychological resources), and on whether they are principle-oriented, status-oriented, or action-oriented. These six groups are the core of the consumer market, and they are explained further next. (Again, which of these types best fits you?)

Principle-Oriented Segment (The purchases of these two groups are guided by views of how the world should be.)

- *Fulfilleds*—High resources. Mature, responsible professionals. High education levels. High incomes, but value-oriented shoppers. Openminded.

- *Believers*—Low resources. Modest incomes, conservative attitudes. Focused on family and the church. Patriotic.

Status-Oriented Segment (The purchases of these groups are guided by the actions and opinions of others.)

- *Achievers*—High resources. Focused on work; successful. Enjoy their jobs and families. Conservative, favor established products. Proud of their success and believe it is important for others to be aware of it.

- *Strivers*—Low resources, but values similar to Achievers. Style is important to them.

Action-Oriented Segment (The purchases of these groups are guided by desire for social or physical activity and risk.)

- *Experiencers*—High resources. Young (median age of 25), and full of energy. Avid consumers, favoring new fashions and designs.

- *Makers*—Low resources. Self-sufficient and narrowly focused on their immediate environment of family, work, and recreation. Favor practical, functional purchases.

Is VALS2 much ado about nothing? Probably not. WISH-TV is certainly happier now that VALS2 shows the station's audience as falling into three major and four minor segments, rather than only two as in the old VALS. More important, however,

SRI has created a new standard that many advertisers and marketers find helpful in visualizing their target markets. And its categories are proving useful to a variety of consumer-products marketers.

It remains difficult, however, to find VALS segments using conventional marketing. But since the first VALS was introduced, considerable progress has been made in targeting individuals and narrowly defined segments. Four firms now specialize in providing what the trade affectionately calls "geodemographic cluster systems." Claritas was profiled previously. CACI, Donnelley Marketing Information Services, and National Decision Systems also specialize in delivering narrowly defined groups of consumers that share a cluster of common characteristics. Their customers, like SRI's, generally purchase annual subscriptions that give their marketing departments full access to the provider's databases and reports. SRI now collaborates with each of these research firms so that VALS2 profiles of their clusters are available to marketers. This means that a marketer can now use one of these databases to actually identify neighborhoods, mailing lists, or other practical groupings that are rich in a targeted VALS segment. VALS has come of age, and so, too, has targeted marketing.[27]

Segmenting the Market by Cohorts

At his company, Lifestage Matrix Marketing, which does consulting work reflecting the aging of American marketplace, Charlie has pioneered a new segmentation approach, called cohort analysis, that not only feels good conceptually but also really works when it is applied. The results of the application of this approach have been showcased in both *Fortune* and *The Wall Street Journal*.[28] It carves out market segments based on similarities held by virtue of being born at a certain time and having common motivations based on widely held values.

Individuals are bound together by being born over a relatively short and contiguous period of time. These people are called a generational cohort and are highly influenced by the era in which they grew up, by the external events that were happening when the group was coming of age, generally between the ages of 17 and 22. The values formed during one's adolescent and early adult years become deeply rooted and are carried through life largely unchanged. During these value programming years, one's life-long and life conduct values are ingrained as the result of, in large part, experiencing major events that produce significant emotional impact on one's mind. These values are referred to as *cohort effects*.

Consider how different cohorts treat spending and saving. Today's older adult generation, those aged 75 to 84 today, began working during the Great Depression. Their conduct with respect to money is very conservative . . . still today. Having experienced the worst of economic times, this age group values security and frugality . . . they save for that rainy day. Those, however, in the 51 to 74 age category were influenced by the Depression but *also* experienced the boom times of the post-World War II period. This group has attitudes toward saving that are less conservative; they are more willing to spend than the older group.

In sharp contrast to the Depression-scarred is the freewheeling generation that grew up during the hippie revolution. This birth group defied the establishment, sought individualism, and was skeptical of everything. This cohort can be characterized as buy-now-pay-later and its members will carry this value (along with their credit cards) into the next century as they journey through middle age and on into old age.

Cohort values are strongly held, deeply rooted, and rather permanent. And buying behavior—desires, preferences, and attitudes—can be expected to mirror these values throughout each individual cohort's lifetime. These values provide the communality for each cohort being targeted as a separate market segment. Since these cohorts can be described by the ages of their constituents, they offer an efficient vehicle for direct marketing.

The terms *cohort* and *generation* are not exactly the same, although both refer to groups that are age-linked. A generation is usually defined by its years of birth and childbirth. For example, a generation is usually 20 to 25 years in length, or roughly the time it takes a person to grow up and have children. But a cohort can be as long or short as the external events that define it. The World War II cohort is only 6 years long, and the Post-War cohort is 18 years.

The Six U.S. Cohorts

American adults can be divided into six distinct cohorts, or market segments, ranging in age from the Depression Cohort (aged 75 to 84) to what many people are calling Generation X (aged 20 to 31). The roughly 4 million people who are aged 85 and older are not included for two reasons. First, this group is much smaller that other cohorts. Also, much of their consumer behavior is controlled by physical need. There are also over 68 million persons under the age of 20. No one knows yet how many of them will belong to Generation X by holding the same cohort values and how many will create new cohorts in the next two decades.

Many companies we have worked with have jumped on the cohort bandwagon and found reflecting the values of cohorts in their marketing rewarding:

- Levi Strauss designed its Slates line of pants for the post-war cohort males that are getting a bit fuller in areas covered by these trousers. Its advertising features a middle-aged man engaging his restaurant waitress in dancing the tango, a dance craze that hits at the heartstrings of 50+ year-olds who ballroom danced their way through their coming-of-age years.

- Nostalgia Television, a cable network, found that the usual 1.5 percent response rate to potential cable subscribers could be ramped up to over 10 percent when photos of Douglas MacArthur and Dwight Eisenhower were put on direct mailings to World War II and post-war cohorts.

- And the Mazda Miata, originally targeted at baby boomers, found its sales gravitating to older buyers that identified with the two-seater convertibles that defined their late adolescence/early adulthood.

It's one thing to develop theories, and quite another to make them work in real-world marketing. Cases like these are therefore extremely exciting to Charlie and his associates at Lifestage Matrix Marketing. They prove that cohort marketing really works.

If you want to design products and promotions for specific cohorts, you need to know a bit more about them. Here is a summary of each cohort and what makes it tick.

- *The Depression Cohort*—Born 1912–1921, coming of age from 1930 to 1939. Currently 13,054,000 people, 7 percent of the adult population.

    This cohort was defined by the Great Depression. Maturing, entering the workforce, trying to build and support families during the Thirties had a profound influence on this cohort in many areas, probably most strongly regarding finances: money and savings. To many of today's business managers, the Depression seems like ancient history, almost apocryphal, like the Great Flood. Yet to this cohort, it was all too real. To put the Depression in perspective, the S&P 400 (the broadest measure of the economy as a whole available at that time) declined 69 percent between 1929 and 1932 in a relentless and agonizing fall. It wasn't until 1953—24 years and a world war later—before the S&P index got back to where it had been in 1929!

    People starting out in this environment were scarred in ways that they carry with them today. (It should be noted, however, that the 10 percent of the population that were attending college during the 1930s don't seem to exhibit the Depression cohort effects nearly as strongly; the theory is that anyone sufficiently well-off to be in college at that time were personally insulated from the Depression to an extent, and while some of the attitude set is similar, it tends not to be nearly as severe.)

    And, while not a cohort-defining event, it's worthy of note that the Depression cohort was the first to be truly influenced by the contemporary media: radio and especially motion pictures. The popularity (and power) of radio was seen in Orsen Wells' 1937 drama "War of the Worlds," which panicked thousands. The first major "talkie" was "The Jazz Singer" in 1927, and by 1933 the number of weekly paid movie admissions was exceeding that of the entire adult population. From this time on mass media have an increasingly important role in shaping cohort attitudes, as we will see with the advent of television.

- *The World War II Cohort*—Born 1922–1927, coming of age from 1940 to 1945. Currently 9,465,000 people, 5.0 percent of the adult population.

    This cohort was defined by World War II. Economically it was not a boom time (the S&P 500 gained 50 percent from 1940 to 1945, but it was still only half of what it had been in 1929), but unemployment was no longer a problem. This cohort was unified by a common enemy, shared experiences, and especially for the 16 million in the military, a sense of deferment and delay. In World War I the average duration of service was less than 12 months; in World War II the average was 33 months. Marriages, careers, children were all put on hold until the war was over.

This sense of deferment made the World War II cohort an intensely romantic one—the yearning for loved ones left behind, and for those who left to fight—is reflected in the music and literature and movies of the time. And while for many the war was an unpleasant experience, for many others it was the apex of their lives. They had a defined role (frequently more important in status than any other they would ever have), a measure of freedom from their particular social norms, and an opportunity to travel, some to exotic foreign shores, others just away from the towns and cornfields of their youth.

World War II profoundly affected more people than those born from 1922 to 1927. But a 25 year old drafted in 1942 had his core values formed about 7 years earlier, in 1935. His life was deeply influenced by World War II, but he is not of this cohort.

- *The Post-War Cohort*—Born 1928 to 1945, coming of age from 1946 to 1963. Currently 42,484,000 people, 22.7 percent of the adult population.

  This cohort is a very long one—18 years span the youngest to the oldest members. They were the beneficiaries of a long period of economic growth and relative social tranquillity. Economically, the S&P 500, which had struggled until 1953 just to get back to where it had been before the Depression, then tripled over the next ten years. There were dislocations during this time—the Korean War in the early 1950s, Sputnik in 1957, the first stirrings of the civil rights movement, a brief recession in 1958—but by and large at least on the surface, things were pretty quiet.

  The tenor of the times was conservative, seeking the comfortable and the secure and the familiar. Perhaps there was a yearning to alleviate in everyday life the global uncertainty spawned by the nuclear bomb, now in the hands of the Russians. In 1954 the words "Under God" were added to the Pledge of Allegiance, and in 1955 "In God We Trust" was put on all U.S. currency, a more benign expression of the fear of godless communism that spawned McCarthyism.

  It was a time that promoted conformity and shrank from individual expression, which is why the overt sexuality of Elvis and the rebellion of James Dean were at once popular and scandalous. But the expectation of good times became ingrained in the national fabric during this period, and although basically conservative, the Post-War Cohort (unlike their Depression Cohort predecessors) has always been willing to spend a little, as well as save for a rainy day.

- *Boomers I*—Born 1946–1954, coming of age from 1963 to 1972. Currently 32,531,000 people, 17.4 percent of the adult population.

  The baby boom is usually defined as the 76 million people born between 1946 and 1964, since this is indeed when the annual birthrate bulged to over 4 million per year. This is one instance when "cohort" and "generation" are very similar, and this is because to a certain extent the baby boom generation was self-defining in terms of cohort. Due to their numbers, the baby boomers have dominated marketing in America since they first appeared on the scene. When they were truly babies, they made Dr. Spock's *Infant and Child Rearing* the second best selling book in the history of the world, after the Bible. As pre-teens, they dominated the media in shows like "Leave it to Beaver" and in merchandising with fads like Davy Crockett caps and Hula Hoops. As teens they propelled Coke and Pepsi and McDonald's and Motown into corporate giants, and made the inventor of Clearasil rich. And they are very well educated and reflect this characteristic in their buying behavior.

The leading-edge boomers are also united by a sociological phenomenon that pre-dates the "coming of age" formative years that otherwise defines cohorts: television. Beginning in the mid-1950s, television's enormous power profoundly influenced this group. Because they were the first to experience it as a uniquely pervasive influence on styles, language, aspirations, even family dining patterns (the TV Dinner), they are forever separated by it from the cohorts that preceded and followed them. For the leading-edge boomers, the "objective correlative" (to use T. S. Eliot's phrase) is "The Mickey Mouse Club," a group event watched Monday through Friday, 4:30 to 6 PM on your local NBC station. The full impact of first-time television immersion as a social norm can be seen in the USSR: the "Evil Empire" fell not from threat of destruction, but from "Dallas," beamed for the first time into the homes of a populace without the slightest conception of the joys of capitalism.

But we have found that there are at least two boomer cohorts. The "Boomer I" Cohort began in 1963, the start of a period of profound dislocations that still haunt our society today. It ended shortly after the last soldier died in Vietnam. The Kennedy presidency seemed like the natural extension of continued good times, of economic growth and domestic stability and a "liberated" and early transfer of power from an older leader to a much younger one.

The Kennedy assassination, followed by that of Martin Luther King and then of Robert Kennedy, signaled an end to the status quo, and galvanized a very large boomer cohort just entering it's formative years. Suddenly the leadership (LBJ) was no longer "theirs," the war (Vietnam) was not their war, and authority and the establishment which had been the bedrock of earlier cohorts disintegrated in the melee of the 1968 Democratic National Convention in Chicago.

However, the Boomer I Cohort continued to experience economic good times. Despite the social turmoil, the economy as a whole as measured by the S&P 500 continued an upward climb. The Boomer I Cohort wanted a lifestyle at least as good as they had experienced as children in the 1950s, and with nearly 20 years of steady economic growth as history, they had no reason not to spend whatever they earned or could borrow to achieve it.

- *Boomers II*—Born 1956–1965, coming of age from 1973 to 1983. Currently 46,794,000 people, 26.0 percent of the adult population.

    The external events that separate the Boomer I from the Boomer II Cohorts were less dramatic than the Depression or World War II, but just as real. It was composed of the stop of the Viet Nam War (it never really ended—it just stopped), Watergate (the final nail in the coffin of institutions and the establishment) and the culmination of a decade of guns and butter which combined with the Arab Oil Embargo to end the stream of economic gains that had continued largely uninterrupted since 1945.

By 1973, something had changed for a person coming of age in America. While faith in institutions had gone, so had the idealistic fervor that made the Boomer I Cohort so cause-oriented. Instead, those in the Boomer II Cohort exhibited a narcissistic preoccupation with themselves which manifested itself in everything from the self-help movement (*I'm OK—You're OK*, various young and aging gurus imported from India) to self-deprecation ("Saturday Night Live," Mary Hartman).

The change in economic fortunes had a more profound effect than is commonly realized. Throughout their childhood and as they came of age, the Boomer I Cohort members experienced good times; their expectations that these good times would continue were thus reinforced, and the cohort mindset that was formed at that time can be seen today in a persistent resistance to begin saving for retirement. Things had been good, and they were going to stay good—somehow.

For the Boomer II Cohort, the money mindset is much different. The Oil Shock of 1973 sent the economy tumbling: the S&P 500 lost 30 percent of its value between 1973 and 1975. At the same time, inflation began to resemble that of a banana republic. The real interest rate (Prime minus the CPI) hit a record low of −4 percent. In those circumstances, debt as a means of maintaining a lifestyle makes great economic sense; and a cohort with a debt imprint will never lose it. Boomers II aren't savers any more than Boomers I; but it's because they assume they can always get a loan, take out a second on the house, get another credit card, and never have to pay the piper.

- *Generation X*—Born 1966–1979, coming of age from 1984 to present. Currently 41,119,000 people, 21.9 percent of the adult population.

  This cohort goes by a number of names—and it is still going on. Demographers call it the "Baby Busters," since the group follows the baby boomers. However, Generation X, despite the negative connotations, seems most appropriate because that appears to be the most commonly accepted nomenclature, at least within the popular media.

  Much has been written about Generation X, most of it derogatory in tone. "Slackers" (from the movie of that name); "Whiners"; "A generation of aging Bart Simpsons, armed and possibly dangerous." That seems to us to be unfair. The generation of F. Scott Fitzgerald was widely characterized as "Lost," and that describes Generation X. This cohort has nothing to hang on to—not the institutions of the Post-War Cohort, not the idealism and causes and institutions to resist of the Boomer I's, not the narcissism of the Boomer II's. These are the children of divorce, and the day-care, latch-key kids of the 1980s, no wonder they have no foundation. That they are searching for anchors can be seen in their seemingly contradictory "retro" behavior—the resurgence of Proms and coming-out parties and fraternities that the boomers rejected.

It can be seen in their political conservatism, which is also motivated by a "What's in it for me?" cynicism that repudiates liberal redistribution tendencies. And they feel alienated, an alienation that is reflected in the violence and brutal sex of their popular culture. They are resigned to a world that seems to have little hope of offering them the lifestyles of their parents.

By the year 2020, there will be but a handful of individuals who may have experienced The Great Depression in their coming of age years. Anyone in this cohort who will be alive will be over the age of 100. The World War II cohort will be similar with anyone still present being at least 97 years of age. Less than 10 percent of the total U.S. population will be from the Post-War Cohort while the two Baby Boom Cohorts will make up about one-third of the marketplace. Furthermore, over 40 percent of the population will be in a cohort as yet unclassified since the external events that shape that cohort are yet unknown; this group of individuals have yet to come of age. So keep an eye on them—they are tomorrow's hot market segments, and any insights you can gain into them will help you win them as loyal consumers before your competitors can!

SEGMENTATION: ADVANTAGE OR ADVERSITY?

Regis McKenna, a prominent Silicon Valley publicist, argued that marketers must operate in a new "age of adversity," and many others seem to agree with his thesis that marketing is increasingly difficult.[29] The proliferation of brands and the growth of targeted marketing make success in most markets more difficult than ever before. A startling possibility is that the very tools that seem to solve our current marketing problems may create worse problems in the future! A continuing drive toward segmentation forces all players to move down this path simply to maintain parity with their competitors. If your competitors adopt segmentation schemes from Claritas and SRI, you may have to as well. And next year you will try to be the one who adopts the new ideas first. Aggressive, innovative pursuit of market segmentation, targeting, and positioning is now a major source of competitive advantage. As Rapp & Collins forecast in the chapter's opening quote, marketing does seem to be driving toward smaller and smaller groups, perhaps even to groups of one where market structure permits.

But, aside from the potential adverse effects on marketers' budgets and database systems, there may be some natural checks on this segmentation trend. In most markets, buying patterns eventually defy the logic of this process. There is often some limit beyond which further breakouts do not improve explanatory power. (Quaker Oat's coupon program may have bumped into one of these limits.) The world may simply refuse to divide neatly into ever-smaller boxes. A clue that this may be the case comes from the on-the-job observation of Larry Gibson, a former research director at General Mills, that "You can never find a way of classifying consumers so one group accounts for all the purchasing . . . there are always a distressing number of other people who use your product." [30] While distressing at first blush, this fact sounds an encouraging counterbeat to the truly distressing vision of ever-increasing market diversity and the adversity it creates for marketers. The tools of segmentation are exciting and in any event requisite in today's markets. But it is encouraging to think there may be some optimal level of segmentation in each market, as opposed to the now popular vision of segmentation ad infinitum, or at least to the smallest possible unit, the single customer.

Come to think of it, the individual might not be the smallest possible unit. One might imagine a further breakdown—for example, one based on role. A company could conceivably target individuals only in their role as grandparents, for instance, to make a personalized pitch for toys or baby clothes. Another pitch might focus on the same individuals, but with different personal information and in a different role. This game might truly go on *ad infinitum!*

PART THREE

APPLYING MARKETING TECHNIQUES

You now have a good strategy and some sound insights into how you can satisfy customers and beat the competition. It took a lot of thinking to get to this point—and a lot of reading to find out how to do it. Unfortunately, it's not yet time to cash the check.

Now you must implement your great ideas. If you are going to reach out to market something to a newly defined market segment, for example, it is time to translate your concept into the right product, at the right time and place, at the right price, to move the market to purchase it.

One more thing: You have to communicate your strategy to customers. If they don't know what you want to do for them, then you'll never have the chance to do it. The promotion of your product to its target buyer is a key part of implementation. Whether it's an ad, a telephone call, a personal visit, or a page on the World Wide Web, your communications must make your offering appealing to the right people.

All these hands-on issues boil down to the need for a well-designed, tightly implemented marketing program. Your program needs to use the tools available to the marketer to their fullest. The product, its pricing, its placement or distribution, and its promotion all add up to effective implementation of your marketing concepts and strategies. That's the four *P*s of the marketing mix, and they will be the focus of this final and vital section of the book. To learn how to use them to your greatest advantage, read on!

8 PRODUCT DEVELOPMENT

The Business of Innovation

They've had a number of limited-run successes with new-product innovations. The problem is they get a tremendous sales spike when the marketing machine is turned on, but it doesn't last. They have to address the problem of their core menu offerings.

—Bill McDowell, senior editor, Chain Leader,
in reference to Pizza Hut products[1]

Good ideas don't begin around the conference table. They begin with the consumer.

—Charles Hooper, executive vice president and chief
operating officer, Helene Curtis[2]

What's usually missing is going to the field and asking dumb questions, and smelling and feeling and getting in bed with the problem so that you understand the other side of it.

—Joe McPherson, director of innovation programs,
SRI International[3]

What we have neglected is the ability to nurture fragile ideas into sturdy products before someone uneasy with the unfamiliar snips the idea at the stem. The nurturing process is called management, and innovation withers without it.

—BusinessWeek[4]

These four opening quotes are a complete lesson in product development. There is the *challenge*—the one the Pizza Hut chain faces as it introduces a new line of pasta dinners and hopes these will prove more popular than previous efforts to expand its menu. Then there is *idea generation*—when you do your best to get into the customer's head and find some spark that will inspire a bold new winner. (And yes, you need to get out of your office and spend some time observing customers if you want high-quality product concepts.) Finally, there is the *nurturing* of the idea, through all the laborious stages of development, through the dangerous time of market introduction, and then, should it take root, through what you hope will prove a long and profitable life.

Make no mistake about it. Products do have a life—and all too often, it is a short one. The greatest challenge of marketing is to develop ideas and nurture them into products that have long, expansive lives, products that grow your company and transform your industry because of their obvious value to customers. Business success is that simple—and that hard!

Proponents of the concept of a product life cycle maintain that every product moves through a series of four life stages, from introduction, to growth, to maturity, and finally to decline and eventual death. In fact, the product life cycle model is one of the most often-cited concepts in marketing. There is a great deal of circumstantial evidence to suggest that the model is valid, but little in the way of hard facts or clear theory to explain why it should be.

As a result, later in the chapter we will examine the model's underlying assumptions with a skeptical eye. The model is too useful as a descriptive framework to abandon. In fact, it not only provides a good starting point for developing product strategies, but it also provides a fine scaffolding for our two chapters on product. This chapter takes the product from development (actually earlier, because how companies first devise product ideas is vital) to introduction (and failure, when things do not work out). Chapter 9 follows the product through its initial growth to

EXHIBIT 8.1. The product life cycle.

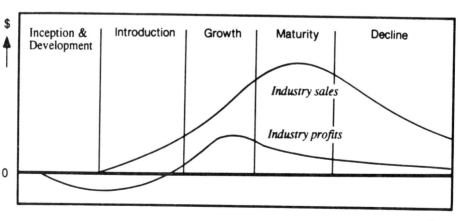

its maturity and decline—or its revival, if innovations in product management and design can be applied successfully. Sometimes it is possible to foil the product life cycle and renew a product. Unlike people, products may have more than one life (Exhibit 8.1 on page 244). In theory, at least, they may even live indefinitely. For instance, people have been selling salt for thousands of years and will probably do so for as long as there are people to buy and sell products.

WHERE PRODUCTS (REALLY) COME FROM

The product life cycle has four stages; however, the first stage of the life cycle is more accurately the inception and development of the new product concept. Often product inception is left out of the model.

The creative process that generates new product ideas is poorly understood and, in most companies, poorly managed. Time and money traditionally go into product development and testing, but not into brainstorming, customer focus groups, and other sources of creative new product ideas. Likewise, until recently, little emphasis has been placed on nurturing and evaluating new ideas within companies.

Before we move on to the exciting topic of inception, let's review what is meant by product. The product is, most simply, the tangible object a customer buys. It can, however, be intangible. In marketing, services such as automobile repair and clerical work also are considered products. It is immensely helpful, however, to broaden this simple view of the product to include a number of abstract concepts.

WHAT PRODUCTS (REALLY) ARE

A product can be viewed as containing a certain amount of potential satisfaction; the full amount is not always realized. Perhaps you have heard the joke: "How do you know if a family has any teenagers living at home?" Answer: "The clock on the VCR isn't flashing." A survey by ad agency Ogilvy & Mather found that a pitiful 3 percent of VCR owners' total viewing time goes to watching programs they prerecorded—the potential for this and other uses is not realized by most VCR owners even though manufacturers compete to cram more programming and other gimmicks into their products every year.[5]

A second way to look at the product is as a set of benefits sought by consumers. Often there is a core need—some primary, overriding desire for satisfaction. Such primary needs and wants provide individual buyers with their most important criteria for making an exchange decision. For instance, if a tennis racket buyer is seeking power as a core benefit, he or she will emphasize attributes such as high-tension strings, a strong metal frame, and a heavy handle above others, such as attractiveness, size of the sweet spot, or lightness. Closely allied to this concept of core need is the idea that the product presents a solution to a problem. In fact, it is through recognition of problems that many products are first conceived. No one would ever think of a paperweight unless they were working at their desk next to an open window on a windy day; there is no problem when the window is closed, and thus no need to be addressed by a new product.

Few marketers have expressed the role of product as solution better than cosmetics maker Charles Revson, who is said to have stated that "in the factory we make chemicals, but in the drugstore we sell hope."

Another perspective portrays the product as a set of tangible and intangible attributes that are assembled into an identifiable form. (You might find it helpful to think of services as being mixes favoring the intangible attributes over the tangible ones.) In this view, each separate product category is defined by a commonly understood descriptive name—pillows, vacuum cleaners, shirts, personal computers. These categories are called *generic products*. The product life-cycle model is most applicable at the level of the generic product. In other words, while individual models of personal computers may be on the market for only a year or two, it is the slower maturation of the category of personal computers in general that fits the descriptive and prescriptive elements of the life-cycle model, as we will discuss shortly.

There are three nested definitions of the product, each a little broader and more elaborate than the preceding: generic product, expected product, and augmented

---

FOR YOUR IMAGINATION

What, Exactly, *Is* a Toilet?

In the chapter on international marketing, we discussed the competition between American Standard and its Japanese toilet-making rival, TOTO, in their drive to bring sitdown toilets to the Chinese market. But you don't have to go to Asia to get in on the new, hot action in this ancient product category. The TOTO brand is also fighting for a foothold in North America, where it often competes with market share leader Kohler. At a few hundred dollars a unit, the roughly ten-million-toilets-per-year U.S. market is well worth fighting over.[6]

TOTO's strategy is to redefine the basic toilet by adding additional functions you didn't know you needed—but will want once you hear the good news. A traditional toilet is expected to flush; not jam or overflow, not leak or break; just flush. But the rest is up to you—including cleaning the thing (most people's least-favorite household chore) and getting rid of any unpleasant odors that are left behind when the flushing is done.

TOTO has a better idea. Actually several. Their top-of-the-line toilets include built-in deodorizers and a control panel to work the soapy jet sprays and the warm, drying blasts of air with which the thing *cleans itself.* The core product concept has just been expanded. And this time, our forecast is a thumbs up. We think these innovations are well-grounded in real customer needs. They give TOTO enough of an advantage to establish itself successfully in North America.

product. Customers have certain expectations about the products they buy, and it is helpful to recognize an *expected* product. The generic product is the core idea of a product. Yet consumers have expectations for it—what it will do, convey, and so forth. This is the expected product. In many cases, the manufacturer tries to offer a product that exceeds the customer's expectations—this is the *augmented* product.

There is, however, an additional necessary layer of complexity. The product actually consists of a great deal more than merely the tangible or intangible item purchased. It has a core benefit or service, but in most cases, this core benefit is supplemented by a series of additional attributes such as packaging, styling, quality, brand name, and so on. These attributes are augmented by services, warranties, postsale service, delivery and installation, and so forth. Although these aspects of the product are trivial for a box of paper clips, they are sometimes of overriding importance for products such as personal computers.

As we think about the conception, development, and introduction of products, we need to think of products in all their complexity. A new product may look and work exactly like an old product, for example, but have a completely different set of associated services and be distributed in a different manner. Or it may simply be a different quantity and packaging of the same core or generic product. These are as much product innovations as the more traditional innovations involving actual modification of the makeup and workings of the core product itself. And all are fair game in the creative stage of the life cycle.

PRODUCT INCEPTION

New product ideas can come from a recognition of need; for example, when 3M sales-people noticed that users of their sandpaper were troubled by the dust in their work-places. From this definition of a problem came the idea for a solution: Sandpaper that can be used wet so that no dust is created. Wet sandpaper is now an important product for 3M. And 3M continues to profit from its need-finding skills, introducing about 500 new products a year![7] 3M's formula is to spot a customer need and develop a product for it. Yet, many marketers forget *whose* need the new product should address, and develop products to fill their *own* needs instead.

That, for example, is probably why Pizza Hut continues to struggle with its new product development launches. The company and its franchisees want to grow sales, and to do so they feel they need to capture a larger share of the dinner business from other restaurants and from the growing to-go selections of grocery stores. That's their need, however, not their customers' need. Customers currently go to Pizza Hut when they need pizza. Not a sit-down meal of chicken primavera. That's something they are more likely to seek at a full-menu Italian restaurant. So our forecast for Pizza Hut's new product launches is trouble ahead. Our hunch is that pizza will continue to dominate their sales, and that they will continue to struggle in their effort to transform themselves into a competitor with Italian restaurants until they refocus on finding a need customers can't fill at those restaurants, and letting that *customer need* direct their marketing imagination.

There is another common exception to product development focused on customer needs. This one is easier to get away with, but also a source of risk. Many new product ideas can be stimulated by *technical developments.* The advances in microchip design and the rapid decreases in their cost have stimulated the development of a host of consumer products with complex internal logic. Everything from personal computers to children's games to toilets takes advantage of this technology, representing creative ways to apply it to offer new benefits to consumers.

Which way is best? Technology-driven or need-driven product development? In theory, technology-driven product development is looking in the wrong direction. Simply because something comes out of the lab does not mean it is the most valuable thing for consumers. It is better to be customer-driven than technology-driven in new product development. But as a practical matter, many companies are strategically dependent on their mastery of certain technologies. The core technologies in which they specialize are what defines them and gives them competitive advantage. If they were to discover customer needs that their technologies did not address, it would probably be a mistake to try to satisfy these needs. The companies would soon find their efforts scattered and without focus, and they would soon lose their competitive strength if they strayed too far from their core technologies. As a practical matter, many companies' new product ideas must be narrowed and focused by issues such as their areas of technical expertise, their distribution capabilities, and their customers' perceptions of them. Ideas are not easily constrained by such boundaries, so in practice, companies evolve dozens of ways—unfortunately many of them unintentional and unmanaged—to discourage the bulk of the clever ideas their people generate. (This is the main obstacle to innovation, both in products and in all the various work processes of the company. But more on this point later.)

Having argued that customer-driven innovation must be tempered by other considerations in technology-based companies, we must now qualify this remark with the observation that in most cases, technology-driven companies could go much farther toward balancing technical innovation with customer input. The evolution of the VCR industry provides a fine example.

Early VCRs were notorious for their complexity and incredibly confusing instruction manuals. The typical first-generation VCR required the operator to hit the "set" and "select" buttons eight times simply to set the clock. Programming, for that 3 percent of the time when owners dared to try it, required the operator to hit the "on/off," "select," and "set" buttons 14 times! Designed by engineers and programmers, these technological nightmares were so unusable that they undoubtedly spread through the U.S. market more slowly than they might have otherwise. (The rate at which a novel product, or idea, diffuses through a market is an important issue in product introductions, and it can be slowed by poor design and marketing.) This article about VCRs concludes, in rather grim tones, that:

> The marketing implications of overwhelming consumers with all these complex and rarely used features may be more profound than companies realize. Manufacturers of

consumer products are not only losing the interest of their customers but they're also alienating them. People have come to believe that somehow it's their fault that they can't master these products. They have been made to feel like technological illiterates. And they don't like it.[8]

Hear, hear! The failure of VCR manufacturers (and many other consumer-products companies) to design to the customer's requirements in the first place has created an opportunity for a second generation of product innovations—driven by customer needs, not technology. A manager with the Japanese VCR manufacturer JVC explains, "We've been getting more and more complaints about the difficulty of using VCRs. All video makers have been working hard to make them simpler."[9] On-screen programming is one innovation that resulted from this effort, and in fact, VCR makers have hardly tapped the rich vein created by the initial user hostility of their products. User friendliness is emerging as a major product attribute—it is on its way to being part of the expected product—and the focus of product innovation is shifting at VCR makers as this dimension becomes more important in brand competition. Customers are now brought into the lab so that engineers can observe their using the machines. Customer complaints and opinions are solicited. The VCR industry is slowly discovering marketing.

A similar process is occurring in other product categories in which marketers switched from simple nobs to sophisticated electronic interfaces when the technology became available to do so. Take the car radio. At the high end of the price range, these formidable pieces of equipment can do almost anything—remember your favorite stations, make recordings, cue up your favorite songs from a deck of CDs, sound an alarm when a stranger fiddles with them, play dead to foil car thieves. But many people use just a few of these features, there are so many buttons and displays. As a result, Volvo decided to introduce a bold new innovation in its car radios in the late 1990s: knobs! Now you can turn a comfortable round knob to tune your Volvo car radio, just like you used to do twenty years ago.

Regis McKenna, the public relations guru of Silicon Valley, has been marketing high-tech companies for decades, and he sees no reason why a technology-based company cannot be marketing oriented. In fact, "marketing oriented" fails to capture the full impact of his vision—the phrase seems to suggest a larger budget for the marketing department, whereas what McKenna envisions is an entire company, even in the labs and product development facilities, that thinks:

> Marketing is not a new ad campaign or this month's promotion. Marketing has to be all-pervasive, part of everyone's job description, from the receptionists to the board of directors. Its job is neither to fool the customer nor to falsify the company's image. It is to integrate the customer into the design of the product and to design a systematic process for interaction that will create substance in the relationship.[10]

Several fascinating concepts are presented in this quote. First, it is clear that the kinds of activities that firms are undertaking—quality improvement programs, employee empowerment, and the like—are in keeping with McKenna's view that marketing ought to be part of everyone's job description. We are seeing the beginning of a revolution, but not a complete revolution—merely a 180-degree turn, putting the customers and the people who interact directly with customers at the top of the organization chart instead of the bottom. This means management must now be at the bottom, providing the support and nourishment needed to sustain these all-important customer relationships, much as the roots of a tree support and nourish its foliage. (See Exhibit 8.2 for a visual representation of this concept that we use sometimes to explain it to our clients.) Traditionally, the company has existed to serve its managers—a feudal model, if you will. (Don't believe the saying that companies serve their shareholders—you don't see shareholders flying around on company planes, do you?) In the traditional model, the company could serve its management either by focusing on customer-defined needs or by focusing on applications of its core technologies. But now the trend is to create firms that exist to serve their customers—surely this is what McKenna means when he refers to "substance in the relationship"—and

EXHIBIT 8.2. Organizing to support customers.

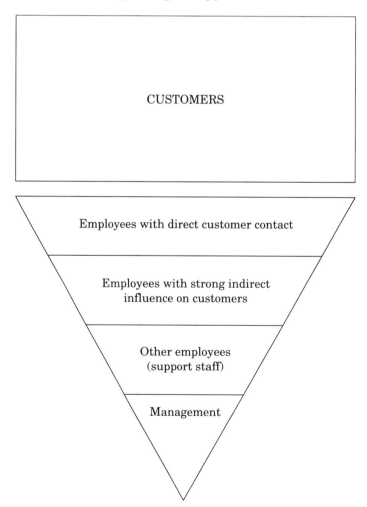

these firms are by nature customer-oriented—or customer-driven—whether or not they have a strong technical base. If this sort of firm's strategy is to nurture a core technology, it is only because this is the best way for customers to obtain improved solutions to a set of problems. The technology is truly secondary from the customer's perspective, and so must be from the company's as well.

Technology-rich DowBrands visualizes the balance of customer and technical considerations in a formula for innovation. According to Rob Grant, the marketing VP for new products, innovation is "the sum of consumer trends, leveraging of technology, and listening." Listening is accomplished through programs such as an Innovator's Club to recognize good new product ideas and the employees who generate them. The judges are typically line employees who use the products at home. Dow also gives awards and recognition to employees for new product ideas and has given away $30,000 to date in what Grant calls "an important investment in the intellect of our people."[11]

Raychem Corporation, maker of electronic and fiber-optic products for telecommunications and other industries, is another example of a very technically-oriented company that nonetheless seems able to stay focused on customer needs with remarkable clarity. Raychem's founder and CEO, Paul Cook, sees a danger in being focused on the market without a complementary focus on the technology. He explains the company's balancing of technology and customer viewpoints as follows:

> Too many American companies are only immersed in their markets. They bring along whatever technology they think is necessary to satisfy a market need. Then they fall flat on their faces because the technology they deliver isn't sophisticated enough or because they don't know what alternatives the competition can deliver. We think of our business differently. Raychem's mission is to creatively interpret our core technologies to serve the marketplace. That means we don't want to be innovators in all technologies. We restrict our charter . . . to niches that can sponsor huge growth over a long period of time and in which we can be pioneers, the first and best in the world . . . Then we draw on those core technologies to proliferate thousands of products in which we have a powerful competitive advantage and for which our customers are willing to pay us lots of money relative to what it costs us to make them.[12]

However, Raychem's customers will be willing to pay high prices only if they reap significant benefits from Raychem's mastery of its core technologies. Raychem adds value from the customer's perspective primarily by virtue of its leading knowledge in various technologies.

Also interesting is McKenna's vision of marketing's purpose as being "to integrate the customer into the design of the product and to design a systematic process for interaction that will create substance in the relationship." The upside-down organization designed to serve the customer is no longer focused on making and selling products. It is, or ought to be, focused on developing products. This is a subtle but profound insight. From the customer's perspective, everything within the organization's walls is transparent and trivial. Only the delivered product and the transactions needed to deliver it matter. Moreover, the delivered product is never good enough. Life is not yet perfect, so customers are eager for new and better products. They wish

---
| **FOR YOUR IMAGINATION** |

The Secrets of Creativity

Marketers—yourself included—need to focus on developing innovative new ideas for their products and services. Good idea. Let's get started. But how? It is impossible to "force" creativity, as the following quote from a chapter on how to be creative in Alex's marketing book, *Marketing for Dummies* (IDG, 1997), makes clear:

> Okay, time to be creative. Ready, set, GO!
> Come up with any good ideas yet?
> No?
> How about now? No?[13]

To be creative, you need to adopt behaviors that lead to creativity. And those are often different from the behaviors you normally engage in at work. For starters, you need to put creativity into your calendar and budget. At P&G, 3.4 percent of sales (or $1.2 billion) is earmarked for innovation each year.[14]

Next, you have to listen to and *encourage your itch*—the urge to solve problems and find better ways to do things. Mary O'Meara, a creative director from Young & Rubicam, provides a classic description of this behavior in the creativity process:

> The drive to solve problems creatively—with new and original solutions—stems from some chronic itch; dissatisfaction with all existing solutions. Even when the latest may be your own.[15]

In other words, don't ever leave well enough alone! Like the people at Billabong, the wetsuit makers. It bugged them that the zippers in their wet suits leaked water, and besides, metal zippers don't stretch like the rubber suits do, which can cramp your surfing style. So they kept scratching this itch, until finally they came up with a way to use Velcro and other materials as a substitute for zippers. The result is a popular new product that won an award from the Industrial Designer's Society.[16]

Third, after devoting resources to creativity and getting itchy all over with problems to solve, you need to engage in *structured creative thinking*. Don't just sit there waiting for lightning to strike. Use some of the many fun methods for generating creative ideas in quantity. Make your own lightening!

You've probably tried brainstorming, where you and a group agree to generate and write down as many ideas as possible, without criticism or ownership, so as to overcome your natural inhibitions against saying stupid things. And there are many useful variations on brainstorming—for example, you can pose questions of relevance to your itch, then brainstorm answers to them. Or you can play the old pass-along game, in which each person in turn adds to a list of ideas on a piece of paper. (Try adapting pass-along to E-mail, too!)

We also like methods that use analogies, either verbal or visual, to stimulate out-of-the-box thinking (itself an analogy for the creative process, by the way). Encourage yourself or a group to think of analogies by posing the itch as a problem, then asking, "What things/situations are similar to this problem?"

These and many other methods for generating creative marketing ideas are covered in *Marketing for Dummies.*

One other thing—*Have fun!* If your efforts to "do" creativity aren't engaging and fun, then something's wrong. Change the process, change the environment, change the mix of people, until it flows. You can't get good ideas out of a bad process.

---

to solve problems more easily and at decreasing cost, and they are open to new problem definitions and new products to solve these problems. This puts the product at the very core of the new marketing-driven company. It also puts greater weight on new product development than ever before, necessitating, as McKenna indicates, a "systematic process" for customer-driven innovation. Thus process, both in its conventional forms and in the newly evolving forms designed for the new customer-driven companies, is the subject of the next section.

DEVELOPMENT

Exactly what is a "new" product? This question can be answered in many ways. From the perspective of management, a new product is anything that an organization believes to be a new product. This approach makes some sense, because in most cases such "newness" results in new research, new organization, new advertising campaigns, and other new ingredients in the marketing mix.

What ultimately matters, however, is whether the customer sees anything new and important in the product's introduction. Many me-too products spark only management's imagination these days. Think for a minute about the new products you noticed on the shelves of your local grocery store last year. A few? Dozens? And how many did you purchase? Whatever the number, it falls incredibly short of the 10,301 new food products and the 2,863 nonfood products introduced to grocery stores during 1990.[17] (And the number of new products grows every year—15,401 were introduced to grocery stores in 1991.)[18] One of Campbell's hard-and-fast rules (one it should have established earlier, as we discuss shortly) is that new products must be substantially better than the old ones with which they compete, from the customer's perspective. This means they must be given a preference rating in consumer tests of 1.6 or more when compared with the competition. This is a substantial difference—and a hurdle that most of those 13,164 new grocery-store products from 1990 would have failed to clear. As Gordon McGovern, CEO of

Campbell's, puts it, "The consumer is ready for improved quality and service. Delivering it is the true secret of new product success."[19]

New products can be modifications, minor innovations, or major innovations. A major innovation is an item that has never been sold by any other organization, as in Intel's introduction of the semiconductor and Searle's development of NutraSweet. But not all innovations need be so astounding. Inspired by a Magic Marker, Chesebrough-Ponds developed a nail polish in a pen. Called Polishing Pen, this product brought quick praise from the cosmetics industry. Said an industry expert, "It's the best concept I've seen in cosmetics in 10 years."[20] But it may also have been the simplest. Rather than offer a new kind of nail polish, the developers simply changed its packaging—and changed the ways the product can be used as a result.

About 70 percent of the new products brought to market by large U.S. firms are modifications; 20 percent are minor innovations, and 10 percent are major innovations.[21] The same study showed that major innovations receive greater support from top management, a key ingredient in the success of new products.

Booz, Allen & Hamilton uses a model that groups new products into six categories:[22]

1. *New-to the-world products.* Products such as digital television and World Wide Web services, which result in entirely new markets.

2. *New product lines.* New categories of products that allow entry into new markets. R.J. Reynolds, for instance, added a chain of bagel stores to its line of cigarettes.

3. *Additions to existing product lines.* Taking an established product line (e.g., Jell-O Pudding Pops) and extending the product or brand (e.g., Jell-O Gelatin Pops).

4. *Improvements in or revisions of existing products.* Providing greater perceived value or satisfaction or replacing existing products with better products. The new generation of "parabolic" or shaped skis are easier to control and thus encourage people to replace old skis—boosting sales in an industry that badly needed reviving.

5. *Repositioning.* Changing the perception of an existing product, as when PepsiCo dropped the hillbilly country image ("Yahoo! Mountain Dew!") for its citrus drink and began positioning it as a drink for daredevil "Dew Dudes"—those bungee-jumping, mountain-biking bunch of guys.

6. *Cost reductions.* Offering similar value at a lower cost. Scott Paper has offered its facial tissues, toilet tissue, and paper towels at prices up to 30 percent lower than competitors' products.

Conventional wisdom has recently shifted toward favoring the bottom half of this list. For example, many managers and expert commentators have been struck by the fact that Japan's competitiveness, and losses by the United States to Japanese manufacturers in many markets, seems to be driven by an emphasis on small, incremental innovations by the Japanese companies. The U.S. companies hit an occasional home run, but the Japanese companies hit single after single and ultimately win the game. As a result, product developers are now urged to add extensions to existing brands or improve their performance rather than to chase fundamental innovations that result in new-to-the-world products. But this is stupid advice, to put it politely.

The Japanese firms may have been weak historically in fundamental R&D, but they compensated for this with better overall product inception and development—better because it is more customer-oriented, more efficiently managed, and far more rapid. Now they are beefing up their research as well, and will soon be hitting both home runs and singles. If U.S. firms bench their heavy hitters in the effort to learn how to hit singles, they will lose much more market share. The issue boils down to leadership, leadership of a market in the customer's eyes, which means advancing the customer's cause through product development more often and consistently than competitors. As McKenna says, in marketing, "What you lead, you own. Leadership is ownership."[23] The successful Japanese companies own their markets because they have led them, and if U.S. competitors mistake the issue and focus on small-scale innovation with an eye toward small-scale market share goals rather than market leadership, they will only strengthen the position of the Japanese leaders in the customer's mind. On the other hand, if they can continue to lead in major innovations, and also learn how to hold onto their lead with continuous smaller innovations, market leadership will be a realistic goal.

Competition, both foreign and domestic, is a major force in spurring innovation. But this incentive is countered by social and governmental constraints (e.g., regulations designed to protect the environment and increase consumer safety), the high costs of research (particularly for small companies), the tendency of firms to emphasize short-term return on investment, and the high cost of borrowing funds. Nevertheless, the key to success in world markets is innovation, and frequently the door to marketing superiority is improved technology.[24] As Richard Swingle, Compaq Computer Corporation's director of strategic marketing, says, "50 percent of our revenues are from products introduced in the last year. We eat our own children. If we don't, someone else will. Last year we introduced twelve new computers."[25]

Older products lose their luster and are withdrawn from the market, creating a need for new products to take their place. New products can renew a faltering image, reduce the firm's overall risk, and open up new markets and distribution channels. It is therefore alarming to see that R&D spending is again shrinking in the United States after a decade of growth.[26] Maybe that's why *The Wall Street Journal* reports that, "Food companies are starving for new ideas. Launches of new foods fell 20% last year [1996], their sharpest decline in at least two decades. After the 1980s round of mergers, food-research departments shrank . . . Kellogg, whose business depends on monitoring the breakfast table, managed to miss the onset of the bagel binge."[27] The same complaint holds true in many industries these days, but that's okay. *You* don't have to overlook major innovations. In fact, this is the best time to be doing them—when the leading companies have forgotten how!

Organizing for New Product Development

At most companies, responsibility for new products takes one of four basic forms. Many companies use the product or brand manager approach. Each manager has complete responsibility for one product or brand—determining objectives, developing strategies, setting prices and advertising budgets, and working with the sales force. The manager is also responsible for creating new product concepts and shepherding them through the development process. Often, however, managing both new and existing products is too extensive a job for one person. Some companies therefore use a system in which each new product is given to another manager after it has been successfully launched.

Other companies form new product committees, generally composed of top managers from several departments. These committees meet to develop new ideas; once the task is complete, their members return to their regular positions. Although this approach has the advantage of getting top managers involved in new products right away, it has certain drawbacks: It takes up valuable executive time, and committee members have a tendency to put their own interests ahead of those of other members.

Also, new product committees tend to take a long time to devise recommendations, and their ideas don't always work. Take Zima—a clear malt beverage from Coors that was supposed to become the hottest product for Generation Xers. Reports on its development agree that "Zima may have been the ultimate created-by-committee product."[28] A large, long-term product development team set out to develop an alternative brew. By the time they finished, the product reflected many people's ideas, but didn't taste very good. Oops!

Other organizations set up permanent, full-time, new product departments. Such a department usually is high in the corporate structure and has considerable power. Sometimes it works in conjunction with a temporary new product committee. Generally, this department plans and coordinates all the activities involved in new product development—from generating ideas to supervising the development process.

A newer approach is the venture team. At larger companies such as Dow Chemical, Monsanto, and Westinghouse, groups of managers, each a specialist in a certain area, are given the task of bringing a specific new product to market. The team combines needed resources and expertise, such as product design, engineering, capital management, market analysis, accounting, and marketing. To promote creativity, members in such a group are usually excused from regular duties and report directly to top management.

The key, but unspoken, issue in any of these structures is how they relate to the customer (the traditional emphasis is unfortunately on how the new product developers relate to the rest of the firm, not to the customer). If they have an arm's-length relationship with customers—for example, through close-ended surveys conducted by the marketing department's subcontractors—then they are unable to play the catalytic role McKenna sees for product development in the new marketing-driven firm.

We next discuss the typical stages in the development of new products: generating ideas, screening ideas, developing and testing the concept, conducting a business analysis, product development, test marketing, and commercialization.

Stage 1: Generating Ideas

The sources of new product ideas are many and varied.[29] Customers sometimes write letters suggesting new products. One study of technological innovation found that in 74 percent of 137 cases studied, the source of the new idea was the customer.[30] Many companies encourage their employees to make suggestions. General Electric gives out $2 million annually in bonuses to employees who contribute successful product ideas, whereas 3M gives trophies and certificates to innovative employees. In addition, a firm's scientists and technicians often make discoveries that lead to new products. There is evidence that innovative companies give their employees a great deal of freedom to tinker with new ideas. At 3M, one story has it that a fired scientist kept sneaking back into the lab to develop an improved asphalt shingle and eventually won a promotion to vice president. Top managers are another source of new product ideas. There are also consulting firms that specialize in idea generation. These "think tanks" assess the client's resources and objectives and devise concepts.

One widely used method for generating ideas is called brainstorming. This approach is based on the recognition that the really new ideas often mix several previous ideas to produce something that is nonobvious and exciting. (Brainstorming is a widely discussed concept, but for some reason, it is seldom practiced, even though it is simple, easy, and beneficial.) Group discussion sessions are held to generate as many new ideas as possible. The group generally consists of six to ten people. A specific problem or goal is set at the beginning of the meeting, but group members are encouraged to be as wild as they want in suggesting solutions. Practicality is not important in a brainstorming session. No idea is criticized, and hence no ideas are held back. As ideas start to flow, one leads to another. Within a short time, hundreds of ideas can be on the table, so it is important to have someone write down the ideas on a chalkboard or pad. Only after ideas are generated freely and noncritically can the group sort out the most promising.[31]

A study of over 700 companies found that firms are increasingly combining the idea-generation step with an analysis of the firm's overall business and new product strategy.[32] In this way, new product ideas are more likely to reflect the company's overall goals. This process includes the establishment of strategic roles for new products, as well as formal financial criteria to be used in measuring their performance. This firmer understanding of the purpose of new products has greatly reduced the mortality rate for new product ideas. In 1968, it took 58 new product ideas to come up with one successful new product. In 1982, the mortality rate was reduced to an average of seven ideas per successful new product,[33] and the mortality rate is thought to be declining gradually.

Although no quantitative studies are available yet to prove it, a trend is occurring toward incorporating customer ideas and evaluation into the idea-generation stage. This is done indirectly when companies such as DowBrands, GE, and 3M encourage employees to generate ideas, for this pushes the employees to think like consumers and to make informal observations of consumers in their daily lives. It is also done directly—many more focus groups and new product testing labs are now used in which customers are directly exposed to new product concepts and even asked to help develop or refine them.

Stage 2: Screening Ideas

Once a large pool of ideas has been generated, the next step is to reduce the pool to a more manageable size. Three general criteria for screening ideas have been suggested.[34] New product ideas should fit into the organization's overall strategy. They should also build on the company's resources and skills—financial, technological, and managerial. Finally, an idea must have sufficient market potential to justify further consideration. (Again, this is the conventional wisdom, but an explicit evaluation by customers does not come into the equation.)

Marketers often establish a formal method for choosing which ideas they want to examine more closely. For example, the Center for Concept Development uses an elaborate new product evaluation form.[35] It rates product ideas on dozens of factors, such as effectiveness, reliability, appearance, design, potential volume, entry position, and regulatory environment. (In general, firms will want to develop their own lists.) Each factor is then grouped with similar ones into a factor group, which in turn is combined with other groups into what this consulting firm calls "major aspects." There are only four of these: item, company, environment, and venture. To understand what they mean, examine the factor groups of which these aspects are comprised:

1. *Item.* Performance, salability, defensibility, marketing.
2. *Company.* Technology, production, market.
3. *Environment.* Competition, suppliers, government.
4. *Venture.* Support, investment, strategy.

If you want to use this structure for rating new product ideas, develop specific criteria for each factor group. For example, list the factors that ought to be related to the performance of the new product. Then rate each idea on each factor using a 1 to 3 (weak to strong) scale, and sum scores across until you know on which major aspects the idea is weak and strong.

Richard Swingle of Compaq explains, "We don't worry about how to save face. Some new products get 'critical mass' that is unstoppable at some companies, no matter what. It's going to market, no matter what. Not at Compaq." He is talking about a powerful force that both limits initial acceptance of ideas and, equally dangerous, limits the company's ability to derail a new product when it isn't holding up to expectations. This force is inertia, the tendency for organizations to resist change. It is much easier to keep going in the same direction than to do an about-face. This is why it is often difficult for companies to become good at recognizing and using novel ideas. Even if they do become innovative in this way, inertia can get them on the backswing by institutionalizing a product development effort. A company must evaluate a new product periodically during development, as if it were under evaluation for the first time. Whatever screening and analysis is performed to select ideas in the first place ought to be repeated as they are developed, perhaps at periodic benchmarks, so that losers can be spotted by management rather than by the market.

Stage 3: Developing and Testing the Concept

Throughout the stages of idea generation and screening, product developers work only with the kernel of an idea, a general concept. In this third stage, they try to make that idea more specific. For example, if they have determined that they will produce a new candy bar, the answers to the following questions might help them formulate a more specific concept from the general idea:

1. *Who will buy the new product?* A candy bar can appeal to children, adults, or the elderly—or to all three groups.
2. *What is the primary benefit of the new product?* A candy bar may appeal as a sweet, a high-energy snack, or an emergency food for diabetics.
3. *Under what circumstances will the new product be used?* A candy bar may be offered to children as a reward, or used as a meal substitute, or eaten by diabetics suffering from too much insulin.

After a concept has been developed, the next step is to test it. Consumer reactions are obtained by using a verbal description or a picture of the product and asking for candid opinions. At this point, the developers want to know how they can improve the product idea, and the best way to find out is to ask the consumer. This is commonly accomplished in the toy industry by inviting kids to come and play in a new toy lab—and watching what they do and don't play with. When the company has a winner, this method makes it obvious. For example, when Huffy's new Street Rocker kid's bike with a radio on the handlebars was tested, new product development manager Wayne Beiser found that the product "was so popular, we eventually had to pull it from the research cells because we couldn't get information on any of the other products we were testing."[36] In the computer industry, the products are brought to business or industrial consumers at designated test sites, and developers work closely with these consumers to spot problems and refine designs. This approach is applicable in any concept-testing effort, and companies increasingly look for ways to use consumers in concept testing.

Stage 4: Conducting a Business Analysis

The next step in the new product development process is to project costs, profits, return on investment (ROI), and cash flow if the product is placed on the market.

Business analysis is not a haphazard process; it is a detailed, realistic projection of maximum and minimum sales and their impact on the company's financial health. Projections of potential sales at various prices need to be made, as well as detailed cost projections for different volumes of production. Start-up and continuing costs, fixed and variable costs, and the impact of economies of scale need to be determined. Tentative marketing plans need to be set, along with the costs associated with them. Finally, a set of full-blown budgets is required to estimate the potential return on the product. The outcome of this analysis is key, for it is not enough to produce a new product that consumers like—it must also be profitable for the company to make and sell the product. Every new product concept must satisfy the parties on both sides of the equation, not only on one side or the other!

The assessment of sales and costs is not an easy task, and sometimes the rules for evaluation can be too stringent. Campbell's Prego spaghetti sauce almost failed in the business analysis stage. Corporate policy required a new product to show a profit in one year, but Prego was not expected to do so for three years. Astute managers, realizing that the one-year policy held back product development, changed the rules—and, luckily for Campbell's, Prego went national.

The business analysis must also include an assessment of the amount of risk the company will face if the new product is introduced. In general, the greater the degree of newness, the greater the risk. Production facilities, because of the huge investment they require, and marketing activities, because of their importance to consumer satisfaction, are two key areas to analyze in terms of risk. If the new product can be produced using existing production and marketing capabilities, the risk is lower. Less investment in new plant and equipment will be needed, and the marketer can benefit from already acquired knowledge of the market. On the other hand, greater tolerance of risk can lead to greater rewards. The study mentioned earlier found that the highest risk ideas (accounting for 30 percent of all new product introductions) provided 60 percent of the "most successful" new products.[37]

Stage 5: Product Development

In the next stage, the new product concept is given a tangible, concrete form: A prototype is made. The prototype can be seen and held, and its benefits and attributes can be demonstrated. Production engineers and R&D specialists construct a model; the marketer develops a brand name to match the idea or concept; packaging is designed; and the major elements of the marketing mix are put together. The positioning strategy is also examined.

The Gillette company uses a unique method to test its shaving products during this stage. Each day about 1,000 men and women in a dozen countries use Gillette prototype products either at home or at the company's facilities. They rate the products in terms of the closeness and comfort of the shave. In addition, numerous testing devices are employed: High-speed cameras and electronic gadgets measure whisker length to within millionths of an inch. Plastic casts of shaved faces are used to compare the closeness of shaves, and technicians measure and weigh the amount of stubble removed. These data—along with reports from physicists, statisticians, and metallurgists—are fed into computers that store knowledge about every aspect of shaving accumulated over some five years.

At the product development stage, many new ideas bog down for months or years, or wander off track completely. At this stage, many different functional areas of the firm are called upon to cooperate in the creation of prototypes and the development of production or delivery processes, marketing plans, and the other elements required to make the idea a reality. The traditional and most logical approach is to move the product from functional area to area sequentially, so that each element of product development is handled in turn. But this approach is no longer viable, as *Business-Week* reported:

> Many laggards have clung to a product development process derisively dubbed the "bucket brigade." Someone in a research lab comes up with an idea. Then it is passed on to the engineering department, which converts it into a design. Next, manufacturing gets specifications from engineering and figures out how to make the thing. At last, responsibility for the finished product is dumped on marketing. . . . Plans are constantly pushed back down the chain to fix problems that could have been avoided. . . . The outcome slow response times, high costs, and shoddy quality. Compare that system to the system most Japanese companies use. They take what's called a "fast cycle" approach to development—whipping out new product and reacting in a flash to shifts in consumer preference. To accomplish that, managers make communication a top priority at the earliest stages of a project. They pull together a team of experts from each business function to anticipate glitches and to guide the project through the organization from start to finish.[38]

Our separation of the product development discussion into stages should not be interpreted as indicating that the product should be developed in a series of separate stages. These various tasks must be accomplished, but they need to be integrated into a whole, to be pursued simultaneously via constant, detailed communication among all parties involved. This is the fast-cycle approach the Japanese have perfected, and one good way to make it happen is to form multidisciplinary product development teams. But how do you create and manage teams so as to achieve a fast product development cycle? According to Derwyn F. Phillips, vice chairman of Gillette, one of the secrets is to avoid heavy top-down management of the process:

> The tendency for walls to exist between functional groups is common. For example, people in the product development cycle may throw an idea over the wall and hope the other functional group will run with it. However, I think that U.S. companies are recognizing this and trying to build more team approaches to new product development. There is a focus on putting individuals together in teams, agreeing to a set of objectives, and letting them get on with it without all of the hierarchical intervention that has gone on in some of the historic structures.[39]

Tom Peters, an advocate of the team-based approach, has proposed a variety of factors that ought to help teams succeed:

- *Multifunctional involvement.* The team needs to include everyone with an interest in the new product, including customers.

- *Simultaneous full-time involvement.* The key team members need to be fully committed to the project, not torn between the new product and their regular tasks.

- *Colocation.* The entire team should work in the same physical location.

- *Constant communication.* Ongoing communication must cross all the functional boundaries, and all team members need to be involved in routine decision making.

- *Fully committed resources.* The team should not have to share resources between the new product development and any ongoing activities of the firm.

- *Outside involvement.* Customers, suppliers, and other external groups with an interest in the product need to be participants in the entire development process.[40]

Note that these rules are likely to strain the average company's organization and culture, which helps explain why product development efforts are commonly fraught with difficulty!

Stage 6: Test Marketing

During test marketing, marketers attempt to measure the reactions of potential consumers of an actual product in a real-world setting. They observe the performance of the product in selected markets and evaluate its probability of success in larger markets. The company can learn about distributors' attitudes toward the product, as well as gauge the reactions of competitors. A test market often provides information that can be used to improve the marketing strategy, such as what type of advertising to use or how to devise point-of-purchase displays.

In a test market, the firm advertises, prices, and distributes the product, just as it will when it goes national. If it finds, for example, that retailers will not give the product the necessary point-of-purchase space, the firm can correct the problem at small expense before encountering it on a national scale. Most companies realize that it is preferable to spend $1 million in a test market than to spend $20 million on a product failure in a national market.

Many marketers have become less enthusiastic about test marketing in recent years. Test marketing is slow, expensive, and open to competitive spying and sabotage. For example, when General Foods tried to test market frozen baby food, Gerber, Libby, and Heinz bought up all the product in the test markets. Thus, many marketers today are avoiding test markets. Quaker Oats grabbed 40 percent of the granola snack market with its Chewy Granola Bars and chocolate-covered Dipps without test marketing these products, and P&G successfully launched its Folgers instant decaffeinated coffee without test marketing. But not all firms are successful in taking this approach. For example, Campbell's Pepperidge Farm Star Wars cookies took a beating when the Star Wars craze faded soon after the product was rushed onto the market without a test.

Stage 7: Commercialization

Once a new product has been tested successfully, it is ready for commercialization, or full-scale production and distribution to the target market. Although the previous steps are expensive, the major investment in terms of both production and marketing is made at this stage. Miller Brewing Company, for instance, invested $247 million to build a highly automated plant in Albany, Georgia, to brew its Lite beer. Fortunately, the company bet on a winner; the light beer market grew rapidly, while regular beer is in no-growth maturity.

Innovation is inherently risky, and any strategies that help innovators minimize their exposure to investment risk during the early stage of the product life cycle are especially valuable. Merck, the New Jersey-based pharmaceuticals company, often invests large sums in manufacturing facilities for a new drug well before the FDA has given it permission to market the product. However, the firm tries to minimize its risk by postponing this kind of gamble as long as possible, even if it means living with difficult and expensive makeshift production at first. For example, rather than erecting a $200 million plant to make Primaxin, a new antibiotic that wipes out most bacteria known to science, Merck produced it in ten complex steps at several of its existing plants.

Companies rarely enter national distribution all at once. Rather, they roll out the new product, going from one geographic area to another. (This can be seen as another way to reduce risk during product introduction.) Rolling out makes it possible to spread the substantial costs of a new product launch over a longer period and provides an opportunity to fine-tune the marketing program as the rollout progresses.

FROM INCEPTION TO BIRTH

When the product is first introduced to the market, it enters the second stage of its life cycle. This move from inception to introduction is a critical transition because the product is now put before customers for the first time, at least outside of the artificial environment of concept evaluation and product testing. To keep with the life cycle analogy, the product is born into its market. The challenges facing the company are many and varied as the focus of innovation expands from the internal product development effort to the challenges of bringing the innovation to life in the market. As Paul Cook of Raychem Corporation sees it:

> Innovation is as much about sales or service or information systems as it is about products. We spend twice as much on selling as we do on research and development, so creativity from our sales force is just as important as creativity from the labs. How do you sell a product no one has seen before? How do you persuade a customer to accept you as a sole source for an important component?[41]

According to the product life-cycle model, sales at introduction are expected to start slowly, then grow at an accelerating rate as early adopters—the innovators in the market—try the product, and others then hear about it and give it a try. If the product has no competitors, as is often the case with a truly novel and original product, it owns the entire market at this stage. But the market is small; that is, the served market is small because the new product has not yet penetrated most of its potential market. How long the first entry has before competitors join it will determine to some extent how much of an advantage the first entrant will have in later competition.

The life-cycle model elaborates even further on the basic situation at introduction. The typical introductory stage is generally characterized by low and gradually growing sales, with high costs and low margins for the producers. The producers are not very experienced at making the product yet, and are not doing it at high enough volume to achieve any potential economies of scale. Fortunately, little competition exists at this stage, although the company usually spends a lot of time worrying about how and when new competition will enter. A protectable product (through patents, trade secrets, or other high barriers to entry) is an obvious advantage in this game.

Because the product is new, the major marketing task is to educate potential consumers. Awareness and knowledge of the new product must be built from scratch in many cases. (You may be accustomed to grabbing a vacuum cleaner when you want to clean the rug, but think for a minute how you might talk people into buying one if they have never used anything but a broom. Would it be difficult to convince them to give you 20 or 30 times the cost of a broom for this unfamiliar contraption?)

Although segmentation and targeted marketing may be all the rage in mature consumer products right now, you are unlikely to see them in introductory stage products. A generalized approach to the marketing task, with a mass-market positioning, is common in the introductory stage. (As the product and its market matures, an increasing number of competitors will begin to carve niches out of the mass market that is created in the introductory and growth stages of the life cycle.)

Much of the most visible marketing in our society is generated in the growth or maturity stages of the life cycle, not in the introductory stage. Marketing budgets are usually low in introduction, and in fact the markets themselves may seem quite small. Who would have guessed the size of the personal computer market back in Apple's early days? And who would have imagined Apple might be buying ad time during the Super Bowl within a decade! Because big U.S. companies seem to have trouble innovating, many of the producers of novel introductory stage products are entrepreneurial and not accustomed to, or financed for, high-profile marketing. As a result, managers rely heavily on word-of-mouth, public relations (for generating news coverage), and, in many markets, direct sales.

The producer of an introductory stage product is generally very close to its customers, at least the few who have discovered it and are willing to take a risk on the new product. This is especially true in business-to-business products and services, but is also true in consumer products. The marketer of an introductory stage product simply cannot afford to be anything but customer-focused. Customers must be found and convinced that the new product is worth a try, which means marketers must really understand what the new product does for a customer, what the switching costs are, and how their product generally fits into the customer's world. These issues are considered vital at this stage, and all of management's attention is focused on how the initial customers react. The product may be modified constantly and extensively, and the sales and marketing strategy may evolve rapidly, in response to this early customer feedback. (Often management is directly involved in customer support and in sales.)

The customer orientation that characterizes most introductory stage products and their managers is of special interest given the current effort in companies to capture this kind of customer orientation in later stages of the product life cycle. The new vision of the corporation, with strong customer ties, little hierarchy, and rapid learning based on market experience, is in many ways a description of the entrepreneurial marketer of growth stage products. This vision can be seen as an effort to return to childhood for many companies and products.

Oddly, this customer orientation that characterizes the introductory stage is not even mentioned in standard write-ups of the product life-cycle model. Yet it is clearly an important and natural element of product introduction—and apparently one that companies lose as their products mature and they begin to jockey for position in a growing field of competitors. At least if a product idea has sprung from recognition of a customer need, management enters the product life cycle with a pure customer orientation. As the concept moves from inception to development and is then introduced to the market, this purely customer-oriented concept is shaped by a variety of practical concerns, many of them adding technical and operational orientations to the concept. But if the core customer benefit has been preserved through this process, it is still there upon introduction, and the task of management is to communicate the benefit and refine the product's ability to deliver this benefit. If the concept has been displaced by internal concerns, or was simply misconceived to begin with, introduction will reveal this fatal flaw rapidly: Customers won't buy the product.

One way to look at the introductory stage of the product life cycle is as the beginning of a fall from grace. Even if customers buy the concept and new product sales start to grow, the practicalities of manufacturing, selling, delivering, and supporting the new product generally take their toll on that initially pure customer orientation. The management begins to worry about cutting costs, building volume, negotiating lower commissions for the sales reps, and so forth, and spends less time thinking and worrying about the customers' needs. The production facilities, product-management hierarchy, and other internal structures that initially were designed to meet customer needs begin to take on a life of their own. In the typical introductory stage, management begins a long, slow, almost imperceptible shift in orientation, from its initial focus on customer needs, to the strong focus on company needs that characterizes the end of the product's life cycle. We suspect that this gradual shift in focus is what makes products mortal. It is something inherent in the way companies manage products, not in the products themselves. But this discussion is jumping way ahead of the chapter and, incidentally, ahead of the existing literature on this model, so it is better left to the end of the next chapter and our critical evaluation of the model.

With introduction comes the threat of failure, which means there are suddenly two paths the product can take. Sales can go up, or they can go down. Results can satisfy management, or they can fall far short of expectations. As in the life cycles of living creatures, product mortality rates are often highest at and shortly after birth. The product life cycle is characterized by high infant mortality.

PRODUCT FAILURES

The reasons for failure are many. Some new products do not match a company's unique skills and competencies. Other times, the firm overestimates the size of a market segment. RCA had forecast annual sales of 600,000 videodiscs by 1984, yet actual sales totaled only 500,000 by the time it scrapped its videodisc player system. RCA's loss can be attributed mainly to competition from VCRs. As a Japanese competitor told *BusinessWeek*, "RCA's problem was they tried to compete with the VCR and focused only on one function—playback."[42] Most frequently, new products fail because there is no need for them; they don't solve a real consumer problem. (What makes a customer problem real? Not whether management or the company's scientists see a problem they want to solve, but whether the customers agree that they have a problem and perceive the company's new product to be a fine solution to it. The only way to verify this is to introduce the product.)

Various studies have shown that the failure rate for new consumer products ranges from a low of 20 percent to a high of 90 percent; new industrial products fare somewhat better.[43] The most recent study we have seen, in which The Conference Board surveyed 148 mid-sized and large U.S. manufacturers, reported a failure rate of one in three for major products launched in the last five years. (Respondents faulted their marketing research, along with technical problems and poor timing of introductions for these failures.)[44] The 33 percent failure rate in this study conforms with another major study, which found that 30 to 35 percent of all consumer goods and 25 percent of all industrial products do not meet the expectations of the firms that develop them.[45] This failure is most likely because the products did not live up to customer expectations—a misunderstanding of customer expectations and needs is probably what lies behind The Conference Board's finding that marketing research was most often at fault in product failures. The chairman of the American Marketing Association (AMA), Calvin L. Hodock, argues that the failure to keep customers in focus while pursuing technology is at the root of many product failures:

> RCA poured millions into the videodisc; Sony chased the Beta format, but VHS won the war. Consumers did not lay down their bag of potato chips for Pringles, because the taste was not as innovative as the packaging. The first smokeless cigarette, Premier, was another good intention that missed. Soft-batch cookies, heralded as tasting like David's and Mrs. Fields, have almost disappeared from grocery shelves. Sony, RCA, Frito-Lay, and Procter & Gamble were victims of technology mesmerization. They became enamored with the sex-appeal of the technology and oblivious to delivering a consumer benefit or need.[46]

These sorts of errors seem the most obvious, yet they can gather incredible momentum within a company. They are the kinds of product developments that catch management's imagination. The way to detect these errors is to keep checking to see if the products catch customers' imaginations as well.

Whereas some products are launched to the dramatic din of a rapid crash, many more are introduced with a whimper. New products do not generally fail immediately or entirely, but they may fail to excite customers, as is the case with many "no-brainer" product line extensions. Hodock observes that the most successful and excellent new products, such as the ones that the AMA recognizes through its Edison Awards, "are truly innovative products rather than warmed-over versions of 'me too.'" Edison winners have included novelties such as Spiffits from DowBrands, the first premoistened towels for household cleaning; Souper Combos from Campbell's, the first microwavable soup and sandwich combination; and Healthy Choice, the first microwavable frozen dinners with low levels of cholesterol, fat, and salt.[47]

What if you have a truly innovative idea, and you develop and introduce it with skill, only to find the new market rapidly filled with competitors? You may never recover the development costs. If you can't hold onto the market for a significant portion of the introductory phase, you are probably in big trouble. The failure to maintain a leadership position for long enough to benefit from the several advantages of being a "first-mover" firm is another common source of disappointing product launches. The advantages to being first include (or ought to include) the technological leadership that comes with being farther down the learning curve than competing firms, the ability to preempt competitors in the acquisition of scarce resources (which often include market niches), and the tendency for buyers to want to stick with first-movers to avoid switching costs.[48] An increasing number of companies seem to be pursuing what is known as the "fast-follower" strategy, which involves rapid imitation of innovating competitors. Fast followers increase the threat that a competitor will steal the thunder—and some of the profits. Given this threat, how can you be sure a new product's competitive advantage will prove durable? What can be done to foil the efforts of those diabolical fast followers?

The advice offered by marketing experts is helpful, but not always consistent. For example, conventional wisdom has it that a skimming strategy is appropriate when rapid competition is not expected, and a penetration strategy when competition is expected. Skimming means a company keeps price and profits high, milking the least price-sensitive customers before pursuing the rest of the market. But if the company expects rapid competition, then it should use a penetration strategy, with lower pricing and aggressive promotion and distribution to capture as much of the potential market as possible at the outset, on the theory that this will give the firm a larger share in the long run. However, one recent academic journal contribution on this question suggests that managers should maximize short-run returns where fast imitation is likely. This strategy requires asking a premium price for a new product where imitation is projected in a relatively short time. Alternatively, a moderate price is warranted where followers are likely to be delayed.[49] In other words, this recommendation is the opposite of the thinking behind the penetration and skimming strategies. For our money, we'd prefer to bet on a penetration strategy when rapid competition is expected, but this boils down to management judgment rather than any firm principle of marketing.

This same journal article identifies the components of a new product that affect the durability of its competitive advantage, and the authors suggest some more logical prescriptive principles on this score. The idea is that management can do a better job both of anticipating the duration of a competitive advantage and of planning so as to maximize its duration by focusing on all the factors that make products easy or difficult to imitate. The factors, with specific ideas for how they can be used to make the product harder to imitate, are as follows:[50]

- *Product form.* Give the product a distinctive form and encourage customers to make inferences about product function from its form.
- *Product function.* Differentiate the product on one or more functional characteristics rather than introduce a generic or nonspecialized product. Consider developing more than one product to give consumers function that is closer to their specific needs.
- *Product intangibles.* Innovate in this area, adding value through warranties, financing, product availability, support to the customer, and so forth.
- *Pricing.* Use penetration pricing, and also price-based sales promotions, if appropriate, to encourage rapid trial and adoption.
- *Promotion.* Use advertising and other promotional efforts to stake out a desirable position within the market, building consumer awareness of this position and signaling possession of it to potential competitors.
- *Distribution.* Minimize transaction barriers (obstacles to customer purchase and use). Invest in building good distribution channels to make the product readily available and to support the user.
- *Firm characteristics.* A unique location or specialized skills and resources can provide the building blocks of durable competitive advantage. Basically, if your firm is less like its competitors, it is more likely to come up with hard-to-imitate innovations.

Perhaps you recognized the familiar four *P*s in this schema: product, price, promotion, and place. Product is broken into three categories, but the rest of the schema is straight out of a textbook (with distribution referring to "place").

The characteristics of the firm that affect ease of imitation include "any unique resource that isolates a new product from rivals."[51] This resource may offer protection because of customer perception—for example, a watch made by a Swiss firm gets a few points in customer perception merely because it is Swiss. The resource also may offer an economic advantage. Most simply, however, the reliance on different resources may minimize the likelihood of another competitor's having hit upon the same idea at almost the same time. This latter problem is, in our opinion, an especially troubling one.

The sad fact is that it is rare to have a completely original idea. Often an insight or invention is a product of circumstance. Both Alfred Wallace and Charles Darwin thought up the theory of evolution in great detail, without knowing about the other's work, at virtually the same time. This kind of concomitant development happens too often in the history of invention for it to be treated as mere coincidence.

You can assume that if a customer need and a novel solution strike you as a natural, they may seem obvious to a competitor as well. No one should really have expected to dominate the laptop computer market, for example, because most PC makers knew that this is the direction their innovations had to go. They did not wait for a competitor to introduce a laptop before beginning their own product development. (Although one wonders why some did not take advantage of the obvious tide of events to swim against it and stake out a novel and unexpected new segment.)

Loel Bleeke of the consulting firm McKinsey and Company has identified a general problem he refers to as look-alike strategy, and it is applicable to product development as well.[52] He finds that companies within an industry often converge on the same or similar strategies without intending to. They do not ask each other what they should do, but all go off and do the same thing, and the end result often looks like they collaborated. They are surprised to find their competitors pursuing the same goals and markets they are, and their strategy is bound to run into trouble as they face unexpected, and unnecessary, competition via the look-alike mechanism. Alternatively, as in the case of laptop computers, the companies all fight it out on the same playing field by tacit agreement, even though only a few are likely to establish significant positions in the game. Look-alike strategy is especially problematic with new product introductions, because the last thing a sane management team wants to do is to introduce a new product at about the same time competitors introduce similar new products. The first-mover advantage is lost to all parties.

Bleeke believes look-alike strategies develop because of five common errors in strategy formation:

1. *Managers tend to focus on where to compete rather than on how to compete.* Where is a two-dimensional issue, whereas how is three-dimensional. Thinking about how can lead to many creative and original ideas. How a company produces and delivers products or services is often a better source of novel new product concepts than where it sells them. Yet a great deal of attention is given to the where's of marketing in new product development and introduction: which markets to serve, which stores or channels to use in reaching markets, where to place products on the stores' shelves, and so forth.

2. *Little emphasis is placed on uniqueness and adaptability.* According to Bleeke, strategic plans ought to be evaluated on the basis of how unique and how adaptable they are, but management usually overlooks these two issues in strategy formulation. The same can be said for new product development and introduction plans. If a company doesn't specify uniqueness in new products, it is unlikely to get uniqueness. Yet most product proposals are evaluated primarily based on financial expectations—what kind of revenues, market share, and profits are forecast in a given period of time. However, because these forecasts are heavily dependent upon the uniqueness of the product, reality will fall short of the projections if similar products appear at the same time. Nevertheless, companies tend to underemphasize the more qualitative assessment of uniqueness in favor of the quantitative projections. The importance of adaptability is even more

obvious. Will the new product prove adaptable enough to survive and profit from unexpected events? Will engineers be able to adapt the basic technical platform to create future generations of the product? Will marketing be able to reposition the product to pursue a segment of the market if a challenger stakes out another segment? These and many similar questions ought to be asked to determine adaptability.

3. *Little attention is given to when to compete.* One of the most common causes for new product failure according to The Conference Board survey is bad timing. As product life cycles shorten (a commonly cited but poorly explained phenomenon), it is increasingly easy for a company to find itself out of step with the market. In technology-driven products, competing technologies can make products out of date rapidly. Products intended to take advantage of a change in public perception may precede the perceptual change and fall on ears that are not yet prepared for the message. Products chasing a demographic trend may similarly be out of step with microlevel change, even though they are on target as far as a long-term trend goes. For example, knowing that the population is aging does not guarantee that a company can succeed today by introducing a line of products or services targeted at the over-60 segment. There must be a self-defined segment consisting of people who see themselves as part of this over-60 cohort. Many people in our society, however, still have mixed attitudes about the elderly, and older people's self-images are often based on the values and images of people a decade younger. Public perception has not yet caught up with the demographic trend, so a product launch based on this trend could be out of step with customer attitudes. Even when the market timing for a new product is precisely right, the company must ask itself whether it is realistically able to be the first entrant and, if not, must modify its investment and development strategy to stake out a second- or third-entrant position.

4. *Companies tend to focus on competing firms instead of competing individuals.* When developing strategy in general, and new product plans in particular, it is easy to limit the competitor analysis to a review of the facts on the major competing firms. But the market shares, growth rates, and financial ratios tell only one side of the story. In predicting competitor behavior, it is vital to incorporate an understanding of the personalities of the decision makers. Who is in charge of new product development at each competitor? What did they study in school, and what kind of products have they developed previously? Are they supported by other managers, or are their hands tied? Are they aggressive or cautious (how many times have they brought out first-mover products)? The personal approach to competitor analysis can even be extended to the companies as a whole by asking what their corporate cultures are like and how they are changing.

5. *Companies use common performance measures.* The fact that the major companies in most industries use the same measures reflects in part the increasing tendency for managers to move from company to company in their career pursuits, taking customs and practices with them. When it comes to strategy in

general, and to new product development in particular, a company is what it measures. For example, a company may decide to strengthen its brand franchise and market share in certain high-growth market segments through its product development and marketing effort. It also may continue to evaluate the key managers according to profitability of products from all segments in the short-term. In such a case, the managers will continue to fight it out for short-term returns in the mainstream segments instead of innovating to pursue the growth segments that the company intended to target for long-term returns. Common performance measures lead to implementation that looks alike, even if the stated goals are divergent.

Academics who study organizations use the term *isomorphism,* which is the tendency toward consistency and constancy within the organization. It is the enemy of innovation and change—the inertia we spoke of early in this chapter. Bleeke's observations suggest that isomorphism can affect not only individual companies, but entire industries. The managers within an industry can be thought of as informal members of an intellectual community. They often come from similar backgrounds, and share ways of looking at and talking about business problems with other managers in their industry. The culture of companies within any industry is often similar. Let's say you were plunked down inside a mystery company and had to guess whether its business was insurance or computers. You would probably guess immediately whether you were in an insurance or a computer company by the dress, manner, and speech of the people around you and the layout and decoration of the building. But you might have trouble guessing which computer company or insurance company, as individual companies differ little on these indicators of culture.

What happens, however, when a foreign company decides to enter the U.S. computer market? The company is not part of this informal industrial community, and it approaches management and marketing differently from U.S. competitors. Its approach to product development also differs. In short, it is not subject to the same isomorphic forces, at least at first. Thus, it is much more likely to generate novel product ideas. It is not subject to the dangers of look-alike strategy.

When U.S. managers talk about innovation, they always look over their shoulders to see if any Japanese companies are creeping up from behind. The subject of innovation, with its related issues of product quality, fast-cycle product development, entrepreneurship, and the like, is high on the management agenda largely because Japanese companies have outperformed U.S. companies in many industries by being better innovators.

The explanations for this phenomenon are many and varied, and some are quite farfetched and convoluted. But the Japanese success may reflect the simple fact that the Japanese companies entered the U.S. market with a fresh perspective, free of the blinders imposed by the U.S. industrial culture. While the big three in Detroit continued to develop autos that offered power and luxury, Japanese companies, with their new and distant view of the market, saw more clearly that fuel economy and reliability were becoming more important to consumers. The time it took for the U.S.

automakers to see what should have been obvious to them from the outset is a testament to the power of the normative forces at work within their industry. They simply could not see what was obvious to the newcomers in their market; they did not understand their own customers.

If there is any overriding concern in the area of new product development, this must be it: The basic scope and direction of the product development effort must be right, and they will not be unless management thought is liberated from the strictures of look-alike strategy and is able to focus on novel opportunities presented by the environment.

We began the chapter with the observation that products can be thought of as living and dying, according to a common architecture as described by the product life cycle. We have followed this life cycle from inception through development and introduction. In the next chapter, we follow it into its growth phase, maturity, and decline. It is also relevant, however, to remember that companies themselves have proven remarkably mortal. How many companies with which you do business have been around for 100 years? And how many are newly formed within the last decade or two? Most companies are young, and many—especially the majority that are privately owned—fail to survive beyond the span of a single generation of managers. One recent survey found that only a few U.S. companies can actually be traced back as far as the Civil War.[53] Why should companies prove so mortal?

One clue to this puzzle is provided by the product life cycle itself, and by the thought that companies seem to have trouble breaking out of traditional ways of thinking to maintain a healthy level of innovation. The isomorphic forces that crystallize organizations and entire industries into rigid, inflexible ways of thinking about their business and their markets put them at risk and open the door to newcomers, whether entrepreneurs from their own country or industrialists from abroad.

No company can live long if it ties itself to a single product. Even the longest lived products die eventually, at least according to theory. The railroads took the myopic view that their product was railroads, not transportation, and that their job was laying track, not moving people and goods the most efficient way.[54] Thus, the railroads went into a long slow decline as automobiles, trucks, and planes began to displace the railroads as the favored form of transportation. But what does the mortality of companies have to do with product development and introduction?

Everything—for it is in this core function of the business that new life is injected, or old life sucked out. The business that allows its product development to degenerate into mindless brand extensions soon has a portfolio of mature and declining products. The company, on the other hand, that is able to break away from the industry—that limits the vision and imagination of its competitors, and manages to introduce a stream of exciting and unique new products, revitalizes itself by keeping its portfolio weighted toward development and growth stage products. Surely this is why some companies now set specific developmental goals for themselves. Rubbermaid insists that 30 percent of sales comes from products developed in the last five years, and 3M reports that 32 percent of its sales come from products that are fewer than five years old.[55]

The vitality of the product development function is directly related to the vitality of the company as a whole. This makes sense, at least if we look at the basic purpose of a business. At its heart, the business exists to produce products and provide them to consumers through an exchange process that is convenient and profitable for both, or all, parties. Business is about products, and it is through products that a business provides value to its customers. As soon as management attention wanders from the customers, rigidity and clouded vision attack the product development efforts, and the company no longer innovates effectively for its customers. The product portfolio shifts toward older goods and services and uneventful extensions of them, and someone else takes the reins to provide the kind of leadership that McKenna was talking about when he said, "in marketing, what you lead, you own. Leadership is ownership."

In the beginning of this chapter, we hypothesized that management attention shifts slowly from customer needs to company needs as the product life cycle progresses. The antidote to the aging of the company via slowed innovation and look-alike strategy is thus a refocusing of management attention on the customer. As Charles Hooper of Helene Curtis states in the chapter's opening quote, "Good ideas don't begin around the conference table. They begin with the consumer." They also *end* with the consumer, as our examination of new product introduction and failure illustrated. In the next chapter, we examine how to keep the company focused on the customer throughout the product's life cycle, as we follow the product from its introduction to the heady growth of its teenage years and on into maturity.

FOR YOUR IMAGINATION

Avoiding New Product Disaster:
A Report from the School of Hard Knocks

The authors have contributed to new products many times, as consultants and researchers and even as marketing managers. New products fail at an alarming rate. Depending upon the study and how failure is defined (usually as failure to meet projections or managers' expectations), the rate of new product failure is between 85 percent and 95 percent. Even if you define failure more rigorously as the withdrawal of the product within the first year or two, rates are still over 50 percent in most industries.

Marketers are used to long odds. After all, 95 percent of most mailings go unread. But when it comes to new products, the effort involved is too great to justify gambling. You need to beat the odds, and beat them hands down. Some companies have failure rates of 25 percent or less, and you can too. Experienced developers we've worked with seem to have a variety of common sense ideas that keeps them out of trouble. They seem to follow some simple but powerful rules of real-world marketing to avoid the quicksand of product development.

(continued)

They know how to avoid those errors that always look stupid in the rearview mirror—but are fiendishly hard to detect in advance!

To help you develop this sixth sense, we've identified what those errors are and given you some real-world guidelines to keep you out of trouble. Here, then, is the advice we give you when wearing our consulting hats. *Do not* make any of the following errors:

1. Getting Ahead of Your Market

It's easier to figure out what the next generation of products should be than to time their introduction properly. Many new product launches fail because they are ahead of their time. Alex remembers in the early 1980s working with a biotechnology company that had what they thought was going to be a really hot new technology. They even had raised enough venture capital to fund its initial development, and all they needed was to enlist some industry partners to help commercialize its various applications. They did their best to interest companies in the technology, but couldn't get anyone to sign on the dotted line. The project died and the technology disappeared. But about a decade later, we began to see references to the same technology as other companies tried to commercialize it. And this time, industry was ready and the companies made a lot of money. Too bad the client had been a decade too early.

The trick is to have enough vision that you can lead your market—but not by a decade. You want to be a year or two ahead, because if you have to wait longer than that for others to catch up, then you won't be able to afford to wait. To avoid this common cause of failure, make sure your new product concept doesn't require other major changes in the industry first—changes that you don't have the time to wait around for.

2. Coming in Late

This is the most obvious way to blow it, but people keep doing it anyway. There isn't much point in waiting for competitors to come up with some great new product, then copying them. Yet that's just what happens, over and over, in most industries. Me-too product launches have a low chance of success. We know many consultants will tell you otherwise—they say to wait and let someone else test the waters, so as not to run the pioneer's risk. But once someone else launches first, then the waters are muddied, not just tested. Your product's potential is limited by the leader's share, so your potential rewards are reduced along with your risks. And in my experience, the reduction in risk rarely justifies the reduction in reward. If you do launch second or third, instead of first, you better have a unique selling proposition—something about your product that is different and better, at least to a segment of the market. Otherwise, who needs you?

3. Not Considering Enough Ideas

Companies develop the best new product concepts they have. And so they are limited by their own ideas. If you increase the quantity and quality of ideas, you will be able to select from a better list of candidates.

Invest the time and effort needed to apply creativity techniques and processes, and also try to incorporate more input from customers, employees, and suppliers. (We describe many such methods in the main text of the chapter on product development.) These sorts of practices will increase your new product success rate in the long run by insuring that you have lots of good ideas to work with. Don't ever develop a dull, boring, me-too idea just because you don't have any better ideas. Keep thinking. You can come up with a winner.

4. Not Screening Ideas Rigorously

If you follow our advice in the previous paragraph, you will take a free-wheeling, creative approach to concept development. Great. Except now you have lots of wild ideas, and if you aren't careful one will slip through without careful evaluation. So it is essential to switch hats and apply rigorous research and analysis to each and every concept before and periodically during the development process. Many companies miss obvious warning signs and waste money developing products that were obviously doomed to failure.

To help insure a careful review of each concept, consider developing formal review criteria such as these from the Gould Corporation, a manufacturer of programmable controls for industrial applications:

- Can the product be introduced within five years?
- Does it have potential to achieve at least $50 million in sales and a 15 percent rate of growth?
- Will it provide a minimum return of 30 percent on sales and 40 percent on investment?
- Will it achieve technical or market leadership?

Many good ideas may fail to pass these four hurdles. But those that do are highly likely to succeed.

5. Making Unrealistic Claims for the Product

Let's say your company invents a new banking service that is designed to prevent people from running out of money. It somehow links up with all sorts of other financial products and services, from credit cards to life insurance policies and mutual funds, in order to manage cash flow automatically. Sounds great. A market-leading product. When you survey customers, they all say they'd love to trade in their current bank account for one that never runs out of money. Yet this product probably will fail in the marketplace for the simple reason that it can't truly keep people from running out of money. What it presumably would do is transform their other financial assets into cash in order to cover their irresponsible spending habits (and surely it would attract the most irresponsible spenders, since these are the people who currently have a problem keeping their bank accounts in balance). And so after a few months, your customers would finally run

(continued)

out of cash and assets you can turn into cash, and then they'd be a lot more broke than they would have been if they had just stuck with a regular bank account.

The problem with this concept is that it was misrepresented—to everybody, not just customers. Once everyone in the company starts thinking that a product can do something like keep people from running out of money, then the analysis and market projections get made on a false assumption. Make sure you test the product's performance very carefully. Does it live up to its claims, or do you need to temper them before evaluating the product's market potential?

6. Developing Too Many Products at Once

This is so obvious we don't need to explain it, only to warn you that marketers fall into the trap despite its visibility. When you have several good concepts, the temptation is to develop all of them. But we doubt you can afford to do them all well. Please resist this temptation. A new product introduction needs all the attention and resources you can give it. Don't divide those resources in half or thirds.

7. Not Investing for the Long-Term

Many product development costs and all new product marketing costs have to be reported right away. They can't be amortized over the expected life of the product. That means your company's financial managers and owners or investors tend to view product development and introduction costs in the short-term, rather than seeing them as the investments in future revenues that they (hopefully) are. As a result, many companies skimp on these costs, trying to develop first-class products on third-class budgets. If you propose to build a new factory, the board will be sympathetic to your desire to do it right. But if you propose to market a new product, they'll try to cut your budget in half. New product developers and marketers must constantly fight for support. One way to eliminate this problem is to do what 3M does, which is to establish specific revenue goals for new products. When a company adopts the goal of generating 50 percent of annual revenues from products introduced in the last three years, for example, this forces everyone to keep thinking about new product costs as investments in future revenues. And it generally frees up some of the resources you need to market new products effectively.

8. Letting Managers Have Pet Projects

In mid-sized and large organizations, individual managers often shelter pet projects in their budgets. The result is that their pet project doesn't get the same kind of scrutiny that other development projects are subjected to. Managers fight efforts to centralize control of new product development efforts because they feel territorial about their pet projects. The failure rate on such projects is high. Their only justification is empire-building in many cases. Bring them into the light and impose the same high standards on them as on all other concepts (see 4 on page 275).

9. Not Thinking about All the Stakeholders

Anyone who might be affected by your new product is a stakeholder. Your company and its investors, along with your customers, are the stakeholders you probably focus on when thinking about new product development. You want to create a transaction between customer and company, after all. But how might that product affect other parties? Will it harm the environment? Will it be abused by kids and do them harm? Will it offend some groups of people? If you don't think about how other stakeholders will view your product, you will encounter unexpected resistance to it. And your new product launch may have a bumpy ride. Or even a dead-end journey.

10. Poorly Designed Marketing Programs

Many a good product concept has been killed by a poor marketing program. It's hard to design the program for a new product because you can't be exactly sure what the issues are. You have to make some assumptions about how the market will react and what concerns or objections customers will have. Make sure you think hard about these issues, and know how your plan will overcome any likely concerns or objections.

When Coca-Cola introduced Minute-Maid squeeze-fresh frozen orange juice concentrate in a squeeze bottle, it thought it had a great concept. And it did! The product was easier to mix with water than competing canned concentrates, and you could dispense just as much as you wanted to make and keep the rest in the freezer. In many households, people drink only one or two glasses of orange juice a day, so why make a whole pitcher? But this packaging-based innovation failed to catch on, largely because consumers had trouble using it. They weren't used to having to figure out how much water to mix with the concentrate. And in practice, it was difficult and messy to squeeze the stuff into your glass. Since nobody anticipated these problems, the marketing program didn't deal with them. If they had known in advance, they could have come up with additional ideas—an easier-to-use package design, educational advertising, or in-store demonstrations, for example. Don't forget that the best new product concept will fail unless it has a good marketing program to go along with it.

New product development is harder than ever and even where it succeeds, the challenges of managing the product are many. In the next chapter, we will look at trends in product management and then revisit product development in an appendix on turbo marketing.

9 PRODUCT MANAGEMENT
Birth, Death, and Sometimes Resurrection

I get up each morning at about 5:30 with a mixture of exhilaration and panic, because one of the first things to pop into my head is: How many Americans will buy and read a Hearst magazine today? Because the fate of my one-thousand-four-hundred employees and our future business depends on how well we inform and entertain the sixty-five million Americans who read our publications.

—*Cathleen Black, president, Hearst Publications*[1]

Managing a product or line of products *is* a stressful business. Your troubles aren't over once you introduce the new product. In a sense, they are just beginning. You need to grow the product's sales and market share, and keep the product vital in the eyes of your customers. Every morning when you wake up, your product's status will be different from the day before. But will things be better or worse? It's up to you—and your competitors, and your customers, and many other forces you have only partial control over at best.

While past success is no guarantee of future success for your products, it certainly helps. And when you combine a successful product launch with good management over the life cycle, that life cycle has a good shot at being long and profitable. In this chapter, we'll show you how to increase the odds of a long, healthy life for your product—and maybe even some good nights' sleep for you!

278

FROM INTRODUCTION TO GROWTH . . . WE HOPE

In Chapter 8, we traced the product's progress from idea through market introduction. As a new product enters the market, its sales usually grow at a modest rate. Sometimes the product is so obviously a great idea that everyone rushes to buy it, but generally, it takes a while for the word to get around. The majority of consumers in most markets do not want to be the first to try something; they wait for opinion leaders to evaluate it, or learn about it when their reference group adopts it. Also, companies rarely flood the market with their new product. They prefer a more cautious rollout, first with regional sales and advertising, allowing less risk on the introduction and greater learning as they proceed.

This caution by consumers and companies gives way to a gradual increase in momentum, presuming that the product is a success, until sales begin to grow at a rapid rate. Imagine that one person tries the product and likes it, then tells two more people about it. They try it, and each tells two more. Soon there is exponential growth. Unfortunately for managers, it is not always this simple to achieve exponential growth! But a successful product introduction generally moves to a rapid growth phase as it begins to penetrate the main portion of its target market. This growth does not accelerate indefinitely, however, because the market comprises a limited number of consumers. Eventually the bulk of the people who are likely to try the product have done so, and new customers become scarcer. If a healthy portion of the people who tried the new product continue to repurchase it, sales will not fall. But sales rarely continue to grow at the same rate. Thus, the growth phase is characterized by sales growth that accelerates at first, then begins to decline. When growth levels off—say to near the rate of growth of the GDP or of the targeted segment itself—the product is said to have moved out of growth and into maturity. At this point, most of the potential market has been exposed to the product, and all but the most conservative laggards have tried it. Because trial does not convert into ongoing usage in every case, however, companies commonly see sales growth flatten out well below 100 percent penetration of the potential market.

The growth phase of the product life cycle is characterized by increased competition. New brands may be launched by competitors who have noted the success of the first-mover's product and rushed to grab some of the market share. There are only two ways to capture market share: A company can take share away from a competitor or convince customers to switch brands. This can be a tough, and costly, fight. Alternatively, a company can convince nonusers to try its product before they have adopted a competing brand. If consumers try and like the company's brand, the job of keeping them as customers is easier than the task of taking them away from a competitor. But if a company lets a first-mover spread a product through the entire market before the company enters with a competitive product, there is no second option—the company is forced to gain share by capturing it from the first-mover. The firm then must overcome any loyalty toward the competitive brand and convince consumers that another product is sufficiently different and better to be worth the trouble, risk, and cost associated with switching brands.

Although marketers and managers find it appealing to think of consumers as dedicated and loyal to their brand and its producer, in fact, brand loyalty is not as strong as it might be. The combination of more products from which to choose and an increasing emphasis on price-oriented promotions has eroded brand loyalty in recent years. Nonetheless, sufficient brand loyalty exists in most categories to support the notion of a first-mover advantage. Exhibit 9.1 reports the results of a survey which asked product users if they were loyal to one brand.

Supporting (and partially explaining) these statistics is another set of numbers collected annually by the Point of Purchase Advertising Institute. Its survey asked consumers whether what they buy (in grocery and mass merchandise stores) was planned or not. The result: A minority of purchases—a quarter to a third depending upon the product—are specifically planned in advance of shopping. A surprisingly small number of purchases are substitutes for something consumers meant to buy but couldn't find—only 3 to 4 percent. And the biggest category by far is unplanned purchases, made on impulse within the store: 60 percent of supermarket sales are unplanned, and 53 percent of mass merchandise store sales are unplanned.[2] If consumers are not planning the majority of their purchases, then they are open to suggestion at point of purchase. They don't have to buy a favored brand—instead, they are willing to experiment with new brands and are also happy to select from many of the leading brands or plausible-looking store substitutes for them. You might say the typical consumer is fickle rather than loyal. What loyalty do they owe you, the marketer? In their minds, none. It's up to you to come up with an offering so compelling that there are real rewards for loyalty. And even then, you cannot assume loyalty will be 100 percent. A more realistic goal is "polygamous loyalty" as per the sidebar on the topic.

EXHIBIT 9.1. Product loyalty.

Product	Percentage of Users Loyal to One Brand
Cigarettes	71
Mayonnaise	65
Toothpaste	61
Coffee	58
Headache remedy	56
Film	56
Laundry detergent	48
Beer	48
Automobiles	47
Shampoo	44
Soft drinks	44
Underwear	36
Television	35
Batteries	29
Athletic shoes	27
Garbage bags	23

FOR YOUR IMAGINATION

Polygamous Consumers

Studies of consumer loyalty characterize three different kinds of relationships between consumers and the goods or services they consume. The first, the one we marketers wish and work for, is *100 percent loyalty*, in which the consumer buys our brand over others all the time. It's a fine dream, but little more than that. Statistics suggest that only 10 percent or so of buyers are 100 percent loyal—and furthermore, that these loyal buyers are typically light consumers of the product, rather than the heavy users most marketers crave.

The second sort of relationship is called *promiscuity*, defined in one academic study as "the butterfly tendency to flit from brand to brand without any fixed allegiance."[3] Coupon-clippers tend to be promiscuous, happy to have one-use stands with whatever brands are available at a favorable discount. And heavy use of coupons and other price-based offers by marketers encourages consumers to be promiscuous—one of those stupid things we can't seem to stop doing in marketing.

But the third sort of relationship, *polygamy*, is actually more common than either of these. Most consumers are polygamous: loyal to a set of products, but happy to switch from one to another within that set. Consumers don't generally marry one brand; they like to keep a harem of brands. The most you can hope for from these polygamists is to be the most popular brand within their harem—say, the one they buy 60 percent to 70 percent of the time.[4] These consumers rarely "get divorced" from a brand by making a definitive decision to switch from one brand to another—even though that is what most marketers hope to accomplish. A more realistic goal for marketing is to get these consumers to buy your brand more often and competing brands less often.

Most discussions of brand loyalty focus on consumer goods, but services are bought in much the same way. That's why the so-called loyalty programs offered by airlines—complete with free miles and first-class upgrades for frequent fliers—fail to generate 100 percent loyalty. Most business travelers—the frequent buyers marketers seek—now belong to multiple loyalty programs, dividing their business among them. In Europe, the average traveler belongs to more than three such loyalty clubs, and the number is rising.[5]

Based on the many statistics suggesting loyalty is a difficult goal at best, one might wonder whether it is wise to focus the majority of a company's marketing expenditures on promoting a brand identity in categories such as televisions and running shoes, in which the majority of consumers do not profess to care about brand loyalty. Perhaps the firm's money would be better spent on product development to create sufficient differences between brands so that consumers would have good reason to become loyal to a brand, or another alternative—focusing on distribution and point-of-purchase displays so as to be "in their face" when consumers make their in-store decisions. Both are, in fact, important strategies for gaining market share. But let's return to discussion of the growth stage, and the strategies available to a second entrant into a new market, because these, too, are important strategies for marketers to master.

What if your product is as good as that of the first entrant into a new market, but not obviously better? If you enter quickly, before the first-mover has captured much of the market, you can attract almost as many first-time customers as the first-mover. But if you wait, you will have to convince consumers who already use the competing product to switch. The longer you wait to enter, the more dramatic the product advantage you need to gain a strong second or third place in the growing market. This is why competition grows so rapidly during the growth phase of the product life cycle. Competitors are eager to reach customers before the consumers have developed affection for any other brand.

Bagels have been around for (almost) ever, but not as a mainstream consumer product. They emerged as a fun, healthy breakfast and snack alternative, then quickly moved onto America's lunch menu, during the 1990s. By 1995, bagels were in the midst of a serious growth phase, with annual sales of $2.3 billion in the United States—up 33 percent since 1990. Forecasts suggested another 50 percent jump in sales by the year 2000.[6] The industry leader is Brueggers Corp., which retails bagels from hundreds of stores around the country. But just about everybody else wants in on the game, from grocery stores to fast-food giants like Dunkin Donuts (which launched its own bagel product in 1997). By the year 2000, market shares in the bagel business will be fairly well settled—and will depend on the skill with which each competitor crafts a growth-stage strategy.

In the competitive environment associated with the growth stage, the life-cycle model prescribes a strategy aimed at establishing brand loyalty and building market share. Also important is the establishment of competition for distribution channels—whoever gets them first has an advantage. If you were to develop a new cola that most people liked better than Coke and Pepsi, you would still face a daunting task of defeating two major companies, whose strong dealer relationships give them a vise grip over shelf space at the retail level.

In response to the increasing competition of the growth stage, managers begin to stake out specific product positioning, the high ground in the consumer's mind from which the company will be able to defend its market share in the future. Companies begin to differentiate their products, in product attributes and consequently in customer perception. The initial single-product, mass-market focus gives way to an increasing number of more specialized products that compete better in the fights for specific segments of the growing market. Pricing is also used to focus offerings on multiple market segments; in fact, one often sees a range of product models, differentiated in large part on the basis of how much they cost and how elaborate they are. The main objective of promotion—the sales, discounts, and advertising used to sell the product—is to build brand loyalty. During introduction, promotion was directed at building primary demand—the desire for the product concept itself. But during the growth stage, promotion shifts toward building selective demand—the specific demand for the company's brand versus the general interest in the new category that is generated during the development of primary demand.

To clarify the impact of these forces, we use three product examples: compact discs, rollerblades, and food processors. These products have two things in common: They are or recently were in growth stages, and they all spin. The latter similarity is quite unimportant, but an interesting coincidence nonetheless.

Compact Discs

Compact discs (CDs) were introduced to Europe and Japan in 1982, and to the U.S. market in 1983. At the time, many industry experts predicted that consumers would refuse to discard their records and tapes, and their turntables and tape players, for the uncertain benefit of digital recordings on compact discs. Some experts saw it differently, remembering that the history of the recorded music industry is one of new standards displacing old with superior sound. An oft-quoted commentary by the editor of a trade magazine comes from 1949, when $33\frac{1}{3}$-rpm (revolutions-per-minute) plastic records were first introduced to a market dominated by shellac 78-rpm records: "I ask readers if they want to feel that their collections of records are obsolete, if they really want to spend money on buying discs that will save them the trouble of getting up to change them, and if they really want to wait years for a repertory as good as what is available now to them?"[7] Much to the expert's surprise, consumers answered yes to these questions, both when long-playing records (LPs) were introduced in 1949 and when CDs were introduced in 1983.

Sales of CD players in the United States started at 35,000 in 1983, a decent showing for the introductory stage of the life cycle. In 1984, sales grew dramatically, to 208,000 units. Although this represents 494 percent growth, the percentage is not particularly important because the base was so small. The next year's growth rate of 188 percent, however, was striking because it represents growth on a fairly large base. This growth brought industry sales of CD players to 600,000 units by 1985, and put the product onto the classic accelerating growth curve characteristic of the first half of the growth stage of the product life cycle.[8] Interestingly, CD players were introduced by several companies at roughly the same time, including the original innovators, Sony and Philips. No single company could claim to have a significant time-lead advantage in this market, although, as the innovators, Sony and Philips turned out to have some advantages that allowed them to hold onto a strong position.

By the mid-1990s, growth was slowing a little in the CD market, suggesting a transition from the first part of growth (with its accelerating growth rate) to the second part—and, eventually, to the maturity stage. For example, 1995 sales were up only 11 percent over 1994 sales; and the 1996 data suggested a further drop to 6 or 7 percent annual growth. However, since CDs still made up only 70 percent or so of total sales—the rest being in cassettes, LPs, and other formats—there was still some room for CD growth. Our best guess at time of writing is a definite transition to maturity around 2000 to 2002—at which time, CDs should make up something like 85 percent of unit sales and their growth will slow to only a little faster than the rate of growth of the U.S. population. (Cassette tape sales fell 26 percent in the same survey of 1996 sales—this product slipped into decline in the early 1990s because of CDs.)[9]

CD players on their own are of no more value than CDs are on their own. The consumer generally will buy neither a CD until he or she has a CD player, nor a CD player without being convinced that CDs are a desirable purchase. Thus, the growth of the CD market is dependent on the growth of the CD player market; their life cycles are linked. In 1983, total unit sales of CDs was 443,320. This is a pretty good showing for the first year in the U.S. market, and it represents about a dozen CDs per CD player. CDs cost consumers about $20 each at the time, so the average owner of a CD player invested about $240 in CDs during 1983. From these statistics, we can also compute that the total sales of CDs was almost $9 million—nothing to sneeze at for an introductory-stage product. Nevertheless, unit shipments of all forms of prerecorded music totaled about 600 million in 1983, which means that CDs accounted for less than one-thousandth of the total market for prerecorded music.[10] The bulk of sales was accounted for by 33⅓-rpm LPs, which accounted for 45 percent of unit sales; by 45-rpm singles, with 20 percent of sales; and by cassette tapes, with a little over 30 percent of sales. Eight-track tapes held only a few percentage points of market share, as cassette tapes had largely displaced them by 1982.

Since 1983, CD unit sales have grown much as the product life cycle might have predicted. Exhibit 9.2 shows CD sales plotted over time. Exactly when the

EXHIBIT 9.2. Compact disc sales, U.S. market (millions of dollars).

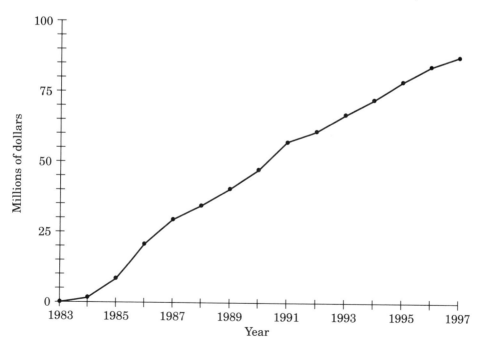

product moved from introduction to growth is difficult to say—the definition of life cycle stage is based on judgment as much as anything—but the curve shifted upward in 1985, making this the first year of a growth phase that is still under way at time of writing. It is worth noting that the total market for prerecorded music did not grow during this time period; it has stayed fairly constant and even declined at times in recent decades, as is typical of a mature market.

A difficult strategic issue for the innovators in this case was how to capture a leading position in the CD market that their innovation had spawned. The innovators were Philips, which developed CD technology for video applications in the 1970s, and Sony, with which Philips entered into a joint venture for the purpose of developing and introducing CDs for prerecorded music. Although these companies focused on developing and marketing the CD players, not the CDs, they also had an active interest in CDs via Philips's record-producing subsidiary, Polygram, and via Sony's acquisition of CBS records. In other words, the joint developers of the CD technology stood to profit handsomely if their record-company subsidiaries could, between them, gain a preeminent position in the market for CDs. Although the companies could have prevented other companies from producing CDs, this would have ensured that the new technology would not become an industry standard.

The CD technology had to be adopted throughout the industry to provide consumers an extensive repertoire of music and to make the new product a viable competitor against the LP standard. In fact, Philips and Sony joined forces specifically to ensure that they would not create competing standards. It was essential to disseminate the new technology widely and encourage record producers to make the new CDs through generous licensing agreements. The necessity of creating an industry standard pushed the innovators to give their technology away, but the desire to profit from CD sales pushed them to maximize their shares of this new market. Further complicating this difficult situation was the fact that CD production capacity must be added in large, expensive increments. Building a new factory is no small investment. Yet, Philips and Sony did not know how successful the new CD standard would be, and thus were not eager to invest in excess capacity. They could have preempted the market by building a huge factory, but they would have lost heavily on this investment had the market not grown as it did.[11] What happened? We will return to this case after discussing our other two products and reviewing some of the principles of product management.

Rollerblades

It's tough to be a 20-year-old entrepreneur in the United States. Ask Scott Olson, who probably had never heard of the product life cycle when he started Rollerblade Inc. in 1980 to manufacture roller skates with in-line wheels. His innovation was to take an old idea—the original design used by Rollerblades was from the eighteenth century—and reproduce it using modern materials. It worked much better with ski boots and skate-board wheels and, after a slow start, the market entered its growth stage in 1987 and reached sales of about $100 million a year by 1990 (see Exhibit 9.3).[12] These sales

EXHIBIT 9.3. Rollerblade growth stage.

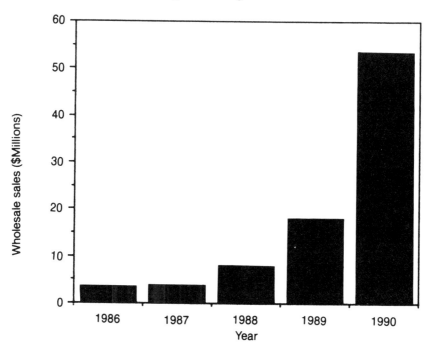

Year

reflected a base of 4.3 million participants in 1990. To project the growth curve past this point, we have to switch to counting participants, since many of the competitors no longer release sales data, even to desperate authors such as ourselves. The next exhibit therefore continues the curve using number of participants per year. It shows rapid growth in the sport continuing through 1996—but at a decelerating pace after 1994.[13] Thus 1994 is probably the inflection point in the growth curve, and we can expect continuing slow down in growth until maturity is reached—our best guess is the market will mature between 2000 and 2005.

The key variable in predicting the end of growth is probably the percentage of households owning in-line roller skates. This is not a product for everyone—it appeals to the young, athletic, and adventurous. In 1996, 19 percent of all U.S. households owned in-line skates, up from 4 percent in 1991. That's a big jump—larger than most marketers would have forecast in 1991. We doubt more than 25 percent of households will ever own this product and use it regularly (about 90 percent of the people who now own skates *do* use them—skating on average 30 times a year). That's why we predict a fairly quick transition to maturity. But we could be wrong. What if the ultimate market is more like 50 percent of U.S. households? Then growth could continue through most of the coming decade—and that would be very nice indeed for this competitive new industry (see Exhibit 9.4).

Olson originally marketed the product to hockey players and skiers for off-season training. From 1980 to 1984, sales were modest and the company stayed small.

EXHIBIT 9.4.   In-line skating: The growth continues (but for how long?).

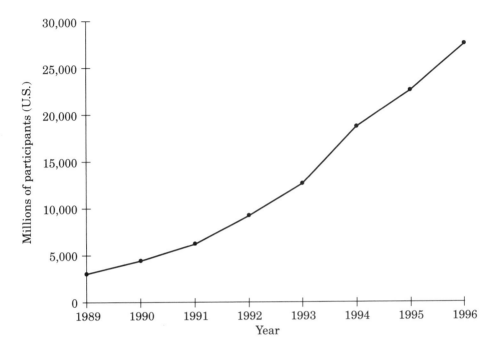

Cash flow problems, that nemesis of entrepreneurial businesses, led Olson to sell 94 percent of his company to a private investor. By 1985, Olson and his investor were not seeing eye-to-eye on how to manage the business, and soon Olson resigned. It is little consolation to him that the company he founded still holds the largest share of the rollerblade market, since Olson now runs one of its eight competitors. Olson's new company, Innovative Sport Systems, holds only 3 percent of the market to Rollerblade Inc.'s 66 percent, demonstrating at Olson's expense the dramatic advantage of being the first-mover in a new market.

From Rollerblade's perspective, Olson's new company is only a minor issue. More troubling is First Team Sports Inc., whose Ultra-Wheels brand was the second to enter, in 1987, and apparently held 22 percent of the market by the beginning of the 1990s. Third came Bauer with only 5 percent. This established maker of hockey skates was a late entrant, but its reputation for quality skates and its strong distribution to sporting goods stores probably worries Rollerblade's president, John Sundet, as much as First Team's large share does.

As the life-cycle model suggests, the rapid growth of rollerblade sales since 1987 has attracted increasing competition, and Rollerblade Inc.'s grasp of the market has slipped as a result. In early 1990, its competitors gained considerably when Rollerblade's production lagged behind demand and store orders were not filled on time. This forced previously loyal retailers to seek other sources, and opened the door to the host of competitors that now crowds Rollerblade for shelf space. What does the life-cycle model prescribe for Rollerblade Inc. at this stage? For starters, it needs to capture distribution channels before competitors do. Its recent move into department stores can be seen in this context. And it needs to begin advertising to build its brand name and establish a strong identity versus its competitors. The competitors are beginning to advertise too; a rush is on to sign up celebrity endorsers.

We wrote the above paragraph in 1991, and have followed Rollerblade's fate with interest since then. It stumbled a bit in the early 1990s, but emerged with a strong marketing campaign, good distribution, and great new products in the mid-1990s. And its market share, though far lower now, seems to be relatively large, and fairly stable.

Market shares are an even harder to chase number than industry sales in this market, and so as we write the second edition (in 1998) we are not exactly sure how competition has played out. But Rollerblade claims (in 1997) to hold a 39 percent market share based on 1996 dollar volume of sales—and they claim no other manufacturer has a greater than 10 percent share. Thus, it appears that Rollerblade's share slipped from 66 percent to 39 percent between our first and second editions—a typical decline for the industry leader during a competitive growth stage. But if it is also true that no other competitor holds a major share, than Rollerblade has accomplished just what you want to in the growth stage of a new market—to maintain a large *relative* share so as to still dominate when maturity is reached.

In the coming years, Rollerblade Inc. needs to maintain its leadership by continuing to lead the market in product development and innovation. When Olson's new company, Innovative Sport Systems, introduced Switchit, the most important thing about the event was that Rollerblade Inc. did not. Switchit skates are combination hockey and roller skates, with interchangeable wheels and blades. Rollerblade's innovations have been minor refinements to its initial product; for example, the addition of a fifth wheel. But can it maintain the kind of leadership that Regis McKenna spoke of in Chapter 8, the leadership that establishes a company's ownership of the market? Without Olson's creativity, this may be Rollerblade's greatest strategic challenge. In the next case, we will find out what can happen to a company that fails to lead the market it created.

Food Processors

At the risk of taking the suspense out of this story, we will start by telling you that Cuisinart, Inc. introduced the food processor to American kitchens in 1973, struggled through two slow years of introductory stage sales, rode the crest of growing sales through the rest of the 1970s and well into the 1980s, but lost share to competitors and ended in bankruptcy court in the fall of 1990.

Carl Sontheimer bought the U.S. distribution rights to Robo-Coupe's restaurant food processor, then adapted the product for the home market. An engineer and passionate cook, Sontheimer kept his company focused on quality and refused to expand the line by offering lower cost, and in his view lower quality, products. His short-line strategy held up better in the introductory phase than it did later, when competing lines from Farberware, Waring, General Electric, Hamilton Beach, and Moulinex entered the market.[14] Instead of expanding the line downward as many companies do during the growth phase, Cuisinart expanded it upward, introducing a more powerful model at $275 retail in 1979 when the competition sold for only $70 on average. Fortunately, Sontheimer's sense of the market was right, and the model fueled Cuisinart's growth. But when Sunbeam introduced a tiny, inexpensive version of the food processor in 1985, the market's mood had changed and the new product's sales went ballistic. However, Sontheimer still refused to compete at the low end.

Advisors and industry experts frequently urged Cuisinart to expand its line and to extend the brand name into related product categories. Sontheimer resisted. He was once quoted as saying, "We could put pebbles in a can, and if we put the Cuisinart name on it, it would sell. But after that, the name would be absolutely worthless."[15] This single-minded vision of the company's mission no doubt avoided cheapening the Cuisinart name in consumers' minds. But it did not position Cuisinart for the end of the growth phase and the onset of maturity, and when sales began to slow Cuisinart ran into big trouble. (Now the brand is back—bought on the auction block by a major appliance maker—but its days of dominance in the industry are probably over for good.)

Lessons Learned?

What can we learn from these three cases? First, they all seem to support the general indications of the life-cycle model. The often-sudden switch to fast growth, the changing competitive picture this brings, the need to alter marketing strategies for growth, the imperative of maintaining market position and leadership for the inevitable growth ceiling and transition to maturity; all these are indicated by the model, and all could have been anticipated by the innovators in each of these three cases. So far, management has not done too poorly. After all, Philips and Sony indirectly control a strong position in CDs, and Rollerblades still holds a majority share. But Rollerblades might have a stronger position if its grasp of distribution channels had not slipped, and its future no doubt depends on how many of the hot new products come out of its labs versus its competitors. That makes two out of three, since Cuisinart failed to hold onto the market it created. A willingness to listen to the market and to jump quickly on the new lightweight processors might well have saved Cuisinart.

The most obvious conclusion is that the growth stage is fraught with peril. It is not easy to take advantage of a high-growth market. Runaway demand puts a lot of strain on a company, making it extremely hard to know what to do next. There is no settled routine in a rapid-growth market, no simple way to look ahead and anticipate future sales, no guarantee that you will not have twice as many competitors next year; or that your sales will not suddenly stop growing. But on the other hand, growth stage products are ultimately manageable, and the same obsession with customers and emphasis on marketing that succeeds in other markets can guide management in a growth market. We will review many of the strategies and tactics that make up the craft of product management in the next section of this chapter, then see how they help define the next steps for each of our case companies. The main focus of strategic choice concerns the nature of the product line—how and how far it is extended, how long it should be allowed to grow before a new generation is introduced—as it moves from introduction toward maturity and into decline. First, however, we will look at some of the product management strategies that are applied in growth and then in maturity.

PRODUCT MANAGEMENT STRATEGIES

It rarely makes sense to limit the company's offering to a single product. As we have seen already, the life-cycle model indicates a tendency toward brand extensions and the creation of lengthening product lines during the growth stage. Most companies have one or more product lines as a result, and companies with many mature brands, like Campbell's, may focus the majority of their development efforts on extending these lines (although this is not necessarily a wise focus, as we saw in the last chapter). Product lines must be managed with care to ensure that viable products are brought out and to ensure the firm's survival and growth. A number of strategies are available to aid in achieving this goal.

Full versus Limited Line

While the terms full and limited are a matter of degree, a full-line strategy refers to a strategy of providing product lines that are both wide in number and deep in assortment. (You can readily see that a full-line strategy is necessary to be a leader in the CD market.) A limited-line strategy entails offering a selected set of products. The full-line strategy has the advantage of greater flexibility to match the market's desires. As an executive of James River Corporation (a paper company) put it, "There's a big advantage in selling to clients from a full wagon."[16]

At the same time, a full-line strategy has some drawbacks. Marketers must be careful not to spread themselves so thin that each line receives less attention than it needs. And they must keep in mind that as product lines are added, the economies of scale associated with mass production (and mass marketing) can be reduced or destroyed. Durk Jager, president and chief operating officer at consumer brands giant Procter & Gamble (P&G), argues that "Consumers are drowning in far too many products." The problem is that, while "variety is good," P&G and other companies tend to offer "too much meaningless variety." As a result, P&G is phasing out about a fifth of its products, and concentrating harder on the remaining ones.[17] Many marketers believe that they must offer a full line of products in order to be successful. A broad mix gives them a competitive advantage, providing greater ability to meet customer needs, increased customer recognition, higher dealer demand, and greater promotional effectiveness. Yet, when this strategy is relied upon in place of managerial judgment, it often results in the addition of inefficient and unneeded products.

American Biltrite's Boston-based Industrial Products Division provides an example. Over the years, this maker of hoses, belting, and shoe soling had tried to be too many things to too many customers. The company had a great many unprofitable products and customers as a result. In one product area, 48 percent of Biltrite's customers provided only 2 percent of its sales. After analyzing its product line strategy, Biltrite reduced the total number of items from 25,000 to 12,000 and eliminated 7,700 of 15,500 customers; revenues and profits benefited from these changes.

The Line-Filling Strategy

Closely allied to the two strategies just described is the line-filling approach. This involves developing products to fill gaps in the market that have not been noticed by competitors or have occurred as a result of changes in consumer preferences. Ideally, the added products will compliment existing ones, perhaps even enhance the sale of present products, and produce a satisfactory return on investment. When Sunbeam studied Cuisinart's market in 1984 and discovered that the majority of food processors were not used by their owners, they saw a gap that needed filling. Their Oskar, introduced in 1985, filled that gap by giving consumers a small, easy-to-use, easy-to-clean food processor that could be used much more casually and easily than the more complicated and bulky Cuisinart. Cuisinart failed to copy this successful strategy. But the real question is why it had not done the market research first, seen the obvious market need, and preempted the competition by innovating to meet that need. You cannot continue with your current strategy if many of your customers have stopped using your products.

Line and Brand Extension Strategies

Armor All is a hundred-million-plus a year product, used by car owners to spruce up their dashboards, bucket seats, and tires. But in 1988, Armor All Products Corporation was a one-product subsidiary of McKesson Corporation. Its product was profitable—1987 profits exceeded $22 million—and its sales continued to grow. But the company had owned the well-known Armor All brand since its introduction in 1972 and never done anything with it. Compare this to Turtle Wax's line of 40 products, and you have a strong case for line extension. Armor All president Jeffrey Sherman decided to extend the brand, but not to the extent his competitors have. He introduced four new products: car wax, protectant, cleaner, and car wash, all of them targeted at the 18- to 49-year-old males who make up Armor All's traditional market, as well as a specially packaged paste wax targeted at women.[18]

Extension strategies are more typical of maturity than growth. Line extensions are new varieties of the same basic product. A different size or new dispenser for Armor All would be a line extension. And Frito-Lay's Max brand, an Olestra (fat substitute) based extension of this potato chip marketer's line, is a good example of why line extensions make sense. Eliminating the calories in potato chips addresses the main objection many consumers have to the product, thus holding forth the potential of a significant market expansion. (But does it raise other objections? Depends on whether Olestra is healthy. It will be interesting to see how this brand fares!)[19]

Brand extensions take the brand name of one product category and extend it to another, as Sherman did when he introduced Armor All waxes, cleaners, and protectants. Brand extensions usually work best when the new categories are closely related to the old in the consumer's mind, as in the Armor All case. Sometimes they are taken much farther, however, as when Coca-Cola and McDonald's licensed their names to clothing manufacturers. These ventures have not been as successful as the companies hoped, probably because the new categories are not mentally linked to the old ones. But sometimes brand names can be extended dramatically, and licensing of brand names continues to increase in popularity. For example, Caterpillar licenses its name to makers of work clothes on the theory that consumers can reasonably be expected to see the relation between them and the earth-moving equipment for which Caterpillar is famous.

The use of a brand or line extension has two distinct advantages. The cost of introduction is much lower because consumer education is not needed. Advertising and other promotional expenditures are more effective because they produce greater awareness and recognition of the brand. Moreover, the risk of introducing the product is reduced because the new product's image is already established. And since the development costs are reduced, the costs of a product failure are lower.

Brand extension is sometimes used by companies that find their competitive situation getting tougher—as typically happens near the end of the growth stage of the product life cycle. A simple way to conceive of this strategy is to imagine that heightened competition encourages consumers to experiment with products different from the one they have grown accustomed to. Since they have more choice, they exercise that choice more often. And in response, competitors add choice to their lines.

All other things being equal, if you offer the most choice within your line, you will capture experimenting consumers most often, and thus keep your competitors from capturing them. And no doubt this simple stratagem would lead to infinite line extensions were it not that all other things are never equal. The limit on this game is shelf space—or catalog space, or salesperson's time. The distribution channels simply cannot handle all this choice. We observed in the previous chapter that about 15,000 new products were introduced to supermarkets in 1991. But on average, only 3,000 of them were pushed to any single grocery store by wholesalers; they know the stores cannot handle all the available products, so focus their efforts where local or regional preferences make them most likely to pay off. Even so, there is no room for 3,000 new products a year in the average grocery store, and most of these get weeded out quickly by store management or by disinterested shoppers.

The limits of brand extension strategies can also be seen in a different sort of statistic—by analyzing the success of new products based on whether they are given new names, or added to an existing brand as a brand extension. When this sort of analysis is performed, it generally reveals little or no advantage to the brand extension strategy. As one research report puts it, "Evidence suggests that brand extension gives little advantage to a new product release."[20] You can't just take a successful brand and use its popularity to force another success. Each product has to stand on its own, regardless of whether you use a novel name or an existing brand identity.

So the real issue is whether a brand extension strategy is good for the *brand* or not. Another academic study concludes that, "Unchecked product-line expansion can

---
| **FOR YOUR IMAGINATION** |

Starbucks Jazzes It Up

The Starbucks chain of coffee shops is a powerful new brand. And its marketers are eager to cash in on this brand's value by extending it to other product categories. Their joint ventures have teamed the Starbucks brand name with other products, often with considerable success. PepsiCo markets a bottled cold coffee using the Starbucks brand identity. Dreyer's ice cream makes an absolutely delicious coffee ice cream for Starbucks. (It's Alex's favorite ice cream—and nobody paid him to say that.) Redhook Brewery is experimenting with a coffee-flavored beer. Then there is the venture with Capital Records, in which the Starbucks name is attached to jazz CDs. We would have forecast failure, but fortunately nobody asked us. The first CD, Blending of the Blues, sold 50,000 units in the first two months—a remarkable performance in the jazz market.[21]

---

weaken a brand's image."[22] When Starbucks puts its name on an excellent coffee ice cream, then the brand is given a boost. But trying to market, say, a mediocre line of Starbucks candy, would just hurt the brand without making the candy a success.

Brand extension is also used in maturity and decline, as an antidote to dwindling markets. Thus Prince Manufacturing, the company that began the oversized tennis racket craze, sought growth in a level market by adding two more Prince lines—one smaller than its standard size and another superlarge racket that has been described as a "garbage can cover." But a caution is in order: Brand extensions often fail to revive flat or falling sales. There generally has to be something new and exciting about the new product introductions for consumers to give them much attention. And unfortunately for Prince, an even larger tennis racket is not it.

Line-Stretching Strategies

Lines are not very stretchable. That is, they tend to resist being traded up or traded down, and it takes considerable marketing effort to stretch them in these directions. However, line stretching is often attempted, perhaps simply because markets are so often segmented on the basis of price and quality. If you want more customers in a market segmented in this manner, the most obvious alternative (although not necessarily the wisest) is to try to pursue both high- and low-quality segments.

When marketers who are known for selling low-priced products offer higher-priced (and presumably higher-quality) products, this is known as trading up. Kmart, long known as the king of mass merchandise discounters, conducted marketing research that found customer preferences shifting toward higher quality. So in 1984, the company began taking down its endless rows of pipe racks and refurbishing its decor. Greater emphasis was put on snappy displays and higher profit national brands.

Electronic centers were added, complete with computers, software, and video-game cartridges. The bed-and-bath areas were refashioned and "Kitchen Korners" were added. But note that this makeover was launched over an 18-month period, and required a huge investment in store redesign and advertising aimed at repositioning the discounter.[23] And furthermore, Kmart did not try to dominate the rock bottom discount position any more, because this would have been too inconsistent with its new image.

Did it work? Well, not really. Certainly not in the 18 months management originally planned on and, in fact, the transformation is still in progress. Since 1984, Kmart has tried many strategies to bring its image upscale, including hiring actress Jaclyn Smith and decorator Martha Stewart to help design and promote apparel and housewares. It has spent millions on advertising to tell consumers about its new position and improved stores. But Louis Stern, a marketing professor at Northwestern who follows the industry, says that the stores do not live up to the advertised image: "Kmarts are depressing. I certainly don't see evidence that they are vastly different." Apparently management agrees, since $1.3 billion in store renovations is currently on the drawing board, along with a $1 billion computer to make Kmart's distribution system competitive with Wal-Mart.[24] Unfortunately, its larger rival is a moving target. Wal-Mart recently unveiled the prototype for its new stores. According to a *Wall Street Journal* report, "Customers expecting the usual warehouse ambiance of discount stores will be shocked." Should they be so shocked as to become disoriented, the store's shopping carts feature video screens that constantly update the shopper concerning location and provide information about products and prices in each department.[25] As Kmart is learning, it is especially hard to trade up when competitors already dominate the desired position.

Trading down occurs when marketers make cheaper lines, and in general it is easy going compared to trading up. It's all down hill, so to speak. But while easy, it is dangerous. The problems come in when the higher priced line is jeopardized by the new, lower-quality line. Tiffany & Co., a marketer of upscale, high-status gift merchandise, was bought by Avon Products and lost its classy image as Avon traded the Tiffany brands down. Regular customers were no longer sure whether Tiffany's was closest to Kmart or Cartier.

In our discussion of segmentation, we reviewed a similar strategy that failed miserably for Jaguar. Its effort to introduce lower priced Jaguar automobiles into the American market damaged its high-end market; the new line had to be withdrawn. It is important to note the relationship between segmentation strategies and line and brand extensions. Research may indicate a new segment worth pursuing, as it did in the Jaguar and Kmart cases. But whether the current product line can be stretched to cover the new segment, and what impact this will have on it in the original segment, is a separate issue and one that management often fails to appreciate fully.

Repositioning Strategies

We have already emphasized the importance of establishing a competitive position in the mind of the consumer. Marketers often attempt to change the consumer's perception of their brand or product. Thus *Playboy* magazine redefined itself as a more "tasteful sex" and "literary quality" publication during its turnaround in the early 1980s. Now Christie Hefner, the CEO, envisions an even more dramatic change. According to a recent profile of her, "Some consuming zeal drives her to attempt to re-fashion her father's sex-based company. She wants it to be a more diversified media concern offering several magazines, videos, television programs, and catalogues: in short, "quality fun for adults."[26] From raunchy sex to quality fun is a tall order, even for a repositioning strategy!

Repositioning generally involves the use of advertising and promotional campaigns to create a changed perception. In using this strategy, however, the marketers must guard against confusing the consumer about the product's position; confusion is likely to accompany *Playboy's* efforts to switch from a sex-based appeal to a wholesome entertainment position, since presumably the magazine itself will continue to feature provocative (or pornographic, depending on your perspective) centerfolds.

Planned Obsolescence

Marketers sometimes use the strategy of forcing a product in their line to become outdated, thereby increasing replacement sales. This strategy, planned obsolescence, takes four forms. Technological obsolescence results when technological improvements are made in the product. Compaq Computers introduces a dozen new products each year because it develops the underlying technology at a rapid rate—and because its competitors will beat it to the punch without this rapid rate of replacement. Postponed obsolescence occurs when technological improvements are available but are not introduced until the demand for existing products declines and inventories are depleted. Gillette follows this strategy in introducing new shaving products; the company held back on the introduction of Teflon-coated razor blades until consumers' interest in chromium blades had peaked. Physical obsolescence results when products are built to last only a limited time. Examples include car batteries, nylon stockings, and light bulbs. Style obsolescence occurs when the physical appearance of a product is changed to make existing versions seem out of date. This strategy is most obvious in the garment and automobile industries. Planned obsolescence—especially style obsolescence—has been strongly criticized because it appears to encourage the purchase of products that are not really needed. It gives the impression that marketers are dictating the buying behavior of consumers. Marketers counter this criticism with the argument that people desire change and that, in some cases, the costs of inventories that no longer sell would only raise the prices of new products. Furthermore, many times the costs associated with higher levels of quality are prohibitive. A car battery that would last as long as a car would probably cost two or three times as much. (Actually, that doesn't sound at all bad!) And, too, the quality should match the intended use—a product need not last forever if the consumer only intends to use it for a season or two.

That's the official response to the standard criticism of planned obsolescence, but one of the great advantages of a book like this is that we can cover the body of marketing knowledge without the reverence required of a standard textbook. And this particular topic deserves to be handled with gloves off. Why? Because marketing has a surly, soiled reputation in some parts, and one of the reasons is the disrespect for the consumer suggested by practices like planned obsolescence. The management team that is dedicated to serving its customers would not make kids' toys that break after a few hours of use; it would never produce automobiles that suffered from innumerable warranty claims, recalls, and malfunctions as new American autos do; it would never build a washing machine using parts that were expected to fail in a few years. And the argument that customers do not care to pay more for better quality is overturned by the success of well-made toys like Lego, by the dramatic in-roads of almost defect-free Japanese autos into Detroit's traditional strongholds; by the success of Maytag's emphasis on long-term reliability in washers and dryers.

On the one hand, consumers are frequently willing to pay a little more for products that they can have confidence in, and feel cheated and gypped when products break down with unseemly rapidity. Every time a child's toy breaks on the day it was bought, both the child and the parent know full well that the manufacturer has ripped them off, and their distrust of marketers and manufacturers in general is increased as a result. These experiences poison the exchange relationship throughout the economy, just as the single bad service encounter poisons the customer's relationship with a single company. In most cases, planned obsolescence makes the job of the manager harder by chipping away at the customer-company relationship; a relationship that is already built on remarkably little trust and information in comparison to personal relationships, as we saw in the introduction to this third section of the book.

On the other hand, while experts debate the extent to which consumers are or are not willing to pay more for better quality, a small group of companies has come to see that better quality can be provided at the same, or lower, cost. Quality guru Philip Crosby has been saying for years that *Quality Is Free*—the title of his bestselling book. Companies like Whirlpool, Florida Power and Light, Xerox, and Corning have thrown themselves into careful person-by-person, process-by-process improvement of their work over the past five years, implementing Total Quality Programs that are loosely modeled on the successful Japanese approach to quality. As was discussed in the chapter on strategy, the early results of these and similar efforts show that when a real commitment is made and the corporate culture can be refocused on the pursuit of perfection, almost unheard of rates of improvement can be achieved. Defect rates can be lowered by orders of magnitude. Processes streamlined to reduce costs. Products redesigned to reduce component costs and improve performance and reliability. These programs are the antithesis of planned obsolescence. They show that if a company wishes to it can give the customer more for less, rather than less for more, which is really all that planned obsolescence boils down to.

Because of technological developments and other innovations, companies must anticipate and plan for product obsolescence. They must even strive to make their own and their competitors' products obsolete through innovation. But they should never plan obsolescence into the product design or packaging, for this is a serious abuse of the consumers' trust; it violates the underlying architecture of the exchange equation. If marketing really is getting harder to conduct—one of the themes that seems to recur as we survey the field—part of the blame must be assigned to the thousands of companies whose acceptance of the notion of planned obsolescence has weakened the foundations of the customer relationship. Innovation does not have to mean an endlessly increasing offering of new bells and whistles, as the rapid growth in new products implies; it can also mean a drive to make a small number of essential products better and better. The success of foreign competitors in the U.S. market can be attributed to the management philosophy that allows ideas like planned obsolescence to gain credence in U.S. companies in the first place, although it is far more often attributed to the allegedly more wily strategies and greater advantages of foreign competitors.

Product Deletion Strategies

As products decline or become obsolete, management must decide when to eliminate them from the line. Not all marketers have a well-defined approach to this situation, and they are often reluctant to phase out products. Since the company must bear the costs of continuing to market weak products, it is important to think through the reasons for retaining products when they have fallen below their point of maximum profitability. In general, products are retained if a segment of the market still prefers them. Often a minority of the market does not adopt new products until well after the majority, and are also laggards when it comes to abandoning them for the next upgrade. But if these customers are important to a company's mission, their needs must be considered when considering how to time product deletion. In other cases, the old product simply confuses customers and competes with the new for access to the distribution channel without really benefiting anyone. If the product was successful, management may be too attached to it to give it the boot. Specifically, the managers who were responsible for its success may find it hard to see their creation die. This decision is probably best given to more impartial members of the management team!

Marketers can choose among three strategies for pruning product lines. The continuation strategy involves following the past strategy until the product is dropped. The milking strategy cuts marketing expenses way back in an effort to reduce costs and secure profits in the product's concluding stages. Finally, a concentrated strategy entails aiming all marketing efforts at the strongest market segment and phasing out the other segments.

MATURITY AND DECLINE

You no doubt noticed that our discussion of product management strategies led us into strategies most suitable for the end of the product life cycle. Perhaps it is fitting that our discussion has moved from the growth stage to maturity and decline without our quite realizing it. This is just what happens to companies like Cuisinart, and perhaps Rollerblade soon as well. The managers in a growth-stage market easily come to take that growth for granted, and when it slows, their companies are strained, sometimes to breaking, by the shortfall in cash flow. One of the problems with the product life-cycle model is that it does not offer any rules for forecasting when the current stage will end and the next one begin.

But once it becomes clear that growth is slowing, the model offers a clear description of what is in store for management. Sales become very sensitive to the ups and downs of the economy, and cost savings become the route to profits. (Cuisinart ignored the fact that new competitors were achieving significant cost savings by producing their machines in Taiwan.) The number of competitors stabilize and the competitive situation can best be described as an oligopoly or monopolistic competition, depending on the number of competitors that remain. As the less efficient and effective competitors disappear from the scene (the victims of increased price competition), the market becomes highly segmented and promotional programs must be designed for each segment. Thus, when the number of male joggers stabilized in 1982, running shoe companies began courting women runners and nonrunners with new, more targeted product offerings and advertising.

During the maturity stage, there are two main strategies: defensive and offensive. The goal of a defensive strategy is to keep the product's market share from being eroded by substitute products. The focus is on cutting production costs and eliminating weaknesses in the product. Some modifications may be made in the marketing mix, such as improved packaging or a change in the promotional theme. Pricing becomes important as consumers become less responsive to promotion.

Promotional efforts are aimed more at dealers than at consumers. Coca-Cola, for example, faced diminished demand for its soft drinks as the teenage market shrank. In response, it began shifting dollars from national media to point-of-sale displays and price promotions designed to increase the loyalty of the more than 500 independent bottlers that produce, warehouse, distribute, sell, merchandise, and market the company's products. (Never underestimate the importance of the distribution channel—especially in maturity.)

An offensive strategy focuses on finding new markets and untapped market segments, new product uses, and ways to stimulate increased use of the product by existing customers. This attempt to break out of a stagnant market is called product relaunch. Attention is given to improving the quality of the product, at least as far as its subjective features are concerned. "Ajax with Ammonia-D" and "Lemon-Scented Mr. Clean" are examples of this approach. But tangible features can be added to the product, too. For instance, in the appliance industry, manufacturers are pushing digital touch-pad controls in the hope that these will create sales growth.

As products approach maturity, management must either revitalize them through an offensive strategy or must look for new products to offset the anticipated decline and death of the existing product. Most companies try to add new, high-growth products regularly so that they have offerings in all stages of the life cycle. But remember that the life cycle applies to the category as a whole, not any particular brand; this means the new products must really be new, not just extensions of brands in a mature category! Although most companies invest in ongoing product development, many fail to allocate their effort appropriately between mature and growth products.

While the onset of maturity sometimes catches management unaware, you can't miss decline. Falling sales are always an attention-getter. However, sometimes companies are uncertain whether their sales decline represents lost share or whether the entire category is actually declining. Good ongoing tracking of competitor performance is a great help in diagnosing the onset of each stage of the product life cycle; without it, companies can miss a life-cycle change for as much as a year or two, and their strategies can be hopelessly out of date as a result.

As product sales turn downward, profits usually decrease and competitors begin to leave the industry. During the decline stage, the typical strategy is to bring in whatever profits can still be made before the product is dropped. In this stage, marketers do little to change a product's style, design, or other features; improvement does not seem worth the investment any more. Prices tend to hold steady; they may even rise if costs go up and there is a loyal segment that will continue to buy the product. On the other hand, prices may go down if the firm wants to reduce inventories. Distribution outlets are phased out as they become unprofitable; promotional expenditures are curtailed; and market information is gathered only for the purpose of identifying the point at which the product should be phased out.

At the beginning of Chapter 8, we postulated that management attention is focused on the customer's needs at the beginning of the product life cycle, and slowly shifts toward a focus on the company's needs by the end. You can easily see how declining sales and profits would draw management's attention away from thoughts of customers and toward the bottom line. Elimination of promotional expenditures makes good sense from a financial point of view, but this eliminates management's primary channel for communicating with customers. Customers' primary channel for communicating with management, through marketing research, is also curtailed to save costs and because management assumes that it would not act on information about customer preferences at this point anyway.

Thus, the cycle is complete: an innovative idea, born of insight into the consumer's condition, develops into a growing product. Competition enters to challenge the first-mover, shifting management attention from the initial concept of consumer need to one of competitive rivalry. Management begins to extend the product and pursue narrower and more defensible niches through segmentation and positioning. Finally, the new market is saturated and, with any luck, management has held on to a dominant share of it. Now its higher volume allows it to drive costs below competitors, and it enters maturity with a strong brand franchise and the likelihood of milking considerable profit before sales head south for the decline phase. Management tightens belts and tries to run an efficient operation in order to control the profit stream it has created. Control means rigidity, ushering in those twin enemies of innovation, routine and procedure. The focus on customers is now a hollow ritual, filtered as it is through computerized sales reports and layers of bureaucracy. When the product enters decline, it is already dead in the sense that the life force provided by the initial consumer focus is gone.

Remember Theodore Levitt's observation (quoted in Chapter 1) that loss of growth reflects "a failure of management?" Management consultant Mack Hanan has found that many mature industrial products can be turned around and given new life with a new management approach. He argues that "maturity occurs when we lose margin control. When customers set our margins, it is they who are marketing to us. It is we who pay the price.[27] Loss of margin control occurs when competitors match your performance and price and you no longer have anything unique and exciting to offer customers. The antidote is simply to start giving customers something unique and exciting again, but the loss of customer focus over the course of the product life cycle makes this simple solution far from obvious in most cases. (Digital controls on the same old washing machine are not unique and exciting.) As Hanan puts it, "In most mature businesses, the most mature component is the manager." The changes in management structure and attitude over the course of the life cycle are what doom products to decline in most cases.

This may sound like a radical thesis at first glance, but there are many examples of product relaunches in which supposedly moribund categories have been given new life and returned to growth. One of the classics is the story of baking soda, which was revived by Arm & Hammer simply by promoting new uses for it. Whereas it's use in baking continues to decline, sales growth and increased profits come from consumer adoption of the product for use as a refrigerator deodorant, rug cleaner and deodorizer, tooth paste, and so on. But it took imagination on Arm & Hammer's part, that particular marketing imagination that is fueled by a creative focus on consumers and their needs, to find and promote these new product uses in the first place. Management had to be revived by a reacquaintance with the customer before the brand and product category could be revived!

Hallmark cards continues to grow in a mature industry because it also understands the secret of reviving the life cycle through refocusing on the customer. Most of the sales in the card industry are made up of special-occasion greeting cards, and this was Hallmark's emphasis as well, at least until two years ago. After (hopefully) exhausting what the cynical consumer might view as an ongoing effort to create more special occasions (did Congress invent Grandparent's Day and National Secretary's Week, or was it really Hallmark?), Hallmark discovered the brave new world of non-occasion cards. Now don't laugh—this is a bona fide market opportunity.

Starting with the observation that "children love to get mail. It builds their self-esteem and it's also supportive," as Christy Wilson of Hallmark puts it, the company developed a line of non-occasion cards for children.[28] The line took off, generating much of the growth in Hallmark's sales. Competitor Gibson entered with a similar line the next year, and now the category makes up 15 percent of total card sales in the United States. This line was successful not only because children love to get mail, but also because demographic trends are straining parent-child communications. When both parents work, the children may not talk to their parents all day. So Hallmark sees a growing social need that it can help address through its card line. What next? Hallmark has just introduced a line of non-occasion cards for adults.

Many years ago, Henry Ford observed that "The man who will use his skill and constructive imagination to see how much he can give for a dollar, instead of how little he can give for a dollar, is bound to succeed." These two extremes can be said to represent the two ends of the product life cycle. Every successful innovation is based on the effort to see how much one can give customers for the dollar. This is what being customer-oriented really boils down to. And as the customer focus is displaced by concern for competitors, and finally in the decline stage, concern for the company itself, the emphasis shifts to seeing how little one can give for the dollar. If you look briefly at the prescriptions of the life-cycle model again, you will notice that the prescribed strategies for the onset of decline are designed to maximize the profits to the company by giving the customer as little as possible. Many of the popular strategies in maturity share this fault, with planned obsolescence being the worst offender. Therefore one way to revive a mature or declining product is to stop and ask, perhaps for the first time since its inception, how the company can give its customers *more* for their dollar.

APPENDIX: TURBO MARKETING—THE NEW APPROACH TO PRODUCT DEVELOPMENT

The traditional new product development process described in Chapters 8 and 9 takes place in one form or another in most companies priding themselves on bringing new products to market. Yet today a number of modern approaches have been introduced to the process and require some description. In the first place, the rush to introduce new products has overshadowed many of the more sequential, plodding through the steps orientation of the past. Today, companies seek speed in bringing new products to customers over all else. This approach has been termed "turbo marketing." And with today's products roaring through their product life cycles, the need for new products is daunting. In the sneaker industry, the product life cycle for shoes is a short-lived 6 months. That means that new product design must be ramped up each 6 months.

More and more companies are recognizing that new product development is a highly integrated problem-solving process rather than merely a set of sequential steps. And with each step, the company can learn from previous experiences in product development. Historically, new product development began with designers developing the concept then handing off the task to engineers who took responsibility until the product was ready for production. Then it landed in the lap of marketing. Today, these steps are conducted in a highly integrated process whereby functional areas—scientists, engineers, designers, accountants, and marketers—are joined early in the process and continue to work together throughout the process rather than in their own functional spheres.

Companies have been stripping away their old new product development organizational structures to unencumber the new product teams. Traditionally the process described above took place within the friendly confines of the company's walls. More recently, new product development teams have been sent offsite to "set them free" of the restrictions of normal corporate policies and procedures. That's what happened when IBM decided in the early 1980s that it wanted to create the PC to compete with Apple's high-flying MacIntosh portable computer. IBM sent its team out of the building with only the charge to bring back a portable computer that would compete with

Apple . . . no holds barred!! And in one year, they did . . . and in one more year, the team's invention outcompeted MacIntosh and grabbed the leading market share. Without the "free rein" given this team, such an unbelievable accomplishment would never have been possible. These offsite, get-the-job-done approaches have been coined Skunk Works by noted guru Tom Peters because they are a location where no one else, other than the "skunk" team members would want to be.

Companies are also involving consumers in the product development process much earlier these days. General Motors' Oldsmobile Division brought to market the wildly successful Aurora by employing both these techniques. Early in 1988, Oldsmobile conducted "customer clinics" with owners of European luxury cars to uncover just what it is that draws them to BMW and Mercedes-Benz. The answers were somewhat as expected initially—performance and quality topped the list. Among their "likes" were the leather seats, wood paneling, smooth acceleration, and four-wheel disc brakes. But what was most fetching to these owners was something difficult to verbalize—the sense of European solidness and quietness that engenders in drivers that feeling of confidence and security.

GM engineers quickly investigated this "European feel," measuring vibration and chassis rigidity in these imports. A fiberglass prototype was designed and loved by consumers in test. Yet the designers had to work with a team of manufacturing engineers to iron out the manufacturing problems associated with achieving the "European feel." To get to this point, the team worked with a rotating group of 50 hourly workers to ferret out the problems and also to develop a production plan that covered a three-year period. These assembly line workers accounted for 80 percent of the major manufacturing changes. Now that's teamwork with a capital C—since it emanates from the Consumer!

To take customer involvement one step further, Boeing designed its 777-200 airplane by actually asking its airline customers to join the design team. Customers made over 1,000 suggestions that lowered the cost, made the plane more "passenger friendly," and reduced maintenance. Because of this extreme involvement of Boeing's customers in the development process, toilet lids no longer crash down, doors are easier to operate, and individual seats have their own video monitors.

The development of the Boeing "Triple 7" used innovative approaches to development and testing. This largest of twin-engine airplanes was developed completely by computer. The project teams were multinational, with employees worldwide taking part in the process. Japanese partners linked via high speed data communications worked on the design of the fuselage from thousands of miles away. And work continued around the clock across the different time zones. Now that's turbo marketing at its finest. This electronic design process resulted in half the usual changes and errors expected in airplane design. Most airplane product development entails very expensive mockups to test the electrical systems. Boeing's computer-aided design system eliminated that step completely. And in the future, more steps will have to go. That's the reality of turbo marketing!

10 THE NATURE OF PRICING

Making Money and Capturing the Customer

The purpose of price is not to recover cost but to capture the value of the product in the mind of the customer.

—*Daniel A. Elmer, president, The DNA Group*[1]

Pricing is a game.

—*Tom Nagle, Strategic Pricing Group*[2]

Ads from Compaq declare in bold, two-page type, "Two bottom-line reasons for buying a Compaq PC." Not surprisingly, No. 1 is that the company "significantly reduced prices." Way down in the far corner if you look hard, comes reason No. 2: "It simply works better." It is clear what the main selling point for PCs is these days. Perhaps the company should change its slogan to "It simply costs less." We saw in Chapter 9 how price comes into play in the maturity stage of the PLC. This price-based competition is a sure sign of maturity.

When Kayser-Roth, the large hosiery maker, introduced its new Sheer Indulgence brand of panty hose, it ran into trouble because its premium pricing deterred consumer trial. According to the trade magazine *Marketing Week*, "Consumers wouldn't try the hose which sold for twice as much as the in-store competition."[3] The company had to relaunch Sheer Indulgence with a coupon on packages that gave buyers one dollar off at the register—a high cost to pay for trial! On average, U.S. coupons give away only about 38 cents off the sticker price—and on average only 3 percent of coupons are redeemed. Deeper discounts cost the company doubly—first, in the discount itself, and second, in higher redemption rates. But if the list price is not doing the trick, then marketers often feel they have no choice but to cut it through a price-based special offer.[4]

Of the four *Ps* (product, pricing, placement, and promotion), pricing is the least visible for the simple reason that marketers feel most competitive with their competitors and with customers themselves when it comes to pricing. As a result, most marketers don't like to talk publicly about pricing (and in the United States, they know they may be charged with illegal price fixing if they talk to competitors about their prices). Pricing is therefore the "secret" component of the marketing mix.

Pricing has plenty of secrets in the auto industry, where the U.S. manufacturers are struggling to increase prices without attracting consumer attention. One *Wall Street Journal* report noted that auto makers are "trying to soft-pedal the price increases by scattering them all over the window sticker, ending discounts on options and putting last year's middle-of-the-lineup name on this year's base model."[5] We don't advocate that sort of approach. Yes, keep your price strategies secret, but no, don't try to trick your customers! Unfortunately, deceptive practices are surprisingly common in pricing.

When Starkist decided it was time to raise the price of its standard 6½ ounces can of tunafish, it faced only one small problem: Consumers did not agree. So it decreased the size of the can to 6⅛ ounces instead. Not enough that most consumers would notice; just enough to increase the effective price per ounce by 5.8 percent.[6] This deceptive practice, called downsizing, is a widespread but little-noticed alternative to direct price increases. And it has been used, at the consumer's expense, in categories ranging from diapers to paper towels.

When President Clinton kept renewing China's "most-favored nation" trade status in spite of continuing human rights abuses, human-rights advocates were shocked. But pricing experts and other cynics (or are they synonymous?) were not. The bottom line is that China has the lowest prices. At a time when U.S. trade deficits have fallen dramatically, imports from China continue to grow by 25 to 30 percent a year (on a dollar basis) and the U.S.-China trade deficit rises almost as fast.[7] But nobody seems inclined to complain about a trend that would provoke calls for war if it characterized the U.S. relationship to Japan. Nobody wants to risk their access to the lowest cost supplier and, as *Fortune* puts it, "a bowl of rice and $2 a day beats wage rates almost everywhere."[8]

TO BUY OR NOT TO BUY? THAT IS THE QUESTION . . . AND IT OFTEN DEPENDS ON PRICE!

How important is pricing? Most managers steer clear of pricing, and on first thought most will rate it far below the other marketing variables—product, place, and promotion—in terms of its ongoing impact on the business. But as soon as you pry the cover off of pricing decisions and issues, as the opening stories and the cereal wars sidebar do, the extent of price's influence seems daunting. This impression is strengthened by most customer surveys, for even in markets considered the least price-sensitive—luxury goods; essential industrial components—consumers consistently rank price as one of the most important variables driving purchase decisions. *Marketing Week* announced with great fanfare at one point that "suddenly, pricing is the hot button." But the truth is that pricing has always been the hot button.[9]

Price is *increasingly* important in many consumer product categories. In spite of the surprisingly consistent health of the U.S. economy during the mid-1990s, survey after survey showed that consumers were not returning to the free-spending ways that characterized previous periods of economic expansion. Instead, we consumers seem to

---

FOR YOUR IMAGINATION

Snap, Crackle, Slip

The Kellogg's brand name has dominated U.S. breakfast cereals for decades. Its top seller, Kellogg's Corn Flakes, now carries the claim on its package, "The Original & Best." Because consumers seem increasingly willing to substitute cheap store brands and other inexpensive substitutes for this venerable brand. Similarly, Kellogg's Rice Crispies brand, famous for its multimillion-dollar television ads featuring the "snap, crackle, pop" jingle, is losing share to lower-priced competitors that don't have to carry the costs of a major national advertising campaign.

Overall, sales barely grow in the $8 billion U.S. cereal market, so newcomers need to steal share from Kellogg's in order to make it big. Their weapon? Similar products, at lower prices. And it's working. Kellogg's held a 40.5 percent share of U.S. cereal sales in 1988, compared to 33.2 percent in 1997.[10]

What should Kellogg's do? It's trying to cut costs—for example, by closing plants and cutting jobs—and it bought the Lender's brand of bagels and introduced several important new products. But it still must do something about the estimated 20 percent of sales that are lost in the expenses associated with its coupons and other discount offers—considerably more than it spends on advertising. And, in the long run, Kellogg's won't be able to do so unless it can differentiate its products as better—so much better that they are worth paying the high list price in most consumers' minds.

Consultant Charles Farkas, a director at Bain & Co., sees Kellogg's struggle against low-priced competitors as a classic marketing problem: "Kellogg is a great company with extraordinary potential, wrestling with issues that other companies, such as Gillette, Procter & Gamble, and Anheuser-Busch, have faced—how to maximize famous brands and retain their premium images without overpricing them. Whether Kellogg will emerge from this struggle stronger or weaker is a question."[11]

be more cost-conscious than ever, more aware of opportunities to buy at discount, and more eager to take advantage of low prices. (Some economists see this oddly cautious approach to spending as the very reason U.S. economic expansion continued for so long without inflation in the 1990s.)

For instance, a survey of 2,500 shoppers conducted by research firm Consumer Network Inc. of Philadelphia revealed that 48 percent of them "agree strongly" and another 23 percent "agree" that "getting the best price is more important to me now than a few years ago."[12]

"Hell no, we won't pay" seems to be the mantra of the 1990s, and it's bad news for us marketers. Pressure to cut prices or at least hold the line against price raises is constant in most industries. For example, A.C. Nielsen Co., another marketing research firm, reports that prices of many grocery store staples have risen more slowly than inflation in recent years.[13]

Breakfast cereal is one of the product categories A.C. Nielsen data show is suffering the most—prices remained steady over a three-year period in which the Consumer Price Index (an indicator of inflation) rose almost 3 percent. At the same time, however, the list prices of some branded breakfast cereals rose so rapidly that members of Congress called for an investigation, suspecting price fixing and unfair profit-taking. Which source is accurate—government data or the Nielsen statistics? Both. The Nielsen figure includes both high-priced brands and their increasingly popular cheap competitors, while government data on leading brands overlook the new competition—and also ignore the deep discounts off list that the leading brands are now forced to offer.

As the sidebar on breakfast cereals reveals, Kellogg's, the leader in branded products, was forced to resort to discounting and coupons during this time period because consumers saw its list prices as too high and began to give their business to cheap store brands and generic competitors instead. Furthermore, Kellogg's market share slipped each year in the decade beginning in 1988—a sure sign that consumers were favoring cheaper alternatives. It is extremely difficult to market high-priced brands, with their need for expensive advertising, when consumers are determined to buy on the basis of price.[14]

What, Exactly, Is a Price?

Prices go by many names—rent, tuition, fare, rate, interest, dues, premium, honorarium, even bribe. But all these names add up to one thing—what one must give up in order to obtain a product. In short, any transaction can be seen as an exchange of something of value, usually money, the price, for some amount of satisfaction, the product. The key to determining the product's price lies in understanding the value that consumers place on the product. And that value results from the consumers' perception of the total satisfaction provided by the product. When the price is higher than the perceived value, the exchange will not take place. When the two sides of the marketing management exchange equation are in alignment, exchanges take place. No one knows this better than Kellogg's marketers, as they struggle to convince consumers that their cereals are of higher value than the new, cheap competitors.

The Kellogg example illustrates an important point: Price is a large part of consumer satisfaction, and a product's value is what consumers *perceive* it to be. Thus buyers help set the values of products. You cannot ignore customer perception—and if enough customers think your leading brand tastes about as good as a cheap store-brand competitor, then the customer is right. At least, you better believe what they say and price competitively or else you will lose market share.

But there is an exception to every rule—at least in marketing. And sometimes price makes no difference to the buyer. This is particularly true in the case of products that are bought on impulse or in an emergency—or with somebody else's money. For instance, when event planners at large companies hire President Bush to speak, they pay between $80,000 and $100,000 to bring him out of retirement.[15] Hard to believe they perceive that much value in a(nother) speech by this well-known politician. Bet they wouldn't pay even a tenth of that price out of their *own* pockets!

In every case, then, you need to think about how important price is—and to market on the basis of price where it looms largest in customer perception.

Because price is a hard number, usually firmly fixed, it is easy to forget that the value it represents is a soft, slippery concept, and thus is seldom represented properly. Value is an action-oriented concept.

The changeable nature of value is expressed in these lines from the poet, Emily Dickinson (who all Amherst-based authors feel obliged to quote at least once in a book since she is our town's most famous deceased resident):

> Undue significance a starving man attaches to food . . . partaken, it relieves indeed, but proves that spices fly in the receipt. It was the distance was savory.[16]

Think about it! If you recall our discussion of Maslow's hierarchy of needs, or more prosaically, to the typical consumption pattern of desire-purchase-gratification, it is clear that "spices fly in the receipt." The perceived value of a product is never so high as just before we buy it, and unfortunately the price commonly reflects this. Once the purchase is made, the need temporarily satisfied, the price would have to be far lower to induce immediate repurchase. This means price usually represents perceived value only to those who happen to be in immediate need of the product. It is misleading to speak of this value as universally accepted; it is tightly linked to the context and condition of each consumer. And it is therefore also misleading to think that a slight drop in price will necessarily lead to a large increase in sales. In fact, the link between price and consumer behavior is a complex one, mediated as it is by perception of value. Perhaps this is what makes many managers wary of pricing; what seems at first to be a hard, quantitative science proves upon reflection to be largely behavioral, not mathematical. As a result, all pricing decisions are complex and difficult.

Because of their intangible nature, services can be even more difficult to price than goods. In the case of services, the tendency to use price as an indicator of quality is more pronounced. When the consumer is especially likely to expect differences in the quality of a service (for example, accountants, investment counselors, or convention speakers), and when the consumer runs greater risks if the service is of poor quality, price becomes even more critical. In marketing services, price is frequently used to build confidence in the quality of the service offered. With these warnings, we will move on to the standard tools and techniques of pricing, even though they often seem too crude for such subtle decisions.

SETTING PRICES

Price-setting starts with an exploration of pricing objectives. There are a variety of possible objectives, and it is helpful to review the options before setting or adjusting prices.

Sales Objectives

Pricing objectives should be tied to the overall strategic objectives of the organization. And since a fundamental goal of most companies is to grow, it follows that sales growth would be a reasonable goal of pricing. Sales growth is often pursued through price reduction. Yet higher sales do not automatically produce higher profits. Too often marketers expect that an increase in unit sales will result in lower cost per unit. In fact, many companies find that the expense of increasing sales volume outweighs the savings in unit costs and that profits actually diminish.

Some companies attempt to avoid sales growth, aiming instead at maintaining sales. Such organizations realize that sales growth and expansion bring increased complexity, greater responsibility, and more problems. Companies that pursue a follower or "me too" strategy realize that aggressive pricing often spurs bigger, more powerful competitors to retaliate. For this reason, companies like Crown Cork & Seal (metal containers) and Union Camp Corporation (paper products) aim to make profits through cost reduction and market share maintenance.

Compagnie Generate des Etablissements Michelin emphasized market share when it attempted to become the world leader in the tire industry. For 30 years, Michelin had stressed the quality of its radial tires and sold them at premium prices. But in the 1980s, it established the goal of increasing its share of the American auto tire market by 6 percent and its share of the truck tire market by 10 percent. To achieve these goals, it slashed its replacement tire prices.

The pricing objective of some companies is simple survival. Organizations that find it difficult to compete may drop their prices—sometimes drastically—in order to generate the cash they need to pay their bills and stay in business, hoping that conditions will change and allow them to regain a firm position in the marketplace.

Profit Objectives

Cost pressures, such as those imposed on U.S. manufacturers by Chinese competitors, lead companies to seek to achieve their financial goals through pricing. One commonly cited profit objective is profit maximization, or obtaining the highest possible profit. Economic models are often used to describe how maximum profits can be attained in theory. In practice, however, this goal is unrealistic, since a firm can never know when it has achieved it. Data about costs and demand are difficult if not impossible to obtain or estimate accurately. In addition, profit maximization is often equated with "profit gouging," and neither consumers nor government officials take kindly to companies that seem to earn excessive profits. Moreover, if a firm's profits are excessive, competitors will be attracted to its markets.

Another profit-oriented objective, a more frequently used and attainable one, is target return on investment. A firm that sets this goal for itself seeks to regain a certain percentage of its investment as income. This return on investment (ROI) is the ratio of profits to invested capital. It may be described as the compensation that the firm expects to receive for the use of its capital. The target return on investment approach has traditionally been used by firms that are monopolies or leaders in their industries— such as General Motors, DuPont, International Harvester, and Union Carbide.

In recent years, the pricing objectives of many companies have emphasized cash flow as well as profits. This involves generating cash as fast as possible and maintaining a steady flow of cash into the company. This emphasis on cash flow is an outgrowth of the poor economic conditions of the 1970s and early 1980s, especially the high cost of borrowing money. To generate cash, many companies pruned their product lines and lowered their prices. It rose again to popularity during the 1990–1991 recession.

Competitive Objectives

Many firms consciously price their products to meet or prevent competition. In a number of industries, there is a definite price leader. At one time, most competitors in the computer industry looked to IBM in setting their prices, although in the last decade IBM has been forced to follow the lead of lower priced competitors like Compaq in its PC line. (Price leadership can be hard to maintain, as Kellogg's also learned during the 1990s!) In other situations, a company may enter a market with extremely low prices in order to discourage other firms from entering the market after it. In still other cases, a marketer may set prices in such a way as to offset the effects of competitors' actions. In the "fare wars" in the airline industry, for example, carriers are often forced to cut their fares in response to the low fares set by their competitors. When fuel prices go up, as they did when Iran invaded Iraq in the early 1970s, these fare wars can drive carriers to below-cost pricing, and even to bankruptcy. The pressure to end such pricing battles through illegal collusion is great.

A price war begins, like a real war, with each combatant believing it is possible to achieve their objectives at the expense of the competitors. But, like real wars, price wars tend to hurt all the parties in the long run. A leading manufacturer in the U.S. adhesive labels industry started a price war by slashing its prices 15 to 20 percent around the country for a two-year period. The reason? A small, regional competitor built a new plant in Florida, a move that the leader feared could lead to the regional brand going national. But this assumption was false, and the deep price cuts were a needless giveaway that hurt profits significantly.[17]

With this introduction to the concepts and objectives of pricing, we are now ready to look at and use specific pricing strategies. A product's price can be compared to a tripod; the initial price generally rests on three foundations: costs, demand, and competition. These are presented in the following sections.

COST-BASED PRICING STRATEGIES

The costs associated with bringing a product to market are a crucial factor in setting prices. Costs represent the floor—the minimum that can be charged in an exchange; prices that are below costs yield no profit (or from the customer's perspective, costs that are above value will not be reimbursed). Some firms do set prices below costs for some products, but only for a short time. In the long run, the price must cover all the costs incurred in producing and marketing the product.

To say that "costs" are the basis of prices is simplistic; there are many kinds of costs, and they are related to price in different ways. We will look at the various kinds of costs and then examine some of the ways in which marketers use them to set the list price for a product (see Exhibit 10.1).

Total fixed costs (TFC) are costs that do not change, no matter what quantity of output is produced. Such costs normally include executives' salaries, plant and equipment depreciation, property taxes, employees' health insurance premiums, and the like. These costs exist whether the firm produces a million units of the product or chooses to produce no units at all. While fixed costs can change in the long run (for example, when a new plant is built), they remain constant in the short run. Yet fixed costs per unit decrease as the quantity produced increases.

Total variable costs (TVC) are costs that fluctuate, depending on the quantity of output produced. Variable costs typically include raw materials, fuel, workers' wages, packaging, sales commissions, freight, and other such charges. If no products are produced, no variable costs are incurred. In practice, variable costs can change as the level of output increases, since suppliers often give discounts for purchases of large quantities of raw materials, and because workers tend to become more efficient at making the product as time goes by.

Total costs (TC) are the sum of total fixed costs and total variable costs. Finally, the marginal cost (MC) is the cost of producing one more unit than the most recent unit produced. This is the extra cost of making just one more unit of the product, the change in the total cost associated with producing one more unit. Since the part of total costs that is fixed remains constant, the only change that takes place is in total variable costs.

In the real world, marketers tend to emphasize costs over all other factors in determining the list price. Although costs cannot always be known exactly, estimates usually are accurate enough to be used as a basis for profitable pricing. It is therefore helpful to examine some frequently used cost-related approaches to setting prices.

Formula Pricing Strategy

Many producers use a simple formula to arrive at a list price. Such formulas are easy to apply, and they eliminate the need for judgment on the part of the price setter (or more accurately, the use of judgment). Pricing formulas emphasize either the cost components just described or the elements that make up the components—such as labor or materials or administrative overhead.

Management consulting firms use a very simple formula in pricing their services: They multiply the daily fees paid to their consultants (a variable cost) by 3. Of the resulting price, one-third covers the salaries of the consultants, one-third pays for overhead expenses (office space, secretaries, phones, and the like), and one-third is profit. Pricing formulas can be more complex than this. For instance, the following formula has been used in the electronics industry:

$$\text{Price} = \begin{array}{c}\text{Material}\\\text{cost}\end{array} + \begin{array}{c}\text{Direct labor cost}\\(\text{to cover overhead})\end{array} + \begin{array}{c}100\% \text{ of}\\\text{direct labor cost}\end{array} + \begin{array}{c}120 \text{ to } 180\%\\\text{of direct labor cost}\\(\text{to cover all other}\\\text{costs and provide a profit})\end{array}$$

Formulas like these are used in the hope that the final price will be sufficient to cover all costs (even though they may not all be used in the computation) and still leave some profit. The main problem with this simple and quick approach, as with all cost-oriented approaches to pricing, is that it does not consider whether the customer will be willing to pay the price charged. In short, demand is ignored. Also, this approach neglects competitors' prices.

Cost-Plus Pricing Strategy

In cost-plus pricing, the list price is determined by adding a reasonable profit to the per unit average total cost. This approach ensures that all costs will be covered and that the desired profit will be achieved. However, it relies on cost forecasts. This can be dangerous, since costs often change rapidly. Moreover, this approach also fails to insure that the quantity of output produced will actually be sold, since the marketer cannot know whether the price is in line with consumers' perceptions of the value of the product. And if fewer units are sold, the firm's profit picture may be bleak at best.

There are situations in which the cost-plus approach is appropriate, but in those cases the nature of demand is known. The level of consumption of some products is stable and not very sensitive to changes in price. Examples of such products are milk, bread, and paper clips.

Scotch whiskey is also priced on a cost-plus basis; the manufacturers typically give the retailers room for a markup of about $7.50 on a $30 bottle of Johnnie Walker Black Label, for example. See Exhibit 10.1, on page 312, for a breakdown of this price into its primary categories.

Cost-Plus Pricing by Intermediaries

In setting their prices, wholesalers and retailers use a version of the cost-plus approach known as markup pricing. The price paid by final consumers is the end result of a series of markups that occur as the product moves through the distribution channel from the producer to the consumer. Let's see how this works.

A wholesaler pays a manufacturer $20 for a product. If the wholesaler adds $5 to the price and then sells the product to a retailer for $25, the markup is $5. This includes an amount to cover all wholesaling costs beyond the manufacturer's price for the product, plus something to ensure a profit. Since the markup is usually expressed as a percentage of the selling price, in this example the wholesaler's markup is 20 percent. (The markup is often computed as a percentage of cost.)

When a retailer purchases the product from the wholesaler, it will also add a markup to the price. The retailer's markup is frequently between 40 and 60 percent, depending on the type of product handled. Assuming a 50 percent markup on a product purchased for $25, the retailer would charge consumers $37.50 for the product.

Some intermediaries use the same markup for all products; others use a variable-markup policy, using different markups for different items. Grocery stores, for instance, use markups of 6 to 8 percent for soap and sugar, 15 to 18 percent for

EXHIBIT 10.1.   Analyzing the cost structure for a bottle of scotch (data for Johnnie Walker Black, as sold in a New York City liquor store).

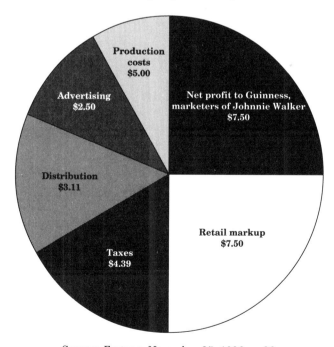

Source: Fortune, November 25, 1996, p. 36.

canned goods, and 25 to 35 percent for meats and produce. These are known as "customary" markups.

Target Return Pricing Strategy

In this popular approach, the marketer seeks to obtain a predetermined or "targeted" percentage return on the capital used to produce and distribute the product, or a specific total dollar return. This method is similar to the average-cost approach. An example will show how it works.

Assume that a company has fixed costs of $50 and must incur an additional $80 in variable costs to produce eight items. (Eight is arbitrarily assumed to be the quantity of an order that management must set a price for.) Also assume that management wants a 10 percent return on its investment of $200 in developing the product; $20 is its targeted profit.

To compute the price, add the targeted profit to the fixed costs:

$$20 + 50 = 70$$

Compute the average:

$$\frac{150}{8} = \$18.75$$

This price will cover all fixed and variable costs plus the targeted return, if all eight units are sold.

This approach, like other cost-related approaches, gets an A for simplicity. And if the company sells all the items it plans to sell, it will achieve its target return. However, this approach also ignores the demand side—as well as competitors' price strategies—and the targeted return is not guaranteed. What happens to return on investment if a firm sells five items rather than the eight items planned? The firm still has three items in inventory and is realizing a loss and, hence, a negative ROI; the calculations are shown in Exhibit 10.2.

EXHIBIT 10.2.   ROI calculations.

Estimated Sales: 8 Items		Actual Sales: 5 Items	
Total revenue (estimated)		Total revenue (actual)	
(8 × $18.75) =	$150.00	(5 × $18.75) =	$ 93.75
Total fixed cost		Total fixed cost	
(excluding target return)	$ 50.00	(excluding target return)	$ 50.00
Total variable cost	$ 80.00	Total variable cost	$ 80.00
Total cost	$130.00	Total cost	$130.00
Profit (loss)	$ 20.00	Profit (loss)	($ 36.25)
Return on investment (ROI)		Return on investment (ROI)	
$= \dfrac{20}{200} = 10\%$		$= \dfrac{(36.25)}{200.00} = -18.12\%$	

Until the early 1980s, the U.S. automobile industry used the target return approach. According to an industry expert, "It was a classic formula dating back to the 1920s. It made pricing a fairly easy task.[18] The car companies had pricing committees that decided how many cars they expected to sell, totaled up costs and threw in a healthy profit, and simply divided these costs by expected unit sales. Whenever costs rose or sales fell, prices were increased to make up the difference.

But the high inflation rates of the late 1970s and fierce competition from Japanese automakers combined to change this pattern. According to a spokesperson for American Motors, "We found out what happens when you try to offset cost with higher prices: You stall the market.[19] In the early 1980s, marketers turned to rebates, savings certificates, contests, extended warranties, low-cost financing—even a money-back guarantee—to lure buyers. In the 1989 and 1990 seasons, the U.S. auto makers were engaged in a costly and unprofitable effort to stimulate demand and grab a share through these price-based incentives. By early 1991, it was clear that auto makers had lost control over their pricing, despite their efforts to disguise price increases. Regardless of sticker price, consumers are buying cars at lower actual prices by waiting to take advantage of promotional deals. So much for formulas.

Now a new move is afoot to return to controlled pricing in the auto industry—this time, through the use of fixed-price superstores that offer a mix of brands as well as used cars. A firm no-haggle policy, combined with attractive sticker prices, will encourage consumers to buy cars at their list price instead of negotiating for a deal. For example, nine of the largest U.S. auto dealerships are combining to open a chain of Driver's Mart superstores. Will this strategy give auto manufacturers an easier task as they try to achieve their targeted levels of return? Probably not—because the main innovation of these superstores is to offer a wider variety of cars, both new and used, from which to chose. But the superdeals may achieve control over their own margins, even if it is at the expense of auto manufacturers.[20]

Breakeven Pricing Strategy

Breakeven pricing focuses on the volume of sales at which total revenue equals total costs, that is, the volume at which no profit or loss is incurred. This approach requires a thorough knowledge of costs. The basic idea of breakeven analysis is that the price of a unit of the product must cover its own variable costs as well as the fixed costs of producing the product. As shown in Exhibit 10.3, the breakeven point is reached when enough units of the product have been sold to cover their own variable costs along with total fixed costs. At sales volumes below the breakeven point, total costs will not be covered and a loss will result. At sales volumes above that point, anything over the variable costs becomes profit.

The breakeven point can be determined by using the following equation:

$$\text{BE volume (units)} = \frac{\text{TFC}}{\text{Fixed - cost contribution}}$$

$$= \frac{\text{TFC}}{\text{Selling price} - \text{Variable cost per unit}}$$

EXHIBIT 10.3.   Computation of the breakeven point.

(1)		(2) Unit		(3)	(4)	(3) = (5)
Unit	−	Variable Cost	=	Contribution to Fixed Cost	Total Fixed Cost	Breakeven Point
23		20		3	50	16.7
29		20		9	50	5.6
32		20		12	50	4.2
42		20		22	50	2.3

Fixed-cost contribution refers to the portion of the selling price that is left over after variable costs have been accounted for, as is indicated in the second equation.

When using this method, the marketer examines a number of different prices, as shown in Exhibit 10.3, and notes the volume of the product that must be sold at each price in order to break even. Breakeven analysis makes two simplifying assumptions:

1. It assumes that the variable cost per unit is constant—but we learned earlier that variable costs depend on the volume produced.

2. Breakeven analysis assumes that any quantity can be sold at a given price.

In reality, however, we know that for any given price there is a maximum quantity that will be sold and that this reflects the upper limit of demand. The marketer therefore must compare the breakeven volumes for various prices with estimates of the maximum volumes that can be sold at those prices. If the estimated maximum volume is below the breakeven quantity, that price is rejected. The price that is finally selected is the one that will yield the greatest amount of profit if the planned volume of sales is achieved.

Experience-Curve Pricing Strategy

In general, the average total cost of a product declines steadily as more units are produced. This decrease is due to a combination of two separate cost-related phenomena—economies of scale and experience. Economies of scale result when fixed costs are spread over more units of the product. Economies of scale can also result from efficiencies that allow average variable costs to decline, such as greater employee skill due to experience. This can be further enhanced if fixed costs can be decreased over the long run.

Analyses of costs in many industries have proven that as the volume of production rises, cost per unit drops at a predictable rate. Specifically, each time the cumulative volume of production doubles, the per-unit cost declines by a fixed percentage. This is a result of learning—in other words, of experience. Producers that benefit from this effect are said to move down the experience curve. An 85 percent experience curve is shown in Exhibit 10.4. This curve, which is typical of many products

EXHIBIT 10.4.   An 85 percent experience curve.

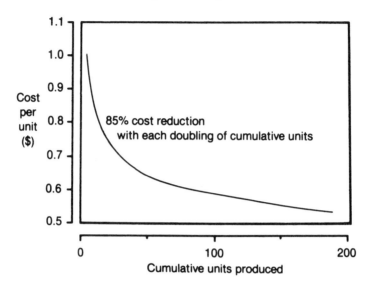

and services, indicates that as cumulative volume of production doubles, costs per unit decrease by 15 percent.

Here we see that higher volumes of production are desirable, since they lead to cost reductions. This is one of the reasons that marketers fight to increase their market share. And when costs decline, the firm can pass on the savings in the form of lower prices, keep it as profits, or do some of both. Texas Instruments rode the experience curve when it brought the prices of digital watches from $2,000 to under $10 in five years. The price reduction followed a 60 percent decrease in production costs as the volume of units produced rose.

Experience curve pricing does not explain the success of Japanese auto firms in American markets. Detroit had (and still has) produced many more units than the Japanese auto makers, but Japanese producers nonetheless learned more rapidly, introducing a series of process and product innovations that allowed them to come into U.S. markets with low prices. Japanese companies quickly took the lead in markets where consumers were particularly price conscious. For example, at the beginning of the 1980s, Japanese cars were priced an average of $2,000 below U.S.-made autos and enjoyed a better quality image to boot. By 1984, Japanese auto producers had a $1,200 to $2,000 cost advantage over U.S. car makers. And a 1990 study shows that productivity is still higher at major Japanese auto makers than in the United States. This illustrates the point that the rate of learning in an organization may be what really drives cost down, and the cumulative experience of the organization is relevant only to the extent that it produces learning. A static, conservative manufacturer may not learn as fast as an aggressive entrepreneur, for example.

Experience curve pricing has the drawbacks of other cost-oriented pricing approaches. It focuses on the cost component without considering what consumers feel is an appropriate price and without taking account of competitors' prices. It has been successful in cases in which the prices charged were in line with demand and the low-price marketer was the market leader. Experience curve pricing works best with products that are entering the rapid growth stage of the product life cycle.

Marginal-Cost Pricing Strategy

In this approach, a firm sells an additional unit of a product for the extra cost of producing that unit. In practice, the seller will not charge precisely the marginal cost, but will charge somewhat more, though still less than the average total cost.

Pricing on the basis of marginal or near-marginal cost is not generally a wise approach, since profits cannot be made unless all costs are recovered. But there are times when such a strategy may be advantageous. For example, marketers that are just beginning to ride the experience curve can afford to price below cost, knowing that as volume expands, the losses will turn into profits as the effects of experience take hold. And if a firm is threatened with a plant shutdown but wants to keep its laborforce employed, this pricing method may produce the volume needed. In addition, marketers that are engaging in a price war may resort to this tactic to drive competitors away. Finally, when a store wants to attract customers it may price a few items below full cost; such low-priced items are called loss leaders.

The McCormick Inn in Chicago used an unusual variation on marginal-cost pricing to secure some publicity and induce people to stay there. In a program called "Rooms by Degree" that was in effect between November 16 and December 30, the room rate was pegged at the outdoor temperature. If the temperature was 20 degrees, the cost of the room was $20. If the temperature dipped to zero, the room was free. Hotels and motels have high fixed costs (the costs of the building, heating, and maintenance) and rather low variable costs (the costs of room cleaning service and laundry). As a result, the rental of a room even at a low rate often covers variable costs and adds something to cover fixed costs. In addition, the temperature rarely dropped below 40 degrees during the time that the program was in effect!

DEMAND-BASED PRICING STRATEGIES

While production and marketing costs set a "floor" for the price, the level of demand establishes its upper limit, or "ceiling." As noted earlier, if the expected satisfaction that will come from the product is less than the price of the product, no exchange will take place. In short, demand reflects the upper limit on what consumers are willing to give up in order to obtain the product.

Demand is very difficult for price setters to estimate; consumers appear fickle, and their attitudes, values, needs, and wants change frequently—often very rapidly. Keeping on top of their moods and whims regarding what they will pay for products is extremely difficult. Marketing surveys can and do help to identify the level of demand, but there is often a big difference between what consumers say they will do and what they in fact do.

As further proof of the difficulty of estimating demand, we note that some high prices are not only accepted, but accepted enthusiastically. General Electric, for example, introduced its Touch 'n Curl mist hair curler for $27, and it outsold a similar hair curler priced at $15 by as much as 45 percent. Litton Industries' best-selling microwave oven-range combination was priced at $1,099 and far outsold similar models priced $400 lower. The difficulty in finding a price that is high enough to meet demand without being too high makes pricing decisions more of an art than a science.

In the typical demand situation facing most firms today, as the price of a product decreases, the quantity demanded goes up. Conversely, as the price goes up, the quantity demanded goes down. There is, in other words, an inverse relationship between price and quantity demanded.

In the real world, marketers need to know with some certainty that a given price will generate a given quantity sold, but this information is rarely available! In order to know that a slightly lower price would generate a specific quantity sold, that price would have to actually be charged, and the marketer would have to monitor purchases of the product. In practice, this kind of testing is not feasible. Furthermore, consumers are very changeable. By the time the experiment was complete, their reactions to various prices could have changed.

One company that has experimented with estimating demand is Noumenon Corporation, a California-based software manufacturer. When it introduced Intuit, a fully integrated program designed to run on an IBM or compatible computer, at a rather typical price of $395, the firm found little consumer interest in the program. Noumenon therefore decided to test-market various prices. It dropped the price to $50 and then raised it by $20 a week. Sales of Intuit rose steadily until the price reached $130. Beyond $130, sales were lower than at the prior price, and at $210 they stopped altogether. Analysis showed that sales were greatest at $90, so the company settled on a price of $89.95. After six months, it had sold 1500 programs.

The Post division of Philip Morris uses demand-based pricing in the breakfast cereals market. Post Cereal's market share is the third biggest in the United States, behind both Kellogg's and General Mills. In the first half of the 1990s, Post lost market share both to these two industry leaders and to the growing number of lower-priced store brands. To realign its prices with demand, Post slashed list prices by an average of 20 percent in 1996.[21] Compare this with Kellogg's strategy, covered in an earlier sidebar, which was to maintain its high list prices but give away more and more through coupons. Both are ways of reflecting the changing nature of consumer demand. But only time will tell which one is best. (Actually, we're willing to make a forecast on this one. We think the entry of low-priced substitute brands, plus the increasingly price-oriented attitudes of consumers, combine to make for a permanently more price-sensitive market. In which case, it's best to bite the bullet, like Post did, and make a big one-time adjustment to prices.)

Prestige Pricing Strategy

Not all products have the traditional downward-sloping demand curve. For some products, higher prices bring higher sales volumes—at least up to a point. Products do not have to be unusually expensive to show this kind of relationship between price and demand. It can be found in such product categories as baby foods and smoke detectors. Consumers tend to believe that a higher price indicates higher quality, especially where safety is a factor. Also, in some product categories, different brands differ greatly in prestige value. Price is also used as a clue to quality when no other information about the product is known.

When high prices are used to signal especially high quality to consumers, the practice is termed price signaling by us marketing nerds. Often, price signaling is used by marketers to create a quality difference, rather than to simply identify one. In other words, the marketers hope that a high price will be its own justification—perhaps a realistic hope in product categories where there are few other clear indicators of quality, making it hard for consumers to base their judgment on more objective indicators than price.

But does it work—can you simply price something higher, and expect people to see it as better? Yes and no. An interesting case study of the cosmetics industry found qualified support for this practice. The report concludes that "consistent and effective application of quality cues such as packaging, advertising, in-store support, and brand-name appeal are necessary for the successful implementation of a signaling strategy."[22] In other words, the high price must be accompanied by lots of other signals of high quality. Consumers aren't that easily fooled!

Price Elasticity Strategy

Consumers are more sensitive to price changes in some product categories than in others. This is even more true at the level of individual brands.[23] This sensitivity to price is termed *price elasticity of demand.* It reflects changes in quantity purchased relative to changes in price. There are three types of price elasticity:

1. *Elastic demand*, in which a percentage change in price brings about a greater percentage in quantity sold (generally in the opposite direction).

2. *Inelastic demand*, in which a percentage change in price brings about a smaller percentage change in quantity sold (generally in the opposite direction).

3. *Unitary demand*, in which a percentage change in price brings about an equal percentage change in quantity sold (again, generally in the opposite direction).

In situations of elastic demand, consumers are quite sensitive to changes in price. For example, in the automobile industry the market was historically quite elastic. Lagging sales were often revived by rebates, savings certificates, and low-cost financing. However, these techniques have not been as effective recently. Demand for autos is becoming less elastic, probably because there is considerable overcapacity in the industry at present.

In situations of inelastic demand, the market is rather insensitive to changes in price. Thus, demand for a product decreases by a relatively small amount as the price per unit increases. This occurs because consumers feel strongly enough about having additional units of the product to purchase it at a higher price. Examples are products for which consumers feel a strong need and for which there are few or no substitutes, such as salt, milk, and postage stamps. Thus sales of domestic postage stamps were hardly affected by the 16 percent increase in the price of stamps in 1991.

Situations of unitary elasticity usually occur when there are many sellers whose products can be readily substituted for one another. No one seller can influence the price to any great extent. The demand for many agricultural products reflects unitary elasticity, since a single farmer cannot control the prices at which farm products will be sold. The prices of these goods rise and fall in accordance with supply and demand.

Three influences have been found to affect the price elasticity of demand for a product. One is the extent to which other products can be substituted for it—the more alternatives there are, the more price elastic the product tends to be. Second, if the product is a necessity, it tends to be price-inelastic—price doesn't matter to the buyer. Third, when the price of the product is a significant portion of one's budget, demand for that product tends to be more price elastic. Cars and houses are price elastic whereas small, routine purchases like canned peaches and cereal are less so.

Products also exhibit "cross elasticity of demand." Changes in the prices of certain products affect sales of other products. For example, as the prices of videocassette recorders (VCRs) dropped to the $200 to $400 range, sales of blank videocassette tapes soared. Why? Many consumers could, for the first time, afford a second VCR, and therefore could copy movies for their own libraries.

Price Range Strategy

Consumers rarely seek products with a particular price in mind. Instead, they typically seek to satisfy a need or want within a range of prices. In fact, it appears that people refrain from buying a product when its price seems to be too low as well as when it seems to be too high. The lower limit on price is tied to the perceived relationship between price and quality. So while we usually talk about demand in terms of setting a ceiling on price, demand may provide a floor, or lower limit, as well. In sum, demand is not tied to a single price; it is related to a range of prices. The marketer's job is to set the price within that range.

COMPETITION

While costs set a floor for prices and are usually used to determine the list price, and demand sets the upper level, or ceiling, for that price, marketers must also consider the prices of competitors that offer buyers other ways of satisfying their needs. Most of the time, the marketer is concerned with direct competitors, but this is not always the case. Some competitors may offer innovative products that satisfy needs in new ways. For example, warm-up suits replaced sweatsuits for joggers and other sports enthusiasts; leather athletic shoes replaced canvas tennis shoes and sneakers; metal tennis rackets replaced wooden ones. In each case, the price of the traditional product could be used as a basis for evaluating the price of the new product.

Most often, though, buyers compare the prices of directly competing products—Federal Express versus Express Mail, Nestle's Souptime versus Lipton's Cup-a-Soup, or Blue Cross/Blue Shield health insurance versus a local health maintenance organization. In many such cases, competitors' prices become the key to price setting. This is especially true in price wars, such as discussed earlier.

Competitors can initiate price changes in either direction. Competitive price reductions are the most frequent maneuver. When this happens, the marketer can respond in a number of ways. It can maintain its price—but this strategy is best only if it has some competitive advantage, some perceived difference in the mind of the buyer that would justify a higher price. With commodities, this strategy would be a mistake. Along the same lines, a competitor can fight back with nonprice competition in the form of higher advertising budgets, improved packaging, or product modification. Most frequently, however, the competitive response to a price reduction is a similar price reduction. This happens constantly in the airline industry. A final approach is a very aggressive one—a price increase with some sort of product improvement. For example, when Heublein was attacked by Wolfschmidt with a $1 per bottle price reduction, it responded with a $1 increase on its Smirnoff brand coupled with additional advertising in an effort to protect its 23 percent market share.

Sometimes competitors take the lead and raise their prices. When the products of competing firms are homogeneous, the reaction to a price rise is to do nothing, since few buyers will pay more for something that they don't see as different from competing products. However, when buyers see differences between products, competitors have more choices open to them. If the price raiser is the market leader, the strategy of maintaining the lower price can create a competitive advantage.

In sum, competitive pressures are extremely influential in setting prices. Competitive pricing is the key marketing tool of discount department stores, cut-rate drugstores, and off-price apparel stores. Their appeal is in offering products at prices below those charged by direct competitors. But for most marketers, strategic pricing requires a solid understanding of the costs of producing and marketing the product and an indication of what consumers are willing to pay for it. The marketer must temper these two inputs with information about competitors' prices and how they are likely to react to price changes.

STRATEGIC PRICING

The tripod concept is helpful in organizing cost-based, demand-based, and competitor-based strategies. However, there are a number of pricing strategies that are more context-specific and best treated outside this scheme. For example, the pricing strategies used for new products are quite different from the typical strategies described previously. For the rest of this chapter, we will review pricing options in specific situations, and then we will close with a look at an emerging theory of pricing that is more closely allied to the marketing concept than are many of the traditional strategies. It is called value pricing. But first, let's quickly review situational pricing strategies.

New Product Introductions

There are two common strategies in this situation, although combinations of the two often are seen. In the skimming approach, the initial price is set at a high level with the goal of selling the product to the people who want it most—and are willing to pay a higher price for it. Later, when the high-demand market segment has been satisfied, the price is reduced to appeal to more price-sensitive customers. In this way, total revenue is maximized.

For a skimming strategy to be effective, a number of conditions must prevail. Demand should be rather insensitive to price. Otherwise the initial high price will not attract enough buyers to make the product profitable. Skimming is more effective when there are different price segments within a market. It works well, too, when consumers know little about the costs of producing and marketing the product—and are unlikely to realize that they are paying a premium for being among the first to acquire it. Finally, skimming works best when there is little likelihood that competitors will enter the market quickly with a similar product. Competition often leads to price cutting, which soon puts an end to the attractive profits that accompany a skimming strategy.

From the marketer's standpoint, skimming offers several advantages. As we have seen, the costs of developing a new product can be substantial, and a skimming strategy can help in recovering these costs. Moreover, if the firm initially produces the product on an experimental basis but plans to produce it on a larger scale later, a skimming policy can be used to limit demand for the product until mass production can be undertaken. And since a high price is often equated with high quality, a skimming policy can develop a prestige image for the product. Finally, marketers know that it is easier to lower the initial price than it is to risk consumer resistance to a price increase. So when the shape of the demand curve is not known, skimming makes sense.

For all its advantages, however, skimming has certain drawbacks. First, it attracts competitors. The initial high price yields high profits, thereby encouraging other firms to introduce similar products. And the higher the initial price, the more likely it is to attract competitors. An inappropriate price may hurt sales throughout a product's life and can even lead to an early death. Another drawback of skimming strategies is that they often make it necessary to revise the marketing mix to serve the new target markets that appear as prices drop. For example, advertising is likely to become more important than personal selling, and the distribution pattern is likely to shift from specialty stores to mass merchandise outlets.

In contrast to the skimming approach, a penetration strategy calls for low prices and high volume. Marketers who choose this approach believe that a low price will lead to such high sales volume that the total profits will be greater than could be achieved with a higher initial price. The idea is to reach the entire market with a low price, thus generating the greatest possible demand.

Penetration is often used when the market is not divided into price segments—when there is no "elite" market that is willing to pay a high price. Such a strategy is appropriate for new products that are not socially visible and do not symbolize high status. The penetration approach is generally useful when consumers are price sensitive and when a lower price will really result in a larger volume of sales. For example, Paramount released the home videocassette of *An Officer and a Gentleman* at a price of $39.95, substantially less than the then standard $59.95 to $79.95 price tag for a hit movie. The cassette took off and sold 80,000 copies at a time when 25,000 copies was considered the equivalent of a gold record. But note this success attracted copycats and helped drive the prices downward in this industry. It could not be done again at this price point—indeed, home videocassettes now typically sell in the $20 to $30 range. For marketers, the party is over!

Penetration pricing is also used in situations in which competitors can enter the market rapidly, since lower prices may make the market less attractive to potential competitors. Finally, penetration pricing is useful when a firm can establish large-scale production plants and reap the benefits of economies of scale.

Like the skimming approach, however, penetration pricing has some disadvantages. Although the tendency to discourage competition is a major benefit of this approach, marketers should never feel that their market position is secure—even when they are offering an attractive low price. In fact, a low price often results in losses during the introductory stage, while the product is gaining consumer acceptance. With a low-price strategy, the breakeven point is not reached until a larger quantity is sold. A penetration approach, therefore, entails more risk than a skimming policy. On the other hand, penetration pricing can open up markets that have not been served before.

Skimming and penetration need not be viewed as either/or alternatives. Sometimes a skimming strategy is followed by a penetration strategy. For example, Texas Instruments was once a price leader in the digital-watch industry, setting both the upper and lower price levels. But once the low-price barrier of $50 was broken by competitive pressures and price cutting, the company quickly adopted a penetration strategy. In the end, it became the first company to introduce a $10 watch.

Skimming and penetration are the major approaches to pricing new products, but they don't cover the full range of strategic options. Let's look at some of the other pricing strategies used by marketers.

Pricing When Intangibles Are Important

We have noted several times that for some consumers the intangible features of a product play a key role in the purchase decision. We have seen, too, that price can be an important element in conveying the product's image. In fact, some marketers make a point of presenting an image of quality through the price tag. Thus certain beers (Beck's and Heineken), automobiles (Cadillac and Lexis), cosmetics (Clinique), and liquors (Chivas Regal Scotch and Jack Daniels Sippin' Whiskey) are given a prestige image through pricing—prestige pricing.

Closely allied to the prestige pricing strategy is the notion of a price-quality relationship. It has been widely assumed that consumers equate high price with high quality and that a low price means low quality. Several studies have explored the validity of this relationship.[24] They have found that when price is the only piece of information used in evaluating a product, different price levels are in fact associated with different quality levels. However, when other information, such as brand name and product features, are taken into consideration, there is little evidence of a close link between price and quality in the mind of the consumer. It appears that consumers also use advertising, brand, store image, and other variables in evaluating the quality of a product. Marketers should not assume that a high price will produce a perception of high quality—or vice versa.

The perceived-value strategy is also appropriate in situations in which intangibles are important. We noted earlier that price should be equated with the consumer's perception of the product's value. This demand-oriented principle is the basis of the perceived-value pricing strategy, in which the price is equated with the amount of value the consumer expects to receive in the exchange. This approach seems sensible and may well be the best way to tap consumers' willingness to buy at the top end of the demand curve. And it avoids the tendency to price solely on the basis of costs.

In this approach, the marketer identifies all the benefits that the buyer will receive in the exchange. Those benefits are then priced individually in accordance with their perceived value. For example, Caterpillar sets high prices for heavy equipment such as bulldozers and tractors. When a customer asks why one should pay a premium price for the product, the Caterpillar dealer will list all the benefits that the customer will receive by buying, say a tractor, from Caterpillar rather from J.I. Case or John Deere. The customer might be informed that a $2,500 premium is being paid for durability, $3,000 more for superior service, $1,500 extra for a better parts warranty, and $2,300 more for reliability. The price of the tractor is $22,000; the extra $9,300 is for the features that are not offered by competitors' products. Often the salesperson follows this speech with the offer of a discount and the shocked customer ends up feeling that the tractor is a bargain!

The value-in-use strategy is similar to the perceived-value strategy except that the benefits supplied by the product are not "unbundled." In this approach, the value that the product will provide when it is used becomes the focus of price setting. Industrial robots, for example, replace humans on an assembly line and reduce labor costs. Word processors do not replace secretaries, but they do make them more productive. A new form of light bulb that saves electricity can be priced to reflect that saving. This is a demand-oriented approach. If price should be equated with perceived value, surely the benefits and cost savings offered by the product ought to be included in the price. Because cost estimates are easier to obtain in industrial than in consumer situations, the value-in-use strategy is best suited to industrial pricing.

Pricing in Oligopolies

In some industries, especially oligopolies, one company sets prices for the entire industry. Such companies tend to be the dominant firms in their industries. Examples include DuPont, Kodak, Hershey, U.S. Steel, National Gypsum, and Gillette.

A price leader must take its role seriously and use care in setting its prices. The firm must be familiar with the cost and demand conditions in its industry. If it is too aggressive in its pricing, it may attract unwelcome attention from antitrust officials. IBM has drawn fire for what critics call "predatory pricing," aggressive low-price tactics that have humbled its competitors. But with the price wars in both PCs and mainframes, IBM's dominance of pricing has slipped. It can no longer use price-leader strategies.

Pricing When Buying Is Habitual

Customary pricing involves sticking to a traditional price level. The marketer tries to avoid changing the price from its accepted level. Instead, it adjusts the size and content of the product in order to hold the price. Candy bars are an example. The traditional 5-cent candy bar has given way to the 25-cent, the 30-cent, and now even the 50-cent bar—but not easily. Between 1949 and 1985, Hershey changed its price only 6 times, but the weight (quantity) of the bar changed over 30 times. As a result, in 1986 chocolate lovers paid 7 times as much for a Hershey bar as they did in 1949, but they got only 45 percent more candy.

Pricing to Reflect Buyer Behavioral Attitudes

In situations when consumers face many potentially confusing choices, it is helpful to adjust prices and their presentation to give them maximum appeal and clarity. This is often done at the retail level with lower-priced consumer products, or consumer nondurables as the economists like to call them. In some cases, the price should take into account certain demand-related considerations. Such considerations usually affect transactions at the retail level rather than those at the manufacturing or wholesaling level. Certain adjustments can make the final price more attractive to consumers and lead to higher sales. Price adjustments reflect how consumers view a product and its price.

   Some prices seem to have greater appeal than others, either because they are traditional or because they match some inner logic of consumers. Thus, prices like $14.31 for a necktie or $38.72 for a toaster may not feel "comfortable." For other products, however, such unrounded prices may be totally acceptable—63 cents for a packet of slivered almonds or $2.69 for Skippy peanut butter. While psychological pricing is often used to make a price more palatable, it can also be used to emphasize the relationship between price and quality. For instance, consumers may not be attracted to a skin lotion that is priced too low. An 8-ounce jar of lotion priced at 49 cents may not be as appealing as the same jar at $2.98. At 49 cents, the link with quality is missing. Let's look at some specific psychological pricing techniques.

   The *odd-pricing form* of psychological pricing is achieved by making the end of the price an odd number or some number just below a round number (for example, 98 or 99). Odd pricing is based on the notion that a price of $9.99 appears lower to consumers than $10.00. This difference of only one cent gives the illusion that the price is in the range of $0.01 to $9.99 rather than in the range of $10.00 to $19.99. While it is customary for marketers to price in this manner, studies of consumers' sensitivity to such price distinctions do not conclusively support this approach.[25] Given these findings, we can conclude that marketers use this pricing technique mostly because others use it.

Some marketers price products at even numbers, such as "3 for $1" for candy bars or $1,650 for a prestige watch. Some even go so far as to work backward so that the even-dollar price includes the sales tax. They believe that consumers feel more comfortable paying even amounts. This is known as the *even-pricing approach.*

Price lining is most often practiced by retailers, but some manufacturers and wholesalers also use this approach. It is based on the fact that most retailers have more than one product to price, and a number of substitute products or brands in each product category. For instance, a women's clothing store may offer a variety of silk scarves. But consumers will not respond to a series of similar prices such as $9.50, $9.60, $9.70, and so on. Instead, buyers prefer to choose among a few prices that sort products into "lines" based on some attribute such as quality, prestige, or style. The retailer therefore may price the scarves at $10, $17.50, and $25. These prices clearly indicate that there are scarves for the economy-minded woman at $10, medium-quality scarves at $17.50, and top-of-the-line scarves at $25.

The theory underlying price lining is that different market segments, or target markets, can be served best through different prices. But this approach raises some important issues for retailers. It is difficult to determine how many segments there are, or which ones it is profitable to serve. In addition, retailers must be careful to establish price lines that match the prices sought by various market segments. The price differences must be large enough so that consumers can distinguish among the various lines. At the same time, however, the lines must not be priced so far apart that some market segments are not served.

Many retailers recognize the appeal of a lower than normal *bargain price.* As a result, they use the price variable to draw customers into the store. The low-priced products are referred to as *traffic builders* or as loss leaders or price leaders. Such products are marked up by less than the usual percentage, and they are chosen for their promotional appeal. Most likely the retailer has large stocks of these items to sell. Price leaders are usually well known, highly desired, somewhat expensive branded goods.

Some marketers use what is known as *bait-and-switch pricing,* in which prices are set low to attract customers, but when they come to buy, an attempt is made to sell them more expensive models. Salespeople attempt to "trade-up" the customer to higher priced, higher margin items. Such pricing is often deceptive—and clearly is not socially responsible. The federal government, through the Federal Trade Commission, has made this practice illegal in interstate commerce.

Consumers often become confused when they try to compare products with different prices. Is a 7-ounce bag of potato chips priced at $1.59 a better buy than a 5-ounce bag at 99 cents? Marketers have responded with *unit pricing,* in which the price of the package is accompanied by the price of the product per ounce, pound, pint, or some other standard measurement of quantity. First used in the early 1970s, unit pricing has been employed extensively for grocery products.

The purpose of unit pricing is to help consumers make more economical purchases. Yet there are costs associated with its use—special labels, computer records, and labor costs for the retailer, as well as reduced brand loyalty as price competition increases. Research has found consumers shifting to store brands as a result of unit pricing. Yet those with the most to gain—the lower income shoppers—tend to use it less than better-educated, higher income shoppers.[26]

Sometimes manufacturers start with the list price that will generate a high enough sales volume for the retailer to make a profit. From that price, they subtract the markups added by each intermediary in the distribution system. In this way, they come up with a price that they, the producers, can charge. This backdoor approach assumes that the manufacturer can correctly assess the demand for the product and that it can compute its own costs so that it can be sure that the price it arrives at will be profitable. The quantity produced has a definite effect on the costs, so the relationship between quantity and the price charged to the customer needs to be known with reasonable accuracy.

PRICING AND THE PRODUCT LIFE CYCLE

Pricing strategies must be adjusted throughout a product's life. Let's look at how pricing differs for new, mature, and declining products in different stages of the life cycle (Exhibit 10.5).

EXHIBIT 10.5.   Pricing over the product life cycle.

The Introductory Stage

Pricing a new product presents a real challenge. Little is known about the costs of making the product, how much consumers will be willing to pay, or how competitors will react. Yet, this initial pricing decision is important, especially in view of the high rate of new-product failures.

The difficulty of pricing a new product depends to a large extent on the degree of newness. Innovative products are the most difficult to price, since they have no reference point in the consumer's mind. Products like Big Bertha golf clubs and voice recognition software are examples. The demand leg of the pricing tripod is particularly troublesome here. Costs can be estimated and sometimes competitors' reactions gauged—but it is often impossible to guess the level of demand. With such unique products, the major choice is between skimming and penetration strategies.

New products that have identifiable substitutes or that replace existing products are classified as imitative products or adaptive replacements. In these cases, the marketer has more to go on. When Gillette's Eraser Mate was the first erasable-ink pen on the market, it still had to compete with regular ball-point and felt-tip pens. The key issue for marketers was how much consumers would pay for perceived differences in the product's function or appearance. When the consumer cannot perceive such differences, the price cannot vary much from the prices of alternative products or brands. For such products, the perceived-value and value-in-use strategies are appropriate.

Sometimes marketers offer an introductory price deal in which the new product is offered at a reduced price for a limited period. This is an attempt to induce trial of the product in the hope of building brand loyalty. This approach should not be confused with penetration pricing.

The Rapid Growth and Slow Growth Stages

The tremendous demand that accompanies the rapid-growth stage encourages a policy of maintaining prices at a high level. Yet a sounder strategy is to reduce prices as the cost savings that come from experience are realized. Holding profit margins at a moderate level has the added benefit of discouraging competitors from entering the market. With consumers eager to buy the product, many price lines can be offered to meet every segment's needs—from low-end to premium models.

In the slow growth stage, as sales start to decrease, the price strategy should aim to broaden the appeal of the product through price reductions. More aggressive pricing is used to boost sales and at the same time fight competition. This pricing strategy has been used extensively by the Japanese in American markets as they have slid down the experience curve with their electronic and automotive products.

The Maturity Stage

When products move from the growth stages into the maturity stage, price adjustments become a major strategic tool. Flexibility is the key to effective pricing at this stage. With mature products, most sales are replacement sales. Price increases are avoided, and when they do occur, they are usually due to increased costs rather than higher demand. If possible, a stable pricing strategy is the best approach at this stage.

While a price reduction may seem to be the logical way to stimulate sales of mature products, this tactic depends on the price sensitivity of consumers and on the competitive situation. With some products—such as paper clips or clothespins—a price reduction is not likely to increase sales and, in fact, would probably lead to lower profits, since the quantity sold is unlikely to change. Moreover, competitors are likely to react by also lowering their prices.

The Decline Stage

Once a product's sales begin to dip, marketers have two pricing options, depending on their long-run plans. If they want to prune the declining product from the line, the appropriate strategy would be to continue to lower the price, preferably in stages, until all inventory has been sold. An alternative is to maintain the price but cut costs. In the latter case, promotional expenditures are often curtailed.

As competitors leave the market, the product becomes less available. Often there is a certain market segment that still needs the product. Since this need can be quite strong, the firms that remain in the market during the later stages of the product's life cycle may actually be able to raise their prices.

VALUE PRICING AND THE MARKETING CONCEPT

A wonderful cartoon appeared in the papers a few years ago, showing a customer at the counter in a small shop. A sign in the window announced "best prices, highest quality." Inside, the storekeeper was talking to the customer, saying, "We got low cost or good quality. Which do you want?"

Not much of a choice for the customer. But often this is just what the consumer faces in the marketplace. Consumers definitely do draw inferences about product quality from price. In general, it makes sense that a higher priced product will be better. One assumes that it is higher priced because it costs more to make, and that it costs more to make because the manufacturer used more expensive (and thus better quality) materials in its manufacture.

This is an appealing tautology, but based on circular reasoning nonetheless. Products are better because they have higher prices. They have higher prices because they cost more to make. They cost more to make because they are made out of better materials. The materials are better because they have higher prices. They have higher prices because they, in turn, are made out of better raw materials, which have higher prices, which . . .

It could well be that a car made out of heavier, larger pieces of metal is better. Detroit always assumed this was so, and paid no attention to the "little sardine cans" imported by foreign auto makers in the 1960s. But the smaller, lighter cars, using less and in many cases less expensive materials, turned out to be superior in many ways.

They were lighter and thus used less gas. They could be made by fewer people, in less time, on a smaller production line. Many of them were better engineered and more fun to drive. The front-wheel drive of many imported cars eliminated the long, heavy, and costly drive train of a rear-wheel-drive car, but gave better traction and handling. By the 1990s, consumers, and Detroit, have come to realize that less is often more when it comes to automobiles. It turns out that you can get better quality for a lower price.

But having said this, we must also point to the obvious counterargument: There is still a large price range in automobiles, with "better" cars generally costing more. Although innovation and marketing imagination have enabled individual manufacturers to introduce individual products that offer better quality for lower price, this happens within the context of a traditional cost-quality continuum. One way to look at this continuum is to draw a value curve, showing different combinations of cost and quality that are acceptable to consumers. As Exhibit 10.6 indicates, the value curve assumes that different combinations of price and quality are available, but that some tradeoff must be made. Further, products anywhere on this line represent different tradeoffs that have the same value to the consumer. At the upper end of this curve is high quality, at the lower end is low cost. Which do you want? Neither, really. What the consumer wants is low cost and high quality, which is not on this value curve.

When an innovator offers more for less, as foreign auto makers did, this does not follow the logic of the value curve. The new combination of cost and quality is *off the curve.* It is a better combination, a better value, from the customer's perspective. In theory, at least, everything on the curve is of equal value, but the innovation that moves beyond the curve is a better value to the consumer. Management has to take a

EXHIBIT 10.6.   Price and quality value curve.

creative, innovative approach to product development and marketing, and when it does, it can truly offer more for less. And that, in the long run, is the best approach to pricing.

If you cannot offer a product that is exceptional—one that lies beyond the value curve—then perhaps it is in your interest to confuse the consumer. Think about the hocus-pocus and smoke screens employed by the average car salesman—they leave the customer uncertain about what the final price will be and what it includes, making it difficult to shop around for the best value. Compare this to Caterpillar's approach. Although its prices are higher than competitors', its strategy is to offer quality in excess of the extra price paid, so the salespeople can use a more information-oriented sale and less of the traditional hocus-pocus. No doubt new products can be sold in a straightforward manner, focusing on communicating the facts rather than conning the buyer. So if you use the value-pricing approach to offer something that really is a better value, then it is in your best interest to cut through noise and confusion and communicate the facts of the product without deception. The value pricing strategy goes beyond pricing, requiring a completely different approach to all the variables in the marketing mix.

A biological analogy is helpful in visualizing the difference between a value-based marketing strategy for a superior product and a persuasion-based strategy, such as might be used for a product that does not offer more value. Among butterflies (and a number of other animals) there are two common forms of mimicry. First, poisonous butterflies that live together tend to look alike, even though they may be of unrelated species. Each has bright warning colors so that predators can learn quickly to avoid it and its kind. And, as evolution has discovered, when all poisonous species use the same warning colors and patterns, the learning is even more effective. The predator is then faced with a very simple rule—don't eat any butterflies that are red with yellow spots (for instance), regardless of their shape, size, or species. They are all poisonous.

The other kind of mimicry involves fakery. Some species that are perfectly delicious have evolved the same warning colors as the poisonous species. Thus predators mistake them for the poisonous ones, and they benefit unjustly from the predators' learning.

But what happens if many good-to-eat butterflies look like poisonous ones? The learning process starts to break down. Say a naive young bird eats a red-with-yellow-spots butterfly, and it tastes great. It may do in any number of the poisonous ones as well before this first experience is overcome with new learning. And the smaller the proportion of poisonous butterflies to good-tasting fakes, the slower and less efficient the learning will be. At some ratio of mimics to models, the whole system breaks down and predators are just confused, but no longer wary of red-and-yellow butterflies. This is bad news for all the predators and butterflies.

This analogy may seem far afield, but the game is the same with the exception that marketers want their products to be consumed, while butterflies take the opposite view. Regardless, the communications objectives are similar, and the problem of consumer learning and choice parallels the problem of predator learning and choice.

And when the proportion of true values is low compared to the mimics or fakes, the system will break down. Perhaps it already has.

Which leads us to an important final point about the value-pricing strategy: It requires consistency to be optimally effective. But to be consistent in its use of the strategy, a firm must consistently innovate and offer superior value to its consumers. It must keep moving the value curve outward, and not resort to smoke and mirrors between moves. This strategy cannot be mixed with other strategies at will since it is predicated on a different relationship with the consumer. The strategy builds trust and adds value—thus it is the purest expression of the marketing concept. But it demands consistent commitment on the part of management, which may be the scarcest commodity of all.

11 THE DISTRIBUTION FUNCTION

Innovative Guidelines for Profitability

Logistics, long an unsung, operations-intensive area, has suddenly become very strategic.

> —*Robert Sabath, Mercer Management*[1]

Moving at the Speed of Business.

> —*UPS slogan*

Moving at the Speed of Life.

> —*Shell Oil slogan*

One of the great inclinations of retailers is to find someone who's doing everything right and try to improve on it.

> —*Allan L. Pennington, president, Pennington Associates*[2]

In the past we have added value to our suppliers' product by buying in large quantities, storing, shipping, receiving and carrying receivables. Today—and more important, tomorrow—the value added is information processing.

> —*W. A. Williamson, former chairman of the board, National Wholesale Druggists Association*[3]

In 1987, the consulting firm Ernst & Whinney announced a revolution in distribution, and nobody paid any attention. The report of their study on the logistics of product distribution, conducted for the Council of Logistics Management, concluded that "logistics . . . can be a critical factor in ensuring the success of new products or other strategic initiatives. As testimony to this fact, the microcomputer industry boasts a graveyard filled with companies offering competitive products backed by fatally uncompetitive distribution/service operations."[4] Their report went on to identify ten fundamental principles of logistics which, they argued, were as critical to the profitability of companies as the principles of excellence enumerated in Peters and Waterman's best-selling book, *In Search of Excellence*. By now, everyone in business knows about the Peters and Waterman book, while hardly anyone has even heard of the Ernst and Whinney report.

We have noted in previous chapters that distribution can be strikingly important, but also that it is often overlooked. (In fact, we have also argued that product development and pricing receive too little of management's attention—perhaps the truth is that all of the marketing activities suffer from lack of upper-level understanding and attention!) Within the field of distribution, two distinct branches are recognized, but neither receives constant management attention. The development and management of the channels of distribution—the chain of intermediaries linking the producer with the ultimate consumer—is considered quite distinct from the logistics of moving the actual material in question. Distribution channels involve relationships between business partners: manufacturers, wholesalers, retailers, sales representatives, and the like. Physical distribution involves the actual movement of products, and thus focuses on how they are transported and warehoused.

From the customer's point of view, this distinction is meaningless. Either the product can be purchased conveniently and delivered quickly and reliably, or it cannot. But from the company's point of view, the activities associated with each branch of distribution are so different that they almost always receive separate treatment. Logistics is run more or less out of the loading docks, and thus has just about the lowest status of any activity. Logistics managers are paid less than other managers. Distribution channels are usually run out of the sales department, which traditionally ranks only slightly better than logistics in the corporate hierarchy. The sales and logistics people rarely talk to each other in the traditional U.S. company, locked as they are in the struggle for last place in the game of interdepartmental politics.

But back to the revolution in logistics. Has anything really changed, or is Ernst & Whinney just trying to drum up business for its National Distribution/Logistics Group? In truth, probably a good measure of both. Certainly a new wind is blowing in statements such as those in our opening quotes, and in the following strategy statement from Howard Gochberg, an executive at Land O'Lakes, the dairy products producer: We want to be perceived as a truly valued supplier—one that really cares about satisfying the needs of its customers. That spirit should be vested in all members of the marketing and logistic channels as well as in our own employees.[5] A *Harvard Business Review* article noted that:

> When communication was limited to telephones and letters, and transportation took weeks or months instead of hours or days, concentrating on a few products—

and the vertical integration that let managers control every step of their production processes—made real sense. Now such traditional strategic formulas no longer hold.[6]

The change in strategic thinking described in Chapter 2 has been driven in large part by these two trends: the increased speed and quality of both communications and transportation. The authors of this article go on to say that managers can now "divide their companies' value chains, handle the key elements internally, outsource others advantageously anywhere in the world with minimal transaction costs, and yet coordinate all essential activities more effectively to meet customers' needs." The result is a new way of organizing the company, in which many of the activities that add value, even in the core manufacturing area, are now spread among suppliers, partners, and subsidiaries all around the world. "Under these circumstances, moving to a less integrated but more focused organization is not just feasible but imperative for competitive success."

This fundamental shift in strategy and organization means, according to these authors, that "managers need to break out of the mind-set that considers manufacturing . . . as separate from (and somehow superior to) the service activities that make such production possible and effective."[7] These service activities include distribution and logistics, as well as many of the other marketing crafts, including the collection and management of marketing information, product inception and development, the management of the customer relationship, and the management and revival of product life cycles. In fact, these activities are increasingly critical to the development and maintenance of a company's market position from the customer's perspective. Again, according to the *Harvard Business Review* paper:

> True strategic focus means that a company can concentrate more power in its chosen markets than anyone else can. Once, this meant owning the largest resource base, manufacturing plants, research labs, or distribution channels to support product lines. Now physical facilities—including a seemingly superior product—seldom provide a sustainable competitive edge. They are too easily bypassed, reverse engineered, cloned, or slightly surpassed. Instead, a maintainable advantage usually derives from outstanding depth in selected human skills, logistics capabilities, knowledge bases, or other service strengths that competitors cannot reproduce and that lead to greater demonstrable value for the customer.[8]

Does this mean we should abandon all the good ideas presented in the product chapter, for example, in favor of yet another new "mindset"? How many times can the poor reader be expected to go through this process? Actually, the revolution in logistics and the revolution in product development are part of the same story—a story that also explains the revolution is strategic thinking by which service management and total quality management programs displaced the planner's traditional organization charts and industry matrices. To find the key that relates these fundamental changes in the nature of management, it is necessary to look among the most prosaic and low-status activities of the organization, the logistics of acquiring raw materials and components on the one hand and of delivering finished goods and services on the other. Here, at the very bottom of the corporate hierarchy, in the warehouses, parts rooms, and loading docks, something fundamental is happening that will remake, or destroy, every business in the country.

The role of logistics is foundational in quality and service improvements, as Joseph Fuller of consulting firm Monitor Company argues in discussing Coca-Cola's marketing strategy: "The driver of service differentiation is logistics. It is well-known, for example, that Coca-Cola has increased its offerings in many ways during the past decade or so: diet Coke, cherry Coke, caffeine-free Coca-Cola. What is less well-known is that the company has also been in the process of differentiating its products along important service dimensions during this time, based on a continual rethinking of its logistic pipelines."[9] Coca-Cola can now compete for access to stores and restaurants based on speed and timing of deliveries, for example.

It started in Japan, and it began with the relationship between a company and its suppliers. As Kaoru Ishikawa, the famous Japanese statistician explains:

> Twenty-five years ago . . . the average Japanese company purchased materials approximating 70 percent of its manufacturing cost from outside suppliers . . . If the parts purchased were defective, no matter how hard the final assembler worked good products would not emerge. Knowing this, we began QC [Quality Control] education among subcontractors in the late 1950s. We also attempted to make these subcontractors specialists in their own fields. Today, Japan's automobiles and electronics are considered to be the best in the world. This is due in part to the excellence of their parts suppliers. In contrast, in western countries companies try to produce all the parts they need in their own factories.[10]

He argues that generalist companies cannot compete with specialized suppliers. Ford's in-house steel mill, for example, "cannot compete against Japanese steel mills, which have many engineers and export everywhere in the world. In terms of quality and effectiveness, there is simply no competition."

Thus, the development of total quality in Japan was not limited to the confines of single factories, but instead was focused in large part on the management of supplier relationships. It required far closer ties at all levels in order to allow for collaborative efforts to engineer quality into products and to produce products more consistently to specifications. And it required a dramatic elevation of the lowly field of logistics, for this greater reliance on specialized suppliers meant that the final assembler had to rely on each supplier delivering the right amounts of the right components at the right times.

This was both a practical and a philosophical change. On the practical level, since most components came from outside the factory, their transportation (the time and place utility provided to the factory by its suppliers) was of necessity a matter of grave concern. On the philosophical level, these suppliers were delivering into factories in which the principles of quality management were being implemented, just as they were at the suppliers' factories. Rather than allowing an inventory of rejected items to pile up at some inspection station at the far end of a production line, the factory tried to build quality into every unit on its way down the line. And, just as this wasteful inventory of rejects was eliminated, so too, were the beginning inventories, those mounds of components that used to cram the factory's warehouses. Management began to see the manufacturing process as including the production and delivery of components by suppliers, and to manage the process all the way through, rather than just on the assembly line. With this new perspective, the costly stockpiling of components at the factory was replaced with just-in-time delivery of just the right components, all of them meeting performance standards. Suppliers became part of the manufacturing process, and sophisticated communication and transportation made it possible to integrate their activities with the company's seamlessly.

The Japanese electronics and auto factories harnessed the new information and transportation technologies to implement the concept of a new strategic focus that, as the authors of the *Harvard Business Review* article put it, provides maintainable advantage derived "from outstanding depth in selected human skills, logistics capabilities, knowledge bases, or other service strengths" instead of from the bricks and mortar investment in some monstrous, fully integrated and self-sufficient plant. Behind the Japanese successes in process management, and their resulting productivity and quality gains, was a simple but revolutionary new approach to logistics. And U.S. companies are now being exhorted to follow a similar strategy.

You have no doubt noticed that the story has so far focused on the logistics of supplier relationships, not customer relationships. From the suppliers' perspective, we are talking about customer relationships; but, even beyond this simple symmetry, the changes in logistics have had a dramatic impact on customer relationships. For as companies developed closer links to their suppliers, they also developed closer links with their customers. The same kind of opening-up happened on the downstream side of the Japanese company, and is now happening at many U.S. companies. The entire purpose of the quality programs was to build in quality for the customer. Quality did not sell if designed to satisfy engineers, managers, or inspectors, or anyone but the person or organization that was expected to purchase the product once completed. To understand how customers defined product quality was no simple task, as you might imagine after our bout with marketing information in Part Two of this book. It required stronger ties and better information flow between customer and manufacturer, and through all the parties involved in distribution who stood in the way of this information flow. Japanese companies began to seek direct contact with customers in much the same spirit that had led to direct contact with suppliers.

And as they asked themselves and their customers penetrating questions about product quality, they came to see the product in a more expanded sense, realizing that it includes all sorts of supporting services, that the product is indeed an action-oriented concept dependent as much upon availability, for instance, as on its more tangible characteristics such as size, power, and so forth. To produce a high-quality product, they had to manage every aspect of it, including its physical distribution, and also including support services like repair and training, even though these might be performed by other parties in the distribution channel. The quest for quality-based competitiveness led management inevitably both up and down the chain of commerce in which it formed the central link, using the new information technologies and a new concept of management to turn the entire process into a single-purpose multicompany organization focused on the customer.

Logistics and distribution become one from this perspective, and their results are inseparable from the product attributes arising from design and production, for

this is the customer's viewpoint seen through management's eyes. While it is convenient to read about these functions, and to manage them, as separate entities, it is
now apparent that they must be envisioned as integral elements of the customer's satisfaction. The links must be so strong, both in how we think of them and in how we
manage them, that they are no longer allowed to go their separate ways. Product development and production is part of the same story as logistics and distribution, and
this story is a new one. There has indeed been at least the beginning of a revolution in
distribution. That no one paid any attention to this argument when Ernst & Whinney
made it in 1987 is indicative of the fact that it is ongoing, and indeed, perhaps still in
its infancy. But with the advantage of hindsight, managers will one day see this revolution for what it is.

It is easy to get carried away by the sweeping changes in management, and to
neglect the fundamentals as a result. If distribution is helping to drive the customer
revolution in management, you can be sure that it will in turn be driven by this revolution as well. The practical, day-to-day issues of distribution and logistics will be
seen in a different light, and the company that can manage these areas effectively will
be better at managing change in all areas. This means that there is more reason than
ever to focus on the fundamentals. Without further ado, our review of the manager's
essential knowledge base in distribution follows.

THE FUNDAMENTALS OF DISTRIBUTION

Distribution involves the movement of products in all stages of development—from
resource procurement through manufacturing and on to final sales. Raw materials
offer little satisfaction until they reach the hands of the producer and are turned into
finished products. From this standpoint, distribution can be seen as adding value, or
satisfaction, to raw materials by moving them to the manufacturer, to intermediaries,
and finally to the ultimate consumer. Distribution accomplishes this by providing
time and place utility, in other words, availability.

Reducing the distance between buyer and seller provides time and place utility.
Consumers do not like to travel long distances or spend a lot of time shopping for
products. In fact, they like it less than ever; surveys show consumer enthusiasm for
shopping is waning. For example, research firm Yankelovich Clancy Shulman reports
that 65 percent of Americans find clothes shopping frustrating, up from 60 percent
just one year earlier. Almost half—47 percent—of shoppers dislike visits to the grocery store.[11] When a product is located close to its potential buyers, the satisfaction it
offers is enhanced. Vending machines and mail-order retailing are excellent examples
of how marketers bridge the time and place barriers to exchange.

Distribution also consists of making sure that products are in the appropriate
place. Having the right product in the right place can help stimulate exchange. Ireland's
Waterford Glass, one of the finest makers of handcrafted crystal, controls 25 percent of
the U.S. market as a result of having created an elite image for its high-quality product.
Ads in such magazines as *Gourmet* and *The New Yorker* and distribution limited to

select department and specialty stores have made Waterford the best-selling fine crystal in America. By maintaining the appropriate places for its product, the company has maintained its upper-class aura; there's little appeal to owning a product that almost anyone can buy.

The broadened view of the product is closely tied to distribution. Services, for example, must be properly located—think about what automatic teller machines have done to make banking services more readily available. Such nonprofit organizations as Goodwill Industries and the Salvation Army understand that a convenient drop-off point stimulates donations—as does home pickup of unwanted appliances and used carpeting.

People also need to be "distributed." Aspiring actors, singers, and comedians know how important it is to be in the right place at the right time. Special kinds of products need to be distributed as well. For example, health and social services are distributed throughout communities to make them more accessible to the public. Doctors, HMOs, and even hospitals are putting up low-cost "urgent care centers" (referred to as "Doc-in-the-Box" or "7-Eleven Medicine" by critics and rivals) at easy-to-get-to locations such as shopping malls. In California, voter registration forms have been distributed through businesses, including fast-food chains like McDonald's.

Intermediaries

Intermediaries make the movement of products efficient and effective. They go by many names: middlemen, retailers, wholesalers, distributors, agents, channel members. Intermediaries provide various services as products move through the distribution system.

There are two types of middlemen who take title to products: retailers and wholesalers. Retailers are intermediaries who sell products primarily to ultimate consumers. They may also buy from other intermediaries as products move through the distribution channel. Wholesalers are intermediaries who distribute products primarily to commercial or professional users: to retailers; to manufacturers (who use the goods to make other products); to the government; and to large institutions that purchase in quantity, like colleges and hospitals. Wholesalers may also function as links in a distribution chain; that is, they buy and sell products among themselves.

Intermediaries exist because there are some real problems in the marketing of products, problems that are best solved by intermediaries. First, there's the matter of geographic distance—the physical separation of buyers and sellers. Second, as we have noted, products must be in the appropriate place in order to stimulate exchange. The process of matching product and market is complicated by distance, because consumers in different locations want different things. Thus a Vermont buyer is likely to want wool sweaters, while a buyer in Arizona would probably prefer polo shirts.

Discrepancies such as this fall into two categories: quantity discrepancies and assortment discrepancies. Manufacturers want to make large numbers of items to benefit from economies of scale. Yet each individual buyer in each region wants only one or a few items. This is the quantity discrepancy. At the same time, manufacturers must understand the assortment that the buyer wants. Buyers throughout the country have a host of unique wants and needs, and manufacturers must attempt to match them. Taken together, these two problems are the assortment problem, that is, the problem of assembling the quantity and assortment of products that will match the wants and needs of different markets.

The first two problems—distance and exchange stimulation—are solved by a process called *sorting*, which consists of two steps: concentration and dispersion. First, products are brought together at one location (concentration). Then they are divided up and moved in smaller quantities to locations closer to the ultimate buyers (dispersion). As an example, consider the wheat grown by farmers in the Midwest. Many buyers in many locations can use this wheat. In Minnesota, Pillsbury uses it for flour and muffin mixes. Dreikorn's bakery in Massachusetts needs it for bread; and Mrs. Paul's in Pennsylvania uses it in pie crusts. How do farmers in Nebraska, Iowa, and Illinois get their crops to these and other companies throughout the nation? Each could load a truck with wheat and drive to all these places to sell it. But this distribution method would be inefficient. Instead, farmers throughout the Midwest pool their crops at a centrally located grain elevator, and then the wheat is shipped in large quantities to various points throughout the country.

By its very nature, sorting is economical. The tasks of concentration and dispersion reduce the number of transactions required to distribute products. Exhibit 11.1 shows the situation with four manufacturers and four consumers. When one intermediary is added, the number of transactions is halved. And since each transaction costs money, the cost of distribution is also reduced. The use of intermediaries allows each producer to transport a quantity of products that is sufficient to meet the needs of all four consumers; without an intermediary, each producer would have to transport a smaller quantity to each of the four consumers. And since the intermediary carries the products of all four producers, the entire assortment is available to each buyer.

Magazines provide an example. They are distributed through two channels—customer subscriptions and single-copy sales at drugstores, newsstands, convenience stores, supermarkets, and chain stores. As postal rates have risen, the single-copy channel has become more important. Ten national wholesalers move more than 33,000 different magazines to about 500 regional wholesalers. The regional wholesalers then distribute the magazines to retail outlets. Since magazines are perishable products, speed is very important. *TV Guide,* for instance, is stocked at more than 150,000 establishments within 36 hours of printing. Thus, concentration and dispersion reduce the complexity of the task of getting magazines into the hands of the reading public.

Because intermediaries are located close to consumers, it is possible for them to assess the needs and wants of a particular market much more accurately than manufacturers can. Since intermediaries, especially retailers, actually talk and work with the buyers of products, they learn first-hand what those buyers want. This knowledge is fed back to the producer so that the appropriate assortment of products can be manufactured. This communication between intermediary and producer helps solve the assortment problem.

In the magazine industry, $200 million worth of magazines are returned unsold each year and must be shredded. Without this cost, the industry could more than

EXHIBIT 11.1.   Product distribution.

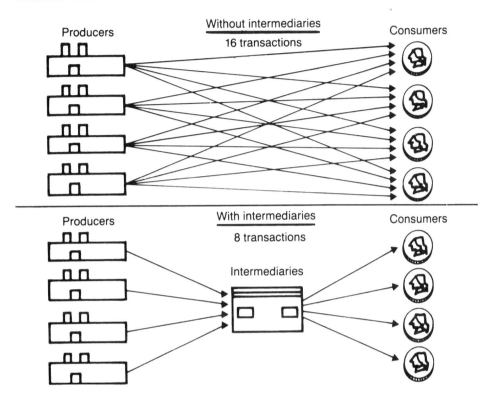

double its profits. In an effort to reduce this loss, wholesalers provide detailed information on returns and sellouts by area and by type of magazines. This information helps publishers regulate the number of magazines shipped and helps wholesalers and retailers select the proper combination of magazines for each area served.

Reducing Total Inventories

Within a distribution system, products must be stored so that they can be made available when the buyer wants them. Paradoxical as it may seem, when intermediaries are used to distribute products, the total inventory stored is lower than would be the case without intermediaries. From Exhibit 11.1, we see that with one intermediary there are five storage locations (four producers plus the intermediary); without that intermediary, there would be only four places in which inventory is stored (the four producers). Although it seems logical that five storage places would contain more inventory than four, this does not hold true. Because the intermediaries are closer to consumers and have a more accurate sense of their needs, they can, in theory, better forecast which products consumers will buy. This leads to fewer products being left in inventory. Without the intermediaries, producers would offer less appropriate assortments, leaving a backlog of products in inventory.

Services Provided by Intermediaries

Intermediaries exist because they perform certain special tasks within the marketing system—and they do so more efficiently and effectively than manufacturers could. Because intermediaries have become experts in distribution activities, they gain economies of scale, become more skillful with experience, and in general do a better job of getting products into the hands of consumers. In doing so, they perform a number of activities, including the following:

- Informal marketing research.
- Buying.
- Selling.
- Bulk breaking.
- Price setting.
- Promotion.
- Transportation.
- Storage.
- Financing (i.e., through credit policies).
- Risk bearing (especially when they take title to products).
- Management services.

The Channel of Distribution

The channel of distribution is the route taken by a product and its title as it moves from the resource procurer through the producer to the ultimate consumer. It is made up of all the intermediaries that perform the functions that put products into the hands of consumers.

As products move from producers to ultimate consumers, various exchange transactions take place. In the process, a number of tangible and intangible items are passed from one channel member to the next. First, there is the product or service itself. Raw materials are sold to manufacturers, which, in turn, produce finished products that are moved down the line to the ultimate user. The product is exchanged for some kind of payment, which usually takes the form of money. But that is not all that is exchanged. In most cases, the title to the product, or legal ownership, also changes hands. In addition, information is exchanged as products pass from one owner to the next. Communication backward through the channel lets manufacturers know consumers' needs, although long channels can filter and limit information. At the same time, information flows in the other direction in the form of promoting, enhancing the desirability of the product, and stimulating exchange. Manufacturers promote not only to consumer markets but also to channel members. Throughout the distribution channel, then, there are a variety of exchanges—product, payment, title, and information—both forward and backward.

The most frequently used channels for distributing consumer products are shown in Exhibit 11.2. Channel A is the shortest, the simplest to manage, and often the quickest way to distribute consumer products. We know it in the form of door-to-door selling of products like cosmetics, magazines, some household items, and vacuum cleaners. Sales representatives come to our doors and present their goods, and industrial salespeople call on purchasing managers. Manufacturers' mail-order catalogs and farmers at roadside stands selling fresh fruits and vegetables are other examples. This channel employs no intermediaries; it is a "direct" or "short" channel, because products move directly into the hands of consumers from those of producers or originators. Avon excels in this type of direct marketing, using a huge sales force to reach directly into the homes of potential customers around the world. And other companies sometimes take advantage of Avon's unique distribution channel. For example, Mattel Inc. distributes three special Barbie dolls through Avon, and Waterford Crystal Ltd. contributes a special crystal vase to Avon's product line.[12]

Channel B is the type of channel that is most visible to us as consumers. We buy many kinds of products through this kind of channel—automobiles, paint, gasoline, and clothing, for instance. Many manufacturers have special outlets that sell directly

EXHIBIT 11.2.   Product distribution channels.

to consumers; some own their own retail stores. Sherwin-Williams and Firestone, for example, use this approach.

Channel C is most often used by small manufacturers and retailers to distribute such products as drugs, lumber, hardware, and food items. Products that have a large market need such a channel, since manufacturers often do not have a large enough salesforce to reach the mass market effectively. Wholesalers provide a large web of contacts that otherwise would be beyond the reach of most manufacturers.

Channel D is the longest and most indirect of the frequently used distribution channels. The agents provide yet another layer of intermediaries with an even more extensive network of contracts. Candy is distributed to wholesalers through agents. This makes sense, since there are so many potential buyers of this impulse item.

Channel E shows that some producers bypass the wholesaler and employee agents to sell to retailers. Food-processing companies that do a great deal of business with large grocery chains don't need the services of wholesalers. Food brokers are very common in the food industry. For example, Ocean Spray, which makes cranberry products and juices, uses 75 food brokers who sell to retail stores, another 20 who sell to food-service buyers, and still another 25 who handle both types of outlets. Recently, it added H.J. Heinz' food-service salespeople, who call on other wholesalers and provide access to the restaurant market.

Exhibit 11.3 shows the distribution channels that are typical of industrial products. Channel F is the most frequently used industrial channel. Because industrial markets usually require personal selling, a short, direct channel is most effective. Many metal manufacturers, conveyor belt producers, and makers of construction equipment use this channel. IBM has built its reputation in the mainframe computer market by selling directly to industrial customers through its expertly trained salesforce.

Industrial distributors are the counterparts of wholesalers. They take title to products and perform the same functions that wholesalers do for consumer products. In Channel G, industrial distributors act as the selling arm for many smaller manufacturers that serve industrial markets.

Channel H shows that industrial producers sometimes need the storage facilities provided by industrial distributors. In this channel, the agent facilitates the sale of products and the industrial distributor stores them until they are needed by users. The distributor thus can provide quick service to users.

In Channel I, industrial distributors are bypassed because their services are not needed. This kind of channel is used to distribute many agricultural products.

A Broadened View of Distribution Channels

The concept of distribution channels is not limited to goods. Services, too, need channels of distribution. Some universities, for example, use telecourses to transmit lectures into the homes of students via dishes or public broadcasting systems. This is an alternative to the familiar on-campus distribution channel. Hospitals, too, are experimenting with alternative channels, such as providing services in clinics separate from the hospital itself.

EXHIBIT 11.3.   Industrial product distribution channels.

Industrial products

```
                          ┌─────────────────────────────────────────────┐
                          │              Originators                     │
                          │ (producers of raw materials, farmers, miners,│
                          │          fisheries, foresters, etc.)         │
                          └─────────────────────────────────────────────┘

                             ┌────────────────────┐
                             │    Wholesalers      │
                             └────────────────────┘

                    ┌────────────────────────────────────────────┐
                    │              Manufacturers                  │
                    └────────────────────────────────────────────┘
                      I   H   G                              F

                    ┌──────────────┐
                    │   Agents     │
                    └──────────────┘

                          ┌────────────────────────────┐
                          │   Industrial distributors   │
                          └────────────────────────────┘

                      I   H   G                          F

                    ┌────────────────────────────────────────────┐
                    │            Industrial users                  │
                    └────────────────────────────────────────────┘
```

Direct mail is another alternative distribution channel, a way to reach customers who do not want to go to the trouble of leaving their homes to shop. The development of alternative channels is one of the most important sources of opportunity for companies. Wholesale clubs are another example. The rapid growth of Costco, Sam's, Price, and other clubs in the past few years has created an alternative channel with the ability to reach most urban markets in the United States. Initially, these clubs picked up the leftovers of the established retail channels, but as they grew they were able to demand special pricing and packaging. Now manufacturers are beginning to design product offerings specifically for the wholesale clubs. For example, Heinz now packages condiments (ketchup, relish, and so on) in special variety packs for distribution in the channel, and also has added oversized ketchup bottles on pallets, ready for the clubs to display on their cement floors.[13]

Multiple Channels of Distribution

Marketers sometimes use more than one distribution channel; this is called *dual distribution*. Appliance manufacturers sell their goods through two very different channels. To reach the housing and mobile-home market (20 percent of industry sales), they submit competitive bids to meet builders' specifications. To reach the larger replacement market, they sell through retail outlets. Computer manufacturers need more than one channel as computers are sold to a growing market of home and business users as well as industrial customers.

Marketers may also choose to serve a single market through several different distribution channels. For example, STP Corporation sells oil and gasoline additives both in service stations and in supermarkets. In this way, marketers reach consumers whose needs are similar but whose buying patterns are different.

Developing a Distribution Strategy

The distribution area of marketing involves both strategic and tactical decisions. The strategic decisions consist of choosing a distribution channel and the intermediaries that will make up the system for moving the product to the market. These decisions set the stage for the tactical decisions, for example, the choice of exactly which firms will serve as intermediaries and how the actual movement of the product will take place.

Remember the Porsche case? It provides a classic example of what *not* to do. In August 1984, with the contract it had reached in 1969 with Volkswagen of America about to expire, Porsche planned to alter the distribution of its sports cars in the United States. The contract between Porsche and VW specified that VW dealers would be the outlets for Porsche products. Porsche's then-president, Peter Shutz, wanted to bring the company closer to the customer by "doing business like no one else." A research study had found that buyers of the pricey, quality cars were not impulse buyers but, rather, saw their purchase as an investment. Shutz did not think they needed the fast-talking sales pitch of a typical dealer's salesforce. However, because he underestimated the power of the dealers, his plan failed.

The new distribution plan called for eliminating dealers completely and using agents in their place. The agents would not buy the cars, and hence would avoid inventory holding costs; instead, they would buy the cars as needed to complete a sale. They would work on an 8 percent commission compared to the 16 to 18 percent markup generally charged by VW. A total of 40 company centers would be established to stock the Porsches—but they would also sell them in direct competition with the agents.

Shutz felt that the mass retailer was the wrong outlet for his low-volume, high-price ($21,400 to $44,000) autos. He had also heard that some dealers who did not have the cars desired by consumers were buying them from other dealers at a large premium that was passed on to the customer, making the cars even more expensive. He also knew that the Japanese would soon introduce a comparable high-performance sports car, and he wanted to set up a stronger distribution system for competitive reasons. Since the VW contract called for all VW dealers to handle Porsche cars, he had no control over the selection of dealers. Hence, the new plan.

Shutz's plan was such a radical departure from the distribution system in America that it met with widespread resistance. In addition, VW dealers were asked to invest in partnerships to finance the Porsche centers. The dealers felt betrayed and insulted by the offer to invest in a distribution system that attacked their traditional franchise system, one that provided them with as much as $40 million in annual sales. Shutz had reasoned that the lower inventory carrying costs would be welcomed and that investment in the centers would foster greater commitment by the dealers. He was wrong.

Three weeks after presenting the plan to what he thought would be an excited and accepting dealer audience, Shutz had to scrap the new distribution system. The dealers were so angered that, with the help of the American International Automobile Association, they started a class action lawsuit. Dealers across the country sought damages of over $3 billion. Shutz issued a letter explaining that the company had decided against the new system. As part of his effort to rebuild the dealer network, Shutz had buttons made with the slogan, "Nobody's perfect."[14]

Strategic Criteria

Marketers are faced with a lot of distribution channel alternatives. How do they choose among them? In the case of products that are new to the firm but not to the marketplace, channels already exist. Given room on the channel member's shelf and sufficient demand, the product can take its place beside those of competitors. Sometimes marketers branch out from the traditional outlets for a particular product. This approach was successfully pursued by Hanes when it took its L'eggs line of pantyhose to supermarkets and drugstores instead of the usual outlets: specialty and department stores. Other products are so innovative (for example, the original Apple Personal Computer or personal telephones once the AT&T monopoly was broken in the early 1980s) that no established channel exists for them. In such cases, channel decisions must be based on an assessment of the organization's goals and resources and an understanding of the market. All distribution strategies, however, are guided by three overall criteria: market coverage, channel control, and costs.

Market Coverage

We have seen how intermediaries decrease the number of transactions that are necessary to reach a particular market. While a producer could make four direct contacts with ultimate consumers, if the producer instead contacts four retailers, each of which makes four contacts with ultimate consumers, the total number of contacts is increased to 16. We can extend this line of thinking to still another layer of intermediary. The longer the channel of distribution, the greater the market coverage. Thus, if the size of the potential market for a product is very large, a larger number of intermediaries is desirable.

Market coverage is an important consideration for many marketers. For example, almost all people in the United States over the age of 15 are potential buyers of Gillette Sensor razor blades. That's a lot of people, and it takes a long channel to ensure that this product is available when and where it is needed. Contrast this with the market for Mack trucks. The total market for heavy trucks is only about 300,000 customers, with 10 percent of them buying 90 percent of all the big rigs sold. In this case, less market coverage is needed. While most buyers of heavy trucks also purchase razor blades, very few razor blade buyers purchase heavy trucks!

Channel Control

The second major criterion in setting distribution strategy is channel control. When intermediaries gain title to a product, they can do almost anything they want with it. They own it. What most manufacturers want is the kind of aggressive selling and promotion by intermediaries that will move the product through the distribution system efficiently and effectively. They may also want to ensure that the product does not fall into the hands of intermediaries whose image does not match the manufacturer's goals. Both concerns were reflected in Porsche's effort to redesign its channel; although in the end, it did not have sufficient power to make any changes.

Costs

Marketers cannot ignore the costs associated with different distribution channels. Many consumers believe that the shorter the channel, the lower the cost of distribution. We have seen, however, that the opposite is true. Intermediaries are specialists that perform the functions of distribution more efficiently and effectively than manufacturers could. Thus, the costs of distribution to the producer are lower when a longer channel is used. A short, direct channel requires a substantial investment by the manufacturer, who must maintain a sizable salesforce and clerical staff for this purpose.

Other Factors

These three criteria—coverage, control, and cost—provide the overall guidelines for choosing a distribution channel. Marketers can analyze the situation more closely, however, using more specific factors like the ones presented in Exhibit 11.4. None of these factors alone should determine the strategy; rather, all relevant factors should be taken into consideration. Some variables will tell the decision maker which channel length is most appropriate. These are referred to as determining factors. Others will indicate whether enough profits will be achieved to offset the higher cost of using a short channel. These are called qualifying factors. Determining factors for a long channel tend to reflect the need for substantial market coverage while determining factors for a short channel reflect the need for control.

Intensity of Distribution

At this point, the basic strategic decisions have been made. The marketer has determined the channel length and what kinds of intermediaries to include or exclude. The next step is to determine the number of intermediaries in the channel. This is known

EXHIBIT 11.4.   Factors that affect the length of distribution channels.

Factors	Explanation	Channel Length
Market Factors		
1. Number of potential exchanges	1. When many individual exchanges are expected, a long channel is indicated. When relatively few exchanges are expected within a given period, as with industrial markets, the manufacturer may be able to serve them directly with a short channel.	1. Many→Long (Determining) Few→Short (Qualifying)
2. Expected size of an exchange	2. When the expected size of an individual exchange is likely to be small, intermediaries will probably be used. When the size of an order is large, it may be economical, in terms of contact cost, to use a short channel.	2. Small→Long (Determining) Large→Short (Qualifying)
3. Geographic concentration of the market	3. When consumers are concentrated within a specific geographic area, as with industrial markets, a short channel is feasible. But if consumers are dispersed across a large region, intermediaries are likely to be used to gain maximum contracts.	3. Concentrated→Short (Qualifying) Dispersed→Long (Determining)
Marketing Mix Factors		
1. Unit Price	1. The per-unit cost of distribution is generally higher with short channels. If the unit price and profit margin are large and can absorb the extra cost, a short channel is feasible. Otherwise a long channel is necessary.	1. High→Short (Qualifying) Low→Long (Determining)
2. Perishability (speed requirements)	2. Short channels are generally quicker than long channels. Products that are perishable generally use short channels.	2. Perishable→Short (Determining) Nonperishable→Long (Qualifying)
3. Width of product line	3. Sometimes other products in a product line throw off excess cash and profit that can be used to support a short channel for a low-cash-producing product in the short run.	3. Wide→Short (Qualifying) Not wide→Long (Determining)
4. Technical, specialized, or customized products	4. Technically complex or specialized products, especially industrial products, often require special service by the manufacturer, such as demonstration, training, customization, or maintenance. This calls for a short channel.	4. Specialized→Short (Determining) Not specialized→Long (Qualifying)

(continued)

EXHIBIT 11.4. (Continued)

Factors	Explanation	Channel Length
5. Product type	5. Some products, such as impulse items or commodities, need intensive distribution so as to make them widely available to consumers. In such situations a long channel is in order. Other products, such as specialty or shopping goods, may require only selective or even exclusive distribution; hence, a short channel may be appropriate.	5. Commodity type→Long (Determining) Specialty type→Short (Qualifying)
6. Promotion	6. When a firm uses a promotional strategy, directed at the final consumer, to build demand, it is hoped that those consumers will then demand that retailers carry the product. This encourages other intermediaries to carry the product as well. In this way longer channels become available for distributing the product. When promotion is directed at intermediaries to gain their support for the product, shorter channels may be used because the producer can expect full cooperation from the few intermediaries it employs.	6. Promotion toward consumers →Long (Qualifying) Promotion toward intermediaries→Short (Qualifying)

Organizational Factors

Factors	Explanation	Channel Length
1. Number of other products or lines	1. When a firm has several products or product lines that can appropriately use the same channel system, together they may be able to support a short channel.	1. Many→Short (Qualifying) One→Long (Determining)
2. Financial resources	2. Distribution generally requires a sales force, transportation equipment, the ability to grant credit, and so on. Financially weak firms cannot establish these on their own and have to use intermediaries.	2. Strong→Short (Qualifying) Weak→Long (Determining)
3. Control desired	3. Firms that want to be able to control the distribution process, so that they may control the final selling price, the level of inventory, sales promotion activities, and activities of the sales force, will want to use a short channel. The shorter the channel, the easier it is for a manufacturer to control.	3. Control desired→Short (Determining) Not desired→Long (Qualifying)

EXHIBIT 11.4.   (Continued)

Factors	Explanation	Channel Length
4. Management skill	4. Channel decisions are strategic decisions that require management know-how. Firms that lack the requisite skills may prefer to turn the job over to an intermediary.	4. Skilled→Short (Qualifying) Not skilled→Long (Determining)

Intermediary Factors

1. Economy in services required	1. For every product, distribution requires certain activities, such as advertising, bulk breaking, sorting, transporting, and storage. The efficiency and effectiveness of intermediaries should be compared with those of the producer itself.	1. Efficient intermediaries →Long (Qualifying) Inefficient intermediaries →Short (Determining)
2. Availability of intermediaries	2. The existence of a distribution structure is an uncontrollable variable. If no intermediaries exist that can accomplish the specific activities and services needed for a product's distribution, the producer will have to establish its own distribution system.	2. Available→Long (Qualifying) Not available→Short (Determining)

Regulatory Environment

1. Regulatory restrictions	1. When an industry is highly regulated, there are often restrictions on the activities in which producers may engage, for example, a prohibition on door-to-door selling. There may also be required activities. For instance, a bottle bill requiring deposits on cans and bottles will call for certain activities aimed at collecting the used containers. In such cases producers will need the assistance of intermediaries to comply with the regulations. In the absence of regulation, producers may be able to work with a short channel.	1. Heavy regulation→Long (Determining) Light regulation→Short (Qualifying)

as the intensity of distribution. There are three alternatives: intensive, selective, and exclusive distribution.

Intensive distribution has the goal of wide geographic coverage. This approach gives products the greatest exposure. At its extreme, intensive distribution means that every appropriate, suitable, available outlet where buyers might shop for the product carries it. This is the latest marketing strategy from Coca-Cola Co., according to its late chairman and chief executive, Roberto C. Goizueta, who says his marketers used to think of distribution in terms of where Coca-Cola is sold. Now, however, "They see where Coca-Cola is not. They see an infinite universe."[15] This means you may soon see Coke for sale in schools, hair salons, churches, and many other nontraditional locations.

Intensive distribution is necessary for convenience items and for some other goods. However, retailers don't always find it so desirable since it means that they have to compete for customers. Current Coke distributors don't want to see new outlets pop up in their territories, for they fear the new distribution will "cannibalize" or eat into their sales. (And it will—but it may also grow total sales a bit. And in mature markets like the soft drink market, even a fraction of a share is highly valued by marketers, so that's why Coca-Cola is willing to risk the ire of existing distributors by seeking new outlets.)

Selective distribution involves the use of a limited set of outlets in a given territory. It is generally used for shopping products and some specialty products—those that are characterized by a high degree of brand awareness and brand loyalty. This is an increasingly frequent approach to distribution as manufacturers have realized that intensive distribution does not always lead to aggressive selling and promotion. With selective distribution, manufacturers gain because channel members are more loyal and cooperative. Retailers, for instance, know that they have some guaranteed sales; they face less competition from other retailers than in the case of intensive distribution. As a result, they are more willing to promote the manufacturer's product aggressively, provide service, and hold more stock in inventory. Peter Shutz's plan for Porsche would have made distribution more selective.

Selective distribution allows producers to choose the best possible channel members, avoiding bad credit risks, unaggressive marketers, poor inventory planners, and others who will not do an adequate job for the producer. At the same time, this strategy puts more pressure on intermediaries to move the product. Manufacturers have higher expectations when only a few intermediaries are included in the channel. Often they place specific constraints on them in order to ensure aggressive selling of their product. For example, retailers may be expected to advertise locally and maintain well-stocked inventories.

In the case of *exclusive distribution*, the number of intermediaries is limited to one for each geographic territory. This is an extreme form of selective distribution, in which producers maintain the greatest possible control in a given market. Retailers are generally tied to the manufacturer by policies that guide their advertising, pricing, and sales promotion. Often, too, they are expected not to carry competing lines. This latter policy is risky. While not illegal per se, it can be interpreted as reducing competition and thereby violating the Clayton Antitrust Act of 1914.

From the intermediary's perspective, exclusive distribution guarantees all sales of the product in that territory. This strategy is generally employed with specialty goods, for which the manufacturer wants to ensure the proper image and buyers will seek out the outlet that carries the product.

An example of exclusive distribution is provided by Nexxus Products Co., the company that markets "polymeric tridimensional" hair conditioners and "botanically fortified" shampoos. Nexxus has chosen to distribute its products almost exclusively through hairstyling salons. To support its distributors, Nexxus keeps them stocked with free samples for salons, copious amounts of sales literature, and annual meetings in beautiful Santa Barbara, California, where the company has its headquarters. Each distributor has an exclusive territory, and over half of the 32 distributors carry only Nexxus products. As one distributor put it, "I feel like one of the family.[16]

Selecting Channel Members

Channel members must be chosen carefully. Not all available distributors can or will do an adequate job. Therefore, marketers must use some specific decision criteria in making their selections:

- Is the intermediary located close to the desired market?
- Is the intermediary able to provide the necessary services to the buyer?
- Does the intermediary have the talents and skills to advertise locally and arrange promotional displays?
- Are the product lines carried by the intermediary compatible with the marketer's product line?
- What competitive product lines are carried?
- Does the intermediary have sufficient financial resources?
- How many years has the intermediary been in business?
- Does the intermediary display a cooperative spirit?
- What is the image and reputation of the intermediary in the market served?
- Does the intermediary have the managerial talent needed to carry the marketer's product line?

The characteristics desired in channel members depend in part on whether the marketer uses a pull or push strategy as part of its overall marketing approach. In a pull approach, the manufacturer spends heavily to create consumer awareness and demand for the product. As a result, consumers request the product from retailers, which in turn request it from intermediaries. Here the promotional flow is a backward one, with consumer demand putting pressure on the intermediaries to carry the product. This strategy has often been used in the packaged-goods industry, where heavy promotional spending by the likes of General Foods, Procter & Gamble, and General Mills has pulled such products through the distribution system. Kellogg's, for example, spends $1.02 on advertising for the typical $3.39 box of cereal.[17] The pull strategy is appropriate when the product is readily differentiated from others, has a mass market, and carries a low price.

In a push strategy, the emphasis shifts to aggressive personal selling by the manufacturer to encourage channel members to stock and promote its product. While promotion to consumers is not ignored, it receives less attention than promotion aimed at gaining the cooperation of distributors and retailers. This strategy is particularly useful for durable goods, for high-priced items, and for products with limited markets.

Channel Management

The distribution channel is a system of channel members—producers, intermediaries, and consumers—that are linked together through the exchange process in order to create time and place utilities. To meet this goal, the distribution system must be viewed as a totality. It is to the advantage of each channel member to cooperate with the other members of the channel, although in practice cooperation is often minimal.

In reality, most channel members operate somewhat independently. Each has its own goals—profits, sales volume, the development of a particular image, and so on—and the goals of one channel member may not be consistent with those of another. Furthermore, each channel member may deal with many others. Under these circumstances, it's difficult, sometimes impossible, for each individual channel member to satisfy all the suppliers and customers involved. In serving the diverse needs of retailers, for example, a food wholesaler may carry canned peas produced by Del Monte, Green Giant, and Stokely Van Camp. Each of these manufacturers would prefer the wholesaler to carry only its brand. Thus, the wholesaler cannot completely satisfy both the retailers and the manufacturers. And most damaging, the wholesaler cannot be an objective conduit for consumer information.

In short, there is often conflict rather than cooperation among channel members. Marketers must anticipate and understand the sources of channel conflict and try to eliminate or minimize them.

Minimizing Channel Conflict

To minimize channel conflict, you must know how it arises. There are two types of channel conflict: vertical and horizontal. Vertical conflict arises between channel members at different levels of the distribution system—between producer and wholesaler, for instance, or between wholesaler and retailer. Each channel member is expected to perform certain functions and behave in certain ways. For example, a manufacturer expects a wholesaler to show its full line of products to a retailer. When this is not done, conflict arises. This is exactly the form of conflict that is depicted between Porsche and the VW dealers, and it currently characterizes the relationship between two other leading marketers as well: Wal-Mart and Rubbermaid. Wal-Mart CEO David Glass complains of Rubbermaid, whose products Wal-Mart sells, "They've lost their momentum, and I'm not sure why. They don't have any good new products." But insiders say the bad blood isn't over new products, but rather stems from Wal-Mart's discovery that Rubbermaid had given another (smaller) retailer a better price on some products. As Rubbermaid's biggest customer, Wal-Mart wants the best prices. But Rubbermaid obviously has much to lose from deep discounts to its biggest customer and tries its best to hold the line on pricing.[18]

Horizontal conflict occurs between channel members at the same level—between two or more wholesalers or two or more retailers. Such conflict can occur between intermediaries of the same type (for example, two competing supermarkets) or between two different types of intermediaries (for example, a department store and a discount store). Generally, the second type of horizontal conflict is more common. So many retailers have turned to carrying a vast array of products, and in so doing have added product lines that formerly were carried by other types of retailers, that they must now engage in intense competition for customers. Drugstores, for instance, must compete with discount stores, supermarkets, small grocery stores, and even department stores. Similarly, specialty paint stores now have to compete with lumberyards, hardware stores, discount stores, and department stores.

Reducing Channel Conflict

Cooperation within a channel often comes from the ability of one channel member to influence the behavior of others, in other words, from the power of one member over the others.[19] Power results in control and thus fosters cooperation. The channel member that has such power is referred to as the channel captain. In most cases, the channel captain is the manufacturer; Procter & Gamble, Gillette, General Electric, and General Motors, for example, are clearly the dominant forces in the distribution of their products. Increasingly retailers or wholesalers are becoming the channel captain. Wal-Mart can pretty much dictate the design, price, and terms of sale of the products they buy from most of the manufacturers in their distribution channels. It certainly tries to do so with Rubbermaid—as we saw above.

In Canada and some European countries, and increasingly in the United States, powerful retailers are requiring "slotting fees" of as much as $30,000 to cover the risk and costs of giving shelf space to new products. And if products do not sell as briskly as expected over say a three-month period, manufacturers are forced to pay failure fees of $2,000 to $5,000. Even more, these are fees demanded for in-store product sampling, promotional ads in circulars, and special displays.[20] A General Mills vice president offered this report: "Seven chains control about 75 percent of the business in Canada, and they are using their power to extract more money from us. So, we're very careful that we have a good new product that will last a long time."[21] The recent consolidation of retailers through acquisitions, failures, and the growth of giant discounters and wholesale clubs is increasing the power of retailers in the United States, too.

Channel leadership requires three conditions: The channel captain must want to exert influence; the other channel members must be willing to accept its control; and there must be significant differences in the power of the various channel members.[22] When a shift in power occurs, there is often disagreement over who should lead, and thus increased conflict.

Knowledge is power in the world of distribution. To maintain its channel leadership, Wal-Mart relies on more than just size. It also makes sure it has the best information—operating a private satellite-communications system that collects and compiles data on daily sales by stock-keeping units in every store. The information is then converted to purchase orders that zip electronically to 4,000 vendors each day. A better information system makes it possible for Wal-Mart to restock twice a week on average, compared to every two weeks at the traditional mass merchandise store. And this information system gives Wal-Mart the power to tell each supplier what to supply, when and where, so as to maximize sales.[23]

A second approach to resolving channel conflict is to integrate the channel members into a single organization called a vertical marketing system. Such a system operates as a whole rather than as a set of individual parts. Also, certain economies of scale can be achieved in this way. For example, marketing research, accounting programs, and advertising personnel can be used by all the members of the channel. At the same time, however, inefficiencies are introduced as the channel is restructured—and the new channel can require a sizable financial investment. Legal restrictions may also interfere, since some vertical systems may be viewed as reducing competition. Nevertheless, more and more such systems are being established both in the United States and in other developed countries.

There are three types of vertical marketing systems: corporate, administered, and contractual. In a corporate vertical marketing system, control is gained through ownership of both production and distribution operations. The corporation can own some or all of the parts of the channel. Firestone, for instance, owns some of the retail outlets that distribute its tires; Coca-Cola owns some of the bottlers that distribute its soft drinks. Not all such systems are owned by the producer, though. Revco D.S., the nation's largest discount drugstore chain, has expanded into the production of drugs and related items.

In an administered vertical marketing system, cooperation results primarily from the economic power of one channel member; in other words, one member is informally designated as captain. This channel member usually has the most resources to invest in channel management and performs functions that win the loyalty of other channel members. Kraft General Foods Corporation, for instance, has developed computer software that will measure retailers' product turnover and should boost their profits. And now with scanner data, many supermarket chains are taking on the captain role; information is their power base.

Contractual vertical marketing systems offer a middle ground between the costly corporate system and the less controllable administered system. In this approach, channel members draw up a legal agreement that specifies the rights and responsibilities of each party. This is the fastest growing type of vertical marketing system. The most common form of it is the franchise system. For a fee, the franchise owner buys the right to sell the franchisers product, but specific guidelines such as using only corporate-sponsored promotions and products and wearing corporate uniforms are set up to ensure a standardized image and level of quality.

The growth in franchising is striking. Over 3,000 companies now distribute through franchises in 60 different industries. A third of all retail sales are made by franchises (on a dollar basis) and at the current rate of growth the figure will be 50 percent in the year 2000.[24] What accounts for this remarkable transformation of distribution channels?

The conventional explanation falls short. Franchisers usually say people buy franchises because the failure rate is only 5 percent. But according to Rupert Bartlett of the American Bar Association's Forum on Franchising, "At best a third are doing very well, a third are in definite financial trouble and a third may be breaking even."[25] The high success rate of franchises is a myth, albeit certainly a useful myth for companies wishing to sell franchises. And the high risk of nonfranchise startups is also a myth. The conventional wisdom says that 9 out of 10 entrepreneurs fail, but the most extensive study to date reported a 77 percent survival rate three years after startup.[26] In fact, the risks of a startup are about the same, whether it is a franchise or not.

While entrepreneurs may select franchises on the basis of myth rather than reality, the real issue is why customers select franchises. More and more consumers are voting for franchises with their wallets, and the most likely explanation is that the franchises offer higher quality. The presence of a concerned owner (and often the owner's spouse and children) behind a retail counter can make a big difference in this era of miserably poor customer service. The franchise owner is management, but this management is on the front lines, interacting with customers daily. The franchise system's organization is inherently more customer-oriented than the centrally-managed chains with which franchises often compete. And while independent stores may also have on-site management, they lack the logistical advantages and economies of scale of a franchise system when it comes to activities like purchasing and advertising. The rise of franchising is a little told part of the story of the marketing revolution in America.

LEGAL ASPECTS OF DISTRIBUTION

Companies that attempt to control the distribution of their products are in danger of violating the Sherman Antitrust Act, the Clayton Antitrust Act, or the Federal Trade Commission Act. Four methods of control are frequently employed—usually by manufacturers. While none is illegal per se, each can be deemed illegal if it has the effect of reducing competition, creating a monopoly, or restraining trade.

In exclusive dealing situations, the manufacturer forbids dealers to carry competitors' products. While not all exclusive dealing is illegal, it tends to be unlawful when such an agreement is reached by a very large manufacturer and a very small dealer. In such cases, the power of the manufacturer is viewed as a restraint of trade.

Exclusive dealing is also deemed unlawful when the manufacturer has a dominant share of a given market. When the exclusive contract actually improves competition—for example, when the manufacturer is small and/or just getting started—exclusive deals may be looked upon favorably by the courts.

Dealer selection involves selecting the dealers to which a manufacturer will sell, and not selling to any others. In 1919, the U.S. Supreme Court firmly established the right of producers to choose the organizations and individuals to whom they will sell—as long as the intent is not to create a monopoly. The courts have also said that dealers cannot be dropped for handling competitors' lines.

In the case of tying agreements, the producer forces the dealer to buy additional products in order to secure one highly desired product—or at least the dealer is restrained from buying that product from another source. Generally, such agreements are viewed as violating the antitrust laws. They are seen as legal when a new company is trying to enter a market, when the producer is trying to maintain a desired level of quality, or when an exclusive dealer is required to carry a manufacturer's full product line.

Manufacturers use exclusive territories to ensure that dealers sell only to customers within a specific territory. Where such arrangements reduce competition and restrain trade, they could be viewed as illegal. Generally, judicial bodies seek to foster competition among intermediaries handling the same brand.

So far we have looked at distribution channels from afar, as would a manager working on a distribution strategy. But it is also helpful to sweep down for a close look at retailing, since this aspect of the channel is of such scale and importance that it is the primary concern of many companies.

RETAILING

Stew Leonard's is a specialty grocery store in Norwalk, Connecticut. But not your average specialty food store; with revenues of $115 million a year, or $3,470 per square foot of selling space, it probably sets the record. Its high sales do not reflect a broader selection; in fact, the store carries only 800 items versus two to three thousand at the typical grocery store. Instead, the store sells more of the items it does stock, simply because they are better. An anecdote told to a reporter by Stew Leonard, Jr., who recently took over the management of the store from his father, illustrates the philosophy that makes this store unique.

> A couple of years ago, Stew, Jr., and his brother, Tom, and some other managers from the store were getting ready to meet with a high-powered, high-priced consultant. Stew, Sr., couldn't attend the meeting, so Stew, Jr., asked him on the phone if there was anything particularly important he wanted discussed. "I bought some corn yesterday," Stew, Sr., replied, "and had it for dinner last night, and it wasn't really sweet."
>
> Stew, Jr., gently remonstrated with his father: "Dad, this isn't that kind of meeting. We're talking about strategy, we're talking about merchandising. Isn't there anything really important that you want me to mention?"
>
> "Yeah. The corn isn't really, really sweet."

From there, Stew, Jr., recalls, their conversation turned immediately to how to get corn into the store the day it was picked. As it wound up, "we had to completely rearrange our trucking, and our farmer had to start picking earlier. But we got fresh-picked corn."[27]

The more limited selection means that the store buys a high volume of what it does sell, getting good prices on it and having enough power to demand quality from its suppliers. To sell better corn, the store had to convince the farmer to pick early in the morning, and had to alter the logistics so that the fresh-picked corn could be loaded and delivered by truck immediately. Even so, the store could not offer fresh-picked corn until 10:00 AM, but you can be sure it now sells a great deal more than the neighboring grocery stores that sell corn that has been in transit for days. So Stew Leonard's is able to sell better corn without buying it at a higher price. Its secret, according to Stew, Sr., is that customers "come here to save money on good stuff." Better quality for a better price—a winning strategy, but only possible if you are willing to innovate and develop new processes. And if you have a better understanding of what customers care about than competitors.

As we saw in our examination of product development, manufacturers offer more products to grocery stores every year. Those "mindless brand extensions" that Campbell's management complained about, and even the hundreds of sincere efforts to innovate, have over the years produced an incredible variety of choice. But have they produced better quality; have they given consumers more value? The Stew Leonard's story suggests that they may have not. As Joseph Palmer, owner of Palmer's Supermarkets in nearby Stamford, Connecticut, explains, "We don't need 16 flavors of health bars. The redundancy is out of control."[28] A quick trip to Norwalk would show him how the retailer can take control over product selection and build a quality-based strategy instead of the typical redundancy-based strategy of grocery stores.

Retailing includes all activities associated with selling goods and services to ultimate consumers. In the case of retailers, one might say, "The buck starts here," since the sale of a product at retail begins the movement of payments back through the distribution channel. Since it sells goods to the final member of the channel, the consumer, the retailer is in the best possible position to understand the specific wants and needs of the markets that drive the entire distribution and production system.

Although we usually think of retailers as merchant intermediaries who own stores, it's also accurate to consider teachers, lawyers, consultants, doctors, and dentists as retailers. Certainly not all retailing requires a store. We buy newspapers at a stand, have our shoes shined on a street corner, buy a hot dog or balloon from a street vendor. A Mary Kay cosmetics representative who comes to our door is a retailer, and so is a mail-order marketer. Anyone who markets to the ultimate consumer, by whatever name, is in the business of retailing. A hospital is a retailer to patients. Colleges are retailers of education, and such organizations as charities, funeral homes, and churches also fall into the retail category. Retailing thus has a very broad scope.

FOR YOUR IMAGINATION

If the Shoe Doesn't Fit, Try One of Our 3,999 Other Styles!

Imagine this: a building the size of a sports stadium filled to bursting, aisle after aisle, with . . . sneakers! Hmm. Kind of a crazy idea. But why not? People are crazy about sneakers these days, and the continual product developments of industry leaders like Nike and Adidas make it possible to stock an endless variety of products.

That's the formula at least for Sneaker Stadium Inc., which specializes in what marketing geeks like to call the "single-category superstore." It's the Staples formula, but for sports shoes instead of office supplies. And because sneakers are supposed to be a lot more fun than office supplies, Sneaker Stadium includes try-out tracks, basketball courts, and other fun attractions in its stores. The idea is to make locations like Sneaker Stadium's 31,000-square-foot store in Paramus, New Jersey a destination for shoppers—the kind of place you can go for an evening of entertainment and hard-core shopping.[29]

What next . . . Ping Pong superstores? We aren't sure. But if we figure it out, we'll stop writing books and get into the retail business in a hurry!

We tend to focus on the time and place utilities that come from the retailing function. But retailers also provide possession utility. By offering desired assortments and prices related to perceived value, the retailer encourages the customer to make a purchase and thereby obtain possession utility. Retailers of services—hairstylists, insurance agencies, landscapers—offer even more; they provide form utility as well as time, place, and possession utilities. Such retailers are virtually inseparable from their highly perishable products. Their services last only as long as they are performed and cannot be performed without the retailer.[30] Moreover, the intangible nature of services makes customer-retailer contact the basis for most of the form utility provided.[31] The cleanliness of the Chemlawn truck that fertilizes your lawn, the personality of the Hertz agent, the professional appearance of the booklet containing your H&R Block prepared tax forms—all of these features contribute to your perception of the product. Service retailers must pay strict attention to such details in order to create the form utility desired by their customers.

Modern Retailing Strategies

In the past, retailers took a "supplier" approach to retailing; they saw themselves essentially as buyers of merchandise for consumers in their locality. But in the late 1970s, the "positioning era" came to retailing. The retail establishment began to be defined in terms of the market segment it served. Initially this segmentation was based on demographic variables, but now life-style segmentation appears to be taking hold as companies provide an image, a merchandise assortment, an entire feeling geared to a well-defined target market.[32] Wal-Mart, for example, has developed product lines, personnel, and policies that reflect the life styles of small-town, rural America. And we saw in an earlier chapter how Kmart tried to change its target market through trading up.

In sharp contrast to these merchandise strategies, other retailers have become specialty stores with a narrow set of product lines and deep assortments. The Gap, Toys 'R Us, B. Dalton, and Radio Shack are examples. In addition, there are numerous approaches that fall somewhere between the mass merchandise and specialty store strategies. In the rest of the chapter, we will take a brief look at some of the strategic options available to modern retailers.[33]

The Value Strategy

A retailer that adopts the value strategy attempts to offer greater overall quality at a lower price than its competitors. While price competition has long been a favorite strategy of retailers, it has become even more important since the inflationary 1970s, and the recent recession has given discount-style retailers a boost as well. Today, consumers are cautious and very value conscious, wanting to get their money's worth. Costco, Sam's, and Price are examples; these wholesale clubs are capitalizing on an opportunity to allow customers to buy leading brands at rock-bottom prices.

The Efficiency Strategy

Americans are time conscious, and many stores have taken advantage of this characteristic. The place in the four *P*s ought to refer to place in time as well as space. Convenience stores emphasize proximity to the customer. Superstores stress one-stop shopping. Catalog and other mail-order retailers combine computer, telephone, and credit card technologies to minimize their customers' shopping effort. Catalog showrooms reduce the time the customer has to spend searching for a desired item. In the future, we are likely to see the expansion of videotext shopping (purchasing via computer) as well as catalogs on videodiscs, interactive cable television, and broadcast teletext, with orders being placed by telephone.

The Personal-Contact Strategy

In the United States today, consumers are increasingly concerned with individual well-being and quality of life. Such consumers crave highly customized and expert personal service. Nordstrom's pampers its customers with personal phone calls and notebooks full of information about their personal tastes. Other retailers are pursuing this strategy by offering a wider array of services. Abraham and Strauss, for example, offers a special department called "The Office," where trained consultants help women executives make decisions about their wardrobes. Stew Leonard's is famous for its numerous well-trained and helpful staff.

The Sensory Strategy

Some retailers emphasize the shopping experience itself. Atmospherics play a large part in this strategy. Excitement is generated by special events and displays and by architectural and lighting effects. Harrod's, the London department store, uses live models in its floor displays. They stand motionless for about 30 seconds and then move just a little, creating a startling effect. Stew Leonard's uses animated model cows to add atmosphere to his dairy goods' lines.

The Future of Retailing

We have looked at several recent developments and trends in retailing. But what is likely to happen in the future? One theory, known as the wheel of retailing, seems to

EXHIBIT 11.5. The wheel of retailing.

be borne out by recent developments.[34] This theory states that each major innovation in retailing begins a cycle. At first the innovation is viewed skeptically, but over time it takes hold, usually because it makes possible lower prices. For example, at the turn of the century, department stores were an innovation based on low cost and high volume, replacing general stores and other small retailers. The first department stores were simple and sparse in their operations. But over time they escalated their services and thus their expenses—and in came the discounters. Now discounters are adding services, and what do we see? In comes the new wave of discounters, the factory outlet malls, the warehouse stores, and the off-price retailers (Exhibit 11.5).

It is easy to imagine continued movement based on the value strategy, with larger and more efficient warehouse stores displacing other forms. But the success of Stew Leonard's stands in contrast, suggesting that the wheel may soon turn in a new direction. The appeal of quality to consumers can obviously be exploited in retailing, for those who are willing to listen hardest to their customers and think more creatively about their operations. After all, why shouldn't every grocery store sell sweet corn?

WHOLESALING AND PHYSICAL DISTRIBUTION

Wholesaling involves all of the activities provided by wholesaling intermediaries engaged in selling merchandise to retailers; to industrial, commercial, institutional, farm, and professional businesses; or to other types of wholesaling intermediaries. Broadly speaking, any transaction between one producer or intermediary and another is a wholesaling transaction. Thus, a retailer selling napkins to a restaurant or paper and pencils to another retailer is engaged in a wholesaling transaction. In the same manner, a manufacturer's representative selling office equipment to a doctor or another kind of professional is also involved in a wholesaling transaction.

Wholesaling is an extremely important part of the distribution channel. Without wholesalers, another member of the channel would have to perform their functions. In some cases, this simply is not possible. For example, many small retailers would not be able to survive if they tried to perform all of the functions that a large chain performs. If food wholesalers did not exist, the grocery industry would be limited to major chain stores that can afford to perform wholesaling functions. Stew Leonard's would be out of business.

In a larger sense, wholesaling is very important to the U.S. economy. Wholesalers have been described as the nation's inventory managers. Wholesaling "helps the economy adjust, both in times of high growth and in times of recession, because of its ability to react rapidly to changing demand and supply."[35]

We have already seen that wholesalers provide a variety of services. In fact, they think of themselves as service providers rather than simply as suppliers of products. The activities of wholesalers include buying and selling, distribution, warehousing, and financing (Exhibit 11.6). Usually the wholesaler can perform these activities more efficiently than either the manufacturer or the retailer.

Types of Wholesaling Intermediaries

There are now a half million wholesaling intermediaries in the United States, which together generate over $2 billion in sales. Roughly five million Americans are employed by wholesaling intermediaries.[36] Wholesaling intermediaries can be subdivided into three major categories: merchant wholesalers, agents, and manufacturers' sales branches.

Merchant Wholesalers

Merchant wholesalers make up the largest segment of the wholesaling industry in terms of both number of establishments and sales volume. They account for 81 percent of all wholesaling intermediaries, and they are responsible for 58 percent of total wholesale trade in the United States. Merchant wholesalers have two distinct features: They take title to the goods they sell, and they are independently owned businesses.

Agent Middlemen

Agents and brokers make up the second major category of wholesaling intermediaries. The main difference between agent middlemen and other types of wholesaling intermediaries is that they do not take title to the merchandise they sell. An agent's or broker's primary function is to bring together buyers and sellers and facilitate exchanges. These intermediaries provide fewer services than other wholesalers and usually work on a commission basis.

Agents can be essential to small manufacturers for which they perform the selling function. This enables the manufacturer to keep expenses down. Normally agents specialize in a particular type of customer or product line. They also tend to have a fairly large customer base within a specific geographic area.

EXHIBIT 11.6.   Services provided by wholesalers.

Service	For Customers	For Suppliers
Buying	✓	
Bulkbreaking	✓	
Warehousing	✓	✓
Transportation	✓	
Financing	✓	✓
Management services	✓	
Provide product/market information	✓	✓
Hold title to products	✓	
Sales and promotion		✓
Risk bearing		✓

Manufacturers' agents are the most frequently encountered type of agent. These are independent sales representatives who work for several manufacturers of related but noncompeting product lines. Manufacturers' agents receive a commission on every sale they make. One of the major benefits of using this type of intermediary is that it spreads the cost of a single sales call over many products. Complementary product lines can be added relatively easily, since a customer base has already been established.

To receive the saving in costs that results from the use of agents, the manufacturer must sacrifice some control over how its product is actually sold.

It is for this reason that Apple Computer at one time made some drastic changes in its distribution system. It dismantled its network of manufacturer's representatives and in its place created a 400-person retail salesforce. It also set up a second salesforce to concentrate on specific market niches, such as business and educational markets. According to an industry analyst, "Apple wants to eliminate layers of marketing and get closer to dealers. . . . That's important because it will enable them to monitor their sales more closely, get dealer input on their marketing strategies, and better gauge what shipment rates and inventory positions should be."[37]

Manufacturer's Sales Branches

Manufacturers' sales branches and offices are the third major type of wholesaling intermediary. These are wholesaling establishments that are owned and operated by manufacturers but are separate from the manufacturers' factories. They account for 9 percent of wholesaling establishments and 31 percent of wholesale sales. The reason for the establishment of sales branches and offices is to improve selling, inventory control, and product promotion. Their relative success is due to the fact they are usually set up in the manufacturer's best markets.

Strategic Problems of Wholesalers

A recent survey of distributors identified five major problem areas; the first is unstable economic conditions. This is a pressing problem that has resulted from apprehension about interest rates, the memory of high inflation rates, plant closings, and government deficits. The next problem cited was the same one that retailers face; intense competition among distributors. Respondents to the survey mentioned numerous unethical practices, intense price competition, and too many distributors per trading area as indicators of this problem. The third major concern of wholesalers is the high cost of making a sales call—both in terms of salaries and in terms of the cost of maintaining cars and paying salespeople's expenses. This is forcing a change in distributors' selling practices.

Declining employee productivity is another problem faced by wholesalers. This cuts into profits because it raises operating expenses. Finally, manufacturer-distributor relationships are a frequently mentioned concern. Wholesalers often come into conflict with manufacturers over such matters as product return policies and discounts. In many cases, the real problem is poor communication.[38]

One strategic tool that is being used to solve some of these problems is computerization. Like retailers, wholesalers are turning to extensive use of computers and automation. More and more wholesalers are applying these technologies to inventory and cost control, warehouse and store design, and a variety of other uses. It has been said that in coming decades wholesalers will be in the information business as well as the distribution business. As one wholesaler has pointed out, "It is important to provide retail accounting services, inventory services, price file services, and computer back-up."[39]

In the not-so-distant past, wholesalers ordered all of their merchandise either by mail or by phone. Now over 40 percent are ordering foods via electronic devices, either directly through a wholesaler-to-manufacturer order entry system or through a computerized clearinghouse. For example, the National Wholesale Drug Association, in conjunction with Informatics Clearinghouse, has set up an order entry system called ORDERNET. In this system, orders from retailers or wholesalers are consolidated at a central location. At certain times during the day, each manufacturer's computer obtains all the relevant purchase orders from the ORDERNET file. This system has significantly cut down the time it takes to order merchandise.

Warehouse automation is another major strategic tool for wholesalers. Fleming Co., a wholesale food merchant, has invested heavily in this approach. Fleming spends as much as $30 million to build computerized warehouses in which orders from different affiliated supermarkets are sorted into categories (breakfast cereals, canned vegetables, etc.). When every item has been classified, a warehouse employee can make a single trip to a specific area for the needed goods. Fleming has also set up a system of laser scanners that will sort one load of, say, green beans and direct the cases to specific loading docks for shipment to different retailers.[40]

PHYSICAL DISTRIBUTION

We have examined in detail the components of the distribution channel, the intermediaries that bridge the gap between the producer and the ultimate consumer. And we have focused on the end of the channel, the retailer. Determining the length and composition of the distribution channel is a strategic decision; it establishes the overall plan for getting products into the hands of consumers. But the job of distribution is not yet complete; still missing are the activities that result in the actual movement of products through the distribution channel.

The physical-distribution system is responsible for actually moving products in such a way as to accomplish the goal of providing time and place utility. The objective of physical distribution is summed up in a statement by Robert Woodruff, late president of Coca-Cola: "Our policy is to put Coke within an arm's length of desire." An effective physical-distribution system can give a company a significant competitive advantage: a survey of 216 industrial purchasing agents showed that physical distribution ranked second only to quality as a factor in their buying decisions.[41]

The economic impact of physical distribution is awesome. It accounts for the largest component of marketing costs—about 20 cents out of every dollar you spend goes to pay for physical distribution. That amounts to over 16 percent of GDP.[42] However, the cost of physical distribution varies dramatically from one industry to another. In the food industry, for example, it accounts for about one-third of each consumer dollar spent; in the textile and wood industries it amounts to only one-sixth of the price of goods.[43]

Physical distribution ensures that the right products are available when consumers want them—in the right place and at the right time. This overall objective can be summed up in one word: service. This applies to the distribution of services as well as goods.

Physical-distribution decisions need to be guided by a strategy. This strategy must reflect the firm's overall marketing strategy. At the same time, the physical-distribution strategy must mesh with all the other activities in the marketing mix. For example, low-priced impulse items with heavy advertising budgets need extensive coverage and therefore must have maximum exposure at the retail level. The physical-distribution strategy, therefore, must concentrate on making the product available wherever it is needed. A long distribution channel may need the support of many warehouses, fast and frequent transportation, and quick order processing. Consumer packaged-goods companies like Procter & Gamble, Frito-Lay, and Kraft General Foods all know the value of such a strategy.

Forecasting Demand

The key to effective and efficient movement of products throughout the physical-distribution system is correctly forecasting the demand for those products. Inaccurate forecasts can result in over- or understocking at intermediate points in the distribution system and may greatly reduce profits. Thus correctly forecasting the level of demand is critical to controlling the flow of products through the distribution system.

Order Processing

At each exchange point within a distribution system, the needs of the next channel are expressed by the placement of orders for products. Thus the retailer orders its inventory from the wholesaler, which, in turn orders replacement products from the distributor or manufacturer, and so on back through the entire channel. How well products flow between channel members depends on how well and how quickly orders are processed at each step along the way. This involves many clerical procedures that may take much time and present many opportunities for mistakes and delays.

Some firms have gained a decided advantage by investing in computerized ordering systems. Bergen Brunswig, a Los Angeles-based distributor of over-the-counter drugs and medical supplies, offers its retail customers a computer-based order entry program designed to speed ordering and delivery. And at Whirlpool Corporation, a major marketer of home appliances, a computerized system allows a distributor to dial into a computer from a dealer's showroom for information about current stock, production, and shipping dates. Orders are taken immediately, and goods can often be shipped straight to the retailer, bypassing the distributor's warehouse. Time and money are saved and damage due to handling is avoided.

Inventory Management

Products must be stored in a way that will make up for any inaccuracies in demand forecasts. Storage of products—that is, inventory management—is a way of safeguarding against inability to meet demand directly from the assembly line. It is an expensive activity, for it involves the costs of storage space, handling, and insurance, as well as costs associated with product obsolescence. These costs can be decreased by reducing the size of the inventory, but then the marketer runs the risk of losing sales when the product is unavailable. In the ideal situation, demand for the product can be forecast correctly and inventory can be built up at an appropriate time to meet that demand. In reality, however, marketers must balance the costs of holding inventory against the costs of lost sales.

As you will recall from the chapter's introduction, Toyota and other Japanese manufacturers have developed a new approach to inventory management. Called just-in-time purchasing, this concept involves buying in small quantities to reduce inventory carrying costs and obtain delivery just in time for use.[44] This system results in lower order quantities, frequent and reliable delivery times, shorter and extremely reliable lead times, and consistently high product quality.[45]

Just-in-time purchasing is now used by Toyota dealers, and has also been used to control inventory at the manufacturing level, but its use is not yet widespread in the United States.[46] To implement this system effectively, the firm must change its manufacturing process. This approach requires tight scheduling, insistence on high-quality materials, simplified materials-handling procedures, and lower inventory levels, all of which make interruptions of production more likely.

Storage

Storage management is concerned with the size, number, and location of facilities to house inventory. To store inventory, channel members can choose between private and public warehouses. Private warehouses are owned and controlled exclusively by their users, while public warehouses are owned by independent contractors that rent space as needed to various channel members. Since public warehouses do not require a large investment on the part of the marketer, inventories can be expanded or contracted as the need arises. This is particularly helpful when the firm markets products for which demand fluctuates widely. Public warehouses have lower unit costs, too, since their fixed costs are spread among a large number of users.[47]

There has been a shift away from storage and toward movement of goods. Distribution centers have replaced warehouses in many cases; these are streamlined storage facilities that are geared to taking orders and delivering products. Automated equipment and computerized inventory systems allow the firm to react rapidly to customer needs. Caterpillar Tractor has a distribution center housing 60 days' worth of inventory—more than 200,000 parts. Its computer network links dealers and other storage points around the world. At Levi Strauss' distribution center, the 48,000 items in inventory come from ten manufacturing plants in the United States and are shipped to 17,000 American retailers as well as to 70 countries. Eastman Kodak maintains its distribution center at Chicago's O'Hare Airport, where products can be shipped anywhere in the world within a matter of hours.

Protective Packaging

Since products that are damaged at any point in the distribution system cause the smooth flow of goods to break down, distribution managers are very concerned about protective packaging. The packages and containers used to ship products should be compatible with the materials-handling system and should fit compactly into transportation equipment in order to reduce freight costs. In addition, shippers should be aware that some modes of transportation may have characteristics that make them unsuitable for transporting a particular product unless it is properly protected. For example, railroad cars are usually very hot, while airplane storage areas get extremely cold; many products that are shipped by either of these methods need to be protected against the temperature.

Transportation

Another major physical-distribution decision is determining the mode of transportation to use in shipping products through the distribution channel. Transportation companies are classified by law into four types: common carriers, contract carriers, private carriers, and exempt carriers.

Common carriers serve the general public by transporting products on a specified schedule and according to regulations and standards established by government regulatory agencies as well as by company rules. Most interstate transportation companies are common carriers. Contract carriers are independent firms that agree to transport a specified number of shipments to specific destinations for an estimated price. Many contract carriers specialize in certain types of goods: household movers and automobile trucking companies are examples. Private carriers are shippers that own the goods they ship. The company employs the drivers and either owns or leases the equipment used. Large grocery chains usually own their own fleets of trucks, for example. Exempt carriers, as their name indicates, are shippers that are exempt from state and federal regulation. They are involved mostly in moving unprocessed agricultural products, usually by truck.

Within these broad categories, there are five main transportation modes: railroad, truck, pipeline, waterway, and airplane. These alternative modes are generally compared on the basis of six characteristics: door-to-door delivery time (speed), number of geographic points served (availability), ability to be on time (dependability), ability to carry various products (capability), number of scheduled shipments per day (frequency), and cost per ton-mile (cost).

The main goal of physical distribution is to ensure that the right products are available when consumers want them—in the right place and at the right time. But this overall goal has several aspects that we should examine more closely.

Availability

The most basic objective of physical distribution is availability. Availability is in fact a key element of any product, although it is often assumed by management and customer alike. Suppliers at each point in the distribution system must anticipate demand and be able to furnish all items ordered by customers. This ability depends on the accuracy of forecasts. When any channel member is out of stock, customers are inconvenienced and must either search for another source or wait until the products have been restocked. In either case, they do not receive the level of service they expected and desired.

Accurate Order Filling

Few things are more maddening than to wait for an order and then receive the wrong items. This can be caused by mistakes made during order writing, order receiving, order filling. Often customers indicate their needs incorrectly, especially over the telephone. Errors also occur in the process of transcribing information from purchase orders to shipping orders, since different intermediaries may misunderstand each other's ordering systems or documents.

Delivering Undamaged Goods

Physical distribution must also pay attention to all activities that could cause damage to goods—materials-handling procedures, packaging, storage, and mode of transportation. Usually, faster transportation results in less damage, although it is more costly.

Speedy and Reliable Delivery

Many physical-distribution activities must be performed between the time when a need for products is recognized by a channel member and the time when those products are received. These activities—order writing and transmitting, order processing, order filling, and shipment—take time. Closely aligned with speed of service is the channel member's dependability. Customers often make plans that depend on the receipt of products as scheduled. But improved speed and dependability usually lead to higher costs. For example, computerized order processing is faster than manual processing, and air transport is faster than truck transport; but each method is more expensive than the alternative. Thus, channel members must be keenly aware of their customers' needs in terms of time and dependability.

The Total-Cost Approach to Physical Distribution

By now it should be clear that there are two main objectives of physical distribution. The level of service is important because it ensures that channel members—and the ultimate consumer—will be satisfied. But as the service level is improved, the costs of distribution increase. Thus, physical-distribution decisions involve a trade-off between minimizing total distribution costs and maintaining a satisfactory level of service.

It is difficult to define a satisfactory level of service; the firm needs to determine its customers' requirements and compare the service levels offered by competitors. Customers want fast, on-time delivery of undamaged goods. They also want to be sure that their emergency needs will be met, and sometimes they expect to have inventory held for them. With respect to the competition, the firm should expect to at least match the level of service offered by others—but going a step further can provide a competitive advantage. The higher costs of providing more service must be studied carefully. An analysis of customer needs may indicate that a low-service, low-price strategy is best, but offering superior service at a premium price may turn out to be a better strategy. And, increasingly, firms are accepting Philip Crosby's argument that "quality is free" and innovating to improve service without raising costs.

12 PROMOTION
The Many Faces of Marketing

A story in every pair.
   or
Levi's. They go on.

*—Competing TV ad themes under consideration
by ad agency FCB for Levi Strauss*[1]

Imagine this. You are a (very highly paid) marketing executive for Levi Strauss, and you have asked Foote, Cone & Belding's San Francisco office (which is conveniently near your company's San Francisco headquarters) to develop a $90 million ad campaign to boost the Levi's brand of jeans.

Why? Because, while U.S. sales of jeans have grown in recent years, your company has not participated actively in this growth. (For instance, while total U.S. jeans sales went up 10 percent in 1996, to $8.7 billion, Levi Strauss sales grew only a few percent during that period.)[2] The problem you face is tough new competition from clothing designers like Calvin Klein, Guess?, and Tommy Hilfinger. They, along with your long-term competitors at The Gap, have been doing some heavy-duty national advertising. Add the recent national ad campaigns designed to establish the house brand jeans of J.C. Penney Co. and Sears, Roebuck & Co., and it all adds up to a lot of advertising in recent years for your competitors. And none for you. For reasons you cannot recall too clearly right now, you and your associates at Levi's decided not to advertise your brand in recent years. Apparently as a result, the Levi's brand is losing market share, and you want to give it a big boost to turn this trend around.

So a major television and print ad campaign makes good sense as a way to reinvigorate the Levi's brand. But now you face a more specific decision—*which* of the two campaigns your agency has designed will work best? They've given you two choices, and you have to decide between them.

The first campaign for the Levi's branding effort is designed around the theme ("themed" as they say in ad agencies), "A story in every pair." It features a series of television ads, each telling a personal story from the life of someone who wears Levi's jeans. The idea is to combine a human interest angle with a diverse collection of individuals to emphasize that Levi's are an integral part of the lives of many different Americans. You think it is a fun idea, and see lots of potential for the human-interest angle. Viewers should identify on an emotional level with the people and their stories.

The second campaign is themed, "Levi's. They go on." This play on words is designed to emphasize two USPs (unique selling propositions). First, that Levi's are designed to be comfortable, to fit well (they go on more easily than competitors' products). Second, that the Levi's brand has a long heritage and a long future—that it goes on and on. The campaign is unusual in its design, featuring whimsical scenes in which unusual characters (in Levi's of course) interact in "slice of life" settings. The first commercial features a cowboy character who is an expert sharp-shooter—and therefore wins all the stuffed animals at carnival shooting galleries. His car is stuffed full of them. And when he runs into a disc jockey in a waffle house on the road, he shares his Zen-style secret for winning stuffed animals at county fairs—to aim "beyond the balloon." Other commercials are equally off-beat, and to add to potential viewer interest, later commercials often recall earlier ones in subtle ways, such as a quick shot of a scene from an earlier commercial, taken from a new angle. You think the ads are a bit bizarre, and you aren't quite sure whether the "They go on" line will be clear to viewers. However, you like the unusual nature of the ads and feel it may be important to differentiate Levi's with a campaign that stands out clearly as being different.

Okay, made your decision yet? Good. Hope you were right.

And we hope the real marketing managers at Levi's were right in their choice. As we wrap up our work on this second edition, the folks at Levi's and FCB have decided to run with the second theme, "Levi's. They go on." Six commercials are scheduled to air, starting in the late summer of 1997 (in time for the back-to-school rush on the jeans shelves).[3] And if they were right, and the campaign really works well, you will know it intimately by the time you read this chapter. Because a successful campaign should run for a long time, and should be extended with many more commercials based on the same theme. *And,* a successful campaign should turn around the Levi's brand, since it is a strong one already, probably permitting Levi's to double its sales growth.

But if they guessed wrong—and that's all too easy to do in the difficult field of promotion—then you probably won't even remember the ads, because the campaign will have to be pulled quickly. And the marketers at Levi Strauss should know fairly quickly whether it works, because they will collect data on how the ads are perceived. Do viewers remember them? Do they like them? Do they hold more favorable attitudes toward the brand as a result of seeing these ads? Not only that, but Levi's can quickly compare monthly sales of jeans with the same month from a year earlier, and if sales aren't up, well, let's just say the "They go on" campaign won't go on.

While we are not involved in this particular campaign, we often help clients with similar decisions. And they are always cliff-hangers. For instance, Charlie and his partner at Lifestage Matrix Marketing, Geoffrey Meredith, worked with one of the larger U.S. cable companies to develop a direct-mail campaign. Their idea was to use the cohort segmentation strategy we discussed in Chapter 7 to design an appeal especially appropriate to older viewers. But would it work? Tests looked good, but the only way to know for sure was to do an expensive mailing to a large list. Then wait for the responses. Typical response rates for direct mail solicitations are in the 0.5 percent to 5 percent range.[4] Could they reach the top of this range? When the dust settled, the mailing had performed over six times as well as expected, coming in far above the normal response range. The theory worked! But not all theories work—in fact, the average promotion is a failure rather than a success, which is why so few commercials stay around for long enough to get well known.

PROMOTION: THE FACE OF YOUR BRAND

Promotion is the face of the company; or its many faces, if it promotes multiple brands and lines, each having a unique identity. The task of promotion is to insure that targeted consumers know and like the company's products. Ads on television and radio, print ads in magazines and newspapers, in the World Wide Web, and on billboards, as well as through event sponsorship, contests and coupons, special packaging, telemarketing, direct mail, in-person sales pitches, and many other vehicles are all available to animate this face and give it meaning in the eyes and minds of consumers. And the cleverness with which the face is drawn is all-important since hundreds of other faces are crowding around every consumer, struggling to be seen and heard.

This image of promotion has a slightly nightmarish quality, and, in fact, promotion has a dark side, both for the company and the consumer. Some people believe that "Advertising has filled in all the cracks of people's lives to the extent that it is seen as an encroachment," as Steven Ewen, a professor of media studies at Hunter College, puts it.[5]

The expansion of ads into all the cracks in our environment certainly strengthens this impression. Ad space is for sale everywhere. Ads now appear over sinks and urinals in public bathrooms. The sponsorship messages on public television and radio are quietly swelling until they sound for all the world like mini-ads. Phones ring off the hook at dinner time with computerized sales pitches. Skiers seeking escape on the slopes are assaulted by small billboards on each post of the ski lift. And when you fill up your car at the gas pump you might be feted with promotional pitches on a CRT monitor. Some supermarkets are now embedding advertisements in the floor. Rotating floor displays. Just the thing! (You can just imagine some ad industry exec. having an epiphany one day at the grocery store. He might have said, "Look at all this blank space on the floors. We've got to fill it up right away!") Next, rotating ad messages painted on the surfaces of roads and highways?

Ambushing the Consumer

Even where ads aren't officially welcome, they find ways to sneak in. Game Show Placements, Ltd. advertises to marketers that giving their products away on game shows is "the ultimate in low-cost mass exposure." "Product placements" in movies are a booming business, with companies paying from thousands to hundreds of thousands to appear in the likes of Batman and Robin, Independence Day, and the smash hit Jerry McGuire. It is become such an integral part of today's promotional landscape that Reebok developed a $1.5 million tie-in promotional campaign focusing on Jerry McGuire's sole client, running back Rod "Show me the Money" Tidwell. The idea was for the Tidwell character to appear in the movie in a scene in which he is making a Reebok commercial. But this scene was left on the cutting room floor, and Reebok was left furious. So much so that the company filed suit against Tri-Star Pictures for breach of promise.

Some managers think advertising has gone too far. Perhaps the Reebok fiasco proves it. Anyway, some movie makers fear it marks a turning point in which advertisers will soon have the upper hand in determining movie content. While Alex Szabo, president of movie theater ad distributor Screenvision Cinema Network crows that "We target viewers entering the theater, exiting the theater. We're taking it to the ultimate step," Richard Cook of Disney Studios says. "Movie ads are an unwelcome intrusion," and Betsy Frank of ad agency Saatchi & Saatchi describes them as one of a number of new "ambush media." (These are media, like restroom and classroom ads, that are designed to play to a captive audience.)

Disney decided not to permit advertising shown with its movies.[6] The protests of managers are not always as convincing, however. While Ashland Oil Inc.'s 592 gasoline and merchandise stores will not be installing television monitors on top of their pumps, they will be using print ads on signs above the pumps and ads in the music piped out of the stores. As John Pettus, president of Super America, puts it, "There's a limit to what you can do to exploit your favorite friend, the customer."[7]

While crassly put, this is the essence of the problem. From the marketer's perspective, the competition for attention intensifies yearly. Alberto Baccari, creative director of Armando Testa Advertising, felt compelled to use a violent image of a man's hand and arm (with advertised Breil watch) grasping and twisting a woman's upside-down head in order to attract attention to the watch in magazine ads. According to Baccari, "I don't believe in violence, but I needed to communicate on the edge. The client had a limited budget, and the ad worked. Sales went up."[8] The proliferation of brands and the incredible redundancy it creates is an obvious source of competition for the consumer's eye and ear, pushing marketers to communicate on, and sometimes over, the edge. The product life cycle may also be at fault—remember the natural proliferation of competition and segmentation of the market that occurs at maturity? There are an awful lot of mature product categories out there, and it seems like the efforts to innovate new ones have pushed introduction rates far higher than withdrawal rates. James Schroer of Booz, Allen & Hamilton published a study concluding that "Most consumer goods markets are static, so to gain a share you have to outspend the competition by a huge amount."[9]

CONSUMER ATTENTION: THE GROWING CHALLENGE

The challenge facing ad agency Saatchi & Saatchi in the introduction of the Salon Selectives line of hair care products from Helene Curtis is typical. As Amy Goldman of Saatchi & Saatchi puts it, "There are more than 250 advertised brands in the hair care category, all of them claiming to deliver beautiful hair."[10] This means an advertiser's "share of voice," or percentage of total promotional spending for the category, is often sickly. And if companies split up share of voice among many participants, they tend to split market share similarly. The alternative is categories like soft drinks in which one or a few large competitors spend so much on their "voices" that no one else can possibly be heard. (Coke and Pepsi hold over 70 percent of the U.S. soda market.)

Ironically, as the clamor for consumer attention swells, many companies are backing off from the conventional emphasis on heavy newspaper and television advertising, shifting to more controversial (and less crowded) media like above-urinal and pre-movie placements. This movement is fueled by the rise in the number of alternative media (cable television and the proliferation of radio station frequencies, for example), which pulls audience away from traditional media. Cost per exposure for advertisers in traditional media like network television are rising as a result.

And there is also a shift away from advertising and toward trade and consumer promotions (such as coupons). Where advertising made up about 40 percent of the ad/promotion budget in the early 1980s, now it only accounts for 30 percent at the average U.S. company.[11] As we discuss later, this shift may represent a nonoptimal effort to maximize short-term sales at the expense of brand equity. But regardless, it is fueling a wave of panic in the ad industry that is made worse by the rising tide of necessary recessionary belt-tightening. As odd as it may sound, at the very time that consumers are complaining about increasingly intrusive advertising, advertisers are desperate for work! Newspapers, television networks (but not cable), magazines, and even billboard companies report loss of advertisers, and the keynote speaker's address at recent conference of the American Association of Advertising Agencies was entitled "Remembering a Year Best Forgotten."[12]

Advertising as Communication

Madison Avenue, no doubt, takes a dim view of Games Gang Ltd.'s promotional strategy. Their favored medium for new game introductions is word of mouth! Gender Bender, for instance, was introduced by salespeople walking populous beaches to demonstrate the game. Rather than press for orders, the salespeople explained the game and handed out mini game packs. Says sales manager Kevin McNulty, "It would be nice if they all bought the game, but our goal is to get them at least talking about it."[13] Are these people crazy? Probably not—this is the company that launched Pictionary with a word-of-mouth campaign that made it the best-selling game for three years running.[14] They seem to take the American Association of Advertising Agencies literally when it defines promotion as "interpreting to the public, or to desired segments of the public, information regarding a legally marketed product or service." Since Games Gang's strategy is to develop a small number of excellent and unique products, all they really need to do is to disseminate information about them and sales will take care of themselves (presuming effective distribution, of course).

Advertising as Persuasion

But what happens if your products are only a little better, or really not much different from hundreds of others—like a new shampoo, for example? You still wish to sell them, but you face an uphill battle before consumers want to buy them. In this (and most) cases, the purpose of promotion goes beyond the official definition as interpreter of information. Promotion has three main objectives: informing, persuading, and reminding. The first job of promotion is to inform the potential buyer about the availability and nature of a product. In the case of new products, the buyer obviously needs such information. But even when a product is not new, many potential buyers may not realize that it exists. And when an existing product is changed in any way, this too needs to be communicated to potential buyers.

Once buyers have been informed, they need to be persuaded that purchase of the product will lead to satisfaction. This is accomplished by transmitting a positive set of beliefs about the key attributes of the product. Promotion is a major force in "the battle for the consumer's mind." As we saw in Chapter 6, marketers strive to create a position for their product vis-à-vis competitive products and brands, and the key to accomplishing this is promotion. Then, knowing that potential buyers are not constantly thinking about its product, the marketer must continually remind them of its existence and availability. This is the purpose, for example, of the "Got Milk" campaign of the National Fluid Milk Processor Promotion Board. It puts print ads of people with milk moustaches in front of consumers to remind them of milk—and also to encourage them to think of the product as a hip thing to drink.[15]

Influencing Demand

At a more specific level, the promotional strategy attempts to influence the shape of the demand curve. The goal is to push the demand curve to the right of its existing position (from D1 to D2 in Exhibit 12.1). This results in the sale of a greater quantity at a given price. Put another way, promotion helps reduce the impact of price on the buyer's decision. It stimulates nonprice competition. Through persuasion, it influences consumers to focus on attributes of the product rather than on its price. In more technical terms, promotion attempts to make the demand curve increasingly inelastic (price insensitive) at high prices and increasingly elastic (price sensitive) at low prices.

EXHIBIT 12.1. Promotion shifts the demand curve.

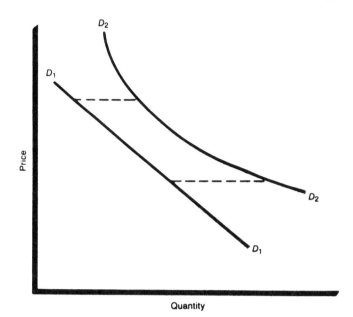

Quantity

| FOR YOUR IMAGINATION |

A Curiously Strong Influence on Sales

Can an ad campaign boost sales of a small, regional brand, making it a national success overnight? Well, it's not the sort of result anybody feels good about promising. But it *can* happen. It certainly did when Kraft General Foods bought Altoids, a British brand of mint candies, and decided to give it national exposure. Previously only popular where it had been "discovered" by the hip set in Seattle, Altoids are now a major player in the U.S. candy market. And all because of an odd print campaign featuring images such as a clean-cut, 1950s-style weight lifter, muscles bulging, holding the tiny metal Altoids tin between his fists. The caption, "NICE ALTOIDS." And under it, in smaller block letters, the simple message, "The curiously strong mints."

It worked. The first year Kraft put $1 million into this print campaign. Pleasing results inspired a pumped up $7 million campaign the next year. After this $8 million investment, Altoids sales reached an estimated $40-plus million across the United States.[16] Not a bad return on an advertising investment!

Promotion versus the Marketing Concept

Informing consumers is not particularly controversial, but when you take the further step of trying to persuade them, you risk irritating and even alienating them. Most promotional campaigns hit more people than they target—it's a symptom of the relative lack of focus of most media. As Steven Star of the Marketing Center at MIT's Sloan School put it, "If a marketing program satisfies a million people, distracts 500,000, and frustrates 300,000, what is the net effect?[17] It may be alienated consumers. And worse, as Star points out, "assuming . . . that one wants to cater carefully to consumer wants and needs" is "not always a justified assumption—there are charlatans and sharpshooters everywhere in all professions." Here the good talk about serving customers can give way to ugly talk like John Pettus' musings on how "to exploit your favorite friend, the customer."

The problem is that you don't exploit your favorite friend, and if the company wants to get truly customer-oriented, it must avoid crossing the sometimes faint line between friendly persuasion and unfriendly exploitation. If the promise of the marketing concept is to be fulfilled, it must carry through to promotion, shaping the face the company presents to its customers as much as the personality behind that face. Persuasion must only be undertaken with the best interests of the customer at heart, and it ought to be management's task to align these interests with the company's so that the customer does not have to feel cheated in order for the company to prosper! But this is a difficult challenge, requiring the active participation of senior management (and perhaps the entire company), not just the efforts of specialists at the ad agency. Promotion can be used to advance the marketing concept, or it can be allowed to conflict with it. At most companies, this key issue has yet to be addressed, let alone resolved. Promotion is still on the frontiers of the marketing concept, despite its being the most visible face of marketing from the customer's perspective.

With these thoughts as a backdrop, it is time to bring the full cast of promotional activities on stage.

Advertising

Advertising is any impersonal form of communication about ideas, goods, or services that is paid for by an identified sponsor. It is usually transmitted by mass media—newspapers, magazines, television, radio, direct mail, outdoor billboards, and transit cards. More than two-thirds of all advertising employs such media; the remainder uses things like matchbooks, circulars, calendars, catalogs, and special-event and trade show advertising. The message channel of advertising is not personal, and it is not as specifically targeted as other promotional methods. Consequently, advertising tends to use rather basic appeals—sex, prestige, hunger, social approval—to get the attention of the receiver.

The feedback from advertising in terms of sales is usually quite slow. While salespeople can get immediate reactions from customers, it is difficult to trace a given sale to any particular advertisement. Advertising offers the advantage of being able to convey a message many times. Moreover, it is offered in a relaxed atmosphere; generally, there is no pressure on the consumer to make an immediate decision. And the combination of creativity with the impressiveness of the mass media can have quite an impact. It has been found that consumers make a strong connection between product quality and use of national advertising.[18]

On the other hand, advertising is not very flexible since it cannot be tailored to each member of the audience. And while mediocre advertising is easy to create, truly good advertising is a much more difficult undertaking. In fact, ad recall is always fairly low, between 25 and 30 percent, for print ads, and it has dropped from a high of 70 percent in 1987 down to 48 percent currently for television ads, according to a tracking study by Video Storyboards Tests, Inc. Mind you, this is the percentage of people who can name an outstanding commercial—any commercial—and it is pretty low considering that anywhere from 1 to 17 percent of most product's price is spent on advertising it (see Exhibit 12.2).

EXHIBIT 12.2.   1997 advertising to sales ratios.

Industry	Ad Dollars as Percent of Sales
Advertising	2.4
Air conditioning, heating and refrigeration	1.5
Apparel	5.8
Beverages	7.6
Books	10.7
Candies	17.4
CDs, tapes and records	10.5
Cookies and crackers	2.7
Cosmetics	8.5
Dolls and stuffed toys	15.3
Eating places	4.0
Engines and turbines	1.7
Food stores	3.9
Greeting cards	2.8
Hospitals	0.9
Jewelry stores	4.3
Mail order catalogs	9.0
Motion picture theaters	3.4
Motor homes	1.8
Newspapers	4.8
Sausage	6.1
Watches and clocks	15.9

Source: Advertising Age, June 30, 1997, p. 35.

Strategic Advertising Management

These statistics conceal complex and, in general, carefully managed advertising campaigns. It is interesting to look briefly at how campaigns are conceived, managed, and executed. This process, while not the direct responsibility of most managers, nonetheless ought to be a direct concern of all managers since it determines the character of the company's public face.

At the heart of advertising management is the concept of a campaign. Rarely is advertising undertaken on a one-time-only basis, or for that matter on a continuous basis either. A campaign is most easily understood as a series of messages with a single theme that are repeatedly conveyed to the target audience over an extended period. The repetition enhances consumer learning and reinforces the message—that is, if the message is appropriate and targeted at a receptive audience.

The development of a campaign starts with the establishment of objectives (which generally flow from the strategic objectives established in the planning processes described in Chapter 2). From one perspective, advertising has the same objectives as promotion in general—to inform, persuade, and remind. But there is more to it than this. Managers advertise in order to generate action in the marketplace, to stimulate the sale of goods and services. This often means immediate action by consumers is an important objective. This means applying the concepts of buyer behavior from Chapter 6 to the development of the campaign. Campaign objectives generally focus on stimulating action over an extended period, first making consumers aware of the brand or product and then building interest, desire, and ultimately intention to purchase. Post-purchase communication with consumers may also be included in the objectives—for instance, management may want to remind consumers about the product or brand.

These are strategic objectives. They cannot be implemented directly, because they do not specify specific actions. They need to be translated into more specific and action-oriented objectives such as the following:

- *Sales objectives.* Sales goals are frequently used despite the difficulty of correlating sales with advertising. Often goals include specific increases in sales dollars, unit volume, or market share.

- *Prepurchase objectives.* Goals are often based on the AIDA hierarchy:

  Awareness $\rightarrow$ Interest $\rightarrow$ Desire $\rightarrow$ Action.

  For instance, a new-product advertiser may set an exposure goal. Lowe's, the leader in the kitty litter industry, budgeted $10 million for an advertising campaign to introduce a new and improved kitty litter. Its goal for the campaign was to reach 95 percent of consumers more than 10 times. To achieve this goal it ran print ads in 18 magazines.

- *Image-building objectives.* Companies often undertake institutional advertising in an effort to improve their image, either with consumers or intermediaries. The "Black and Decker . . . ideas that work" campaign is an example of this kind of advertising.

FOR YOUR IMAGINATION

Ha, Ha, Ha, Neat!! . . . But, No Thanks

Great Ad . . . But no clout in the showrooms. That's what they have determined for the Nissan advertisement known in the industry as the "Toys" ad. It's the one where the "hip hunky" toy soldier (as a doll) drives his "cool" top-down car (looking like a remote control toy) on the living room floor to the dollhouse of the girl he is pursuing. Upon seeing him, she sheds her tennis clothes for a party dress, descends the stairs and slips into the car with the gentleman . . . while her apparent other suitor, in tennis togs, sadly gazes upon the one-upmanship of the man in the car as they ride off amid the sounds of Van Halen's "You Really Got Me." Then we see a real person of apparent Japanese descent bearing a short-brimmed cap, small round glasses, and a big smile with the tag line "Life's a Journey. Enjoy the Ride."

Time magazine and *Rolling Stone* gave it "two thumbs up" and named it best ad of the year. The creators of the commercial at Los Angeles' TBWA Chiat/Day were showcased on Oprah Winfrey's talk show. And Sony even plans to turn the concept for the ad into a television series.

Research by the advertising agency showed that consumers really hated the usual automobile advertisements. So TBWA Chiat/Day set out to make their mark. To create a "brand connector," the agency chose an actor to portray Yutaka Katayama, the unusual head of Nissan's U.S. operations. And they wanted to spotlight a car that resembled the first affordable Japanese sports car, the Datsun 240Z. The creative department jumped on the idea of dropping "Mr. K" into a series of commercials and he pops up repeatedly without mention of the car company's name, the brand, or even who he is . . . only a sign indicating "Smile."

In September 1996, when the commercial was first aired, U.S. sales of Nissan cars dropped 2.7 percent over those for September 1995. The next month sales plummeted 10.2 percent . . . and then 4.2 percent in November and 1.6 percent again in December. What happened was clear. Many consumers loved the ads, others enjoyed them . . . but they were not motivated to buy a new car. As a dealer in Texas said, "It isn't anything that makes anyone go out and say, 'Hey, I need to go buy a Nissan.'" In short, the agency created a real buzz in the marketplace and in the industry but it was ineffective in gaining sales for its client.

TWBA Chiat/Day's explanation was clear and simple. The agency was never counting on Mr. K to sell cars in the short-term. Rather, the advertisements were intended to improve the value of the Nissan brand. And its research showed that Nissan's "advertising awareness" and "brand likeability" rose while the ads were aired.[19]

The core of effective advertising is translating the objectives into a specific message concept. The advertising message is based on an "advertising platform," which is a concise statement of the issues and benefits the advertiser wishes to convey. It may include a specific positioning strategy, as discussed in Chapter 7.

If all else fails, conventional wisdom has it that one can develop an advertising platform by answering three questions:

- What features are unique to the marketer's product or brand?
- What criteria do consumers employ to evaluate different products or brands?
- How does the marketer's product or brand rate vis-à-vis those of competitors on these criteria (where is it strong or weak)?

The selling points that come out of the platform form an advertising theme, a message that is repeated in various forms throughout the advertising campaign. How this theme is expressed has a lot to do with the effectiveness of advertising. If stated clearly but unimaginatively, the theme may not cut through the clutter and make its way into the target's cerebellum. This is where the art in advertising comes in. Creativity, humor, surprise, excitement—something must be used to animate the theme, but care must be taken not to lose the underlying message in the pursuit of memorable advertising. It is a delicate balance, often missed. Here are some of the most common and successful message strategies:

- *Testimonials.* These use an authority to present the message strategy. Athletes and movie stars are often used for testimonials because their notoriety attracts viewer attention—but if their public image is inconsistent with the message strategy and product positioning, their testimonials will not be effective. Bill Cosby (for Jell-O) and Candice Bergen's dime lady always get great marks for their endorsements.
- *Humor.* Good humor can be particularly effective; poor humor can sometimes be devastating. There's nothing like a really humorous campaign to excite special-interest groups and generate negative publicity. The classic "Where's the beef?" campaign of Wendy's, for example, led many groups to complain that the elderly woman in it was a demeaning stereotype. Even well-received humor is not necessarily successful—some of the funniest campaigns ever, including the long series of humorous Alka-Seltzer campaigns in the 1980s, have had little measurable effect on sales or market share. But although it is hard to control, humor is nonetheless a popular message strategy because of its power to attract and hold attention. Rold Gold pretzels commercials, like those featuring Seinfeld star Jason Alexander, are examples of ads popular with consumers.
- *Sensual/sexual message strategies.* Sex is often used in advertising messages. However, research shows that it generally is not very effective in getting the message across. Consumer attention may be captured, but it is difficult to focus on the message.
- *Comparative messages.* Pepsi strikes at Coca-Cola. Burger King attacks McDonald's. Until the mid-1970s, marketers viewed such comparisons as

ill-mannered and risky. Naming competitors in an ad gives the competitor free exposure. However, the FTC took the novel position in 1973 that such ads could lead to better products, lower prices, and more information for consumers, and in 1981 the National Association of Broadcasters abolished their guidelines that restricted use of comparative advertising. Now comparisons are quite common, although they can still backfire. The 1990 television campaign from Volvo that showed an oversized pickup driving over a line of cars, crushing all but the Volvo, was persuasive—until it came out that the Volvo had been secretly reinforced.[20] A successful comparison campaign is the long-standing one used by Visa to position its credit cards as more widely usable than American Express with themes such as, "Bring your Visa Card because they don't take American Express."

- *Slice-of-life messages.* These use a popular song and a brief scene from life to position a product. The music is often key; for example, baby boomers may be targeted with an old Marvin Gaye song or something else from their teens, along with an appropriate fictional scene, in order to create a brand identity for the product. MCI's "Friends and Family" commercials are an example, as are the commercials by Levi's that we discussed in the beginning of this chapter.

- *Fantasy messages.* These stress the ideal self-image of the buyer. They relate a product or brand to some desirable person or situation, implying that the use of the product or brand will help the consumer achieve the desired state.

- *Infomercials.* Slick, half-hour broadcasts using fictional story lines, real actors, and Hollywood quality production. Most offer toll-free 800 numbers for convenient telephone ordering. Infomercials have become popular with marketers because they are popular with consumers. Some consumers even tape late night infomercials for viewing at another time. And an effective infomercial (say, for a drink that is supposed to help you lose weight) will pull hundreds of orders over the 800 line with each airing.

The choice of a medium to transmit the message obviously has a major influence on the way advertising ideas are carried out. We will look briefly at the issues involved in selecting a message channel, but first it is helpful to look at the common elements of advertising. Whatever medium is used, a typical ad includes copy, illustrations, and several other elements. Copy consists of all the written or spoken elements of the message. The headline tends to be the focal point of an advertisement—this may in fact be the only part of the ad the consumer sees or hears. Body copy (and sometimes sub-headlines, extend the headline and elaborate on it). The body copy presents the major points of the message. Here the basic problem to be solved is set forth, the advantages of the focal point or brand are explained, a claim of superiority over competing brands is made, and a plea for action is made. Finally, the ad should contain a signature, the identifying name and other symbols of the sponsor of the ad. The signature needs to be distinctive and attention-getting; in television and radio, it must be repeated to insure retention.

The illustrations in an ad consist of photographs, graphs, charts, drawings, cartoons, and any other visual devices that accompany the copy. They are used to gain attention, arouse interest and desire, and even stimulate action. The illustrations should be clearly related to the appeal and wording of the copy. This sounds like obvious advice, but we guarantee that you can open any magazine and find that the majority of ads violate this rule.

The layout of an ad is its overall structure—the positions assigned to various elements of the copy and illustrations. The placement of headlines, copy, illustrations, and the marketer's signature are critical to the overall effect of the ad and also determine how, and how well, the ad will lead the viewer through the message. The same is true for a television or radio ad, except that the timing can be more tightly controlled by the advertiser. But in either case, the ad is not digested immediately. There is a sequence and timing to the ad that has a great deal of impact on its effectiveness.

In general, illustrations seem to be displacing copy in ads. The typical print ad has fewer words of copy and a larger, brighter illustration today than ads did thirty years ago. Ron Jackson, the CEO of ad agency Jackson/Ridey & Co., argues that "We don't read copy like we used to. We find out at the store. What we're seeing is a copyless generation."[21]

Hogwash. More likely, we don't *write* copy like we used to. After all, consumers still read plenty of novels and newspaper articles! So if you can write wonderful copy, we are convinced it will sell better than an ad that is all header (or jingle) and illustration, because body copy can communicate a great deal more information. It can engage the consumer over a longer period of time, more meaningfully. According to ad guru David Ogilvy (who *can* write wonderful copy), "All my experience says that for a great many products, long copy sells more than short."[22] (Alex discusses how to write good print ads in Chapters 4, 5, and 8 of his book, *Marketing for Dummies*, if you need in-depth assistance at this task.)

Let Us Show You What We Mean

To illustrate the points about elements of an advertisement and to show how they can be used to convey a powerful message, we have included Exhibit 12.3, a two-page magazine advertisement by Omon New York, Ltd. created for their client, Toyota, by art director Rodd Martin and copywriter Paul Bernasconi.

This ad illustrates the power of copy; the majority of the space is taken up by the copy and, to draw the eye strongly to the beginning of the body copy, the header is placed at the bottom instead of the top. The illustrations are small and treated almost like snapshots in a journal. They focus attention on the fish the children caught while out on Chesapeake Bay. This fish is used to symbolize the learning about nature and the environment that the Chesapeake Bay Foundation provides to inner-city kids. The body copy picks up the fish theme and expands on it powerfully.

But what does this foundation and the students and teacher it worked with have to do with Toyota? What is the campaign's message? What objective did Toyota have in mind, and is it accomplished?

EXHIBIT 12.3.   Toyota magazine advertisement. (Reproduced courtesy of OMON New York, Ltd.)

THERE'S BEEN A LOT OF TALK about the environment lately. But out on Chesapeake Bay, sailing around on a vintage skipjack, a group of school kids are learning that when it comes to the environment, actions speak louder than words.

Myrtha Allen, Environmental Sciences teacher at P.S. 405, Baltimore, explains, "Most of my kids are city born and bred. They live in apartments, they get their milk in cartons, their eggs in those styrofoam containers. They were about as interested in the environment as they are in

> "IT WAS THE FIRST FISH Jawan had seen that WASN'T SURROUNDED by french fries."
>
> MYRTHA ALLEN, Teacher

(continued)

EXHIBIT 12.3. (Continued)

homework." She smiles at a nearby eight-year-old. "And who can blame them? Some of them, like Jawan here, had never even seen a live fish before."

That's where the Chesapeake Bay Foundation stepped in. Since 1966, when it started in Annapolis, Maryland, with a rented fishing trawler and little else, the Foundation has taken more than 300,000 students out into the Bay to experience the environment first hand. And at the same time making them aware of how important their contribution is to the future of the planet.

Myrtha puts it simply. "To get these kids wanting to clean up the world, we've got to get their hands dirty."

And they do. They get very dirty.

"Oh yeah," chuckles Myrtha, "we do it all. Once we threw a net in just to see what we'd get. When we pulled it up, sure enough there were the milk cartons, the soda cans, the egg containers. And flapping around in the middle of it all was this big, cranky striped bass. You should've seen their faces.

"We took 20 little consumers out on a boat that day. We came back with 20 budding environmentalists."

At Toyota, we're proud that through the support we give to the Foundation more kids like Jawan will be able to experience our fragile environment first hand. And hopefully start playing an active part in preserving it.

Is the program working? "These kids are organizing neighborhood recycling drives,

they're writing letters to Senators. Take a look at these posters some of my students have been doing."

The classroom walls are alive with crayon and pencil. Bright orange crabs. Smiling oysters. Families of ducks.

And one poster that stops everyone. It's of a smiling little boy holding hands with a big striped bass. And boldly scrawled above both their heads is one word: "Brothers".

And it's signed by Jawan. Age eight.

TOYOTA
INVESTING IN THE INDIVIDUAL

This is an example of corporate advertising. It's objective is to build Toyota's image by highlighting socially-responsible investments made by the corporation. Toyota gave money to the foundation—this is implied without being discussed specifically in the ad. And it is interesting to speculate to whom the socially responsible image is targeted. What group of consumers is Toyota courting in such a round-about manner? Probably baby-boomers, who are increasingly concerned about the environment, poverty, and other social problems.

This is an effective ad, but it uses the various elements of advertising very differently than most ads. Contrast it with Toyota's typical slice-of-life television advertising, which focuses on the good feelings associated with owning a Toyota. Why are the ads so different—how do the objectives and messages differ? (This is a good question for readers to apply the principles of marketing to.)

You can see why Omon selected magazine spreads for their corporate image campaign (which includes profiles of other nonprofits supported by Toyota as well). They need the full two pages to tell the story. These ads present their message—that Toyota is a responsible corporate citizen, involved and helpful in the United States—through interesting but lengthy stories. The copy takes a few minutes to read, and because it is about interesting nonprofits and their work, Omon can count on people wanting to read it. The slower pace of the magazine is perfect for story-telling. The message channel was well-chosen for this campaign.

Each channel has unique characteristics that provide both advantages and disadvantages. Marketers must understand these characteristics in order to select the proper channel. Newspapers claim the largest share of advertising expenditures, but their ad revenues have not grown in recent years. They offer extensive market coverage on a local level; almost every household receives a newspaper every day. They permit flexible scheduling and the cost per contact is relatively low. But in general they do not permit the advertiser to target any narrowly defined segments. If you want to say something to cat-owners in the newspaper, you will have to say it to everyone else as well. Magazines give more specificity, and their better print quality makes possible a wider range of visual effects in advertising. Television advertising is split between the fast-growing cable channels and the slow-growth network advertising. Television offers the choice of national or local (or spot) exposure, and the video medium permits a wide range of techniques and effects. A good television ad can have tremendous impact and high recall (although most do not). But television is very expensive by comparison with other media. Prime time ad spending on the Big Four U.S. networks alone in 1997 was $6 billion. A 30-second commercial aired on Seinfeld cost $500,000.

Less common, but also important, are radio, outdoor, and direct mail. Radio offers extensive coverage of local markets, and can be highly selective. For example, rock stations appeal to young people while classical stations tend to attract mature listeners. Radio is also a relatively inexpensive and flexible medium. Our society's preoccupation with television has probably blinded many managers to the power of radio advertising. Outdoor advertising options are growing, as we have already noted critically, but they do present a useful medium in some cases. Outdoor is great for awareness-building, since it can offer a large number of exposures at low cost. But it generally does not allow complex messages—who can read more than a few words while driving past a billboard? The more conventional outdoor ads, such as roadside billboards, are not at all selective. Newer types, such as those at ski resorts or in men's bathrooms, offer selectivity at the likely expense of irritating the customer. In general, there is considerable wasted exposure and the risk of negative connotations with this medium. Direct marketing is the most rapidly growing medium at present, and it is sufficiently important to justify its own section (coming in a moment—after we introduce you to the important concept of how to schedule ads and other promotions in the media).

Media Scheduling Strategies

Most advertising campaigns run for a stated period of time, often a year. Three broad approaches are available: the continuity, flighting, and massed (or concentration) strategies (see Exhibit 12.4). In the continuity strategy, advertisements are spread

EXHIBIT 12.4.   Advertisement strategy approaches.

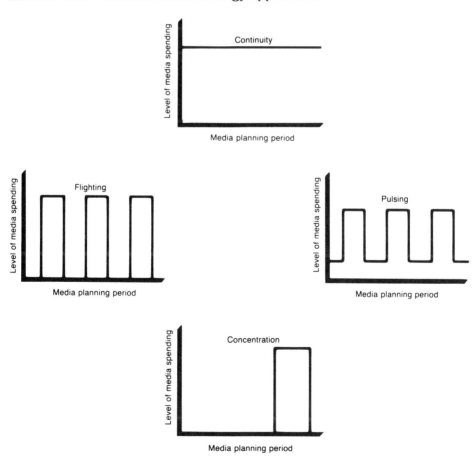

out over the entire planning period. When demand for the advertised product is evenly disbursed throughout the year, this strategy often works best.[23] Convenience items and other products with high repeat purchase rates warrant this approach. When demand for the product has distinct and identifiable peaks and valleys, the flighting strategy can be used. In this case, advertising follows a stop-and-go pattern. Typically, there is heavy advertising during some days, weeks, or months, and no advertising in between. A special form of flighting, called the pulse strategy, combines a continuous campaign with short bursts of heavier advertising. Supermarkets, for example, know that shopping is heaviest on Fridays and Saturdays, so they do most of their newspaper advertising on Thursdays and Fridays. Finally, in the concentrated strategy, the marketer bunches all of its advertising into specified periods and does no advertising in between. Makers of swimming pools, charcoal, and snow blowers use this approach. These contrasting strategies are illustrated in Exhibit 12.4.

Direct Marketing

In recent years, marketers have made increasing use of a form of advertising called direct marketing, defined by the Direct Marketing Association as "any direct communication to a consumer or business recipient that is designed to generate a response in the form of an order (direct order), a request for further information (lead generation), and/or a visit to a store or other place of business for purchase of a specific product(s) or service(s) (traffic generation)."[24] This definition is helpful in that it makes the aims of direct marketing clear. It is any marketing that aims to generate an order, lead, or store traffic through direct communication with the end customer.

But there are other approaches to defining direct marketing (it's exact definition is a point of contention because it is an emerging field). One authority gives the following definition—which we also find helpful: "An interactive system of marketing which uses one or more advertising media to effect a measurable response and/or transaction at any location."[25] The key words in this definition are *measurable response*. Direct marketing uses various kinds of message channels—coupons, catalogs, direct mail, consumer and business magazines, newspapers, telephone, television, and radio—to communicate an offer that will elicit an almost immediate response. And when that response is measurable in orders placed, leads generated, or traffic produced, then the direct marketer can learn from his or her direct contact with consumers. This learning process often takes the form of statistical testing of different offers and media, and it allows direct marketers to take a fairly scientific approach to their craft.

Direct marketing is distinguished from general advertising by the following characteristics (see Exhibit 12.5):

1. A definite offer is made.
2. All the information necessary to make a decision is provided.

EXHIBIT 12.5. Comparison of direct marketing and general advertising.

Direct Marketing	vs.	General Advertising
• Selling to individuals. Customers are indentifiable by name, address, and purchase behavior.		• Mass selling. Buyers identified as broad groups sharing common demographic and psychographic characteristics.
• Products have added value or service. Distribution is important product benefit.		• Product benefits do not always include convenient distribution channels.
• The medium is the marketplace.		• Retail outlet is marketplace.
• Marketer controls product until delivery.		• Marketer may lose control as product enters distribution channel.
• Advertising used to motivate an immediate order or inquiry.		• Advertising used for cumulative effect over time to build image, awareness, loyalty, benefit recall. Purchase action deferred.
• Repetition used within ad.		• Repetition used over time.
• Consumers feel high perceived risk—product bought unseen. Recourse is distant.		• Consumers feel less risk—have direct contact with the product and direct recourse.

Source: Bob Stone, *Successful Direct Marketing Methods,* 5th ed. (Chicago: NTC Business Books, 1994), p. 2.

3. A response mechanism is given—a toll-free telephone number or a mail-in coupon, for example.

In 1978, direct marketing accounted for $60 billion in annual sales; by 1985, the figure had shot up to over $200 billion. By the mid 1990s, sales through catalog/direct mail alone stood at over $250 billion annually in the United States. Per capita annual direct sales were a whopping $461.[26] Jumping on the bandwagon, companies like General Foods, Nestlé, Thomas J. Lipton, Sunkist, Whitman's Chocolates, and R.J. Reynolds began marketing premium products via catalogs and toll-free 800 numbers. Lipton, for instance, mailed out more than a million catalogs touting its Sir Thomas Lipton Collection of exotic teas, teakettles, and shortbreads.

Direct Marketing in a One-to-One Environment

Don Peppers and Martha Rogers wrote a book, *The One to One Future: Building Relationships One Customer at a Time,*[27] that has revolutionized promotional thinking and its execution. With the advent of electronic media came the opportunity to literally communicate directly with customers on a personal, collaborative basis. Instead of sending out mass messages, marketers now have the opportunity to speak with individuals via various method that allow a two-way communication process. Customers can actually ask for information from marketers. They can make fax requests, click on Web sites, or even choose to listen to specific advertisements chosen from a menu of options delivered to one's computer.

The 1:1 future of advertising has some basic tenets. First, the electronic media are individually addressable. Before, the postal service was the only way to deliver a single, separate message to a consumer. It is slow, cumbersome, and expensive. But with electronic media, this is no longer true. Second, electronic media are two-way, not one-way. The new media allow the customer to talk to the marketer . . . in the past, the marketer did all the communicating. Finally, electronic media are inexpensive. The cost of sending electronic messages to fax machines, computers, and other receivers is insignificant when compared to traditional mass media.

FOR YOUR IMAGINATION

Catching Car Buyers in the Web

Sure, the World Wide Web is a great new direct marketing medium. But there must be limits to what you can sell on it. Books are good, financial information, stuff life that. But how could you sell something big and nonvirtual, like a car? Here's how.

First, create a Web site that allows prospective buyers to shop for the features and prices they want. Second, sign up a network of auto dealers all around the United States, so as to be able to deliver what those car buyers want, when and where they want it. Follow these two simple steps, and you have a powerful lead-generation system for new and/or used car sales, one that is more efficient at matching buyers and sellers than the traditional walk-in approach offered by retail car dealerships.

Oh, but there is one other thing you need to know before you get started. Somebody has done it already. The company is called ABT (stands for Auto-By-Tel Corp.). They've signed up about 2,000 car dealers for their network, so they really can offer consumers a wealth of alternatives. And it works. In their first month on line, February 1995, ABT generated 5,000 purchase requests. Not bad. But nothing compared to the monthly total of 60,000, just a couple years later.[28] Need a new car? Or just curious about how to make a whole lot of money through direct marketing on the Internet? Then visit the ABT site: http://www.autobytel.com. They can teach you all you need to know about real-world direct marketing.

This new approach to advertising concentrates on building unique relationships with individual customers on a one-to-one basis. Some of these relationships will be more valuable since some customers will interact more frequently. Customers will dialogue back and forth electronically to present a clear picture to the marketer of what they want. Instead of being "sold to," customers increasingly will "sell themselves." Customers will view, for example, used cars for sale on their CRT and request further information about those they are most interested in . . . via fax or a click of a mouse. This approach to advertising insures greater responsiveness by the customer since each one has self-selected the information desired based wants and needs.

Can you imagine getting an advertisement over your telephone before you place each of your calls? And pay a one-time fee of $24.95 to have this pleasure? Well, you can and you might because for each advertisement you listen to, you will receive 15 cents. On average, each participant listens to enough calls to receive a monthly check in the amount of $18, roughly the cost on your basic service. Hence the service is called FreeFone. And FreeFone has signed up over 60,000 Seattle subscribers. Part of the allure is the money, but part is the fact that the ads are highly targeted. So listeners, having filled out an extensive questionnaire on themselves, get mostly advertisements that benefit them. And if they are in a hurry, they can punch in a code and bypass the commercial. The system can really target, too. For example, only callers who have a Bon Marche credit card but haven't used it in the past six months get the store's ads. For a local Ford dealership, only callers who have called a rival dealership would get their ads. Marketers pay $1.95 to $3.20 per subscriber for ten messages a month, a cost far below the cost of direct mail. Now how does that sound? That's one-to-one advertising at its best.

Marketing in the New Millennium: Electronic Commerce

The wave of today and of the future is the online channel that connects the customer to the marketer via a computer and a modem and a telephone line. The customer/user can reach various online information sources and choose, one-to-one style, messages that one wants to hear and read. This communication channel includes commercial online channels such as CompuServe, Prodigy, and America Online. These channels offer subscribers five main services: information, entertainment, shopping services, dialogue opportunities, and E-mail. And this online channel provides access to the Internet.

Online marketing is clearly convenient for customers to use since access is available 24 hours a day and right in one's home. Customers can find tons of information on products, companies, and competitors without ever leaving home. And not having to face salespeople, customers find online marketing to offer fewer hassles in gaining information and purchases.

From the marketers standpoint, quick adjustments can be made to messages as market conditions change. Lower costs are realized compared to other media and online marketing can be great for building relationships, as we saw with one-to-one marketing above. And because "hits" on a Web site can be counted, marketers can get some idea of the popularity of their messages. Online marketing is terrific for small companies with small budgets. No limit exists on advertising space and information access and retrieval is swift, faster in fact than overnight mail. And it offers shopping privacy for customers.

Today, you can find thousands of products for sale online. You can order clothes, flowers, or books. The speed at which technological changes are occurring create new opportunities at light speed today. In fact, by the time this book hits your hands, new opportunities will have made those of today obsolete. In the beginning, marketers would create Web sites with colorful pictures of products and extensive information . . . and wait for a response by telephone or by E-mail. The risk of giving credit card authority over the computer was too great so easy transactions were not an option generally. Few Web sites became commercial successes. But changes in security allowed greater instant purchase. And rich productions needed to engage users with video, sound, animation, and interactivity to produce a worthwhile number of "hits" or Web site visits.

Then came PointCast. PointCast is a screensaver that broadcasts, or "webcasts," news, sports, weather, and industry information when the computer monitor is idle for a period of time. And it also broadcasts advertisements. Levi Strauss & Co. was an early convert. Shortly after the launch of Slates, the line of trousers for men over the age of 50, Levi's marketing manager signed up for $100,000 worth of 30-second commercials delivered to excellent prospects right in their offices. "It's like reaching through someone's television screen when they're hungry and giving them popcorn," she told *The Wall Street Journal*.[29] Some believe that the conversion of the Web into a broadcast medium is as big a technological progression as the Web itself.

To get greater hit rates, some marketers are buying better Web site locations from online merchants and paying commissions to the services. Said a CEO of an online support company, "For the last two years you've heard that content is king. But to me, distribution is king. If you have a terrific service but no eyeballs, it's likely the service will fail."[30] Consider these deals. CUC International Inc. pays AOL $50 million and a fee for each new customer in exchange for becoming its exclusive discount shopping service, while 1-800-FLOWERS pays AOL $25 million and shares revenue to become its exclusive flowers merchant.

And the beat goes on!! Now software companies will allow Web marketers the use of huge warehouses of consumer databases to overlay on Web sites that will allow marketers to identify computer users and target more directly and precisely electronic advertising. Adfinity, for example, allows advertisers to link up to direct marketing databases and target ads to Web users based on user characteristics such as location and income. DoubleClick sells ads for Web sites and then uses software to place those ads on those pages of a Web site where users have visited. Cybergold offers to pay Web users cash or premiums such as frequent flyer miles in exchange for viewing ads. There seem to be an infinite number of possibilities in the arena of electronic advertising . . . and they are coming fast and furious. And they are changing the fabric of advertising forever.

Personal Selling

Personal selling is person-to-person communication in which the receiver provides immediate feedback to the source's message through words, gestures, expressions, and the like. Since personal selling is a conversation between two or more parties, the message can be tailored to the audience. This permits more precise customer targeting than advertising, but it limits the total number of contacts that can be made. Another disadvantage is that the cost of each contact is much higher than in the case of advertising. Even so, because of its adaptability and its "personal" nature, personal selling has a much greater persuasive impact than advertising.

Personal selling is especially appropriate when the unit of sale is large enough to support the cost of the contact; when the product is rather complex, so that detailed explanation or demonstration is needed; and when the product benefits have to be carefully matched to the customer's desires. Personal selling has the greatest potential to close the sale—the salesperson is there to complete the order or get the customer's promise to make the purchase.

What makes the difference between effective personal selling and wasted time? A great many salespeople make calls every day, but many of them have relatively low closure rates. Part of this is personal technique, and experience and training can make a difference. But much of it comes down to how well the salesforce is managed. Every year the trade magazine *Sales & Marketing Management* uses a survey to identify the best salesforces in America. The categories against which salesforces are rated are:

1. Recruiting top salespeople.
2. Retention of top salespeople.
3. Quality of training.
4. Opening new accounts.
5. Product and technical knowledge.
6. Reputation with customers.[31]

These are the yardsticks against which many managers judge a sales program. But it is interesting to listen to managers from one year's winners talk about their sales strategies (in fact, winning strategies are fairly constant from year to year). While they do indeed excel on these attributes, they seem to emphasize *building long-term, mutually-beneficial customer relationships* over any of the specific items on the list. They actually use personal selling in the spirit of the marketing concept, to benefit customers over the long term, rather than just .to write orders more rapidly.

Procter & Gamble (P&G) is winner in the Health & Beauty Aids category. Here is Shelly Zimbler, P&G's general sales manager for this category. "It's a matter of survival. The old way of doing business—good products with good advertising copy—is history. We need to work creatively with customers to find out what they need to move our products. We've moved from a confrontational period of doing business to understanding that five different retailers may have five different ways of selling."[32] This required a reorganization of the salesforce. P&G now uses category selling, in which a single salesperson handles an entire category for certain retail buyers—P&G's direct customers. It used to be that every retailer would see dozens of different salespeople, each specializing in specific product lines. But with the new organization, the customer works one-on-one with just a single salesperson, one who can afford to work closely with the customer in a problem-solving, cooperative manner. For big customers, this salesperson is backed up by a team of people from finance, manufacturing, and distribution, making it possible for P&G to make significant changes in response to the customer's needs.

Working with the customer is also a theme at Nabisco Biscuit Company, a winner in the Food Products category. This RJR Nabisco subsidiary focuses on the basics—it makes sure deliveries are timely and shelves stocked. But senior vice president of sales Harry Lees believes their success comes from their effort to make life easier for their retail customers. "First of all, we deliver product to the back door so they don't have to go through a warehouse. Then, we literally set up the biscuit department. We help our customers pick the best location—even the best aisle and shelves—for the products. Our salesperson can sit down with a customer and, using a laptop computer, share our information on what the retail outlet's position is in a market, who its customers are, what its average purchase is, and how to create the most effective merchandise mix for that environment." He adds that, unlike many competitors, Nabisco does not pay slotting fees, and is able to stick to this policy because of the high level of attention it gives to customers.[33]

Note the added value both these companies get from direct sales. They are not only taking advantage of the personal contact to make a lengthier, more personalized and more persuasive sales pitch. They are taking advantage of the relationship to build a long-term relationship in which their expertise and data is used to help the customer's business. They profit by selling soaps or cookies, but the customer profits by improving their business overall as well as by selling specific products. This kind of relationship goes far beyond anything possible with arms-length alternatives such as advertising and direct mail (see Exhibit 12.5).

Personal Selling Skills

Our discussion of personal selling treats it from the strategic perspective—that is, by examining how to do it well and what its role should be in the marketing mix. But there is another perspective—the personal one. Personal selling comes down to the individual efforts of one or more people to go out and meet with and try to influence prospects. You will play this role yourself in the future, and have in the past, for we all do some personal selling in our work and lives, whether we chose to make it our profession or not. (For instance, when you apply for a job or negotiate to trade in your used car for a new one you are doing personal selling.) We believe every reader should work on developing their selling skills, and we have provided a two special appendices to this chapter to help you do so.

The first appendix, *Measuring Your Sales Ability*, is a simplified version of the kind of assessment and training tools that Alex develops for use in corporate training, and markets through the Human Interactions Assessment & Management product line. This assessment is helpful because it not only estimates your current sales ability, but it also diagnoses that ability by identifying your weaknesses and strengths in a number of component skills that are fairly easy to work on if you want to build your effectiveness in personal selling. It only takes a few minutes to complete this assessment, so we recommend you give it a try.

The second assessment is one of several in the *Flex Style Negotiating* line of products, which are used by trainers and dispute resolution specialists as tools for preparing to negotiate and for planning specific negotiations. They are published by HRD Press (in Amherst, MA). At first blush, negotiation may not seem directly relevant to personal selling. But personal selling is increasingly a negotiation itself since many customer relationships are consultative and flexible—leaving it to the marketer or salesperson to work out details of the sale with the customer. Consultative selling is always a negotiation process, and even a simple one-time sale often includes some negotiation over price and discounts, timing of payments and deliveries, and many other variables.

What style of negotiating is most appropriate? Where you care about the long-term relationship (as in consultative selling), then a cooperative approach is best. Where you are trying to maximize short-term returns, then a competitive approach may be best. And there are other alternatives as well, as described in this second appendix.

But knowing which style is best and using that style well are two quite separate things. We all have a natural style, one that unconsciously structures our approach to negotiations and sales encounters. That natural style may be just right in some circumstances, but it is not going to be right all of the time. At best, it suits us for a minority of sales situations. Thus the negotiation appendix is especially helpful in that it helps identify your natural negotiating style, making any unconscious bias toward one style apparent. Use it not only to diagnose your natural style, but to study the other styles as well so as to be able to adopt one of them when necessary. People who learn to take a flexible approach, using the best style for the circumstances, become far more able at negotiated sales, and at personal selling in general!

SALES PROMOTION

The American Marketing Association defines sales promotion as "those marketing activities, other than personal selling, advertising, and publicity, that stimulate consumer purchasing and dealer effectiveness, such as displays, shows and expositions, demonstrations, and various nonrecurrent selling efforts not in the ordinary routine."[34] This very broad definition embraces many kinds of activities, including in-store displays, sampling, coupons, contests, trading stamps, trade shows, price-off deals, premiums, refund offers, sweepstakes, and rebates. Annual expenditures for such activities have been found to exceed total spending on advertising and to be increasing in importance.[35]

Sales promotion is typically used at the point of purchase to motivate consumers to complete an exchange. It is not a substitute for a promotional program; instead, it is used to supplement other promotional activities. Sales promotion, however, can go a long way toward creating awareness and favorable attitudes—generally the domain of advertising.

Sales promotion offers additional ways of reaching customers. It is generally used at infrequent intervals, since the response tends to diminish over time; this is called *wearout*. Advertising and personal selling, on the other hand, are used on a more continuous basis. Sales promotion is usually intended to increase sales over a short period, while personal selling and advertising have a long-term sales goal. Exhibit 12.6 depicts the "ratchet" effect of a short-term sales promotion carried out in conjunction with an advertising program.

Public Relations

Public relations (PR) is a promotional activity that aims to communicate a favorable image of the product or its marketer and to promote goodwill. Every organization deals with many important groups, called publics, such as stockholders, the government, intermediaries, the community at large, employees, suppliers, customers, and the news media. Public relations activities are directed toward these publics.

An activity that is usually considered to be part of public relations is publicity. This term refers to any message about the organization that is communicated through the mass media but is not paid for by the organization. Although public-relations personnel can send press releases, feature stories, and photographs to the media, marketers have much less control over publicity than they do over advertising, personal selling, and sales promotion. Perhaps for this reason, audiences tend to find such information more believable than information that comes from an identified sponsor.

Publicity can result in negative images as well as positive ones. Adverse publicity has affected companies that market breast implants, artificial sweeteners, tampons, products containing asbestos, and flammable sleepwear. Unfavorable publicity often leads to the banning of such products, or at least to consumer reluctance to use

EXHIBIT 12.6.   Short-term sales promotion "ratchet" effect.

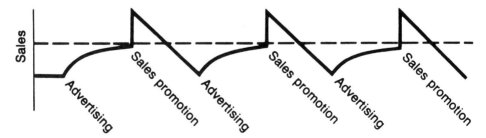

them. Thus, Ford's Pinto, accused of having an unsafe gas tank, was taken off the market even though Ford was vindicated in the courts.

Advertising, personal selling, sales promotion, and public relations are the tools that marketers have available to them as they plan their promotional strategies and communication campaigns. In the next section, we will see how these tools are used in designing promotional strategies.

The conventional paths to successful promotion of a product or service no longer guarantee a safe arrival, and an increasing number of innovators are succeeding through creative bushwhacking. That is because promotion has become more difficult and challenging in recent years, driven as we have seen by many of the same factors that make management in general more difficult, factors that are behind the new wave of emphasis on the customer: increased competition, globalization, saturation of advertising and distribution channels, and proliferation of products. Consider these examples of nontraditional efforts to communicate with the customer:

Wily General Mills captured a PR coup when at the 1997 Super Bowl, the company dispatched two marketing managers armed with a suitcase each filled with boxes of Wheaties. One suitcase had its packages emblazoned with pictures of the New England Patriots, the other with the Green Bay Packers. When the game's conclusion became evident, the PR men sped to news broadcasters and dispensed the boxes with the victorious Packers photographs as the Champions. What happened? Sportscasters showed the boxes on Fox, the network carrying the game. CNN, ESPN, and a scad of local stations also offered the free promotion.

And when General Mills found that Seattle Mariner Jay Buhner favored Cheerios, the company stuffed his locker with 162 boxes of the cereal, filmed his reaction and provided the video to television stations around the country. Stations in 12 major markets showed it. The beauty is that these PR tactics are relatively costless. While a 30-second commercial on the Super Bowl ran $1.2 million, sending the General Mills PR employees to New Orleans cost a mere couple of thousand dollars. PR pays.

Other companies agree and follow suit. Grand Metropolitan PLC's Pillsbury division received publicity on CNN when it introduced a new low-fat dessert on Fat Tuesday, the last day of Mardi Gras. Gillette sponsored a million dollar putting contest along with another one for shooting basketballs. And Hershey Food Corp. paid an amateur for kicking a field goal in the NFL's Pro Bowl. The media loved the event and gave it superior airing . . . and the kicker was wearing a shirt with the Hershey name all over it. Said a consultant, "A third-party endorsement is almost always more effective than a paid commercial."[36]

DESIGNING PROMOTIONAL STRATEGIES

Putting together a promotional strategy involves considering the various promotional activities as a whole. The main task of the strategic planner is to determine the blend of activities that will achieve the organization's promotional goals. Rarely will only one of those activities be used; usually a combination of activities is more effective. But even though several promotional tools may be used, one of those tools will receive the greatest emphasis.

There are many kinds of promotional strategies. Each can be defined in terms of how it allocates funds and effort among the various promotional activities. Any firm can have its own unique promotional program in which it uses promotional techniques differently than any other firm. The choice of particular techniques is determined mainly by the objectives of the promotional strategy itself and by the situation analysis, an evaluation of the internal and external factors that affect the strategy's chances of success. In the remainder of this section we will explore these key strategic considerations.

Promotional Objectives

The basic objective of promotion is to bring about an exchange. Yet that exchange may not be a sale in the usual sense. For example, we see marketers attempting to get consumers to accept an idea ("Friends don't let friends drive drunk"): And even when a sale is the ultimate goal, promotional efforts may not be aimed toward achieving immediate results. In general, then, we can say that the objective of promotion may be to communicate information as well as to stimulate sales.

The objectives of promotion follow the "hierarchy of effects" decision model, known as **AIDA: A**wareness leads to **I**nterest, which in turn fosters **D**esire, which ultimately leads to **A**ction. Thus, creating awareness must be the first goal of promotion. By providing information, the marketer arouses the interest of consumers; more persuasive communications arouse desire, and finally this leads to action in the form of an exchange. The various promotional tools are applied in different ways to achieve each of these goals.

Readers with previous training in marketing may recall the AIDA model as one of those dreadful multiple-choice favorites, and others may skim over it on the assumption that it is just another silly mnemonic. Wait! For all its simplicity, it is an essential concept, and a great many promotional efforts fail by trying to generate action before systematically building awareness, interest, and desire. If you research nothing else before planning a promotion strategy, at least find out how many consumers in the target market are currently in each stage, and identify the inter-stage transition at which the most potential customers are lost. There is no point in spending money on awareness—generating ads if awareness is high but poor distribution limits conversion of desire to action, for instance.

Some generalizations can be made about the relative effectiveness of each of the four promotional tools. Advertising, because of its mass market coverage, is thought to be highly effective in creating awareness, but it becomes less persuasive as time goes by. Personal selling with its lower contact rate is less effective in creating mass awareness but is most effective in creating desire and action. Sales promotion is most effective in getting consumers to complete an exchange; its impact is greatest at the point of purchase. Finally, public relations and publicity are helpful in creating awareness, but they have little immediate effect on sales.

Potential buyers are more receptive to some promotional tools than to others. Their desire for information causes them to seek out particular promotional tools or media—a fact that can be very useful to marketers. Exhibit 12.7 charts various promotional tools according to their value as providers of information as well as the immediacy of their sales effect. Some promotional tools are not sought out, but when consumers and intermediaries become aware of them, they readily use them to gain information (for example, to find out if they have won a contest). In the figure, this is represented by a dotted line moving these techniques to the left.

What is the practical value of this insight? Simply put, if consumer information-seeking can be accommodated, the information, persuasion and reminder goals of promotion can all be accomplished far more easily. Best to try to communicate with the consumer when he or she wishes to communicate with you! So, for example, if you know that people read computer magazines when thinking about buying a new PC, you will focus your promotional efforts at them via public relations and display advertising in this medium, and you may also want to use reader service cards to establish

EXHIBIT 12.7. When to use promotional tools.

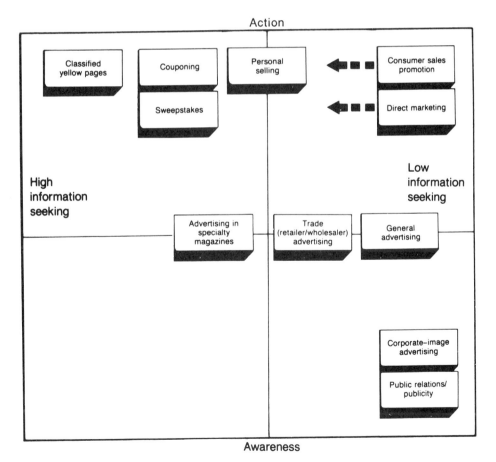

direct contact with them in order to focus sales or telemarketing on these interested readers as well.

ANALYZING STRATEGIC ISSUES

Most companies have a mixture of promotional activities but usually one is emphasized. The main emphasis of the promotional strategy is determined by the external environment as well as by certain aspects of the marketing organization and its product. Let's take a look at some of the key issues that affect development of promotional strategy and determine which activity will be emphasized.

The Nature of the Market

Like other marketing decisions, promotional decisions should be based on a firm understanding of the market. Its size and nature can actually dictate the strategy. For instance, a widely dispersed market like consumer packaged goods requires a large number of contacts. Mass media advertising is the most cost-effective means of accomplishing this. Good mass media exposure and persuasive appeals can be so effective that little personal selling is necessary. Small geographically concentrated markets warrant greater emphasis on personal selling. Since less distance needs to be covered in making contacts, it is less expensive to reach potential customers. This is why personal selling is used extensively to market industrial products. Industrial markets are clustered in relatively few locations, generally close to waterways.

When the promotion is aimed at retailers and/or wholesalers, the use of personal selling is also common. Large orders, concentrated markets, and small numbers of potential customers all require emphasis on personal contact. And as in the case of industrial buyers, the buying motives tend to be rational. Personal selling is better suited to rational appeals than advertising, which tends toward more emotional appeals. On the other hand, promotional efforts aimed at intermediaries often includes sales promotions—especially contests—and advertising in trade publications.

Push versus Pull Strategies

The push-versus-pull distinction refers to the ways in which a manufacturer tries to get intermediaries to carry its products. In a push strategy each channel member attempts to persuade the next member in the system to handle and promote the product. Thus, the product is "pushed" through the channel, often by means of personal selling. (We saw this in the last chapter when we discussed channel loading.) In a pull strategy, the producer uses mass promotion to stimulate demand in the consumer market, thereby causing intermediaries to want to carry the product so that they can satisfy customers who request it. This is the strategy that cosmetics companies like Maybelline have begun to emphasize—they are spending heavily on advertising to "pull" the product through the channel.

The Nature of the Product

The nature of the product also affects the methods used to promote it. Personal selling is emphasized when a product has a high unit value, since consumers often need to be prodded into making the exchange. When a demonstration is needed to show the product's main features, personal selling is far more effective than advertising. Personal selling is also important for goods and services that must be tailored to the needs of the customer, such as investment securities, insurance portfolios, industrial conveyor systems, or electrical or legal services.

Advertising is a more effective promotional tool for products that are purchased frequently, like convenience goods. Marketers of specialty and shopping products can use advertising to create awareness, but usually some personal selling is needed to point out the advantages of the product over competing ones. Advertising is also appropriate for products that have hidden qualities (for example, the lack of phosphates in Tide detergent). Advertising helps, too, in communicating highly emotional appeals (for example, the U.S. Army's "Be all that you can be" and AT&T's "Reach out and touch someone") and in differentiating a product from competing products.

In addition to advertising, much sales promotion is directed toward consumers. Sales promotion is particularly effective for impulse items whose features can best be judged at the point of purchase. For example, many magazines need exposure at supermarket and drugstore checkout counters, where people can leaf through them while waiting to make their purchases.

Stage in the Product Life Cycle

In the introductory stage of the product life cycle, the promotional mix must provide information in order to create product (as opposed to brand) awareness. The marketer must stimulate primary demand, or demand for the product category itself. Consumers must understand the nature of a compact disc, rollerblade, or food processor. They must know that the product exists and must learn about its attributes. Exposure is the key, and advertising is usually the best way to get it.

Also during the introductory stage, a product may need to be pushed through the distribution system. Getting intermediaries to accept the product may require a substantial investment in personal selling. Trade shows, fairs, and conventions are often a good way to sell the product to channel members, greatly reducing the number of contacts needed to make the product familiar and desired.

As the product enters the maturity stage of the cycle, the promotional mix calls for a shift from building primary demand to creating selective demand, or demand for a particular brand. As marketers face stiffer competition, the focus shifts toward persuasion. Promotion must stress the benefits and advantages of the product over those of competitors. In this stage, more and more consumers are responsive to product promotion; thus the promotional costs per contact are reduced. While mass advertising generally continues to get heavy use, personal selling is necessary in order to push the product through the distribution system.

In the maturity stage, organizations with strong brand recognition can use reminder advertising to keep the brand name in the consumer's consciousness. During the decline stage, new products overtake old ones, which are ultimately abandoned. Unless sales can be revived by repositioning the product or innovating to improve it, promotional expenditures will be reduced significantly or eliminated completely. Advertising, in particular, is ineffective when a product's primary demand takes an unfavorable turn. Any promotion that is undertaken is usually targeted toward consumers who still have a strong preference for the product.

Stage in the Adoption Process

New ideas and new products have been found to spread through society in a predictable set of five stages that parallel the AIDA model to some extent. The adoption curve in Exhibit 12.8 shows this process.[37]

Each stage of the adoption process requires a different promotional emphasis. In the first stage, a group of consumers known as innovators adopt the new idea. These risk-takers tend to be young, well educated, mobile, and sophisticated. They tend also to have a wide network of social contacts outside their immediate reference groups. They have less difficulty understanding and applying technical information than most people. They employ nonpersonal sources of information, especially technical and scientific journals, and generally read advertisements for information, especially ads in specialty magazines and newspapers.

In the next stage, the product is bought by early adopters (also known as "opinion leaders"). Other people tend to be highly influenced by these individuals. Early adopters, like innovators, tend to be young and mobile. However, they have smaller networks of social contacts than innovators have. Salespeople are very useful in reaching this group, and the mass media are also important. Because of its size and influence, this is an important group from the standpoint of promotional strategy.

The early majority are less venturesome in adopting new products. This cautious group waits and watches others before accepting a new idea. Typically the product is in the rapid-growth stage of the product life cycle before these consumers will buy it. They need loads of information from as many sources as possible—salespeople and mass media advertising as well as early adopters among their friends and associates.

The late majority are skeptical of new ideas. They are older and more committed to familiar ways of doing things. This group usually needs strong social pressure to purchase something new. Its members have little contact with salespeople and are not greatly influenced by advertising. Getting to them generally means getting to early adopters or the early majority, who in turn influence these consumers.

The final group to adopt a product consists of the laggards or nonadopters, who are strongly oriented towards the past and very suspicious of new concepts. They are generally lower in social-class status and less educated than other consumers. They depend on other laggards for ideas and are very difficult to reach via promotional activities. In fact, it may well be that promotional efforts should avoid this group, since when its members are ready to buy, the marketer is likely to have newer products on the market.

EXHIBIT 12.8. Adoption curve.

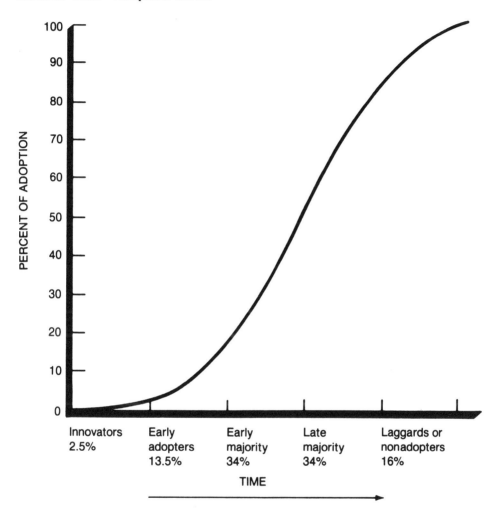

Stage in the Buying Decision Process

We have seen how the individual goes through the process called AIDA. And in Chapter 6 we saw how the consumer first becomes aware of a problem and then searches for information, makes a decision, and finally evaluates that decision. If we collapse these processes into "prepurchase time" and actual "purchase time," we find that different promotional activities have varying degrees of effectiveness at different points in the process.

Corporate-image advertising, general consumer advertising, and publicity all are effective in creating prepurchase awareness but diminish in effectiveness as the sale becomes imminent. At that point, personal selling and sales promotion techniques such as point-of-sale displays have greater impact. But in the postpurchase stage, the mass media become useful for reminder purposes and as an aid in positive evaluation. Many other forms of sales promotion remain effective throughout the process. Retailers' circulars, for instance, stimulate awareness, interest, and desire—and are often referred to after the sale.

In the case of trade promotion, what seems to be most effective are price deals and sales contests. Personal selling is continuously effective with trade buyers as is being listed in trade catalogs. In the case of direct marketing, techniques such as telemarketing and door-to-door selling are most effective in the purchase period. Catalogs, direct mail, and broadcast advertising create awareness and often lead to direct responses, as well as reminding consumers of the value of a purchase. Thus, they are effective in both prepurchase and postpurchase periods.

DEVELOPING A PROMOTION MIX

After evaluating strategic issues such as the nature of the market and product, the applicability of push or pull strategies to the distribution channel, the stage of the product life cycle, the stage of the adoption process, and the stage of the buying decision process—deep breath now!—management should have sufficient insight to develop a promotion strategy.

At least the broad brush strokes should become apparent. For example, an early stage of the product life cycle for an innovative and exciting product, low awareness and interest, and a resulting desire to focus initially on the prepurchase period will all point toward general consumer advertising and publicity. If the channel is very competitive and retail shelf space hard to obtain, a pull strategy will be favored, with consumer promotion emphasized over trade promotion. The selection of advertising medium will depend on which media best reach consumers when they are already seeking information and whether the sale is complex or simple, emotional or rational. And if these broad brush strokes are well executed, a decent result is highly likely. (The inverse is unfortunately also true.) The plan can (and must) be further refined by detailed consideration of the message to be communicated—this goes back to the product's positioning and how to make it clear and exciting—and also by the specifics of a promotional budget. Several common techniques are applied in budgeting.

Percentage of Sales

In the percentage-of-sales approach, the marketer first determines the percentage of sales revenue that has been allocated to promotion in the past. The next year's promotional budget is determined by applying this percentage to the past year's sales, to some level of anticipated sales, or to some combination of the two. This approach is easy to use and provides a handy means of comparing the firm's expenditures with those of competitors. But it ignores the fact that promotion is intended to stimulate sales. When this approach is used, promotional expenditures are reduced when sales go down! At best, this approach should be used in making preliminary calculations; it should not determine the final budget. Yet because of its simplicity it is used by over 50 percent of major advertisers.[38]

Competitive Parity

Marketers—especially those with mature products—often match what competitors are spending on promotion. This approach adds a measure of competitiveness to the strict percent-of-sales approach. However, it assumes that competitors know what they are doing and that all the firms in the industry have the same goals. That, of course, often is not the case.

The Market Share Approach

Some promotional budgets are based on the assumption that market share is directly proportional to proportional expenditures. A firm with an 8 percent share would allocate an amount equivalent to 8 percent of the industry's total promotional expenditures to its promotional budget. Evidence shows, however, that this approach is ill-founded since it is rarely true that share of promotion is equal to share of market.[39] But, on the other hand, if your share of voice is far lower than your targeted market share, it is likely to limit your performance.

All Available Funds

In some cases, the marketer allocates all available funds to promotion. While this is an easy solution, it too has its drawbacks. "All available funds" essentially means all profits. But profits have little relationship to promotion, since they are a function of the firm's total costs, including manufacturing, executives' salaries, administrative overhead, and so on. Moreover, this approach may result in lost opportunities if promotional expenditures still fall below the amount needed to generate a sizable change in sales. That is, the investment of just a bit more in promotion (even if it means borrowing) could have a dramatic effect on sales.

The Task (Objective) Approach

In setting a promotional budget, marketers should first establish what they would like to accomplish; then they can decide what level of investment in promotion is needed to reach their goals. As noted earlier, sales goals are difficult to relate to promotional expenditures, but that approach makes the most sense. And some firms can arrive at a reasonable estimate of what they will require to reach certain objectives. Marketing research and past experience are good guides. Test markets provide an experimental setting in which various levels of promotional spending can be tested. Finally, long experience allows some marketers to make a reasonable estimate of the costs involved in reaching certain promotional goals. This approach, in fact, is the one that is used most frequently by large advertisers.[40]

IN SEARCH OF EXCELLENT PROMOTIONS

Talking about promotion strategy is one thing, but doing it is quite another. The problem is that the process alone cannot guarantee results—it takes a little inspiration as well. Many, probably most, promotion plans produce mediocre results even if the planners considered the situation thoroughly in advance. The truly excellent promotional campaign is terribly rare. Most ads are zapped or forgotten, most coupons ignored or lost, most telemarketing callers hung up on, most direct mail thrown out. Even personal sales calls often fail to close the sale. So when a promotional effort really works, it is as if a little magic has been thrown into the equation. And marketing magic is hard to capture in general principles or rules—it is best communicated through a successful case history instead. The following case concerns Samsung's effort to establish its products in the U.S. market, and a campaign that proved a major turning point in the company's history.

Samsung Semi-Conductors, a large Korean manufacturer, hired ad agency Curtin Emerson Ransick in the spring of 1988 with the goal of establishing its semiconductors in the U.S. market. At the time, Samsung was an ugly duckling, ranking a sorry twentieth or worse in market share among suppliers of semiconductors (the chips out of which computers and the like are built). But its investment in high-capacity production facilities gave it swan potential—it was capable of supplying large volumes of high-quality products at very competitive prices.

Awareness of Samsung was low among electronic design engineers, purchasers, and management at the companies that buy semiconductors in the United States. According to Neil Ransick of Curtin Emerson Ransick, "Research indicated that Samsung's standing was low," and it was considered weak on technology and thought of as a low-price, low-quality, impersonal and unfriendly company. "Overall, the company just wasn't anyone the prospect wanted to hear about."[41]

The promotion mix favored personal selling when Neil Ransick and his agency took Samsung on. Most sales were made by independent sales rep firms and distributors, and 10 percent of products were sold direct by Samsung's own salesforce. The agency could have focused on pushing products through these two personal sales-oriented channels, since personal selling is obviously important, at least with the more complex and expensive semiconductors. But the low recognition and negative image among customers suggested the necessity of a strong image-building pull strategy as well. As a compromise, the promotion plan used pull advertising and sales promotions to generate leads (not sales), and emphasized personal selling for closing sales, servicing customers, and building and maintaining the customer relationship. To complicate the task, the promotion budget was determined by a method that, although common, was not included in our earlier list of "official" techniques: management dictum. Samsung gave the agency a "modest advertising budget for the job to be done," according to Ransick.

The pull advertising had to succeed in a "highly cluttered media environment." There are lots of trade magazines read by the purchasers and purchase influencers, and they are bursting with competitive advertising. However, the agency noted that most competing ads were detailed, dull recitations of product features. But Samsung did not need to communicate details of its products, so much as it needed to communicate a new, "sophisticated, up-to-date" image and also convince customers it was a "supplier that you'd want to do business with," again according to Ransick.

To achieve this goal, and to stand out from the clutter, the agency chose a "benefit-oriented concept, addressed with an illustration by an eminent illustrator . . . something almost unknown in the industry." Translated (agency-speak is unintelligible to most managers), this means large, bold ads in trade magazines using humorous cartoons. Ransick explains that "the idea behind wit and fun as a key ingredient was, of course, to provide a friendly demeanor and build a sense that Samsung was a company you'd want to do business with."

Because of the budget constraints, the agency negotiated a special rate with "one of the giant trade publication organizations" that gave it access to magazines reaching electronics engineering management, engineers, and purchasing agents (these three members of the buying group read different magazines). They used a combination of two-page spreads and 12-page freestanding inserts (in order to provide more detailed coverage of the broad product line). In addition to the image-building cartoons and copy, ads included coupons designed to stimulate readers to contact Samsung. Ransick explains:

> Lead generation was a major objective. In the advertising inserts, we used a prominent coupon promising specific pieces of literature and sample products, with prompts [on each page inviting the reader to turn to the coupon . . . page.] An easy-to-find address and 800 phone number closed each spread ad.

Samsung's case illustrates the value of different promotional techniques at each stage of the purchase. Corporate image advertising, followed by coupons for free samples and literature, targets prospects in the prepurchase period. Personal selling takes over in the purchase period (using leads generated by the prepurchase promotions). Advertising continues to keep the company visible to provide reminders (and to reduce any post-purchase dissonance) after the sale. This is good promotion; the broad brush strokes are right. But it achieves excellence because it is executed with originality and care. The almost magical first-year results speak to this point:

- Awareness improved 13 percent.
- Attitude improved 11 percent.
- Purchase intent up 73 percent.
- 50,000 inquiries generated.
- Solid support for campaign in a survey of the salesforce.
- Samsung moved up to 11th place in its industry.

The program also had something very important going for it—a message that benefited both Samsung and the customer. As customers became aware of the breadth of products, quality, and low prices, and once they overcame their initial prejudice against the company, they were eager to use Samsung as a supplier. Perhaps this is the best promotion strategy in this age of adversity for marketers and managers—to communicate a message the customer will be pleased to receive!

APPENDIX: TESTING AND DEVELOPING YOUR SALES ABILITY

How good are you at personal selling? Are there some areas that need improvement? Here is a quick, fun way to find out. Answer each of the following questions as honestly and thoughtfully as you can, then follow the instructions to key out your score and diagnose your sales ability. (Based on an assessment developed at Alexander Hiam & Associates, Amherst, MA, 1997.)

INSTRUCTIONS: If a statement fits you well, *check* it. If not, don't.

1 ____ I feel good about myself much of the time.

2 ____ I usually say the right thing at the right time.

3 ____ People seek out my company.

4 ____ I don't get discouraged, even if I fail repeatedly.

5 ____ I am an excellent listener.

6 ____ I can read people's moods and body language with ease.

7 ____ I project warmth and enthusiasm when I first meet people.

8 ____ I am good at sensing and bringing out the real reasons behind a "no" answer.

9 ____ I can see many ways to define a problem and understand its causes.

10 ____ I am skilled at drawing out other people's concerns and problems.

11 ____ I know enough about business to help others solve their problems with ease.

12 ____ I am so trustworthy and helpful that I quickly convince people to work with me in true collaborations.

13 ____ I manage my time so well that I am able to get to everything important.

14 ____ I keep focused on the "big picture" goals that matter most to me and my company, instead of always reacting to the latest crisis or chore.

15 ____ I can balance the need for finding new customers with the demands of maintaining and strengthening all existing customer relationships.

16 ____ I keep looking for and finding ways to be more effective and efficient.

17 ____ I find that for me, a sense of accomplishment is even more rewarding than money.

18 ____ My internal standards and expectations are higher than any imposed on me by others.

19 ____ I don't care how long it takes—I know I'll succeed in the end.

20 ____ I feel I deserve the respect and admiration of my customers and associates.

Scoring

A. Positive Personality?
   Total number of checks on questions 1 through 4: ____
   (Less than 3 checks = Need improvement on personal attitude, emotional resiliency, and self-confidence.)

B. Interpersonal Skills?
   Total number of checks on questions 5 through 8: ____
   (Less than 3 checks = Need improvement on communications and listening skills, including your ability to control your own non-verbal communications and read others' body language.)

C. Solution-Finding Skills?
   Total number of checks on questions 9 through 12: ____
   (Less than 3 checks = Need improvement on problem-finding, creative problem-solving, and collaborative negotiating skills.)

D. Self-Management Skills?
   Total number of checks on questions 13 through 16: ____
   (Less than 3 checks = Need improvement on organization, strategy, and focus skills.)

E. Self Motivation?
   Total number of checks on questions 17 through 20: ____
   (Less than 3 checks = Need to build your personal motivation and learn how to find rewards in the pleasures of doing a job well and accomplishing a difficult goal.)

F. Overall Level of Sales Ability?
   Total Number of Checks
   Sales Ability Score

0–5	F	Guaranteed to Fail
6–9	E	Low sales ability. Not likely to succeed.
10–12	D	Low sales ability. With improvement, may be moderately capable.
13–15	C	Moderate sales ability. Capable of improvement.
16–18	B	High sales ability. Capable of improvement.
19–20	A	Guaranteed to succeed. Superstar potential.

Interpreting Your Overall Score

If your grade is a C or higher, you have enough ability to be out there on the road making sales calls right now. However, if your score is anything less than an A, you should work on your weak areas—and when you do, your sales success rate should go up.

Working on Your Sales Ability

Some people believe that you can't do much about sales ability—that you are "stuck" with whatever you have. We think that's a ridiculous attitude, and that a far more empowering and helpful approach is to identify specific components of sales ability that need work—and work on them! Look back to your subtotals to see which of the six component scores are low enough that you want to work on them. For example, if you scored low on "positive personality," then this needs your attention—and your success in personal selling should increase if you work on it. But how? The clues lie in the four questions you totaled to measure your positive personality score. Each question describes some aspect of the positive personality construct. For example, take the very first item in this assessment, "I feel good about myself much of the time." If you don't, then you probably do not have the kind of positive personality usually associated with a high level of sales success.

But don't let that upset you. At least you have a clear focus, and a definite idea of what to work on. What you need (assuming you disagreed with that first statement) is to work on a more positive outlook. Think about when and how you form opinions about yourself. Are you being overly critical or anxious? Are you beating yourself up and knocking yourself down? And if so, ask why. Did a parent or older sibling always criticize you when you were young, for example? A little self-analysis can help get at the root causes of any lack of confidence that might make you vulnerable to the rejections one tends to encounter in personal selling. And it is certainly good news to many people to learn that the best thing they can do to build their sales ability is to work on feeling more positive about themselves. This permits all sorts of pleasant self-indulgences in the name of professional improvement. Go have some fun! Work out, visit a spa, treat yourself to a relaxing massage. You deserve it—and if it helps you feel better about yourself, you will be a better marketer as a result.

APPENDIX: FLEX STYLE NEGOTIATING SELF-ASSESSMENT

Here is another self-assessment instrument that is helpful in improving your sales and marketing performance. Use it by filling in the assessment below, then reading the instructions to diagnose your style. You will find that the diagnosis applies not only to negotiating situations, but to your personal selling style more generally as well. For example, if you find you have a tendency to withdraw from or avoid conflict situations (one of the possibilities in the following assessment), then you probably are not very aggressive about making cold sales calls or handling difficult situations like customer service problems and complaints. Knowing you have such a bias is, however, the first and most important step toward overcoming it!

The assessment on pages 413–423 are reproduced from the Flex Style Negotiating line of products Alex designed for HRD Press. (They have kindly agreed to let us reproduce this in our book, but please don't make unauthorized copies of it. The original is inexpensive and easily obtained through them if you want to use it in training.) Contact them at 800-822-2801 if you want additional copies of this assessment, or want to learn more about the additional assessments and training manuals in the product line. We find that negotiation training is a useful component of sales force development, and also relevant to the training and development of marketing managers.

Instructions

Below are 21 pairs of statements. To complete this self-assessment, circle the letter of *the one statement from each pair* that you agree with most strongly. (Don't worry about the meaning of the letters right now; that will be discussed later.)

Even if neither statement describes exactly how you feel, *you must choose one statement over the other.* Weigh the statements as accurately and honestly as possible.

In all cases, *both statements represent common attitudes in the population as a whole.* There is no right or wrong answer, just the one that you feel is most descriptive of you.

Example:

A. I prefer to work with others.
B. I prefer to work by myself.

Style Assessment Statements

A. I prefer to work with others.
B. I prefer to work by myself.

C. My personal motto is, "Do unto others as you want them to do unto you."
D. My personal motto is, "Do unto others, before they do unto you!"

E. Life is like a game in which some people are dealt better cards than others.
F. Life is like a game in which anyone can win if they are clever and motivated.

A. I'd rather be popular than rich.
B. I'd rather be successful than well liked.

C. I don't mind letting someone cut in line ahead of me, because I know that "what goes around, comes around."
D. I don't let anybody cut in line ahead of me.

E. Sometimes you just have to make hard choices.
F. If I don't like the alternatives, I make up my own.

Published by Human Resource Development Press, Inc., 22 Amherst Road, Amherst, Massachusetts 01002, 1-800-822-2801 (U.S. and Canada), 1-413-253-3488, 1-413-253-3490 (fax), http://www.hrdpress.com. All rights reserved. It is a violation of the law to reproduce, store in a retrieval system or transmit, in any form or by any means, electronic, mechanical, photocopying, recording or otherwise, any part of this publication without the prior written permission of HRD Press, Inc. Excerpted from *Flex Style Negotiating,* by Alexander Watson Hiam, 1997.

(continued)

Style Assessment Statements

A. I am fascinated by how other people behave.
B. I am not concerned about what other people think.

C. If I saw a twenty-dollar bill in the hall, I'd try to figure out who dropped it and return it to the owner.
D. I think that if anyone is dumb enough to lose their own money, they have no claim on whoever finds it.

E. An attention to detail and a knowledge of the facts are essential to problem solving.
F. A creative approach and an understanding of the bigger picture are essential to problem solving.

A. It feels good to know that other people owe you favors.
B. It is safest to rely on yourself.

C. When people beg money from me on the street, I often give them something.
D. I think people who beg money on the street don't deserve our attention because most of them are taking advantage of our feelings.

E. I don't know why people can't stay focused.
F. I don't know why people can't see the connections between things.

A. If people are rude to me, I let them know their behavior is unacceptable.
B. If people are rude to me, I avoid them.

C. When somebody wants a favor from me, I do what I can to help out.
D. I am careful to do favors only when I can reasonably expect the person would do something for me in return.

E. Some people will do anything to avoid facing facts.
F. I believe there is always a better way to look at a problem.

A. A good reputation is a person's most important possession.
B. Experience is a person's most important possession.

Style Assessment Statements

C.   I feel that the world has been good to me.
D.   I figure the world owes me one.

E.   For every winner there must be a loser.
F.   There is always some way to make sure everybody wins.

A.   What I value most from my school years is the time I spent with my friends.
B.   What I value most from my school years is the time I spent learning essential skills.

C.   Work and personal relationships usually turn out favorably in the long run.
D.   You have to be very careful in work or personal relationships to avoid getting burned.

E.   I don't see why I should be flexible about meeting my essential needs.
F.   I prefer to take a flexible approach, especially when others are flexible.

(continued)

Scoring Sheet

Instructions

Please transfer your letter scores from the Style Assessment Statements and fill in the blanks below.

How many A's did you circle?   _____ A's

How many B's did you circle?   _____ B's

How many C's did you circle?   _____ C's

How many D's did you circle?   _____ D's

How many E's did you circle?   _____ E's

How many F's did you circle?   _____ F's

Check your scores, totaling your counts of each letter.   _____ Total

The total should be 21. If you have not received this total, count again.

Finding Your Default Negotiating Style

Check the appropriate item in each pair listed below to find out which end of the three negotiation behavior dimensions fits you best.

Note that these dimensions are intended to predict your *natural*, or *default*, negotiating style. The findings should *not* be considered relevant to any other aspect of behavior.

Example:

    ✔ I circled four or more A's. I am **A Oriented**   =   Engage ✔

    ____ I circled four or more B's. I am **B Oriented**   =   Avoid ____

Social Dimension—A/B

Check one:

    ____ I circled four or more A's. I am **A Oriented**   =   **Engage** ____

    ____ I circled four or more B's. I am **B Oriented**   =   **Avoid** ____

Emotional Dimension—C/D

Check one:

    ____ I circled four or more C's. I am **C Oriented**   =   **Give** ____

    ____ I circled four or more D's. I am **D Oriented**   =   **Take** ____

Cognitive Dimension—E/F

Check one:

    ____ I circled four or more E's. I am **E Oriented**   =   **Accept** ____

    ____ I circled four or more F's. I am **F Oriented**   =   **Redefine** ____

Now turn the page to find your default negotiating style.

(continued)

The Default Negotiating Style Table

Look at the three words you have checked in the right-hand column on the previous page; then find their combination in the table below. Circle the number next to them and the strategy across from them. For example, if you checked "Engage," "Give," and "Redefine," you would circle number 4 below, read across the fourth row, and circle "Collaborate" as your default style.

Example:

4.	Engage, Give, Redefine	Collaborate

	If your pattern is:	Your default style is to:
1.	Engage, Take, Accept	Compete
2.	Engage, Take, Redefine	Con
3.	Engage, Give, Accept	Borrow
4.	Engage, Give, Redefine	Collaborate
5.	Avoid, Take, Accept	Compromise
6.	Avoid, Take, Redefine	Rob
7.	Avoid, Give, Accept	Accommodate
8.	Avoid, Give, Redefine	Withdraw

Interpreting Your Default Style(s)

The eight styles identified by this assessment are briefly described below. Note that they fall into two categories: legitimate negotiating styles and illegitimate negotiating styles. Training and study will prepare you to use the five legitimate negotiating styles more effectively. You will not practice the three illegitimate styles, because they are not generally considered socially acceptable or effective.

However, you may have an inclination toward one of the illegitimate styles, and if so will need to recognize that your first instinct in a negotiation may be unhelpful to you. You will need to train yourself to consciously select a more appropriate strategy—just as we all do whenever our default strategy is not the best one for a particular negotiating situation.

Most people studying negotiation find that their default style is one of the five legitimate styles, or at least that they can easily learn to use these legitimate styles. And so there is no reason to focus on the illegitimate styles in training. However, do remember that other parties you negotiate with may utilize an illegitimate style. You can use the *Behavioral Style Assessment/Other* to make an educated guess about others' default negotiating styles. And if it indicates that they are inclined to use one or more illegitimate styles, you should either avoid the negotiation or, if that is impossible, utilize an extremely cautious competitive strategy.

Now let's examine the eight possible styles.

Legitimate Styles

These are the five classic negotiating styles that you need to master in order to be an effective negotiator in any situation. Some negotiation training courses focus on just one strategy (the Compete strategy is the most frequent focus of single-strategy courses); other training courses cover all five.

Compete

This is the classic negotiation style in which both parties try to better the other through tough bargaining. It is sometimes termed *win-lose* because what one person gains, the other gives up. A "poker face" is helpful as you don't want the other party to know every detail of your position.

(continued)

In behavioral terms, people who are naturals at this strategy tend to be social and good at engaging others. They tend toward the take end, rather than the give end, of the emotional spectrum—which means they do not feel bad about asking for, and receiving, more for themselves than they are willing to give others. On the cognitive dimension, they tend to accept existing rules and problem definitions and do their best to win within these constraints; they fight over the pie rather than try to figure out how to bake a bigger one.

Collaborate

This is the opposite of the Compete strategy in that the parties work cooperatively, problem-solving in order to meet both of their needs. They try to redefine the problem—which requires that they share details of their needs and positions—and then collaborate to find a creative way to make everybody happy. The collaborative strategy requires trust and good-faith behavior; if one party switches to a competitive approach part of the way through, the other will be hurt.

In behavioral terms, this strategy is a natural for someone who is socially engaged, thus willing and able to work collaboratively. It is also associated with a giving or generous emotional nature, and with a cognitive tendency to redefine the situation rather than to accept the current constraints.

Compromise

The Compromise strategy uses the traditional "let's split the difference" approach. It is competitive in the sense that it accepts there is a pie of limited size to fight over, but it shortcuts the competition by adopting a simple, fair way to reach a generally acceptable division. It is often adopted by negotiators when they do not care enough about the outcome to go through a lengthy negotiation yet want to ensure they do not lose too much as a result of taking a shortcut.

The behavioral model portrays the compromise negotiator as someone whose social tendency is to avoid others rather than to engage them. Compromise gets you out of the negotiation encounter quickly and with a minimum of social effort. This strategy is also consistent with an emotional tendency toward take rather than give, as it protects the negotiator's position by applying common rules of fairness. On the cognitive dimension, it is accepting of the given constraints in a negotiation; the strategy does not show a tendency to redefine the problem.

Accommodate

In this strategy, the negotiator gives in and accepts the other party's demands. Why? Generally because the outcome is of little importance or the relationship is of great importance, or both. For instance, in order to avoid an argument a wife may agree to her husband's suggestion that they buy a red car, even though she hates the color. Of course, not all spouses would accommodate this position, and those who do might regret it later!

People who have a natural tendency to accommodate tend to avoid social interaction—it is, after all, a great way to avoid the intimacy of any of the more engaged styles. They are emotionally giving, or else they would not be willing to accept the poor outcomes that this strategy produces. And they are cognitively accepting of the situation; their inclination is to accept the way in which the other party has framed the negotiating situation.

Withdraw

This strategy is employed by someone who sees the negotiation as a waste of time and effort, or as too unpleasant to be worth the investment of time and effort. Some negotiations are best avoided. But the strategy can result in a loss to both parties if there was anything for them to gain through negotiation.

Some people just don't like to negotiate, and would rather not bake a pie with another party, even if it means that neither of them will get to eat a piece of it! Behaviorally, they tend to avoid people rather than to engage socially. They are more inclined toward emotional giving than taking, since the strategy requires some sacrifice of potential outcome. And they are cognitively inclined to redefine the situation rather than accept it—the act of withdrawal is a rejection of the other party's definition of the negotiating situation.

Details of when and how to use each of these five strategies are contained in the *Flex Style Negotating* training products from HRD Press and in *Think Before You Speak: The Complete Guide to Strategic Negotiation*, by Roy J. Lewicki, Alexander Hiam, and Karen Olander, (John H. Wiley & Sons, 1996).

(continued)

Illegitimate Styles

These negotiating styles are sometimes viewed as extreme or unethical variations on the competitive style. They are not taught in negotiation training for obvious reasons, but you need to be aware of them in order to guard against them. And in some cases their use is legal and condoned by society, so you may well encounter them on the job or elsewhere.

Con

This negotiation style involves taking advantage of the other party through deception and the creation of misplaced trust. The accountant who talks little old ladies into giving him their life savings to invest, then keeps it, is using the Con strategy. It requires a keen sense of the other party's personality and needs, plus a willingness to deceive. Not all examples of the Con strategy are blatant or illegal, however. A great many business and political relationships have an element of this strategy somewhere within them. And it is not always obvious to the other party that they have been conned—the most successful users of this strategy rely on information that the other party never discovers.

Behaviorally, people who are naturally good at this strategy are socially engaged—it demands excellent people skills. They are emotional takers rather than givers, feeling that the world owes them something rather than the other way around. And they are cognitively creative, good at redefining the situation in order to end-run normal negotiating conventions and skillful at finding some way to take advantage of the other party without the other realizing it.

Borrow

This strategy is exemplified by Wimpy, the gluttonous sidekick in the old Popeye cartoons, whose opening line in most negotiations is "I'll gladly pay you Tuesday for a hamburger today." Of course, there is nothing wrong with offering debt as part of your compensation to the other party—but people like Wimpy are very hard to collect from! The Borrow strategy trades future concessions for current ones without much concern for how those future concessions will be made. In the long run, the other party is likely to feel taken advantage of. But the borrower may be perfectly sincere, if slightly unrealistic, when sitting at the negotiating table. You might think this a rare strategy, but in fact most of us have friends who habitually borrow our things and never seem to return them.

Behaviorally, this strategy is most natural for people who are socially engaging—they must gain the temporary trust of the other party just as in the Con strategy. They tend to be generous, and are more likely to be emotionally giving than taking. (Although what they give in this strategy is not always what it appears, they believe in it wholeheartedly themselves.) And they are cognitively accepting, trying to make the existing situation work in their favor rather than finding ways to redefine it.

Rob

This strategy takes advantage of the other party through the use of power to reach an outcome that the other party, and any objective observer, would consider unjust. It flirts with illegality but is not always as brazen as a hold-up. For example, a boss may take advantage of his position power to force an employee to accept an unreasonable workload or an unpleasant task that is not in the job description. Similarly, information power can be used for the Rob strategy, as when one party suggests a compromise with the other without revealing that the half she keeps is actually worth far more. (To give a concrete example of that, let's say a sister and brother inherit two pieces of property, and the sister finds out that one piece is above a newly discovered oil field. Without sharing this knowledge, she suggests that they each take one of the properties, and carefully works it so that she gets the one with oil.)

Behaviorally, this strategy is associated with a tendency toward independence, along with a strong inclination toward emotional taking rather than giving. It is also associated with a cognitive tendency to redefine the situation rather than to accept norms and expectations of conduct.

> **Note:** All three illegitimate negotiating strategies lend themselves to unethical, even illegal actions, but that does not mean a person inclined toward one of them will act unethically. This assessment does not explore the ethical dimension of behavior, and so it cannot predict whether someone with an inclination toward one of these strategies will actually use it unethically or not. Obviously, someone with a strong set of ethical beliefs and values is not going to negotiate unethically, even if they have a natural tendency toward one of these strategies

NOTES

CHAPTER 1

1. Edgar Woolard, "Creating a New Company Culture," *Fortune*, January 15, 1990, pp. 127–131.

2. "Does Customer Satisfaction Go Down with Downsizing?" *On Q*, July/August 1997, p. 5.

3. Ibid.

4. L.L. Bean company catalogs and literature.

5. Howard Schlossberg, "Baldridge Winner Aims for 100% Satisfaction," *Marketing News*, February 4, 1991, pp. 1, 12.

6. Howard Schlossberg, "Author: Consumers Just Can't Wait to Be Satisfied," *Marketing News*, February 4, 1991, p. 13.

7. Grahame R. Dowling and Mark Uncles, "Do Customer Loyalty Programs Really Work?" *Sloan Management Review*, Summer 1997, pp. 71–88. Also see A.S.C. Ehrenberg, *Repeat-Buying: Facts, Theory, and Applications*, 2nd ed., Oxford University Press, 1988.

8. Peter M. Senge, "The Leader's New Work: Building Learning Organizations," *Sloan Management Review*, Fall 1990, pp. 7–23.

9. Ibid.

10. Howard Schlossberg, "Author: Consumers Just Can't Wait to Be Satisfied," *Marketing News*, February 4, 1991, p. 13.

11. Brian Dumaine, "The Bureaucracy Busters," *Fortune*, June 17, 1991, pp. 36–50.

12. Howard Schlossberg, "Baldridge Winner Aims for 100% Satisfaction," *Marketing News*, February 4, 1991, pp. 1, 12.

13. Brian Dumaine, "The Bureaucracy Busters," *Fortune*, June 17, 1991, pp. 36–50.

14. Cited in Theodore Levitt, "Marketing Myopia 1975: Retrospective Commentary," *Harvard Business Review*, September–October 1975.

15. Ibid.

16. Ibid.

17. Michael Miller, "Lawmakers Are Hoping to Ring Out Era of Unrestricted Calls by Telemarketers," *The Wall Street Journal*, May 28, 1991, p. B1.

18. Steven Star, "Marketing and Its Discontents," *Harvard Business Review*, November–December 1989, pp. 148–154.

19. "Shareholder Superstars," *Fortune*, June 23, 1997, p. 83.

20. Dick Berry, *Marketing News*, December 24, 1990, p. 10.

21. Brian Dumaine, "The Bureaucracy Busters," *Fortune*, June 17, 1991, pp. 36–50.

22. Henry Ford, *My Life and Work*, New York: Doubleday Page & Co., 1923, pp. 146–147.

CHAPTER 2

1. Paul Schoemaker, "Strategy Complexity and Economic Rent," *Management Science*, 36(10), October 1990, pp. 1178–1192.

2. "The New Breed of Strategic Planner," *BusinessWeek*, September 17, 1984, p. 63.

3. Gary Reiner, "Getting There First: It Takes Planning to Put Plans into Action," *The New York Times*, March 12, 1989: Business Forum.

4. Ronald Hentcoff, "How to Plan for 1995," *Fortune*, December 31, 1990, pp. 70–77.

5. David A. Aaker, *Strategic Market Management*, 4th ed., Wiley, 1995, p. 12.

6. "Stanley Works Posts a $64.5 Million Loss Tied to Restructuring," *The Wall Street Journal*, July 21, 1997, p. A4.

7. Michael Dertonzos, Richard Lester, and Robert Solow, *Made in America: Regaining the Competitive Edge*, New York: HarperCollins, 1989, p. 46.

8. Janice Castro, "Making It Better," *Time*, November 13, 1989, pp. 78–81.

9. "How to Plan for 1995," *Fortune*, December 31, 1990, p. 70.

10. Alice Z. Cuneo, "Starbucks Readies Supermarket Invasion," *Advertising Age*, June 9, 1997, p. 1.

11. "Levi Strauss Is Stretching Its Wardrobe," *Fortune*, November 19, 1979, p. 89.

12. "It's Back to Basics for Levi's," *BusinessWeek*, March 8, 1982, p. 77.

13. Andrew Feinberg, "The First Global Generation," *Adweek's Marketing Week*, February 6, 1989, pp. 18–27.

14. Susan Faluti, "Levi Strauss's Net Surged 30% in 2nd Quarter," *The Wall Street Journal*, July 11, 1991, p. C13.

15. Andrew S. Grove, *Only the Paranoid Survive: How to Exploit the Crisis Points That Challenge Every Company and Career*, Doubleday, 1996, pp. 152–153.

16. "How Do You Follow an Act Like Bud?" *BusinessWeek*, May 2, 1988, p. 119.

17. Alice Z. Cuneo, "Starbucks Readies Supermarket Invasion," *Advertising Age*, June 9, 1997, p. 1.

18. H. Igor Ansoff, Measuring and Managing for Environmental Turbulence: The Ansoff Associates Approach, in Hiam, *The Portable Conference on Change Management*, HRD Press, 1997, pp. 67–83. Also see Hugh Courtney et al., "Strategy Under Uncertainty, *Harvard Business Review*, November–December, 1997, pp. 67–79, for a similar scale.

19. Tom Peters, *Thriving on Chaos: Handbook for a Management Revolution*, Harper & Row, 1987, pp. 8, 477, 478.

20. Vicki L. Spagnol, "The Criteria: A Looking Glass to Americans' Understanding of Quality," *Quality Progress*, July 1997, pp. 78–84.

21. Ibid.

22. Laurie J. Bassi and Mark E. Van Buren, "Sustaining High Performance in Bad Times," *Training*, June 1997, p. 35.

23. Robert Buzzell and Bradley Gale, *The PIMS Principles: Linking Strategy to Performance*, New York: The Free Press, 1987, p. 9.

24. Statistics for 2nd quarter 1990, from a September 24, 1990, report by Diana Temple of Salomon Brothers.

25. "Diversified Gillette Still Depends on Blades," *The New York Times*, February 25, 1990.

26. Data for this example are from Mart-Charlier, "Brewers Shake Off a 3-Year Hangover," *The Wall Street Journal*, January 15, 1991, and originally collected by the trade magazines *Impact* and *Beer Marketer's Insights*.

27. Vijay Vishwanath and Jonathon Mark, "Your Brand's Best Strategy," *Harvard Business Review*, May–June 1997, pp. 123–129.

28. For an explanation of other approaches, see Yoram Wind and Vijay Mahajan, "Designing Product and Business Portfolios," *Harvard Business Review*, 60(1), January–February 1981, pp. 156–165.

29. Based on telephone conversations with Bruce Bunch and William Rothschild. See Alexander Hiam, *The Vest-Pocket CEO: Decision-Making Tools for Executives*, Englewood Cliffs, NJ: Prentice-Hall, 1990, pp. 377–384.

30. "The New Breed of Strategic Planner," *BusinessWeek*, September 17, 1984, pp. 62–66.

31. Ibid.

32. Ibid.

33. Ibid.

34. This case based on Brian Dumaine, "How Managers Can Succeed Through Speed," *Fortune*, February 13, 1989, pp. 54–59.

35. Ibid., 56.

36. "The New Breed of Strategic Planner," *BusinessWeek*, September 17, 1984, pp. 62–66.

37. Frank Sonenberg, "Customer Satisfaction: The Strategic Edge for the 1990s," *Adweek's Marketing Week*, September 3, 1990.

38. Andrea Gabor, "The Front Lines of Quality," *U.S. News & World Report*, November 27, 1989, pp. 57–59.

39. Janice Castro, "Making It Better," *Time*, November 13, 1989, pp. 78–81.

40. Brian Dumaine, "The Bureaucracy Busters," *Fortune*, June 17, 1991, pp. 36–50.

41. Hideki Kaihatsu, "TQC in Japan," *Making Total Quality Happen*, New York: The Conference Board, 1990.

42. Robert Camp, "Competitive Benchmarking," *Making Total Quality Happen*, New York: The Conference Board, 1990.

43. Ibid.

44. Ibid.

45. Janice Castro, "Making It Better," *Time*, November 13, 1989, pp. 78–81.

46. Ibid.

47. Roy Stata, "Organizational Learning—the Key to Management Innovation," *Sloan Management Review*, Spring 1989, pp. 63–73.

48. Ibid., 64.

49. Nine senior managers worked with Peter Senge and Jay Forrester at MIT; the group is called the New Management Style Project.

50. Roy Stata, "Organizational Learning—the Key to Management Innovation," *Sloan Management Review*, Spring 1989, pp. 63–73.

51. Elliot Carlisle, *Mac: Managers Talk About Managing People*, New York: Penguin Books, 1982, p. 12.

52. Chris Argyris, "Teaching Smart People How to Learn," *Harvard Business Review*, May–June 1991, pp. 99–109.

53. Rosabeth Moss Kanter, "The New Managerial Work," *Harvard Business Review*, November–December 1989, pp. 85–92.

54. Brian Dumaine, "The Bureaucracy Busters," *Fortune*, June 17, 1991, pp. 36–50.

55. Patricia Sellers, "Pepsi Keeps on Going After No. 1," *Fortune*, March 11, 1991.

56. Henry Mintzberg, *The Rise and Fall of Strategic Planning: Reconceiving Roles for Planning, Plans, Planners,* The Free Press, 1994, p. 397.

57. Ibid., 110.

58. Gayle Sato Stodder, "Painting the Town," *Entrepreneur,* February 1997, p. 135.

CHAPTER 3

1. Steve Glain, "Top Toilet Makers from U.S. and Japan Vie for Chinese Market," *The Wall Street Journal,* December 19, 1996.

2. Koichi Noda, President of Toto Ltd.'s China Unit, Ibid.

3. Roger Thurow, "In Global Drive, Nike Finds its Brash Ways Don't Always Pay Off," *The Wall Street Journal,* May 5, 1997, pp. A1, A10.

4. Alexander Hiam, *Quality Profile: Whirlpool Corporation,* The Conference Board, January 1995, p. 7.

5. *U.S. News & World Report,* December 3, 1990, p. 62.

6. Robert L. Rose and Carl Quintanilla, "More Small U.S. Firms Take Up Exporting, With Much Success," *The Wall Street Journal,* December 20, 1996.

7. Susan V. Lawrence, "The Revolt of the Chinese Consumer," *U.S. News & World Report,* December 3, 1990, p. 62.

8. "Expatriate Gaps," *Training & Development,* July 1997, p. 7.

9. Regina Fazio Maruca, "The Right Way To Go Global: An Interview with Whirlpool CEO David Whitman," *Harvard Business Review,* March–April 1994, p. 136.

10. John Templeman, "A Troubling Barrage of True Sanctions from All Across America," *BusinessWeek,* February 24, 1997, p. 59.

11. "Asking for Protection Is Asking for Trouble," *Harvard Business Review,* 65(4), July–August 1987, pp. 42–47.

12. Ibid.

13. "PepsiCo Accepts Tough Conditions for the Right to Sell Cola in India," *The Wall Street Journal,* September 20, 1988, p. 44.

14. "U.S. Products Still Hot in Philippines," *Advertising Age,* November 18, 1985, p. 70.

15. Directory of Trade Statistics Yearbook, International Monetary Fund, 1985, p. 6.

16. P.S. Raju, "Consumer Behavior in Global Markets: The A-B-C-D Paradigm and its Application to Eastern Europe and the Third World," *Journal of Consumer Marketing,* 12(5), 1995, pp. 37–56.

17. Ibid.

18. Many of the following examples are excerpted from David A. Ricks, *Big Business Blunders,* Homewood, IL: Dow Jones-Irwin, 1983.

19. Vern Terpstra and Kenneth David, *The Cultural Environment of International Business,* Cincinnati: South-Western, 1991.

20. Edward T. Hall, "The Silent Language in Overseas Business," *Harvard Business Review,* 38(3), May–June 1960, pp. 87–96.

21. Jeffrey A. Fadiman, "A Traveler's Guide to Gifts and Bribes," *Harvard Business Review,* 86(4), July–August 1986, pp. 122–136; "The New Export Entrepreneurs," *Fortune,* January 4, 1988.

22. Ernest Dichter, "The World Customer," *Harvard Business Review,* 4(4), July–August 1962, pp. 113–123.

23. Kathryn Rudie Harrigan, "Strategic Alliances: Their Role in Global Competition," *Columbia Journal of World Business,* 22(2), Summer 1987, pp. 67–69.

24. White, Heather, Amherst, MA, January 1998.

25. See J. J. Boddewyn, Robin Soehl, and Jacques Picard, "Standardization in International Marketing: Is Ted Levitt in Fact Right?" *Business Horizons,* 29(6), November–December 1986, pp. 69–75; W. Chan Kim and R. A. Mauborgne, "Cross-Cultural Strategies," *Journal of Business Strategy,* 7(1), Spring 1987, pp. 28–35; "The Issue Globalists Don't Talk About," *International Management,* 42(9), September 1987, pp. 37–42; James F. Bolt, "Global Competitors: Some Criteria for Success," *Business Horizons,* 30(1), January–February 1988, pp. 34–41.13.

26. Theodore Levitt, "The Globalization of Markets," *Harvard Business Review,* 61(3), May–June 1983, pp. 92–102.

27. Hidea Sugiura, "How Honda Localizes Its Global Strategy," *Sloan Management Review,* Fall 1990, pp. 77–82.

28. Ibid., 78.

29. Ibid., 82.

30. Christopher Bartlett and Sumantra Ghoshal, "Organizing for Worldwide Effectiveness: The Transnational Solution," *California Management Review,* Fall 1988, pp. 54–74.

31. Ibid., 73.

32. Hiam, *Quality Profile: Whirlpool Corporation,* 6.

33. Bartlett and Ghoshal, "Organizing for Worldwide Effectiveness: The Transnational Solution," *California Management Review,* Fall 1988, p. 66.

34. Warren Keegan, "Multinationals Product Planning: Strategic Alternatives," *Journal of Marketing,* 33(1), January 1969, p. 59.

35. Michael Porter, "Why Nations Triumph," *Fortune,* March 12, 1990, pp. 94–108. Also see Michael Porter, *The Competitive Advantage of Nations,* New York: The Free Press, 1990.

36. "Have We Lost Our Faith in Competition?" (an interview with Michael Porter), *Across The Board,* September 1990, pp. 37–46.

37. Ibid., 39.

CHAPTER 4

1. Justin Martin, "Ignore Your Customer," *Fortune,* May 1, 1995, p. 121.

2. Joshua Levine, "Desperately Seeking 'Jeepness,'" *Forbes,* May 15, 1989, pp. 134–138.

3. John Paul Newport, Jr., "American Express: Service That Sells," *Fortune,* November 20, 1989, pp. 80–94.

4. Laurie Hays, "Using Computers to Divine Who Might Buy a Gas Grill," *The Wall Street Journal,* August 16, 1994, p. B1.

5. Ibid.

6. Alexander Hiam, *The Portable Conference on Change Management,* HRD Press and Lakewood Publications, 1997, pp. 300–301.

7. Betsy Morris, "He's Smart. He's Not Nice. He's Saving Big Blue," *Fortune,* April 14, pp. 68–81.

8. Francis J. Gouillart and Frederick D. Sturdivant, "Spend a Day in the Life of Your Customers," *Harvard Business Review,* January–February 1994, pp. 116–125.

9. Newport, Jr., "American Express: Service That Sells," pp. 80–94.

10. Jim Bessen, "Riding the Marketing Information Wave," *Harvard Business Review,* September/October 1993, pp. 156–157.

11. William Rathje and Cullen Murphy, "Garbage Demographics," *American Demographics,* May 1982, pp. 50, 54.

12. Bruce G. Posner, "The Future of Marketing Is Looking at You," *Fast Company,* October 1996, p. 105.

13. Ronald B. Lieber, "Storytelling: A New Way to Get Close to Your Customer," *Fortune,* February 3, 1997, p. 104.

14. "Big Brother Is Grocery Shopping with You," *BusinessWeek,* March 29, 1993, p. 60.

15. Terence P. Pere, "How to Find Out What They Want," *Fortune,* Special Issue, Autumn/Winter 1993, p. 39.

16. Ibid.

17. Maryanne E. Rasmussen, "Measuring Bottom-Line Impact of Customer Satisfaction; Making Total Quality Happen," New York: The Conference Board, 1990, pp. 55–59.

18. Ibid.

19. Sources: "How to Snoop on your Competitors," *Fortune,* May 14, 1984, pp. 29–33; "George Smiley Joins the Firm," *Newsweek,* May 2, 1988, pp. 46–47; "Strategies for Playing the Global Game," *The New York Times,* June 26, 1988, p. F3.

20. Vern Terpstra, *International Marketing,* 4th ed., Chicago: The Dryden Press, 1987, pp. 178–185.

21. Charles S. Mayer, "The Lessons of Multinational Marketing Research," *Business Horizons,* 21(6), December, 1978, pp. 7–13.

22. David Kilburn, "Putting Out Feelers: Japanese 'Antenna Shops' Aid Research," *Advertising Age,* January 2, 1989, pp. 3, 25.

23. Donald F. Cox and Robert E. Good, "How to Build a Marketing Information System," *Harvard Business Review, 45*(3), May–June 1967, p. 145.

24. John D. C. Little, "Decision Support Systems for Marketing Managers," *Journal of Marketing, 43*(3), Summer 1979, p. 9.

CHAPTER 5

1. Ellen Graham, "When Terrible Twos Become Terrible Teens," *The Wall Street Journal,* February 5, 1997, p. B1.

2. Peter F. Drucker, *Innovation and Entrepreneurship: Practice and Principles,* New York: Harper & Row, 1985, p. 90.

3. Elizabeth Lesley and Robert Hof, "Is Digital Convergence for Real?," *BusinessWeek,* June 23, 1997, p. 42.

4. Demo Memo, *American Demographics,* April 1997, p. 24.

5. Graham, "When Terrible Twos Become Terrible Teens," B1.

6. Andrew Feinberg, "Bust or Boom?" *Adweek's Marketing Week,* December 5, 1988, pp. 20–30.

7. C. Northcote Parkinson, *Parkinson's Law,* New York: Random House, 1957, pp. vii–viii. By the way, Parkinson's law is, "Work expands so as to fill the time available for its completion."

8. Joel R. Evans and Barry Berman, *Marketing,* 7th ed., Englewood Cliffs: Prentice-Hall, Inc., 1997, p. 185.

9. Hugh Pope, "Turkish Mustaches, or the Lack Thereof, Bristle with Meaning," *The Wall Street Journal,* May 15, 1997, p. A1.

10. Susan Mitchell, "Are Boomers Their Parents?" *American Demographics,* August 1996, pp. 40–45.

11. "Teen-Age Shoppers; Desperately Seeking Spinach," *The New York Times,* November 29, 1987, p. F10.

12. "Marketing Briefs," *Marketing News,* September 9, 1996, p. 2.

13. Samuel H. Preston, "Children Will Pay," *The New York Times Magazine,* September 29, 1996, p. 97.

14. Ian Murphy, "'Downscale' Luxury Cars Drive to the Heart of Baby Boomers," *Marketing News,* October 7, 1996, p. 1.

15. Sid and Bruce Good, "Boomers Need Security Blanket," *Marketing News,* September 30, 1996, p. 6.

16. Charles D. Schewe, "Gray America Goes to Market," *Business: The Magazine of Managerial Thought and Action, 35*(2), April–June 1985, pp. 3–9; Hale N. Tongren, "Determinant Behavior Characteristics of Older Consumers," *Journal of Consumer Affairs, 22*(1), Summer 1988, pp. 136–157.

17. Ganesan Visvabharathy and David Rink, "The Elderly: Neglected Business Opportunities," *Journal of Consumer Marketing, 1*(4), 1984, p. 39.

18. "Soon, Most People May Have 'Lived in Sin,'" *The Wall Street Journal,* June 13, 1988, p. 37.

19. *Statistical Abstract of the United States 1996,* U.S. Dept. of Commerce, Bureau of the Census, p. 67, Table No. 84.

20. Ibid, p. 15, Table No. 14 and p. 67, Table No. 84.

21. "The Future of Households," *American Demographics,* December 1993, pp. 27–40.

22. *Statistical Abstract of the United States 1996,* pp. 393, 399.

23. "Breaking Through," *BusinessWeek,* February 17, 1997, p. 64.

24. Chad Rubel, "Marketers Giving Better Treatment to Females," *Marketing News,* April 22, 1996, p. 10.

25. Charles D. Schewe, "Marketing to Blacks: Research Implications for Managers," *Atlanta Economic Review,* 36(5), September–October 1976, pp. 34–40.

26. Henry Assael, *Consumer Behavior and Marketing Action,* Boston: Kent, 1981, p. 274; David Loudon and Albert J. Della Bitta, *Consumer Behavior: Concepts and Applications,* 2nd ed., New York: McGraw-Hill, 1984, pp. 210–216.

27. Kelly Shermach, "Infomercials for Hispanics," *Marketing News,* March 17, 1997, p. 1.

28. "Fast Times on Avenida Madison," *BusinessWeek,* June 6, 1988, p. 64.

29. *Statistical Abstract of the United States 1996,* p. 199.

30. "Proceeding with Caution," *Time,* July 16, 1990, p. 60.

31. David Leonhardt, "Two-Tier Marketing," *BusinessWeek,* March 17, 1997, p. 82.

32. Marshall Fisher, Janice Hammond, Walter Obermeyer, and Ananth Raman, "Making Supply Meet Demand in an Uncertain World," *Harvard Business Review,* May–June 1994, p. 83.

33. Niknil Deogun and Sally Goll Beatty, "New Ads Aim to Make Diet Sodas Cool Again," *The Wall Street Journal,* May 14, 1997, p. B1.

34. Ibid.

35. Peter F. Drucker, *Innovation and Entrepreneurship,* New York: Harper & Row, 1985, p. 91.

36. David M. Georgoff and Robert G. Murdick, "Manager's Guide to Forecasting," *Harvard Business Review,* 86(1), January–February 1986, see table.

37. John Naisbitt, *Megatrends,* New York: Warner Books, 1982; John Naisbitt and Patricia Aburdene, *Re-Inventing the Corporation,* New York: Warner Books, 1985.

38. Herb Brody, "Great Expectations: Why Predictions Go Awry," *Journal of Consumer Marketing, 10* (1), 1993, pp. 23–27.

39. "Back Issues," *Census '90, The Wall Street Journal Research Reports,* March 9, 1990, pp. R7, R27.

40. "For Better or Worse?" *Newsweek Special Issue: The 21st Century Family,* Winter–Spring 1990, p. 18.

CHAPTER 6

1. Abraham Maslow, *Motivation and Personality,* 3rd ed., New York: Harper & Row, 1970, p. 7.

2. As quoted in Robert Johnson, "In The Chips," *The Wall Street Journal,* March 22, 1991, pp. B1–2.

3. Malcolm Gladwell, "The Science of Shopping," *The New Yorker,* November 4, 1996, p. 67.

4. Johnson, "In The Chips," pp. B1–2. Many of the details in this chapter concerning Frito-Lay and chip marketing come from the above article.

5. Ibid.

6. Peter Samuel, "Chipping Away at the Champ," *Forbes,* April 25, 1994, pp. 107–116.

7. "Children's Hour: As Kids Gain Power of Purse," *The Wall Street Journal,* January 19, 1988, p. 1.

8. Matt Murray, "Hey Kids! Marketers Want Your Help!" *The Wall Street Journal,* May 6, 1997, p. B1.

9. Alfred L. Kroeber and Talcott Parsons, "The Concepts of Culture and of Social System," in Gardner Lindzey and Elliot Aronson, *Handbook of Social Psychology,* Vol. 2, New York: Random House, 1985, p. 994.

10. Michael J. McCarthy, "Marketers Zero in on Their Customers," *The Wall Street Journal,* March 18, 1991, pp. B1, B8.

11. Lorraine C. Scarpa, Ph.D., "Fast, Flexible, Computerized: That's Today's Analytic World," *Brandweek,* November 15, 1993, p. 28.

12. Ibid., 32.

13. McCarthy, "Marketers Zero in on Their Customers," pp. B1, B8.

14. Ibid.

15. Janice Castro, "The Simple Life," *Time,* April 8, 1991, pp. 58–65.

16. Ibid.

17. Rebecca Piirto Heath, "Life on Easy Street," *American Demographics,* April 1997, p. 33.

18. Elaine Underwood, "Luxury's Tide Turns," *Brandweek,* March 7, 1994, p. 20.

19. Laura Parker, "Cigar-and-Martini Town Echos Nation's Prosperity," *USA Today,* May 30, 1997, p. A1.

20. Benjamin DeMott, *The Imperial Middle: Why Americans Can't Think Straight about Class*, New York: Morrow, 1990.

21. Andrew Hacker, "Class Dismissed," *The New York Review of Books*, March 7, 1991.

22. "Class in America," *Fortune*, February 7, 1994, p. 116.

23. William O. Bearden and Michael J. Etzel, "Reference Group Influence on Product and Brand Purchase Decisions," *Journal of Consumer Research*, 9(2), September 1982, pp. 183–194.

24. Full page ad in *The Wall Street Journal*, May 15, 1997, p. B3.

25. Robert Berner, "The Rolls-Royce of Leather Jackets Is Hard to Come By," *The Wall Street Journal*, November 22, 1996, pp. A1, A8.

26. Rochan D. Ahuja and Mary Walker, "Female-Headed Single Parent Families," *Journal of Consumer Marketing*, 11(4), 1994, pp. 41–54.

27. Isabella Cunningham and Robert Green, "Purchasing Roles in the U.S. Family, 1955 and 1973," *Journal of Marketing*, 30(4), October 1974, pp. 61–64.

28. Marilyn Lavin, "Husband-Dominant, Wife-Dominant, Joint: A Shopping Typology for Boom Couples?," *Journal of Consumer Marketing*, 10(3), 1993, pp. 33–42.

29. Charles M. Schaninger and W. C. Buss, "Intergenerational Transfer of Task Allocation within the Family," paper presented at the American Marketing Association Winter Educators' Conference, Fort Lauderdale, Florida, 1984.

30. John B. Ford, Michael S. LaTour, and Tony L. Henthorne, "Perception of Marital Roles in Purchase Decision Processes: A Cross-Cultural Study," *Journal of the Academy of Marketing Science*, 23(2), pp. 120–131.

31. Jean Halliday, "Saab Spotlights Heritage in Ads Planned by Martin," *Advertising Age*, May 26, 1997, p. 12.

32. Cheryl Russell, "Birth Order and the Baby Boom," *American Demographics*, March 1997, p. 10; Frank J. Sulloway, *Born to Rebel*, Pantheon Books, 1996.

33. Christina Duff, "Two Family Budgets: Different Means, Similar Ends," *The Wall Street Journal*, April 14, 1997, p. B1.

34. "If I Have the Doctor . . .," *Forbes*, March 30, 1981, p. 64.

35. Abraham H. Maslow, *Motivation and Personality*, New York: Harper & Row, 1954.

36. Lisa Miller, "This Spring Break, The Hottest Thing Is Unprotected Skin," *The Wall Street Journal*, March 7, 1997, pp. A1, A6.

37. Paul A. Herbig and Hugh Kramer, "The Effect of Information Overload on the Innovation Choice Process," *Journal of Consumer Marketing*, 11(2), pp. 45–54.

38. According to Michael Rothschild of the University of Wisconsin, in Michael J. McCarthy, "Mind Probe," *The Wall Street Journal*, March 22, 1991, p. B3.

39. Sally Goll Beatty, "Whose Ad Is This Anyway? Parodies Amuse, Bemuse," *The Wall Street Journal*, April 14, 1997.

40. William M. Casey, "Whole Lotta Shakin' Has Some Owners Rattled at Mercedes," *The Wall Street Journal*, June 7, 1995, pp. A1, A7.

41. John B. Hinge, "Critics Call Cuts in Package Size Deceptive Move," *The Wall Street Journal*, February 5, 1991, pp. B1, B8.

42. James Ryan, "Tom Waits Wins 'Sound-Alike' Suit," *Billboard*, May 19, 1990, pp. 6, 82.

43. John Deighton, Daniel Romer, and Josh McQueen, "Using Drama to Persuade," *Journal of Consumer Research*, 16, December 1989, pp. 335–343.

44. Kathleen Deveny, "Copycat Cold Medicines Proliferate, Creating Confusion among Consumers," *The Wall Street Journal*, February 1, 1991, pp. B1, B8.

45. For more on low involvement, see Harold H. Kassarjian, "Low Involvement: A Second Look," in Kent B. Monroe, Ed., *Advances in Consumer Research, 8,* Ann Arbor, Michigan: Association for Consumer Research, 1981, pp. 31–34; Michael J. Houston and Michael L. Rothchild, "Conceptual and Methodological Perspectives on Involvement," in Subash C. Jain, Ed., Research Frontiers in Marketing: Dialogues and Directions, Chicago: *American Marketing Association*, 1978, pp. 184–187.

46. Sue Shellenbarger, "McDonald's Low-Fat Burger to Go National," *The Wall Street Journal*, March 13, 1991, p. B1.

47. Jon Bigness, "Bag Trends: Convertibles, Four-Wheelers," *The Wall Street Journal*, November 22, 1996, pp. B1, B6.

48. "Problem Recognition: The Crucial First Stage of the Consumer Decision Process," *The Journal of Consumer Marketing*, 5(1), Winter 1988, pp. 53–63.

49. Joseph W. Newman, "Consumer External Search: Amount and Determinant," in Arch Woodside, Jagdish Sheth, and Peter Bennett, Eds., *Consumer and Industrial Buying Behavior*, New York: North-Holland, 1977, p. 86.

50. William B. Locander and Peter W. Hermann, "The Effect of Self-Confidence and Anxiety on Information Seeking in Consumer Risk Reduction." *Journal of Marketing Research*, 16(2), May 1979, pp. 233–246.

51. Jennifer Lawrence, "Frito Heavies Up on 'Light' Items," *Advertising Age*, August 1988, p. 42; also "Frito-Lay Tests Low-Oil Doritos," *Advertising Age*, January 18, 1988, p. 91.

52. Michael J. McCarthy, "Marketers Zero In on Their Customers," *The Wall Street Journal*, March 18, 1991, pp. B1, B8.

CHAPTER 7

1. Stann Rapp and Tom Collins, *MaxiMarketing*, New York: McGraw-Hill, 1987.

2. Don Peppers and Martha Rogers, *The One to One Future: Building Relationships One Customer at a Time,* New York: Doubleday, 1993, p. 5.

3. Scott Adams, *The Dilbert Future*, New York: HarperCollins, 1997, p. 166.

4. Cleveland Horten, "Porsche 300,000: The New Elite," *Advertising Age,* February 5, 1990, p. 6.

5. For its beginning, see Wendell R. Smith, "Product Differentiation and Market Segmentation as Alternative Marketing Strategies," *Journal of Marketing,* 20(3), July 1956, pp. 3–8.

6. Reid P. Claxton, "Birth Order as a Market Segmentation Variable," *Journal of Consumer Marketing, 12*(3), 1995, pp. 22–38.

7. Douglas L. Fugate, "Evaluating the U.S. Male Homosexual and Lesbian Population as a Viable Target Market Segment," *Journal of Consumer Marketing, 10*(4), 1993, pp. 46–57.

8. Kate Fitzgerald, "MCI Rings Up Gays via Direct Marketing," *Advertising Age,* June 5, 1995, p. 50.

9. Rebecca Piirto Heath, "You Can Buy a Thrill: Chasing the Ultimate Rush," *American Demographics,* June 1997, pp. 47–51.

10. "Global Marketing: How Marketing Executives Really Feel," *Ad Forum,* April 1985, pp. 30–31.

11. Franklin B. Evans, "Psychological and Objective Factors in the Prediction of Brand Choice, Ford versus Chevrolet," *Journal of Business,* October 1959, pp. 340–369; Ralph Westfall, "Psychological Factors in Predicting Product Choice," *Journal of Marketing, 26*(2), April 1962, pp. 34–40; Shirley Young, "The Dynamics of Measuring Unchange," in Russell I. Haley, Ed., *Attitude Research in Transition,* Chicago: American Marketing Association, 1972, pp. 61–82.

12. Fred D. Reynolds and William R. Darden, "An Operational Construction of Life Style," in M. Venkatesen, Ed., Proceedings of the 3rd Annual Conference for Consumer Research, 1972, pp. 482–484.

13. Arnold Mitchell, *The Nine American Lifestyles: Who We Are and Where We Are Going,* New York: Macmillan, 1983.

14. Judith D. Schwartz, "What Is A Family Today? For Hallmark, a Challenge," *Brandweek,* June 14, 1993, p. 22.

15. Based on research reported in "People's Choice," *Advertising Age,* January 16, 1984, p. 10, and "The Touch Is Light on Women's Market," *Advertising Age,* January 16, 1984, pp. 14–16.

16. Kevin J. Clancy and Mary Lou Roberts, "Toward an Optimal Market Target: A Strategy for Market Segmentation," *Journal of Consumer Marketing, 1*(1), Summer 1983, p. 66.

17. Adam Zagorin, "Sub-Prime Time," *Time,* November 4, 1996, p. 67–68.

18. Kathleen Deveny, "Segments of One," *The Wall Street Journal,* March 22, 1991, p. B3; Stan Rapp and Tom Collins, *The Great Marketing Turnaround,* Englewood Cliffs, NJ: Prentice-Hall, 1991.

19. Ibid.

20. B. Joseph Pine II, Don Peppers, and Martha Rogers, "Do You Want to Keep Your Customers Forever?," *Harvard Business Review,* March–April 1995, pp. 103–114.

21. Kathleen Deveny, "Segments of One," *The Wall Street Journal,* March 22, 1991, p. B3; Stan Rapp and Tom Collins, *The Great Marketing Turnaround,* Englewood Cliffs, NJ: Prentice-Hall, 1991.

22. Al Ries and Jack Trout, *Positioning: The Battle for Your Mind,* New York: Warner Books, 1982.

23. Yoram J. Wind, *Product Policy: Concepts, Methods, and Strategy,* Reading, MA: Addison-Wesley, 1982, pp. 79–81; David A. Aaker and J. Gary Shansby, "Positioning Your Product," *Business Horizons, 24*(3), May–June 1981, pp. 56–62.

24. Teresa Domzal and Lynette Unger, "Emerging Positioning Strategies in Global Marketing," *The Journal of Consumer Marketing, 4*(4), Fall 1987, pp. 23–40.

25. Patricia Sellers, "Pepsi Opens a Second Front," *Fortune,* September 30, 1996.

26. "Marketing Firm Slices U.S. into 240,000 Parts to Spur Clients' Sales," *The Wall Street Journal,* November 3, 1986, p. 1.

27. References: Arnold Mitchell, *The Nine American Lifestyles: Who We Are and Where We Are Going,* New York: Macmillan, 1983; Martha Farnsworth Riche, "Psychographics for the 1990s," *American Demographics,* July 1989.

28. Faye Rice, "Making Generational Marketing Come of Age," *Fortune,* June 26, 1995, pp. 110–114; Michael Phillips, "Selling by Evoking What Defines a Generation," *The Wall Street Journal,* August 13, 1996, B1, B2.

29. Regis McKenna, "Marketing in an Age of Diversity," *Harvard Business Review,* September–October 1988. (And Alexander Hiam, "Adversity and Market Diversity," *Harvard Business Review,* March–April 1989, for the influence of marketing and other factors.)

30. Aimee Stern, "Tired of Playing Mind Games," *Adweek's Marketing Week,* July 13, 1987, pp. 1, 6.

CHAPTER 8

1. Judann Pollack and Laura Petrecca, "Pizza Hut Turns to Pasta to Boost Dinner Business," *Advertising Age,* July 21, 1997, pp. 1, 35.

2. Howard Schlossberg, "Experts Share Formulas for Innovative Success," *Marketing News,* April 15, 1991, pp. 11, 26.

3. Michael Ray and Rochelle Myers, *Creativity in Business,* New York: Doubleday, 1986, p. 93.

4. "Nurturing Those Ideas," *BusinessWeek: Innovation in America 1989,* pp. 105–118.

5. "I Can't Work This Thing!" *BusinessWeek,* April 29, 1991, pp. 58–66.

6. "TOTO vs. Kohler: Attack of the Japanese Toilets," *Time,* November 11, 1996, p. 56.

7. Brian O'Reilly, "The Secret's of America's Most Admired Corporations: New Ideas New Products," *Fortune,* March 3, 1997, pp. 60–64.

8. "I Can't Work This Thing!" pp. 58–66.

9. Yuichi Okomura, general manager of the product-planning unit at JVC's Video Products Division.

10. Regis McKenna, "Marketing Is Everything," *Harvard Business Review,* January–February 1991, pp. 65–79.

11. Howard Schlossberg, "Experts Share Formulas for Innovative Success," *Marketing News,* April 15, 1991, pp. 11, 26.

12. William Taylor, "The Business of Innovation: An Interview with Paul Cook," *Harvard Business Review,* March–April 1990, pp. 97–106.

13. Alexander Hiam, *Marketing for Dummies,* Foster City, CA: IDG Books, 1997, pp. 57–58.

14. Ronald Henkoff, "P&G:New and Improved!" *Fortune,* October 14, 1996, pp. 151–161.

15. Hiam, *Marketing for Dummies,* p. 59.

16. "To Surf and Protect," *BusinessWeek,* January 13, 1997, p. 78.

17. "Marketing Briefs," *Marketing News,* April 15, 1991, p. 26 (quoting Gorman's New Product News).

18. "Another 15,000 New Products Expected for U.S. Supermarkets," *Marketing News,* June 10, 1991, p. 8; "Fewer New Products in '91," *Marketing News,* January 20, 1992, p. 1.

19. Alexander Hiam, "Campbell's New Product Rules," in *The Vest-Pocket Marketer,* Englewood Cliffs, NJ: Prentice-Hall, 1991.

20. *New Product Management for the 1980s,* New York: Booz, Allen & Hamilton, 1982, p. 9.

21. "How Chesebrough-Ponds Put Nail Polish in a Pen," *BusinessWeek,* October 8, 1984, p. 196.

22. *New Product Management for the 1980s: Phase I,* New York: Booz, Allen & Hamilton, 1981.

23. Regis McKenna, "Marketing Is Everything," *Harvard Business Review,* January–February 1991, pp. 65–79.

24. Actually, we argued in Chapter 3 that a strong home base, plus a "think globally, act locally" strategy, was key to global success. They are, but in large part because they improve the quality of innovation.

25. Howard Schlossberg, "Experts Share Formulas for Innovative Success," *Marketing News,* April 15, 1991, pp. 11, 26.

26. "The Brakes Go On in R & D," *BusinessWeek*, July 1,1991, pp. 24–46.

27. Michael J. McCarthy, "Slim Pickings," *The Wall Street Journal*, May 6, 1997, p. A8.

28. Richard A. Melcher, "Why Zima Faded So Fast," *BusinessWeek*, March 10, 1997, pp. 110–114.

29. See Tom W. White, "Use of Internal, External Sources to Garner and Screen New Product Ideas," *Marketing News*, September 16, 1983, Sec. 2, D 2.

30. Eric van Hippel, "Has a Customer Already Developed Your Next Product?" *Sloan Management Review*, 18(4), Winter 1977, p. 63.

31. *New Products: Best Practices—Today and Tomorrow*, New York: Booz, Allen & Hamilton, 1982.

32. See "Osborn's Brainstorming" and "Crawford Slip Writing" for detailed instructions on two brainstorming methods, in Alexander Hiam, *The Vest-Pocket CEO: Decision-Making Tools for Executives*, Englewood Cliffs, NJ: Prentice-Hall, 1990.

33. *Management of New Products*, 4th ed., New York: Booz, Allen & Hamilton, 1968, and *New Products: Best Practices*.

34. David B. Montgomery and Glen L. Urban, "Screening New-Product Possibilities," in Robert Rothberg, (Ed.), *Corporate Strategy and Product Innovation*, 2nd ed., New York: The Free Press, 1981.

35. Alexander Hiam, "Center for Concept Development's Evaluation Form," *The Vest-Pocket Marketer*, Englewood Cliffs, NJ: Prentice-Hall, 1991, pp. 104–106.

36. "Bik 'n' Bop," *Marketing News*, April 15, 1991, p. 26.

37. *New Product Management for the 1980s: Phase I*, New York: Allen & Hamilton, 1981.

38. "Bucket Brigade vs. Fast Cycle Development," *BusinessWeek*, Innovation in America, 1989, p. 107.

39. "Product Development: Where Planning and Marketing Meet" (Interview), *The Journal of Business Strategy*, September–October 1990, pp. 13–16.

40. Tom Peters, *Thriving on Chaos: Handbook for a Management Revolution*, New York: Harper & Row, 1987, Chapters 1–2.

41. As quoted in William Taylor, "The Business of Innovation: An Interview with Paul Cook," *Harvard Business Review*, March–April 1990, pp. 97–106.

42. "RCA's Rivals See Life in Videodiscs," *BusinessWeek*, April 23, 1984, p. 88.

43. C. Merle Crawford, *New-Product Management*, Homewood, IL: Richard D. Irwin, 1983, pp. 25–28.

44. As reported by *Marketing News*, February 8, 1990, p. 1.

45. C. Merle Crawford, "New-Product Failure Rates—Facts and Fallacies," *Research Management*, September 1979, pp. 9–13.

46. Calvin L. Hodock, "Strategies Behind the Winners and Losers," *The Journal of Business Strategy*, September–October 1990, pp. 4–7.

47. Ibid.

48. Marvin B. Lieberman and David B. Montgomery, "First-Mover Advantages," *Strategic Management Journal,* 9, 1988, pp. 41–58.

49. Michael W. Lawless and Robert J. Fisher, "Sources of Durable Competitive Advantage in New Products," *Journal of Product Innovation Management,* 7(1), March 1990, pp. 35–44.

50. Ibid.

51. Ibid.

52. "Making Strategy Look Different," *Management Briefing: Marketing,* February–March 1988, The Conference Board.

53. "America's Oldest Companies," *Nation's Business,* July 1976, pp. 36–37.

54. Theodore Levitt, "Marketing Myopia 1975: Retrospective Commentary," *Harvard Business Review,* September–October 1975. Levitt points out in this important article (probably the most important article ever written on marketing) that "The railroads are in trouble today not because the need [for transportation] was filled by others (cars, trucks, airplanes, even telephones), but because it was not filled by railroads themselves." Here lies the key issue in determining whether product decline and death is inevitable. This issue is addressed in detail in the next chapter.

55. "Masters of Innovation," *BusinessWeek,* April 10, 1989, pp. 58–67.

CHAPTER 9

1. Cathleen Black, president, Hearst Publications, *Speech to the Economic Club of Indianapolis,* Indianapolis, IN, March 4, 1997.

2. Alexander Hiam, *Marketing for Dummies,* Foster City, CA: IDG Books, 1997, p. 291.

3. Grahame R. Dowling and Mark Uncles, "Do Customer Loyalty Programs Really Work?" *Sloan Management Review,* Summer 1997, pp. 71–82, quote, p. 74.

4. A.S.C. Ehrenberg, *Repeat-Buying: Facts, Theory, and Applications,* 2d ed., Oxford University Press, 1988.

5. Dowling and Uncles, "Do Customer Loyalty Programs Really Work?" p. 74.

6. "Fad Food: Gimme a Bagel—with Legs," *BusinessWeek,* November 13, 1995, p. 82.

7. Compton MacKenzie, Editor of *The Gramophone,* as quoted in E. Levin, "CDs: To Buy or Not To Buy," *People Weekly,* March 11, 1985, p. 11.

8. "Compact Discs Now the Hottest Sound in Town," *U.S. News and World Report,* June 17, 1985, p. 62.

9. Industry Surveys, *Leisure Time,* April 18, 1996, p. L36.

10. These calculations are based on data collected by Anita M. McGahan in "Market Segmentation and Capacity Commitment in the American Compact Disc Industry," Working Paper, Harvard Business School, October 1990.

11. This issue is addressed in Anita McGahan's working paper, noted above, and our discussion relies heavily upon this source for information and ideas.

12. "A Craze May Outsprint Its Creator," *The New York Times*, August 7, 1990, pp. D1, D6.

13. Data from In-Line Skating Industry Facts: 1996 Statistics, Compiled by Rollerblade, Inc.

14. This case is based largely on N. R. Kleinfield, "How Cuisinart Lost Its Edge," *The New York Times Magazine*, April 15, 1990, pp. 46, 66–67.

15. Ibid.

16. "Fort Howard: New Marketing Muscle from Maryland Cup," *Business-Week*, July 18, 1983, p. 132.

17. Raju Narisetti, "P&G, Seeing Shoppers Were Being Confused, Overhauls Marketing," *The Wall Street Journal*, January 15, 1997, p. A7.

18. Julie Schlax, "A Good Reason to Mess With Success," *Forbes*, September 19, 1988.

19. Annetta Miller and Karen Springem, "Will Fake Fat Play in Peoria?," *Newsweek*, June 3, 1996, p. 50.

20. Byron M. Sharp, "Managing Brand Extension," *Journal of Consumer Marketing, 10*(3), 1993, pp. 11–17.

21. "Starbucks Does Not Live by Coffee Alone," *BusinessWeek*, August 5, 1996, p. 76. "Play It Again, Starbucks," *Time*, January 13, 1997, p. 58.

22. John A. Quelch, "Extend Profits, Not Product Lines," *Harvard Business Review*, September–October 1994, pp. 153–160.

23. "Kmart: The No. 2 Retailer Starts to Make an Upscale Move—At Last," *BusinessWeek*, June 4, 1984, p. 51.

24. David Woodruff, "Will Kmart Ever Be a Silk Purse?" *BusinessWeek*, January 22, 1990, p. 46.

25. Kevin Hellikee, "Wal-Mart's Store of the Future Blends Discount Prices, Department-Store Feel," *The Wall Street Journal*, April 17, 1991, p. B1.

26. Roger Cohen, "Ms. Playboy," *The New York Times Magazine*, June 9, 1991, pp. 32, 55–56, 84.

27. Mack Harlan, *Re-Competitive Strategies: How to Regain Growth Profits for Mature Businesses*, American Management Association (AMACOM), 1986.

28. Isadore Barmash, "Sending the Very Best, For No Particular Reason," *The New York Times*, June 9, 1991, p. F12.

CHAPTER 10

1. "Pricing for Profit: The 1% Solution," HIDA Management Seminar, Boston, September 1983.

2. David R. Henderson, "What Are Price Wars Good For? Absolutely Nothing," *Fortune*, May 12, 1997, p. 156.

3. Dan Koeppel, "A Panty Hose That Couldn't Make the Stretch," *Adweek's Marketing Week*, June 19, 1989, p. 28.

4. Alexander Hiam, *Marketing for Dummies*, Foster City, CA: IDG Books, 1997, p. 234.

5. Joseph P. White, "Car Makers Seek to Mask Price Increases," *The Wall Street Journal*, August 16, 1989, p. B1.

6. John B. Hinge, "Critics Call Cuts in Package Size Deceptive Move," *The Wall Street Journal*, February 5, 1991, pp. B1, B8.

7. Ford S. Worthy, "Making It in China," *Fortune*, June 17, 1991, pp. 103–104.

8. Ibid.

9. John Berry, "Suddenly, Pricing Is the Hot Button," *Adweek's Marketing Week*, November 5, 1990, p. 5.

10. Linda Grant, "Smart Managing: Where Did the Snap, Crackle & Pop Go?" *Fortune*, August 4, 1997, pp. 223–226.

11. Ibid., 224.

12. Fred R. Bleakley, "Why Shoppers Think Food Is a Rip-Off," *The Wall Street Journal*, March 6, 1997, pp. B1, B7.

13. "America's Grocery Cart," *The Wall Street Journal*, March 6, 1997, p. B1.

14. Grant, "Smart Managing: Where Did the Snap, Crackle & Pop Go?" pp. 223–226.

15. Jeffrey Taylor, "As Speechmakers Go, Few Can Say They Are in Bush's League," *The Wall Street Journal*, May 5, 1997, pp. A1, A6.

16. From Poem CXXXI, *Collected Poems of Emily Dickinson*, Avenel Books, 1982.

17. David R. Henderson, "What Are Price Wars Good For? Absolutely Nothing," *Fortune*, May 12, 1997, p. 156.

18. "Auto Makers Rethink Pricing Policies to Woo Still-Reluctant Buyers," *The Wall Street Journal*, October 23, 1981, p. 1.

19. "Detroit's Merry-Go-Round," *BusinessWeek*, September 12, 1983, p. 75.

20. Jesse Bimbaum, "No Need to Kick the Tires," *Time*, February 19, 1996.

21. John Greenwald, "Cereal Showdown," *Time*, April 29, 1996, p. 60.

22. Frank Alpert, Beth Wilson, and Michael T. Elliot, "Price Signaling: Does It Ever Work?" *Journal of Consumer Marketing*, 10(4), 1993, pp. 4–14.

23. Scott A. Neslin and Robert W. Shoemaker, "Using a Natural Experiment to Estimate Price Elasticity: The 1974 Sugar Shortage and the Ready-to-Eat Cereal Market," *Journal of Marketing*, 47(4), Winter 1983, pp. 44–57.

24. J. Douglas McConnell, "Effect of Pricing on Perception of Product Quality," *Journal of Applied Psychology*, 52(4), September 1968, pp. 331–334; Ben M.

Enis and James Stafford, "The Price-Quality Relationship: An Extension," *Journal of Marketing Research, 6*(4), November 1969, pp. 256–258; Jacob Jacoby, Jerry Olson, and Rafael Haddock, "Price, Brand Name, and Product Composition Characteristics as Determinants of Perceived Quality," *Journal of Applied Psychology, 55*(6), December 1971, pp. 470–479; David M. Gardner, "Is There a Generalized Price-Quality Relationship in an Experimental Setting?," *Journal of Advertising Research, 21*(4), August 1981, pp. 49–52.

25. Zarrell V. Lambert, "Perceived Price as Related to Odd and Even Price Endings," *Journal of Retailing, 51*(3), Fall 1975, pp. 13–22.

26. Kent B. Monroe and Peter J. LaPlaca, "What Are the Benefits of Unit Pricing?" *Journal of Marketing, 36*(3), July 1972, pp. 16–22; Michael J. Houston, "The Effect of Unit Pricing on Choices of Brand and Size in Economic Shopping," *Journal of Marketing, 36*(3), July 1972, pp. 51–54; David A. Aacker and Gary T. Ford, "Unit Pricing Ten Years Later: A Replication," *Journal of Marketing, 47*(4), Winter 1983, pp. 118–122.

CHAPTER 11

1. Ronald Henkoff, "Delivering The Goods," *Fortune,* November 28, 1994, p. 64.

2. "Boom Times in a Bargain-Hunter's Paradise," *BusinessWeek,* March 11, 1985, p. 120.

3. "Computers Are the Key to Wholesalers' Strength," *American Druggist,* December 1983, p. 16.

4. Ernst & Whinney, "Corporate Profitability & Logistics: Innovative Guidelines for Executives," *Council of Logistics Management,* 1987, p. vii.

5. "True Partners Operate on a Handshake and Shared Values," *Marketing News,* June 24, 1991, p. 29.

6. James Brian Quinn, Thomas L. Doorley, and Penny C. Paquette, "Beyond Products: Services-Based Strategy," *Harvard Business Review,* March–April 1990, pp. 58–68.

7. Ibid.

8. Ibid.

9. Joseph B. Fuller, James O'Connor, and Richard Rawlinson, "Tailored Logistics: The Next Advantage," *Harvard Business Review,* May–June 1993, pp. 87–98.

10. Kaoru Ishikawa, "What Is Total Quality Control? The Japanese Way," Translated by David J. Lu, Englewood Cliffs, NJ: Prentice-Hall, 1985, p. 32.

11. Patricia Sellers, "Winning Over the New Consumer," *Fortune,* July 29, 1991.

12. Tara Parker-Pope and Lisa Bannon, "Avon's New Calling: Sell Barbie in China," *The Wall Street Journal,* May 1, 1997, p. B1.

13. Patricia Sellers, "Winning Over the New Consumer," *Fortune,* July 29, 1991, pp. 113–124.

14. "Porsche's Civil War with its Dealers," *Fortune,* April 16, 1984, pp. 63–68.

15. Nikhil Deogun, "A Coke and a Perm? Soda Giant is Pushing Into Unusual Locales," *The Wall Street Journal,* May 6, 1997, pp. A1, A8.

16. "The King of Shampoo," *Fortune,* September 2, 1985, p. 48.

17. John Greenwald, "Cereal Showdown," *Time,* April 29, 1996, p. 60.

18. "The Customer With Clout," *Fortune,* October 2, 1995, p. 100.

19. Robert F. Lusch, "Sources of Power: Their Impact on Intrachannel Conflict," *Journal of Marketing Research, 13*(4), November 1976, pp. 382–390.

20. "Want Shelf Space at the Supermarket? Ante Up," *BusinessWeek,* August 7, 1989, pp. 60–61.

21. "Retailers Exert More Influence in Selling of Packaged Goods," *The Wall Street Journal,* April 25, 1985, p. 33.

22. Adel I. El-Ansary, "Perspectives on Channel System Performance," in Robert F. Lusch and Paul H. Zinszer, eds., *Contemporary Issues in Marketing Channels,* Norman, OK: University of Oklahoma Press, 1979, p. 50.

23. Ken Blanchard, Charles Schewe, Bob Nelson, and Alex Hiam, *Exploring the World of Business,* New York: Worth Publishers, 1996, p. 490.

24. Lisa J. Moore, "The Flight to Franchising," *U.S. News & World Report,* June 10, 1991, pp. 68–71.

25. Ibid.

26. National Federation of Independent Business, *Profiles of Success: An American Express Study of New Business,* 1989 (available from Ketchum Public Relations).

27. Michael Barrier, "A New Sense of Service," *Nation's Business,* June 1991, pp. 16–24.

28. "Another 15,000 New Products Expected for U.S. Supermarkets," *Marketing News,* June 10, 1991, p. 8.

29. Joseph Pereira, "New Sneaker Superstores Aim to Step on Their Competition," *The Wall Street Journal,* March 19, 1997, pp. B1, B5.

30. Richard M. Bessom and Donald W. Jackson, "Service Retailing: A Strategic Marketing Approach," *Journal of Retailing, 51*(2), Summer 1975, pp. 75–76.

31. Theodore Levitt, "Marketing Intangible Products and Product Intangibles," *Harvard Business Review, 59*(3), May–June 1981, pp. 94–102.

32. Roger D. Blackwell and W. Wayne Talarzyk, "Life-Style Retailing: Competitive Strategies for the 1980s," *Journal of Retailing, 59*(4), Winter 1983, pp. 7–27.

33. Leonard L. Berry, "Retail Positioning Strategies for the 1980s," *Business Horizons, 25*(6), November–December 1982, pp. 45–50.

34. Malcolm P. McNair, "Significant Trends and Developments in the Postwar Period," in A.B. Smith, ed., *Competitive Distribution in a Free, High-Level Economy and Its Implications for the University,* Pittsburgh, PA: University of Pittsburgh

Press, 1958, pp. 1–25. For a refinement of this theory, see Stanley C. Hollander, "The Wheel of Retailing," *Journal of Marketing, 26*(3), July 1960, pp. 47–42.

35. U.S. Department of Commerce, *1985 U.S. Industrial Outlook,* Washington, D.C., 1985, p. 53–1.

36. Ibid.

37. "Apple-Polishing the Dealer," *Sales and Marketing Management,* September 10, 1984, p. 47.

38. "Key problems Facing Industrial Distributors" in James A. Narus, N. Mohan Reddy, and George L. Pinchak, *Industrial Marketing Management, 13,* September 1984, pp. 139–147.

39. "What Makes Retailers Switch," *Supermarket Business,* March 1985, p. 24.

40. "Fleming's Fast Rise in Wholesale Foods," *Fortune,* January 21, 1985, p. 54.

41. William D. Perreault, Jr., and Frederick A. Russ, "Physical Distribution Service in Industrial Purchase Decisions," *Journal of Marketing, 40*(2), April 1976, pp. 3–10.

42. U.S. Bureau of Economic Analysis, "Survey of Current Business," November 1993, pp. 442, 773.

43. Ronald H. Ballou, *Basic Logistics,* Englewood Cliffs, NJ: Prentice-Hall, 1978, pp. 17–18.

44. Richard J. Schoenberger and Abdolhossein Ansari, "'Just-in-Time' Purchasing Can Improve Quality," *Journal of Purchasing and Materials Management,* Spring 1984, pp. 2–7.

45. Chan K. Hahn, Peter A. Pinto, and Daniel J. Bragg, "'Just-in-Time' Production and Purchasing," *Journal of Purchasing and Materials Management,* Fall 1983, pp. 2–10.

46. Richard C. Walleigh, "What's Your Excuse for Not Using JIT?" *Harvard Business Review, 86*(2), March–April 1986, pp. 38–54.

47. Louis W. Stern and Adel I. El-Ansary, *Marketing Channels,* 2nd ed., Englewood Cliffs, NJ: Prentice-Hall, 1982, p. 167.

CHAPTER 12

1. Alice Z. Cuneo, "Levi's Unleashing New Image Ads," *Advertising Age,* July 28, 1997.

2. Ibid.

3. Ibid.

4. Alexander Hiam, *Marketing For Dummies,* Foster City, CA: IDG Books, 1997, front matter.

5. Mark Landler, "Consumers are Getting Mad, Mad, Mad, Mad at Mad. Ave.," *BusinessWeek*, April 30, 1990, pp. 70–72.

6. Joshua Hammer, "Advertising in the Dark," *Newsweek*, April 19, 1990, p. 44.

7. "Had it up to Here with Ad? Better Not Fill'er Up," *The Wall Street Journal*, February 2, 1990, p. B1.

8. Thaddeus Rutkowski, "Unnecessary Roughness," *Adweek*, January 11, 1988, p. BR22.

9. James C. Schroer, "Ad Spending: Growing Market Share," *Harvard Business Review*, January–February 1990, pp. 44–48.

10. American Marketing Association & American Association of Advertising Agencies, 1990 Winners: The Effie Gold Awards, 1991.

11. Robert Buzzell, John Quelch, and Walter Salmon, "The Costly Bargain of Trade Promotion," *Harvard Business Review*, March–April 1990, pp. 141–149.

12. Joanne Lipman, "Executives Tackle Biggest Marketing Task," *The Wall Street Journal*, May 16, 1991, p. B6.

13. John Duggleby, "Games Gang Ltd. Finds That Talk Is Cheaper," *Adweek's Marketing Week*, July 17, 1989, pp. 46–47.

14. Ibid.

15. Andrew Wallenstein, "Milk Producers Fight Fat Fatalism," *Advertising Age*, May 22, 1995, p. 1.

16. Pat Wechsler, "A Curiously Strong Campaign," *BusinessWeek*, April 21, 1997, p. 134.

17. Steven H. Star, "Marketing and Its Discontents," *Harvard Business Review*, November–December 1989, pp. 148–154.

18. Arch C. Woodside and James J. Taylor, "Consumer Purchase Intentions, Perceptions of Product Quality and National Advertising," *Journal of Advertising*, Winter 1978, pp. 48–51.

19. Sally Goll Beatty, "Nissan's Ad Campaign Was a Hit Everywhere But in The Showrooms," *The Wall Street Journal*, April 8, 1997, pp. 1, 14.

20. Howard Schlossberg, "The Simple Truth: Ads Will Have to Be Truthful," *Marketing News*, December 24, 1990, p. 6.

21. Ibid.

22. David Ogilvy, *Ogilvy on Advertising*, New York: Vintage Books, 1983, p. 84.

23. Julian Simon, "What Do Zielske's Real Data Really Show About Pulsing?" *Journal of Marketing Research*, 16(3), August 1979, pp. 415–420.

24. Economic Impact: U.S. Direct Marketing Today: Direct Marketing Association, Inc., October 1995, p. 3.

25. Bob Stone, *Successful Direct Marketing Methods*, 3rd ed., Chicago: Crain Books, 1985, p. 1.

26. *Arnold Fishman's Guide to Mail Order Sales,* August 1994, pp. 26–28.

27. Don Peppers and Martha Rogers, Ph.D. *The One to One Future: Building Relationships One Customer at a Time,* New York: Currency Doubleday, 1993.

28. Edward O. Welles, "Burning Down the House," *Inc.,* August 1997, pp. 67–73.

29. David Bank, "How Net Is Becoming More Like Television to Draw Advertisers," *The Wall Street Journal,* December 13, 1996, p. 1.

30. Jared Sandberg, "Retailers Pay Big for Prime Internet Real Estate," *The Wall Street Journal,* July 8, 1997, p. B1.

31. William Keenan Jr., "America's Best Sales Forces: Six at the Summit," *Sales & Marketing Management,* June 1990, pp. 62–82.

32. Ibid., 72.

33. Ibid., 75–76.

34. American Marketing Association, *Committee on Definitions, Marketing Definitions: A Glossary of Marketing Terms,* Chicago, 1960, p. 20.

35. Roger A. Strang, "Sales Promotion—Fast Growth, Faulty Management," *Harvard Business Review,* 54(4), July–August 1976, pp. 115–124.

36. Kevin Helliker, "Old-Fashioned PR Gives General Mills Advertising Bargains," *The Wall Street Journal,* March 20, 1997, p. 1.

37. "New? Improved?" *BusinessWeek,* October 21, 1985, p. 109.

38. Charles H. Patti and Vincent Blasko, "Budgeting Practices of Big Advertisers," *Journal of Advertising Research,* 21(6), December 1981, pp. 23–29.

39. "Advertising and Sales Relationships: A Current Appraisal," *Nielsen Researcher,* 1(1980), pp. 2–9.

40. Patti and Blasko, "Budgeting Practices of Big Advertisers," pp. 23–29.

41. This and the following case history is based on 1990 Winners: The Effe Gold Awards, AMA/New York and AAAA, 1991.

GLOSSARY

ADMINISTERED VERTICAL MARKETING SYSTEM: A vertical marketing system in which one member is informally designated as captain.

ADVERTISING: Any impersonal form of communication about ideas, goods, or services that is paid for by an identified sponsor.

ADVERTISING CAMPAIGN: A set of messages with a single theme that is repeatedly conveyed to the target audience over an extended period.

ADVERTISING PLATFORM: The issues and product benefits that a marketer wishes to convey in an advertising message.

ADVERTISING TARGET MARKET: The specific audience toward which an advertising message is aimed.

ADVERTISING THEME: The parts of an advertising message that are repeated throughout the campaign.

AFFECTIVE COMPONENT (OF AN ATTITUDE): The emotional feeling of favorableness or unfavorableness that results from a person's evaluation of an object.

AGENT: A wholesaling intermediary that does not take title to merchandise but serves primarily to bring buyers and sellers together and facilitate exchanges.

ANNUAL PLAN: A plan in which the organization's managers set goals for a single year.

AREA SAMPLE: A probability sample in which respondents are chosen at random from a complete list of the population in a specific geographic area.

ATTITUDES: Feelings that express whether a person likes or dislikes objects in his or her environment.

AUCTION COMPANY: A wholesaling intermediary that sells merchandise on an agency basis by means of auctions.

AUGMENTED PRODUCT: An expected product that has been enhanced by a set of benefits that consumers do not expect or that exceed their expectations.

449

BACKTRANSLATION: A process in which a questionnaire is translated into a second language and then translated back into the original language.

BAIT-AND-SWITCH PRICING: A pricing strategy in which a product is given a low price in order to lure customers into a store, where an attempt is made to persuade them to buy a more expensive model or product.

BANNER: A box holding one to several lines of text, displayed on a Web page. A new form of paid advertising. (Also, Banner Headline in print advertising is a large Headline.)

BAROMETRIC TECHNIQUES: Forecasting techniques that use analyses of past trends to predict the future.

BARTER: The exchange of one good for another without using money as a means of valuation.

BASING-POINT PRICING: A geographic pricing policy in which the seller designates one or more geographic locations from which the rate that a buyer will be charged is calculated.

BRAINSTORMING: A method of generating new-product ideas that consists of holding group discussions in which a specific problem or goal is set and no suggested solution is criticized.

BRAND: A name, term, symbol, design, or combination of these elements that is intended to identify the goods or services of one seller or group of sellers and differentiate them from those of competitors.

BRAND COMPETITOR: An organization that competes with others to satisfy consumers' demand for a specific product.

BRAND EXTENSION: A new product category that is given the brand name of an existing category.

BRAND MARK: The portion of a brand that consists of a symbol, design, or distinctive coloring or lettering.

BRAND NAME: The portion of a brand that consists of words, letters, or numbers that can be vocalized.

BREAKDOWN METHOD: An approach to salesforce design in which the size of the salesforce is determined by dividing the forecasted annual sales volume by the expected sales volume per salesperson.

BREAK-EVEN PRICING: An approach to pricing in which the price of a unit of the product is set high enough to cover the variable costs of producing that unit as well as the fixed costs of producing the product.

BROKER: A wholesaling intermediary whose primary function is to supply market information and establish contacts in order to facilitate sales for clients.

BUSINESS DEFINITION: The way an organization answers the questions, "What business are we in?" and "What business *should* we be in?"

BUYER: In the exchange process, the purchaser of a product.

BUYING CENTER: All the individuals and groups participating in the buying process that have interdependent goals and share common risks.

CALL CENTER: A managed or subcontracted facility where calls from customers are answered. Typically handles orders, requests for catalogs, questions, and complaints.

CASH-AND-CARRY WHOLESALER: A limited-service wholesaler that sells on a cash-only basis and does not provide delivery.

CASH COW: An SBU that has a higher market share than its competitors and is in a low-growth market.

CASH DISCOUNT: A discount that is offered to buyers who pay their bills within a stated period.

CASH FLOW: The flow of cash into a company; maintaining a steady cash flow is sometimes used as a pricing objective.

CATALOG SHOWROOM: A discount store at which customers review catalogs and then place orders and wait for delivery.

CAUSAL STUDIES: Research in which the cause-and-effect relationships between various phenomena are explored.

CHAIN STORE: A retail organization that consists of two or more units under a single ownership.

CHANNEL CAPTAIN: A channel member that is able to influence the behavior of the other members of the channel.

CHANNEL MANAGEMENT: The activities involved in anticipating and understanding the sources of channel conflict and trying to eliminate or minimize them.

CHANNEL OF DISTRIBUTION: The route taken by a product and its title as it moves from the resource procurer through the producer to the ultimate consumer.

COGNITIVE COMPONENT (OF AN ATTITUDE): A person's evaluation of the characteristics of an object.

COGNITIVE DISSONANCE: The state of anxiety or uneasiness that follows a purchase decision and creates a need for reassurance that the decision was the best one.

COMBINATION STORE: A type of superstore that places emphasis on nonfood items and on services.

COMMISSION MERCHANT: An agent that performs selling functions for manufacturers, normally on a one-time basis.

COMMON CARRIER: A transportation company that transports products on a specified schedule and according to regulations and standards established by government regulatory agencies.

COMMON COSTS: Costs that must be allocated among two or more functional areas.

COMMUNICATION: The process of exchanging meaning.

COMP: The comprehensive layout of a print ad that an ad agency or designer shows the marketer for final approval of the design.

COMPARATIVE ADVANTAGE: A theory that states that if a country has a relative cost advantage in a particular product, specializes in the production of that product, and trades it for products in which other countries have a relative cost advantage, more products will be available at lower prices than would be the case without specialization and trade.

COMPETITIVE ADVANTAGE: Differential access to resources (such as distribution channels, expertise, or technology) that can give a firm cost and quality advantages compared to its competitors.

CONATIVE COMPONENT (OF AN ATTITUDE): The intention or tendency to act that results from a person's evaluation of an object.

CONCENTRATED STRATEGY: A media scheduling strategy in which the marketer limits its advertising to specified periods.

CONCENTRATION STRATEGY: A marketing strategy that aims at a single market segment.

CONCLUSIVE STAGE: The stage of the research process in which the researchers develop a plan for collecting data, implement the plan, and provide the resulting information to decision makers.

CONSOLIDATED METROPOLITAN STATISTICAL AREA (CMSA): A population unit that contains a major metropolitan area and has a total population of more than 1 million.

CONSUMER: In the exchange process, the person who uses a product.

CONSUMER MARKET: A market in which goods and services are actually used up.

CONSUMER PANEL: A variation of the mail survey in which respondents are given some form of remuneration for participating in an ongoing study by filling out a series of questionnaires or keeping detailed records of their behavior.

CONTAINERIZATION: The use of large, standardized, easy-to-handle containers in which smaller packages can be loaded for shipping.

CONTEST: A sales promotion technique in which consumers are offered prizes for performing a task such as making up a slogan.

CONTINUITY STRATEGY: A media scheduling strategy in which advertisements are spread out over the entire period of the campaign.

CONTINUOUS IMPROVEMENT: Frequent incremental improvements driven primarily by customer requirements and competitor actions. Requires active organizational learning.

CONTRACT CARRIER: A transportation company that agrees to transport a specified number of shipments to specific destinations for an estimated price.

CONTRACTUAL VERTICAL MARKETING SYSTEM: A vertical marketing system in which channel members draw up a legal agreement that specifies the rights and responsibilities of each party.

CONTRIBUTION MARGIN TECHNIQUE: An approach to cost analysis that ignores non-traceable common costs.

CONTROL: The process of monitoring action programs, analyzing performance results, and, if necessary, taking corrective action.

CONVENIENCE PRODUCTS: Inexpensive, frequently purchased goods and services that consumers want to buy with the least possible effort.

CONVENIENCE SAMPLE: A nonprobability sample in which respondents are selected to suit the convenience of the researchers.

CONVENIENCE STORE: A store that is located near the residences or workplaces of its target customers and carries a wide assortment of products.

COOPERATIVE ADVERTISING: Store advertising featuring a marketer's product or line, and designed and paid for cooperatively by marketer and retailer.

COOPERATIVE ORGANIZATION: A retail organization that consists of a set of independent retailers that combine their resources to maintain their own wholesaling operation.

COPY: The words (or other printed characters) of a print ad.

CORE COMPETENCY: A constellation of closely related areas of expertise that, combined, give a firm a long-term advantage over competing firms.

CORPORATE CULTURE: A set of values that create a distinct pattern that is reflected in all of an organization's activities.

CORPORATE MISSION: A statement of an organization's overall goals, usually broadly defined and difficult to measure objectively.

CORPORATE VERTICAL MARKETING SYSTEM: A vertical marketing system in which one member gains control through ownership of both production and distribution systems.

COST-PER-THOUSAND: The dollar cost of an advertisement per 1000 readers or viewers.

COST-PLUS PRICING: An approach to pricing in which the list price is determined by adding a reasonable profit to the cost per unit.

COUPON: A certificate that entitles a consumer to a price reduction or a cash refund.

CROSS ELASTICITY OF DEMAND: A situation in which a change in the price of a product affects sales of another product.

CUE: An environmental stimulus that is perceived as a signal for action.

CULTURE: A set of values, ideas, attitudes, and other meaningful symbols created by human beings to shape human behavior and the artifacts of that behavior as they are transmitted from one generation to the next.

CUMULATIVE QUANTITY DISCOUNT: A quantity discount that is applied to a buyer's total purchases over a set period.

CUSTOMARY PRICING: A pricing strategy in which the marketer maintains a traditional price level.

CUSTOM RESEARCH FIRM: A research firm that assists a marketer in designing a study, collecting information, and preparing a report.

DATA BANK: The component of an MIS that stores raw data that come in from both the external environment and internal records.

DATABASE: Any organized collection of names, contact information, and other information useful in predicting purchase patterns. Computerized databases are essential for direct marketing, but small-scale databases are sometimes managed on index cards as well.

DEALER BRAND: A brand that is created and owned by an intermediary.

DECIDER: In the exchange process, the person who chooses an alternative that will satisfy a want or need.

DECISION INFLUENCER: Any individual who affects the purchaser's decision as to what or whether to buy.

DECODING: The process whereby a receiver extracts meaning from a transmitted message.

DELEGATION: Assigning specific responsibilities to specific people.

DELPHI TECHNIQUE: A forecasting technique in which a panel of experts is asked to assign rankings and probabilities to various factors that may influence future events.

DEMAND: The composite desire for particular products as measured by how consumers choose to allocate their resources among different products in a given market.

DEMARKETING: A marketing tool whose objective is to persuade consumers to use less of a product while maintaining the same level of satisfaction.

DEMOGRAPHICS: Statistics about a population, such as sex, age, marital status, birthrate, mortality rate, education, income, and occupation.

DEPARTMENT STORE: A store that offers a wide variety of product lines and is divided into departments to facilitate marketing and merchandise management.

DERIVED DEMAND: Demand that is dependent on the demand for another product.

DESCRIPTIVE LABEL: A label that explains the important characteristics or benefits of a product.

DESCRIPTIVE STUDIES: Research that focuses on demographic information about markets and their composition.

DETERMINING (BEHAVIORAL) VARIABLES: A set of variables that determine whether or not a consumer is a member of a particular market segment.

DIFFERENCE THRESHOLD: The smallest change in the intensity of a stimulus that can be noticed.

DIFFERENTIATED MARKETING: A marketing strategy that aims at several market segments, varying the marketing mix for each segment.

DIRECT COSTS: Costs that can be assigned to a specific functional area.

DIRECT MARKETING: An approach to marketing that uses one or more advertising media to effect a measurable response directly from the customer.

DISCOUNT: A deduction from the list price in the form of cash or something else of value.

DISCOUNT STORE: A self-service general-merchandise store that combines low price with high volume.

DISCRETIONARY INCOME: The amount of disposable income that is left over after spending on essentials such as food, shelter, and clothing.

DISPLAY UNIT: The component of an MIS that permits the user to communicate with the system.

DISPOSABLE INCOME: The amount of income available for spending after taxes have been deducted.

DISTINCTIVE COMPETENCIES: Activities that a firm can perform better than other firms.

DISTRIBUTION: The process of making sure that a product is available when and where it is desired.

DISTRIBUTION CENTER: A storage facility that takes orders and delivers products.

DOG: An SBU that has a low relative market share and is in a low-growth market.

DRIVE: A strong motivating tendency that arouses an organism toward a particular type of behavior; see also *motive.*

DROP SHIPPER: A limited-service wholesaler that sells goods but does not stock, handle, or deliver them.

DUMPING: A situation in which a product is sold at a lower price in a foreign market than in a domestic one, or at a price below the cost of production.

EARLY ADOPTERS: Consumers who buy a product early in its life cycle and influence other people to buy it.

EARLY MAJORITY: Consumers who wait and watch others before adopting a new product.

ECONOMIC ORDER QUANTITY: The optimum quantity of a product to order at a given time.

ECONOMIC SYSTEM: The way in which society organizes its resources to produce goods and services that will satisfy its members' wants and needs.

ECONOMIES OF SCALE: The savings that result when fixed costs are spread over more units of a product.

EFFECTIVE DEMAND: The combination of desire to buy and ability to buy.

80/20 RULE: A term used to refer to the fact that a large percentage of a company's sales and profits may come from a relatively small percentage of its customers or products.

ELASTIC DEMAND: A situation in which a percentage change in price brings about a greater percentage change in quantity sold.

EMERGENCY PRODUCTS: Goods or services that are needed to solve an immediate crisis.

ENCODING: The process whereby a source translates a message into words and signs that can be transmitted, received, and understood by the receiver.

ENGEL'S LAWS: A set of statements concerning the proportional changes in expenditures that accompany increases in family income.

ENVIRONMENT: A set of forces external to the organization that the marketer may be able to influence but cannot control.

ENVIRONMENTAL SCANNING: A set of procedures for monitoring the organization's external environment.

EVALUATOR: In the exchange process, an individual who provides feedback on a chosen product's ability to satisfy.

EVEN PRICING: A form of psychological pricing in which the price is an even number.

EVENT MARKETING: Promotion of special events by a marketer with the goal of generating positive publicity for the marketer. When events are put on by social change organizations, they are termed Cause-related Events.

EVOKED SET: The set of alternatives that come immediately to mind when a consumer seeks a solution to a problem.

EXCHANGE: An exchange occurs when two or more individuals, groups, or organizations give to each other something of value in order to receive something else of value. Each party to the exchange must want to exchange; must believe that what is received is more valuable than what is given up; and must be able to communicate with the other parties.

EXCLUSIVE DEALING: A method of control over distribution in which the manufacturer forbids dealers to carry competitors' products.

EXCLUSIVE DISTRIBUTION: An approach to distribution in which the number of intermediaries is limited to one for each geographic territory.

EXEMPT CARRIER: A company that is exempt from state and federal transportation regulations.

EXPECTED PRODUCT: A generic product plus a set of features that meet additional expectations of consumers.

EXPERIENCE CURVE: A graphic representation of the effect of experience on the per-unit cost of producing a product.

EXPERIMENT: A research method in which the effect of a particular variable is measured by making changes in the conditions experienced by a test group with respect to the variable and comparing the results with those of a control group that did not experience the change.

EXPLORATORY STAGE: The stage of the research process in which the problem is defined, objectives are set, and possible solutions are explored.

EXPRESS WARRANTY: A statement that specifies the exact conditions under which a manufacturer is responsible for a product's performance.

EXPROPRIATION: A situation in which a host country denies a foreign corporation the right to engage in business there and seizes its assets.

EXTENDED FAMILY: A nuclear family plus aunts, uncles, grandparents, and in-laws.

EXTENSIVE DISTRIBUTION: An approach to distribution that seeks the widest possible geographic coverage.

FACTORY OUTLET MALL: A shopping center that focuses on quality, name brand items offered at lower than usual prices.

FAMILY OF ORIENTATION: The family into which a person is born.

FAMILY OF PROCREATION: The family that a person establishes through marriage.

FEEDBACK: Information that tells an organization's managers about the performance of each marketing program.

FIXED-COST CONTRIBUTION: The portion of a selling price that is left over after variable costs have been accounted for.

FLEXIBLE-PRICE POLICY: A pricing policy in which the marketer offers the same products and quantities to different customers at different prices, depending on their bargaining power and other factors.

FLIGHTING STRATEGY: A media scheduling strategy in which there is heavy advertising during some parts of the campaign and no advertising in between.

F.O.B. PRICING: A geographic pricing policy in which buyers pay transportation costs from the point at which they take title to the product.

FOCUS GROUP: A form of personal interview in which a group of 8 to 12 people are brought together to offer their views on an issue, idea, or product.

FORM COMPETITOR: An organization that competes with others to satisfy consumers' wants or needs within a specific class of products or services.

FORM UTILITY: The satisfaction that buyers receive from the physical characteristics of a product (e.g., its shape, function, or style).

FRANCHISE: A legal contractual relationship between a supplier and one or more independent retailers. The franchisee gains an established brand name and operating assistance, while the franchisor gains financial remuneration as well as some control over how the business is run.

FREIGHT ABSORPTION: A geographic pricing policy in which the seller charges the same freight rate as the competitor located nearest to the buyer.

FREIGHT FORWARDER: A transportation company that pools many small shipments to take advantage of lower rates, passing some of the savings on to the shippers.

FREQUENCY: The average number of times that the average prospect will be exposed to a specific advertisement in a specified period.

FULL-COST APPROACH: An approach to cost analysis that takes both direct and common costs into consideration.

FULL-SERVICE WHOLESALER: A merchant wholesaler that performs a full range of services for its customers.

FUNCTIONAL ACCOUNT: An accounting category that reflects the purpose for which money is spent.

FUNCTIONAL SATISFACTION: The satisfaction received from the tangible or functional features of a product.

GENERAL-MERCHANDISE RETAILER: A retailer that carries a wide range of products.

GENERAL-MERCHANDISE WHOLESALER: A full-service wholesaler that carries a wide variety of product lines.

GENERIC COMPETITOR: An organization that competes with others to satisfy consumers' wants or needs within a general category of products or services.

GENERIC NAME: A brand name that has become associated with a product category rather than with a particular brand.

GENERIC PRODUCT: A set of tangible or intangible attributes that are assembled into an identifiable form.

GLOBALIZATION: The tendency for markets to expand across national boundaries, leading to increasing competition among firms from different nations and a growing dependence on diverse, multinational and multicultural customer bases.

GOVERNMENTAL MARKET: A set of federal, state, county, or local agencies that buy goods and services for use in meeting social needs.

GRADE LABEL: A label that identifies the quality of a product by a letter, number, or word.

GROSS RATING POINTS: The reach of an advertisement multiplied by its frequency.

HEADLINE: The large-sized text in a print ad that is designed to first catch the eye and draw the reader into the ad's copy.

HORIZONTAL CONFLICT: Conflict that occurs between channel members at the same level of the distribution channel.

HORIZONTAL COOPERATIVE ADVERTISING: Advertising in which marketers at the same level in the distribution system advertise jointly.

HORIZONTAL MARKET: A market that is made up of a broad spectrum of industries.

HORIZONTAL PRICE FIXING: A form of price fixing in which marketers at the same level of the distribution system get together and decide the price at which all of them will sell the product.

HYPERMARCHE: A combination department store and supermarket.

HYPOTHESIS: A statement about possible relationships between objects or events.

IDEAL SELF-IMAGE: Our mental picture of ourselves as we would like to be.

IMPLEMENTATION: The actual execution of a strategic plan.

IMPLIED WARRANTY: A legal promise that a product will serve the purpose for which it is intended, whether stated by the manufacturer or not.

IMPRESSIONS: The total number of exposures to a specific advertisement in a specified period.

IMPULSE ITEMS: Convenience products that are purchased not because of planning but because of a strongly felt need.

INDEPENDENT RETAILER: A retailer that owns a single outlet that is not affiliated with any other retail outlet.

INDUSTRIAL DISTRIBUTOR: An independently owned operation that buys, stocks, and sells industrial products.

INDUSTRIAL MARKET: A producer market that consists of firms that engage in the manufacture of goods.

INDUSTRIAL MARKETING: The process of anticipating, discovering, and designing product and service specifications that will satisfy the requirements of industrial customers.

INDUSTRIAL MARKETING RESEARCH: The systematic gathering, recording, and analyzing of data for use in solving problems related to the marketing of industrial goods and services.

INELASTIC DEMAND: A situation in which a percentage change in price brings about a smaller percentage change in quantity sold.

INFLUENCER: In the exchange process, an individual who provides information about how a want or need may be satisfied.

INFORMATIVE LABEL: A label that advises consumers about the care, use, or preparation of a product.

INITIATOR: In the exchange process, the person who first recognizes an unsatisfied want or need.

INNOVATORS: Consumers who are ready and willing to adopt a new idea.

INSTITUTIONAL ADVERTISING: Advertising that develops and maintains a favorable image for a particular industry or company.

INSTITUTIONAL MARKET: A set of not-for-profit organizations that buy goods and services for use in achieving a particular goal or mission.

INTENSIVE DISTRIBUTION: An approach to distribution that seeks the largest possible number of outlets in a given territory.

INTERACTIVE MIS: A computer-based marketing information system that allows managers to communicate directly with the system.

INTERMEDIARY: An independent or corporate-owned business that helps move products from the producer to the ultimate consumer.

INTERMEDIATE MARKET: A set of wholesalers and retailers that buy goods from others and resell them.

INTRAPRENEURSHIP: An approach to new-product development in which a small team of employees is set apart from the rest of the organization and freed from ordinary bureaucratic requirements long enough to develop a particular product.

JOINT DEMAND: Demand for two products that are complementary.

JUDGMENT SAMPLING: Nonprobability sampling in which respondents are selected on the basis of criteria that the researchers believe will result in a group that is representative of the population being surveyed.

JURY OF EXECUTIVE OPINION: A forecasting technique in which executives from various departments of the company are asked to estimate market potential and sales and then try to reach a consensus.

JUST-IN-TIME PURCHASING: An approach to inventory management in which products are bought in small quantities to reduce inventory carrying costs and obtain delivery just in time for use.

LABEL: A tag or part of a package that supplies information about a product or its seller.

LAGGARDS: Consumers who are strongly oriented toward the past and very suspicious of new concepts; they are the last to adopt a new product.

LATE MAJORITY: Consumers who are committed to familiar ways of doing things and skeptical of new ideas.

LAYOUT: The design of any two-dimensional advertisement, including print ads, Web pages, banners on the Web, billboards, catalog pages, and brochures.

LEAD: The name of any individual or organization that may be a potential customer.

LEARNING: The process by which people's experiences produce change in their behavior.

LEVELING: A cognitive process in which the information retained becomes shorter and more concise.

LIMITED-LINE RETAILER: A retailer that offers only one or a few lines of related merchandise.

LIMITED-SERVICE WHOLESALER: A merchant wholesaler that performs a limited number of services for its customers.

LINE EXTENSION: A new variety of a basic product.

LIST PRICE: The initial price of a product; also termed the *base price*.

LONG-RANGE PLAN: A plan in which the organization's managers set goals for a period of more than one year.

LOSS LEADER: A product that is given a lower than normal price in order to attract customers to a store.

MACROMARKETING: Bringing about exchanges between individuals and/or groups so as to provide satisfaction of a society's wants and needs.

MACROSEGMENTATION: A process in which an industrial market is divided into segments based on types of buying organizations.

MAIL INTERVIEW: A survey technique in which questionnaires are mailed to potential respondents.

MAIL-ORDER WHOLESALER: A limited-service wholesaler that sells to industrial, institutional, and retail customers by means of catalogs.

MAJOR INNOVATION: An item that has never been sold by any other organization.

MANUFACTURER'S AGENT: An independent sales representative who works for several manufacturers of related but noncompeting product lines.

MANUFACTURER'S BRAND: A brand that is owned and marketed by the manufacturer that produces it.

MANUFACTURER'S SALES BRANCH: A wholesaling establishment that is owned and operated by a manufacturer separately from its factories.

MANUFACTURER'S SALES OFFICE: A wholesaling establishment that is similar to a manufacturer's sales branch except that it does not carry inventory.

MARGINAL COST: The cost of producing one more unit than the most recent unit produced.

MARKET: A group of people with unsatisfied wants and needs who are willing to exchange and have the ability to buy.

MARKET AGGREGATION: A marketing strategy that uses a single marketing program to offer the same product to all consumers.

MARKET ATOMIZATION: A marketing strategy that treats each individual consumer as a unique market segment.

MARKET BREAKDOWN TECHNIQUE: A forecasting technique in which the sales forecast for a large unit is broken down into forecasts for smaller units.

MARKET BUILDUP TECHNIQUE: A forecasting technique in which information on a few specific market segments is aggregated to arrive at a total sales forecast.

MARKET-DRIVEN ECONOMY: An economic system in which supply, demand, and price determine what products will be produced and who will receive those products.

MARKETING AUDIT: A comprehensive, systematic, independent, and periodic examination of an organization's marketing environment, objectives, strategies, and activities.

MARKETING CONCEPT: The management philosophy that recognizes that the consumer should be the focal point of all activity within an organization.

MARKETING CONTROL CHART: A chart that combines trend analysis with the performance standards set by the organization.

MARKETING DECISION SUPPORT SYSTEM: A coordinated collection of data, models, analytic tools, and computing power by which an organization gathers information from the environment and turns it into a basis for action.

MARKETING INFORMATION SYSTEM (MIS): A set of procedures and methods for regular, planned collection, analysis, and presentation of marketing information.

MARKETING INTELLIGENCE SYSTEM: Within a marketing information system, the set of activities whose purpose is to monitor the external environment for emerging trends or events.

MARKETING MIX: The combination of activities involving product, price, place, and promotion that a firm undertakes in order to provide satisfaction to consumers in a given market.

MARKETING RESEARCH: A systematic, objective approach to the development and provision of information for decision making regarding a specific marketing problem.

MARKET SEGMENT: A group of buyers within a market who have relatively similar wants and needs.

MARKET SEGMENTATION: A marketing strategy in which a large, heterogeneous market is broken down into small, more homogeneous segments and a separate marketing program is developed for each segment.

MARKET SHARE: The total number of units of a product (or their dollar value) expressed as a percentage of the total number of units sold by all competitors in a given market.

MARKET SHARE ANALYSIS: A forecasting technique in which it is assumed that the firm's market share will remain constant and sales forecasts for the firm are based on forecasts for the industry.

MATRIX ORGANIZATION: An organizational structure in which projects are assigned to task forces made up of people drawn from various functional departments.

MEAN: The sum of all the numbers in a set of scores divided by the number of scores.

MEDIAN: In a list of numbers, the number above which half of the numbers in the list fall and below which the other half fall.

MERCHANT MIDDLEMAN: An intermediary that takes title to the products it distributes.

MERCHANT WHOLESALER: A wholesaling intermediary that is an independently owned business and takes title to the goods its sells.

MESSAGE: An idea that is to be conveyed from a source to a receiver.

MESSAGE CHANNEL: A vehicle for delivering a message.

MICROMARKETING: Strategically managing human and organizational exchange relationships so as to provide socially responsible want and need satisfaction throughout the world while achieving the marketer's objectives.

MICROSEGMENTATION: A process in which industrial market segments are subdivided on the basis of characteristics of the buying center and individual participants.

MILL SUPPLY HOUSE: A general-merchandise wholesaler that operates in an industrial setting.

MINIWAREHOUSE MALL: A type of shopping center in which a large warehouse offers space to a variety of sellers, including both retailers and wholesalers.

MINOR INNOVATION: A product that was not previously sold by the company but has been marketed by some other company.

MODE: In a set of data, the number that occurs most frequently.

MODEL BANK: The component of an MIS that contains mathematical marketing models that show relationships among various marketing activities, environmental forces, and desired outcomes.

MODIFICATION: Any adjustment of an existing product's style, color, or model; any product improvement; or a brand change.

MODIFIED REBUY: A purchasing situation in which the organization has bought the good or service before, but some aspect of the situation has changed.

MONOPOLISTIC COMPETITION: A competitive situation in which there are many buyers and sellers, imperfect market information, some barriers to entry, and differentiated products.

MONOPOLY: A competitive situation in which there is only one seller of a product and entry to the market is restricted.

MOTIVE: A need or want that is activated by a particular stimulus and initiates behavior toward some goal.

MULTINATIONAL CORPORATION (MNC): A corporation that operates in more than one country and makes all of its decisions within a global framework.

NATIONALIZATION: A situation in which a national government becomes involved in the ownership or management of a business organization.

NATURAL ACCOUNT: An accounting category that reflects how money is actually spent.

NEED: Something that is lacking that is necessary for a person's physical or psychological well-being.

NEW-TASK PURCHASE: A purchasing situation in which the organization is making the purchase for the first time.

NOISE: Any distraction that interferes with the effectiveness of a communication.

NONCUMULATIVE QUANTITY DISCOUNT: A quantity discount that is offered on each sale made to a particular buyer.

NONPROBABILITY SAMPLING: A sampling technique in which respondents are selected partly on the basis of researchers' judgment.

NONTRACEABLE COSTS: Common costs that are assigned to functional areas on an arbitrary basis.

NORMS: Rules that tell the members of a particular cultural group what behavior is correct in certain situations.

NUCLEAR FAMILY: A husband and wife and their children.

NUTRITIONAL LABELING: A form of labeling in which consumers are informed of the amounts of protein, fat, carbohydrates, and calories in a processed food product.

OBSERVATIONAL APPROACH: A research method in which researchers observe people's behavior and record what they see but avoid direct interaction.

ODD PRICING: A form of psychological pricing in which the price is an odd number or a number just below a round number.

OFF-PRICE STORE: A discount store that buys manufacturers' overruns and end-of-season goods at below-wholesale prices and resells them at prices significantly lower than the regular department store price.

OLIGOPOLY: A competitive situation in which a few firms account for a large percentage of the industry's sales and in which there are substantial barriers to entry.

ONE-PRICE POLICY: A pricing policy in which the marketer assigns a price to the product and sells it at that price to all customers who purchase the same quantity of the product under the same conditions.

OPEN DATING: A form of labeling in which consumers are informed of the expected shelf life of a product.

OPPORTUNITY: An unsatisfied want or need that arises from a change in the organization's environment.

ORGANIZATION: All the activities involved in getting ready to carry out a strategic plan.

ORGANIZATIONAL LEARNING: The process whereby individuals within an organization learn as a group and apply that learning to their work. Traditionally thought to vary with amount of experience (as measured for example by number of units produced), but increasingly seen as an independent variable that can be managed as a source of competitive advantage.

ORGANIZATIONAL STRUCTURE: A set of relationships among individuals with different responsibilities.

ORIGINAL-EQUIPMENT MANUFACTURER (OEM): An organization that purchases industrial goods to incorporate into other products.

OTHERS SELF-IMAGE: Our mental picture of ourselves as we believe others see us.

PACKAGING: All activities that are related to designing and producing the container or wrapper for a product.

PENETRATION: A pricing strategy in which the initial price is set at a low level in order to generate the greatest possible demand for the product.

PERCEPTION: The process by which a person attaches meaning to the various stimuli he or she senses.

PERFECT COMPETITION: A competitive situation in which there are many buyers and sellers, perfect market information, few or no barriers to entry, and homogeneous products.

PERSONAL INTERVIEW: A survey technique in which respondents are questioned in a face-to-face setting.

PERSONAL SELLING: Person-to-person communication in which the receiver provides immediate feedback to the source's message.

PHANTOM FREIGHT: A term used to refer to the difference between the true freight cost and the cost charged to the buyer in situations in which the buyer is charged an amount greater than the actual cost.

PHYSICAL DISTRIBUTION: All the activities that provide for the efficient flow of raw materials, in-process inventory, and finished goods from the point of procurement to the ultimate consumer.

PHYSICAL OBSOLESCENCE: Obsolescence that results when products are built to last only a limited time.

PIGGYBACK SERVICE: A transportation service in which loaded trucks are taken directly onto railroad flatcars.

PLACE UTILITY: The satisfaction that buyers receive from having a product available at the appropriate place.

PLAN: A written document that specifies resource requirements, costs, expected benefits, and activities necessary to achieve a goal.

PLANNED OBSOLESCENCE: A product management strategy in which a marketer forces a product in its line to become outdated, thereby increasing replacement sales.

PLANNING: The process of predicting future events and using those predictions to set courses of action that will achieve the organization's goals.

POINT-OF-PURCHASE PROMOTION: A sales promotion technique that consists of locating an attention-getting device at the place of actual purchase.

POSITIONING: A process in which a marketer communicates with consumers to establish a distinct place for its product or brand in their minds.

POSSESSION UTILITY: The satisfaction that buyers receive from having the right to use or own a product.

POSTPONED OBSOLESCENCE: Obsolescence that occurs when technological improvements are available but are not introduced until the demand for existing products declines.

PREMIUM: A product that is offered free or at less than the regular price in order to induce the consumer to buy another product.

PRICE: That which the buyer gives up in exchange for something that provides satisfaction.

PRICE LINING: A pricing strategy in which prices are used to sort products into "lines" based on an attribute such as quality, prestige, or style.

PRICE-OFF: A price reduction that is used to induce trial or increase usage of a product.

PRIMARY DATA: Data that are collected specifically for use in a particular research project.

PRIMARY DEMAND: Market demand for a product class rather than a particular brand.

PRIMARY DEMAND ADVERTISING: Advertising in which the marketer attempts to create awareness of and provide information about a type of product.

PRIMARY GROUP: A group that is small and intimate enough so that all of its members can communicate with one another face to face.

PRIVATE CARRIER: A company that owns the goods it transports.

PRIVATE WAREHOUSE: A warehouse that is owned and controlled by its users.

PROBABILITY SAMPLING: A sampling technique in which all members of the population being surveyed have a known chance of being included in the sample.

PRODUCER COOPERATIVE: A member-owned wholesale operation that assembles farm products to sell in local markets.

PRODUCER MARKET: A set of buyers that purchase goods and services and use them to make other products.

PRODUCT: A combination of functional and psychological features that provides form utility; the entire set of benefits that are offered in an exchange, including goods, services, ideas, people, places, and organizations.

PRODUCT DIFFERENTIATION: A marketing strategy that uses promotion and other marketing activities to get consumers to perceive a product as different from and better than those of competitors.

PRODUCT LIFE CYCLE: A sequence of stages in the marketing of a product that begins with commercialization and ends with removal from the market.

PRODUCT LINE: Within a company's product mix, a broad group of products that are similar in terms of use or characteristics.

PRODUCT MIX: The various products that a company offers to consumers.

PRODUCT PORTFOLIO: A company's product mix viewed from a strategic perspective; a set of products or brands that are at different stages in the product life cycle.

PRODUCT RELAUNCH: A product management strategy that focuses on finding new markets and untapped market segments, new product uses, and ways to stimulate increased use of a product by existing customers.

PROFESSIONAL ADVERTISING: Advertising that focuses on the benefits offered by professional services.

PROGRAM EVALUATION AND REVIEW TECHNIQUE (PERT): An implementation technique that uses detailed flowcharts showing which tasks can be carried out only after certain other tasks have been completed and which tasks can be done simultaneously.

PROMOTION: Any technique that persuasively communicates favorable information about a seller's product to potential buyers; includes advertising, personal selling, sales promotion, and public relations.

PROMOTIONAL DISCOUNT: A discount that is offered to intermediaries as compensation for carrying out promotional activities.

PROSPECTING: The process of locating and classifying potential buyers of a product.

PROTECTIONISM: The erection of barriers to trade in an attempt to protect domestic industries from foreign competition.

PSYCHOLOGICAL PRICING: A pricing strategy in which the product is given a price that is psychologically appealing to consumers.

PSYCHOLOGICAL SATISFACTION: The satisfaction received from the intangible benefits of a product, such as a feeling of self-worth.

PUBLICITY: Any message about an organization that is communicated through the mass media but is not paid for by the organization.

PUBLIC RELATIONS: A promotional activity that aims to communicate a favorable image of a product or its marketer and to promote goodwill.

PUBLIC WAREHOUSE: A warehouse that is owned by an independent contractor, which rents space to users.

PULL STRATEGY: A promotional strategy in which each channel member attempts to persuade the next member in the system to handle and promote the product.

PULSING STRATEGY: A media scheduling strategy in which a continuous campaign is combined with short bursts of heavier advertising.

PUSH STRATEGY: A promotional strategy in which the producer uses mass promotion to stimulate demand in the consumer market, thereby causing intermediaries to want to carry the product.

QUALIFYING (DESCRIPTIVE) VARIABLES: A set of variables that allow or qualify an individual to be a member of a particular market segment.

QUALITY CONTROL: The traditional approach to quality in which problems are detected after manufacturing and an effort is made to remove sub-standard products before shipping to customers.

QUANTITY DISCOUNT: A discount offered to buyers that purchase larger than normal quantities of the product.

QUESTION MARK: An SBU that has a low relative market share and is in a high-growth market.

QUOTA: A specific limit on the number of items of a particular kind that may be imported.

QUOTA SAMPLING: A form of judgment sampling in which the population is divided into subgroups on the basis of one or more characteristics and a specified proportion of respondents are chosen from each subgroup.

RACK JOBBER: A limited-service wholesaler that supplies nonfood products to supermarkets, grocery stores, and drug retailers.

REACH: The percentage of total prospects that are exposed to a specific advertisement in a specified period.

REAL INCOME: Income that has been adjusted for the effects of inflation.

REAL SELF-IMAGE: Our mental picture of ourselves as we think we really are.

RECEIVER: The audience that is the target of a message.

RECRUITING: The activity of locating skilled salespeople and inducing them to apply for employment.

REFERENCE GROUP: Any set of people that influences an individual's attitudes or behavior.

REINFORCEMENT: The extent to which satisfaction is derived from a response to an aroused need.

RELATIVE MARKET SHARE: An organization or SBU's market share divided by that of its largest competitor.

REPATRIATION: The transfer of profits to a parent firm from an affiliate in a foreign country.

RESEARCH DESIGN: An overall plan for conducting a research project, including the choice of the method that will be used to achieve the goals of the research.

RESPONSE: Whatever occurs as a reaction to an aroused need.

RETAILER: An intermediary that sells products primarily to ultimate consumers.

RETAILING: All activities undertaken by intermediaries whose primary function is to sell goods and services to ultimate consumers.

RETENTION: The extent to which one remembers what one has learned.

REVERSE ELASTICITY: A situation in which anticipation of a steady increase (decrease) in price causes buyers to make more (fewer) purchases of a product.

ROLE EXPECTATIONS: The rights, privileges, duties, and responsibilities that are associated with a particular role.

ROLE THEORY: An approach to the study of group influence that recognizes that people conduct their lives by playing many roles, each of which is accompanied by a certain range of acceptable behaviors.

ROLLOUT: An approach to new-product introduction in which the product is launched in a series of geographic areas over an extended period.

SALES MANAGER: The person who designs and manages the activities of an organization's salesforce.

SALES POTENTIAL FORECAST: A forecast of total potential sales for the firm for a specific time period.

SALES PROMOTION: The array of techniques that marketers use to stimulate immediate purchase.

SALES VARIANCE ANALYSIS: A method of data analysis in which data on actual sales are compared with quantitative sales objectives.

SAMPLE: A group of respondents who are representative of the population being surveyed.

SAMPLING: Giving free samples of a product to consumers or offering a trial size at a very low cost.

SCENARIO ANALYSIS: A forecasting technique in which researchers develop a subjective picture of several possible futures by identifying cause-and-effect relationships and following them to their logical conclusions.

SCIENTIFIC METHOD: A research process that involves the development of a hypothesis that can be confirmed, modified, or rejected on the basis of information gathered by objective means.

SCRAMBLED MERCHANDISING: The practice of carrying any product line, however dissimilar from other lines carried, as long as it yields a profit.

SEASONAL DISCOUNT: A discount that is offered to customers who purchase a product during a season when demand for that product is low.

SECONDARY GROUP: A large group whose members have a shared goal but do not engage in face-to-face communication.

SECONDARY SOURCE: Data that have been collected for a purpose other than the research project in question.

SELECTIVE DEMAND: Demand for a particular brand.

SELECTIVE DEMAND ADVERTISING: Advertising in which the marketer attempts to create awareness of and provide information about a specific brand.

SELECTIVE DISTRIBUTION: An approach to distribution that involves the use of a limited set of outlets in a given territory.

SELF-LIQUIDATING PREMIUM: A premium for which the buyer pays all or part of the cost.

SELLING: The process of assisting and/or persuading a prospective customer to buy a good or service or to act favorably on an idea.

SELLING AGENT: An agent that handles the entire marketing function for a manufacturer.

SENSORY THRESHOLDS: The upper and lower limits on the ability of human sensory processes to perceive increases or decreases in the intensity of a stimulus.

SERVICE: A deed, act, or performance.

SHARPENING: A cognitive process in which the information retained becomes more vivid and important than the event itself.

SHIPPERS' COOPERATIVE: A group of shippers that pool shipments of similar items in order to benefit from lower freight rates.

SHOPPING CENTER: A group of retail stores at a single location that is planned, developed, and controlled by one organization.

SHOPPING MALL INTERCEPT: A form of personal interview in which respondents are approached or intercepted as they pass a particular spot in a shopping mall.

SHOPPING PRODUCTS: Goods and services about which consumers will seek information before making a purchase.

SHOPPING STORE: A retail outlet that is favored by consumers who are shopping for a certain type of product.

SIMPLE RANDOM SAMPLING: Probability sampling in which respondents are chosen at random from a complete list of the members of the population.

SIMPLE TREND ANALYSIS: A forecasting technique in which managers review historical data and use the rates of change to project future trends.

SINGLE-LINE WHOLESALER: A full-service wholesaler that carries only one or two product lines but offers considerable depth in each.

SKIMMING: A pricing strategy in which the initial price is set at a high level with the goal of selling the product to people who want it and are willing to pay a high price for it.

SLICE-OF-LIFE ADVERTISING: Advertising that portrays consumers in realistic situations that are consistent with consumers' perceptions of their own life styles.

SOCIAL CLASS: A relatively permanent and homogeneous category of people within a society. The members of a class have similar values, life styles, interests, and behavior.

SOCIALIZATION: The process by which we learn the values and norms of our culture.

SORTING: A process in which products are brought together at one location and then divided up and moved in smaller quantities to locations closer to the ultimate buyers.

SOURCE: The originator of a message.

SPECIALTY LINE SUPPLIER: A research firm that specializes in one aspect of the marketing research process.

SPECIALTY-LINE RETAILER: A limited-line retailer that carries only one or two product lines, but offers substantial depth and expertise in those lines.

SPECIALTY-LINE WHOLESALER: A full-service wholesaler that carries a limited number of products for customers with specialized needs.

SPECIALTY PRODUCTS: Goods and services for which there are no acceptable substitutes in the consumer's mind.

SPECIALTY STORE: A retail outlet for which customers develop a strong preference based on the assortment of products offered, the service, or the store's reputation.

SPOKESPERSON: The person who delivers the message in a testimonial.

STANDARD METROPOLITAN STATISTICAL AREA (SMSA): The Census Bureau's standard urban population unit. An area is classified as an SMSA if it contains a city with a population of at least 50,000 or an urbanized area of 50,000 with a total metropolitan population of at least 100,000.

STAPLE ITEMS: Convenience products that consumers plan to buy.

STAR: An SBU that has a high growth rate and a high relative market share.

STATISTICAL BANK: The component of an MIS that offers statistical techniques to be used in analyzing data.

STATISTICAL PROCESS CONTROL: The use of statistical analysis (usually by line employees) to measure and manage specific work processes. Commonly used in total quality programs.

STRAIGHT REBUY: A purchasing situation in which the organization has bought the good or service before and is likely to reorder from the same vendor.

STRATEGIC BUSINESS UNIT (SBU): One or more products, brands, divisions, or market segments that have something in common, such as the same distribution system. Each SBU has its own mission, its own set of competitors, and its own strategic plan.

STRATEGIC INFORMATION SCANNING SYSTEM: A formal structure of people, equipment, and procedures to obtain and manage information to support strategic decision making.

STRATEGIC MARKET PLANNING: The managerial process of developing and implementing a match between market opportunities and the resources of the firm.

STRATEGIC PLAN: A long-term plan covering a period of 3, 5, or sometimes 10 years.

STRATEGIC PLANNING: The process of developing a long-range plan that is designed to match the organization's strengths and weaknesses with the threats and opportunities in its environment.

STRATIFIED RANDOM SAMPLING: Probability sampling in which the total population is divided into subgroups, or *strata,* and a random sample is chosen from each subgroup.

STRUCTURED QUESTION: A question that limits respondents to a specific set of replies.

STYLE OBSOLESCENCE: Obsolescence that occurs when the physical appearance of a product is changed to make existing versions seem out of date.

SUBCULTURE: A smaller cultural group within a society that reflects geographic, religious, and ethnic differences.

SUPERMARKET: A large self-service store that carries a full line of food products and, often, a number of nonfood products.

SUPERSTORE: A combination of a general-merchandise discount operation and a supermarket.

SURVEY APPROACH: A research method in which researchers use personal interviews, telephone interviews, or mailed questionnaires to question a group of people directly.

SWEEPSTAKES: A sales promotion technique in which prizes are tied to chance and consumers are encouraged to buy a product as part of the entry procedure.

SYNDICATED SERVICE: A research firm that periodically compiles specific types of data for sale to marketers.

TACTICAL PLAN: A short-term plan that specifies the activities necessary to carry out a strategic plan.

TARGET MARKETING: A process in which the marketer evaluates a number of market segments, decides which one or ones to serve, and develops and implements a unique marketing mix for the targeted segment(s).

TARGET RETURN ON INVESTMENT: An amount of income equivalent to a certain percentage of the firm's investment; this amount is set as a goal to be achieved through pricing.

TARGET RETURN PRICING: An approach to pricing in which the marketer seeks to obtain a predetermined percentage return on the capital used to produce and distribute the product.

TARIFF: A tax on imported goods.

TECHNOLOGICAL OBSOLESCENCE: Obsolescence that results when technological improvements are made in a product.

TELEMARKETING: The sale of goods and services by telephone.

TELEPHONE INTERVIEW: A survey technique in which respondents are questioned by telephone.

TESTIMONIAL: An advertising message that is presented by someone who is viewed as an expert on the subject.

TEST-MARKETING: The controlled introduction of a new product to carefully selected markets for the purpose of testing market acceptance and predicting future sales of the product in that region.

THREAT: An unfavorable trend or situation that could prevent the organization from satisfying a want or need.

TIME UTILITY: The satisfaction that buyers receive from having a product available at the appropriate time.

TOTAL FIXED COSTS: Costs that ordinarily do not change over time, no matter what quantity of output is produced.

TOTAL QUALITY PROGRAM: The most common rubric for Japanese-inspired efforts to build quality into a product or service as it is produced or performed. Quality may be defined as closeness of fit to specifications, customer needs, or (in the most sophisticated programs), fit to latent customer needs. Total quality programs require the active involvement of the line workers themselves, which generally is best achieved via a radical change in corporate culture led by the chief executive.

TOTAL VARIABLE COSTS: Costs that fluctuate, depending on the quantity of output produced.

TRACEABLE COSTS: Common costs that can be assigned to two or more specific functional areas.

TRADE DEFICIT: The amount by which a nation's total imports exceed its total exports.

TRADE DISCOUNT: A discount that is offered to intermediaries as compensation for carrying out various marketing activities.

TRADEMARK: A brand that is given legal protection because it has been appropriated exclusively by one marketer.

TRADING DOWN: A product management strategy in which a marketer that is known for selling high-priced products offers lower-priced products.

TRADING STAMPS: A sales promotion technique in which customers receive stamps in quantities depending on how much they purchase, and can redeem the stamps for merchandise.

TRADING UP: A product management strategy in which a marketer that is known for selling low-priced products offers higher-priced products.

TRANSACTION: An exchange between two or more parties.

TRANSFER PRICING: Raising the price of a product shipped to a foreign affiliate in order to increase the amount of profit transferred from the affiliate to the parent firm.

TRIAL: The consumer's initial purchase and use of a product or brand.

TRUCK WHOLESALER: A limited-service wholesaler that specializes in selling and delivery services.

TRUE PROSPECT: A lead that can benefit from the use of the product, can afford to buy it, and has the authority to do so.

TYING AGREEMENT: A method of control over distribution in which the producer forces the dealer to buy additional products in order to secure one highly desired product.

UNIFORM DELIVERED PRICING: A geographic pricing policy in which the seller offers the same delivered price to all buyers, regardless of their location and the actual freight expense.

UNITARY DEMAND: A situation in which a percentage change in price brings about an equal percentage change in quantity sold.

UNIT PRICING: A form of pricing in which the price of the package is accompanied by the price of the product in terms of some standard measure of quantity.

UNSOUGHT PRODUCTS: Goods and services for which consumers have no felt need.

UNSTRUCTURED QUESTION: A question that allows respondents to answer as they wish and does not limit the length of responses.

VALUE-ADDED TAX: A tax that is levied every time a product is sold to another member of the distribution channel.

VALUE PROPOSITION: The reasons why a product is of sufficient value to the customer to be well worth its price. This term is often used in ad agencies as they formulate their pitch for use in promoting a product.

VALUES: The deeply held beliefs and attitudes of the members of a particular society.

VARIETY STORE: A retailer that offers a wide assortment of low-priced items.

VERTICAL CONFLICT: Conflict that occurs between channel members at different levels of the distribution system.

VERTICAL COOPERATIVE ADVERTISING: Advertising in which marketers at different levels in the distribution system advertise jointly.

VERTICAL MARKET: A market that consists of a single industry.

VERTICAL MARKETING SYSTEM: A distribution channel whose members are integrated into a single organization.

VERTICAL PRICE FIXING: A form of price fixing in which marketers at different levels of the distribution system get together to set retail prices.

VOLUNTARY CHAIN: A retail organization that consists of a set of independent retailers that agree to buy most of their merchandise through a single wholesaler.

WANT: Something that is lacking that is desirable or useful. It is formed by a person's experiences, culture, and personality.

WAREHOUSE CLUB: A no-frills, cash-and-carry discount store that operates in a poor location; to shop there, the customer must become a member and pay dues.

WAREHOUSE SHOWROOM: A discount store that follows a strategy based on low overhead and high turnover; customers pay cash and must transport the merchandise themselves.

WAREHOUSE STORE: A no-frills supermarket that stocks a wide variety of food and nonfood items and sells them at lower prices than the typical supermarket price.

WARRANTY: A manufacturer's promise that a product will serve the purpose for which it is intended.

WEAROUT: The tendency of consumer response to a sales promotion to diminish over time.

WEB PAGE: A publicized address on the World Wide Web that offers any information the designer wishes the public to see. Often used by marketers to provide background information to customers, to entertain customers with interactive displays, or to create "on-line catalogs" to sell products.

WHOLESALER: An intermediary that distributes products primarily to commercial or professional users.

WHOLESALING: All of the activities provided by wholesaling intermediaries involved in selling merchandise to retailers; to industrial, institutional, farm, and professional businesses; or to other types of wholesaling intermediaries.

WHOLESALING INTERMEDIARY: Any firm that engages primarily in wholesaling activities.

WORKLOAD APPROACH: An approach to salesforce design in which the size of the salesforce is determined by dividing the total workload in hours by the number of selling hours available from each salesperson.

WORLD WIDE WEB: The computerized network accessed via computer modem on which millions of people and companies post information, and others search for entertainment or information. A growing medium for advertising, sales promotions, and direct selling.

ZERO-BASED BUDGETING: An approach to budgeting in which each part of the organization must justify each item in its budget before it will be granted the funds it needs.

ZONE PRICING: A geographic pricing policy in which the seller divides a geographic area into zones and charges each buyer in a given zone the base price plus the standard freight rate for that zone.

RESOURCES

Karl Albrecht and Ron Zemke. *Service America!* New York: Warner Books, 1990.

H. Igor Ansoff. *The New Corporate Strategy,* New York: John Wiley, 1988.

Leonard L. Berry and A. Parasuraman. *Marketing Services: Competing Through Quality,* New York: The Free Press, 1991.

Ken Blanchard and Sheldon Bowles. *Raving Fans: A Revolutionary Approach to Customer Service,* New York: William Morrow and Co., 1993.

Robert W. Bly. *Advertising Manager's Handbook,* Englewood Cliffs, NJ: Prentice-Hall, 1993.

Robert D. Buzzell and Bradley T. Gale. *The PIMS Principles: Linking Strategy to Performance,* New York: The Free Press, 1987.

Jan Carlson. *Moments of Truth: New Strategies for Today's Customer-Driven Economy,* New York: Harper & Row, 1987.

C. Merle Crawford. *New Product Management,* Homewood, IL: Richard D. Irwin, 1983.

Philip B. Crosby. *Quality Is Free: The Art of Making Quality Certain,* New York: McGraw-Hill, 1979.

Richard Cross and Janet Smith. *Customer Bonding: Pathways to Lasting Customer Loyalty,* Chicago, IL: NTC Business Books, 1995.

William H. Davidow and Bro Uttal. *Total Customer Service: The Ultimate Weapon,* New York: Harper & Row, 1989.

Michael Dertouzos, Richard Lester, and Robert Solow. *Made in America: Regaining the Productive Edge,* New York: HarperCollins, 1990.

Peter F. Drucker. *Innovation and Entrepreneurship: Practice and Principles,* New York: Harper & Row, 1985.

Peter F. Drucker. *Management: Tasks, Responsibilities, Practices,* New York: Harper & Row, 1973.

Leonard M. Fuld. *Competitor Intelligence: How to Get It—How to Use It,* New York: Ronald Press, 1984.

Gary Hamel and C. K. Prahalad. "Corporate Imagination and Expeditionary Marketing," *Harvard Business Review*, 69(4) (July–August 1991) pp. 81–92.

Harvard Business Review paperback No. 90089. *Unconditional Quality* (a collection of HBR articles), Boston: Harvard Business School, 1991.

Alexander Hiam. *The Vest-Pocket Marketer: Classic Marketing Tools for Executives*, Englewood Cliffs, NJ: Prentice-Hall, 1991.

Alexander Hiam. *Closing the Gap: How America's Leading Companies Are Responding to the Quality Challenge*, Englewood Cliffs, NJ: Prentice-Hall, 1992.

Alexander Hiam. *Marketing for Dummies*, Foster City, CA: IDG Books, 1997.

Alexander Hiam. *The Manager's Pocket Guide to Creativity*, Amherst, MA: HRD Press, 1998.

Kaoru Ishikawa. *What Is Total Quality Control? The Japanese Way*, Englewood Cliffs, NJ, Prentice-Hall, 1985.

JIAN. *Marketing Builder: Complete Sales and Marketing Planning, Implementation & Analysis Software*, Mountain View, CA: JIAN Tools for Sales, Inc., 1995.

Thomas C. Kinnear and James R. Taylor. *Marketing Research: An Applied Approach*, New York: McGraw-Hill, 1987.

Theodore Levitt. "Marketing Intangible Products and Product Intangibles," *Harvard Business Review*, 59(3) (May–June 1981), pp. 94–102.

Allan J. Magrath. *The 6 Imperatives of Marketing: Lessons from the World's Best Companies*, New York, NY: AMACOM, 1992.

Thomas T. Nagle. *The Strategy and Tactics of Pricing*, Englewood Cliffs, NJ: Prentice-Hall, 1987.

Tom Peters and Nancy Austin. *A Passion for Excellence: The Leadership Difference*, New York: Random House, 1985.

Thomas J. Peters and Robert H. Waterman, Jr. *In Search of Excellence: Lessons from America's Best-Run Companies*, New York: Harper & Row, 1982.

Michael E. Porter. *Competitive Advantage: Creating and Sustaining Superior Performance*, New York: The Free Press, 1985.

Michael E. Porter. *Competitive Strategy: Techniques for Analyzing Industries and Competitors*, New York: The Free Press, 1980.

C. K. Prahalad and Gary Hamel. "The Core Competence of the Corporation," *Harvard Business Review*, (May–June 1990) pp. 79–91.

Stan Rapp and Thomas L. Collins. *MaxiMarketing*, New York: McGraw-Hill, 1987.

Al Ries and Jack Trout. *Marketing Warfare*, New York: McGraw-Hill, 1986.

Al Ries and Jack Trout. *Positioning: The Battle for Your Mind*, New York: Warner Books, 1982.

Everett M. Rogers. *Diffusion of Innovations*, New York: The Free Press, 1983.

F. G. "Buck" Rogers. *The IBM Way: Insights into the World's Most Successful Marketing Organization*, New York: Harper & Row, 1985.

Ernan Roman. *Integrated Direct Marketing*, New York: McGraw-Hill, 1989.

William E. Rothschild. *How to Gain (and Maintain) the Competitive Advantage*, New York: McGraw-Hill, 1984.

W. Earl Sasser, Jr., Christopher W. L. Hart, and James L. Heskett. *The Service Management Course: Cases and Readings,* New York: The Free Press, 1991.

Leon G. Shiffman and Leslie Lazar Kanuk. *Consumer Behavior,* Englewood Cliffs, NJ: Prentice-Hall, 1987.

Louis W. Stern and Adel I. El-Ansary. *Marketing Channels,* Englewood Cliffs, NJ: Prentice-Hall, 1988.

Michael Treacy and Fred Wiersema. *The Discipline of Market Leaders,* Reading, MA: Addison-Wesley Publishing Co., 1995.

Lynn B. Upshaw. *Building Brand Identity: A Strategy for Success in a Hostile Marketplace,* New York, NY: John Wiley & Sons, 1995.

Valerie A. Zeithaml, A. Parasuraman, and Leonard L. Berry. *Delivering Quality Service: Balancing Customer Perceptions and Expectations,* New York: The Free Press, 1990.

INDEX